CONTEMPORARY GOVERNMENT AND BUSINESS RELATIONS

CONTEMPORARY GOVERNMENT AND BUSINESS RELATIONS

Fourth Edition

Martin C. Schnitzer

Virginia Polytechnic Institute

HOUGHTON MIFFLIN COMPANY   Boston

Dallas   Geneva, Illinois   Palo Alto   Princeton, New Jersey

Library of Congress Catalog Card Number: 89-80907

ISBN: 0-395-43364-9

CDEFGHIJ-CS-998765432

Contents

**Chapter 3   Extension of Government Control Over Business:
The New Deal to the Present** **49**

PART III

INDUSTRIAL CONCENTRATION AND ANTITRUST

**Chapter 4   Market Structure: Competition, Monopoly,
and Oligopoly** **75**

PART IV

SOCIAL REGULATION OF BUSINESS

Chapter 10   Issues of Social Regulation 237

Chapter 11   Equal Employment Opportunity Policies
           and Their Impact on Business 258

PART V

DEREGULATION OF BUSINESS

Chapter 14   Deregulation and Airline Competition 369

PART VI

THE UNITED STATES IN THE POST-REAGAN ERA

List of Cases

Preface

The purpose of this book is to fill a void in government and business courses: the lack of coverage of all areas of government regulation that directly affect business operations. Some books on government fail to show or do not sufficiently emphasize the fact that government influence has expanded into a number of areas totally unrelated to antitrust policies and public utility regulation. In fact, most business firms are far more likely to be affected by the federal government's environmental and affirmative action policies than by its antitrust policies. The federal government has expanded so greatly that today it has become the largest purchaser of business products. Moreover, government economic policies exercise a powerful influence over business; for example, the deficit in the federal budget and the tax reform legislation of 1986, have or will have a direct impact on business operations.

The composition of this book reflects the many and diverse areas in which government and business interact. Chapter 1 is about how government affects business—in public finance, regulation and control, as an employer, and as an owner of industry. Chapters 2 and 3 present the background of the development of government and business relations in the United States. Chapters 4, 5, 6, 7, 8, and 9 cover market models, industrial concentration, and antitrust laws. Chapters 10, 11, 12, and 13 deal with the very important subject of social regulation of business and include such areas as affirmative action and comparable worth, consumer protection, and environmental policy. Chapters 14 and 15 cover the results of deregulation of air transportation and banking. Chapters 16 through 20 cover the problems of the United States economy. They deal with the subjects of the decline in United States industrial competitiveness, the United States as the world's leading debtor nation, the trade deficit, the budget deficit, and business and the Bush administration.

I have updated this book to include as many changes as possible in a subject area that is constantly changing. Approximately 50 percent of the material is new when compared with the 1987 edition. Included in this edition are three major 1988 Supreme Court decisions on affirmative action and sexual harassment. The most important product liability ever entered against the tobacco industry is included in the chapter on consumer protection. The leveraged buyout of RJR Nabisco, which received front-page attention in *Time, Newsweek,* and the newspapers, is included in the new edition as are several new cases involving price fixing. Major attention is given to the collapse of the savings and loan industry and the bailout plan of the Bush administration. The results of deregulation of the airline industry is covered in a chapter, and the Exxon Valdez environmental disaster is discussed in a special case in the Appendix.

The coverage of the book has been broadened to cover other subjects of paramount importance to business. The United States has become a part of a global economy in which economic competition is fierce. Is the position of the United States as the world's leading economic power declining and, if so, can this decline be reversed? The United States started the 1980s as the world's leading creditor nation; now it is the world's leading debtor nation. The federal budget runs a deficit that has an impact on savings and investment, and the federal debt has almost tripled in the 1980s. There continues to be a deficit in the merchandise trade account, and Japan is being blamed for our trade problems. There is also concern that foreigners are buying too many U.S. assets.

I have utilized the most current data available and have relied where possible on firsthand sources. I am indebted to William Young of the Washington law firm of Hunton and Williams who provided me with most of the new antitrust cases used in the book, the Attorney General's Office of Florida, Congressman Rick Boucher of Virginia, various persons on the Senate and House banking and judiciary committees who sent me committee reports, and the office of Peter W. Rodino who was chairman of the House Judiciary Committee. I would also like to thank Judith Johnson, Director of Equal Employment Opportunity/Affirmative Action programs at Virginia Tech for providing me with the most current Supreme Court cases, and Greg Campbell, a local lawyer, who provided me the materials on the tobacco liability suits. Above all, I would like to thank my wife, Joan, for her assistance in typing the manuscript.

M.C.S.

CONTEMPORARY GOVERNMENT AND BUSINESS RELATIONS

PART I

INTRODUCTION TO GOVERNMENT AND BUSINESS RELATIONS

No U.S. company or industry is immune from the impact of decisions made in Washington. But many corporate executives still act as if politics is an exercise in crisis management—something to worry about after trouble comes. Ignoring Washington may have worked twenty-five years ago. Today it is a prescription for failure.*

This statement, taken from a recent *Harvard Business Review* article, defines quite well the significance of the relationship between business and government in the United States. Today no business firm is free from some form of government control. Not more than two decades ago, most American business firms were unregulated. They were free to design the kinds of products they pleased, subject to product acceptance. They were also free to practice personnel policies of their own choosing. But now business firms are subject to detailed government regulations in which almost all phases of design, marketing, management, personnel, and at times even pricing policies are responses to requirements that were laid down in Washington. Therefore, the subject of business-government relations is even more important to students because there is an enormous amount of interaction between these two major institutions in U.S. society, and it is necessary to establish a framework within which a discussion of this interaction can take place.

*David B. Yoffie, "How an Industry Builds Political Advantage," *Harvard Business Review*, 66 (May–June 1988) pp. 77–91.

Chapter 1

The Influence of Government on Business

To use a botanical analogy, government and business are two genera of the social and economic system of the United States. Each genus contains various species, such as federal, state, and local political bodies in the case of government, and corporations, partnerships, and proprietorships in the case of business. Sometimes there are even hybrid species, joint government–business or public–private enterprises such as the Communications Satellite Corporation (COMSAT). These two genera interrelate because government provides the institutional foundation on which business rests, the legal framework within which it functions, and many of the instruments through which its activities are carried out. The economic system within which business functions is also shaped by government, and its performance depends on decisions made by government. The system's expectations of profit or loss depend to some extent on the policies adopted by central banking authorities to control the volume of credit and on the policies pursued by the federal government to balance its budget, to accumulate a surplus, or to run a deficit.

To be more specific, government relates to business in at least the following ways: it regulates the particular functions of all businesses, such as competition, foreign trade, product safety, the issuance and sale of securities, labor relations, and the impact of a business on the environment. Government participates in the management of the so-called public utilities by regulating entry, service, output, investment, prices, and other variables of the utilities' operation. Government also sells or regulates a wide variety of goods and services, including postal services, nuclear fuel, electricity, and police and fire protection. It taxes business, and it makes business a collector of taxes such as those levied on alcohol, gasoline, and tobacco. In addition, it purchases many kinds of equipment, supplies, goods, and services from business. Government also subsidizes some business enterprises, particularly those connected with

3

farming and shipbuilding; it finances other enterprises through direct loans, loan guarantees, and insurance. Finally, and perhaps most important, government attempts to stabilize the economic environment within which business must operate through its use of fiscal and monetary policies.

The government's participation in U.S. business life has grown enormously. From the beginning of the republic in 1787, the federal government has been interested in promoting manufacturing, and it soon passed tariff laws to protect American business interests. Subsidies were used to develop canals, roads, and various forms of transportation, from which business benefited directly. As industrialization and business concentration increased, the government passed laws to regulate specific segments of business—for example, railroads—or to control business practices. This trend began in the latter part of the last century and continued, with some interruptions, until 1940. After World War II, government participation in business took the form of increasing consumption of a wide variety of goods and services, the bulk of which have been items considered essential for the national defense. One result of this process is that many industries and enterprises have become dependent on government spending.

In recent years, U.S. society has made a shift in emphasis from market to political decisions, largely in response to increased societal problems. Not much more than a decade ago, most business firms were largely unregulated, free to produce whatever kinds of products they pleased, as long as consumers would accept them. Today, these firms are subject to detailed government regulations in almost all phases of their operations. One example is the controversial affirmative action programs set in motion by the federal government, which apply to business firms and unions alike. Protection of the environment is another area in which the government has encroached on the activities of most business firms. The prime example is the automobile industry, which must now comply with emission control standards that require a radical reduction in the amount of hydrocarbons and carbon monoxide emitted by motor vehicles. Safety standards require automobile designers to accommodate various restraints, including safety belts and buzzer systems, specifications for brakes, safety glass, and the padding of bumpers. Government constraints on business can be expected to increase in the future in accordance with new social and ideological demands. One example is probably closer supervision of the savings and loan industry. Another example may be a law providing maternity and parental leave from employment. It is possible that there will be some reregulation of the airline industry.

AREAS OF GOVERNMENT INTERVENTION

For the purpose of organization, government intervention and participation in the U.S. economy can be divided into four areas, which provide the subject matter of the remainder of this chapter. First, there is public finance, in which government is a purchaser of goods and services as well as a tax collector. Government economic stabilization policies may also be considered a part of this area. Second, government regulation and control prescribe specific conditions under which private business activity can or cannot take place. Government may interpose itself as a part of management in certain industries, such as public utilities, and regulate rates and the provision of services. It may also influence private business operations both directly and indirectly through antitrust and other laws. Third, government is the single largest employer in the U.S. economy and, as such, competes directly with private industry for labor. The government also affects the level of wages and salaries. Fourth, government owns and operates business enterprises and is a major provider of credit. In fact, few, if any, changes in the market structure of the U.S. economy have as much social and political significance as does this movement of government into areas previously reserved for private enterprise.

THE ROLE OF PUBLIC FINANCE

Public finance is the clearest and probably the most important example of the extent of government participation in the "mixed" economy of the United States. Taxes give the government control over the nation's resources and also affect the distribution of income. Government expenditures for goods and services divert resources from the private to the public sector of the economy. Through its own expenditures, the government has literally created business firms and whole industries, has conducted much of the basic research in certain industries, and has given impetus and direction to technological change. Indeed, the direct subsidies and indirect benefits offered business by government are too numerous to mention. In addition, preferential tax treatment is accorded to some firms and industries. So great is the impact of taxes and so great are the benefits of favorable tax treatment that businesses take immense interest in, and attempt to influence the writing of, tax legislation. Examples of special tax treatment include the investment credit, depletion allowances, and accelerated depreciation.

The importance of the public sector to business can be explained in three ways. First, the general level of government expenditures and taxation, in relation to the gross national product (GNP), is high. Economists prefer, however, to use changes in the share of the GNP taken off the market rather than total government expenditures as a guide to the public sector's economic influence. Second, the actual composition of expenditures and taxes affects the status of the public sector. For example, direct government expenditures for goods and services would have an impact on business different from that exerted by transfer payments, which return no equivalent value in either products or services. The composition of taxes is also important, and in recent years more attention has been paid to the role of tax policies in promoting economic growth. Third, public policy measures designed to maintain a high level of employment, economic growth, stable prices, and other economic and social goals have all been generally accepted. Both fiscal and monetary policies have thereby become important to the management of the U.S. economy.

The Level of Expenditures and Taxation

The importance of the federal government's budget to the business community cannot be overemphasized. The budget exerts an influence on the national economy and also on business, regarding the level of expenditures and taxes, whether or not it is balanced, and the specific expenditures and taxes it authorizes. The federal budget tends to be the focal point of the presentation and implementation of the government's economic policy, and it is often used as a means of publicizing the government's policies toward particular sectors, groups of people, or industries, either in an attempt to improve the chances of success of the proposed measures or, at times, as a substitute for any specific measures. Moreover, the budget can be used to alter the level of economic activity. Taxes represent a withdrawal of income from the income stream, whereas government expenditures represent an injection of income into the stream.

The significance of the federal budget can be measured by its size in relation to GNP. Budgetary receipts for 1989 are estimated at $1,059.3 billion, and expenditures are estimated at $1,151.9 billion.[1] When these tax revenues are compared to the estimated GNP for 1989 of approximately $5.1 trillion, it is

---

[1]*Budget of the U.S. Government, Fiscal Year 1990* (Washington, D.C.: U.S. Government Printing Office, 1989), p. I-5.

apparent that the federal budget diverts approximately 21 percent of GNP from the private to the public sector. The budgetary outlays of around $1,150 billion take the form of direct expenditures for goods and services, most of which are provided by business firms, and of transfer payments and subsidies of various types, many of which also benefit business firms. Government purchases of goods and services also directly increase the total demand for output in the economy; government transfer payments and taxes exert a more indirect influence on total demand.

State and local expenditures also must be considered. In 1987, for example, total receipts, including taxes, for all levels of government amounted to $1.5 trillion and total expenditures amounted to $1.6 trillion.[2] However, some of the state and local receipts are federal grants-in-aid. In the same year, total government purchases of goods and services amounted to $955.7 billion, in comparison with a GNP of $4.8 trillion.[3] Of the total $923.8 billion, federal government expenditures on goods and services accounted for $380.6 billion and state and local government expenditures accounted for $543.2 billion. It can be said that in regard to the actual purchases of goods and services, state and local governments have more impact on business than the federal government does.

The economic influence of the public sector has intensified steadily throughout this century and has become particularly pervasive during the last thirty years. To some extent, this increase in influence can be attributed to a growing acceptance of the government's taking charge of public welfare. But in fact, government expenditures for the national defense have been the most important single factor in the growth of public expenditures during the last three decades. Indeed, in 1987 this type of expenditure accounted for about 32 percent of the total purchases of goods and services by all government units. Economic growth has also spurred a trend toward urban living. As a larger proportion of the nation's population has concentrated in urban areas, the inevitable result has been a greater demand for services that must be provided through the public sector. Increased industrialization has changed the size and complexity of business enterprises, and the government's regulatory operations have had to be expanded. But regardless of the causes, the growth of both the absolute and the relative importance of the public sector is clear, as

[2] *Economic Report of the President 1989* (Washington, D.C.: U.S. Government Printing Office, 1989), table B-80, p. 402.

[3] Ibid., table B-1, p. 249.

TABLE 1-1   Government Expenditures on Goods and Services Compared to Gross National Product for Selected Years

Year	Gross National Product (in billions)	Government Expenditures on Goods and Services (in billions)
1929	$ 103.4	$ 8.9
1939	91.3	13.6
1950	289.3	39.9
1960	515.3	100.6
1970	1,015.5	219.9
1980	2,732.0	530.3
1981	3,052.6	588.1
1982	3,166.0	641.7
1983	3,405.7	675.0
1984	3,772.2	735.9
1985	4,010.3	818.6
1986	4,235.0	869.7
1987	4,496.2	923.9
1988	4,823.8	955.3

Source: *Economic Report of the President 1988* (Washington, D.C.: U.S. Government Printing Office, 1989), table B-1, pp. 248–249.

Table 1-1 indicates. (The table excludes government transfer payments to individuals and business firms.)

The Composition of Taxes and Expenditures

The pie charts in Figure 1-1 present a breakdown of government taxes and expenditures by categories. To business firms, the actual composition of taxes and expenditures is more important than the level of taxes and expenditures. Taxes represent an outflow of revenue from business firms and individuals to the government, and expenditures represent an outflow from the government to individuals and business firms. As the chart indicates, the three major sources of government revenues are individual income taxes, social insurance receipts, and borrowing. Government expenditures include direct payments to

FIGURE 1-1   The Budget Dollar (Fiscal Year 1990 Estimate)

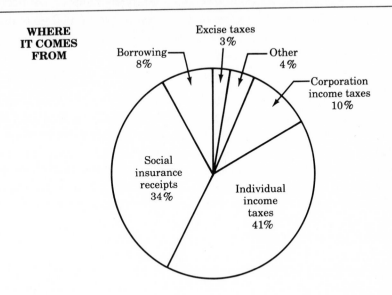

WHERE IT COMES FROM

Excise taxes 3%
Borrowing 8%
Other 4%
Corporation income taxes 10%
Social insurance receipts 34%
Individual income taxes 41%

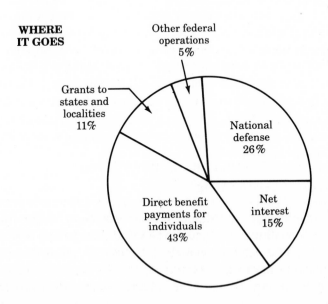

WHERE IT GOES

Other federal operations 5%
Grants to states and localities 11%
National defense 26%
Direct benefit payments for individuals 43%
Net interest 15%

Source: *Budget of the U.S. Government, Fiscal Year 1990* (Washington, D.C.: U.S. Government Printing Office, 1989), p. M-2.

individuals and business firms, which includes subsidies and transfer payments, national defense expenditures, and interest payments on the national debt. Interest payment, when expressed as a percentage of total government expenditures, have more than doubled since 1975.

The Composition of Taxes

The composition of taxes is important to business firms. Government expenditures are normally covered by taxes, including taxes on business; thus, where taxes are levied ultimately determines who will pay for government expenditures. Many public policymakers believe that variations in the rate of economic growth can be attributed to tax policies. A hallmark of the Reagan administration was a shift in tax policy to stimulate economic growth. The Economic Recovery Tax Act of 1982 was designed to stimulate the rate of savings and capital formation by cutting both individual and corporate income taxes. Various tax breaks can be used to encourage specific types of economic activity. An example is the investment credit, which has been used both in this country and abroad to stimulate investment in the capital goods industries.

Taxes can be used manipulatively by granting exemptions and special tax cuts to certain types of people, corporations, and activities. An example is the corporate income tax, which is used by the federal government. The maximum tax rate on all corporate income is 34 percent as a result of the Tax Reform Act of 1986, though favorable treatment of particular types of income has been used to influence shifts in corporate behavior by reducing the income on which the tax has to be paid. One such example is the provision in the corporate income tax law that allows firms in certain extractive industries to deduct an allowance for depletion before computing taxable income. This allowance reduces the amount of taxes that these industries have to pay, which often results in additional investment in this area.

The Composition of Expenditures

Many types of government expenditures provide income to business firms. National defense expenditures, estimated to be $303 billion for the 1990 fiscal year, are important to the defense industries.[4] Defense Department expenditures for the procurement of various types of weapons are estimated at $79 billion. In addition to procurement expenditures, outlays for research and

[4] *Budget of the U.S. Government, Fiscal Year 1990* (Washington, D.C.: U.S. Government Printing Office, 1989), pp. 5–6.

development are projected to be around $37 billion. Almost all these expenditures help the high-technology industries. Operation and maintenance expenditures, estimated to be $89 billion, include expenditures for ship and aircraft fuel, overhaul of ships, aircraft, other weapons, and medical supplies and services, thus providing income for still other industries. Expenditures on the construction of military bases and family houses, projected at $8.9 billion, benefit the construction industry. Atomic energy defense activities, conducted by the Department of Energy, also provide revenue to business firms.

Business firms are also the beneficiaries of other types of government expenditures—shipbuilding, for example. The cost of building a ship in the United States is about twice what it would be elsewhere, and if it were not for the subsidies and the various laws confining U.S. commercial shipping to U.S.-built and -operated ships, there would be no shipbuilding in this country. In 1990, expenditures for ship construction and operating differential subsidies are estimated at around $500 million.[5] Then there are the business development loans made by federal agencies at interest rates lower than those prevailing at the usual lending sources. The federal government sponsors and encourages the development of small businesses through loans financed out of budget revenues. The Export-Import Bank (Eximbank) makes direct loans to U.S. exporters and importers.[6]

Economic Stabilization Policies

It is generally accepted that the economic objectives of U.S. society are a high level of employment, price stability, economic growth, and a balance-of-payments equilibrium. Each goal does not lend itself to precise definition, and the attainment of one may not help achieve the others. Considerable government intervention is necessary. This intervention takes the form of macroeconomic stabilization of fiscal and monetary policies that are implemented by the government's use of taxation, transfer payments, and purchases, and by the Federal Reserve's control over the money supply and interest rates.

Fiscal Policy

The term *fiscal policy* refers to the tax and expenditure policies of the federal government. Its objective is to increase or decrease the level of aggregate

[5] Ibid., pp. 9–132.
[6] Total guaranteed loans of Eximbank are estimated at $10 billion for 1989.

demand through changes in the level of government expenditures and taxation. For example, an expansionary fiscal policy would stimulate economic
growth and employment through an increase in government spending, decreases in taxes, or both. Conversely, fiscal policy can be used to contract the
level of aggregate demand. Taxes can be raised, expenditures can be reduced,
or a combination of these tactics can be used. The federal budget is the fulcrum
of fiscal policy. It provides a system of planning and control over government
activities by the executive and legislative branches of government. The
budget, because of its sheer dollar size, exercises a potent influence on the
economy.

Monetary Policy

Monetary policy is used by the Federal Reserve to control the level of national
output and the price level through variations in the money supply.[7] An increase in the money supply will lower interest rates and stimulate private and
public spending; a decrease in the money supply will raise interest rates and
reduce private and public spending. The Federal Reserve cannot fix the
amount of credit and its cost independently. If it wants to restrain the rate of
growth in the money supply, it must allow interest rates to rise as high as possible. If it wants to keep interest rates low, it has to accept the consequences of an
increase in the money supply. Monetary policy differs from fiscal policy in
that control over it is not in the hands of the federal government.

Impact on Business

Government economic policies provide parameters within which both U.S.
domestic and multinational business firms have to operate. Monetary policy
affects the cost of credit available to domestic and multinational corporations.
Changes in interest rates can affect currency exchange rates between countries. Exports or imports can be stimulated, which will either positively or
negatively affect the U.S. balance of payments. Fiscal policy also has an impact on both domestic and multinational corporations. On the tax side of the
government budget, changes in tax rates can affect earnings; on the expend-

---

[7] The money supply is the total quantity of money existing in an economy at a particular time. It
consists of coins and currency, demand deposits, and other checkable account balances. It includes M_1, which represents the more liquid types of money, and M_2, which represents less liquid assets such as savings and certificates of deposits. $M_1 + M_2$ equals the total money supply.

iture side, changes in expenditure can affect earnings. Whether or not the budget is balanced can also affect business. The deficit in the budget, which is around $147 billion as of 1988, has kept interest rates high and has contributed to a negative balance in the U.S. merchandise trade accounts with other countries, particularly Japan.

GOVERNMENT REGULATION AND CONTROL OF BUSINESS

The regulation and control of business is a second area in which government has become firmly entrenched. This sphere of public sector activity has developed sporadically. The demand for some form of government regulation or control arose as various crises or problems occurred. In the 1880s the trust movement threatened to envelop much of U.S. industry, which brought out a demand for some sort of government control over the trusts. The result was that the Sherman Antitrust Act was passed in 1890. The Depression, which began with the stock market crash of 1929 and continued until the wartime mobilization of the early 1940s, was a crisis. In response, many new government agencies were created, most of which encroached in some way on the activities of business firms. By the end of the Depression, the federal government extensively regulated and controlled business. But after that time there was little increase in government intervention until the late 1960s and early 1970s, when environmental protection, employment of minorities and women, and consumer protection became dominant issues.

Government regulation and control of business became necessary for several reasons, all of which are associated with certain failures of the market system, Over time, many industries came to be dominated by a relatively few large firms, instead of the many small firms that create the strict competitive conditions required for a pure market economy. In some cases, a single large firm or trust achieved control of a large part of an industry's productive capacity, or a few large firms were able to act together to achieve monopolistic control of output. Thus it follows that the results of operating under monopoly or oligopoly can be quite different from those anticipated under a true market system. One reason is that firms operating under monopoly or oligopoly have some control over output and are able, within limits, to ask a price that does not reflect market forces.

The distribution of income and wealth can be considered a second flaw in the market system. In a purely competitive market economy, market forces are supposed to enable people to be compensated on the basis of their contributions to total output. In regard to reward for labor, those people, whose skills are scarce in relation to demand would enjoy a high level of income, whereas those people whose skills are not scarce would not. But this concept of reward had to be modified when it became apparent that large incomes accrued to some people not on the basis of their contributions to national output but through inherited wealth and other accidents of birth or through the exercise of special privileges. Moreover, capricious economic and social factors often impeded the most productive individuals. The Social Darwinist concept of "survival of the fittest" made little sense when a depression put millions of efficient and productive people out of work.

Finally, the market system, with its price mechanism, failed to furnish individuals or society with a satisfactory means for achieving certain wants, for example, the desire for a clean environment. Although great importance is attached to this want, it is difficult to achieve on the basis of price-cost relationships in the market. Initiative for the provision of a clean environment therefore falls to public agencies, which use controls that inevitably have a major impact on the operations of business firms. There are also certain services, such as education, that are not suitable for production and sale on a private basis and are provided by the public sector.

Antitrust Laws

In a market economy, competition is necessary to provide the discipline needed for the efficient allocation of resources. Any departure from competition can work against the public welfare. A prime example was the development of trusts and other forms of business combinations in the United States in the latter part of the last century. The trusts were aimed at eliminating competitors and many industries fell under the control of a single trust. Discriminatory pricing and other anticompetitive business practices were numerous, and companies colluded to restrain competition. For these reasons, antitrust laws were passed to protect the public. These laws are designed to maintain competition by limiting monopoly power, whether achieved by internal growth or by mergers. They are also directed at specific business practices: anticompetitive price fixing, price discrimination against buyers or sellers, tying agreements, interlocking directorates, and other coercive practices. Each device can be used to restrain competition. For example, the aim of a price-fixing agreement, if successful, is the elimination of price competition. The power to fix prices, whether exercised reasonably or not, also involves the power to control the market.

Public Utility Regulation

Public utilities are enterprises that are in some degree characterized by monopoly. In these enterprises, government accepts monopoly as being natural or desirable and establishes maximum rates to protect the public against unreasonable charges. In some instances, the government may also set minimum rates to ensure that a given utility will not arbitrarily reduce rates to injure other enterprises. Public utilities are recognized by the courts as being affected with a public interest, and as such, their property is subject to regulation. If they do business intrastate, they are subject to control by the public service or public utility commission in the particular state. Utility companies engaged in interstate commerce are subject to regulation by the federal government.

Social Regulation

There is also government social regulation of business—hiring of the handicapped, occupational safety, consumer protection, environmental protection, affirmative action, and so forth. The rationale for social regulation is that the market system does not work to solve such problems as sex and race discrimination, negative wants, and externalities created by rising living standards. For example, pollution is an externality. No price was imposed on business for using the air or water to store or discharge its waste, and so the cost to society of polluting the air or water was not taken into consideration by market forces. Thus the federal government stepped in to improve regulation and to create the Environmental Protection Agency. It and other social regulatory agencies have come to have a great influence on business for the simple reason that few business firms can avoid dealing with them.

GOVERNMENT AS AN EMPLOYER

One measure of the public sector's size and its impact on business is the number of people employed by governmental units. When the armed forces are included, some 16 percent of the total labor force is employed by the public sector, and since the demand for social services is likely to increase, so is this percentage likely to, particularly at the state and local levels of government.[8] In addition, many other jobs are related indirectly to government employment. An army base, defense plant, or state university often supports the economy of a whole town or area.[9] In many areas, the public sector sets the wage standards and competes against the private sector for labor and other resources. This control can have an adverse effect on productivity. Although comparisons with the private sector are difficult to make, the available evidence suggests that productivity in the federal government sector has risen less rapidly than that in the private sector.[10]

Two sets of administrative hierarchies, one public and the other private, have grown at different times for different reasons to carry out different functions. The public hierarchy developed much later than the private hierarchy. In 1929, the federal government's working force in Washington was a great deal smaller than that at U.S. Steel or General Motors; today it is much larger than both companies combined. Numerous federal agencies have been created, and a new administrative culture has developed. The work, attitudes, and perspective of the business administrator and the government administrator have become and will remain almost as distinct and separate as those of the scientist and humanist. The attitudes of these two hierarchies define business and government relations. This relationship over time has been anything but amicable. One reason is cultural: business leaders are usually older and have different educational and career backgrounds from those of the public officials with whom they must deal.

GOVERNMENT OWNERSHIP OF BUSINESS

In the United States, all levels of government own and operate productive facilities of many kinds. Airports, but not railway terminals, are usually govern-

---

[8] A major objective of the Reagan administration was to reduce the role of the federal government in the U.S. economy. If he was successful over the long run the role of state and local governments in the U.S. economy may increase. The likelihood, at least for the immediate future, is for a more rapid increase in state and local government employment than in federal government employment.

[9] An example is Blacksburg, Virginia, where Virginia Tech is by far the largest employer in the area.

[10] U.S. Congress, Joint Economic Committee, *Productivity in the Federal Government* (Washington, D.C.: U.S. Government Printing Office, May 1979).

ment owned. Government units own and operate the plants that provide water, gas, and electricity to thousands of cities and towns, as well as owning local transportation systems, heating plants, warehouses, printing companies, and many other facilities. The government also produces, either directly or indirectly, all of our artificial rubber, atomic power, and many other goods, and it runs projects connected with reforestation, soil erosion, slum clearance, rural electrification, and housing. All this does not mean that government ownership and operation is necessarily preferred to private ownership and operation. In many cases, the resources required were too large, the risks too great, or the likelihood of profit too small to attract private enterprise, and so the government was compelled to perform the tasks.

One example of this is the Tennessee Valley Authority (TVA), a major public enterprise for the production and distribution of electrical power in the southeastern United States. At one time, the area adjacent to the Tennessee River was among the most impoverished in the United States. Flooding and soil erosion were common, and almost all homes in the area were without electricity. The area was also generally unattractive to industry, and so TVA was created to erect dams and hydroelectric plants to provide electric power, to improve navigation on the Tennessee River, to promote flood control, to prevent soil erosion, to reforest the land, and to contribute to the nation's defense through the manufacture of artificial nitrates. It was opposed by private companies, in particular the utility companies, because it was empowered to sell electricity in direct competition with them, even though the utility companies in the Tennessee Valley area had never considered it profitable to provide any but the most minimal amount of service. TVA was also supposed to serve as a yardstick of efficiency, though government ownership and operation of power facilities do not always mean lower rates or greater efficiency. Opinion on TVA's efficiency is mixed: TVA is efficient compared with other government agencies, but not so compared with private business.

Government credit programs are a gray area in that they do not involve outright state ownership of industry. Federal credit programs, however, do have an impact on private industry that should be mentioned. Direct, insured, and federally sponsored agency loans passed the $500 billion mark in 1980 and have continued to increase. These programs have three main functions: the elimination of gaps in the credit market, the provision of subsidies to encourage socially desirable activity, and the stimulation of the economy. The first two of these functions are microeconomic in that they are supposed to affect the types of activity for which credit is made available, the geographical location of that activity, and the types of borrowers who have access to credit. For example, Federal Housing Administration (FHA) and Veterans' Administration (VA) mortgage insurance programs have resulted in a greater demand for housing. The third function is macroeconomic in that federal lending affects the level of economic activity on a large scale, in particular the gross national product and employment.

THE BUSINESS–GOVERNMENT INTERFACE

President Calvin Coolidge once said that the business of America is business. But that was long ago when business was supreme and government was small, and business firms had the power to shift business–government relations in their favor.[11]   Presidents were usually probusiness, and businessmen were appointed to cabinet positions and to other key government jobs where they could gain approval of such measures as a protective tariff and could transform the Federal Trade Commission and other federal government regulatory agencies into having a more probusiness attitude. These businessmen were not necessarily the "greedy capitalists" who inspired government regulations in the first place. Often they were like evangelists who believed in the fervor of their cause.[12]   Many saw success in business as a service to society, not just as the pursuit of private gain.

But times have changed. Not only does government now control a significant share of the national product, but its expenditures and regulatory and redistributive activities also affect virtually every kind of private activity. Even though business firms have been the beneficiaries of many government activities, many business leaders and some politicians would like to reduce the role of the federal government in the marketplace. They believe that a responsibly managed private sector can solve many social problems more efficiently than government.[13]   They feel that government intrusion into private decisions, bureaucracy, and the uncertainty of political and economic policy all frustrate capital investment planning.[14]   This involvement reduces the capacity of the private sector to create jobs, products, and services. Moreover, many

[11] The time was the 1920s, which has been called the golden age of American capitalism.

[12] Evangelism was a powerful religious force during the 1920s. Aimee Semple MacPherson and Billy Sunday were the counterparts of Billy Graham and Oral Roberts today.

[13] Private enterprise is now running prisons and hospitals.

[14] They have some justification here, as witnessed by the inability of President Reagan and Congress to balance the budget.

government regulatory agencies are regarded as too intrusive into business affairs.

Conversely, it can be argued that much of the government regulations and intervention that business wants to remove was brought about by business itself. This regulation occurred because business failed either to recognize or to accede to the public's stake in its activities. Business would always react when compelled to do so, but would never act to solve a problem. Despite the desire of the public for clean air and water, safer goods and working conditions, and truthful advertising, government legislation and regulation were needed to make business respond. Moreover, many people see business as being willing to use its power to frustrate the public interest and to oppose social change, so that government intervention in the process of business decision making is mandatory if the public interest is to be served.

It is necessary to go back at least to the last century to understand the current relationship of government and business. The coming of the large railroads and then of large industrial enterprises brought about government regulation. The regulation of business became the paramount domestic issue in U.S. politics for the period from 1880 to 1920. In the 1930s, business—in particular big business—took much of the blame for the Depression. Then in the 1960s and 1970s, business was blamed for the depletion of resources and the pollution that resulted, as well as for other social problems of the day. By then the standard response to complex economic problems was to pass laws creating regulatory commissions to monitor the activities of the businesses involved. During the 1980s, the Reagan administration made an attempt to reduce the extent of government regulation of business and the overall role of the federal government in the U.S. economy. Whether this trend continues remains to be seen.

SUMMARY

Some government intervention is necessary for the establishment of even the freest type of economic system. The very atmosphere for the conduct of business is created by the ability of government to establish and maintain private property, freedom of enterprise, money and credit, and a system of civil laws for adjudicating the private disputes of individuals. Such institutions make possible an elaborate system of private planning in which individuals, rather than government, organize and direct the production of goods and services in response to the desires of consumers.

Government regulation of business has been established for a number of reasons. One reason is the failure of the market mechanism to allocate resources properly. When there is a breakdown in competitive market forces, monopoly, oligopoly, and otherwise imperfectly competitive market structures cause inefficient resource allocation and socially undesirable market performance. Antitrust policies are designed to deal with industry conduct, such as price fixing, and with industry structure that might foster monopolistic powers. There is also government regulation of the so-called natural monopolies—industries so large or so vital that competition is simply not feasible. Another area of regulation is the use of public resources such as air and water. There are two issues here: (1) balancing the amount of tolerable pollution against the value of the goods or services produced and (2) choosing the appropriate instruments to minimize the cost of achieving this balance. Government regulation can also intervene between sellers and consumers to protect either or both from certain conditions that might emerge in the absence of regulation. Since research is expensive to conduct, the government itself often collects data rather than having the market participant do so. The government then uses the research data to determine whether or not a product should be available to the public. For example, it is unlawful to market certain drugs unless they have been approved by the Federal Drug Administration (FDA).

QUESTIONS FOR DISCUSSION

1. Discuss the various ways in which the activities of government have an impact on business.
2. Explain the reasons for the increase in the government's intervention in business affairs.
3. "Government expenditures and taxes affect almost every business firm in the U.S. economy." Discuss this statement.
4. Explain the reasons for the increase in expenditures at all levels of government.
5. In what ways has the U.S. government helped business firms?
6. Why is it important for students to learn about the relationship between business and government?
7. What is government social regulation of business?
8. "Government ownership of business in the United States is limited to a few areas." Discuss this statement.

PART II

HISTORICAL BACKGROUND OF GOVERNMENT AND BUSINESS RELATIONS

Government regulation of business can be divided into three periods. The first period, which is the subject of Chapter 2, lasted from 1870 to 1930. During this time, government intervention in business was sporadic and essentially microeconomic. This intervention was in the form of laws to regulate railroads and to curb the power of monopolies. Only when the competitive, self-adjusting market mechanism broke down did the government undertake to correct its most serious failings. The first laws to protect the interests of consumers were also passed during this period. Those laws regulating the railroads and monopolies usually were initiated by the state governments and only later by the federal government. Laws were also passed to improve the lot of laborers, particularly with respect to working conditions and tax income and wealth. But for the most part, the laws directed against industrial concentration and the accumulation of wealth did not have much effect, and by 1920 industrial concentration was more pronounced than it had been in 1880.

The second period covers the Depression of the 1930s, probably the most active period ever in business–government relations, during which much legislation was passed to stimulate business recovery. Because people believed that certain defects in the business system were at least partly responsible for causing the Depression, laws regulating business were enacted in a number of areas, and the number of regulatory agencies multiplied. It was evident, when the decade of the Depression ended, that the federal government had begun extensive regulation of most segments of business activity. The Depression marked the decline of laissez faire and the advent of the mixed economy, which was reflected in increased governmental intervention in all spheres of business activity. The federal debt, which had been reduced to less than $2

billion by 1929, had increased to $40 billion by 1939. The machinery
for the government's macroeconomic intervention was started during
the 1930s and was completed with the passage of the Employment Act
of 1946. The third period of increased government control of business
extends from roughly 1960 to the present. Before this period, most legislation affecting business was economic in nature. The Sherman Antitrust Act, the Clayton Act, the Federal Trade Commission Act, the
Robinson–Patman Act, and many other acts all dealt with specific economic issues: monopoly power, pricing, concentration of industry, and
corporate economic power and its uses and abuses. The focus of more
recent legislation, however, has been on the attainment of certain social
goals: environmental protection, consumerism, employment of minorities and women, job safety, and so forth. These goals are associated
with a change in societal values that is characterized by the terms "rising entitlements" and "a better quality of life." Examples of such legislation include the Clean Air Act of 1970, the Consumer Product Safety
Act of 1972, and the Equal Employment Opportunity Act of 1972. This
kind of legislation also has created a new type of regulatory agency that
has a broader-based control over business activities and is more oriented toward accomplishing social objectives than the older regulatory
agencies were. For example, the Environmental Protection Agency can
regulate any type of business that pollutes the atmosphere.

Chapter 2 provides a historical framework to explain why government intervention into business affairs became necessary. Because
there was a concentration of economic power in many industries, terms
like *competition* and *free enterprise* had ceased to have much meaning.
In addition, there were great inequalities in the distribution of income
and wealth, since no countervailing forces opposed big business. Labor
unions were weak because they were denied due process under the law,
and the authority of government was circumscribed by its adherence to
the philosophy of laissez faire. The concentration of economic power in
the hands of a few people and corporations hindered the democratic
process because it tended to promote the concentration of political
power; many economic and political abuses worked to the detriment of
the country's social welfare. These abuses angered farmers, consumers,
and small business owners, who felt at a disadvantage compared with
big business, trusts, and the eastern banks. Organized pressure from
these groups eventually resulted in government regulation of railroads
and government action against the industrial monopolies.

Chapter 2

The Development of Government Regulation of Business

This chapter and the following one provide the historical background necessary to understand the reasons for government intervention into business affairs. Once this background has been presented, it will be possible to explore in more detail the role of government in today's business world. It can be said that business-government relations as they exist today have evolved from the last century as the United States began its transformation from an agrarian to an industrial society. Following the Civil War, industry became increasingly complex, and mass production techniques enabled producers to expand their output. The industrial capitalists began to rise above those who were so much a part of the U.S. economy before the war—merchants, shippers, farmers, and artisans. The economic pendulum, which before the Civil War had favored competition among a large number of sellers, swung over to the large-scale enterprise with an ever-increasing need for capital.

Various business abuses followed that contributed to a decline in competition. Industrial and railroad monopolies were formed around 1880 and continued into this century. The primary reason for the creation of this type of combination was the manufacturer's desire to restrict or eliminate competition and thus establish monopoly prices. This strategy was accomplished through control of supply. A monopoly price is likely to be higher than a competitive price, for the monopolist can limit supply and in this way prevent prices from falling to the level determined by competition. A second reason for business monopolies was the development of the business cycle. As recessions became more severe, business firms merged to achieve some sort of control over the market. A third reason for monopolies was that those organizing them hoped they would achieve the economies of the trust: a trust could almost always secure raw materials more cheaply than would be possible in a state of competition.

INDUSTRIAL CONSOLIDATION AND THE DECLINE OF COMPETITION

The period from the end of the Civil War to around 1890 can be called the golden age of laissez-faire capitalism. Business had just about everything its own way. The government, in particular the federal government, did nothing to intervene until business abuses of the market system became so prevalent that some form of intervention became necessary. Business, after a period of fierce competition, was characterized not only by the rise of the corporation as the dominant business unit but also by the growth of large-scale production and the beginning of business combinations. These combinations, of which the trust was the most important, were organized to eliminate competition and to regulate output and thereby stabilize prices, control production, and acquire greater profit. They were united under one central management of a large number of production units either turning out the same product or operating different stages of the process necessary to prepare the final product for market.

The growing concentration of economic power also created another problem—extremes of poverty and wealth. The new aristocracy of the country was made up of wealthy entrepreneurs and business leaders whom some called the robber barons. The prototypes of the industrial capitalists were John D. Rockefeller and Andrew Carnegie. They epitomized the Protestant work ethic, success in a competitive race in which victory went to the swift and resourceful. They also were not particularly scrupulous, taking advantage of every loophole, corrupting government officials, and bribing rivals' employees in a no-holds-barred effort to ruin competitors. But they were supported by a philosophy that helped explain and justify their preeminent position—social Darwinism. Put simply, social Darwinism was the application of Darwin's biological theory to economics.[1] It was the "survival of the fittest" principle applied to the business world. The Carnegies and the Rockefellers reached their positions through a competitive selection process, proved themselves the fittest, and were therefore entitled to the fruits of their labor. Society was the beneficiary of their efforts. Social Darwinism opposed government intervention in the operation of the economy and upheld industrial capitalism as a system in which each contributing group received a just reward.

---

[1] Social Darwinism was conceived by the English philosopher Herbert Spencer. His disciples in the United States were William Graham Sumner and John B. Clark. Sumner, a professor of moral philosophy at Yale, had a particularly strong influence on American thought.

There is some merit in social Darwinism. Carnegie, Rockefeller, and others of their type possessed certain attributes that encouraged success.[2] They were energetic, shrewd, and resourceful men who worked hard and expanded their business by plowing profits back into it. But there also were hardworking people at the opposite end of the income spectrum. In 1890, Marshall Field's income was calculated at $600 an hour; his shopgirls, earning salaries of $3 to $5 a week, had to work more than three years to earn that amount.[3] The working conditions for almost all workers were deplorable, and working twelve hours a day, seven days a week, was not uncommon. Wages were low, and there was no government intervention in the form of laws designed to provide unemployment benefits, worker's compensation, or any form of social security taken for granted in the industrial societies of today. There were no child labor laws—children eight years old and even younger worked in the mills and coal mines. Social and economic inequities divided the United States, and by 1890, 1 percent of the population owned as much of the nation's wealth as the remaining 99 percent did.

The Decline of Competition

Edward Bellamy, a social critic of the time and the author of the well-known utopian novel *Looking Backward,* offered some rather incisive insights into the industrial society that existed in the United States during the latter part of the last century.[4] He feared the consequences of the ever-increasing concentration of business in the hands of fewer and fewer individuals—individuals responsible neither to society nor to government. He saw that smallness was no remedy for bigness, however, and that as the concentration of business continued, government control would be the only means of protecting the public from exploitation. The following excerpt from *Looking Backward* summarizes conditions as they existed at the time.

> The next of the great wastes was that from competition. The field of industry was a battleground as wide as the world, in which the workers wasted in assailing one

[2] Hacker, *The Triumph of American Capitalism,* p. 401.

[3] Cited in Otto L. Bettman, *The Good Old Days—They Were Terrible* (New York: Random House, 1974), p. 67.

[4] Edward Bellamy, *Looking Backward* (New York: NAL, 1963). The main protagonist in the story is a wealthy young Bostonian named Julian West who is transported in time from the year 1887 to the year 2000. There has been a complete transformation of society during the interval.

another, energies which, if expended in concentrated effort would have enriched all. As for mercy or quarter in this warfare, there was absolutely none of it. To deliberately enter a field of business and destroy the enterprises of those who had occupied it previously, in order to plant one's own enterprise on their ruins, was an achievement which never failed to command popular admiration. . . . [5]

This description of competition during the late nineteenth century was not far from the truth. Competition among companies took many forms, including physical violence. For example, an independently owned railroad, the Albany and Susquehanna, had been constructed between Albany and Binghamton, New York. One of its major objectives was to haul coal between the Pennsylvania coal fields near Binghamton and the New England users of coal beyond Albany. The line was adjacent to the territory served by the Erie Railroad, which saw the desirability of possessing the Albany and Susquehanna. First the Erie tried to buy a majority of the shares of stock in the line but failed. It then attempted through legal maneuvering to gain a clear majority on the line's board of directors but failed in this, too. The Erie finally tried by armed assault to gain control of the Albany terminus of the line but was repulsed, though it did succeed in taking the line's facilities at the Binghamton end. The Albany and Susquehanna planned to retaliate by sending out several hundred men from Albany to retake the terminus. The Erie Railroad sent out its own men from Binghamton. The trains carrying the two factions met head-on, and passengers in both trains were killed. A battle between the two groups of men ensued. The Erie group lost and retreated, tearing up tracks and bridges as they went. Only then did the Erie group give up trying to gain control of the Albany and Susquehanna.[6]

The market system, if working well, can produce many generally good results. It can play on self-interest to produce results in the interest of others. It can use the lures of profits, income, and material rewards to induce individuals and business enterprises to behave in ways that are supposed to benefit others. The market system does not, however, eliminate all the disadvantages of economic interdependence among people and groups. At times it is a hard taskmaster, exacting heavy penalties on those who fail to conform to its demands. Thus there are not only winners under a market system but losers, too, and many manufacturers learned the hard way that competition can have the effect

[5] Ibid., pp. 156-157.
[6] For a detailed description of this and other practices, see Matthew Josephson, *The Robber Barons* (New York: Harcourt, Brace & World, 1934). The Erie Railroad was controlled by the Erie Ring, a combination put together by Jay Gould.

of reducing prices and profits. At least to some extent, the more some win, the more others lose. A business, for example, may lose its local market to a distant rival now able to compete because of a new mode of transportation. Therefore, business firms began to seek ways to make sure that they, rather than someone else, were the winners. In the absence of laws and government regulation to force them to play the free enterprise game by the rules, it became easy for business firms to circumvent competition through collusive practices and various forms of combinations.

Modern technology was partly responsible for the decline of competition. As mentioned previously, many inventions after the Civil War made possible the use of highly specialized and sometimes quite elaborate and complex machinery. Efficient ways to organize production in large units were also being discovered. One outcome of this was an increase in the average size of many businesses and a decline in the number of firms in many industries. Many of these larger firms had a considerable investment tied up in durable and highly specialized equipment. Interest, maintenance, and depreciation costs were incurred regularly, whether or not the equipment was being used. Fixed costs were beginning to be very large and therefore very important for some firms. When the volume of output was below capacity, additional amounts of product could be produced without any increase in fixed costs and, therefore, with relatively little total additional cost. In these circumstances, the managers of these firms were eager to find ways to sell all the output that could be produced at full capacity.

A third factor leading to the decline of competition was the business cycle. As the United States became an industrial nation, there were more and more periods of boom and bust. During a business depression, competition for survival led to falling prices and output. Business firms learned that the reductions in the price of goods they offered for sale often did not encourage consumers to buy more of them, particularly when the demand for the goods was inelastic—in other words, when a change in price was accompanied by a less than proportionate change in the quantity demanded. The small increases in the volume of sales of these goods also were accompanied by declining profits. An advantage of the business combine or monopoly was that output could be controlled and prices stabilized. Business consolidation was facilitated by the depressions. In the depression of 1893, Andrew Carnegie was able to take advantage of his competitors' economic distress to acquire a wide variety of holdings. He bought iron deposits, ore ships, ports, docks, warehouses, and railroad lines to link his coal, coke, limestone, furnaces, and mills into a single chain. The end of that depression saw the Carnegie Company, later the U.S.

Steel Corporation, in control of the heavy steel field and the fixer of prices for the finished steel manufacturers.

Devices for Achieving Monopoly Power

The era of industrial expansion that began after the end of the Civil War resulted in two related developments important to policy. The first was a trend toward the concentration of production in the hands of a limited number of firms. This trend was in part a logical concomitant of changing technology: as the technically optimum size of firms grew larger, some firms went under. The high proportion of fixed costs associated with the elaborate equipment that the new technology had made possible increased the efforts of each firm to take over the market sales of other firms. In many industrial fields, competition was virtually unimpaired, but in others a few enterprises came to dominate enough of the market to allow them to control prices. The second development, which had more important implications for public policy, was a trend by business firms to limit competition through various types of combinations designed to promote monopoly power.

These combinations usually came in cycles. The first cycle, lasting roughly from 1870 to 1890, used the pool and the trust as monopoly devices. The pool was devised first but was superseded by the trust, which proved to be a more effective type of combination. A wave of federal and state antimonopoly legislation, culminating with the Sherman Antitrust Act, made the trust a rather unpopular vehicle for combination. The trust began to decline in popularity, and by the end of the last century the holding company had achieved dominance. The second cycle was the period of the holding company. An intensive phase of consolidation was facilitated by the holding company device, lasting from 1897 to 1903. A third cycle of industrial combination occurred during the 1920s, when mergers in the form of holding companies or outright mergers between companies were used to consolidate and reduce the number of firms in new industries such as radios, automobiles, and electrical appliances. The fourth cycle of the combination movement, which came after the end of World War II and continued into the 1950s, was characterized by horizontal and vertical merger arrangements.

We should emphasize that the results of various business combinations were often disappointing. There were many reasons for this. Combinations were unable to increase profits or even to perpetuate them in industries subject to stagnation; yet accelerated growth in a new industry created an industrial climate in which combinations were able to prosper. Industrial combinations were also affected by the vagaries of the business cycle and were often incapable of forestalling sharp decreases in profits in years of general business depression. When combinations acquired unmanageable financial structures that subjected them to fixed charges above their minimum earnings capacity, they were often unable to readily adapt themselves to new situations. Many of the earlier combinations were made up of equal producers who sought to curb the excesses of cutthroat competition by allocating production and fixing prices; sooner or later, however, almost all such arrangements ended in failure because one of the participants violated the agreements. The large corporation had to appear first, based on horizontal and vertical integration, before combinations could be truly effective. Finally, combinations did not automatically guarantee competent management.

Pools

The pool was used widely in the 1870s among the railroads and in some manufacturing companies. Under this arrangement, all or almost all the producers of some good or service reached an agreement, usually informally, to share customers, sales, profits, or territories in some fashion. In this way, they hoped to avoid price reductions and the more ruthless kinds of competition among themselves. Pooling arrangements took a number of forms. Two railroads could decide to divide freight revenues evenly, regardless of which one actually transported the freight. For example, in the 1870s the five or six railroads that controlled the shipment of anthracite coal in the five counties of northeastern Pennsylvania divided the total shipment among themselves. Some pools attempted to corner the market for a given product; often, though, pooling agreements were violated soon after their initiation, when one or more of the parties found it irresistible to undercut the others. Other reasons for the short duration of the pools were that competition from a large number of small firms operating in local markets made pooling agreements ineffective and the pools could not adapt rapidly to changing market conditions.

Trusts

In the 1880s, trusts began to replace or exist alongside pools as the primary means for eliminating competition. Under a trust arrangement, owners of a controlling interest in all or almost all of an industry's firms would agree to entrust their ownership shares to the control of one or a few people, called *trustees,* and to receive trust certificates in return. These certificates were issued on the basis of the amount of stock held in trust, and the board of trustees controlled the business policies of the combination. The trustees would direct all firms in the trust as though they were one large firm. With monolithic power, they confronted the competition. They maximized profits, not by being best, but by being biggest. Trusts had a highly centralized form of management in which the trustees were able to elect members of the board of directors of the operating companies whose common stock was deposited with them. Although the trust eventually gave way to other arrangements, it first gave its name to the general government campaign against monopolies.

The trust par excellence was the Standard Oil Trust formed in 1879, forever to be associated with John D. Rockefeller. By 1884, Standard Oil was selling more than 80 percent of all the oil that flowed out of domestic wells. It controlled not only the refining of petroleum but also its retail sales. The trust was organized to eliminate competition at these two levels of operation. In areas in which the competition with the products of other oil companies was keen, the trust reduced the retail prices of its products to attract customers from competing retailers. In many cases, these outlets were unable to compete and sold out to Standard Oil. In areas in which there was no competition, Standard Oil would charge artificially high prices. The trust also tried to control the transportation of petroleum. It was able to negotiate secret rebates from railroads, which were eager to carry Standard's petroleum, and was even able to force one railroad to give it a rate of 10 cents a barrel and to charge other companies 35 cents a barrel, of which 25 cents went back to Standard Oil.[7]

Holding Companies

Holding companies replaced trusts as a device to ensure the firms' survival and to prevent economic warfare among them. A holding company is a corporation that has among its assets shares of stock in other corporations. Controlled corporations are subsidiaries of the holding company, which may be a managing company or an operating company. Those who control a holding company are able through their ownership of stock in other companies to dictate business policies. Competition among companies can be controlled by the holding company. As a direct corporate entity, it can issue stock and borrow

[7] Ida M. Tarbell, *The History of the Standard Oil Company* (New York: McClure, Phillips, 1904).

money through the issuance of corporate bonds. The proceeds from the sale of either or both of these types of securities have often been used to purchase common stock in other holding companies, thus creating a pyramid arrangement. In the 1920s, pyramiding corporate issues in public utility companies channeled power and control over vast corporate empires into the hands of a few utility magnates.

Mergers

The merger is another device used to eliminate competition. Mergers may take several forms. One company may purchase the physical assets or the shares of stock of a previously competing company. Two companies may exchange their stock, and a new company may be formed to buy up the assets or shares of two or more older companies. The General Electric Company, the American Sugar Refining Company, and the International Harvester Company all were born of mergers. The results of mergers are similar to those of holding companies. The power to make decisions about such things as production techniques and selling arrangements is transferred to a single group of people, among whom coordination is achieved largely by central command. As a method of controlling large industries, the merger was somewhat impractical, because it required the consent of each class of security holder to the merger and involved complex negotiations on the terms of exchange.

Mergers also can be classified on the basis of horizontal and vertical arrangements. A horizontal merger is one between firms engaging in the same or similar activities—a union of railroads, bakeries, or shoe manufacturers, for example. There is nothing illegal about a horizontal merger unless it is used to restrict competition, which all too often has been the case. A vertical merger is one between firms engaging in different parts of the producing and selling process. An example would be the union of a shoe manufacturer and a shoe retail store. A steel mill could acquire a coal mine and use its entire output in its own furnace. In a vertical merger, various phases of the production and distribution process are integrated. Again, there is nothing illegal about a vertical merger unless it can be demonstrated that competition is lessened. During the last century, both types of mergers were common, and no laws controlled their impact on competition. The merger arrangement itself did not guarantee success, for profits were often affected by other factors, including business recessions, over which a combination had no control.

Cartels

Cartels are international associations of firms in the same industry established to allocate world markets among their members, regulate the prices in those markets, eliminate competition, and restrict output. The cartel arrangement was less a product of the period that produced the trust and the holding company than of a later period when business firms had more global operations. Almost all cartels have been made up of companies in the production of chemicals, electrical equipment, and synthetic products such as plastics. Their control is usually over the cross-licensing of patents, which has often led to worldwide control of production and trade by what almost amounts to a private government. The cartels may also control the use of trademarks, with each cartel member granted the exclusive right to use a trademark in its own territory.

Interlocking Directorates

An interlocking directorate is an arrangement in which one person sits on the board of directors of two or more companies. In a complex network of many interlocking directorates, it is possible for the interlocked firms to eliminate or reduce competition. The interlocking device has been used not only by industrial firms but also by banks. The latter would place one of their members on the board of directors of companies with which they did business, and thus the banks were in a position to dictate corporate policy and regulate competition. Thus, supposedly independent firms collaborated rather than competed with each other. Although it is now illegal for one person to serve on the board of directors of two companies that produce the same goods and services, interlocking directorates are still used, with interlocks between competitors and between companies and their suppliers or customers.

Anticompetitive Business Practices

A variety of anticompetitive business practices began during the last century, and many still remain in effect. As laws were passed to correct existing abuses, new abuses would arise; some of the devices used to eliminate competition are presented here. It should be emphasized that trusts, pools, and other monopoly arrangements were *originally* devised to circumvent some of the more ruthless kinds of competition, but this certainly did not mean that the trust was free from anticompetitive business practices; if anything, the trust refined such practices.

Preemptive Buying

One tactic that has been used to eliminate competition is preemptive buying. Using this technique, a company would buy up all the supplies or resources needed to make its product. The company does not necessarily need all that it buys, but in this way it can deny vital supplies to its competitors. In the last century, the Southern Pacific Railroad, in an attempt to ensure for itself a monopoly on rail transport eastward out of the state of California, bought up land and constructed rail lines in the few suitable passageways through the Sierra mountains. It did this not to provide services through these places but to block the construction of competing lines. More recently (during the 1920s and 1930s), the Aluminum Company of America (Alcoa) acted similarly. According to the government charges levied against it, Alcoa acted to acquire bauxite deposits, water power sites, and plants in excess of its needs with the intent of denying their use to competitors.[8]

Exclusive Sales Arrangements

In exclusive sales arrangements, manufacturing companies agree to allow distributors and retailers to handle their products only if they agree not to handle similar products made by other manufacturers. A case in point is the American Tobacco Trust, a trust comparable in power and ruthlessness to the Standard Oil Trust. During the latter part of the nineteenth century, the trust controlled distributors at the wholesale and retail levels by offering large discounts to jobbers who agreed to handle exclusively the products of American Tobacco. A commission of 2.5 percent was paid to jobbers who agreed to sell only to the retail trade and only at prices fixed by the trust. If they agreed to handle only the products of the trust, they received an additional 7.5 percent commission. The objective of the arrangement was to leave no room for the products of

---

[8] Robert F. Lanzilloti, *The Structure of American Industry: Some Case Studies,* ed. Walter Adams, 3rd ed. (New York: Macmillan, 1961), chap. 6.

other tobacco manufacturers. American Tobacco was able to do this because of its economic power: it almost completely controlled the supply of cigarettes and other tobacco products.

Tying Agreements

Tying agreements are somewhat similar to exclusive sales arrangements. In a tying agreement, a company requires a buyer to purchase one or more additional products as a condition for purchasing the desired product. For the tying agreement to be successful, the desired product must have few substitutes and must also be relatively less interchangeable than the tied item. In one well-known case, the International Salt Company, which had patents on two salt-dispensing machines, would lease the machines only if the lessee would agree to buy all salt to be used in the machine from International Salt. The United Shoe Machinery Company once compelled shoemakers to purchase other materials and intermediate products from it as a condition for purchasing shoe machinery, which limited the other sellers of the tied products from competing in the market. But the courts have generally disallowed tying agreements in which the end result is the lessening of competition, particularly when the tied product is a legal monopoly such as a patent.

Patent Control

To stimulate invention, the federal government grants patents, which give exclusive control over articles and processes for seventeen years. These legal grants sometimes have been used to establish and maintain a monopolistic position. Patent rights are property and can be rented with conditions of use specified. They thus have formed the basis of agreements to maintain prices, allocate markets, and restrict production. Patents promote invention by granting temporary monopolies to inventors, but they have often had the effect of subverting competition. An example of this was the Ethyl Gasoline Corporation, jointly owned by Standard Oil of New Jersey and General Motors, which held the patent on tetra-ethyl, "antiknock" gasoline. It licensed all refiners and eleven thousand independent retail distributors, forcing them to agree to maintain a price differential over ordinary gasoline and to follow the big oil companies' price policies before they would be allowed to make and use tetra-ethyl.

Price Discrimination

Discriminatory pricing policies are almost too numerous to describe. One example is the basing point system. To avoid giving mills located near a consuming center an advantage in obtaining business, steel corporations adopted the idea of selling all iron and steel products, except rails, at delivered prices only. The delivered prices were the sum of the base price added to the cost of transportation from Pittsburgh to the destination, regardless of the origin of the shipment or the actual freight cost. Thus the "Pittsburgh-plus" system was born. Prices were quoted on the basis of Pittsburgh, even though the product may have been made in Chicago. Buyers in the Chicago area, for example, were required to pay $7.50 a ton in phantom freight—the freight "plus" from Pittsburgh—on steel produced in Chicago by the local subsidiaries of U.S. Steel. In 1948, the Supreme Court declared that the basing point system was a monopolistic form of pricing.

In attempting to eliminate competition, business firms have also used predatory pricing practices. Firms with several products or with sales in more than one market area were able to use predatory pricing. A firm with a chain of grocery stores, for example, might lower prices at one of its outlets that was in close competition with an independent grocery store. It could sustain the resulting temporary losses at the one outlet by relying on the profits it received from other outlets. In this way, the chain could drive the independent store out of business. Then it could raise its prices in what had become its own local monopoly. Firms with many products used similar tactics to eliminate rival firms with one product. Price discrimination occurs when a seller charges different prices to the same or different buyers for the same good. This in itself is not necessarily unfair, for it may be more economical for a firm to sell in bulk, and those economies can be passed on to the consumer. But often discriminatory pricing has been used to undercut the competition of other firms.

Business firms also have resorted to price fixing. This approach has always been tempting because firms can reduce or even eliminate the risk of economic loss. The power to fix prices requires having the power to control the market. Price fixing may take two forms, either overt collusion between business firms to set prices or price leadership, in which one firm sets the price. Collusion may occur when several firms agree to fix bids on government contracts, with each firm taking its turn in submitting the lowest bid. In some industries there is a relatively small number of firms, and one dominates the market by virtue of its size and economic power. The dominant firm acts as the price leader, and the others set their prices accordingly, because of fear of the consequences if they do not or because of the benefit of the price stability that will occur if they do. Price competition disappears, and often the prices are higher than they would be in a competitive market. The potential harm to price competition from adopting the same prices as those of the industry leader appears to be as great as that stemming from an outright conspiracy to fix prices.

Reciprocal Agreements

Reciprocal agreements are arrangements in which firms agree to purchase certain products from each other. This kind of thing happens all the time, and there is nothing inherently wrong with reciprocal agreements unless the end result is the lessening of competition. This may well happen. Company A may refuse to buy products from Company B unless it in turn agrees to buy Company A's products. Company A may be able, through the volume of its purchases, to compel Company B to reciprocate by buying its products, and Company A can threaten to purchase its goods elsewhere unless such an arrangement is made. In one case, Consolidated Foods was able to use its buying power to force its suppliers to purchase products from one of its affiliates. In another case, General Motors told the railroads that unless they bought GM locomotives, GM would take its shipping business to other lines. In both cases, the courts found these activities to constitute a substantial lessening of competition and ordered them stopped.

RAILROAD REGULATION

In his novel *Giants in the Earth,* O. E. Rölvaag describes the coming of the railroad to South Dakota:

> One fine day a strange monster came writhing westward over the prairie, from Worthington to Luverne; it was the greatest and most memorable event that had yet happened in these parts. The monster crawled along with a terrible speed, but when it came near, it did not crawl at all; it rushed forward in tortuous windings, with an awful roar, while black, curling smoke streaked out behind it in the air. People felt that day a joy that almost frightened them; for it seemed now that all their troubles were over, that there could be no more hardships to contend with— at least, that was what the Sognings solemnly affirmed. For now that the railway

had come as far as this, it wouldn't take long before they would see it winding its way into Sioux Falls.[9]

Few inventions have had more impact on American life than the railroad. To the farmers, the railroads brought many blessings. They enabled the farmers to get their produce to market, supplied them with agricultural implements, catalogues, and other accoutrements of the outside world, and ended rural isolation as passenger trains connected the farms with the cities. The railroads contributed to the development of mass transportation and distribution and to large-scale corporations in their modern form. They also helped urbanize the U.S. economy by carrying laborers and supplies to newly built factories in the cities. Many railroad innovations and inventions improved the economy—for example, the Pullman car and the creation of a standard gauge, which enabled the integration of the nation's rail system. Methods of financing and promoting railroad expansion also influenced the economy. Railroad securities were one of the largest outlets for the U.S. peoples' savings. State and local governments also extended financial aid to the railroads in the form of loans, grants, and property tax exemption. Almost all railroads tended to rely on bonds for financial expansion; however, the heavy fixed interest charge they incurred often led to financial disaster.

The railroad industry had many of the same characteristics of industrial capitalism that were previously described—increasing costs leading to large-scale production, keen competition, and a resulting tendency toward monopoly. But it was in the railroads that the country first encountered the problems that arise under such conditions. There was a period of competition that eventually degenerated into a struggle for the survival of the fittest. One condition that contributed to undesirable practices by the railroads was the high ratio of fixed to operating costs. In addition, the railroads' total fixed costs bore no relation to the volume of traffic once these fixed costs had been incurred or once the railroads had been constructed. Rate wars were common, and in response, railroad operators began to expand and consolidate their holdings in order to operate more efficiently and secure greater profits. The earliest type of combination is exemplified by the railroad empire created by Cornelius Vanderbilt, who bought control of competing lines operating from New York City to Albany and from Albany to Buffalo, and formed the New York Central system.[10]

[9] O. E. Rölvaag, *Giants in the Earth* (New York: Harper & Row, 1927), p. 327.

[10] Matthew Josephson, *The Robber Barons* (New York: Harcourt, Brace & World, 1934), pp. 134–138.

A later form of railroad combination was the pool, formed to apportion business, fix rates, and thus avoid ruinous competition. For example, the five or six railroads that controlled the shipment of anthracite coal in northeastern Pennsylvania allocated to each of themselves certain percentages of the total shipment of coal. Fines were collected from those railroads that exceeded their allocations, and in turn, the money from the fines was distributed among the railroads that had carried less than their allocated portions of coal.

Reasons for Railroad Regulation

In the railroads' early days, the prevailing government policy was one of aid rather than regulation. The promise of swift transportation, industrial development, and access to market enhanced the value of the railroads, and the public interest was identified with the railroads' interests. But there were a number of abuses, resulting in part from cutthroat competitive practices in which railroads disregarded the interests of consumers and shippers. Rate discrimination was one abuse, which entailed setting different rates for different places, for different commodities, or for different firms. Railroads charged more for short hauls than for long hauls, and rates were higher between local, noncompetitive points. Deviations from published tariffs were a common means of rate discrimination, and rebates were given to favored shippers and localities. One of the reasons for these practices was the high ratio of fixed costs to operating costs. Traffic attracted by charging rates that brought in anything at all over operating costs, was better than no traffic at all; at least it brought in something to help defray fixed costs.

Immediately after the Civil War, the farmers and small businessmen began pressing for railroad regulation. The farmers were particularly hard hit because they were absolutely dependent on the railroads, which, unregulated by any government body, practiced various forms of price discrimination, the money from which often went to pay dividends on watered stock. The prices for agricultural products fluctuated widely in domestic markets, and a high protective tariff prevented foreign manufactured goods from competing effectively with U.S. manufactured goods, whose prices remained high. The farmers' discontent coalesced in the Grange movement, which became an important political force at the state level.[11] The Grange wanted the regulation of

[11] Broadus Mitchell, *American Economic History* (Boston: Houghton Mifflin, 1947), p. 697.

railroads to bring about lower freights and fares and to ban discriminatory rates for different places and people. It also wanted cheap money, an income tax, and a reduction of the protective tariff except on agricultural products. But the Grange's main impact was on the passage of laws which would regulate the railroads.

State Regulation of Railroads

The Grange, together with its allies—merchants and other small businessmen who also resented rate discrimination—gained control of a number of midwestern state governments and enacted a series of regulatory laws since known as "Granger legislation."[12] In 1871, Illinois created a railroad and warehouse commission authorized to fix maximum rates for intrastate freight and passenger service on the railroads, as well as rates for storing grain in public warehouses and grain elevators. The commission was empowered to prosecute when a railroad charged a higher rate for a short than for a long haul over the same line in the same direction. Also in 1871, the Minnesota legislature prescribed maximum rates for passengers and freight and appointed a railroad commission to enforce the railroad laws. In 1874, a board of railway commissioners was authorized to fix maximum rates. The Iowa Railroad Act of 1874 followed the Minnesota model of setting maximum rates, with provisions for a railroad commission empowered to reduce rates below the maximum when that could be done without injury to the railroad. Wisconsin and other states followed the Minnesota and Iowa examples.

Federal Regulation of Railroads

The farmers' anger over railroad abuses also affected the federal government. The railroads continued to combine and strengthen, and the farmers continued to find themselves exploited, suffering from high rates and rate discrimination. Stock watering and manipulation and bribing of state legislatures injured a further section of the population. Between 1875 and 1880, pooling arrangements spread rapidly all over the United States. Whenever competition promised to regulate railroad rates through supply and demand, the pool was used to preserve dividends on watered stock and interest on fixed obligations. To a

---

[12] Ibid., p. 701.

certain extent, the railroads were caught up in a frenetic round of speculation and overbuilding, and they resorted to frequent issues of common stock to provide investment funds. Competition on interstate rail routes brought rate wars: in one year, the rate for fourth-class mail from New York to Chicago fell from $1.80 a pound to $.25 a pound.[13] In turn, the rate wars, particularly on trunk lines, led to the first pooling arrangement in 1874 when, at the Saratoga Conference, the owners of the Erie, Pennsylvania, and New York Central railroads met to devise a means for suppressing competition in trunk line traffic. But the pools, far from being a remedy for the evils of excess competition, only aggravated the problem they attempted to cure. The high rates they were able to maintain often attracted the attention of speculators and led to the creation of rival roads. After prolonged railroad wars, in which competing promoters neglected the interest of the shippers and others, E. H. Harriman achieved control of the Union Pacific and Southern Pacific, and James J. Hill, with Morgan backing, gained control of the Great Northern and the Northern Pacific. The New York Central and the Pennsylvania Railroad established a community of interest between themselves; the Pennsylvania Railroad obtained stock control of the Baltimore and Ohio and the Norfolk and Western, and the New York Central acquired the Lake Erie and Western and leased the Baltimore and Albany. These two major roads also controlled the Chesapeake and Ohio. These railroad combinations were possible because stock ownership had become so diffused that often a comparatively small block of shares was enough to give one railroad decisive control over the management of another railroad.

Federal government regulation of the railroads began with the passage of the Interstate Commerce Act of 1887. It created the Interstate Commerce Commission, the first major federal regulatory agency. It outlawed certain discriminatory acts used by railroads against shippers; for example, the act made it unlawful for railroads to charge a higher rate for short hauls on shipments on the same line in the same direction. Schedules of freight rates and passenger rates alike had to be made public to prevent discrimination against shippers, and rate increases could be made only after ten days' advance public notice had been given. The Interstate Commerce Act was followed by the Hepburn Act of 1906, which broadened the jurisdiction of the Interstate Commerce Commission to cover other forms of transportation such as pipelines and

[13] Chester W. Wright, *Economic History of the United States,* 2nd ed. (New York: McGraw-Hill, 1949), p. 597.

express companies. The Mann–Elkins Act of 1910 extended this jurisdiction further to include telephone, telegraph, and cable and wireless companies engaged in interstate commerce.

GOVERNMENT REGULATION OF TRUSTS

As mentioned previously, the enormous growth in the size of business units, often with consequent damage to competition, took place in the period following the end of the Civil War and continued unabated until the end of the century. To circumvent competition, various types of business combinations were formed—the pool, the trust, and the holding company. These combinations engaged in various forms of abuses that aroused the general public. Freedom of enterprise was threatened as combinations were able to restrict entry into many business fields. Consumers were at the mercy of the trusts, for through control over markets, they were able to set prices on many basic necessities. In particular, there was public resentment against the Standard Oil Trust and the Sugar Trust. The former was criticized for its goal of monopoly and for the practices it used to eliminate competition; the latter was charged with fixing prices and eliminating competition. The Standard Oil, Sugar, and other trusts were able to apply political pressure to achieve their goals; e.g., the Sugar Trust engineered the passage of protective tariffs to protect itself against foreign competition. Then it was free to raise the domestic prices of sugar.

The Influence of Populism

Public indignation by itself was not enough to enact antitrust laws, but the same political force was present that had contributed to the passage of federal and state laws to regulate railroads. Even though the influence of the Grange had declined by 1880, various farm–labor parties, the most important of which was the Farmers' Alliance, were created as part of the general political movement known as *populism*. Populism expressed the anger of the farmer, the factory worker, and the small businessman against the trusts, railroads, and big banks. The trusts, they felt, overcharged them for the necessities of life they had to buy, the railroads overcharged them for what they had to transport, and the banks charged them usurious rates when they had to borrow. These groups felt that the politicians of both the major political parties represented vested business interests; therefore, it would be better for them to elect their own representatives. The farmers, together with the nascent labor movement, were able in the decade between 1880 and 1890 to elect many senators, congressmen, and state legislators supporting their interests. A national third party, the Populist party, emerged in the presidential election of 1892.[14] Pragmatic Republican and Democrat politicians took notice and concluded that the best way to defeat a competing political movement was to incorporate some of its more important ideas.

State Antitrust Laws

We should emphasize that the state courts rather than the state legislatures were the first to regulate trusts under the provisions of common law, which is a system of unwritten law not necessarily expressed in written statutes. Until 1889 there were no state laws covering industrial combinations and trusts, but there was a large body of common doctrine on which courts could rely. Early in English law it was established that contracts or agreements in restraint of trade were void and, therefore, unenforceable. English common law was carried over into U.S. law and generally accommodated the rising American antitrust movement; in fact, the state courts used the common law to outlaw trusts. In what is probably the most important common law antitrust case, the Ohio Supreme Court in 1892 declared the Standard Oil Trust to be illegal.[15] The state charged that the Standard Oil Company of Ohio had violated the law by placing the control of its affairs in the hands of trustees, nearly none of whom were residents of the state. In its decision, the court ruled that the Standard Oil Trust, domiciled in New York, exerted a virtual monopoly over petroleum production, refining, and distribution all over the country and ordered the Standard Oil Company of Ohio to dissociate itself from the trust.

The first antitrust laws were enacted by the states rather than by the federal government because the impact of populism was felt first at the state level. In 1889, the state of Kansas passed a law outlawing trusts, which were defined as combinations formed to restrict trade, fix prices, or prevent competition. In the same year, similar laws were passed in Michigan, Tennessee, and Texas. By 1895, seventeen states had passed various types of antitrust laws. These laws

[14] The Populist party gained twenty-two electoral votes and more than a million popular votes in 1892.

[15] *State v. Standard Oil Company,* 49 Ohio 137 (1892).

varied considerably in content, but almost all forbade monopolies and combinations in restraint of trade and provided criminal penalties and administrative machinery for prosecution. In addition, they attacked particular forms of agreements and specific practices that were thought likely to bring about control of the market. The state antitrust laws, however, were limited, because in the U.S. system of government the states can regulate only intrastate commerce.

Federal Antitrust Laws

The application of common law to business combinations did little to slow down their growth. Remedies were difficult to enforce and rarely succeeded in restoring competition. What is more, these applications of common law were statewide only, and a large combination could operate in other states even after being declared illegal in one. States varied in their interpretation and application of the law, and there was no all-encompassing federal law. State antitrust statutes were at best in an embryonic stage and applied only to intrastate commerce. Thus the movement toward industrial concentration was viewed with concern by many people, and this concern crystallized in the populist reform programs. In 1888, both the major political parties referred in their presidential platforms to the dangers inherent in trusts, and in 1890, during President Benjamin Harrison's administration, the Sherman Antitrust Act was passed.

The Sherman Act is the most important of all the federal antimonopoly laws, and it probably is one of the most important measures ever passed by Congress. It marked a major milestone in business–government relations, for with the passage of the act there was no turning back to full laissez-faire capitalism, and the federal government began the long task of regulating business. In 1914, the Clayton Act and the Federal Trade Commission Act were passed concurrently. Both acts increased the federal government's role in the area of antitrust policy.

The Standard Oil Trust[16]

The Standard Oil Trust, the most powerful monopoly in the history of the United States, was created as the Standard Oil Company of Ohio in 1870 by

[16] The sources used are Matthew Josephson, *The Robber Barons* (New York: Harcourt, Brace & World, 1934); Ida M. Tarbell, *The History of the Standard Oil Trust*, vols. 1 and 2 (New York: Macmillan, 1925); and *U.S. v. Standard Oil of N.J.*, 221 U.S. 106 (1911).

the consummate industrial capitalist of the last century, John D. Rockefeller. He was the living embodiment of the Protestant work ethic that was associated with John Calvin, the religious reformer who preached a doctrine of salvation that later proved to be consistent with the principles of a capitalist system. According to Calvin, hard work, diligence, and thrift were earthly means through which people would fully use the talents given to them by God. Salvation was associated with achievement on this earth, and Rockefeller was an achiever. In 1856, at the age of sixteen, he went to work as a bookkeeper at a salary of $15 a month; by 1880, he was the richest man in the world. In three years of work as a bookkeeper, he saved $800, with which he eventually created the Standard Oil Company. Rockefeller was pious. He read the Bible every night.

When Rockefeller created Standard Oil in 1870, it was one of thirty oil companies in Cleveland alone.[17] By 1880, his was the only oil company left in Cleveland; indeed, left in Ohio. Expanding into Pennsylvania, Standard Oil gained control over the oil fields in that state.[18] It became not only a refiner, but a producer of oil. Thus it could control and direct the flow of crude petroleum into its refineries. By doing so, it could drive out competitors and compel customers to buy oil at its prices. It could also compel the railroads to give it special freight rates. Before Standard Oil gained control over the Pennsylvania oil fields, cutthroat competition was the order of the day. Prices on a given day could vary from 5 to 15 cents a gallon for crude oil. By gaining control of the supply of oil, Standard Oil changed that; it set prices at 20 cents a gallon.

By 1880, Standard Oil was on its way to becoming a national entity. To do this, it had to attract more capital and expand. In 1881, the Standard Oil Trust was created. All companies that were a part of Standard Oil conveyed their "in trust" to Standard Oil. For the shares they deposited, they received trust certificates. The trustees then became the direct stockholders of all the companies in the system and were empowered to serve as directors. They could dissolve any corporation within the system and form new ones. The trust arrangement enabled Standard Oil to get its hands on large amounts of capital, which it used to expand its control over the oil industry. In 1886, net earnings amounted to $15 million on invested capital of $70 million, a return of better than 20 percent. The earnings of the Standard Oil Trust provided it with the capital to gain control of oil production in other parts of the United States.

[17] Rockefeller had a partner named Henry M. Flagler who later became a railroad tycoon and a Florida real estate developer. Standard Oil originally was a refiner of oil.

[18] The U.S. oil industry had its start in Pennsylvania when oil was discovered there after the Civil War. Pennsylvania was the major oil-producing state until oil was discovered in Texas.

The Standard Oil Trust was directly responsible for the passage of antitrust laws, first at the state level and then, when the Sherman Act was passed in 1890, at the federal level. Investigations took place in Ohio and New York. Standard Oil was accused of blowing up the refinery of a competitor in Buffalo. Standard Oil, though sued for damages, was acquitted. Nevertheless, hearings held by the State of New York indicated that the refinery was blown up by Standard Oil. In Ohio, Standard Oil was accused of bribing politicians and violating the state charter laws by creating a trust. When a prosecuting attorney in Cleveland began a suit to annul the charter of the Standard Oil Company, he was told by the state chairman of his political party, "You have been in politics long enough to know that no man in public office owes the public anything." Nevertheless, the charter was revoked, and the company moved to New Jersey.

After the Ohio decision of 1892, the Standard Oil Company reorganized itself as a holding company. This holding company, the Standard Oil Company of New Jersey, was given voting control over the other companies of the Standard Oil group, and it exchanged its stock for the stocks of the firms that formerly had been controlled by the Standard Oil Trust. Through this process of exchange, the holding company obtained $97 million in stock, practically the same amount of trust certificates as had been issued at the time the Standard Oil Trust was dissolved in 1892. Standard Oil of New Jersey had massive economic power. In 1906, the Bureau of Corporations reported that about 91 percent of the refining industry was directly or indirectly under Standard control.[19] In 1904, the Bureau of Corporations reported that Standard Oil controlled 85 percent of domestic sales of refined oil.[20] In the same year, the total production of refined oil in the United States was 27.1 million barrels; of this total, Standard Oil and its affiliates produced 23.5 million barrels, or around 86 percent of domestic output.[21]

Some indication of the Standard Oil Trust's economic power can be seen in Table 2-1, which presents the ratio of net earnings to the value of Standard Oil's property from 1890 to 1906. The net earnings of Standard for the ten years ending in 1906 averaged more than 25 percent of the average value of its property. During the same ten-year period, the ratio of net earnings to capital ranged from 48.8 percent to 84 percent, the average for the period being more than 61 percent. The ratio of dividends to capital ranged from 30 percent to 48

[19] *Brief for the United States,* vol. 1, no. 725 (1909): 8.

[20] Ibid., p. 9.

[21] *Brief for the United States,* vol. 2 (1909): 18.

TABLE 2-1   Dividends and Profits of the Standard Oil Company, 1890-1906

Year	Percent Rate of Dividends	Percent of Net Earnings to Capital Stock	Percent of Net Earnings to Property
1890	12.0%	19.7%	17.6%
1891	12.0	16.8	13.8
1892	12.2	19.7	15.4
1893	12.0	15.9	11.9
1894	12.0	10.0	11.6
1895	17.0	24.8	17.3
1896	31.0	35.0	23.5
1897	33.0	48.8	27.6
1898	30.0	48.8	27.6
1899	33.0	48.8	27.6
1900	48.0	57.0	27.6
1901	48.0	53.7	25.1
1902	45.0	66.3	29.2
1903	44.0	83.5	32.4
1904	36.0	62.6	21.7
1905	40.0	58.4	18.7
1906	40.0	84.5	24.6

Source: *Brief for the United States,* 1, no. 725 (1909): 6; 2, 8–9.

percent, with the average for the period being more than 40 percent. The ratio would have been much higher if allowance had been made for the fact that Standard was overcapitalized by $30 million.

Theodore Roosevelt distinguished between "good" trusts and "bad" trusts. A good trust was one that gained its position through economies engendered by large-scale operations short of complete monopoly and took no unfair advantage of competitors or consumers. A bad trust competed unfairly and abused its monopoly power. Standard Oil was in the latter category. It had perpetrated a number of abuses on competitors and consumers. It had secured rebates and other discriminatory favors from the railroads, and it had bribed railway and other employees for information about competitors. Through its ownership of almost all the oil pipelines in the United States, Standard controlled the flow of crude oil and was able to fix prices. The independent refiners were unable to obtain crude oil except from Standard itself, and Standard would allow them only as much crude oil as it chose and thus was able to prevent them from expanding their business. Standard allocated sales areas among its subsidiaries so as to eliminate competition among them. Because of the rebates and other favors it obtained from the railroads, Standard was able to sell oil in competitive areas at prices that were profitable to it but that left no profit for its competition. And then, when it had eliminated the competition, Standard raised its prices.

SUMMARY

Industrial and railroad monopolies were created around 1880 and continued into this century. The primary reason for instituting the various types of combinations was the manufacturers' desire to restrict or eliminate competition and thus to establish monopoly prices. This was done by having business monopolies control supply. A monopoly price is likely to be higher than a competitive price, for the monopolist can limit supply and by this means prevent prices from falling to the level they would if determined by competition. A second reason for establishing monopolies was the hope of those organizing them that they would thus achieve the economies of the trust. This is because a trust can almost always secure raw materials more cheaply than would be possible in a state of competition. A trust can often save money by vertically integrating so that it is assured of an ample supply of raw materials at cost. A trust is also supposed to achieve certain economies of production through specialization of plant and machinery and also of business talents.

QUESTIONS FOR DISCUSSION

1. The philosophy of social Darwinism was used as a rationale to justify the accumulation of great wealth by Carnegie, Rockefeller, and other industrial magnates of the nineteenth century. Define social Darwinism, and explain how it was used as a justification by such magnates.
2. Discuss the factors that led to the decline of competition in many industries during the latter part of the nineteenth century.

3. Differentiate among the following types of business combinations: pools, trusts, and holding companies.
4. What is preemptive buying?
5. What prompted railroads to form combinations such as pools?
6. Discuss the methods used by the Standard Oil Company to eliminate competition.
7. What is a reciprocal agreement?
8. What was the "Pittsburgh plus" system?

RECOMMENDED READINGS

Burns, Arthur. *The Decline of Competition*. New York: McGraw-Hill, 1936.

Chandler, Alfred D., Jr., ed. *The Railroads: The Nation's First Big Business*. New York: Harcourt, Brace & World, 1965.

Clark, John D. *The Federal Trust Policy*. Baltimore: Johns Hopkins Press, 1931.

Faulkner, Harold V. *The Decline of Laissez Faire, 1897-1917*. New York: Holt, Rinehart & Winston, 1951, chaps. 5, 8, and 15.

Hofstadter, Richard, *Social Darwinism in American Thought*. Boston: Beacon Press,1969.

Jones, Edward. *The Trust Problem in the United States*. New York: Macmillan, 1921.

Josephson, Matthew. *The Robber Barons*. New York: Harcourt, Brace & World, 1934.

Mitchell, Broadus. *American Economic History*. Boston: Houghton Mifflin, 1947.

Chapter 3

Extension of Government Control over Business: The New Deal to the Present

During the Depression decade of the 1930s, government regulation and control of business greatly expanded. By the end of the decade, much of the legislative framework for government's current relations with business had been completed. Direct government regulation was extended over the electrical power and airline industries. Antitrust laws were strengthened by the passage of new legislation, including the Robinson–Patman Act, and consumer protection, particularly in the area of false or misleading advertising, also was improved with the passage of the Wheeler–Lea Amendment. A number of changes were made in the banking system, including the creation of the Federal Deposit Insurance Corporation to insure individual deposits against loss in the event of a bank failure. The position of the individual investor was also improved by federal legislation designed to regulate the securities market. Moreover, there was direct government intervention to support business. In 1932, the Reconstruction Finance Corporation was created and financed by the federal government to make loans to business firms in economic difficulty. The first effort at national economic planning occurred in 1933 when the National Industrial Recovery Act was passed. The federal government also entered the mortgage market through the creation of the Home Owners Loan Corporation to refinance the mortgages of financially distressed homeowners.

Other New Deal measures had a more indirect impact on business. The National Labor Relations Act, passed in 1935, greatly enhanced the bargaining power of unions and made them a countervailing force to business. New Deal efforts to regulate hours, wages, and working conditions culminated in the passage of the Walsh–Healey Act and the Fair Labor Standards Act. The

Walsh–Healey Act illustrated the leverage that the federal government could use to enforce compliance with an economic or social goal. It required business firms with federal contracts for $10,000 or more to limit working hours to eight per day or forty per week and to pay wages that were no less than the industry's minimum. The Fair Labor Standards Act enacted minimum wages and maximum hours for labor engaged in interstate commerce or in the production of goods sold in interstate commerce. In the area of social welfare, the Social Security Act provided for federal pensions for people sixty-five years and older and for survivors' benefits to widows and orphans. The cost of social security was financed in part by a payroll tax on employers.

Until the 1960s, almost all government legislation affecting business was economic. Within the past twenty years, however, the pattern of legislation has changed to reflect shifts in societal values. These shifts have occurred in several areas—ecology, consumerism, civil rights, and women's liberation. The legislative approach that has been used attempts to influence private decision makers to achieve specific social ends. New government regulatory agencies have been created in such areas as affirmative action, consumer protection, and environmental protection, and their regulatory efforts have cut across virtually every form of private industry. Changes in societal values also have caused an increase in the amount of federal funds allocated for social welfare programs. The federal government, through a variety of programs, has made a commitment to alleviate social inequalities but, in the process, has drastically altered the distribution of the federal budget. In 1950, federal budget outlays for social welfare amounted to one-fourth of the total outlays; by 1981, the outlays for social welfare had increased to one-half of what had become a much larger total of the budgetary outlays.[1]

THE GREAT DEPRESSION

The Great Depression was an economic and social catastrophe with no previous parallel in U.S. history. Before the 1930s, there had been periods of unemployment and falling prices, but they were rarely of long duration, and they were generally followed by a reasonably prompt recovery. But all this changed with the Depression, which began with the collapse of the stock market in the fall of 1929 and continued until 1941, when preparation for war

[1] Executive Office of the President, Office of Management and Budget, *The Budget of the United States Government, 1982* (Washington, D.C.: U.S. Government Printing Office, 1981), p. 480.

eventually created full employment in the U.S. economy. Prolonged mass unemployment became the norm for the decade of the 1930s. At its worst, 25 percent of the labor force was out of work.[2] But the Depression meant more than unemployment; it also meant idle production capacity, loss of profits, business bankruptcies, a fall in the standard of living, decreases in the value of property, the closing of many banks, and considerable social unrest. It can be said that the Depression did more to reshape the U.S. economic system than any other event of the nineteenth or twentieth centuries, with the possible exception of the Civil War, for the government's efforts to alleviate it changed the market system.

The Causes of the Depression

Economists disagree on the causes of the Great Depression.[3] One theory suggests that during the 1920s many business firms enlarged their productive capacity at a rate that was too rapid to be sustained into and through the 1930s. These businesses expanded by ordering and installing new equipment, building additional floor space, and adding to their inventories of materials and products. As long as the spending continued, jobs were plentiful and times were prosperous. Indeed, the 1920s was a period of prosperity, with the mass production of the automobile stimulating the development of a number of related industries. But beginning in 1929, business firms discovered they had been creating too much productive capacity, and consequently, decreased their spending. Workers who had jobs necessitated by the previous expansion were either discharged or required to work fewer hours for lower wages. Earning less income, these workers inevitably spent less. A cumulative decline in employment, earnings, and income, in spending on the expansion of productive capacity, and in expenditures on products ensued.

Still, the Depression might have been avoided, at least in part, if the market system had functioned the way it was supposed to. In an ideal market economy, the forces of supply and demand should have caused price readjustments, and there should have been a series of reactions to price changes. Consumer and capital goods in oversupply would have declined in price, and those types of labor and other resources in oversupply would also have declined in

[2] *Economic Report of the President, 1976* (Washington, D.C.: U.S. Government Printing Office, 1976), p. 380.

[3] John Kenneth Galbraith, *The Great Crash* (Boston: Houghton Mifflin, 1972), chap. 9.

price. The fall in the price of consumer goods would eventually have induced buyers to purchase larger quantities of them, and the fall in the price of labor would have prompted business firms to hire more labor. In other words, an ideal market system would have been self-correcting because all markets were assumed to be competitive and labor and capital able to go wherever needed. Competition among sellers or buyers would have set an equilibrium price that would have cleared the market of any surplus product or resource. It can be argued that the pattern of response was defective. There was resistance to reducing prices because business firms held monopolistic power over their products and chose not to permit their prices to fall. Instead, they restricted the volume of physical output of their products to amounts that could be sold at prices higher than would prevail in a purely competitive market. Holding companies controlled large segments of the utilities and railroads and curtailed investment in operating plants to maintain dividends, the interruption of which meant default on bonds and the collapse of the holding company structure. Unionized labor, although at that time lacking the economic power of big business, did try to resist wage cuts, even though the consequence was unemployment. Income was also distributed unequally, with the top 1 percent of all income earners in 1929 receiving 14.5 percent of the total income and the top 5 percent receiving around a third of the total income.[4] This unequal income distribution meant the economy depended on a high level of investment or a high level of luxury consumer spending, or both. In contrast, the top 20 percent of all income earners received 42.7 percent of the income in 1987.

The Depression's Effect on Public Policy

Regardless of the cause or causes of the Great Depression, however, forces were set in motion that produced an increase in federal economic and political power unequaled in scope and purpose. As the Depression grew worse, public policy was pushed far beyond the traditional regulatory techniques that had been devised for railroad regulation and antitrust. The principal concern became the stability of the nation's whole economy; the problems that called for action transcended the boundaries of any single industry. Public policy was increasingly forced to cope with the broader issues of large-scale unemployment and poverty and with ways of stimulating production and new invest-

---

[4] Maurice Leven, Harold G. Moulton, and Charles Warburton, *America's Capacity to Consume* (Washington, D.C.: Brookings Institution, 1934), chap. 5.

ment. The Depression also changed the country's political and social milieu. Politically, as the prestige of corporate managers and financiers declined, the federal government became more sensitive to the claims of labor, farmers, and small business firms. President Franklin D. Roosevelt's New Deal provided a vehicle for the organization of these groups, thereby counterbalancing the power of the large business firms. In addition, the New Deal instituted new laws to regulate business.

When Franklin D. Roosevelt became president in March 1933, the nation was near economic collapse. Industry was operating at less than half its full capacity, the rate of unemployment had reached 25 percent, prices were at their lowest point during the whole Depression, the banking system was on the verge of disintegration, and the gross national product of the country had declined 50 percent from its 1929 level. A number of economic measures were enacted, some of which were temporary and cosmetic, but others of which permanently restructured the U.S. economy. New Deal measures related directly to business can be divided into several broad categories: increased regulation and control of industry, reforms of the banking system, closer government control of the securities market, regulation of public utilities and airlines, and consumer protection.

GOVERNMENT REGULATION OF BUSINESS

It should not be assumed that increased government intervention in business began with the New Deal, for some changes were initiated by the Hoover administration. In the early stages of the Depression, President Herbert Hoover followed the traditional policy of laissez faire and waited for the self-correcting forces of the market to work. Gradually, however, he began to use governmental powers and influence to relieve economic distress.[5] The Reconstruction Finance Corporation was organized to assist banks, railroads, insurance companies, and other enterprises threatened with insolvency. The federal government contributed $500 million in capital, and the corporation was empowered to borrow an additional $1.5 billion through the sale of debenture bonds. The creation of the corporation put the federal government in the business of making loans to private firms and set a precedent for a later time when the government would decide to make loans to firms faced with bankruptcy,

[5] Herbert Stein, *The Fiscal Revolution in America* (Chicago: University of Chicago Press, 1969), pp. 6–26.

such as Lockheed and Penn Central. By 1933, the Reconstruction Finance Corporation had advanced more than $2 billion to business, and during the Roosevelt administration it was enlarged so that it could also make loans to newly created public financial institutions. During its twelve-year life, the corporation lent $50 billion to businesses.

The National Industrial Recovery Act, 1933

The purpose of the National Industrial Recovery Act (NIRA) was to relax antitrust policies designed to promote competition and instead to permit business firms to modify or even to eliminate competition. The devices used included restricting an industry's total production and assigning quotas to individual producers. Although deliberate attempts to reduce competition and restrict output were socially unjustifiable, it was felt that once the industrial system was stabilized an economy of abundance would result. But the NIRA did not work as well in practice as it did in theory. One effect it had was the creation of a price structure unfair to the interests of consumers. It was also felt that the codes of fair competition were breeding monopolies, and large firms did engage in price fixing under the codes. Moreover, the degree of government control necessary to prevent abuses of the codes was immense, beyond what business and the general public were willing to accept. In May 1935, in the Schechter Poultry case, the Supreme Court held the NIRA to be unconstitutional on the grounds that it had provided for an unconstitutional delegation of legislative power to the president in his code-making authority and that the wages and hours of employees working in local plants were not subject to regulation because the processes of production did not come under the constitutional meaning of interstate commerce.[6]

Revival of Antitrust Policies

With the end of the NIRA, there was renewed interest in enforcing measures designed to promote competition and to halt various types of price-fixing arrangements. There now was a new trend in U.S. business, namely, the development of large-scale organizations in the area of distribution. Of particular importance was the creation of chain stores. Chain stores were organized around the turn of this century to take advantage of discounts offered to them

[6]*Schechter v. U.S.*, 295 U.S. 495 (1935).

by manufacturers in return for purchasing in volume. Chain stores also standardized the packaging and labeling of consumer goods, which tended to lower production costs. The next step was the introduction of self-service, so as to lower the cost of handling goods. Particularly during the 1920s, chain stores began to multiply, and their impact on retailing and wholesaling was significant: many types of specialty stores disappeared entirely or became much fewer in number. And as chain stores increased, the wholesale function of the marketing process was absorbed by the chain itself, and independent wholesale outlets were eliminated. Chain stores were the focus of independent stores' resentment, which was partly caused by the various forms of price discrimination used by the chains.[7] One form of price discrimination was the manufacturers' awarding discounts for volume purchases by the chains that could not be justified on the basis of a lower cost for selling and delivering the larger quantity. A second form of discrimination took the form of "loss leaders." The chains would often sell nationally advertised products or unbranded staples familiar to the buying public at a price below cost. These loss leaders would entice buyers into the chain stores where they would buy other products as well. The device had a particularly deleterious effect on single-line independent stores, which might lose their entire trade to multiline chains using the same line of merchandise as a loss leader. Independent druggists and tobacco stores were particularly hurt by the loss leaders employed by drug and food chains. A third form of price discrimination was what is called *whipsawing*. When a chain, or any large seller, operated in several geographic markets, prices were cut in one market but maintained in others. This device was used to eliminate local sellers who, unlike the chains, could not make up a portion of their losses in other geographic areas. The chains also had a competitive advantage in that manufacturers would grant advertising and promotional allowances for large-scale purchases—allowances that were not granted equally to independent buyers.

The Depression created all sorts of demands for government assistance to small business firms. The growth of the large chain stores, like A&P and Peoples Drugs, placed great competitive pressures on individual business firms engaged in distribution, particularly the independent retail groceries and retail drug stores, and also attracted the hostility of the state legislatures, which enacted legislation to regulate the chains. To some extent, A&P became a

---

[7] The history of the anti-chain store movement is summarized in Frederick M. Rowe, *Price Discrimination Under the Robinson–Patman Act* (Boston: Little, Brown, 1962), pp. 8–11.

symbol similar to that presented by Standard Oil earlier.[8] The Roosevelt administration passed two laws designed to help small business firms. The first was the Robinson–Patman Act, commonly known as the Chain Store Act. Its objective was to limit certain unfair pricing practices and to aid competition.[9] The second law, the Miller–Tydings Act, legalized resale price maintenance agreements covering branded goods. It permitted the manufacturer or distributor of a branded product to set the minimum retail price at which the product would be sold. The purpose was to protect independent retail stores against the chains.[10]

FEDERAL REGULATION OF THE SECURITIES MARKET

The stock market crash of 1929 was a traumatic experience for many Americans. Millions of investors lost their savings, and many were forced into bankruptcy. After a decade of unprecedented prosperity, during which investors hoping for quick profits speculated feverishly in stocks, the economy began to sour. By autumn, the indexes of industrial and factory production had turned downward. The stock market, which is a mirror of economic conditions, began to reflect investors' deepening concern about the state of the economy. On October 24, 1929, more than 12 million shares were traded on the major exchanges. October 29 was the most devastating day in the history of the stock market; 16.4 million shares changed hands, as the average price of fifty leading stocks fell forty points.[11] This crash was followed by repeated declines in stock prices throughout the period from 1929 to 1932; the average value of fifty industrials fell from $252 to $61 per share, that of twenty railroads from $167 to $33 per share, and that of twenty public utilities from $353 to $99 per share.[12]

---

[8] There was no reliable evidence of widespread monopoly abuses by the chains during the 1930s, and they were largely exonerated by the Federal Trade Commission from the charges of anticompetitive practices.

[9] The Robinson–Patman Act will be discussed in detail in Chapter 6. It is regarded by some experts as protecting inefficient companies at the expense of consumers.

[10] The Miller–Tydings Act was repealed by Congress in 1976.

[11] Galbraith, *The Great Crash,* pp. 103–110.

[12] Ibid., p. 146.

Business Abuses of the Securities Market

The stock market crash eventually brought to light many corporate abuses that had occurred during the 1920s.[13] Some of these abuses involved the issuance of securities to the general public. Business firms were caught up in the general optimism of the time, and, undoubtedly, U.S. capitalism was at its productive best: automobile production alone increased from 2.3 million new cars in 1921 to 5.4 million in 1929.[14] The general public, traders on the exchanges, and investment trusts found the stock market an appropriate vehicle for investment, and the demand for securities was high. To capitalize on the demand for securities, business firms would often continue to issue stock until it was so "watered down" as to be almost worthless in book value. Another abuse was the use of various accounting methods to overstate the value of assets or to understate the extent of liabilities. Many business firms issued stock far beyond their need for financing and would use the proceeds to invest in the stock market through loans to brokers. The public also lacked adequate information to make rational buying decisions, for firms often did not reveal relevant data or, when they did, often misrepresented the facts.

Other abuses were not necessarily related to business firms. Insiders on the stock exchanges who could learn about corporate earnings in advance were able to make financial gains by manipulating the market. They would run up the price of stocks to induce buying by the general public and then sell out, thus causing prices to decline. They would also depress the price of stocks by selling "short," thus prompting the public to sell. Then, of course, they would repurchase the stocks at a lower price. Brokers were usually unlicensed and unregulated, and their records were not subject to inspection.

Banks, too, were guilty of unsound practices with respect to the stock market, for they often made loans to brokers and investors to buy securities. When the stock market crashed, the banks were caught short because they were unable to recoup their loans and to pay their depositors on demand.

Investment banking practices also contributed to the stock market crash. Senate hearings conducted from 1932 to 1934 revealed many instances of irresponsibility and abuse of trust by investment bankers, particularly in the

[13] See U.S., Congress, Senate, Committee on Banking and Currency, *Stock Exchange Practices,* 73rd Cong., 2nd sess., 1934.

[14] Galbraith, *The Great Crash,* p. 7.

flotation of foreign securities, which often turned out to be worthless. Investment banks would get large underwriting margins for handling the securities and the public enthusiastically purchased them. Competition among banks to handle the securities was very keen, and the bribing of foreign officials was considered a way of life. In one case, the son of the president of Peru was paid $450,000 for services rendered to a New York investment bank in the notation of a $50 million loan for the Peruvian government.[15] There was never any attention paid to the fact that Peru had a bad debt record, with defaults on previous loans, and an unstable economic and political situation. A similar pattern held true for other Latin American countries. About one-half of all foreign securities floated by investment banks ended in default. The Depression particularly wreaked havoc on the Latin American countries, because their economies were almost wholly dependent on world prices for their exports.

The distribution of domestic securities by investment banks often did not fare much better. It is estimated that U.S. investors lost some $25 million on worthless domestic and foreign securities acquired from 1923 to 1929.[16] One source of abuse, since terminated by legislation, was in the interrelationship of commercial and investment banking. Large commercial banks would organize affiliated investment companies and use them to speculate in stock and to manipulate the market price for securities. In numerous instances, investment bankers sponsored the flotation of issues that created unsound and unsafe corporate structures. In fact, the promoters of business mergers and consolidations during the 1920s were often investment bankers, who would profit from the result because these mergers would create new securities for notation. Perpetual option warrants were issued, which enabled the sponsoring banker to purchase common stock at a fixed price over an unlimited time. In 1929, for example, J. P. Morgan and Company received, for $1 apiece, 1,514,200 option warrants on United Corporation stock.[17] Within two months, Morgan and Company was in a position to sell these warrants at $40 each, and netted a profit of $60 million.

[15] Ibid., p. 187.

[16] U.S., Congress, Senate, Committee on Banking and Currency, *Regulation of Securities,* Senate Report no. 47, 73rd Cong., 1st sess., 1933, p. 2.

[17] U.S., Congress, Senate, Committee on Banking and Currency, *Stock Exchange Practices,* U.S. Government Printing Office, 1933, p. 115.

Reforms of the Securities Market

The stock market crash, and the abuses that led to it, created a need for reforms in the securities market. A series of laws were passed to achieve such reforms, beginning with the Securities Act of 1933, which prohibited the public sale of securities in interstate commerce or through the mails unless detailed information concerning the securities had been filed with the Federal Trade Commission. In 1934, the Securities and Exchange Act extended federal regulation to the securities market through the creation of the Securities and Exchange Commission (SEC), with which information about securities had to be registered. In 1935, the Public Utility Holding Company Act extended the power of the commission into the field of public utility holding companies. Subsequently, the commission was given broadened authority with respect to over-the-counter markets, was enabled to participate in corporate reorganizations, and was authorized to regulate trust indentures and investment trusts.

The Securities Act, 1933

The Securities Act—commonly known as the Truth-in-Securities Act—was passed in 1933. Its objective was to protect the unwary investor from the sale of fraudulent securities through the mail and by door-to-door salesmen who peddled "get rich quick" schemes in such things as Florida real estate ventures and Nevada silver mine stock. Various states had enacted legislation, later called " blue sky laws," to regulate the sales of securities. The laws varied widely in their scope and character, with some providing penalties for fraud and others requiring the registration of security salesmen, but not the registration of securities. State laws were limited in their effectiveness because they did not have adequate provisions for enforcement. Thus more comprehensive federal legislation became necessary to protect the public.

The heart of the Securities Act is the requirement that new securities offered for sale in interstate commerce, unless exempted, be registered with the Securities and Exchange Commission (SEC). The registration statement must contain all the information about the issuing company and its business that the SEC considers necessary to the investors' interest. Although the requirements for different types of issuers vary, they generally include a full description of the kind of business conducted, the services or products sold, the physical assets owned, the identity of the directors and officers, detailed financial statements for the past three years, the terms of the issuer's contract with investment bankers, and many other details.

The Securities Exchange Act, 1934

As mentioned previously, widespread and flagrant abuses in the securities markets existed during the 1920s. Through such abuses, prices of securities were either pushed up or forced down for the benefit of those in control, with corresponding losses for investors. Uncontrolled margin requirements, in which a buyer puts up only a small percentage of the cost of securities and has his or her broker use the purchased securities as collateral for loans to finance the rest of the cost, caused much speculation and accentuated the instability in the stock market. When market prices declined, there was a deflationary spiral in which falling prices reduced collateral values, causing loan liquidations, which put a further downward pressure on prices.

The Securities Exchange Act created the Securities and Exchange Commission, consisting of five members appointed by the president with the consent of the Senate, and each holding office for five years. The act condemns a number of manipulative practices and gives the SEC the authority to check their use. Manipulation of stock prices in any manner is outlawed. Under the act, corporate directors, officers, and insiders are not permitted to sell their company's stock short, and they must make public any intent to exercise stock options; furthermore, willful violation of an unfair practice is punishable by a fine of not more than $10,000 or imprisonment for not more than two years, or both. The act also requires that all securities listed in national securities exchanges be registered with the SEC by the issuer, and that the financial reports contained in the registration of securities be in a form prescribed by the SEC.

The Public Utility Holding Company Act, 1935

There were several reasons for the passage of the Public Utility Holding Company Act. One was to protect investors from a recurrence of what had happened during the 1920s, namely, the loss of billions of dollars in the collapse of the public utility holding companies. Another reason was the inability of state regulatory commissions to exercise any effective control over rate making. The magnitude of the holding company systems put them beyond the reach of the state commissions. The ease with which inflated property values could be worked into the rate base and the lack of access to holding company books led state commissions to accept almost any valuation put on properties by the holding companies. Proponents of public utility holding company regulation also wanted to reduce the concentration of control of the electric and gas industries. In 1930, for example, the nineteen largest holding company groups received 77 percent of the gross revenues for electricity in the United States, and in 1932, thirteen holding companies controlled three-fourths of all privately owned public utilities.[18] This concentration, it was felt, circumvented the natural processes of a free enterprise economy.

The Public Utility Holding Company Act declared gas and electric holding companies to be responsible for the public interest because of their sale of securities in interstate commerce. The act requires public utility holding companies to register with the Securities and Exchange Commission. The registration statement must include copies of the charter of incorporation, and it must show the organization, financial status, directors and officers, balance sheets, and related information. Unless a holding company is registered, it is unlawful for it to sell, transport, or distribute gas or electricity across state lines. The act also has an antipyramiding provision, in that it requires the dissolution of holding companies above the second degree. In other words, there can be no more than two tiers of holding companies above the operating companies: the first-degree holding company, which controls the operating companies directly through stock ownership, and the second-degree holding company, which controls the first holding company.

Reforms of the Banking System

The collapse of the banking system was one of the cataclysmic results of the Depression. In 1929, the banking system was inherently weak, in part because of the large number of speculative loans made by bankers during the 1920s and in part because of the large number of independent banks free from any form of government control.[19] When the economy collapsed, these loans went into default, as the market value of the borrowers' goods or the value of their collateral declined. When debtors defaulted on their loans, banks were unable to satisfy the demands of depositors who came to claim their deposits. Whenever one bank failed, it would act as a warning to depositors to go to their other banks and withdraw deposits. Thus, one bank failure would lead to other bank failures, and these spread, domino-like, throughout the country. As income, employment, and property values fell as a result of the Depression, bank failures quickly became epidemic, and the eventual collapse of the entire banking

---

[18] Galbraith, *The Great Crash,* p. 106.

[19] Paul Studenski and Herman E. Krooss, *Financial History of the United States* (New York: McGraw-Hill, 1952), chap. 25.

system became a real possibility. In March 1933, President Roosevelt declared a moratorium on bank operations until ways could be found to resuscitate the banking system. Congress passed an Emergency Banking Act providing for the inspection of banks and the reopening of licensed solvent banks.

The Glass–Steagall Act, 1933

The Glass–Steagall Act was an effort by the Roosevelt administration to place the banking system under more centralized government control. The act was designed to strengthen the commercial banks, weaken the link between speculation and banking, and give added power to the Federal Reserve system. It created the Federal Deposit Insurance Corporation (FDIC) to guarantee bank deposits.[20] The purpose of this guarantee was to prevent runs on banks by depositors fearful of losing their money. It required commercial banks to give up their securities affiliates and to abstain from investment banking. It also limited the investment securities that member banks in the Federal Reserve system could have in their investment portfolio. To prevent a recurrence of speculative transactions in corporate securities, real estate, and commodities financed by commercial banks, Federal Reserve banks were required to supervise the use of credit made by them. The act also created an Open Market Committee, which was given control over commercial bank policies.

The Banking Act of 1935

The Banking Act of 1935 marked a further extension of government control over banking. With the passage of this act, the banking structure became inseparably connected with federal government monetary and fiscal policy, and the Federal Reserve and the U.S. Treasury operated in tandem. The act is also important because it provided for certain forms of centralized credit and monetary controls. It made the president's power to appoint and remove members of the Federal Reserve Board practically unlimited. The old Federal Reserve Board was dissolved and replaced by a board of governors composed of seven members appointed by the president. The board was given broader rediscounting power and mandatory power over legal reserve requirements against customer demand and time deposits. Each reserve bank was required to restate its rediscount rate every two weeks, and approval of the rate had to be given by the board.

[20] The original guaranteed amount was up to $2,500. The amount today is $100,000.

REGULATION OF PUBLIC UTILITIES

Public utility regulation began in the 1870s when various states passed special laws and granted charters for the railroads. The first federal law regulating the railroads was the Interstate Commerce Act of 1887, which created the Interstate Commerce Commission. Subsequent acts reinforced the powers of the commission. The regulation of transportation was expanded to include motor carriers, first at the state level. State regulation of trucks and buses, introduced in the 1920s, was at first concerned with safety, physical characteristics of vehicles, licensing of drivers, and the number of hours that a driver might work. Soon, however, the states began to regulate the rates and services of common carriers. To prevent the evasion of such regulation, these controls were extended to contract carriers. But the impossibility of the states' regulating interstate motor carriers led to the federal regulation of motor carriers through the Motor Carrier Act of 1935.

Government regulation of the electric power industry also began at the state level. As with the railroads, early public policy was largely promotional, primarily concerned with encouraging the development of the industry. Later, as abuses ensued, particularly in the form of high rates, consumer dissatisfaction laid the groundwork for state regulation. Starting in 1907, regulatory commissions were established in New York and Wisconsin and spread rapidly to other jurisdictions. With the growing importance of interstate transmission of electricity, federal intervention became inevitable. In 1920, the Federal Power Commission (FPC) was established, with the authority to issue permits or licenses for private and public power projects involved in interstate commerce. In 1935, by which time about 18 percent of all generated electric power was used in interstate commerce, the authority of the FPC was extended to cover the regulation of rates, earnings, financial transactions, and accounting practices. In 1938, control over the interstate transmission of natural gas, as well as planning control over all river basins, was also placed under the FPC.

The New Deal and Public Utility Regulation

The large-scale entry of the federal government into the field of public utility regulation began with the New Deal. This move was not primarily a result of any change in the government's philosophy; it was merely a recognition of the forces of the time. The utility industries had crossed state lines and were beyond the power of the state regulatory commissions. The rapidly growing communications industry had always been national or international. At the same time, the arrival of the air age introduced a new facet to the regulation of transportation, and two important acts were passed, the Motor Carrier Act of 1935 and the Civil Aeronautics Act of 1938, which created a major regulatory commission, the Civil Aeronautics Board.

The Motor Carrier Act of 1935

The Motor Carrier Act of 1935 extended the jurisdiction of the Interstate Commerce Commission (ICC) to motor carriers engaged in interstate commerce. But the ICC cannot interfere with the exclusive rights of the states to regulate intrastate motor carriers, and permission from the ICC to engage in interstate commerce does not thereby convey any right to do intrastate business. The act established different degrees of regulation for common carriers, contract carriers, private carriers, and transportation brokers. A common carrier may operate only under a certificate from the ICC, after a finding that it is able to perform the proposed service and that the proposed service is required for public convenience and necessity. Rates and fares must be published and must not be discriminatory. The ICC is also charged with enforcing safety standards. Although general publication of rates is not required, minimum rates must be made public and filed with the ICC, which can prescribe minimum but not maximum rates. Private carriers, not available for hire and carrying their own goods, are subject only to controls over hours of service for employees, safety, and equipment. Brokers must be licensed by the commission.

The Civil Aeronautics Act, 1938

After 1918, the federal government had indirect control over air routes, and types of planes allowed through its granting of conditional airmail contracts. The airmail acts of 1934 and 1935 gave the postmaster general the power to regulate schedule frequencies, departure times, stops, speed, load capacity, and so forth. Regulation of air transportation, however, culminated in the passage of the Civil Aeronautics Act, which created the Civil Aeronautics Board (CAB) and gave it regulatory authority over entry, routes, rates, airmail payments, and subsidies of common carriers. The Civil Aeronautics Board (no longer in existence) was authorized to issue a certificate of convenience and necessity, which gives an air carrier the right to serve a particular route. Rates had to be approved, published, and observed by the board. Pooling, combinations, intercorporate relations, and abandonment of services were subject to control, but the CAB had no authority over security issues. The Civil Aeronautics Act was modified by an executive order in 1940 that created within the Department of Commerce a Civil Aeronautics Authority (CAA), which maintains the national airway system, plans and administers the airport program, and enforces safety, licensing, and traffic control regulations.

Communication facilities were also made subject to federal government control. The first federal regulation of communications was authorized by the Post Roads Act of 1866, which encouraged the construction of telegraph lines. In 1888, Congress gave the Interstate Commerce Commission the power to require telegraph companies to interconnect their lines. Regulation of rates and practices of communications carriers was introduced in the Mann–Elkins Act of 1910, which also extended certain provisions of the Interstate Commerce Act to cover wireless service. When the radio became the principal form of mass communications, regulatory problems arose, for the ICC had been created to regulate railroads, not telephone and telegraph services and radio broadcasting. So in 1927 Congress created the Federal Radio Commission, and in 1934 passed the Communications Act.

The Communications Act, 1934

The Communications Act of 1934 created the Federal Communications Commission (FCC) to regulate interstate and foreign commerce in wire and radio communications. The commission replaced the Federal Radio Commission and was given the jurisdiction over communications previously held by the ICC. The FCC has control over the telephone and telegraph industries as well as over radio and television broadcasting. The latter is not a utility, and its regulation is based on the principle of competition. The FCC has power over rates, services, accounts, interconnections, facilities, combinations, and finances. For example, the FCC grants licenses to radio stations, assigns them frequencies, fixes their hours of operations, and prevents interference among stations. With respect to rates, the FCC has control over interstate and foreign telephone and telegraph companies but not over broadcasting charges. Telephone and telegraph companies must file their rates with the FCC and make them available for public inspection. Notice must be given of rate changes. If a new rate is filed, the commission may suspend it for a period not exceeding three months and hold hearings on its reasonableness. The burden of proving reasonableness is on the company.

The Federal Power Act, 1935

The Federal Power Act of 1935 gave the Federal Power Commission jurisdiction over securities, combinations, and the interstate rates and services of all interstate electric utilities. The commission was also empowered to make special studies of electric rates, the interstate transmission of electricity, national defense problems, and other matters. A corollary act, the Natural Gas Act of 1938, enlarged the commission's responsibilities by also giving it jurisdiction over the interstate transportation and wholesaling of natural gas. These powers were similar to those exercised over the nation's interstate electric utilities. In subsequent acts, the commission was authorized to make water basin studies and was given control of the Tennessee Valley Authority's accounting and use of bond proceeds.

THE NEW CYCLE OF GOVERNMENT REGULATION OF BUSINESS

A new wave of federal government regulation of business began during the 1960s and continued into the 1970s. This cycle is marked by the appearance of social goals in business legislation: eliminating discrimination in employment, ensuring better and safer products for the consumer, reducing environmental pollution, creating safer working conditions, and so forth. These goals resulted in the creation of a number of new federal agencies with regulatory functions—the Consumer Product Safety Commission, the Environmental Protection Agency, the Equal Employment Opportunity Commission, the Federal Energy Administration, the Occupational Safety and Health Administration, and a myriad others. These new agencies follow a fundamentally different pattern from that of the older regulatory agencies such as the Interstate Commerce Commission. They are broader in scope, and they are not limited to a single industry. Their jurisdiction extends throughout most of the private sector and, at times, into the public sector. There are advantages as well as disadvantages in this type of federal regulation. An advantage is that the wide range of these agencies makes it impossible for any one industry to exercise a controlling influence on their activities. A disadvantage is that these new types of agencies are concerned only with the limited segment of operations that falls under their jurisdiction. This limitation often results in an agency's lack of concern or understanding about the effects of its actions on an entire company or industry. More recent government legislation is the subject of Chapters 10, 11, 12, and 13. Almost all the legislation falls into three categories—consumer protection and safety, environmental protection, and equal employment opportunities. These laws have specific objectives, including reduction of product hazards, elimination of job discrimination, and environmental cleanup. Many of these laws are meritorious on the surface, but they are not without their costs. For example, the basic purpose of the Occupational Safety and Health Act of 1970 is to achieve a higher level of job safety. This act gives to the employer the responsibility for safeguarding a person's well-being. In some cases, investment in employees' safety and health can add up to a considerable part of an industry's total capital spending.

Consumer Protection

Several consumer protection laws were enacted between 1962 and 1975. These laws, and a summary of what they are supposed to accomplish, are presented in Table 3-1. They were the manifestation of a consumer movement that has fluctuated in intensity from the beginning of the twentieth century but that has never coalesced into an organized pressure group. Occasional waves of popular indignation and, more frequently, identity of common interest between consumers and organized groups have produced several kinds of special government protection for the consumer—protection against adulteration or misrepresentation of foods, drugs, and cosmetics; labeling of consumer products; product safety; and so forth.

Environmental Protection

Concern about the quality of the environment, which has come from the ecology movement, is a second area currently affecting government and business relations. Although laws to protect the environment against industrial pollution have been on the books for many years, it was not until the 1970s that any major legislation was passed. Protection of the environment is partly a reflection of changing societal values, the new emphasis on the quality of life as opposed to mindless material consumption. More and more citizens have come to object to the increasing annoyances and assaults on health and esthetic sense that result from various forms of pollution. The probability that

TABLE 3-1   Consumer Protection Laws, 1962–1975

Year of Enactment	Law	Purpose
1962	Food and Drug Amendments	Requires pretesting of drugs for safety and effectiveness.
1965	Cigarette Labeling Act	Requires labels disclosing hazards of smoking.
1966	Fair Packaging and Labeling Act	Requires producers to state what a package contains and how much it contains.
1967	Wholesome Meat Act	Offers to states federal assistance in establishing inspection standards.
1968	Consumer Credit Protection Act	Requires full disclosure of terms and conditions of finance charges in credit transactions.
1968	Wholesome Poultry Products Act	Increases protection against impure poultry.
1970	Public Health Smoking Act	Extends warnings about hazards of cigarette smoking.
1970	Poison Prevention Packing Act	Authorizes creation of standards for child-resistant packaging of hazardous substances.
1972	Consumer Product Safety Act	Establishes commission authorized to set safety standards for consumer products.
1975	Consumer Product Warranty Act	Establishes warranty standards to which business firms must adhere.

pollution causes health hazards, some of which may endanger life itself, and the possibility that pollution may in time upset the balance of nature to such an extent that Earth can no longer support human life create anxiety and have led to demands for stringent regulation of pollution.

The most important pollution laws are quite new. The Air Quality Act of 1967 directed the federal government to establish atmospheric areas for the country and created the Presidential Air Quality Advisory Board. The Clean

Air Act Amendments of 1970 set air quality standards and required that by 1975 new cars be virtually pollution free.[21] The National Environmental Policy Act of 1970 created a permanent Council on Environmental Quality, consisting of three members and a professional staff, whose functions are to advise and assist the president in environmental matters. The act also requires all federal agencies to consider the effect of their actions on the environment. In 1970, the Environmental Protection Agency was established to enforce the environmental protection laws and to assume responsibility for environmental functions previously given to other federal agencies. In 1972, the Water Pollution Control Act was passed to regulate the discharge of industrial pollution into navigable waters, and in the same year the Noise Pollution and Control Act was passed to regulate the noise limits of products and vehicles. In addition to these major laws, a number of minor laws, mostly concerned with relatively limited matters such as the effluents from navigable vessels, have also been enacted.

Affirmative Action

A third new area that touches the operations of business firms is affirmative action. This policy also reflects a shift in societal values, which was prompted by three movements: the civil rights movement, the women's liberation movement, and an increased emphasis on egalitarianism. The civil rights movement was begun to end economic and social discrimination based on race or color. Because a large proportion of minority members have among the lowest incomes in our society, the movement also advocates the concept of entitlement, based on the idea that since society over time has deprived certain groups of their rights, the members of these groups are now entitled to compensatory incomes and education, more representation at all levels of management, and so forth. The women's liberation movement is somewhat similar to the civil rights movement. It asks for the elimination of sex discrimination, and it also advocates entitlement. Egalitarianism is somewhat more difficult to define. Essentially, it rejects merit as a desideratum for promotion and reward and instead stresses equality of result. An example is the use of mandatory quotas for minority groups, including women, in hiring and promotion policies, education, and job training.

[21] These amendments have subsequently been amended several times.

These movements have resulted in the passage of laws that affect business. In 1963, the Equal Pay Act was passed to eliminate wage differentials based on sex when the type of work performed by either sex was the same. In 1964, the Civil Rights Act was enacted to eliminate job discrimination based on such factors as sex, race, color, or religion, and it created the Equal Employment Opportunity Commission to investigate charges of job discrimination. In 1967, the Age Discrimination in Employment Act was passed to prohibit job discrimination against people aged forty to sixty-five. In 1972, the Equal Employment Opportunity Act broadened the authority of the Equal Employment Opportunity Commission so that it could sue employers accused of job discrimination. In addition to these laws, a series of executive orders have extended the federal government's authority to cover the personnel practices of business. These executive orders are the framework for affirmative action, which seeks to redress any racial, sexual, or other imbalance that may exist in an employer's work force. Affirmative action applies to all nonconstruction contractors and subcontractors of the federal government and to all government entities.

SUMMARY

Legislation affecting government and business relations tends to come in cycles. One cycle occurred during the Depression of the 1930s, when much of the existing government regulatory framework was created. New Deal legislation, for the most part, was crisis oriented. The banking system was in a state of collapse, and so it was necessary to pass laws to preserve and support banking. Abuses in the securities market contributed to the stock market crash of 1929, and a thoroughgoing reform of the market followed. Massive unemployment and an increase in business failures stimulated a shift in emphasis in government antitrust policy and a reliance on a form of state planning under the National Industrial Recovery Act, which was to influence market conditions in ways previously prohibited by the antitrust laws. But the desire, especially of small business firms, for protection against the rigors of competition was reflected after the demise of the NIRA in their pressure for such measures as the Robinson–Patman Act. The New Deal also provided a vehicle for the organization of labor and other groups, thereby counterbalancing the power of big business. The federal government assumed greater responsibility for the functioning of the economy and for overall coordination of economic activity.

The second cycle of government-business legislation began in the 1960s but has run its course. This cycle was the result of several factors, including ecology, consumerism, and civil rights. Legislation was concentrated in three areas—consumer protection, ecology, and employment. A new set of regulatory agencies was created that has had a rather broad effect on business, in that their functions are not limited to a specific industry. With the new legislation, no business firm can operate today without contending with a multitude of government restrictions and regulations. Moreover, virtually every major department of a typical industrial corporation in the United States has one or more counterparts in a federal agency that controls or strongly influences its internal decision making. As will be pointed out, government regulation can have many adverse effects on business and consumers—a stultification of incentives and innovations by business and an increase in the costs that consumers pay for products, as government regulation increases the cost of production. Because these costs are not the result of any measurable output, they are reflected in a lower rate of productivity.

QUESTIONS FOR DISCUSSION

1. In what ways did the New Deal change business–government relations?
2. The National Industrial Recovery Act represented an attempt by the Roosevelt administration to relax the antitrust laws. Was it successful?
3. Discuss the reasons for the passage of the Robinson–Patman Act.
4. What is meant by *whipsawing* and *loss leader*?
5. Describe the activities of the Securities Exchange Commission.
6. "The epidemic of bank failures between 1929 and 1932 can be attributed to basic defects in the banking system." Discuss this statement.
7. Explain the reasons for the New Deal's regulation of air and motor carrier transportation.
8. Discuss the purposes of the Communications Act of 1934 and the Federal Power Act of 1935.

RECOMMENDED READINGS

Allen, Frederick Lewis. *The Big Change: America Transforms Itself, 1900–1959*. New York: Harper & Row, 1952. Chap. 10.

Elias, Erwin A. "Robinson–Patman: Time for Rechiseling." *Mercer Law Review* 26 (1975): 689-697.

Galbraith, John Kenneth. *The Great Crash*. Boston: Houghton Mifflin, 1972.

Mitchell, Broadus. *Depression Decade: From New Era Through New Deal*. New York: Rinehart, 1941.

O'Connor, James F. *The Banking Crisis and Recovery Under the Roosevelt Administration*. Chicago: Callaghan, 1938.

Posner, Richard A. *The Robinson–Patman Act*. Washington, D.C.: American Enterprise Institute for Public Policy Research, 1976.

Rowe, Frederick M. *Price Discrimination Under the Robinson–Patman Act*. Boston: Little, Brown, 1962.

Studenski, Paul, and Herman E. Krooss. *Financial History of the United States*. New York: McGraw-Hill, 1952.

PART III

INDUSTRIAL CONCENTRATION AND ANTITRUST

The concentration of many industries in the hands of a few firms is a fact of life in the United States and other major industrial countries, although attitudes toward concentration may vary from country to country. In the United States, there is a deeply rooted tradition dating back to the last century that concentrated wealth in any form was bad, and that big business would eliminate the small firms. It is not surprising that by statute and common law our legal system has been concerned with the maintenance of a competitive market system. This concern is reflected in the existence of antitrust laws that have several major objectives—the promotion of competition by outlawing monopolies and prohibiting unfair competition, the protection of consumer welfare by prohibiting unfair business practices, and the protection of small business firms from economic pressures exerted by large firms.

Antitrust policy in the United States has had an uneven course. Historically, enforcement has had political overtones, with laws resulting from political reaction to a problem considered pressing at the time. The Sherman Act was passed in 1890 in response to public (including business) reaction to the economic power of the trusts. The Clayton Act was passed in 1914 in part as a result of public concern over the power of the investment banks. The Robinson–Patman Act was passed in 1936 in response to pressure exerted by small firms that wanted protection against the large chain stores. Since that time, antitrust policy has moved in spurts, with long interim periods in which there has been little activity. Moreover, attitudes toward antitrust regulation of business have changed. There is less worry about the size of companies and the degree of concentration in an industry and more attention to their actual impact on economic efficiency and productivity.

U.S. antitrust laws also must be considered within the framework of global market competition. Once unassailable U.S. industries are losing their edge in foreign competition. The mystique of U.S. management superiority has been shaken by such events as the Japanese rise to prominence in the world auto industry. International considerations have come to the fore in reference to U.S. antitrust laws. There has been a broadening of the focus of antitrust policy, away from a narrow legal attempt to curb anticompetitive business behavior to a broader policy of promoting the competitive position of U.S. industry at home and abroad. Put into practice by the Reagan administration, this policy involves a more relaxed approach toward corporate size, concentration, and corporate mergers.

Chapter 4

Market Structure: Competition, Monopoly, and Oligopoly

In a market economy, business firms are supposed to make most of their economic decisions on the basis of prices, price changes, and price relationships. Demand and supply forces acting in several separate market situations are supposed to determine prices. In any given market situation, some degree of competition is assumed to exist, although the degree of competition varies considerably from one situation to another. In one market situation, there may be a large number of sellers and buyers of a given product; in another situation, a few sellers and a number of buyers; and in a third situation, one seller and a number of buyers. In price theory, pure competition and monopoly can be considered opposite points on the competitive spectrum. The essential feature of competition is that there are so many sellers and buyers of a good that no one seller or buyer is able to influence prices in the marketplace; the essential feature of monopoly is control over supply by a single seller. This control can be translated into control over the price of a good in the marketplace.

COMPETITION

Clearly, competition in the economic sense is not a natural thing but is a social pattern produced by the operation of various supporting institutions, including private property ownership and freedom of enterprise. Its justification, like that of the other capitalistic institutions, is that it contributes to the social welfare. When the industries and markets of an economy are organized competitively, certain supposedly desirable results will ensue.

First, competition should bring about efficiency in the operation of industry and business by granting economic success to those firms efficiently operated and by relentlessly eliminating those inefficiently and wastefully operated.

Thus to survive, each enterprise must use the best machines and productive methods available and eliminate waste at all points in its organization. The removal of inefficient producers from the market is meant to leave the productive factors in the hands of those firms that use them most effectively.

Second, competition should lead to innovation and technological progress. Better productive methods, machines that increase efficiency or lower cost, or a product that appears to satisfy a human want more effectively than similar products from other business firms give certain firms a greatly prized advantage over the others with respect to income. But such advantages tend to be lost sooner or later in a competitive industry, and the continuing result should be the consumers' ability to obtain better and better products at lower and lower prices.

Finally, competition is said to be a regulator of economic activity, a means by which the productive efforts of numerous business firms are correlated through prices with the desires of consumers as expressed in the market. Success in competition depends on the ability to give consumers the right amount, quality, and kinds of goods, at the right price. Firms that supply goods not suited to consumers' desires or that cost more than similar products of other firms, usually fall by the wayside. If the total output of a good is small in relation to the demand for it, the possibility of making a profit will stimulate a competitive industry to expand production and, if necessary, its plant facilities. But if competitive producers turn out far more goods than are demanded, the lack of profits will force some firms out of the industry and adjust output to demand.

Economic Concepts of Competition

Competition as an economic concept can mean a number of things, the most common of which is pure competition. Certain elements must be present for pure competition to exist in a market. First, there must be a large number of buyers and sellers of a standardized product. Second, there must be complete freedom of entry and exit into and out of the market. Third, no one buyer or no one seller can influence the price of the product sold. Fourth, there must be no collusion of any form between the buyers and the sellers. Finally, there can be no interference in the market from outside forces—government, labor unions, and so forth.

Pure competition is a theoretical concept. It can be used to define a desirable market situation, which, if it existed, would redound to the advantage of the consumer for the simple reason that supply and demand forces acting in a given market would determine the price and output of a product. No single seller or buyer could affect the market in any way. The hallmark of competition is the existence of many producers, each of which contributes only a small part of the output traded in the market. A competitive market price is decided by an equilibrium of supply and demand, which is determined independently of the actions of any single seller or buyer. Sellers may sell all they please, and buyers may buy all they please, but only at the price set in the market by supply and demand.

Figure 4-1 illustrates price and output determination under conditions of pure competition. The supply curve, labeled S, indicates the quantity that sellers are willing to provide at each price. There is a direct relationship between the amount supplied and the price: the higher the price, the greater the amount supplied, The demand curve, labeled D, indicates the quantity that buyers are willing to purchase at each price. The relationship between the amount demanded and the price is inverse: the higher the price, the lower the amount demanded. Equilibrium is reached when the quantity that sellers are willing to sell is equal to the quantity that buyers are willing to buy. The market price is set by this equilibrium point. At any point above the equilibrium point, supply exceeds demand; at any point below the equilibrium point, demand exceeds supply. In the diagram, the price OP is the market price, and the quantity OA is what is sold.

Competitive prices are explained mainly as the supply and demand for two different periods: first, a short-run period during which sellers can vary supply only as is possible using existing production facilities and, second, a long-run period during which sellers can freely vary their actual production capacity. In the short run, sellers can sell all they please, but only at the equilibrium price that clears the market. This equilibrium price bears no relation to the cost of production for an individual seller, which may be higher or lower than the price. In the short run, some firms can make profits, and others can sustain losses.

Demand, supply, or both can change in the short run. For instance, an increase in demand means buyers are willing to purchase more at each of a series of prices than they were formerly. In the diagram, the demand line would shift to the right, as indicated by the curve D_1. A decrease in demand means just the opposite. An increase in demand, with supply remaining constant, would result in an increase in both price and quantity; a decrease in demand would have the opposite effect. An increase in supply means sellers are willing to offer more at each of a series of prices than formerly. In the diagram, the supply

FIGURE 4-1 Supply and Demand Analysis

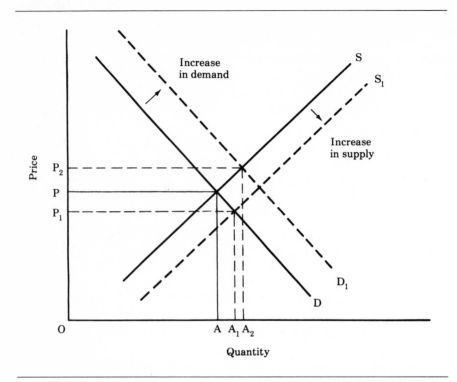

curve would shift to the right. The result would be a decrease in the equilibrium price and an increase in the quantity bought. A decrease in supply would
have the opposite effect.

Demand originates with the consumer. It implies a desire for a good or service that can be expressed, usually through willingness to pay money for it. The
demand schedule assumes its shape, first, because individual incomes are limited, and second, because as the quantities of a given commodity increase at a
given time, they become less useful to the consumer. In other words, the consumers' desire for a particular product tends to diminish as they acquire more
of it. This is the principle of diminishing marginal utility. Marginal utility is
the amount by which total utility would be changed with the addition of one
unit to a stock of goods. The principle of diminishing marginal utility states
that marginal utility varies inversely with the number of units acquired. When

TABLE 4-1

Output	Selling Price	Average Revenue	Total Revenue	Marginal Revenue
1	$20	$20	$ 20	$20
2	20	20	40	20
3	20	20	60	20
4	20	20	80	20
5	20	20	100	20
6	20	20	120	20

expenditures are increased for a given item, successive increments will make smaller and smaller additions to total satisfaction. The basis for the principle is that any physical want is probably satiable.

Price and Output Determination—Short Run

Under conditions of pure competition, the individual firm must accept the price established in the market by market supply and market demand. Since the firm has no effect on or control over price, it must try to maximize profits or minimize losses by adjusting its output to this price. The average revenue curve is a horizontal line, indicating that the firm can sell varying amounts of output at the established price (see Figure 4-2 on page 83). Average revenue is the total revenue divided by the number of units of output and is synonymous with the price per unit. For a competitive firm, average revenue and price are the same. Since the price remains unchanged as more units are sold, each additional unit sold increases the total revenue by an amount equal to the price. This is illustrated in Table 4-1. There is also the economic concept of marginal revenue, the amount by which the total revenue is increased by the sale of one more unit of product. As shown in the table, marginal revenue, average revenue, and selling price are the same.

The firm can sell all it can produce at the selling price of $20, and so we shall figure how much it will produce under conditions of pure competition in the short run. Output is based on the cost of production. In the short run, there are both fixed and variable costs. Fixed costs are those that remain constant regardless of the amount of output. Variable costs are those that vary in amount in accordance with changes in the volume of output. From the standpoint of cost, the firm can adjust its output by changes in variable factors, such as labor, but cannot change its affixed physical factors. The key cost concept, however, is marginal cost, the amount by which the total cost is increased when an additional unit of output is produced. Given these cost concepts, the basic economic principle governing the behavior of the firm in the short run is that output will be adjusted to the point at which marginal cost and marginal revenue are equal. The firm must do this to maximize its profits or, for that matter, to minimize its losses. Whenever marginal revenue is greater than marginal cost, total profit can be increased by expanding production, but whenever marginal cost exceeds marginal revenue, total profit is increased by reducing production.

Table 4-2 shows the principle of profit maximization in the short run under conditions of pure competition. The price, as determined in the marketplace by supply and demand, is assumed to be $20, and total fixed costs are assumed to be $10, regardless of the number of units of output produced. Profit maximization occurs at ten units of output. If a firm stopped producing before this point, it could still add more to unit revenue than to unit cost; if it went beyond this point, the cost of producing an additional unit of output would more than offset the addition to revenue.

Reaching the point of equality of marginal cost and marginal revenue does not imply that a firm always makes a profit. Whether or not it does make a profit depends on the relation between total cost and total revenue, or average cost and price. The equality between price and marginal cost guarantees that a position of maximum profit or minimum loss has been attained, but it does not offer any information about the absolute profit or loss position. If a firm has decided what to produce and has constructed a single plant to house a certain quantity of physical resources, its ability to change output is limited. It can change the inputs of its variable factors and thus adjust output somewhat, but it cannot change its overall scale of operations, since that would require changing fixed as well as variable factors. The marginal cost function represents the rate of change in total cost as output is changed within a given plant. Since for the individual seller in a purely competitive market, price does not vary as output varies, the marginal cost function becomes, in the short run, the supply function for the competitive firm, that is, the quantities that will be supplied at all possible prices.

TABLE 4-2

Output	Fixed Cost	Variable Cost	Total Cost	Marginal Cost	Price	Total Revenue	Marginal Revenue
1	$10	$ 15	$ 25	$15	$20	$ 20	$20
2	10	28	38	13	20	40	20
3	10	39	49	11	20	60	20
4	10	50	60	11	20	80	20
5	10	59	69	9	20	100	20
6	10	67	77	8	20	120	20
7	10	81	91	14	20	140	20
8	10	97	107	16	20	160	20
9	10	115	125	18	20	180	20
10	10	135	145	20	20	200	20
11	10	160	170	25	20	220	20

It is also desirable to think in terms of average costs rather than total costs, since this approach allows costs to be related directly to prices. Corresponding to the concepts of total cost, total variable costs, and total fixed cost, are average total cost, average variable cost, and average fixed cost. The average total cost is the sum of the average fixed costs. Average variable cost is derived by dividing total variable costs by output, and average fixed cost is derived by dividing total fixed cost by output. Marginal cost is neither a total nor an average cost but is simply the additional cost incurred as a result of producing an additional unit of output. The marginal and average cost concepts are presented in Table 4-3. Average fixed costs show that fixed costs per unit decline continuously as output increases. Average variable costs decrease, then reach a minimum value, and thereafter increase. The initial decline in average variable cost is because, within limits, the more units of variable factors there are, the more effectively fixed factors are put to use.

The concepts of marginal revenue (MR), average revenue (AR), marginal cost (MC), average variable cost (AVC), and average total cost (ATC) are given in Figure 4-2. As mentioned earlier, the marginal curve is the short-run supply curve for a firm operating in a purely competitive industry. We should qualify this, however: the marginal cost curve represents the supply curve of

TABLE 4-3

Output	Total Fixed Cost	Total Variable Cost	Average Fixed Cost	Average Variable Cost	Marginal Cost
1	$10	$15	$10.00	$15.00	$15
2	10	28	5.00	14.00	13
3	10	39	3.33	13.00	11
4	10	50	2.50	12.50	11
5	10	59	2.00	11.80	9
6	10	67	1.67	11.16	8
7	10	81	1.43	11.57	14
8	10	97	1.25	12.12	16
9	10	115	1.11	12.77	18
10	10	135	1.00	13.50	20

the firm only above a certain price. A firm that cannot cover its variable costs should shut down. No sensible firm would supply any amount of goods at a price below that which would bring in enough revenue to cover variable costs. This point can be shown in the diagram. AVC is the firm's average variable cost curve. No quantity will be supplied at any price below OP_1. If the price falls below this point, the firm should shut down. Thus, the marginal cost curve (MC) becomes the supply curve at all prices above OP_1. As long as the price is above OP_1, the firm will continue to operate even though it is not covering total costs. At prices above this level, it will be more than covering variable cost; it will also be making some return on its fixed investment.

The diagram shows three price levels: OP_1 is the minimum price a firm can receive and remain in business; OP_2 is the breakeven point, at which the firm would make neither a profit nor a loss; and any point above OP_2—for instance, OP_3—is a price at which a firm would make a profit. Using OP_3 as one price, the quantity supplied is OQ_3. At the point L, where MC = MR, profit is maximized and the firm is in short-run equilibrium. At the price OP_3, the average revenue per unit, LQ_3, multiplied by the number of units of output, OQ_3, equals total revenue, which is the area of the large rectangle OP_3LQ_3. Similarly, average total cost, KQ_3, multiplied by the number of units of output,

FIGURE 4-2   Alternative Price Levels, Pure Competition in Short Run

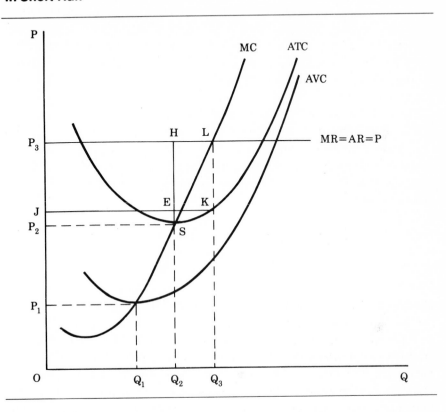

OQ_3, equals total cost, or the area of the rectangle $OJKQ_3$. The net profit rectangle, is the total revenue rectangle less the total cost rectangle, or JP_3LK.

Price and Output Determination—Long Run

In the long run, firms operating under conditions of pure competition can adjust both output and capacity to a given demand and price. In the short run, a firm can adjust output only by changing the amounts of the variable factors of production, but plant capacity remains fixed. In the long run, there may also be a change in the total number of firms in the industry. Assuming firms are free to enter into and depart from a market, new firms will be attracted to a given industry if existing firms are making an above-normal profit. In other words, if the price is above the short-run average cost, there is an incentive for new firms to enter the industry. Inefficient firms, those sustaining losses, will be eliminated. A long-run equilibrium price is then achieved at the point at which marginal revenue equals not only marginal cost but also the average cost of the firms in the industry. This is possible only at the lowest point on the long-run average cost curve, since this is the only point at which marginal cost and average cost are equal.

Figure 4-3 shows the long-run equilibrium for a firm operating under pure competition. The firm is operating at an output level at which its average total costs (ATC) are lowest, but all its economic profit has disappeared. Marginal cost (MC), marginal revenue (MR), and price (P) are equal at the equilibrium point. The industry itself is in equilibrium because it has reached a point at which for all the firms in the industry the price just covers their average total cost. There is no incentive for new firms to come into the industry, and each firm will find itself in an equilibrium position. Marginal revenue equals not only each firm's marginal cost but also its average cost. This balance is possible only at the lowest point on the long-run average cost curve, since this is the only point at which marginal cost and average cost are equal. Under pure competition, each firm will in the long run produce at the lowest point on the long-run average cost curve.

The long-run equilibrium price can be called a normal price that brings sellers a normal profit—that is, enough profit to keep them from leaving the industry, but not enough to entice other sellers to stop producing other things and shift into this industry. Normal profit may be considered a cost of production, a rate of return on the resources a firm owns, including the labor of the owner. It also means that the rate of return on all a firm's resources, including internally owned labor and other factors of production, is no greater than can be obtained elsewhere in the economic system. Excess, or economic profit, which is considered a surplus over and above all costs of production and which can attract new firms into a competitive industry, would be eliminated in the long run under pure competition.

Economic Significance of Pure Competition

From the standpoint of the consumer, the most desirable condition under which a free enterprise market economy can operate is pure competition. Under this condition, different goods are usually supplied at a minimum price. In

FIGURE 4-3 Long-Run Equilibrium for Firm Under Pure Competition

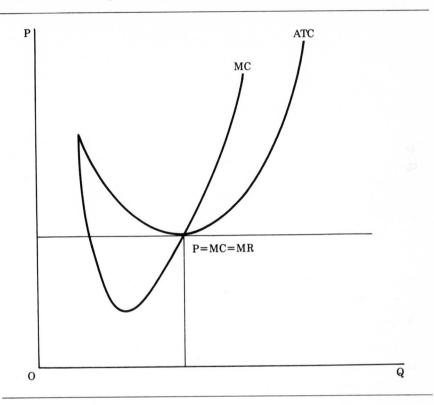

such a market, the numbers of buyers and sellers are so large that no one of them can influence the price; buyers and sellers are completely aware of market conditions; and firms may move freely in and out of an industry. An individual firm operating within the framework of pure competition, however, is confronted with several limiting factors. Since it is such a small part of the total market, it cannot by any individual action in any way affect prices. It must accept the market price and must adjust its production to this price if it is to maximize its profits. The firm therefore can have no price policy of its own, since price is fixed by market forces. But this protects the consumers, for only impersonal market forces can determine price. The market price presumably also reflects consumer preferences, because it measures the marginal utility to the consumer of the final unit of the commodity produced. In a long-run equilibrium position, price is equal to marginal cost for each firm in a purely competitive industry. An optimum allocation of resources within the industry has been reached. If all industries in the economy were purely competitive, an optimal use of resources in the entire economy would occur; there could not be an excess of profits in any one industry, since new firms would be attracted into it as the margin of profit grew. Wages could not remain higher in any one occupation than in others, for workers would be attracted to the high-paying occupation, with the consequence that the pay level would come more into line with that in other occupations. Therefore, an equality of marginal cost and price in all industries would mean that resources could be used in no better way. No improvement in economic well-being could be obtained by shifting resources from one industry into another. Consumers would be satisfied because their marginal utilities for each of the various products would be approximately equal. In the theoretical equilibrium position, consumers cannot improve their satisfaction by changing any one of their expenditures for goods and services.

The ideal market situation epitomized by pure competition is almost never achieved, except perhaps approximately in the buying and selling of some farm products. But even in agriculture, farmers have created marketing cooperatives for some crops and have obtained special legislation in the form of price support and acreage allotment programs. In retailing, in which pure competition is sometimes approached, retail price maintenance laws, usually referred to as "fair trade laws" by their supporters, have prevented price competition. Almost all other markets are characterized by imperfect competition, in which sellers or buyers have some control over price. In such situations, the price policy of one seller depends on the expected reaction of rival sellers. Price wars, the elimination of rival competitors, collusion, and combinations all are possible. Instead of regulating prices, the government may try to enforce competition through prosecution based on antitrust laws.

Pure competition should be regarded as one of several economic models developed both to describe a particular structural arrangement within a market economy and to enable economists to predict the consequences of certain changes in variables within that structure. The other models are monopoly, oligopoly, and monopolistic competition. Pure competition is an ideal that can serve as a frame of reference when it is necessary to evaluate whether or not there is viable competition in a given marketplace situation. Actually, many different concepts and subconcepts of competition depart from pure competition; for example, the concept of effective or workable competition has a pragmatic legal-economic orientation. The economic idea underlying effective competition is that no seller or group of sellers acting in concert has the power to choose its level of profits by giving less and charging more. So competition means different things to different people.

MONOPOLY

Pure monopoly, or having only one seller of a commodity for which no close substitutes exist, is a rare market situation. But some of the industries classified by law as public utilities are in approximately this situation, and their prices are regulated by the government. Such monopolies avoid duplication of facilities and achieve the low costs made possible by large-scale production that would not be possible under purely competitive conditions. Whether this regulation is effective is debatable, but it does attest to a deep-seated and well-founded suspicion of the U.S. public about what might happen if it were absent. A monopoly may exist in part because of the decreasing costs resulting from an increased scale of production that reduces the number of sellers in a market or allows a few to agree to avoid price competition. Patents are also the basis for many different monopolies.

A monopolist can fix prices by gaining control of the supply of a given commodity, for the individual firm and the industry are, in effect, identical, and the market demand curve for the industry is the same as the average revenue or sales curve for the monopolist. The demand schedule for the product of a monopolist is the same type as shown in Figure 4-1. There is no supply schedule, for the monopolist has the entire supply, and there is no substitute for the product, so the monopolist need not be concerned with the possibility of consumers shifting to substitute commodities or rival firms. This effect could be the result of the monopolist's complete control of some strategic raw material or the possession of a specific franchise or patent. The monopolist is primarily interested in regulating supply so as to obtain a maximum profit. Demand and cost of production form the basis for the amount of output. The maximum profit is tied to the quantity sold and to the difference between cost and price per unit of output.

Monopoly prices are frequently higher than the prices that would prevail under competitive conditions because a monopolist can sometimes charge different prices to different customers. The individual firm in a purely competitive market can only react to the price set in the market by supply and demand. It need not consider the effect of variations in its output on price, since it is such a small part of the total market. Its average revenue line is horizontal, and it cannot charge different prices to different customers. But the monopolist must examine the effects of pricing policies, for the demand curve for its product, which is also its average revenue curve, slopes downward to the right, This means that a monopolist must consider the effect on the price of changes in its output. A larger output can be sold only at a lower price, the degree to which it is lower depending on the elasticity of demand. If the price is raised, consumers will reduce the amount of the product they purchase, but they cannot shift to substitute commodities or rival producers.

Price and Output Under Monopoly—Short Run

When the objective is maximization of profit, price and output determination under conditions of monopoly follows basically the same rules as those applying to the firm operating under pure competition. The general rule for maximizing profits is usually stated as the output at which marginal cost equals marginal revenue. Net profit for a monopolist depends on the quantity of output sold and the difference between cost and price per unit of output. Operation at the point of greatest difference between cost and price per unit of output may not yield the monopolist the highest total net profit because added sales beyond that point may more than offset the decline in profit per unit. Demand and the cost of production form the basis for the monopolist's choice of output. In more precise terms, profits are at a maximum when marginal costs equal marginal revenue. When the two amounts become equal, further expansion is not profitable. Up to that point, expansion of output adds more to receipts than to costs; past that point it is the other way around. But when there are finite changes in output, marginal cost will seldom exactly equal marginal revenue.

The monopolist's price and output determination is shown in Table 4-4. Remember that in a monopoly, unlike the conditions prevailing under pure competition, the average revenue line is not horizontal; the price declines as the output increases. The demand average lines are the same, sloping downward from left to right. The average revenue column shows the prices at which various quantities of output can be sold, whereas the marginal revenue column shows the increments to total revenue that result from selling additional units of output. In the short run, some costs are fixed and others are variable. In the table, total fixed costs are assumed to be $500, regardless of the volume of output, and total variable costs have been given assigned values.

TABLE 4-4

Output	Price	Total Revenue	Marginal Revenue	Fixed Costs	Variable Costs	Marginal Cost	Profit
10	$100	$1,000	$	$500	$483	$	$17
11	99	1,089	89	500	544	61	45
12	98	1,176	87	500	598	54	78
13	96	1,248	72	500	659	61	89
14	94	1,316	68	500	725	66	91
15	90	1,350	34	500	802	77	48
16	85	1,360	10	500	890	88	–30

At all outputs up to the fourteenth unit, marginal cost is less than marginal revenue. The cutoff point is the fourteenth unit, for the production of this unit will add $2 to net profits. At a volume of fourteen units, marginal revenue is $68, marginal cost is $66, total revenue is $1,316, and total costs are $1,225. The difference, or profits over and above all costs, is $91, which is greater than at any volume of output less than fourteen. Beyond fourteen, marginal cost is greater than marginal revenue. To produce the fifteenth unit, the additional cost is $77 and the additional revenue is $34. Profit declines from $91 to $48. The point of maximum profit is at a price of $94 and at a volume of fourteen units.

The same analysis is presented in Figure 4-4, which shows the monopolist's average revenue or demand curve (D), marginal revenue curve (MR), short-run marginal cost (MC), and average total cost (ATC) curves. The marginal cost and marginal revenue curves intersect at a volume of OQ. For the monopolist to expand up to this point would be profitable, since at all smaller volumes the marginal cost curve lies below the marginal revenue curve. Beyond this point, however, marginal cost rises above marginal revenue. To determine the price at which this volume can be sold, it is necessary to use the average revenue curve, which is also the monopolist's demand curve. The average revenue is the price column in the table, and the curve shows the prices at which various outputs can be sold, whereas the marginal revenue curve shows the increments to total revenue that result from selling additional units of output. The price that will maximize profits is OP, the total revenue is represented

FIGURE 4-4   Short-Run Price and Output for Firm Under Monopoly

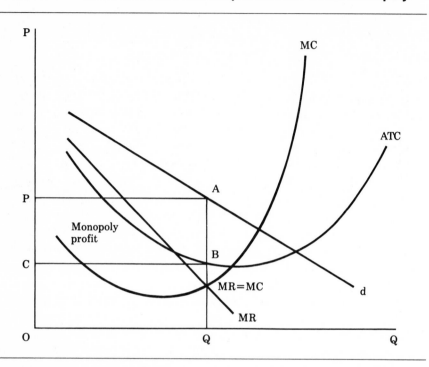

by the rectangle OPAQ, and the total cost is represented by the smaller rectangle OCBQ. The total profit over and above all necessary costs is represented by PABC, the difference between the revenue and cost rectangles.

Monopoly profit is usually higher than that which would prevail under pure competition, since the monopolist has control over supply, whereas the individual firm operating under conditions of pure competition is only one among many and so has no control over total output. The individual firm can only react to the price set in the marketplace by supply and demand, but the monopolist can set price and hunt for the point on the demand curve at which profit is maximized. Monopoly profits over and above all necessary production costs do not call forth the type of effective adjustment that would be needed under pure competition. In other words, there is no free movement of resources into and out of a monopoly industry. Typically, output would also be at a level lower than that which would prevail under pure competition.

Long-Run Adjustments

In the short run, the price may be below the average total cost, but this cannot continue in the long run because if it did, the firm would cease operation. If the price is above the average total cost, there will be excess profits, and in a monopoly market nothing can correct this automatically because of barriers to the entrance of new firms. In the long run, a monopoly is able to adjust its scale of operation because all costs are variable, whereas in the short run it can determine the most profitable rate of operation only for its existing fixed and variable factors of production. The most profitable scale of operation in the long run is the one that equates marginal cost and marginal revenue. The monopoly, like the purely competitive firm, has a U-shaped long-run average cost curve; that is, if the firm is either too small or too large, its production cost per unit will be higher than if it is of optimum size. The actual size of the firm will depend on the expected demand for its product. This size may happen to be that at which the cost per unit is minimal, but because the monopolistic firm does not have to compete, it is more likely that the firm will be either too large or too small to minimize cost.

Economic Significance of Monopoly

Pure monopoly, like pure competition, is a rare market situation and should be regarded as a theoretical framework in which to decide regulatory policies. The main defect in a monopolistic market situation, unlike pure competition, is that nothing automatically protects the consumer. The existence of monopolies and their consequent excessive profits obviously would affect the personal distribution of income in the economy and result in a misallocation of resources. Monopoly prices are frequently higher than the prices that would prevail under competitive conditions because a monopolist can charge different prices to different customers. There are no competing sellers to whom buyers may go in case of price discrimination. Moreover, there is less incentive for a monopoly to organize its plant most efficiently because it may make profits that are greater than in competitive industries merely by restricting supply. Modernization of facilities, experimentation with lower prices and larger output, and managerial incentives may be retarded by the lack of competition. In some instances, the monopolist may be unwilling to experiment and expand, even though greater profits are possible.

But in some cases, monopoly prices may be as low as or lower than competitive prices. For instance, when the scale of production is much larger and the level of costs much lower than they would be under competition, a monopoly price may be lower than a competitive price. Furthermore, a greater long-run efficiency of production sometimes may be achieved under monopoly conditions when the economy is highly unstable. A monopoly can operate at a more uniform rate and maintain an inventory to carry it through the changes in demand. Under competition, firms must estimate demand and also their competitors' probable supplies. The accumulation of an inventory is risky; consequently, many firms may operate beyond capacity at one time and below capacity at another time. High prices encourage expansion, which may result in very low prices. And very low prices may bankrupt many firms, which will result in very high prices from the firms that remain in business. The average competitive price may very well exceed the monopoly price.

OLIGOPOLY

The term *oligopoly* refers to a market situation in which there are a few sellers of a differentiated product. Many American industries have oligopolistic qualities, such as the steel, automobile, and cigarette industries. In fact, oligopoly seems to be a characteristic of industries to which modern methods of production are applicable. The pattern of oligopolistic industries is for there to be a few giant firms that account for one-half or more of the total industry output, followed by smaller firms that produce the rest. For example, General Motors and Ford account for at least two-thirds of the automobile sales by U.S. car manufacturers. Typical of most oligopolistic industries is mass merchandising, which means distinguishing a firm's products from those of its competitors by means of branding and trademarks, and creating a preference for the brand by means of advertising. Some industries, however, approach pure oligopoly. Here the firms in the industry produce virtually identical products. Buyers have little reason to prefer the product of one firm to that of another except on the basis of price. Examples of nearly pure oligopolies are the cement, aluminum, and steel industries.

Oligopoly markets have several important characteristics. First, no one firm can profit by adhering to price competition. For example, if a firm raises its price and other firms do not, its sales usually will suffer. Second, prices are identical or almost identical in oligopoly markets. Finally, without price competition, firms reach some sort of agreement, tacitly or otherwise, about what the set price will be. There may be a leader, usually the largest firm in the industry, that sets the price, and the other firms merely follow it. What little competition there is takes the form of product differentiation. The products of all firms in an oligopolistic industry are nearly interchangeable, but each firm's products have their own distinguishing characteristics, either real (as in quality or design) or fancied (as in brand names).

Price and Output Under Oligopoly—Short Run

The basic tools for analyzing price and output under conditions of oligopoly are the same as those used in analyzing pure competition and pure monopoly. If a firm seeks to maximize its short-run profits, price and output will be set at the point at which marginal cost equals marginal revenue. Under oligopoly, the average revenue curve slopes downward from left to right and in general appearance is similar to that under monopoly. The total sales of a product sold under oligopoly, however, are divided among a number of firms. The average revenue curve of each firm, therefore, reflects not only the change in total sales that accompanies a change in price but also the shifts in sales among the various firms resulting from the price change. If one firm reduces its price, this will increase somewhat the industry's total sales, and it will also attract some sales from its competitors. The extent of the shift in sales will depend on the reactions of its rivals to the initial price reduction. Other firms may leave their prices unchanged, reduce their prices by varying amounts, increase sales promotion activities, or introduce product changes. Firms operating under conditions of oligopoly are faced with much uncertainty; instead of a single determinate average revenue curve, as there is under monopoly, there is a family of average revenue curves, each indicating a different reaction by rival firms.

This reasoning means that the very nature of an oligopoly frequently rules out price competition. Firms in oligopoly know that price competition is unlikely to yield any significant gain in either sales or revenue. So each firm is likely to practice some form of product differentiation, such as advertising, to increase the demand curve for the firm's product. The individual firm's profit will be increased, too, because a shift to the right in the demand curve increases the differential between price and average total cost. Economies of scale would affect the part of the cost curve in which the average total costs are still declining. Since relatively few oligopolistic firms exist, any successful product differentiation by one firm will have significant effects on the sales of its rivals. These rivals will seek to offset this by trying to differentiate their own products. In estimating the effectiveness of a new advertising program, therefore, each firm must gauge the likely reactions of its rivals.

Price and Output—Long Run

In the short run, an oligopolist can make a profit or a loss. If its losses continue, the firm will be forced to leave the industry. In the long run, all the oligopolist's costs can vary, as existing plant facilities can be expanded. Economies of scale can result from decreases in a firm's long-run average total costs as the size of its plant increases. This, of course, is also true of firms operating in the long run under conditions of pure competition or pure monopoly. Those factors that produce economies of scale or decreasing long-run average costs as plant size increases are reduced input unit costs, greater specialization of resources, and more efficient use of equipment. Economies of scale shift all short-run cost curves to a lower level as the scale of operations becomes larger.

In the long run, the excess profits of firms operating in an oligopoly market situation can be maintained if there are restrictions on the entry of new firms into the market. Entry into an oligopolistic industry may be restricted in many ways, large capital requirements being one. The automobile industry is an example. Few companies have the resources to enter the industry, which was demonstrated after the end of World War II when the highly successful Kaiser Industries, the maker of various defense products, attempted to capitalize on an increased demand for automobiles by entering the market. Its effort ended in failure. There may be legal barriers in the form of patents, licenses, tariffs, or franchises, and it also may be difficult to counter the reputations of established firms. If the entry of new firms is restricted, which is likely in a typical oligopolistic situation, the prices may remain permanently above the average total costs, with excess profits both for the individual firms and the industry.

Economic Significance of Oligopoly

The economic and social losses from oligopolists' collusive practices are similar to those connected with monopoly. Output in such industries tends to be restricted; prices are maintained at high levels; and too few resources are employed when compared with the more competitive areas of the economy. Nonetheless, oligopoly itself does not necessarily contradict the social interest, since it may be based on the economies that can be obtained by large-sized firms. These economies may be so great in relation to the market served that they leave room for only a limited number of firms in an industry. When, however, oligopoly results from the exclusion of new, potentially efficient firms by such means as patent holdings, withholding of needed materials, or any form of collusion, the situation is clearly contrary to the public interest. Even when the small number of sellers can be traced to the economies of scale, this efficiency does the public little good if no real price competition ensures that the prices reflect that efficiency.

In summary, in a free enterprise market economy, theoretically the most desirable goal is pure competition because goods purchased by consumers usually are supplied at a minimum price under these conditions. The forms of competition in the real world, however, are far more numerous than the simple price and output adjustments that occur in the classical model of pure competition. In addition to price, real-world competition includes, among others, the variables of product quality, product performance, and product financing and marketing. Business firms' planning and controlling activities are efforts to adjust to external economic and market conditions, including the strategies of rival firms. The use of standard costing, target pricing, market share measurements, and similar practices are common to small and large firms and are part of the competitive process rather than evidence of monopoly power. Competition can occur in oligopolistic industries, and large firms can enable society to benefit from important economies of scale.

APPLICATION OF ECONOMIC MODELS TO ANTITRUST LAWS

Economic models have been developed to help describe our economic structure and to enable economists to predict the consequences of certain changes in variables within that structure. Although very few industries in the United States come close to the market structure of pure competition or monopoly, they provide a frame of reference for policy decisions. They represent opposite extremes. Pure competition represents a desirable market situation that, if it existed, would result in the maximum welfare of consumers. Both price and output would be market determined. In a purely competitive market, there would be no excessive concentration of economic power and no barriers to market entry. Many U.S. industries can best be described as oligopolies. An important social welfare question that must be asked is whether or not an oligopolistic market is able to allocate resources well enough to meet the wants of consumers and to provide effective competition. Since there are a few firms in oligopolistic industries, they may restrict competition through certain practices, such as agreements to limit output to be able to charge higher prices.

Collusion among such companies can be used to lessen or eliminate competition. In this way they act like monopolies. Oligopolies with rather high levels of economic concentration and high entry barriers are more likely to act in a collusive way than are oligopolies with lower levels of economic concentration and low entry barriers.

To understand the purpose of antitrust laws, it is first necessary to examine the subject of industrial concentration in the U.S. economy. By *concentration* we mean the control of the whole supply of a given class of goods by a small number of business firms. It may result from the growth and extension of a single enterprise, or more likely, from the acquisition of separate firms. Mainly in the field of large corporations is the government faced with the problem of creating and preserving competition. The realization of actual competition depends on the creation and maintenance of competitive conditions through the use of antitrust laws. The subject of industrial concentration is discussed in detail in Chapter 5.

SUMMARY

There are several types of markets. In a purely competitive market, output prices always tend to be equal to marginal costs of production. This equality between price and marginal cost means the consumer is required to pay for a product an amount equal to the additional costs of producing an additional unit of that product. This cost represents the amount that would have been produced elsewhere in the economy by the resources used in the production process. Output prices in the short run may be above, equal to, or below average costs of production. In the long run, prices tend to equal average costs of production. Furthermore, average costs of production tend to be forced to the minimum level by the pressure on firms to operate at the most efficient scale.

From a social point of view, monopoly—with some exceptions—is the most objectionable type of market structure. A given sum spent on a good produced by a monopoly gives the consumer a smaller amount of productive services than if the same sum had been spent on a good produced in a competitive market. This is because price under pure competition tends to equal marginal cost of production, whereas price under monopoly exceeds marginal cost. However, in some industries the economies of a large firm are so great that monopolies are desirable. Examples are the electric power and gas industries, In such cases, it is socially desirable to permit monopolies and regulate rates through publicly appointed commissions.

In oligopolistic markets, the number of firms is small relative to the total output. This type of market best describes the market conditions for many U.S. industries. Pricing policies of firms operating in an oligopolistic industry depend to a large degree on an estimate of what other sellers will do as a result of such action. When one firm is substantially larger than other firms, it is likely to be the price leader. This means it is usually the first to announce a price change, and its rivals will follow. Competition in an oligopolistic industry may take the form of product differentiation, where firms try to capture large shares of the market through brand names and advertising. A good example is the competition between Coca-Cola and Pepsi-Cola in the soft drink industry.

QUESTIONS FOR DISCUSSION

1. Do the economists' models of market structure have any validity in the study of antitrust enforcement?
2. What is the economic rationale for competition in the marketplace?
3. What is the economic significance of pure competition?
4. How are prices determined under conditions of monopoly?
5. Is it possible for monopoly prices to be lower than prices determined under purely competitive conditions? Discuss.
6. Why are oligopolistic industries often characterized by uniform action?
7. "Oligopoly seems to be the market type that accurately describes almost all major industries in the United States." Do you agree with this statement? Discuss.
8. Price leadership can take place in oligopolistic markets. What is price leadership?
9. "Oligopoly, like monopoly, contradicts the public interest." Do you agree with this statement? Why or why not?
10. "Prices in oligopolistic markets would always be higher than prices in purely competitive markets." Do you agree with this statement? Explain.

Chapter 5

Industrial Concentration
in the United States

The industrial development of the United States accelerated during the period following the end of the Civil War. Many factors contributed, one of which was an abundance of natural resources such as coal, oil, iron, lead, and silver. Railroad construction widened the domestic market, opened up new areas for settlement, and was itself a prime mover in stimulating demand for coal and iron. Population growth was accelerated by an influx of immigration, which provided a cheap supply of labor. Technological advances in transportation and industry opened the way to mass production, increased labor productivity, and large-scale economic organization. The institutions and goals of society were uniquely favorable to the individual entrepreneur. Agriculture, too, was undergoing a process of mechanization and expansion; the increasing emphasis on cash crops helped to provide export balances to pay interest and dividends on the imported capital that was furthering economic growth.

A trend toward industrial concentration began in the last century when many industries came to be dominated by a few relatively large firms or even by only one firm. The development of the corporation in the latter part of the century facilitated the concentration of control in many industries because corporations were able to buy the common stock of other corporations. Various anticompetitive business practices also enabled firms to drive their competitors out of business. By 1884, Standard Oil was selling more than 80 percent of the oil that flowed out of U.S. wells. In 1891, the American Tobacco Company controlled 88 percent of the total output of cigarettes, and by 1901, the U.S. Steel Corporation controlled 65 percent of the nation's steel capacity. This concentration continued unabated into the twentieth century. A contributory factor was the rising power of the investment banker, who supplied the funds to finance industrial expansion. In 1914, firms with an annual output valued at a million or more dollars constituted only 2.2 percent of the total

99

number of manufacturing firms, but they employed 35.3 percent of all manufacturing workers and produced, in value, 48.7 percent of all manufactured
products.[1]

In the 1920s an extraordinary expansion of industrial concentration occurred. In part this concentration was an inevitable concomitant of a rapidly
developing industrial society in which the use of large specialized machines
and facilities and assembly-line methods of production necessitated large
firms. A case in point is the automobile industry. In 1900, 4,192 automobiles
were built in the United States. By 1910, the number of cars produced increased to 181,000, and by 1920, automobile production had increased to
1,900,000.[2] During the 1920s, the automobile industry forged rapidly ahead,
bringing along with it such related industries as rubber, oil, glass, steel, and
road building. However, a consolidation took place in the automobile industry
so that in 1911 Ford and General Motors had 37.7 percent of the automobile
market, and by 1923 their share had increased to 66.3 percent. The rewards
went to the companies that could turn out the most cars. The higher the volume
of production, the lower the cost of turning out each individual automobile.
But this method required the building or acquisition of vast manufacturing and
distribution facilities.

Industrial concentration in the United States was accentuated by events during and immediately after World War II. Large corporations emerged from the
war in a much stronger position, whereas small businesses were weakened.
War contracts had been given mainly to large firms, most likely because large
firms had the capacity to mass-produce the thousands of airplanes and tanks
necessary for the war effort. Indeed, the U.S. industrial might was probably
the decisive factor in the Allied victory over the Axis powers. War contracts
were instruments of economic power that guaranteed their holders marked and
sizable profits, gave them priority in obtaining parts and raw materials, and
gave them the right to take advantage of favorable depreciation and tax carry-
back provisions. During the war, the federal government spent about $600
million a year on industrial research, over one-third of all the research funds
going to large corporations. And even when the large firms subcontracted
work, three-fourths of their subcontracts went to other large firms. The federal

---

[1] Solomon Fabricant, *The Output of Manufacturing Industries, 1899–1937* (New York:
National Bureau of Economic Research, 1940), pp. 84–85.

[2] *Facts and Figures, 1985* (Detroit: Motor Vehicle Manufacturers of the United States, 1985),
p. 6.

government also financed new production facilities, which also benefited the largest corporations most.

In the 1960s and 1970s, there arose a new form of business combination called the *conglomerate,* which represents a union of unrelated companies. Conglomerates are multiproduct, multimarket companies that are the result of an amalgam of unlike companies. The conglomerate became the most popular form of business combination when companies hastened to acquire other companies with different products and markets. An example of a conglomerate merger was the acquisition of Columbia Pictures by Coca-Cola. Moreover, conglomerates have taken over other conglomerates; for example, the acquisitions in 1985 of Nabisco by Reynolds Industries, and General Foods by Philip Morris. In attempting to diversify their product lines, oil companies have acquired chain retail stores and a copper company, and U.S. Steel acquired an oil company.

MERGERS

Typically, large firms have become larger through mergers. A classic example is General Motors, the largest manufacturing firm in America, which was formed in 1908 by William Durant as a holding company. Buick, Cadillac, and Oldsmobile were joined together in the holding company, which by 1910 controlled ten automobile, three truck-making, and ten parts and accessories firms.[3] The Chevrolet automobile company was acquired in 1915. In 1916, General Motors purchased makers of roller bearings, radiators, horns, and starting ignition, and lighting systems. General Motors then became a corporation, and the various holding company subsidiaries became divisions. It acquired companies making tires, leather, aluminum, gears, casting, and machine tools. From its original inception in 1908, General Motors acquired more than sixty companies by 1920. The whole strategy of General Motors was predicated on capitalizing on the potential mass market for automobiles by combining the production, assembly, and distribution facilities of many existing companies.

The same conditions of industrial concentration prevail in the United States today as in the past. A case in point was the twenty-fifth anniversary of *Fortune* magazine's annual list of the 500 largest manufacturing corporations in

---

[3] Alfred D. Chandler, *Giant Enterprise: Ford, General Motors, and the Automobile Industry* (New York: Harcourt, Brace & World, 1964), pp. 44–63.

the United States. Of the top 500 companies when the list was first published in 1953, only 262 were still around by 1980.[4] Almost all the departed 238 were acquired by mergers or acquisitions by other large firms; only four of them actually went out of business. Since 1980, there have been many more mergers involving firms in *Fortune*'s 500. One example was Du Pont's acquisition of Conoco in 1981. This merger, the largest in the history of the United States up to that time, involved two of the twenty-five largest industrial corporations in America, with combined sales of $32 billion. Two larger mergers were consummated in 1984 when Standard Oil of California (Chevron) acquired Gulf Oil and Texaco acquired Getty Oil.[5]

Types of Mergers

On the basis of the economic interrelationship between the firms involved, mergers may be classified into three basic types—horizontal, vertical, and conglomerate. The last one can also be divided into three types of mergers—market extension, product extension, and pure conglomerate.

Horizontal Merger

A horizontal merger involves the merger of two competing firms at the same stage of the production or distribution process. Examples would be the merger of two beer companies or two shoe companies. Of the three kinds of mergers, a horizontal merger has the most immediate effect on competition. The unification of two firms producing the same product will increase concentration within an industry no matter how small the firms are. The merger may be insignificant with respect to its effect on competition, or it may be patently anticompetitive. In a horizontal merger, there is the question of what constitutes an anticompetitive share of the total market. The factors considered are the number of firms, the degree of industry concentration, the conditions of entry, and product characteristics.

---

[4] *Fortune,* May 5, 1980, Vol. 101, No. 9, p. 88.

[5] Pennzoil sued Texaco over this acquisition and won in court. Texaco had to make financial restitution to Pennzoil.

Vertical Merger

A vertical merger brings under one ownership control over firms engaged in different stages of production and distribution. The acquisition of a shoe retail outlet by a shoe manufacturer is an example. A vertical merger may serve to give a firm access to essential raw materials and outlets for its products. It is often based on projected realization of economics in distribution. In other instances, it may be used to ensure sources of supply for a manufacturing firm, particularly in industries in which the availability of essential supplies may vary erratically. A manufacturer having difficulty in obtaining retailers to handle its product line may acquire a retail chain to enable it to directly market its product. A vertical merger may stem from the difficulty of preventing partial excess capacity in multifunctional firms.

Conglomerate Merger

The conglomerate merger unites firms producing diverse and unrelated product lines in which the end products bear no similarity. An example would be the acquisition of a bank by an oil company. The conglomerate merger does not entail firms in direct competition with each other, nor are there usually any extensive vertical relations between the firms. Many large American firms have attained their size through the conglomerate merger. An example is the International Telegraph and Telephone Company (ITT), which originally operated almost exclusively as a telephone, telegraph, cable, and wireless public utility. Through mergers, ITT acquired companies in such areas as book publishing, baking, hotels, fire insurance, vending machines, and consumer financing.

There are three types of conglomerate mergers:

1. *Market extension.* A market extension merger is one in which a conglomerate wants to get a toehold in a particular industry through the acquisition of an existing firm in the industry. An example was the acquisition of the Miller Brewing Company by Philip Morris.

2. *Product extension.* A product extension merger is one firm's acquisition of a second business producing a product closely related to the acquiring firm's product line. The classic example of a production extension merger was the attempted takeover of Clorox, a maker of liquid bleach, by Procter & Gamble, the largest manufacturer of household cleaning supplies in the United States.

3. *Pure conglomerate.* A pure conglomerate merger is a merger of two totally unrelated firms. An example would be the acquisition of Avis, a
rental car company, by ITT, a manufacturer of telecommunication equipment.

Development of Mergers

Mergers tend to come in cycles, the first coming around the turn of the century.
The Sherman Act had little effect on curbing industrial concentration in the
United States in the first decade after its passage. By 1900, after ten years of
enforcement of the Sherman Act, the number of industrial combinations in the
United States with capital of $1 billion or more had increased from ten to three
hundred.[6] The catalyst in the merger movement was an economic depression
that occurred between 1893 and 1896. The merger was one way to protect
against a decline in economic activity, for if a firm could gain control over
competing plants in its principal line of commerce, it would have a better opportunity to fix prices and control output. The mergers consummated at the
end of the century were in such industries as petroleum, iron and steel, copper,
sugar, lead, and salt.

A second cycle of mergers was completed during the prosperous 1920s,
with the peak occurring in 1929, when some 1,245 mergers were formed.[7]
During that entire decade, there were around seven thousand mergers, primarily in the mass production and entertainment industries—automobiles, automobile parts, motion pictures, movie theaters, and appliances. The mass production of the automobile effected certain economies of scale that could be
best achieved through mergers. Automobile companies acquired medium-
sized firms that could produce such things as parts and components used in the
automobile industry. The stock market itself had an influence on the merger
movement of the 1920s. This was a period of rapidly rising securities prices,
which provided an opportunity for selling new securities to brokerage houses,
and mergers were a way of stimulating speculative interest in securities.

A third cycle of mergers began in the middle 1950s and continued up to the
latter part of the 1970s. There was a significant increase in the number of con-

---

[6] Temporary National Economic Committee, *Competition and Monopoly in American Industry,* Monograph No. 21 (Washington, D.C.: U.S. Government Printing Office, 1940), p. 88.

[7] Ibid., p. 105.

TABLE 5-1   Corporate Acquisitions, Including Takeovers 1979–1988

Year	No. of Acquisitions	Value (in bill.)	No. of Takeovers	Value of Takeovers (in bill.)
1979	1526	$ 34.2	3	$ 6.2
1980	1565	33.1	3	6.5
1981	2326	67.0	8	20.6
1982	2295	60.4	9	24.0
1983	2345	52.3	7	10.4
1984	3064	125.2	19	55.2
1985	3165	139.1	26	60.8
1986	4022	190.0	34	68.8
1987	3701	167.5	30	62.2
1988 (Jan.-July)	1656	82.1	14	32.4

Sources: Data provided by Peter W. Rodino, Chairman, Committee on the Judiciary, U.S. House of Representatives, and from "Deals of the Year" by Ronald Henkoff, FORTUNE, Vol. 119, No. 3, pp. 162–163. ©1989 The Time Inc. Magazine Company. All rights reserved. Reprinted by permission.

glomerate mergers, a movement that cut across different types of industries, such as manufacturing, mining, banking, insurance, trade, and service. The reasons for the continued growth of mergers were varied and included the desire to meet foreign competition, the need to control the various stages of product flow, to diversify, and to improve access to credit. Certainly a widespread, unstated motive may have been the desire to restrict competition. However, an acquiring firm may also gain from a merger by securing the acquired firm's personnel, marketing facilities, and trade reputation.

A fourth cycle of mergers began in the 1980s. What differentiates this cycle from the others is the size of the firms involved in the mergers. The biggest wave of corporate acquisitions in U.S. history contributed to the rise in stock prices to historic highs, and increased the debt of many corporations so that they could finance their multibillion-dollar takeovers of other companies. A new kind of corporate acquisition developed during this time—an acquisition not for the purpose of expansion or diversification but for liquidating a company and making an immediate profit. The fourth cycle of mergers also reflects the free market policies of the Reagan administration.

TABLE 5-2   Major Acquisitions, Including Takeovers, for 1988

Buyer	Company Bought	Value (billions)
Kohlberg Kravis Roberts*	RJR Nabisco**	$24.5
Philip Morris	Kraft	12.9
Campeau	Federated Department Stores	6.5
BAT Industries	Farmers Group	5.1
Eastman Kodak	Sterling Drug	5.1
F. H. Acquisition	Fort Howard**	3.6
News Corp.	Triangle Publications	3.0
Bridgeton	Firestone Tire & Rubber	2.6
Chevron	Gulf of Mexico	2.6
Maxwell Communications	Macmillan	2.6
ASI Holdings	American Standard**	2.5
Sony	CBS Records	2.0

* This deal was not consummated in 1988. It will be completed in 1989. Also pending is Grand Metropolitan's acquisition of Pillsbury for $5.7 billion.

** Leveraged buyouts.

Source: From "Deals of the Year" by Ronald Henkoff, FORTUNE, Vol. 119, No. 3, pp. 163–164.
©1989 The Time Inc. Magazine Company. All rights reserved. Reprinted by permission.

Table 5-1 presents the number and value of acquisitions consummated during the period 1979–1988. The dollar value of acquisitions increased from $34.2 billion in 1979 to $167.5 billion in 1987. The number of acquisitions also hit an all-time high of 4,022 in 1986. Included in the acquisitions are takeovers. Some companies and individuals are simply in the business of buying other companies. They do not intend to run a company on a day-to-day basis; they will either keep existing management or hire a new management team to run the company. They have financed acquisitions through the sale of high-yield junk bonds to wealthy people and institutional investors. Some companies make money by acting as an intermediary to the merger of other companies. Table 5-2 presents some of the major acquisitions consummated in 1988. The largest acquisition of the year involved Kohlberg Kravis

Roberts' acquisition of RJR Nabisco for $24.5 billion. Foreign firms were active in their acquisition of U.S. firms. The most important reason was the discount in the value of the dollar relative to foreign currencies. It is also important to point out the fact that financial intermediaries take in money in the form of advisory fees. For example, Goldman Sachs, representing Kraft, and Wasserman Parella, representing Philip Morris, charged fees of $42 million.

TAKEOVERS

The takeover is an important type of corporate acquisition. The term is imprecise, referring to the transfer of control of a firm from one group of shareholders to another. Unlike a merger, which represents a pooling of interests, the firm that is taken over can disappear. Takeovers can be "hostile" in that management of a firm will fight the attempted takeover, usually because they stand to lose their jobs; or "friendly" in that management is in favor of it. Takeovers can be done by firms or individuals, such as T. Boone Pickens and Carl Icahn, who have earned the sobriquet "corporate raiders." In 1987 takeovers accounted for 40 percent of the value of all corporate acquisitions. Thirty takeovers had values of more than $1 billion.[8] Takeovers are quite controversial, and there is strong pressure on regulators and legislators to enact restrictions that would curb this type of business activity. Legislatures in a number of states have passed antitakeover laws.

Benefits of Takeovers

Proponents of takeovers argue that they represent productive activity that improves the control and management of assets and helps move assets to more productive uses.[9] They help keep managers on the ball through fear that they will lose their jobs. Acquiring firm shareholders gain more from takeovers than they do from mergers. T. Boone Pickens has claimed to be the champion of the small stockholder, asserting that his raids on four major oil companies

[8] Data furnished by the Committee on the Judiciary, U.S. House of Representatives, June, 1988.

[9] Michael C. Jensen, "The Takeover Controversy: Analysis and Evidence," *Midland Corporate Financial Journal* 4, no. 2 (Summer 1986).

added some $6.5 billion to the value of their stocks. Another alleged benefit of takeovers is that they do not waste credit or resources; instead they generate substantive gains—historically, 8.4 percent of the total value of both companies. Finally, takeovers generally occur because changing technology or market conditions require a major restructuring of corporate assets.

Criticisms of Takeovers

One major criticism of takeovers is that they add to the concentration of economic power in the hands of a few people or firms. A second criticism involves the two-tiered tender offer, in which a corporate bidder offers a substantial premium over the market for a bare majority of a target company's shares.[10] Once the deal is consummated, the remaining stockholders receive a price well below the cash bid price. A third criticism of takeovers, particularly the hostile ones, is that the acquirer is often more interested in making money than running a business. There is no concern for the employees of the acquired firm. Often the most lucrative assets of the business are sold to make money for the corporate raider. Finally, targeted companies that have successfully fought a takeover attempt find themselves financially weakened.

Leveraged Buyouts and Junk Bonds

The leveraged buyout is associated with the takeover. It is a way in which to raise cash to buy out a company. An investor group, which can be headed by a company's top managers or by buyout specialists, can put up a small percentage of the bid price in cash, borrow against the company's assets in secured bank loans, and issue junk bonds. Junk bonds are low quality bonds with a Standard & Poor's rating of B or less.[11] They carry a high rate of interest and are purchased by individuals, insurance companies, and anyone who wishes to assume the risks of buying them. The group then buys all of the outstanding common stock shares of the company, taking the company private. It then sells off parts of the company to reduce the debt. It cuts costs to increase profitability and to ensure that the company can meet payments on its debts. It may lay

[10] William J. Carney, "Two-Tier Tender Offers and Shark Repellents," *Midland Corporate Financial Journal* 4, no. 2 (Summer 1986).

[11] Standard & Poor's rates bonds from AAA (the best), AA, A, BBB, BB, B, CCC, and so forth. BBB and below carry low ratings and can be considered junk bonds.

off workers, close losing divisions, and reduce spending on new plants and equipment. Finally, the company can earn high returns by taking the stream-lined company public again.

THE EXTENT OF CONCENTRATION BY INDUSTRY

The extent of concentration in the United States varies considerably by industry. In some industries, one large firm is clearly dominant, in that it contributed 60 percent or more of total output. General Motors, with more than 60 percent of America's domestic output of automobiles is an example. In other industries, a few firms may account for the bulk of shares, with no one firm clearly dominant over the others; for example, the dominance of the tobacco industry by RJR Nabisco and Philip Morris, and of the soft drink industry by Coca-Cola and PepsiCo. Both industries correspond to an oligopolistic market. Also, some industries have little or no concentration and thus come fairly close to approximating a purely competitive market situation. The shoe, concrete products, and women's clothing industries are examples.

There are several ways of measuring the extent of industrial concentration. One way is concentration by firm size, which divides firms on the basis of such criteria as number of employees, payrolls, and value added by manufacturing. A second way is to measure changes in the share of value added by manufacturing for large companies over various periods. A third way is to compare shares of value added by manufacturing, value of shipment, and other measures of concentration for large companies over different periods. And a fourth way is to measure the extent of concentration for each industry by dividing its market output for the four largest firms. If 80 percent of the output of an industry is contributed by the four largest firms, it can be said that the industry possesses a high degree of industrial concentration.

Concentration by Firm Size

Table 5-3 presents payrolls, value added by manufacturing, and capital expenditures for a distribution of firms based on number of employees. The data are for 1982. Firms employing a thousand or more workers accounted for 0.6 percent of all firms, but accounted for 25.2 percent of total employment in manufacturing, 33.1 percent of total value of payrolls, 31.5 percent of value added by manufacturing, and 34.6 percent of new capital expenditures. However,

TABLE 5-3   Distribution of Industry in the United States by Employment Size, 1982

Item	Total	Under 20	20–99	100–249	250–999	1,000 and Over
			Employment Size			
In thousands:						
Establishments	348	230	84	21	11	2
Employees	17,818	1,405	3,662	3,287	4,977	4,486
In millions:						
Payroll	$341,406	$20,404	$59,103	$55,708	$93,125	$113,068
Value added by manu- facturing	824,117	45,997	135,932	134,379	247,729	260,081
New capital expenditures	74,562	3,639	9,469	12,323	23,331	25,800

Source: U.S. Department of Commerce, Bureau of the Census, *1982 Census of Manufacturers: General Summary* (Washington, D.C.: U.S. Government Printing Office, 1986), pp. 1–8.

these percentages show a decline when compared to statistics for 1977. The respective percentages for 1977 were employment in manufacturing, 28 percent; total value of payrolls, 35.4 percent; value added by manufacturing, 34.2 percent; new capital expenditures, 35.8 percent. However, approximately only 2 percent of all industrial firms in the United States produced about half of the value added by manufacturing and about all new capital expenditures for 1982.

There also have been no discernible long-run trends toward greater concentration of output from a smaller number of firms; in fact, the opposite appears. When 1954 is used as a base year, firms with a thousand or more workers employed 32.6 percent of the labor force in manufacturing compared to 25.2 percent in 1982. The percentage of payrolls provided by these largest firms declined from 37.3 percent of the total in 1954 to 35.4 percent in 1982. The contribution made to total new capital expenditures by the largest firms decreased from 38.3 percent in 1954 to 35.8 percent in 1982, and the contribution of the largest firms to value added by manufacturing declined from 37.0

TABLE 5-4   Percent Share of Largest Companies of Total Value Added by Manufacturing, 1947–1982

Company Rank Group Based on Value Added by Manufacturing	Year									
	1947	1954	1958	1963	1966	1967	1970	1972	1977	1982
50 largest	17%	23%	23%	25%	25%	25%	24%	25%	24%	24%
100 largest	23	30	30	33	33	33	33	33	33	33
150 largest	27	34	35	37	38	38	38	39	39	39
200 largest	30	37	38	41	42	42	43	43	44	43

Source: U.S. Bureau of the Census, 1982 Census of Manufacture, *Concentration Ratios in Manufacturing*, (Washington, D.C.: U.S. Government Pritning Office, May 1986) Table 1, p. 7.

percent in 1954 to 34.2 percent in 1982. Also note the decline in the number of workers employed in manufacturing.

Concentration Based on Value Added by Manufacturing

Table 5-4 presents the percentages of the share of total value added by manufacturing of the largest companies over several periods, with 1947 as the base year. The trend during the earlier periods was toward greater concentration of output. The largest fifty companies, as measured by their contribution to value added by manufacturing, contributed 17 percent of value added in 1947 to 24 percent in 1982. But from 1954 to 1982, the percentage share of the fifty largest firms has remained virtually unchanged. The percentage share of the two hundred largest firms of total value added by manufacturing was 30 percent in 1947 compared to 43 percent in 1982. However, almost all this increase was during the period from 1947 to 1963, and there has been little change since. A large overall relative gain was made by the second fifty largest firms in the top one hundred, which increased this share of value added from 6 percent in 1947 to 9 percent in 1982. It is important to note that the largest fifty companies contributed more to the total value added by manufacturing in 1947 and 1982 than the next largest 150 firms did.

TABLE 5-5 Share of Value Added, Employment, Payroll, Value of Shipments, and Capital Expenditures Accounted for by the 200 Largest Companies, 1982

Company Rank Group Based on Value Added by Manufacturing	Year	Value Added by Manufacturing	All Employees		Production Workers			Value of Shipments	Capital Expenditures, New
			Number	Payroll	Number	Labor Hours	Wages		
50 largest	1982	24	17	24	14	14	20	23	27
	1977	24	16	25	16	17	24	25	28
	1967	25	20	25	18	18	23	25	27
51 to 100 largest	1982	9	7	8	6	6	8	9	10
	1977	9	7	8	6	7	7	9	11
	1967	8	6	7	5	6	6	8	13
101 to 150 largest	1982	6	5	6	4	4	5	7	7
	1977	6	5	5	5	5	5	6	6
	1967	5	4	5	4	4	4	6	6
151 to 200 largest	1982	4	4	4	3	3	4	5	6
	1977	4	4	4	4	4	4	4	5
	1967	4	4	3	3	3	3	4	4
200 largest	1982	43	33	41	28	28	37	44	49
	1977	44	33	42	31	32	40	45	49
	1967	42	34	40	30	31	37	43	51

Sources: U.S. Bureau of the Census, Census of Manufacture, 1982, *Concentration Ratios in Manufacturing* (Washington, D.C.: U.S. Government Printing Office), Table 4, May 1986; Census of Manufacture, 1977, *Concentration Ratios in Manufacturing* (Washington, D.C.: U.S. Government Printing Office), Table 4, May 1981.

Concentration as Measured by Share of Value Added by Manufacturing and Other Criteria

Table 5-5 compares the shares of value added by manufacturing, employment, value of shipment, and capital expenditures by the two hundred largest manufacturing firms for three periods, 1967, 1977, and 1982. The dominance of the sixty largest firms is apparent. In 1982, the fifty largest firms accounted for 24 percent of the total value added by manufacturing; the next largest fifty firms contributed only 9 percent; and the remaining largest one hundred firms accounted for 10 percent. The fifty largest firms employed 17 percent of all manufacturing workers in 1982; the next largest one hundred fifty firms employed 16 percent. The fifty largest companies accounted for 23 percent of the total value of shipment in 1982 compared to 21 percent for the next largest one hundred fifty companies. With regard to new capital expenditures, the fifty largest firms were responsible for 27 percent of the total in 1982 compared with 22 percent for the next largest one hundred fifty companies. However, there was very little change in the firms' relative shares in each classification for the three periods, 1967, 1977, and 1982; if anything, there is a slight decline in the shares of the fifty largest companies. In 1982, the fifty largest companies contributed 24 percent of the value added by manufacturing compared to 25 percent in 1967. They employed 17 percent of all manufacturing workers in 1982 compared to 20 percent in 1967, and they contributed 23 percent of the total value of shipments in 1982 compared to 25 percent in 1967.

Concentration Based on Share of Industry Output

A common measure of industrial concentration is the total output of the four largest firms within an industry. Table 5-6 compares the output of the four largest firms in a number of high- and low-concentration industries. The extent of concentration is highest in the production of motor vehicles, car and truck bodies, household laundry equipment, and cereal breakfast foods, and lowest in women's and misses' dresses, concrete products, and fur goods. However, a high degree of concentration does not necessarily indicate a monopoly or a lack of competition. For one thing, the concentration data offered by the Bureau of the Census cover only U.S. production and omit foreign imports. Omitting this foreign competition leads to a significant overstatement of economic concentration in some U.S. markets. A case in point is the U.S. car market. Although the four largest U.S. firms produce more than 90 percent of

TABLE 5-6 Percentages of Industry Output Produced by the Four Largest Firms in High- and Low-Concentration Industries (output measured by value of shipment)

High-Concentration and Low-Concentration Industries	*Percent of Industry Output Produced by Four Largest Firms*
High-Concentration Industries	
Motor vehicles and car bodies	92%
Household laundry equipment	91
Cereal breakfast foods	86
Cigarettes	84
Organic fibers	77
Malt beverages	77
Photographic equipment	74
Sewing machines	72
Tires	66
Primary aluminum	64
Aircraft	64
Motor vehicle parts and accessories	61
Soap and other detergents	60
Metal cans	50
Low-Concentration Industries	
Meat packing	29
Petroleum refining	28
Pharmaceutical products	26
Men's and boys' suits and clothes	26
Millinery	24
Radio and TV equipment	22
Poultry dressing	22
Canned fruits and vegetables	21
Sawmills	17
Fluid milk	16
Wood household furniture	16
Fur goods	12
Concrete products	10
Women's and misses' dresses	6

Source: U.S. Bureau of the Census, 1982 Census of Manufacture, *Concentration Ratios in Manufacturing* (Washington, D.C.: U.S. Government Printing Office, 1986), Table 5.

domestic-made cars, 25 percent of all cars sold in the United States are foreign imports. Consumers are free to choose from a variety of cars, domestic and foreign. There have been some shifts in concentration ratios by industries over time. For example, in 1967, the four largest tire companies had 73 percent of their industry output compared to 66 percent in 1982. Conversely, the four largest car companies had 52 percent of industry output in 1967 compared to 77 percent in 1982. The four largest cereal breakfast food companies had 90 percent of industry output in 1967 compared to 86 percent in 1982. For less concentrated industries, the four largest meat-packing companies contributed 22 percent of total industry output in 1967 compared to 29 percent in 1982. The four largest firms in petroleum refining contributed 24 percent of industry output in 1967 compared to 28 percent in 1982. On the other hand, the share of output of women's and misses' dresses produced by the four largest firms declined from 9 percent in 1967 to 6 percent in 1982.

INDUSTRIAL CONCENTRATION AND GLOBAL MARKETS

Almost all U.S. and foreign industrial corporations do not confine themselves to domestic sales but participate in business activities outside the boundaries of their countries. These corporations are called *multinationals* because they transcend national boundaries. They have contributed to the internationalization of production. Many foreign companies sell in the United States, and in some markets they have more than 50 percent of the market share. Realistically, market definitions should be reappraised because the change to a global economy means that traditional measures of industrial concentration understate the existence of competition. Many U.S. industries appear highly concentrated when measures of concentration are limited only to domestic markets, but fall far short of this concentration when world markets are considered. The U.S. auto industry is a case in point.

The U.S. Automobile Industry

The U.S. automobile industry is highly concentrated when only domestic automobile output is used to measure industrial concentration. In 1986, General Motors, Ford, and Chrysler produced 95 percent of all cars manufactured

TABLE 5-7 Leading World Automobile Producers and Their Share of Total Worldwide Output, 1987

Company	Passenger Cars (in thousands)	Percent of World Production
General Motors (USA)	5,605	16.9%
Ford (USA)	4,000	12.1
Toyota (Japan)	2,796	8.4
Nissan (Japan)	2,017	6.1
Peugeot (France)	2,301	6.9
Volkswagen (West Germany)	2,338	7.1
Chrysler (USA)	1,186	3.6
Renault (France)	1,742	5.2
Fiat (Italy)	1,675	5.1
Honda (Japan)	1,362	4.1
VAZ (USSR)	725	1.8
Mitsubishi (Japan)	595	1.8
World Output	33,007	

Source: From *Facts & Figures, 1988* (Detroit, MI: Motor Vehicle Manufacturers Association), p. 31. Used by permission.

in the United States.[12] Their shares of domestic auto production were respectively 55 percent, 23 percent, and 17 percent. However, when imports of foreign cars are taken into consideration, the market shares changed. Of the more than 11 million cars sold in the United States in 1986, General Motors accounted for 40 percent, Ford 18 percent, Chrysler 10 percent, and Toyota 10 percent.[13] Total foreign imports of cars accounted for around 29 percent of the automobile sales in the U.S. market, giving American consumers a variety of choices when it came to buying automobiles.

The automobile market has to be viewed in terms of a global market. There are some forty automobile producers in the world, and almost all sell in a number of foreign markets. Ford sells as many cars outside the United States as it does in it. Table 5-7 presents the total number of passenger cars produced

[12] *Facts & Figures,* 1987 (Detroit: Motor Vehicle Manufacturers Association, 1988), pp. 14–15.
[13] Ibid., p. 16.

for the twelve largest automobile companies in the world. These twelve companies accounted for 85 percent of all automobiles produced in the world in 1987. The four largest automobile producers accounted for around 49 percent of the world output. Japan was the world's largest producer of motor vehicles in 1987; the United States was second, West Germany third, and France fourth. Approximately 60 percent of all cars manufactured in Japan were shipped to foreign markets, with the United States being the largest of those markets.

THE ISSUES IN INDUSTRIAL CONCENTRATION

In some industries, a certain amount of industrial concentration apparently is inevitable, since some types of business organizations lend themselves to large-scale production. For example, in some industries the product itself is highly complex and can be constructed only by a large and diversified organization. Automobiles and computers are examples. Also in some industries the product is large in size, requiring complex equipment for construction and large capital investments; for example, shipbuilding. And some industries require a large capital investment, particularly in plants and equipment. The steel industry is an example. Finally, in some industries a natural resource is required that is available only in limited amounts and in specific geographic locations. An example is the petroleum industry.

Industrial concentration may also be an inevitable concomitant of advancing technology in all major industrial countries, regardless of their ideologies. For example, data show that for some industries, concentration ratios are generally higher in other Western countries than in the United States; that the foreign industries in which concentration is high are generally the same as those in which concentration is high in the United States; and that the industries that are not highly concentrated in other Western industrial countries are generally the same as those industries that are not concentrated in this country. In Japan and West Germany, the steel, chemical, and rubber industries are more concentrated than they are in the United States.[14] In France, Peugeot and Renault produce 100 percent of all French cars.[15] These data suggest that technological

[14] The President's Commission on Industrial Competitiveness, *Global Competition: The New Reality,* vol. 2 (Washington, D.C.: U.S. Government Printing Office, 1985), p. 190.

[15] Motor Vehicle Manufacturers Association, *Facts & Figures, 1988,* p. 31.

and economic factors determine somewhat the degree of concentration of industry in all market economies.[16]

Advantages of Concentration

Large-scale production offers several advantages. An expansion of a firm's production unit often permits greater specialization in the use of both labor and capital equipment. Overhead cost may be spread over a larger output, which results in a lower unit cost. Economies can result from new lower minimum-cost combinations of production factors; that is, land, labor, and capital. Specialized labor and capital equipment frequently can be added to a production unit only in large indivisible amounts, and because of the inability of specialized factors to diversify, they cannot be used profitably in small-scale operations. In many industries, smaller business units may well result in higher unit costs, and hence the answer to the problem of monopoly may not necessarily be the breaking up of the firms. Market power can be based on underlying economies of scale and technological or managerial leadership; in some cases, large firms are the price of efficiency and innovation.[17]

Disadvantages of Concentration

In a competitive market economy, the interests of producers and consumers coincide because the way to larger profits for producers is through greater efficiency, price reductions, and increased sales volume, all of which naturally benefit consumers. In a monopolistic or oligopolistic market, profits may be maximized at the expense of consumers by selling a smaller quantity of goods at a higher price than under competitive conditions. Also, evidence shows that small or medium-sized firms are often more innovative than larger firms. Apple Computer Company, for instance, was created in the 1970s by two men in their twenties who started their operations in a garage. Although the computer (data processing) industry was and is dominated by IBM, Apple became the leading exponent of technology for the masses. Finally, industrial concentra-

---

[16] Industries in the centrally planned economies of the Soviet Union and Eastern Europe are even more concentrated.

[17] In a case involving Alcoa, the Supreme Court was unwilling to split up the company for fear of losing substantial economies of scale in production and research and development.

tion can and has resulted in the growth of unfair business practices designed to eliminate competition and exploit consumers.

Market Power and Barriers to Entry

The idea of entry has for a long time been used by economists as an important part of economic theory. In pure competition, freedom of entry and departure bring about the long-run equilibrium of an industry. In the short run, if profits are high in an industry, new firms will enter and compete away profits. In the long run, all firms in the industry will receive a price equal to their average total costs. Conversely, firms will leave less profitable industries. Market power exists in any industry when there are significant barriers to entry. The extent of this market power varies considerably by industry. In some oligopolistic industries, entry would be extremely difficult, if not impossible—the automobile and cigarette industries, for example. There have been no new domestic producers of automobiles in the last forty years. However, although IBM dominates the computer and data processing industry, six new firms entered the market during the 1970s.

Several barriers can block entry into a market. One barrier is product differentiation. The greater the degree of product differentiation, the higher the barrier to entry. An example is the soft drink industry, which is dominated by Coca-Cola Company and PepsiCo. Coca-Cola and Pepsi-Cola are well-known products. In February and March 1988, Pepsi-Cola had 18.4 percent of total soft drink sales compared with 14.9 percent for Classic Coke and 2.4 percent for New Coke.[18] A number of other soft drinks each company makes are differentiated on the basis of taste, caffeine, or calories. Examples are Diet Coke, Cherry Coke, Diet Pepsi, Tab, Pepsi-Free, Slice, Sprite, and so forth. Consumer acceptance of these products makes entry of new soft drink firms very difficult. The same would hold true for other industries where products are differentiated and there is a high degree of consumer acceptance. Examples are the breakfast food, cigarette, and detergent industries.

Another barrier to entry can occur when firms in an industry possess an absolute cost advantage over potential entrants into the market. This advantage can arise in several ways. First, existing firms may already possess the best natural resource—coal, timberland, or iron ore deposits. Second, the existing firms may already have patents on the most popular products. Third, they may have access to capital at lower rates of interest than would be available to new

---

[18] *Birmingham Post-Herald,* June 4, 1988, Section B11.

entrants into the market. Fourth, they possess management and marketing advantages over potential rivals who have to hire skilled managers. These advantages would give existing firms a lower average total cost advantage over potential competition at a whole range of output that could be supplied.

A third barrier to entry is capital requirements. The reason there have been no entrants into the automobile industry in many years is that an enormous amount of money would have to be invested in plants and equipment to compete with the existing automobile companies. In 1988 the assets of General Motors, the world's largest automobile company, amounted to $164 billion.[19] Entry is made difficult because auto company assets are durable and specialized. Moreover, any market entrant would have to achieve a substantial market share to realize economies of scale. The established Japanese and European automobile companies have successfully penetrated the U.S. market because they already have plant facilities and can mass-produce cars.

INDUSTRIAL CONCENTRATION—BANKING

The structure of the U.S, banking system is undergoing changes of unprecedented magnitude.[20] To some extent these changes reflect the impact of rapid technological change. They also reflect the passage of laws that have eliminated many of the regulatory constraints on the management of commercial banks, as they have allowed many other institutions to alter the nature of deposit and lending services offered to their customers. For example, Merrill Lynch offers credit for real estate and related purposes and for the purchase of securities. Furthermore, with its Cash Management Account (CMA) Merrill Lynch has created a financial instrument directly competitive with checking accounts offered by commercial banks. Money market mutual funds also provide another example of the growth of nondeposit financial institutions that provide competition to commercial banks. Moreover, many offer a number of convenient services, the most attractive of which is the ability to write checks against the value of the account. The elimination of interest rate ceilings has stimulated the growth of money market funds.

Changes have also taken place within the banking system itself. The development of branch banking means that banks are permitted to branch through-

---

[19] *Fortune,* April 24, 1989, p. 354.

[20] Kerry M. Cooper and Donald R. Fraser, "Banking Deregulation and the New Competition in Financial Services" *The Fortune 500* (Cambridge, Mass.: Ballinger, 1984), Vol. 117, No. 9, Chaps. 1 and 2.

out a state. The advent of automatic teller machines (ATMs) is a second change. They allow a bank to offer deposit and check-cashing services without constructing and staffing a branch. Placing ATMs across state lines is economically feasible and—where economic communities or metropolitan areas spread over state lines—desirable. Furthermore, in an effort to provide twenty-four-hour service at minimal cost in many locations, banks have created interbank ATM networks. Because of the strength of market forces, banks anticipate further liberalization of laws governing branch banking and the geographic extension of services. The growing acceptance of regional banking has resulted in a momentum encouraging national banking.

Mergers

Bank mergers have become common in the United States, and the prospect is for mergers to increase among the larger banks. There are several reasons for the increase in bank mergers.[21] First, branch banking has provided the impetus toward mergers in which large banks create branches by mergers with smaller ones. Second, if a bank wishes to offer a new form of service, a merger can be the easiest way to acquire the facilities. Third, economies of scale provide a motive for bank mergers. Spreading overhead costs over a larger volume of business reduces unit costs. Fourth, mergers allow banks to increase their capitalization and deposits. This factor is significant because legal limits on the size of loans made to one borrower are based on the size of the bank's capital. With a merger, the newly enlarged bank has a larger capital base and can make larger loans.[22]

Holding Companies

Bank holding companies are an important feature of the banking industry. They have evolved in response to the increasingly competitive operating environment of the banking system and to increasing demands by consumers for

---

[21] Emmanuel N. Roussakis, *Commercial Banking in an Era of Deregulation* (New York: Praeger, 1985), p. 54.

[22] Smaller banks may also find it advantageous to be acquired by larger ones. To avoid failure, financially weak banks may agree to acquisition. Another reason for agreeing to be absorbed is the problem of management. Small banks are often at a disadvantage in attracting skilled management personnel.

varied financial services. The growth of the holding company has been phenomenal. At the end of 1957, fifty bank holding companies were registered with the Federal Reserve System, and they held 7.5 percent of all bank deposits. By the end of 1986, there were 3,702 bank holding companies, and they held 89 percent of all the deposits in the United States.[23] Bank holding companies can be divided into two categories—multibank holding companies and single-bank holding companies. In 1986 they controlled 37.1 percent of all commercial banks and 72.7 percent of the branch banks in the United States.

Table 5-8 presents the number of bank mergers consummated during the period 1980–1987. Included are only those mergers where both the acquirer and acquired banking organizations have deposits of over a billion dollars. The rapid increase in the number of mergers, particularly interstate mergers, can be attributed to the Garn–St. Germain Act of 1982, which relaxed geographic and institutional barriers that had constrained interstate bank mergers. States also passed laws that facilitated an increase in mergers, particularly by holding companies. As the table indicates, the number of bank mergers has rapidly increased. The largest merger consummated in 1987 was between two bank holding companies, First Interstate and Allied Bankshares, with combined deposits of $47.5 billion.

Issues of Bank Concentration

Certain advantages accrue to large-scale bank operations that can benefit their customers. Their size enables them to afford the most advanced computer technology to facilitate immediate withdrawal of funds by depositors. They can hire highly specialized experts, such as economists and engineers, whose expertise can be used to advise their clients; management specialists can also provide bank customers with expertise on portfolio management. In addition, large banks often have access to inside information of value to their customers, they can provide capital to their clients at a lower cost, and they are able to offer a variety of consumer services including discount brokerage accounts.

There also can be disadvantages to the public from bank concentration: for instance, trial agreements among banks on such matters as price fixing and terms of service, and unspoken agreements not to encroach on each other's territory. Evidence indicates that bank mergers do not improve the perform-

---

[23] Data provided by Stephen A. Rhoades of the Financial Research Department of the Board of Governors of the Federal Reserve System (Unpublished, June, 1988).

TABLE 5-8   Number of Approved Mergers of Large (both over $1 billion) Banking Organizations and Deposits by Year, 1980–1987

Year	Number of Mergers Total	Interstate	Deposits of Acquiring Firms (in billions)	Deposits of Acquired Firms (in billions)	Total (in billions)
1980	0	0	$ 0	$ 0	$ 0
1981	1	0	1.0	1.0	2.0
1982	2	0	6.5	3.1	9.6
1983	6	1	78.9	16.1	95.0
1984	14	5	95.9	35.7	131.6
1985	7	3	26.8	19.0	45.8
1986	20	12	167.8	49.7	217.5
1987	20	13	238.2	84.8	323.0
Total	70	34	$615.1	$209.4	$824.6

Source: Data provided by Stephen A. Rhoades, Staff, Board of Governors of the Federal Reserve System, June, 1988.

ance of the acquired firm.[24] Such evidence undermines the view that mergers, at least in banking, rid the system of poor performers or generally result in net public benefits in the form of gains in efficiency or significantly improved prices or services. Acquired banks are neither more nor less efficient than other banks before or after acquisition. Innovation in banking has generally been slow; in fact, most innovations have been introduced by firms outside of the banking system. Computer handling was prepackaged by computer firms, and sidewalk push-button transaction units also were an outside innovation.

However, it is important to point out that a myriad of competitors offer financial services in direct competition with commercial banks. Insurance companies, securities dealers, retailers, manufacturers, credit unions, and savings and loan banks are also in the business of providing credit, although the importance of S&Ls as a source of credit has declined. The impact of other firms on competition has affected the share of credit provided by commercial banks. In

[24] Stephen A. Rhoades, *The Operating Performance of Acquired Firms in Banking Before and After Acquisition* (Washington, D.C.: Board of Governors of the Federal Reserve System, 1988), pp. 1–18.

1973, commercial banks provided 45.6 percent of all credit in the United States; by 1987, the share had declined to 25.8 percent.[25] Even though the banking industry is getting more concentrated, the market shares of total credit outstanding for both commercial banks and S&Ls has declined.

INDUSTRIAL CONCENTRATION—COMMUNICATIONS

A generation ago, nearly every U.S. city had two or more newspapers. Almost every small town had its weekly newspaper, locally owned and operated. But today virtually all city newspapers have the same owner and thus no competition, and almost all the daily newspaper circulation is controlled by companies that publish two or more dailies. Weekly newspapers also have become part of the newspaper chains; today, it is rare to find a locally owned, independent weekly newspaper. Newspaper companies own commercial radio and television stations as well. The *Washington Post* owns *Newsweek* magazine, various television stations, and other newspapers. So a single newspaper can have a monopoly of news and information in its circulation area.

Obviously, the communications industry has forms of communication other than newspapers. CBS, the leader in the broadcasting industry, owns Holt, Rinehart, & Winston, a major book-publishing company, and ABC, which was acquired by Capital Cities in 1985, also owns movie theaters and publishing companies. Thus, there is much cross-pollination in the communications industry, with newspaper chains owning magazines and television stations, broadcasting companies owning book-publishing companies and movie theaters, and book-publishing companies owning magazines and television stations. There is also a trend toward concentration in the publishing industry,[26] facilitated by high advertising and publishing costs. In the advertising industry, there have been global mergers of advertising companies. Whether all this is good or bad is a matter of opinion. Economies of scale can result from this concentration, and firms such as General Cinema have been able to revive the once moribund movie theater business by showing as many as ten or twelve pictures under the same roof.

---

[25] Board of Governors of the Federal Reserve System, *Flow of Funds Accounts,* Dec. 1987, p. 5

[26] McGraw-Hill bought Random House in 1989.

INDUSTRIAL CONCENTRATION—RETAILING

The general store was once the most important retail outlet in America. But when the country became urbanized and living standards increased, the general store was supplanted by more specialized stores—grocery stores, dress shops, shoe stores, drug stores, and so forth. Until the 1930s and early 1940s, the majority of these stores were owned by local merchants who were someone's next-door neighbor. But all this has changed: the local drug store is now part of the Peoples Drug chain; the local grocery store is now a Winn-Dixie; and the locally owned department store has gone the way of a Sears Roebuck or a K mart store. These changes are not necessarily bad; they reflect the continuing change in the evolution of distribution and the transformation of the United States from a rural to an urban society. Economies of scale can be affected by mass volume sales, and lower prices redound to the consumers' advantage.

There is also concentration in retailing. In 1960, the ten largest retail firms accounted for 56.4 percent of total retail sales of *Fortune*'s fifty largest retail companies. In 1979, the ten largest retail firms accounted for 54.5 percent of total retail stores among *Fortune*'s top fifty. The top twenty retail firms accounted for 74.4 percent of the top fifty's total sales in 1960 and 73.7 percent in 1979.[27] In 1987, the ten largest retail companies accounted for 51.8 percent of total retail sales of the largest fifty companies, and the top twenty firms accounted for 72.1 percent of total sales.[28] The trend from 1960 is toward a little less concentration of retail sales by the largest companies. There were also many shifts in and out of the top ten and top fifty. McDonald's and Eckerd Drugs were not in the top fifty in 1960, but both were in 1987. K mart was not in the top fifty in 1979, but ranked second in total sales in 1987. Wal-Mart barely made the top fifty in 1979 but was fifth in total sales in 1987.

SUMMARY

The U.S. economy is characterized by the control of a large share of the output in particular industries by comparatively few large firms. This control has been typically accomplished by mergers, which are of three types—horizontal, vertical, and conglomerate. Mergers tend to come in cycles, the latest of

---

[27] *Fortune,* July 14, 1980, Vol. 111, No. 14, pp. 154–155.

[28] *Fortune,* June 6, 1988, Vol. 17, No. 12, pp. 2–9.

which has occurred during the 1980s. More large mergers have taken place during this period than at any other time since the merger movement began, with dramatic increases in the total value of all mergers occurring in 1986 and 1987. In part, these mergers can be attributed to the acquirer's desire for speculative gain. Some firms have become specialists on mergers. But mergers have occurred for other reasons, including the desire to expand into a new market or to diversify into a new product line. Since competition has become global, mergers can help firms to better compete in international markets. Industrial concentration varies considerably by industry, with some industries being far more concentrated than others. In the automobile industry, for example, the four largest U.S. auto companies accounted for 92 percent of the domestic output of automobiles in 1984. However, the most current Bureau of the Census data on concentration in manufacturing indicate there has been little change in concentration over the last several decades, and some measures of concentration have actually showed a decline. In the banking industry, deregulation, financial and technological innovations, and economic change have clearly transformed the nature of competition. An increase in outside competition from nondepositor financial institutions and from brokerage firms and insurance companies has contributed to an increase in the number of bank mergers. Concentration also has occurred in a variety of other U.S. industries, including communications and retailing.

There can be problems in industrial concentration, such as barriers to entry of new firms. Large firms can restrict competition and impede the rate of capital investment, and large firms' economies of scale are limited. Large firms also do not necessarily excel in productive efficiency in comparison with medium or small firms. Increasing corporate size can create managerial problems, for the top management of a large firm cannot know all the details of the business and must rely on the support of subordinates. Finally, large firms in certain situations can exercise discretionary power over prices and entry into markets. This power to engage in restrictive practices forms one of the bases for U.S. antitrust policy, which is the subject of Chapter 6.

QUESTIONS FOR DISCUSSION

1. What is a conglomerate merger? Give examples.
2. What are some barriers to entry into concentrated markets?
3. Discuss the reasons for the recent number of bank mergers.

4. What is meant by economies of scale?
5. What are the advantages and disadvantages of large-scale production?
6. It is argued that industrial concentration is an irreversible trend that is occurring in all industrial societies. Do you agree?
7. Using the various measures of industrial concentration, has there been an increase or a decrease in concentration in recent years?
8. How does the cycle of 1980s mergers differ from previous cycles?
9. How can individuals such as T. Boone Pickens benefit from acquiring companies?
10. Industrial concentration can also be measured in terms of global markets. Discuss.

RECOMMENDED READINGS

Crane, Dwight B., and Robert G. Eccles. "Commercial Banks: Taking Shape for Turbulent Times." *Harvard Business Review* 65, No. 6 (November–December 1987): 94–100.

Henkoff, Ronald. "Deals of the Year." *Fortune,* January 30, 1989, Vol. 119, No. 3, pp. 162–170.

Icahn, Carl C. "Icahn on Icahn." *Fortune,* February 29, 1988, Vol. 117, No. 5, pp. 54–58.

Jensen, Michael C. "The Takeover Controversy: Analysis and Evidence." In John Coffee, Louis Lowenstein, and Susan Rose Ackerman, eds., *Takeovers & Contests for Corporate Control.* New York: Oxford University Press, 1987.

Kumpe, Ted and Piet Bolwejn. "Manufacturing: The New Case for Vertical Integration." *Harvard Business Review* 66, No. 2 (March–April 1988): 75–83.

Neal, Alfred. *Business Power and Public Policy.* New York: Praeger, 1982.

Rhoades, Stephen. *The Operating Performance of Acquired Firms in Banking Before and After Acquisition.* Washington, D.C.: Board of Governors of the Federal Reserve System, 1988.

Scherer, Frederick M. *Testimony Before the Subcommittee on Monopolies and Commercial Law.* Committee on the Judiciary, U.S. House of Representatives, February 24, 1988.

Chapter 6

Antitrust Laws in the United States

Antitrust legislation in the United States rests on two premises. The first is the English common law as it evolved through court decisions over a long time. In general, these decisions held that restraint on trade or commerce is not in the public interest. In interpreting the common law, courts in both England and the United States ruled that contracts or agreements to restrain or attempt to restrain trade were illegal. The second premise is the belief that competition is an effective regulator of most markets and, with a few exceptions, that monopolistic practices can be stopped by competition. This premise is based on the economic theory espousing pure or perfect competition as the ideal, since according to the theory competition forces firms to be efficient, cut costs, and receive no more than normal profits. The theory assumes that in a state of pure or perfect competition, economic decisions would be made on the basis of prices, price changes, and price relationships, all of which are determined by the market-related forces of supply and demand.

Ideal competition of the pure or perfect type does not exist, nor can it, given the impact of modern technology and the economies of scale resulting from this technology. Modern attitudes toward industrial concentration assume that when a few firms dominate an industry they are in a position to set prices higher than would prevail in more competitive pricing situations and are therefore able to gain profits higher than total competition would allow. It is presumed that concentration and competition are inversely related. So some form of competition requiring sellers in a given industry to compete against one another in terms of prices is desired. In addition, there should be no natural or artificial barriers to entry so that there will be a flow of sellers in and out of markets that will reflect market changes. Each seller would then be limited in his or her ability to control prices. Unfortunately, competition has many facets, and it is likely to mean different things to different people. And as an objective of national economic policy, it may have even more meanings. Thus, many of the federal regulatory laws are concerned with different definitions of competition and may not be totally compatible with one another. The U.S. economy is characterized by its heterogeneity, and no one model or set of normative criteria can be used to explain or evaluate overall economic performance. Therefore, the issue for those responsible for regulatory policymaking must necessarily be to determine whether consumers have realistic alternatives rather than to engage in a quixotic search for perfection in marketplace competition.

A REVIEW OF ANTITRUST LAWS

Although we discussed the major antitrust laws, with the exception of the Celler–Kefauver Act of 1950, in Chapters 2 and 3, our aim then was largely to set them in their historical context. Now we shall review these laws in some detail, for they are complex and constantly subjected to changes in interpretation, but not to changes in principle. These laws contain sweeping provisions directed against private restraints that might threaten a competitive market economy. There has been no meticulous itemization of these restraints by Congress because it is possible for a specific type of conduct to be prohibited in most settings, although the public interest could be served by permitting it in others. For example, defining an illegal monopoly as a firm seeking to control 90 percent of the output of a product might be justified for large producers of basic commodities competing in a national market, but such a determination would be unrealistic for the only movie theater in a small town. To catalogue a list of antisocial restraints invites evasion by ingenious firms, for what is applicable to one industry may not be applicable to another.

The Sherman Act, 1890

The Sherman Act is, of course, the original and most basic of the antitrust laws. Its most important provisions are summarized here. Section 1 prohibits agreements, expressed or otherwise, conspiracies, or combinations between two or more parties, who may be individuals or corporations, that unreasonably restrain the trade or commerce of the United States. This trade or commerce may be domestic, interstate, or foreign. This section's provisions are relevant only if the facts—when weighed by the courts—reveal either an unduly restraining effect on trade or an intent so to affect it.

The Supreme Court has held that certain types of agreements, conspiracies, or combinations are in and of themselves so restrictive of competition as to be conclusively presumed unreasonable restraints of trade. In other words, the Court has declined to inquire into whether or not such arrangements cause any public injury or are justified for business reasons and has not considered the amount of interstate trade and commerce affected so long as it is clearly beyond a small level. Any of these arrangements is unlawful if it limits the import of products into the United States or the export of products from the United States or if it impedes commerce within the United States. The government need not prove any more than that the parties to such arrangements have in fact entered into them. Among these offenses, called *per se violations,* are the following:

1. *Price fixing.* This offense is any agreement or understanding between two or more competitors to fix, stabilize, or in any way affect the price of a product. The courts are here concerned about the inhibition of price competition. Arrangements that tamper in any way with the price structure have been determined to constitute price fixing.

2. *Division of customers, markets, and volume of production.* This category pertains to agreements or understandings between two or more corporations to divide or allocate the markets in which each will sell a product and to arrangements to divide, limit, or maintain the production of a given product at a certain level. The courts have consistently struck down arrangements between two or more competitors in which they agree to divide customers, allocate markets, or in any way control the output of goods.

3. *Boycotts or concerted refusals to deal.* An agreement or understanding among competitors to boycott or refuse to deal with any third party is unlawful. Moreover, a single seller may not agree, directly or indirectly, with one or more of its independent distributors to refuse to deal with anyone else desiring to purchase the product for sale.

4. *Tie-in sales.* Any type of tying arrangement may be a per se violation; for example, when the tied product is patented or the seller has a dominant economic position in the sale of the product. Unlawful tie-in sales usually occur when the seller seeks to force or induce a buyer to purchase one or more less desirable products in order to purchase the desired product over which the seller has significant economic control.

In addition to these per se violations, the courts have applied "a rule of reason" approach to deciding which other types of conduct may be unlawful under Section 1 of the Sherman Act. As a general proposition, this rule results in legalizing certain types of conduct, even though there is some restraint of trade when the restraint is ancillary to the main business purpose of an arrangement. In this situation, a corporation may defend a challenged course of conduct on the ground that there is a sound business justification for it and that any restraint of trade is ancillary or incidental to the main business purpose. Under this rule, the legality of business conduct may be determined on the basis of the duration of the agreement, the percentage of the market affected by it, the relative bargaining power of the parties involved, and the size of the geographic market affected.

Section 2 prohibits any single company from monopolizing, or attempting to monopolize, any part of interstate trade and commerce in any relevant market. A relevant market is defined both by the geographic area in which a product competes and by the products with which the product in question can reasonably be interchanged in its end use. This section also makes it unlawful for two or more competing firms to agree to, or to conspire to, monopolize any part of trade or commerce. No exact minimum percentage of a relevant market has been fixed by the courts as constituting monopoly; the real test is whether a company has the power to control prices or to exclude competition. If that power is proved, the company is a monopolist. Note that Section 2 prohibits even attempts to monopolize; that is, a company could violate the law if it engaged in conduct intended to result in monopoly, even if it did not succeed.

Civil Remedies

The enforcement of the Sherman Act is entrusted to the Justice Department, which in 1903 created a special antitrust division for this purpose. The punishments for violating the act are spelled out in Sections 1 and 2. Section 4 provides for the use of civil suits, giving the attorney general the right to enforce the act by using civil proceedings to prevent and restrain violations. Dissolution, divestiture, or divorcement proceedings can be used to prevent combinations and to promote competition. Another civil remedy is to use an injunction, a restraining order used by a judge to prevent unfair business practices. A third method of court action against violators of the act is given in Section 7, which provides for damage suits by private parties injured by other private parties acting in a manner forbidden or declared unlawful by the act. If successful in their suit, the injured parties can recover three times the amount of damages sustained.

Criminal Remedies

All violations of Sections 1 and 2 of the Sherman Act are subject to criminal penalties, and provision is made for punishment by fine, not to exceed $100,000 for each violation, or by imprisonment, not to exceed three years, or by both. On conviction, the fine may be levied against each party indicted and for each charge in the complaint. Criminal cases are essentially punitive; they seek to penalize past illegal conduct—mainly conspiracies—and to prevent a repetition of such conduct. In criminal cases, a defendant may plead *nolo contendere,* with the consent of the court. This plea means the accused party makes no contention about whether or not he or she is guilty and agrees to accept the decision of the court. If the court accepts the plea, it may impose criminal penalties according to the provisions of the law.

Two major antitrust acts were passed in 1914, the Clayton Act and the Federal Trade Commission Act. Both were designed to strengthen the Sherman Act by adding teeth to its enforcement provisions. By 1914, the Sherman Act, through judicial interpretation, had lost much of its efficacy. There was no legislation to prevent holding companies, interlocking directorates, price discrimination, or other abuses designed to lessen competition, and the trend toward the concentration of economic power in the hands of a few business firms and investment banks continued unabated. The Sherman Act was surrounded by a cloud of uncertainty because it failed to state precisely which kinds of abuses or actions by business were prohibited. Without being specific, the Sherman Act emphasized the punishment of abuses, whereas the Clayton and Federal Trade Commission acts tried to define and prevent abuses. In particular, these two acts were aimed at the practice of unfair competition, including price discrimination, exclusive and tying agreements, and interlocking directorates.

The Clayton Antitrust Act, 1914

The Clayton Act was passed almost concurrently with the Federal Trade Commission Act. It represented an attempt to modify the Sherman Act by specifying unfair business practices and thus eliminating some of the uncertainty introduced by the concept of the rule of reason. The act dealt with a wide range of activities, most of which can be organized into three categories: (1) provisions prohibiting various forms of business abuses, such as price discrimination and tying agreements; (2) provisions providing various kinds of remedies against these abuses, and (3) provisions relating to labor unions.

Probably the most important provision of the Clayton Act is Section 2, which deals with primary-line price discrimination. This type of price discrimination involves a geographic price differential; that is, the sale of goods at a higher price in one area and a lower price in another area, to the injury of a local seller. However, this kind of discrimination may also occur within the same geographic area. Section 2 prohibits price discrimination in the sale of goods of like grade or quality when the effect is to injure or prevent competition. Price discrimination is identified by considering variations in the net prices charged by a seller and in the selling price of the same class of goods under the same circumstances.

Section 3 of the Clayton Act prohibits tying contracts and exclusive dealing arrangements. The tying contract, as mentioned in Chapter 2, makes the lease or sale of a particular product conditional on the lessee's or purchaser's use of associated products sold by the same manufacturer. In the exclusive dealing arrangement, one firm induces another not to deal with the former's competitors. The prohibition of the tying contract was designed to prevent the extension of a partial monopoly into a wider field. The decision of the Supreme Court in the A. B. Dick case of 1912 made the passage of Section 3 imperative.[1] In this case, the Supreme Court had allowed the A. B. Dick Company to compel purchasers of its patented mimeograph machines to use only ink paper sold by it. Tying contracts and exclusive dealing arrangements have generally been condemned by the courts only when a seller enjoys substantial market power and they result in a lessening of competition.

Section 7, which pertains to mergers and acquisitions, is another important provision of the Clayton Act. A wave of mergers had taken place in the United States during the period 1894–1904. In an effort to stop them, the federal government brought action against the American Sugar Refining Company in 1895, charging it with a violation of Section 2—the antimonopoly provision, of the Sherman Act. This company had gained control of more than 98 percent of the refined sugar capacity of the United States. However, the Supreme Court ruled that manufacturing was not commerce and that industrial monopolies could be prosecuted only by the states.[2] The effect was to give firms

[1] *Henry v. A. B. Dick Co.*, 224 U.S. 1 (1912).
[2] *U.S. v. E. C. Knight Co.*, 156 U.S. 1 (1895).

seeking monopoly power a new way to bring scores of competitors under control. Since the Sherman Act had made the trust form of combination illegal, mergers would serve just as well to control competition. Mergers took place in a wide variety of industries, ranging from petroleum to whiskey. By 1900, companies such as American Tobacco and Standard Oil controlled some 90 percent of the output of their products.

Section 7 prohibits any corporation engaged in commerce from acquiring the stock of another corporation when the effect may be to reduce competition substantially or to create a monopoly in any line of business and in any section of the country. It should be emphasized that Section 7 applies to firms engaged in either interstate or foreign commerce. The acquisition by a U.S. firm of a major interest in a foreign firm that threatens actual or potential competition to firms in the United States would almost certainly be scrutinized, as would any joint venture by a U.S. firm and a competing foreign firm.[3] Section 7 does not exclude all mergers; it excludes only those that substantially lessen competition. From its application, it exempts those acquisitions in which one of the two parties is an individual or a partnership or in which the acquired firm is not engaged in interstate commerce. It also exempts the acquisition of stock when that acquisition is made solely for investment and therefore is not used to restrain trade.

Section 8 pertains to interlocking directorates. The interlocking directorate arrangement was a device commonly used to gain control over the activities of competing corporations. It was associated with investment banks, in particular J. P. Morgan and Company, a major New York investment banking firm. Investment banks would gain control over the financial affairs of corporations as a condition for issuing investment credit. They achieved this control by having one or more of their executives appointed to the board of directors of corporations with which they did business. At the peak of its control, J. P. Morgan and Company held directorates in sixty-three corporations with assets of $74 billion.[4] Section 8 of the Clayton Act provides that no person shall be a

---

[3] Joint ventures involve a partnership arrangement between two firms or between a firm and a government. An example is the General Motors–Toyota arrangement to build subcompact cars in a General Motors plant in California. This arrangement was challenged by both Ford and Chrysler on the grounds that it lessened competition in the automobile industry. However, the joint venture was approved by the Federal Trade Commission by a three-to-two vote. Joint ventures between U.S. and foreign firms will increase in importance.

[4] National Resources Committee, *The Structure of the American Economy* (Washington, D.C.: U.S. Government Printing Office, 1939), pp. 306–317.

director in two or more corporations if they are competitors and if they have capital, surplus, and undivided profits in excess of $1 million. The act does not require the government to find that the interlocking directorate reduces competition. The fact of the interlock itself makes for illegality.[5]

Violations of the Clayton Act are civil offenses. The government can sue defendants for actual damages, and private plaintiffs are entitled to sue for triple damages. In dealing with violations, Section 14 provides that individual directors or officers of a corporation can be fined as much as $5,000, or sentenced to prison for up to one year, or both. The Federal Trade Commission was given joint responsibility with the Justice Department for the enforcement of Sections 2, 3, 7, and 8 of the act. Section 15 invests the U.S. district courts with the power to prevent and restrain violations of the act, and Section 16 permits any person or firm to sue for and have injunctive relief against potential loss or damage by violations of Sections 2, 3, 7, and 8 of the act.

The Federal Trade Commission Act, 1914

The Federal Trade Commission Act was passed in September 1914 to replace the Bureau of Corporations with the Federal Trade Commission, consisting of five members, each holding office for seven years. It was hoped that the commission, which was made independent of the president, would be a specialized body that would aid in law enforcement and supervise and apply guiding rules to the competitive market system. Application of the Sherman Act to specific competitive practices had proved unsatisfactory to business groups and the general public, since victims of predatory business acts felt that the law should intervene before such acts had been committed. Moreover, many business-people wanted clearer guidelines about what constituted unfair methods of competition. The premise of the Federal Trade Commission Act is that fair competition should stand as the basic economic policy for the nation, and that unfair competition should be prohibited.

The Federal Trade Commission Act supplements the Sherman and Clayton acts by using sweeping prohibitions of unfair methods, acts, and practices to foster competition. It provides that these prohibitions are to be interpreted and

---

[5] Section 8 has not been actively enforced, and the few attempts that have been made to carry out its provisions have resulted in judicial emasculation. The section prohibits interlocks only where two companies produce the same items. It is still possible for competitors to have interlocking directorates and interlocks between sellers and buyers, and between manufacturers and bankers.

enforced in administrative proceedings brought by and before the Federal Trade Commission, subject to review by the courts. Section 5 of the act empowers the FTC to prevent unfair methods of competition and unfair or deceptive acts or practices in or affecting commerce. Generally, this section is used to stop practices before they develop into other violations of the antitrust laws. As a consequence, the FTC has used it to attack alleged price fixing that would not necessarily be a violation of the Sherman Act, as well as mergers, tie-in sales, exclusive dealing, and other actions that the commission deems are unfair methods of competition. For example, a suit was brought in 1972 against the major cereal companies for alleged price fixing, even though the FTC admitted publicly that there was no charge of agreement or conspiracy, which would be essential to a Sherman Act case. The suit has since been dropped.

It can be said that Section 5 has been interpreted to go further than the other antitrust laws do to reach all unfair business practices, whether or not they have an impact on competition. Section 5 gives to the FTC and the courts the power to prohibit present and potential trade restraints proscribed by the Sherman and Clayton acts and also allows the commission to proceed against other antisocial conduct. The current aim of the commission's enforcement activities under Section 5 is both to protect fair competition and to assure that the consumer is not subjected to unfair or deceptive practices, without regard to their effect on competition. One example of the latter is the commission's attack on false or misleading advertising.

The Robinson–Patman Act, 1936

The Robinson–Patman Act is commonly known as the Chain Store Act. It is an amendment to the Clayton Act, in particular to Section 2, which had sought, among other things, to outlaw price-cutting practices by large firms that were designed to eliminate competition from smaller firms. But Section 2 had not been widely used, even though the Federal Trade Commission had on occasion attempted to apply it to discriminatory discounts and to geographic discrimination resulting from the use of basing-point price systems, under which uniform delivered prices were charged regardless of the origin of the shipment. In one case, the commission condemned a manufacturer who granted discounts to chains for the combined purchases of their separate stores while refusing to grant a similar privilege to associations of independent stores, even though selling costs did not vary between the two.[6] The commission was rebuffed in its attempt by a circuit court of appeals on the grounds that the Clayton Act applied only to the reduction of competition in the seller's own line of commerce.

The most important provision of the Robinson–Patman Act is Section 2(a); it amends Section 2 of the Clayton Act to prohibit secondary-line price discrimination; that is, the sale of the same good to different buyers in the same geographic area at different prices when there is no cost difference. The impact of this kind of discrimination falls on small buyers who, because of their size, are unable to obtain discount concessions that large buyers are able to obtain from sellers. It does permit a seller to show that lower prices to some buyers are based on cost differences related to different methods or quantities involved in the sale or delivery of the product. Section 2(a) also prohibits any form of price discrimination when the end result is to lessen competition; also, when it tends to create a monopoly in any line of commerce, or when it injures, destroys, or prevents competition with any person who either grants or knowingly receives the benefits of such discrimination. It was not only restraint of competition but also injury to competitors that became a test of illegality.

The remaining subsections of the amended Section 2 of the Clayton Act enacted prohibitions not included in the original Clayton Act. For example, the payment of brokerage fees when no independent broker was involved became illegal. This provision was designed to eliminate the practice some chains had of demanding the regular brokerage fees as a discount when they purchased directly from the manufacturers. This compensation normally went to a broker, traditionally a seller's agent who assembled the output of a number of small producers for shipment to the distributor. Advertising allowances also were prohibited. These, which normally were made for point-of-sale advertising of goods manufactured by the seller and sold at retail by the buyer, could no longer be given unless the allowances were made on equal terms to all competing purchasers. Advertising allowances and the remission of brokerage fees were considered forms of secret rebates secured because a buyer was in a strong position to extract them from a seller. The Standard Oil Trust was thought to owe its rise to a monopoly and its continuance in that position in

---

[6] *National Biscuit Co. v. FTC,* 299 Fed. 733 (1924).

part to its ability to extract secret discounts from the railroads. The authors of the Robinson–Patman Act felt that price discrimination in the form of secret brokerage fees or advertising allowances should be forced into the open, where it would come under Section 2(a).

The Celler–Kefauver Act, 1950

The Celler–Kefauver Act was passed in 1950 to plug a loophole in Section 7 of the Clayton Act. Section 7 specifically forbade the acquisition of one firm's stock by another firm when the end result was to reduce competition substantially in interstate or foreign commerce. But over time the courts had generally emasculated this provision through judicial interpretation: in 1926 the Supreme Court distinguished between acquisition of stock and acquisition of assets, holding the latter to be beyond the reach of the Federal Trade Commission even if the merger of physical assets had been based on an illegal acquisition of voting stock. Moreover, the Supreme Court in several other cases had held that such mergers were not illegal under the Clayton Act if a corporation used its stock purchases to acquire assets before the FTC issued a complaint or before it issued its final order banning the stock acquisition. Thus the number of mergers based on the acquisition of firm assets steadily increased, and it was not until the late 1940s that federal legislation to plug the loophole was considered seriously. There had been a wave of post-World War II mergers, leading to the fear by Congress that greater industrial concentration would lead to a significant decline in competition.

Section 7 of the Clayton Act was amended to make it illegal for one corporation to acquire the stock or assets of another corporation when the end result might be to lessen competition substantially or to tend to create monopoly. Celler–Kefauver also tightened the constraints against business mergers by making a merger illegal if there was a trend toward concentration in an industry, thereby creating a presumption of tendencies toward monopoly. It delineated markets more narrowly by defining them as "a line of commerce" in any section of the nation. The intent of Congress in passing the Celler–Kefauver Act was that competition be maintained. Small firms that merge to improve their competitive position are generally not challenged, but mergers that would ordinarily be allowed in nonconcentrated industries may well be challenged if a large firm acquires a small competitor. For example, Alcoa, which accounted for 27.8 percent of all aluminum conductor production, acquired

Rome Cable, whose market share was 1.3 percent.[7] The merger was disallowed in 1964 on the grounds that Alcoa would increase its market share through the acquisition and thus competition would be substantially reduced, since Rome had been an aggressive competitor in the aluminum conductor field. It has been said that Celler–Kefauver has virtually stopped horizontal and vertical mergers between large companies.[8]

The Hart–Scott–Rodino Act, 1976

The Hart–Scott–Rodino Act[9] made a number of procedural changes in antitrust law. It gives the Justice Department the authority to issue civil investigative demands to third parties, such as competitors of those companies under investigation, and to compel oral testimony and answers to written questions. It also requires notice to the antitrust division of the Justice Department and to the Federal Trade Commission thirty days in advance of mergers involving large companies. The law covers companies with stock or assets of $100 million or more that plan to merge with companies worth $10 million or more when the transaction involves acquisitions of more than $15 million in stock or assets. This gives the Justice Department or the Federal Trade Commission time in which to challenge the merger. The act also authorizes state attorneys general to bring triple damage suits in federal court on behalf of state citizens injured by violations of the Sherman Act. This provision has had the effect of increasing the amount of antitrust enforcement by state governments.

Before the passage of the act, it was often difficult for the Justice Department or the Federal Trade Commission to stop a merger once the union had been consummated. When mergers were contested, decisions often took time, and firms were able to consolidate their assets. The Hart–Scott–Rodino Act enables the government to act quickly against many proposed mergers. Firms know before the completion of a merger whether or not it will be challenged, thus eliminating from their minds any uncertainty about any future antitrust action after the merger had been consummated. The act requires that firms

[7] *U.S. v. Aluminum Co. of America*, 377 U.S. 271 (1964).

[8] George J. Stigler, "The Economic Effects of the Antitrust Laws," *Journal of Law and Economics* 9 (October 1966): 235–236.

[9] The full name of the act is the Hart–Scott–Rodino Antitrust Improvements Act of 1976. It is Public Law 94-435.

contemplating a merger provide the government with extensive information pertaining to the merger. The government then decides whether or not to challenge the merger. It may decide to approve the merger subject to certain conditions; for example, it may require the acquiring firm to divest itself of part of the assets of its new acquisition.

Section 301 of the act amends the Clayton Act to permit *parens patriae* actions by state attorneys general. Any state attorney general may bring a civil action on behalf of people residing in the state to secure monetary damages for injuries sustained as a result of any violation of the Sherman Act. The state attorney general may sue in any district court having jurisdiction over the defendant. For example, residents in certain states have had to pay more for a product as a result of a price-fixing agreement involving regional distributors. The attorney general of each state can initiate *parens patriae* action for damages. Section 301 strengthens state antitrust enforcement. A district court will exclude from the amount of monetary relief any amount duplicating an award for the same injury, and it can award a state as monetary relief triple damages for the antitrust violation.

ANTITRUST ENFORCEMENT

The antitrust laws are enforced by the Antitrust Division of the Justice Department and by the Federal Trade Commission. Table 6-1 on page 142 summarizes important antitrust provisions. The Antitrust Division, exclusively, is responsible for enforcing the Sherman Act and, with the Federal Trade Commission, is responsible for enforcing the Clayton Act. The FTC has exclusive jurisdiction to enforce the Federal Trade Commission Act and has primary responsibility for enforcing the Robinson–Patman Act. Both public agencies can make use of the following four basic remedies to enforce the antitrust laws:

1. They may use an injunction to prohibit a specific action such as false advertising.
2. They may use an order for specific performance requiring action on the part of the party against whom the order applies. An example would be divestiture of certain designated firm assets.
3. Criminal sanctions can also be used. Violation of the Sherman Act is a misdemeanor and may result in imprisonment for up to three years.
4. Fines of up to $100,000 per violation are provided for in the Sherman Act.

The majority of antitrust cases initiated by the federal government are settled by an agreement between it and the defendant.[10] This method saves the
government time and money. After the terms of a proposed settlement have
been agreed on, the government must take the proposed settlement to the judge
before whom the case was initially filed to obtain approval. This second check
ensures that the public's interests are being served under the terms of the settlement. If the judge approves, a consent decree is filed with the court. Violations of the terms of a decree will mean the offending party is in contempt of
court. There is one major drawback to the use of the consent decree: had the
government litigated and won the suit against the defendant, the victory would
have constituted *prima facie* evidence of the antitrust violation and would be
used by a private plaintiff in a triple damage suit.

Exemptions from Antitrust Laws

The Sherman Act, as well as other antitrust legislation, is applicable in principle to all forms of private business enterprise carried out in interstate and foreign commerce. The Sherman Act itself makes no exceptions and declares that
every restraint of trade and commerce is unlawful. However, certain industries
and organizations are exempt from the antitrust laws. The reasons for exemption are as varied as the industries and organizations exempted. Each exemption is supposed to accomplish some specific objective that in the minds of a
particular group is necessary to its interests. Over time, moving forces or interest groups have demanded relaxation of the antitrust laws. Some of the more
important industries and organizations and the reasons for their exemption
from antitrust laws are presented here.

Labor Unions

Section 6 of the Clayton Act exempts labor unions from antitrust laws. There
were two main reasons for this exemption. First, the Sherman Act had been
used on occasion to break up labor unions. In the Danbury Hatters Case of
1908, for example, a labor union was convicted of restraint of trade when it

---

[10] It is also necessary to point out that companies can bring action against other companies to
obtain compensation for injuries they have suffered as a result of violation of the antitrust laws.
An example is the Pennzoil suit against Texaco charging it with wrongdoing in acquiring Getty
Oil, a company Pennzoil had planned to acquire. A judge awarded Pennzoil $11 billion in
damages.

TABLE 6-1 Important Antitrust Provisions

Act	Provisions
Sherman Act (1890)	*Section 1* prohibits contracts, combinations, and conspiracies in restraint of trade in interstate or foreign commerce, including price fixing, group boycotts, and tie-in sales. *Section 2* prohibits monopolies and attempts to create monopolies in interstate or foreign commerce.
Clayton Act (1914)	*Section 2* prohibits primary-line price discrimination lessening sellers level of competition. *Section 3* prohibits exclusive dealing and tying arrangements that substantially lessen competition. *Section 7* prohibits mergers when the effect is to substantially lessen competition or to tend to create a monopoly.
Federal Trade Commission Act (1914)	*Section 5* prohibits unfair methods of competition and defines powers of the FTC.
Robinson–Patman Act (1936)	*Amends Section 2* of the Clayton Act to prohibit secondary-line price discrimination.
Celler–Kefauver Act (1950)	*Amends Section 7* of the Clayton Act to include the acquisition of assets of one firm by another firm when the result is to substantially lessen competition.
Hart–Scott–Rodino Act (1976)	*Section 301* permits *parens patriae* actions by state attorneys general to secure monetary relief for any violation of the Sherman Act. It also requires advance notice of proposed mergers.

1908, for example, a labor union was convicted of restraint of trade when it organized an interstate boycott against the hat manufacturers of Danbury, Connecticut.[11] The court found the members of the union liable for triple dam-

---

[11] *Loewe v. Lawlor,* 208 U.S. 274 (1908).

ages of $240,000 for the boycott. The end result of the conviction was the dissolution of the union. Second, it was felt that labor had a bargaining position far inferior to that of business; therefore, collective action by labor was necessary to improve this position. Today, labor unions retain their exempt status as long as they do not combine with nonlabor groups to restrain trade.[12]

Natural Monopolies

The so-called natural monopolies exist in those industries that possess special conditions inherent to the nature of their operations that would make competition self-destructive and hence incompatible with the public interest. Since they provide an indispensable service to the public, however, they are subject to government regulation in the interest of the public. Such industries include transportation, electricity, gas, and broadcasting. A public utility is usually given a monopoly over a particular area. The purpose is in part to prevent the wasteful and duplicating competition that prevailed at one time. During the nineteenth century, the railroads built duplicating lines in a desire to surmount their competition. The end result was cutthroat competition and a great waste of resources.

In return for its control over a given service area, a natural monopoly is subject to the regulation of rates, services, and other functions by federal and state agencies to ensure the protection of the public interest. Regulation is designed to prevent public utilities from making too much profit. Because these industries are so strictly regulated, there is no particular need to subject them to antitrust laws.

Export Trade Associations

The Webb–Pomerene Act of 1918 specifically exempts export trade associations from the Sherman Act. The rationale for this exemption was the existence of cartels and monopolies in other countries actively engaged in international trade. Countries such as Germany and the United Kingdom encouraged the formation of these cartels as a matter of public policy. The purpose of the Webb-Pomerene exemption was to enable U.S. firms to compete more effectively with foreign companies belonging to cartel arrangements. The act permits the formation of export associations, which are required to file outlines of their organization with the Federal Trade Commission. The commission is then supposed to investigate association activities to see that there is no viola-

[12] *U.S. v. Hutcheson,* 312 U.S. 219 (1941).

tion of the law, since the Webb–Pomerene Act was intended to promote competition rather than collusion in the world markets.

Agricultural Cooperatives

Agricultural cooperatives were exempted by the Clayton Act from antitrust laws provided they issued no capital stock and were not run for a profit. The Capper–Volstead Act of 1922 amended the Clayton Act to allow the formation of cooperatives issuing capital stock; it also legalized action by the members of a cooperative marketing association to enhance the prices of their products. The Capper–Volstead Act provides agricultural producers with a substantial exemption from antitrust laws in giving their associations the power to set prices. However, this power has limits, for the price must not be increased unduly. A single cooperative association also may enter into contracts with many farmers that require them to market their products only through the association.

Other Exemptions

There are also other exemptions from antitrust laws. Transoceanic shipping rates established by shipping conferences have for years been exempted from the antitrust laws on certification by the U.S. Maritime Board. Combinations and mergers were sanctioned by Congress in the case of the railroads in 1920, telephone companies in 1921, motor carriers in 1935, and water carriers in 1940. Combinations of marine insurance companies were exempted from the antitrust laws in 1920. There is also an antitrust exemption for small businesses in that the Small Business Act of 1953, as amended, provides that voluntary agreements may be made by small business concerns for joint programs in research and development and for joint participation in national defense contracts. The McCarran Act of 1945 partially exempts insurance companies from the antitrust laws in that it leaves their regulation up to the states. The Reed–Bulwinkle Bill of 1948 specifically authorizes the Interstate Commerce Commission to approve railroad traffic association agreements with respect to rates and fares. The Miller–Tydings Act and the McGuire Act extended antitrust exemptions to retailers so as to maintain resale prices. But the Consumer Goods Pricing Act of 1975 repealed these provisions, mainly because they sanctioned a form of price fixing that was having a perceptibly adverse effect on consumer purchasing power.

State Antitrust Laws

As mentioned in Chapter 2, the first antitrust laws were passed by the states in the latter part of the last century. The development of trusts and other kinds of business combinations created much popular discontent, which was translated into state laws. Kansas enacted the first antitrust law in 1889, and at least thirteen states had antitrust laws before the passage of the Sherman Act in 1890. The first state laws came from the farming states in the Midwest, where populism was influential. In fact, the Sherman Act was intended to supplement, rather than supplant, state power. The federal courts were supposed to cooperate within the limits of their constitutional power with the state courts in curbing and controlling any form of business combination that threatened U.S. commerce.

By 1900, thirty states had antitrust laws that varied in content but, in general, restricted monopolies and combinations in restraint of trade, prohibited specific unfair business practices, and provided criminal penalties and other sanctions. These laws fell into disuse after the turn of the century, however, and the enforcement of antitrust was left almost entirely to the federal government. There were several reasons for the decline in state activity. First, state antitrust law was attacked and often invalidated on the grounds of vagueness. Second, the laws were subjected to a prolonged series of constitutional challenges. State statutes were often attacked on equal protection and due process grounds. Third, the courts set severe restrictions on the extraterritorial jurisdiction of state enforcement efforts. Fourth, the enforcement of state laws was generally haphazard and poorly financed, and it was difficult for the states to deal with national or international economic institutions through their limited jurisdiction.

State antitrust activities picked up during the 1960s and accelerated even more during the 1970s. From 1970 to 1974, twelve states, one territory, and the Commonwealth of Puerto Rico enacted or reenacted antitrust statutes.[13] This resurgence of antitrust enforcement can be attributed to a number of factors: protecting state and local governments from the collusive bidding practices of some business firms, combatting the efforts of organized crime to take over legitimate business interests, and protecting the general business community from the predatory actions of a few firms. In some states, organizations of small businesspeople lobbied successfully for the state's enforcing its own

[13] Unpublished data furnished by the Antitrust Division, Department of Justice, Washington, D.C., 1986.

antitrust laws once again. There was also a growing belief that the federal government could not and should not bear sole responsibility for the enforcement of antitrust. And there was an increasing recognition that the state attorney general, as the people's advocate, must combat abuses of the marketplace through antitrust as well as consumer protection programs. Finally, there had been a great growth in state procurement of goods and services and an accompanying belief that a vigorous antitrust program could save money on government purchases.

Example of State Antitrust Laws

State antitrust laws may differ in form and content, but basic patterns have been followed. The antitrust laws of Connecticut and Virginia can be used as examples. Connecticut was one of the first states to pass an antitrust law. Modeled after the Sherman Act, it prohibits various forms of price fixing, including agreements among competing business firms to fix or lower prices, bid rigging, and resale price maintenance.[14] The antitrust laws of Connecticut also prohibit competing firms from agreeing to divide geographic areas in which each will do business. It prohibits tying arrangements where the seller conditions or ties the sale of a popular product to the purchase of a less popular product when the intent is to lessen competition. The law prohibits group boycotts where business firms conspire to deny a competitor access to supplies or services. Price discrimination is also illegal when the intent is to lessen competition.

The Virginia Antitrust Act was passed in 1974. Its provisions are somewhat similar to those of Connecticut's antitrust law.[15] Any contract in restraint of trade in Virginia is unlawful. Monopolies and combinations that restrain the commerce of Virginia are illegal. Various discriminatory practices are also illegal, including secondary-line price discrimination where a seller discriminates in price between different purchasers of products or services when any of the purchasers are in direct competition with one another. Tying arrangements are also illegal when the intent is to lessen discrimination. Price fixing, including bid rigging, is illegal, as are boycotts. The Virginia antitrust law is

[14] State of Connecticut, Office of Attorney General, *Antitrust Law in Connecticut,* Hartford, 1966.

[15] Information provided by the Office of Attorney General, Commonwealth of Virginia, Richmond 1986.

considered a fair trade law, and practices that discriminate against trade are illegal.

Importance of State Antitrust Laws

State antitrust law is important because much business is strictly intrastate. In the federal system, the regulation of intrastate or local commerce is left to the state governments, which perform the same kind of economic regulation that the federal government performs at the national level. Moreover, the Department of Justice and the Federal Trade Commission prosecute only a small fraction of the complaints they receive; their efforts are concentrated on the restraints and abuses that are national in scope. This focus leaves the states with jurisdiction over a wide area of economic activity within interstate commerce; for example, the production and sale of food and beverages, fuel oil, lumber, used cars, hotels and housing facilities, building and road construction, recreational facilities, local transportation, and banking services. The kinds of abuses and anticompetitive business practices that occur nationally can also occur locally. State governments also have such functions as prohibiting false advertising and preventing monopoly and unfair competition.

State antitrust enforcement can be expected to increase in importance in the future for two reasons. First, the Hart–Scott–Rodino Act of 1976 authorizes the attorneys general of the fifty states to bring suits against companies that fix prices or engage in other forms of anticompetitive business practices, and to recover damages for consumers injured by such practices. Second, the Reagan administration has attempted to reduce the role of the federal government in the U.S. economy. Emphasis has been placed on increasing the responsibility of the states in all areas of economic and political activity. That there will be an increase in the role of the state attorneys general when it comes to the enforcement of state antitrust laws can therefore be assumed.

SUMMARY

Antitrust laws are designed to protect and encourage vigorous and open competition—the hallmark of a free enterprise market economy. Competition creates incentives for business firms to reduce costs while improving products or services. Business firms offering the highest-quality products or services at the lowest price will thrive in a competitive environment. Because competition leads to higher quality at a lower price, the consumer is the ultimate beneficiary. The benefits of competition disappear when business firms agree on prices or engage in other illegal activities that may unfairly force competitors out of business or discriminate against consumers. However, not every restraint on competition violates antitrust laws; rather, courts have consistently held that only unreasonable restraints on competition violate the antitrust laws.

The antitrust laws of the United States are used to prevent certain business practices considered economically harmful. The laws are designed to maintain a competitive market structure by challenging monopoly power, whether achieved through internal growth or through mergers. The laws also are directed at specific business practices considered anticompetitive. Examples are price fixing, group boycotts, and tying arrangements. These and other practices have been defined by the courts over time and have become an integral part of the legal environment in which the modern business manager has to operate. Obeying the antitrust laws is not always simple. The laws are complex, and there is often a hazy line between legal and nonlegal conduct. In most cases, the marginally illegal acts that a business manager engages in are not likely to be challenged, but there is always the risk that some action will violate federal or state antitrust laws.

QUESTIONS FOR DISCUSSION

1. What is meant by a per se violation of the Sherman Act?
2. What is a tying agreement? When is it illegal?
3. How do state antitrust laws differ from federal antitrust laws?
4. Distinguish between primary-line and secondary-line price discrimination.
5. What is the difference between a civil remedy and a criminal remedy in antitrust enforcement?
6. What is the purpose of the Hart–Scott–Rodino Antitrust Improvements Act?
7. Summarize the methods of enforcing the antitrust laws.
8. What is a consent decree?
9. Company A, located in the northern part of a state, sells office equipment throughout the state. Company B, located in the southern part of the state, also sells office equipment throughout the state. The owners

meet at a trade association convention and agree that they each will sell office equipment in three different parts of the state. Does this violate antitrust laws?

RECOMMENDED READINGS

Asch, Peter. *Industrial Organization and Antitrust Policy*. New York: Wiley, 1983.

Bock, Betty. *Continuation and Discontinuation in Antitrust*. New York: The Conference Board, 1982.

Calvani, Terry, and John Siegfried. *Economic Analysis and Antitrust Law*. Boston: Little, Brown, 1980.

Demsetz, Harold. *Economic, Legal and Political Dimensions of Competition*. New York: Elsevier Science Publishing, 1982.

Kintner, Earl. *An Antitrust Primer*. 3rd ed. New York: Macmillan, 1978.

Singer, Eugene M. *Antitrust Economics and Legal Analysis*. Columbus, Ohio: Grid Publishers, 1983.

Van Cise, Jerrold G. *The Federal Antitrust Laws*. 4th ed. Washington, D.C.: American Enterprise Institute for Public Policy Research, 1983.

Waldman, Don E. *The Economics of Antitrust*. Boston: Little, Brown, 1986.

Chapter 7

Application of Antitrust Laws
to Market Power

On the basis of their economic models, both oligopoly and monopoly can generally be regarded as indicators of market power. Certainly in an oligopolistic industry, the barriers to entry can be formidable. Oligopolistic industry structure, in which four or fewer firms make up 70 percent or more of all sales in a particular product market, accounts for a significant amount of all manufacturing in the U.S. economy. The dominant firms in these industries are usually characterized by uniform pricing practices, which means that if one firm in an oligopolistic industry raises its prices and the others do not, consumers will quickly shift to purchasing the less expensive product; conversely, if one firm lowers prices and the others do not, all the firms not lowering their prices could lose business.[1] The product differentiation, advertising, and vertical integration of dominant firms also provide barriers to entry.

In Chapter 5, we pointed out that large firms in the United States have achieved their growth either through internal growth or, more often, through mergers. This is not necessarily bad. To a considerable extent, industrial growth and concentration is a logical concomitant of an advanced industrial society. Large business size has certain advantages, one of which is the mass production of one or a few products, such as automobiles or rubber tires. In addition, there can be economies of scale in mass production, including division of labor and specialization in particular operations, and economics of large-scale buying and selling. However, large firms can restrict competition and impede the rate of capital formation. In certain situations, they can exercise discretionary power over price and entry into market.

Antitrust laws can be applied to the market power achieved by a particular firm. This dominance can be achieved in a single product market or in a geo-

---

[1] This can be theoretically explained by the so-called kinked demand curve.

graphic market. One problem that has arisen over time is there has been no set test of market power within a particular relevant competitive market. In applying Section 2 of the Sherman Act, a variety of tests can be used. One is the existence of an intent to monopolize; another is the committing of specific anticompetitive acts; and a third is the attainment of an illegal absolute or relative size. The last test comes closest to meeting the economic test of a monopoly. However, in applying Section 2 of the Sherman Act, the courts have been unable to rely on the economic model of monopoly because it is based on the concept of one firm being protected from the entry of others into the market and thus, in the absence of competitive products, does not represent a practical legal standard.

ANTITRUST LAWS AS APPLIED TO MONOPOLIES

In applying the antitrust laws, especially Section 2 of the Sherman Act, the courts have not used a clear definition of monopoly based on economic concepts. Generally, they have focused their attention on predatory acts, exclusion of competitors, conspiracies to monopolize, and the impact of mergers on competition. In particular, enforcement of the monopoly provision of the Sherman Act has been based on determining whether or not the industry structure in question rose out of any wrongdoing. Under the act, monopoly and the offense of monopoly have two characteristics: (1) the actual possession of monopoly power in a market and (2) the maintenance of that power or its willful acquisition. The following court cases illustrate how the courts have applied Section 2 of the Sherman Act to monopoly power.

The Northern Securities Company Case, 1904

The Northern Securities Company was a holding company for three large railroads—the Northern Pacific, the Great Northern, and the Chicago, Burlington, and Quincy. Involved in its formation were some of the nation's largest finance capitalists and railroad tycoons, including J. P. Morgan and Company, the Rockefeller interests, James J. Hill, and E. H. Harriman. To Morgan, the holding company combination represented stability and the removal of wasteful competition. The holding company acquired, by giving its own stock in exchange, more than nine-tenths of the stock of the Northern Pacific and three-fourths of the stock of the Great Northern. The effect of this arrangement would have been to end competition between those two rail-roads; the former stockholders in the two roads, as common stockholders in the holding company, would have an interest in preventing competition.

The federal government instituted a suit to have the Northern Securities Company dissolved as a combination in restraint of interstate commerce and to have the railway stock returned. The case reached the U.S. Supreme Court, which by a vote of five to four ordered the company dissolved.[2] The case was significant because it condemned the holding company as a method of control over previously competing companies and because it included this type of stockholding within the scope of the commerce clause.

The Standard Oil Case, 1911

The Standard Oil Company was a classic example of what President Theodore Roosevelt called a "bad" trust.[3] After the Ohio decision of 1892,[4] it had reorganized itself as a holding company to hold the stock of seventy different corporations engaged in operating oil refineries, oil wells, pipelines, storage plants, and distribution facilities. Almost all the facilities had been united under central control by means of a trust. As early as 1882, the trust had secured control of about 90 percent of the oil-refining business, and this control had been maintained in the new organization. Its record of operations was replete with examples of predatory practices designed to injure, eliminate, or buy up competitors to secure monopoly control over oil production. Among other things, it was found that the Standard Oil Company had pursued a policy of cutting prices in areas where there was competition, while maintaining or increasing them in areas where there was no competition.[5] It bribed railway and other employees for information on competitors, and it controlled pipelines to the detriment of competitors.

In 1906, the government initiated action against the Standard Oil Company, charging it with conspiracy to restrain trade and commerce in crude oil, refined oil, and other petroleum products in interstate and foreign commerce. In 1911, the U.S. Supreme Court unanimously affirmed a circuit court decision

---

[2] *U.S. v. Northern Securities Co.,* 193 U.S. 197 (1904).

[3] The development of the Standard Oil Company was discussed in Chapter 2.

[4] The Ohio decision of 1892 resulted in the dissolution of the Standard Oil Trust.

[5] This behavior is primary-line or seller's discrimination.

to dissolve Standard Oil.[6] In its decision, the Supreme Court ordered the holding company to transfer to the original holders the stock that had been turned over to it in exchange for holding company stock. Each owner of one share of stock in Standard Oil of New Jersey received securities in thirty-three companies; in addition, each retained control in the parent company, which continued as a producing concern. Since a few persons owned a large proportion of the stock of Standard Oil of New Jersey, the decree resulted in giving these same persons a controlling interest in all thirty-four companies. The effect of this decree was to divide Standard Oil into a series of companies, each of which was supreme in a given geographic area.

The American Tobacco Case, 1911

The American Tobacco Company was also a "bad" trust. Before 1890, competition existed in all branches of the tobacco trade: snuff, plug, cigarettes, and cigars. The Tobacco Trust differed from its contemporaries in that it was formed to hold property, whereas the others held securities. It exchanged its shares directly for the plants, business, brands, and goodwill of the five companies that manufactured cigarettes. The trust was originally formed as a horizontal combination, but then it expanded and absorbed the MacAndrews and Forbes Company, which had an almost complete monopoly of the manufacture of licorice, a substance used in processing tobacco. Other concerns that did not process tobacco but made related products were bought by the trust, including those that manufactured tinfoil, the cotton bags in which tobacco was packed, and wooden boxes. The trust controlled the companies that made the machinery used in the manufacture of tobacco as well as those that held the patents for these machines.

The American Tobacco Trust was formed to check a decline in the price of tobacco products, and this it set out to do by controlling competition in foreign and domestic markets. To control foreign markets, a cartel was formed, and to eliminate domestic competition, the trust used its financial power. In 1889, it bought and closed thirty competing companies engaged in the manufacture, distribution, and sale of tobacco. Price wars were entered into freely to force the manufacturers of competing cigarette products to agree to terms set by the trust. The trust also required vendors, stockholders, and employees to promise to use only its products. While buying up the tobacco companies, American

[6] *U.S. v. Standard Oil of N.J.*, 221 U.S. 106 (1911).

Tobacco also seized the plug tobacco trade. It approached the leading manufacturers of plug tobacco and sought to bring about a combination of plug tobacco interests. Failing in this, it simply tried to ruin the competition by lowering the price of its plug tobacco to below cost. It was successful.

In 1907, the government initiated a suit against the American Tobacco
Company, charging it with violations of Sections 1 and 2 of the Sherman Act.
The lower courts dismissed the suit, but the government appealed the case to
the Supreme Court. In May 1911, the trust was dissolved by order of the
court.[7] The dissolution did little to promote competition in the tobacco industry because subsidiary companies of the American Tobacco Company were
reorganized into new companies. The American Snuff Company, which had a
monopoly on the manufacture of snuff, gave part of its facilities to two new
snuff companies, George W. Helme and Weyman-Burton. American Tobacco
gave to its common stockholders the stock it held in R. J. Reynolds Company,
a manufacturer of plug and pipe tobacco. American Tobacco was then split
into three full-line companies making cigarettes, small cigars, plug, pipe, and
fine-cut tobacco. These companies were American Tobacco, Liggett and
Myers, and P. Lorillard.

The Rule of Reason

The Standard Oil and American Tobacco cases represent a landmark in the Supreme Court's interpretation of antitrust laws. In these cases, the legal concept
of rule of reason—that is, the guidelines by which to distinguish good trusts
from bad trusts—was drawn up. In the mind of the Court, the size and power of
a combination created only the presumption of an attempt to dominate an industry. Before the Sherman Act could be applied, proof that predatory acts—
such as price discrimination, allocation of markets, or other devices designed
to achieve market dominance—had been committed was needed. In other
words, size could be achieved through the normal methods of industrial development or through the commission of predatory acts designed to eliminate
competition. Only the latter, the Court believed, imposed unreasonable restraints on competition.

In deciding these two cases, the Supreme Court essentially distinguished
between good and bad trusts. Large firm size in itself was not illegal; illegal
was the commission of predatory acts. The Supreme Court adopted the famous rule of reason. Since the Sherman Act did not specifically define those

[7] *U.S. v. American Tobacco Co.*, 221 U.S. 106 (1911).

acts that were in restraint of trade, the courts had to do so. Rule of reason meant that in applying a statute condemning restraints on trade, a court could use flexibility and discretion. Two criteria were used to determine the kind of business practice that would be in violation of the Sherman Act. First, there had to be unworthy motives or predatory acts designed to harm competitors, and second, there had to be such overwhelming control of an industry that competition had virtually ceased to exist.

The U.S. Steel Case, 1920

Later, during the 1920s, the Supreme Court, acting under the rule of reason doctrine, held that the existence of monopoly power that was not abused did not violate the Sherman Act. The U.S. Steel case of 1920 is an example of the application of the rule of reason doctrine.[8] U.S. Steel, then the nation's largest industrial enterprise, was a holding company formed in 1901 to merge concerns that were themselves amalgamations of smaller companies. It had been set up to forestall a threat of overexpansion and ruinous competition at a time when other manufacturers of heavier semifinished products had been about to integrate forward into the finished lines, and other manufacturers of finished products had made plans to integrate backward. The U.S. Steel Corporation brought under its control in one financial unit a series of corporations that had already secured control over the principal plants in their respective lines of business in the steel industry. These and other acquisitions gave U.S. Steel control of 65 to 75 percent of all lines of steel manufacturing in the country and also more than 80 percent of the best iron ore reserves, bringing together major companies that were themselves competing with one another.

The Justice Department brought action against U.S. Steel in 1912, accusing it, among other things, of a conspiracy to fix prices in the steel industry. The corporation had made it a practice to meet with its competitors to set prices. These became the official prices for all iron and steel products. When U.S. Steel changed prices, its competitors followed suit. In 1920, the Supreme Court reached a final decision in the case and refused to allow a dissolution of the company.

There were several reasons for the Court's decision. One was that the meetings of U.S. Steel and its competitors had been discontinued before the government suit. In its approach to competition, a majority of the Court

---

[8] *U.S. v. U.S. Steel Corporation,* 251 U.S. 417 (1920).

emphasized the legal rather than the economic concept. Competition had not been restrained, for U.S. Steel had made no effort to suppress other companies by unfair means. The Court also held that the corporation did not have sufficient power to control prices in the industry and that size in itself did not constitute a violation of the Sherman Act. To violate the act, overt predatory actions were required. The decision of the Supreme Court gave rise to the so-called abuse theory of monopoly. In other words, in the absence of abusive market practices, the Sherman Act did not make mere size an offense.

The Alcoa Case, 1945

The Alcoa case is considered a landmark case in that it broke sharply with antitrust cases of the past.[9] In this case, Judge Learned Hand, speaking for the Supreme Court, declared monopolies illegal per se, thus abandoning the rule of reason. A government suit had been initiated in 1937 charging that Aluminum Company of America (Alcoa) had violated Section 2 of the Sherman Act by monopolizing virgin aluminum production. At the time of the suit, Alcoa controlled more than 90 percent of the production of aluminum ingots. It had become a monopoly originally through its exclusive control over patent rights and then by its control over bauxite deposits and generation sites for the hydroelectric power needed in aluminum manufacture. Moreover, Alcoa was able to anticipate and forestall virtually all competition in the production of aluminum ingots by stimulating demand and producing new uses for the metal. Thus the company could hardly maintain it was a passive beneficiary of a monopoly that had come about from an involuntary elimination of competitors by automatically operating market forces.

The significance of the Alcoa case lies in the identification and condemnation of monopoly in and of itself, without respect to abuses, predatory acts, injuries to competitors, or intent to monopolize. In initiating the suit, the Justice Department asked for the dissolution of Alcoa. A district court ruled in favor of Alcoa, finding no abuse of power. The case was then appealed, and Judge Hand ruled against Alcoa. The test of a monopoly, he emphasized, is the existence of that size that gives a firm the power to fix and manage prices. Alcoa's control of 90 percent of all aluminum ingots was sufficient in itself to constitute monopoly power. The mere existence of such a monopoly gave the firm as much or more power to fix prices as would an illegal combination or contract

[9] *U.S. v. Aluminum Co. of America,* 148 F. 2d, 416 (1945).

among firms. Monopoly power, even though not abused, was now to be considered a violation of the Sherman Act. The good behavior of the company, which before 1945 would have been acceptable defense to the court, was no longer valid, for Congress, according to the Supreme Court, in passing the Sherman Act, did not condone "good" trusts and condemn "bad" trusts; it forbade all. Therefore, Alcoa was required to divest itself of certain facilities, which were given to other aluminum companies in order to encourage more competition.[10]

Subsequent court decisions have not reversed the thinking advanced in the Alcoa case. At this time, the judgment of monopoly is based on such factors as the number and strength of the firms in the market, their effective size from the standpoint of technological development, their ability to compete with similar domestic and foreign industries, and the public's interest in lower costs. But the Alcoa case also indicated that the courts would not apply Section 2 of the Sherman Act to a firm with overwhelming market power when that position was "thrust on" the defendant. So a firm could achieve market power legitimately in one of several ways: through historical accident, by lawful use of government-granted patent protection, or by uncontrollable factors in the marketplace.

The AT&T Case, 1974–1982

The AT&T case, perhaps the most important antitrust case of all time, was also resolved in January 1982. Not since the breakup of Standard Oil in 1911 has there been a more complex and potentially revolutionary restructuring of a U.S. corporation, which in 1982 happened to be the largest in the world. In 1980, AT&T had total assets of $137 billion, and its total operating revenues amounted to $51 billion.[11] In contrast, the next largest public utility, General Telephone & Electronics, had assets of $21 billion and operating revenues of $10 billion. In fact, AT&T's assets and operating revenues were larger than the nine next largest public utilities combined. The company's stock is owned by more stockholders than any other company in the world, and the stock has always been regarded as the bluest of the blue chips.

---

[10] There was a second Alcoa case in 1950. The Justice Department accused Alcoa of price fixing and asked that the company be required to divest itself of more facilities. The court decision favored Alcoa this time, however, on the grounds that there was strong competition in the industry.

[11] *Fortune,* May 31, 1981, p. 124.

In its suit against AT&T, the Justice Department sought to separate owner-ship of AT&T's local operating phone companies, its long-lines department, and its equipment-manufacturing subsidiary, Western Electric, which by it-self ranked nineteenth among the five hundred largest industrial corporations in the United States. This situation presented the anomaly of a regulated public utility owning an industrial firm not subject to regulation. The Justice Depart-ment charged that AT&T's subsidiaries bought equipment from Western Electric even when other companies were developing better and cheaper equipment. It contended that AT&T set unreasonable restrictions on the con-nection of terminal equipment produced by other companies and that AT&T either refused to deal with competitors of its long-lines department who wanted to connect with local phone networks or subjected them to discrimina-tory terms and prices. Finally, the Justice Department wanted a realignment of AT&T's research unit, Bell Laboratories.

AT&T, however, contended that the government was attacking policies the company developed under comprehensive state and federal regulation. The company argued that its policies were reasonable responses to regulation and were subject to change by the regulators and therefore should be immune from antitrust laws. It maintained that restrictions on the connection of some equip-ment were necessary to protect the telephone network from harm. It defended its opposition to competitors in long-distance service as a way to prevent "cream-skimming" by competitors—that is, taking the most lucrative lines of business and leaving AT&T as a utility, with an obligation to supply the most costly services. AT&T also contended that competition in the communica-tions industry increased dramatically during the 1970s. A side argument, ad-vanced by the Department of Defense, was that fragmentation of AT&T might well prove detrimental to the national defense. The company argued that its telecommunications system produced an important contribution to the na-tion's missile, defense, space, and scientific programs.

Results of the AT&T Settlement

The results of the AT&T settlement were as follows:

1. AT&T had to divest itself of the local telephone services of its twenty-two Bell Operating Companies. They became a part of seven independent holding companies.
2. Western Electric, Bell Laboratories, and the long-distance division of AT&T were retained by AT&T. All intrastate long-distance service was turned over to AT&T by the local companies.

3. AT&T is no longer barred from offering unregulated nontelephone service, thereby opening the way for the corporation to enter the computer data processing and information service business.
4. Local telephone companies divested by AT&T are required to share their facilities with all long-distance telephone companies on the same terms.
5. Local companies are barred from discriminating against AT&T's competitors in buying equipment and planning new facilities.
6. AT&T's stockholders retained stock in AT&T and were issued proportionate shares in the local companies.

Figure 7-1 presents the organization of AT&T before and after the divestiture of its twenty-two operating companies. The divestiture, the largest in antitrust history, amounted to $87 billion. The settlement leaves AT&T partially regulated (Long-Lines Division) and partially unregulated (Bell Labs, Western Electric). The local telephone companies are regulated. AT&T is also able to enter the highly profitable computer and information industries, such as cable television and electronic newspapers. But working against AT&T is its lack of marketing expertise; as a regulated monopoly, the company never really had to sell anything.

Benefits of the AT&T Divestiture

Certain benefits are supposed to accrue to the U.S. economy as a result of the AT&T divestiture. New competition is lowering prices paid by phone companies for equipment and by customers for long-distance service. Competition is also supposed to stimulate the growth of new technology. This growth could prove crucial as telecommunications becomes vital to an increasingly information-based U.S. economy. The divestiture has also had some drawbacks: higher costs for equipment installation and service provided by the short-distance phone companies and more customer confusion over telephone bills, for example. Many customers have become dissatisfied with local phone service. They believe that it costs more than it should and that the quality of service is deteriorating.

The Aspen Skiing Company Case, 1985

Aspen Skiing Company owns three of the four major mountain facilities for downhill skiing in Aspen, Colorado. Aspen Highlands owns the fourth. In

FIGURE 7-1 AT&T Before and After the Divestiture

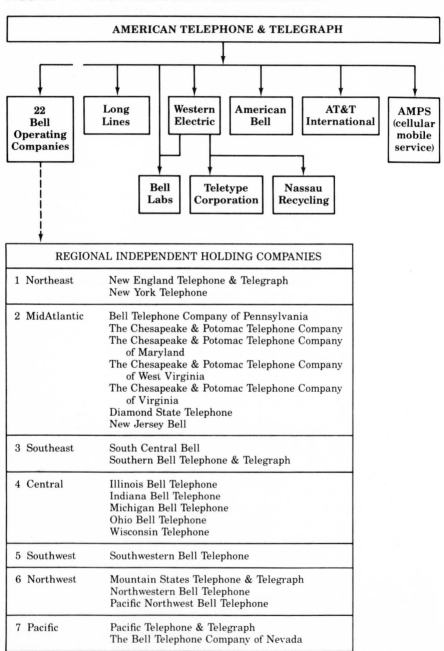

earlier years, each company offered its own ticket for daily use of its mountains, and they both offered an interchangeable multiday, all-Aspen ticket. Allocations from the multiday, multiarea ticket were based on samples of the number of skiers on each mountain. However, Aspen Skiing refused to continue offering the multiday, multiarea ticket unless Aspen Highlands accepted a fixed percentage of the revenues. Aspen Highlands accepted but refused to take a lower percentage a year later. Aspen Skiing then tried to eliminate Aspen Highlands from the joint ticket arrangement, and the latter went to court, alleging that Aspen Skiing was monopolizing the market in violation of Section 2 of the Sherman Act.

A jury ruled that Aspen Skiing had used exclusionary means to enhance its monopoly position and awarded the plaintiff triple damages of $7 million. This was affirmed by a circuit court, which held that the multiday, multiarea ticket had become an essential facility of the Aspen downhill skiing market and that Aspen Skiing had a duty to make that essential facility available to its competitor. The U.S. Supreme Court affirmed the decision and also held that Aspen Skiing's refusal to cooperate with its business rival, combined with the absence of any justification of efficiency whatsoever for its conduct, demonstrated an intent to monopolize in violation of Section 2 of the Sherman Act.[12]

ANTITRUST LAWS AS APPLIED TO MERGERS

The foundation of merger law is Section 7 of the Clayton Act, which states a merger is unlawful "when in any line of commerce or in any activity affecting commerce in any section of the country, the effect of such acquisition . . . may be substantially to lessen competition, or to tend to create a monopoly."[13] By 1950, the original language of Section 7 was considered inadequate. The courts had ruled it inapplicable to mergers by the acquisition of assets, and many people believed that it only proscribed mergers between direct competitors (horizontal mergers) but not between firms in a buyer-seller relationship (vertical mergers). A number of mergers occurred during the period after World War II, and Congress produced the Celler-Kefauver Amendment to Section 7 in 1950 to include asset acquisition. All types of mergers are banned provided it can be shown that the effect may be a substantial lessening of

[12] *Aspen Skiing Co. v. Aspen Highland Skiing Corp.*, 53 U.S.L.W. 4818 (June 19, 1985).

[13] U.S. House of Representatives, Committee on the Judiciary, *Compilation of Selected Antitrust Acts,* 95th Cong., 2nd sess., 1978, pp. 14–15.

competition or a tendency to create a monopoly. The prohibition of the law depends on market effects.

Economic analysis can be used in the application of Section 7 to specific mergers. This proceeds from the concepts of competition and monopoly discussed in Chapter 5. These concepts describe diametrically opposite results that can occur when society allocates limited resources in the free market. Under perfect competition, sellers produce and sell goods in an open market. In the long run, production results in maximum efficiency: goods are produced with the least possible expenditures of resources and the lowest possible cost per unit, and they are sold at the lowest possible price. Conversely, a monopolist has complete control over production of a good and need not produce at the lowest cost or sell at the lowest price. In maximizing profits, the monopolist can sell at a price above that which would have prevailed under perfect competition. Consumer well-being is not maximized, for fewer units of a good will be sold. However, real markets rarely conform to either model, and most industries fall within a continuum of each.

Mergers are of three types: horizontal, vertical, and conglomerate. All have the potential to lessen competition by increasing industrial concentration in the hands of fewer firms and preventing market entry by new firms. Nevertheless, some mergers stimulate competition; therefore, it is necessary to restrain only those mergers that can lessen competition. That judgment depends on the facts and circumstances of each merger within the context of a particular industry and market. In the remainder of this chapter, the antitrust laws are applied to horizontal, vertical, and conglomerate mergers. But first we discuss what factors condemn a merger as anticompetitive or monopolistic. These factors determine market power, which enables firms to keep prices above competitive levels. They are barriers to entry and market structure, and they are mostly applicable to horizontal mergers.

In a market characterized by pure competition, there are no barriers to entry. New firms can enter a market and compete against existing firms. Any barrier to entry protects existing firms against increased price competition and increases the possibility of collusion. In a monopolistic market, however, there would be a complete barrier to entry of another firm; in an oligopolistic market there also can be barriers to entry. For example, Coca-Cola and PepsiCo dominate the soft drink industry. The two companies dominate the soft drink market through advertising, product differentiation, and control over display space. Whether a new firm could enter the soft drink market today is doubtful.

The term *market structure* refers to the number of firms and the degree of concentration in an industry. A basic distinction is made between oligopolistic industries and less concentrated industries. Mergers that would ordinarily be allowed in nonconcentrated industries may be challenged in oligopolistic industries. Decisions to challenge a merger may turn primarily on the answers to two questions: How concentrated would the market be after the merger? And how much of that concentration will result from the merger? However, even in concentrated markets mergers may not be precluded from occurring when it can be demonstrated that economies of scale would be achieved or that competition could in some way be enhanced.

Horizontal Mergers

The horizontal merger is an economic arrangement between companies performing similar functions in the production or distribution of comparable goods. Almost all early mergers in the United States were horizontal, and Section 7 of the Clayton Act had them specifically in mind when it stated that no corporation shall acquire the stock of another corporation when the effect may be to substantially lessen competition. The factors that have been considered over time are the number of firms, the degree of industrial concentration, the product line, the conditions of entry, and the geographic market. The following cases illustrate some of the factors that have been weighed by the courts in arriving at decisions in horizontal merger cases.

The Brown Shoe Case, 1962

The Brown Shoe case was a landmark case with regard to the application of Section 7 of the Clayton Act, as amended by Celler–Kefauver.[14] The Justice Department challenged the acquisition of the Kinney Shoe Company by the Brown Shoe Company. At the time of the acquisition, Brown was the third largest shoe retailer and the fourth largest shoe manufacturer in the United States, and Kinney was the eighth largest shoe retailer and the twelfth largest shoe manufacturer. Between them, Brown and Kinney had about sixteen hundred retail outlets but produced only 5 percent of the total national output of shoes. The Justice Department challenged the merger on the grounds that competition would be lessened substantially vertically and horizontally—vertically because Brown Shoe would use the Kinney retail outlets to sell Brown Shoes exclusively, thus excluding independent firms from using the same

---

[14] *Brown Shoe Co. v. U.S.*, 370 U.S. 294 (1962).

outlets, and horizontally because the former retail store competition between the two shoe companies would be eliminated.

There were also other issues in the Brown Shoe case. An important one, often considered in merger cases, was the determination of the relevant market area. To determine a merger's effect on competition, the relevant market area can be subdivided into a geographic market and a product market. The latter is determined by the reasonable interchange of products or the cross-elasticity of demand between the product itself and the substitutes for it. Within the product market are submarkets whose boundaries may be defined by examining industrial customs and practices. Regarding the vertical arrangement in the case, the relevant geographic market was the United States, and the product market was various lines of shoes. The geographic market involved in the horizontal arrangement was cities with a population of ten thousand or more and their environs in which both Brown and Kinney retailed shoes through their own outlets. The horizontal product market was men's, women's, and children's shoes sold in all retail stores.

We should emphasize that the merger had both horizontal and vertical aspects. There was a horizontal combination at both the manufacturing and the retail outlet level. The ruling of the district court, which was upheld by the Supreme Court, was that the merger at the manufacturing level was too insignificant to affect competition adversely. But at the retail level the ruling was different. It was ruled that as a result of the merger competition was reduced in those cities in which both Brown and Kinney had retail outlets. In some 118 cities with populations of ten thousand or more, the combined retail outlets exceeded 5 percent of the total market. Even though there was a lack of concentration in the shoe retailing industry, the court felt that a merger resulting in 5 percent market control could have an adverse affect on competition, particularly since future merger efforts by Brown's competitors might be encouraged. It was also ruled that a vertical restraint existed, specifically that Brown would use its control to force its shoes into the Kinney retail stores, thus excluding other manufacturers.

The Von's Grocery Case, 1966

Von's Grocery acquired Shopping Bag Food Stores. At the time of the acquisition, Von's and Shopping Bag were respectively the third and sixth largest retail grocery chains in the Los Angeles area. Their combined share of annual retail grocery sales in the Los Angeles market was 7.5 percent in 1960. Both companies had enjoyed great success before the merger. From 1948 to 1958, the number of Von's stores had increased from fifteen to thirty-four. During the same period, Von's share of the Los Angeles market almost doubled, and Shopping Bag's share of the market tripled. The merger of the two successful supermarket chains created the second largest grocery chain in Los Angeles after Safeway, which had around 10 percent of the market.

The government brought action in a federal district court, alleging that the merger violated Section 7 of the Clayton Act and asking that the merger be enjoined. The district court ruled in favor of the defendants, and the case was appealed to the Supreme Court. The latter, by a vote of six to two, found the merger violated Section 7 and ordered it dissolved.[15] Von's argued that the merger would enable it to compete more effectively against Safeway. However, the Supreme Court found that the number of individual competitors in the Los Angeles market area had decreased. In 1950, there were 5,365 single grocery store owners in the market area; by 1963, the number of stores decreased to 3,590. During the same period, the number of chains with two or more stores doubled, with small stores being absorbed by mergers. This, in the minds of the majority of the justices in the decision, made it necessary to prevent economic concentration in the U.S. economy by keeping a large number of small competitors in business.[16]

Times have changed since the Von's Grocery case, and it is doubtful whether the government would challenge a merger between two small firms today. The total sales of the two grocery chains at the time of their merger was $173 million. Compare this to two horizontal mergers consummated in 1984: Texaco acquired Getty, and Standard Oil of California (Chevron) acquired Gulf Oil. The combined sales of Texaco and Getty after the merger were $50 billion, and the combined sales of Chevron and Gulf were $36 billion. Merger guidelines have changed to reflect a more lenient government attitude. The standards that the antitrust agencies have applied in reaching a prosecutorial determination can be illustrated by presenting the Justice Department's merger guidelines for 1968 and 1984.

---

[15] *U.S. v. Von's Grocery,* 348 U.S. 270 (1966).

[16] The district court and a minority on the Supreme Court found that there was no increase in market concentration before or after the merger. Entry barriers appeared to be nonexistent, for 173 new retail grocery chains had entered the Los Angeles market between 1953 and 1962. Between 1948 and 1958, the market share of Safeway had fallen from 14 percent to 8 percent. Many of the stores that had gone out of business were small "Mom and Pop" stores, inefficiently run and with prices higher than those charged by the supermarkets.

Merger Guidelines

The Justice Department has emphasized market structure in establishing the boundaries of allowable horizontal mergers. In 1968, it issued its first set of merger guidelines, which were based on the four-firm industrial concentration ratio. Markets were classified as highly concentrated and less highly concentrated depending on the concentration ratio. In new guidelines, first issued in 1982 and revised in 1984, the Justice Department adopted a measure of concentration called the Herfindahl–Hirschman index. It reflects both the distribution of the market shares of the top four firms and the composition of the market outside the top four firms. The index also gives proportionately greater weight to the market shares of the larger firms by the technique of squaring all market shares. A comparison of the two sets of guidelines follows.

The 1968 Merger Guidelines

The 1968 merger guidelines emphasized market structure in establishing the boundaries of allowable horizontal mergers. A basic distinction was made between oligopolistic industries and less concentrated industries. Mergers that ordinarily would have been allowed in less concentrated industries could have been challenged in oligopolistic industries. The following examples show the postacquisition market shares of horizontal mergers that ordinarily would have been challenged by the Justice Department.

| *Concentrated Markets (four firms with 75 percent of market)* | |
Acquiring firm	*Acquired firm*
5%	4%
10%	2%
15% or more	1%

| *Less Concentrated Markets* | |
Acquiring firm	*Acquired firm*
5%	5% or more
10%	4% or more
15%	3% or more
20%	2% or more
25% or more	1% or more

Vertical Mergers

The basic problem in applying the antitrust laws to vertical mergers is that since direct competition is not involved, it is difficult to apply such criteria as market shares, ease of entry, or concentration indexes. Direct competition is not involved because in a vertical merger the firms operate at different stages of the production or distribution process. Somehow it has to be demonstrated that the merger has an anticompetitive effect. In the Brown Shoe case, the Supreme Court was concerned that independent shoe manufacturers would be denied access to retail shoe store outlets because of the number of retail stores that Brown–Kinney would control after acquisition. Generally, action against vertical mergers is taken when the result is likely either to raise barriers to entry in an industry or to foreclose equal access to potential customers or suppliers.

The Du Pont Case, 1956

A case involving the Du Pont Corporation illustrates the application of Section 7 of the Clayton Act to a vertical merger, even though technically the merger was never consummated.[17] In 1919, when General Motors was just getting a major start in the automobile industry, Du Pont acquired ownership of 23 percent of its stock. The primary issue in the case, which was initiated by the Justice Department in 1949, was whether or not Du Pont had used this stock ownership to ensure a market for many of its products, including automobile finishes, fabrics, and chemicals. Not only was General Motors dominant in the automobile industry, it also was first in sales among all industrial corporations in the United States, so its link with America's largest chemical company was significant with respect to the alleged anticompetitive effects of the stock acquisition. In this case, the complaint was originally issued some thirty years after the stock acquisition, showing that Section 7 can be applied to both past and current mergers.

In 1956, the Supreme Court reversed a ruling by a lower court and ordered that Du Pont divest itself of its General Motors stock. Even though Du Pont and General Motors were not competitors, Du Pont enjoyed a commanding position as a General Motors supplier in a particular line of commerce, namely, automotive finishes and fabrics. In 1946, Du Pont furnished General Motors with 67 percent of its requirements for automotive finishes and, in

---

[17] *U.S. v. Du Pont and Co.*, 353 U.S. 588 (1956).

1947, 68 percent. In fabrics, Du Pont furnished only 52 percent in 1946 and 38 percent in 1947. The court ruled that anticompetitive effects were created by the stock acquisition because Du Pont was able to use its stock to become the primary supplier of General Motors in these two fields, thus negating the principle of free competition and creating an element of monopoly.

Conglomerate Mergers

Conglomerate mergers do not entail firms in direct competition with each other, nor are there usually any extensive vertical relations between the firms. They do not affect the structure of any market but merely alter the identity of firms already in the market. There are many different types of conglomerate mergers, and thus many different economic effects of them. Because no readily available criteria exist that may simply be applied to determine their legality, the courts have had to analyze each specific merger to evaluate its particular economic effect. So antitrust law governing conglomerate mergers has had to develop case by case. Case precedents have identified the types of conglomerate mergers most likely to be found in violation of Section 7 of the Clayton Act as amended by Celler–Kefauver.

The Procter & Gamble Case, 1966

A product extension merger is one type of conglomerate merger. It occurs when one firm acquires a second firm producing a product closely related to the acquiring firm's product line. The classic example of a product extension merger, which was not allowed, was when Procter & Gamble, the largest manufacturer of household cleaning supplies in the United States, entered the liquid bleach market through the acquisition of Clorox.[18] At the time of the merger, in 1957, Clorox was the leading manufacturer in the liquid bleach industry, with 48.8 percent of total sales. Its market share had been steadily increasing for the five years before the merger. Its nearest rival was Purex, which accounted for 15.7 percent of the liquid bleach sales in an industry dominated by the two companies. Liquid bleach is chemically identifiable, so no patentable difference among brands existed to exploit. Clorox spent around $3.7 million in advertising, almost one-tenth of its total sales in 1957. Heavy expenditures on advertising had enabled Clorox to gain such a large share of

[18] *FTC v. Procter & Gamble Co.*, 386 U.S. 568 (1966).

the liquid bleach market, even though its product was no different from rival brands.

Clorox fitted into Procter & Gamble's production plans. The products were complementary in use, employed the same methods of distribution and advertising, and were sold to the same customers. The merger was challenged by the Federal Trade Commission on the grounds that it was a violation of Section 7. Competition was lessened for several reasons. First, the acquisition would raise the barriers to entry by new firms wanting to make liquid bleach. Procter & Gamble's advertising budget, which was several times larger than Clorox's yearly sales, would be used to promote Clorox bleach at the expense of Purex and other liquid bleach producers. Second, the acquisition of Clorox by Procter & Gamble eliminated the former as a potential competitor. Liquid bleach was a natural avenue of diversification since it complemented Procter & Gamble's products. The company could enter the liquid bleach market and compete against Clorox. The Supreme Court, reversing the decision of a circuit court of appeals, dissolved the merger.

The ITT Case, 1970

In 1969, the Justice Department filed suit against the International Telephone & Telegraph Company (ITT), America's largest corporate conglomerate, to force it to divest itself of the Hartford Fire Insurance Company and two other subsidiaries.[19] The Justice Department initiated action against ITT for two reasons. First, it felt that the ITT acquisition of the Hartford Fire Insurance Company, Sheraton, Avis, and a wide variety of other companies would encourage the existing trend of large corporations to acquire dominant firms in concentrated markets, thereby increasing the concentration of control of manufacturing assets. The ITT acquisition of the Hartford Fire Insurance Company was a case in point. With assets of $1.8 billion, it was one of the five largest fire and casualty insurance companies in the United States.

Three separate acquisitions of ITT were challenged by the Justice Department. The first was the acquisition of the Canteen Corporation; the second was the acquisition of the Grinnell Corporation; and the third was the acquisition of the Hartford Fire Insurance Company. The government's case against these mergers was based on several forms of alleged competitive damage—reciprocity, geographic foreclosure of markets, financial resources, and the combination of the automatic sprinkler (Grinnell) and fire insurance (Hartford)

---

[19] *U.S. v. International Telephone & Telegraph Co.*, 324 F. Supp. 19 (1970).

business. The record of the ITT–Canteen case documented how ITT promoted reciprocity with banks. As for geographic foreclosure of markets, it was felt that the acquisition of Grinnell, a major producer of automatic sprinkler systems, would enable ITT to capture an expanding share of the foreign market. Finally, there was the interrelationship between Grinnell and Hartford, for insurance rates are related directly to the presence of automatic sprinkler systems. There was the possibility that Hartford insurance agents would recommend Grinnell sprinkler systems to their customers, thus eliminating competition from a segment of the sprinkler market.

There were three judgments in the ITT case:

1. In the judgment involving the Canteen Corporation, ITT was ordered to divest itself, within two years, of all its interest, direct and indirect, in the company.
2. ITT was ordered to divest itself, within two years, of all its interest, direct and indirect, in the fire protection division of Grinnell.
3. ITT was ordered to divest itself, within three years of the final judgment, of all its interests, direct and indirect, in Levitt, Avis, and Hamilton Life or, alternatively, to divest itself of all its interests, direct and indirect, in Hartford.

Joint Ventures

Section 7 of the Clayton Act applies to most forms of joint venture, which is broadly defined as a combination of two or more firms for a particular business objective. A joint venture often results in the formation of a new entry, but this is not essential; the parties may simply agree by contract to cooperate. Each party contributes to the venture—production facilities, personnel, technology, and funding. Joint ventures are becoming particularly important in the area of international business. Their advantage, domestic or international, is that they allow companies to combine complementary resources, develop new products, or pool capital and share risks where the project is costly or the likelihood of success small. Projects beyond the individual reach of each company may be feasible through a joint venture. But they also can be anticompetitive because potential entry into the market by other firms can be blocked, and collaboration by the partners in the venture can lead to illegal agreements between them to fix prices or divide markets.

The Penn-Olin Chemical Company Case, 1964

Pennsalt Chemicals Corporation, a producer of industrial salt, and Olin Matheson Chemical Corporation, a manufacturer of industrial chemical products, formed a joint venture, Penn–Olin, to produce and market industrial salt in the growing southeastern market. The product, which is used to bleach wood pulp, was produced in a concentrated market dominated by three firms, including Pennsalt. Before the joint venture with Olin Matheson in 1960, Pennsalt's product was marketed in the southeast through an agreement with Olin. The market at that time was dominated by two of Pennsalt's competitors, Hooker Chemical and American Potash, which together had more than a 90 percent share of the market. Pennsalt formed the joint venture with Olin to enter the market.

The government challenged the joint venture on the grounds that either or both companies could have entered the southeast market independently, or that either could be a potential entrant. In its decision, the Supreme Court, reversing the lower courts, held that they should have considered the ongoing effect of both firms standing on the edge of the market as potential competitors and should have determined whether their decision to enter the southeastern market through the venture could have resulted in a substantial lessening of competition. The case was sent back for further review to a district court, which found that no reasonable probability existed that either company would have entered the market on its own and dismissed the case.[20]

ANTITRUST ENFORCEMENT AND THE REAGAN ADMINISTRATION

The area of merger enforcement was one of the areas of greatest change in the Reagan administration. On the whole, merger guidelines were more lenient than those that were applied in the past. For years the structural approach was used to decide antitrust cases. This approach, as mentioned previously, placed emphasis on market concentration. It held that the structure of the marketplace is a reliable indicator of monopoly power. The more concentrated the market, the greater was the market power of those firms in it. Excessive concentration of market power gave firms the power to fix prices, regulate output, and make

[20] *U.S. v. Penn-Olin Chemical Co.*, 378 U.S. 158 (1964).

excessive profits. The way to reduce market power was to prevent mergers of firms in concentrated industries. So, for example, a firm with 10 percent market share in a concentrated market (four firms with 75 percent of the market) would probably have been challenged if it attempted to acquire another firm with 2 percent of the market.

A new attitude toward mergers began in the 1970s. Economists and the courts felt that industrial concentration in itself did not necessarily mean a lack of competition. In this view, the notion that increasing the number of competitors in an industry will add to competition is conjectural. Nothing proves that the number of competitors guarantees efficiency or increases the likelihood of improved decision making. It was argued, with considerable justification, that in certain industries large companies and concentration are essential because of the heavy capital investment needed to do business. Bigness is often a result of efficiency, and efficiency contributes to economic growth. Also, as the United States is becoming more of a part of a global economy, U.S. firms have to compete against very large foreign multinational firms that are not subject to the same antitrust regulations. What counts is the performance of an industry, not its market structure.

The Herfindahl–Hirschman Index

New horizontal merger guidelines were introduced by the Justice Department in 1982. As noted earlier, it departed from traditional concentration ratios and adopted another measure of market power called the Herfindahl–Hirschman Index. The index can take into consideration a larger number of companies and their relative sizes in determining market concentration. The index is obtained by squaring and summing the market shares of a given number of firms. If there is only one firm, the index would attain its maximum value of 100 percent squared, or 10,000 percent, because the firm would be a pure monopoly. If four firms have an equal share of the market, the index would be $25\%^2 + 25\%^2 + 25\%^2 + 25\%^2 = 2,500\%$. By squaring market shares, the index is weighted more heavily in favor of firms with large market shares than firms with smaller market shares. If one firm has a 50 percent market share, and four firms have an equal share of the remaining 50 percent, the index would be $50\%^2 + 12.5\%^2 + 12.5\%^2 + 12.5\%^2 + 12.5\%^2 = 3,130\%$.[21]

[21] The Herfindahl–Hirschman Index is discussed in more detail in Thomas W. Brunner, Thomas J. Krattenmaker, Robert A. Skitol, and Ann Adams Webster, *Mergers in the New Antitrust Era* (Washington, D.C.: Bureau of National Affairs, 1985), pp. 21–24.

The following guidelines are applicable to horizontal mergers.[22]

1. If the postmerger index is below 1,000 percent, the merger will not be challenged by the Justice Department or the Federal Trade Commission. Price fixing and other forms of collusion prohibited by Section 1 of the Sherman Act is unlikely to occur because the market is not concentrated.

2. If the postmerger index is between 1,000 and 1,800, and the increase in the index is less than 100, the merger is not likely to be challenged; if it is more than 100, it is likely to be challenged.

3. If the postmerger index is greater than 1,800, the merger is likely to be challenged if (a) the increase in the index is greater than 50 or (b) the merger will substantially lessen competition.[23]

An application of the Herfindahl–Hirschman Index to horizontal mergers follows. Assume that the five largest firms in a market have 30 percent, 20 percent, 10 percent, 8 percent, and 5 percent. The third largest firm wants to acquire the fifth largest firm. The premerger and postmerger indexes are computed below.

Premerger Index				*Postmerger Index*		
Firm A	$(30\%)^2$	=	900%	Firm A	$(30\%)^2$	=	900%
Firm B	$(20\%)^2$	=	400%	Firm B	$(20\%)^2$	=	400%
Firm C	$(10\%)^2$	=	100%	Firm C	$(16\%)^2$	=	225%
Firm D	$(8\%)^2$	=	64%	Firm D	$(8\%)^2$	=	64%
Firm E	$(5\%)^2$	=	25%			
	Index	=	1,489%		Index	=	1,614%

[22] *U.S. Department of Justice Merger Guidelines*, July 14, 1984, section 3.11, pp. 9–10.

[23] The Justice Department is likely to challenge the merger of any firm with a market share of at least 1 percent with the leading firm in the market, providing the leading firm has a market share of at least 85 percent. For example, the index of two firms with market shares of 36 percent and 2 percent would be $(36\%)^2 + (2\%)^2 = 1,300\%$. If the two firms merged, the index would be $(38\%)^2 = 1,444\%$.

MERGERS, TAKEOVERS, AND THE REAGAN ADMINISTRATION

There is one thing that can be said with absolute certainty about the Reagan administration: it never met a merger or takeover it didn't like. It maintained a laissez-faire attitude toward them and thousands of mergers were consummated during the eight years he was in office. The period also witnessed the rise of the corporate raiders such as T. Boone Pickens, Carl Icahn, and Donald Trump who financed their acquisitions through the sale of high-yield junk bonds to institutions and wealthy investors. Some companies were simply in the business of buying out other companies. The classic example was the leveraged buyout of RJR Nabisco by the Wall Street firm of Kohlberg, Kravis and Roberts (KKR) for $24.5 billion. This was the largest corporate acquisition of any type in American history. Seldom since the period of the 19th century Robber Barons has corporate behavior been so open to question as it was during the wave of takeovers that marked the last years of the Reagan administration.

The laissez-faire attitude of the Reagan administration toward mergers and acquisitions was reflected in the enforcement of the antitrust laws by the Department of Justice and the Federal Trade Commission. Their approach toward mergers and acquisitions was: "Just say yes." Table 7-1 presents federal merger enforcement activity through the period 1979–1987. Included in the table are premerger transactions and enforcement action expressed as a percentage of premerger transactions. Enforcement actions include all court complaints filed by the Justice Department and all cases in which the Federal Trade Commission has issued an administrative complaint, filed a court petition for a preliminary injunction, or both. As the table indicates, enforcement action expressed as a percentage of premerger transactions reported declined by 2.30 percent in 1979 to a low of .52 percent in 1985.

KKR RJR Nabisco: The Takeover to End All Takeovers

The capstone on the Reagan administration's antitrust enforcement policies was put in place on December 1, 1988 when KKR announced that it had offered $24.5 billion for RJR Nabisco. It was the biggest acquisition, takeover or otherwise, ever consummated in the history of the United States, that is, until KKR or Carl Icahn conclude a leveraged buyout of Fort Knox. The leveraged buyout of RJR Nabisco concluded a bidding war between RJR's president,

TABLE 7-1   Federal Merger Enforcement, 1979–1987

Year	Premerger Transactions Reported	Enforcement Actions			Percent of Transactions
		DOJ	FTC	Total	
1979	868	10	10	20	2.30%
1980	824	10	13	23	2.79
1981	1,083	4	14	18	1.66
1982	1,144	9	7	16	1.40
1983	1,128	3	3	6	.53
1984	1,400	7	6	13	.93
1985	1,749	4	5	9	.52
1986	2,406	7	6	13	.54
1987	2,254	6	8	4	.62

Source: Information provided by Peter W. Rodino, Chairman, Committee on the Judiciary, U.S. House of Representatives, Washington, D.C.

Ross Johnson, and KKR in which the former offered stockholders $108 a share and the latter offered them $109 a share. To many, including *Time,* the size of the buyout and the fortunes to be made represented the consummate epitome of greed, an example of capitalism gone haywire.[24] What KKR is getting for its money is one of the nation's largest consumer goods companies that provides a range of products, such as, Oreo cookies, Ritz crackers, Camel cigarettes, Planters peanuts, Baby Ruth candy bars, and Del Monte fruits and vegetables. It is expected that KKR will sell off most of the Nabisco divisions.

Who Gained and Who Lost?

As is true of most takeovers, leveraged buyouts or otherwise, those who could most afford to gain, gained, and those who could least afford to lose, lost. There were a number of winners in the leveraged buyout of RJR Nabisco. One obvious winner is KKR whose co-founder Henry Kravis, in a statement made

---

[24] *Time*'s cover on its December 5, 1988 issue was entitled "Game of Greed." On page 62 there is a caricature of a bloated capitalist that would do justice to the *Daily Worker*.

after the acquisition, said that greed turned him off.[25] Another group of winners were the stockholders who saw the value of their shares double. Lawyers, of course, gained, because they had to make sure everything was legal. Junk-bondholders benefitted from the high interest rates paid on their bonds, which will accrue to them if nothing happens to the economy. Leveraged buyout investors may get rich, particularly since KKR is involved. Return on LBO funds managed by KKR can yield as much as 40 percent annually.[26] Another attractive feature of the LBO is that it can give managers a sizable share of equity in newly structured companies created out of RJR Nabisco. By using borrowed money to buy out stockholders, executives can cash in their old shares at a profit even as they become owners of the firm. Finally, Ross Johnson, the president of RJR Nabisco, stood to make at least $100 million from the buyout.[27]

However, there is a reverse side to the LBO of RJR Nabisco. First, there is the potential loss of employment for workers who work for the company. There was no dancing in the streets of Winston-Salem, North Carolina, long the home for the tobacco division, when the buyout was announced.[28] Workers were concerned about their jobs and what would become of them if the company were split up and sold. Managers, too, are not exempt, for the *Winston-Salem Journal* reported that KKR planned to get rid of whole layers of managers and install a whole group of its own. Second, Metropolitan Life decided to sue RJR Nabisco on the grounds that its holding of RJR Nabisco's bonds had lost over $1 billion in value as a result of the buyout.[29] It claimed that the action of Ross Johnson and others converted high quality investment grade RJR Nabisco bonds into junk bonds. Third, the RJR Nabisco leveraged buyout and others like it represented a loss of revenue to the U.S. Treasury.

---

[25] Henry Kravis, "Greed Really Turns Me Off," *Fortune,* Vol. 119, No. 1. January 2, 1989, 69–72. Greed, like beauty, is in the eyes of the beholder.

[26] Carol J. Loomis, "Buyout Kings," *Fortune.* Vol. 118, No. 1, July 4, 1988, p. 54.

[27] *Time,* "Where's The Limit?" December 5, 1988, p. 69. Also see cover.

[28] Needless to say, the headlines in the *Winston-Salem Journal* probably rivaled those when Japan surrendered in 1945. It was page 1 news for two weeks. On Tuesday, November 22, 1988, the top page 1 headline said, "RJR Nabisco Brass Reaped Millions, SEC Documents Indicate." Another heading stated that North Carolina could lose more than $100 million a year in taxes as a result of the leveraged buyout. Finally, in large type, the banner "RJR Sold to Kohlberg Kravis" and under it, "Cutbacks Expected Under KKR."

[29] This suit was initiated before the final consummation of the buyout of RJR Nabisco by KKR.

Interest on borrowed debt has been tax deductible, making it easier to issue junk bonds and claim the interest paid on them as a deductible expense.

Junk Bonds and Corporate Equity

The use of junk bonds in the LBO of RJR Nabisco and other firms has become highly controversial. The result is that debt is replacing equity as a part of corporate capital structure. In the period 1984–1988 nonfinancial corporations retired more stock than they issued, for a net loss of $442 billion in equity. At the same time, they increased their debt by $800 billion. Interest payments consumed one-fourth of their internal cash flow in 1988. Thus, many companies are not able to build new plants, since much of their earnings have to go to pay interest. They are also more vulnerable to bankruptcy during a recession. Table 7-2 presents the growth in the use of junk bonds relative to total public bond issues by U.S. corporations for the period 1979–1987.

Regulation

The "anything goes" attitude of the Reagan administration toward mergers, acquisitions, takeovers (hostile or friendly), and leveraged buyouts, for example, caused concern on the part of the public. A *Washington Post* poll of August 1988 showed that 73 percent of those persons polled felt that large corporations had too much power.[30]

The cover of *Time* for December 1, 1988, titled "A Game of Greed" in reference to the RJR Nabisco takeover, was hardly reassuring to the public. What they have been seeing is a rather indiscriminant attempt on the part of firms and individuals to grab other firms. The term "corporate raider" which is applied to T. Boone Pickens, Carl Icahn, Donald Trump, and others, has a pejorative connotation analogous to buccaneers of the Spanish Main forcing their unwanted attentions on the maidens of a sacked town. Their takeovers are called "hostile" because they are opposed by the target's board of directors.[31]

[30] The *Washington Post,* August 14, 1988, p. A30.

[31] In a hostile takeover, a bid is made directly to the shareholders of the targeted firm rather than to the target's management. The acquirer gets the needed votes, gains control, and replaces existing management.

TABLE 7-2   A Comparison of Junk Bond Issues to Total Bond Issues by U.S. Corporations, 1979–1987 ($ billions)

Year	Public Junk Bonds	Public Bond Issues	Percent Relationship
1980	1.4	41.6	3.4
1981	1.4	38.1	3.7
1982	2.7	44.5	6.1
1983	8.0	47.6	16.8
1984	14.8	73.6	20.1
1985	15.4	119.6	12.9
1986	34.5	232.5	14.8
1987	28.9	219.1	15.2

Source: Kevin J. Perry and Robert A. Taggart, "The Growing Role of Junk Bonds in Corporate Finance," *Journal of Applied Corporate Finance,* Vol. 1, No. 1, Spring 1988, p. 58. Reprinted by permission.

Then, there are the "white knights" who, like Sir Lancelot riding to save Guinevere from the evil Mordred, charge to the corporate rescue, consummating a "friendly takeover," meaning that the target's board of directors approve of them.

The enormous publicity given to the LBO of RJR Nabisco will probably force the Bush administration and Congress to take some sort of action before even larger buyouts occur. Taxwriting committees in the Senate and House of Representatives can be expected to hold hearings. There are a number of possibilities that could occur.[32] One is to restrict the deduction of interest on junk bonds used to finance LBO's. A second is to reduce taxes on dividends to encourage corporations to rely more on equity financing and less on debt financing. A third approach is to limit investment banks' financial stakes in LBO's by prohibiting them from underwriting junk bonds. A corollary of this approach would subject LBO specialists like KKR to the same disclosure requirements imposed on managers who attempt buyouts of their own firms. A fourth approach would be to give bondholders the explicit right to sue if an LBO diminishes the value of their bonds.

[32] Ann Reilly Dowd, "Washington's War Against LBO Debt," *Fortune,* February 13, 1989, Vol. 119, No. 4, pp. 91–92.

SUMMARY

Power over a market can be achieved through forming monopolies and making mergers. The latter is the more typical way of gaining market power. By reducing the number of firms in a market and enlarging the merged firms' share of market sales, a merger can result in higher prices for consumers and the reduction of competition. The federal statute that deals with monopolies is Section 2 of the Sherman Act. Tests of market power when applied in monopoly cases have varied. In the 1911 decision that broke up the Standard Oil Company, the Supreme Court established a rule of reason approach, in which it looked for an intent to monopolize and actual instances of predatory conduct representing the exercise of this intent. In the Alcoa case of 1945, market power was measured by Alcoa's share of the market. Size alone became an offense because the possession of power could not be separated from the abuse of that power.

Mergers come under the jurisdiction of Section 7 of the Clayton Act, which was later amended by the Celler–Kefauver Act. The enforcement of Section 7 is done by the Justice Department through its Antitrust Division as well as by the Federal Trade Commission. Private actions to enforce Section 7 may also be brought in federal district court. Merger enforcement in the United States has gone through shifts in philosophy. Many mergers during the 1950s and 1960s, following the passage of the Celler–Kefauver Act, were excluded between companies that were almost microscopic in competitive terms. The 1980s are different from the 1960s. Mergers were treated more in terms of their potential for desirable effects on the economy. As noted earlier, the new measure of industrial concentration called the Herfindahl–Hirschman index is now used. Focus is being placed on market power, barriers to entry, and enhancement of allocative and productive efficiencies.

A tidal wave of acquisitions and takeovers of any form inundated America during the Reagan years, but probably the one thing that caught the attention of the American public was the leveraged buyout of RJR Nabisco by Kohlberg, Kravis, and Roberts. It represented the largest acquisition in any form consummated in the United States. It also created concern on the part of the American public that a more sophisticated version of the 19th century Robber Barons had been reincarnated. It is entirely possible that even larger takeovers will be consummated in the future. The buyout craze, coupled with scandals on Wall Street, the Chicago futures market, and on defense procurement contracts, has not done the image of business much good. It is likely that some form of regulation of leveraged buyouts will be introduced in Congress.

QUESTIONS FOR DISCUSSION

1. What was the "thrust on" defense used by Alcoa?
2. Why are oligopolistic industries often characterized by uniform action?
3. How can a vertical merger be anticompetitive?
4. How can a conglomerate merger be anticompetitive when by definition it involves noncompeting and nonrelated firms?
5. Discuss the "legal concept" of rule of reason.
6. Is it necessary to keep a large number of small firms in business to prevent economic concentration?
7. Discuss some of the results of the AT&T case.
8. Why is the AT&T settlement one of the most important antitrust decisions of all times?
9. What is a product extension merger? Why was the acquisition of Clorox by Procter & Gamble disallowed?
10. Discuss the issues in the Von's Grocery case.
11. Discuss the criticism of the Reagan administration's policy concerning mergers.

RECOMMENDED READINGS

Baldwin, William L. *Market Power, Competition, and Antitrust Policy*. Homewood, Illinois: Irwin, 1987.

Brunner, Thomas W., Thomas G. Krattenmaker, Robert R. Skitol, and Ann Adams Webster. *Mergers in the New Antitrust Era*. Washington, D.C.: The Bureau of National Affairs, Inc., 1985.

Dowd, Ann Reilly, "Washington's War on LBO Debt," *Fortune*. Vol. 119, No. 4. February 13, 1989, pp. 91–92.

ers and the Market for Corporate Control," *Economic Perspectives*. Federal Reserve Bank of Chicago. January–February 1989, pp. 2–16.

Jensen, Michael C. "The Takeover Controversy: Analysis and Evidence," in John C. Coffee, Jr., Louis Lowenstein, and Susan Rose Ackerman, eds.,

Knights, Raiders, and Targets: The Impact of the Hostile Takeover. New York: Oxford University Press, 1988.

Labich, Kenneth. "Was Breaking Up AT&T a Good Idea?" *Fortune.* Vol. 119, No. 1. January 2, 1989, pp. 82–86.

Loomis, Carol J. "Buyout Kings," *Fortune.* Vol. 118, No. 1, July 4, 1988, pp. 53–60.

Perry, Kevin J. and Robert A. Taggart. "The Growing Role of Junk Bonds in Corporate Finance," *Journal of Applied Corporate Finance.* Vol. 1, No. 1. Spring 1988, pp. 37–45.

Pickens, T. Boone. *Boone.* Boston: Houghton Mifflin, 1987.

Porter, Michael E. "From Competitive Advantage to Corporate Strategy," *Harvard Business Review.* Vol. 65 (May–June 1987), pp. 43–59.

Ravenscraft, David J. and Frederick M. Scherer. *Mergers, Sell-Offs, and Economic Efficiency.* Washington, D.C.: The Brookings Institution, 1988.

Time. "A Game of Greed." December 5, 1988, pp. 66–70.

Chapter 8

Antitrust Laws and the Regulation of Anticompetitive Practices

The rationale for U.S. antitrust policies has been to promote competition between business firms in the marketplace by prohibiting monopolies and other activities that result in restraint of trade. The essence of competition is for a business firm to try to take business from its rivals. If it succeeds by virtue of superior efficiency or other legitimate advantages, the rivals have no legal recourse. All too often, however, business firms have tried to gain an advantage over their competitors through various practices that have come to be considered unfair. Over time, laws have been developed to confine competition within the framework of a set of rules. The historical development of public policy to regulate certain unfair or anticompetitive business practices began with common law, which is simply a set of legal precedents that have been established over time.

Certain types of practices were condemned by common law as violating standards of common morality. Unfair competition was defined as representing one's goods as those of another's. By adeptly copying a brand name or a style, one firm could trade on the goodwill established by a rival. The rival could go to court and seek damages. Similar relief could be obtained when one firm maligned the reputation of, or engaged in commercial espionage against, a rival. Common law also extended the concept of unfair competition to apply to infringements on patents and trademarks. But common law provided poor protection against the infinite variety of anticompetitive business practices that developed with the growth of business combinations in the last century. These practices included attacks on small rivals through local price cutting, tying arrangements, exclusive dealing contracts, and other acts.

Common law was supplemented by the Sherman Act of 1890. Among the unfair practices covered by the act were excessive price cutting and local price discrimination when clearly intended to eliminate competition. The Sherman

Act was applied to concerted efforts of distributors to preserve the traditional channels of distribution from manufacturer to wholesaler to retailer. Efforts of wholesalers to boycott manufacturers who sold directly to retailers or to circulate blacklists with this objective were prohibited, as were efforts of retailers or manufacturers to boycott other retailers or manufacturers. The Sherman Act delegated to the courts broad powers to interpret and apply the proscriptions against certain anticompetitive practices, case by case, in civil and criminal actions brought by the Justice Department and by private persons.

Application of the Sherman Act to specific anticompetitive practices was unsatisfactory to many groups. Victims of predatory actions felt the law should intervene before the practices had taken effect. Others felt the courts had not gone far enough. Tying contracts and exclusive dealing arrangements, for example, were often upheld as legitimate extensions of patent rights. Among localities or different types of customers, the permissible limits of price discrimination were uncertain. The Sherman Act was criticized on the grounds that its provisions against unfair restraint of trade were too general. Some business groups favored the creation of a new commission to review potentially illegal acts, and other groups wanted a clearer definition of what constituted an illegal act.

To satisfy these and other complaints, the Clayton and Federal Trade Commission acts were passed in 1914. Their objectives were to modify the Sherman Act by specifically prohibiting certain types of unfair practices and to create new administrative machinery to aid in law enforcement. However, no set of statutory definitions can ever be drawn to include the infinite range of industrial and commercial practices that can be used to prevent competition. As soon as one set of prohibitions are laid down, new methods, or new variations on old methods, invariably spring up to circumvent them, which is why the courts have had to constantly reinterpret the antitrust laws throughout the years. Because they are ultimately responsible for the interpretation and application of the antitrust laws, the courts have been vested with a wide range of discretion in construing their statutory provisions and in molding their remedies. The remainder of this chapter is devoted to a discussion of various types of anticompetitive practices and how the courts have dealt with them.

ANTICOMPETITIVE BUSINESS PRACTICES

Anticompetitive business practices cover a multitude of sins—price fixing, reciprocity, exclusive dealing, price discrimination against buyers or sellers, territorial restrictions, tying agreements, interlocking directorates, boycotts, preemptive buying, and other coercive practices. Each device can be used to restrain competition. For example, the aim of a price-fixing agreement is to eliminate one form of competition. The power to fix prices, whether or not reasonably exercised, includes the power to control the market. Reciprocity can also be used to restrain trade. When a buyer uses its power to compel sellers to buy from it as a condition for doing business, it is a restraint on free trade. Any restrictive agreement can be regarded by the courts as a conspiracy of firms that results in a restraint of trade among separate companies. Usually the restrictive agreement is understood to entail some direct or indirect, overt or implied, form of price fixing, output control, market sharing, or exclusion of competitors.

The antitrust laws apply to various forms of restrictive agreements. Section 1 of the Sherman Act has been used to prohibit both vertical and horizontal price-fixing arrangements. With respect to price fixing, the courts have applied, with few exceptions, an absolute prohibition. Pricing discrimination would generally come under Section 2 of the Clayton Act, as amended by the Robinson–Patman Act. This legislation attempts to foster competition by prohibiting both primary-line and secondary-line price discrimination. Tying arrangements that restrain trade would come under the Clayton and Sherman acts. Exclusive dealing arrangements would come under Section 3 of the Clayton Act, and boycotts or concerted refusal to deal would come under Section 1 of the Sherman Act. Preemptive buying would also come under the Sherman Act.

Price Fixing

Agreements among competing firms to fix, stabilize, raise, or lower prices constitute illegal price fixing. These agreements have always had an allure to business firms because they reduce, perhaps even eliminate, the risks of economic loss. But price fixing destroys the right of each business firm to determine independently the prices of goods and services and often leads to higher prices for consumers. Horizontal price fixing occurs when business firms compete directly against each other. For example, Company A and Company B are competitors. The presidents of each company, Smith and Jones, are friendly and often meet for lunch. At one lunch, Smith suggests there is enough business for both companies without a need for price competition.

Jones agrees, and both companies decide not to charge less than $75 for their product. Vertical price fixing occurs among firms that operate at different levels in the distribution channels of particular goods.

Bid rigging is a form of price fixing in which business firms interfere with the integrity of the bidding process. State and local governments, as well as many private firms, purchase products by inviting businesses to submit competitive bids. The firm submitting the lowest bid is awarded the contract to sell its product or service to a buyer. When business firms agree on which one will submit the winning bid or agree to submit the same price bid, the process breaks down, and the buyer pays a higher price for the product or service. For example, companies A and B are invited by a city to bid on the sale of stationery. The president of A asks the president of B to submit a high bid so that A can win the contract. The president of B agrees but in return asks the president of A to submit a high bid on stationery bids being solicited by another city. The president of A is agreeable, and both of the businesses win a government contract.

Another form of price fixing is resale price maintenance, in which a manufacturer or distributor of a product enters into an agreement with, or pressures, a retail dealer to sell the product at a specific retail price. This is vertical price fixing because the agreement is made between business firms at two different levels of distribution (wholesale and retail). For example, Sweaters Inc., which manufactures sweaters, sells to two retail merchants, Mr. Black and Ms. Brown. To attract more customers, Mr. Black decides to sell sweaters at a 10 percent discount. Ms. Brown is upset because this discount will likely attract some of her customers. She calls Sweaters Inc., to complain. The company then calls Mr. Black and tells him to sell at the suggested retail price or else he might not be allowed to sell the company's products at all. Both Sweaters Inc. and Ms. Brown have conspired to fix prices by attempting to force Mr. Black to maintain his prices at the suggested retail level.

An effective price-fixing agreement permits firms to set a price as if they were one company—a single-firm monopoly. It constitutes a per se violation of Section 1 of the Sherman Act, which states that a contract, combination, or conspiracy in restraint of trade in interstate or foreign commerce is illegal. It is a per se violation because its aim is the elimination of price competition. Price fixing is also illegal under Section 5 of the Federal Trade Commission Act, which is designed to prevent unfair methods of competition in commerce. It may be added that, since collusion or conspiracy to fix prices is illegal under the antitrust laws, firms closely guard any agreements on price that they may make. Price-fixing agreements are usually made in secret, and all sorts of subterfuge can be used. The following case involving General Electric, Westinghouse, and other makers of electrical equipment is a good illustration.

The Electrical Equipment Case, 1961

The Electrical Equipment case of 1961 is a good example of a restrictive business practice, specifically price fixing by a number of firms in the electrical equipment industry.[1] Agreements to fix prices violate Section 1 of the Sherman Act and are illegal per se, for they vitiate the essence of competition in the marketplace. The case involved a conspiracy by a number of companies, including General Electric and Westinghouse, to fix prices and rig bids in the sale of heavy electrical equipment to private and public utilities. Markets were also divided up among the companies, with General Electric and Westinghouse getting the biggest shares. The conspiracy had been going on for nearly twenty-five years, and the companies were accused of fixing prices and rigging bids on the sale of $7 billion of heavy electrical equipment between 1953 and 1960.

The conspiracy followed an elaborate pattern. Executives of the various electrical equipment companies would meet at conventions, hotels, and private homes to work out arrangements to divide markets and to rig bids on contracts. The companies would take turns in submitting low bids. The executives used false names and blank stationery to correspond and phases of the moon to determine which company would put in the low bid on a contract. Using the moon-phase system, each firm knew when to bid high and when to bid low. With twenty-nine different companies taking part, including the two largest, the conspiracy was about as complete as possible. Over the period of the conspiracy, millions of extra dollars were charged to utilities and their customers. The conspiracy directly or indirectly affected almost every dam built, every power generator installed, and every electrical distribution system set up in the United States. Eventually, the TVA became suspicious of the similarities of a series of bids and notified the Justice Department.

The fines, penalties, and loss of business prestige resulting from the outcome of the suit, which was initiated by the Justice Department, were

---

[1] *U.S. v. General Electric et al.,* 209 F. Supp. 197 (1961). For discussions of the case, see John G. Fuller, *The Gentlemen Conspirators* (New York: Grove Press, 1962), and Walter Jensen, "The Light of the Moon Formula—Some Whys and Wherefores," *Western Business Review* 5 (May, 1961): 27–33.

enormous. Both the Clayton and Sherman acts provide for triple-damage suits by private citizens. Both fines and jail sentences are provided for in the Sherman Act. Convictions by a federal court led to the thirty-day imprisonment of seven executives, the greatest number of jail terms ever in an antitrust proceeding, and suspended thirty-day jail sentences for twenty-one other executives. A total of $1.9 million was levied against both the companies and their executives. In addition, by the end of 1967, a series of private triple damage suits filed against the major companies had cost General Electric $225 million and Westinghouse $125 million. Although the victims of this price-fixing conspiracy were able to recover hundreds of millions of dollars, the triple-damage remedy generally has not been an effective tool for victimized individuals, who often have found antitrust litigation too costly and time consuming.

The Spray-Rite Case, 1984

Monsanto is a large chemical company. It manufactures many chemical products, including agricultural herbicides. Spray-Rite, an authorized Monsanto distributor, engaged in a discount operation. Following complaints from other Monsanto distributors that Spray-Rite's prices were too low, Monsanto refused to renew Spray-Rite's one-year distributorship term. Spray-Rite brought suit under Section 1 of the Sherman Act, claiming, among other things, that Monsanto and some of its distributors had conspired to fix the retail prices of herbicides and that Spray-Rite was terminated as a result of the conspiracy. The case went to a trial court where the jury was instructed that Monsanto's conduct was illegal per se if it furthered a vertical conspiracy to fix prices. The jury so found. A court of appeals and the U.S. Supreme Court affirmed the decision.

The Supreme Court enunciated a standard of proof required to find the existence of a vertical price-fixing conspiracy.[2] It stated that evidence of complaints from other distributors, or even that termination came about in response to these complaints, is not enough to show the existence of a conspiracy. According to the Court, evidence must reasonably tend to prove a producer and others had a conscious commitment to a common scheme designed to achieve an unlawful objective. To clarify its standard, the Court stated that the concept of a common scheme means more than showing the nonterminated distributors conformed to Monsanto's suggested price. It also

---

[2] *Monsanto Co. v. Spray-Rite Corp.*, 52 U.S.L.W. 4341 (March 20, 1984).

means showing that the distributors communicated their agreement and that this agreement was sought by the producer. The Spray-Rite case reaffirms the per se illegality of vertical price-fixing agreements and raises the burden of proof necessary to show the existence of such agreements.

The Milk Companies Case, 1988

The Attorney General of Florida has charged that eleven milk companies conspired in a bid-rigging scheme that inflated the price of lunchroom milk in Florida schools by at least $10 million over a decade.[3] The suit was filed against seven major milk producers and four Florida distributors alleging that high-level officials of the companies established production levels, divided the Florida market among themselves and fixed an inflated price on half-pint cartons of milk. The price of each carton of milk was inflated by more than one penny. More than one billion cartons of milk were sold during the ten-year period. The state of Florida is seeking more than $30 million from the companies, or three times the amount of the alleged overcharges. If the state is awarded damages, the money will be distributed to the public school boards of thirty-two Florida counties that bought the milk and resold it to students.

Dairy processors named in the suit were Southland Corporation, which settled out of court for $10 million; Borden of Columbus, Ohio; Flavorich of Louisville, Kentucky; Dean Foods Products Company of Chicago; Pet of St. Louis, Missouri; Kraft of Chicago; and Hart's Dairy of Fort Myers, Florida. The distributors named in the suit were Florida firms: Marshall Simmons Enterprises of Mango; Pierson Distributors of Opa Locka; H&T Distributors of Homestead; and Butter Foods in Naples. The federal civil suit involving these companies was filed in Tampa by Florida Attorney General Robert Butterworth. It represents the largest antitrust action ever taken against the milk industry, and bears some similarity to the highway bid-rigging scandals that occurred in Georgia and other southern states in the late 1970s.

The Business Electronics Case, 1988

Business Electronics Corporation was the exclusive retailer of Sharp Electronics's calculators in the Houston area until Sharp appointed Gilbert Hartwell as a second retailer for the area. Like many other manufacturers,

[3] The data for this case were provided by the Attorney General's Office of the state of Florida, Tallahassee, FL, July, 1988.

Sharp published a list of suggested minimum retail prices, but neither retailer was obliged to follow them. Business Electronics often sold below the suggested prices and usually below Hartwell's prices. Hartwell complained to Sharp, arguing that BEC was free-riding on his investment in product promotion and other sales-related services, and also complained to Sharp about BEC's cost cutting. Eventually Hartwell threatened to terminate his own dealership with Sharp unless Sharp terminated BEC within thirty days. Sharp responded by terminating BEC, claiming it was due to the latter's poor sales performance.

BEC sued Sharp, claiming that Sharp had committed a per se violation of Section 1 of the Sherman Act by agreeing with a competing dealer to terminate BEC because of price cutting. A jury awarded BEC $600,000 in damages. Sharp appealed to the Fifth Circuit Court of Appeals, which reversed the verdict. The court held that in order for a manufacturer's termination of a distributor to be illegal per se, it must be pursuant to a price maintenance agreement with another distributor. That distributor must expressly or implicitly agree to set its prices at some level, though not a special one. The distributor cannot retain complete freedom to set whatever price it chooses. BEC then appealed to the Supreme Court, which upheld by a six-to-two majority the ruling of the Fifth Circuit Court. Justice Scalia, writing for the majority, stated that there was nothing to indicate that an agreement between a manufacturer and a dealer to terminate a price cutter (without an agreement on the price to be charged by the remaining dealer) almost always tends to restrict competition and reduce output.[4]

Tying Arrangements

When a seller conditions or ties the sale of a popular product or service (the tying item) to a buyer's purchase of another less popular product or service (the tied item), the seller has engaged in a tying arrangement. Such sales are illegal if the seller has economic power in the tying product or is successful in conditioning the sale of the tying item on the purchase of the tied item. A tying arrangement interferes with a competitive marketplace because the seller is able to sell the tied item without regard to its price or quality but solely because the buyer needs to purchase the tying item. By tying, the seller can sell a

---

[4] *Business Electronics Corp. v. Sharp Electronics Corp.,* 56 U.S. L. W. 4887 (1988), affirming 780 R1213, 1218 (5th, Cir 1986).

greater quantity of tied items and thus take business away from other firms that sell the tied item or a similar product. Tying also directly harms the consumer by forcing the purchase of an unwanted item as a condition of purchasing a desirable item.

An example of a tying arrangement is as follows: a company called Stereco manufactures a popular high-quality stereo record player. All retail stores carry the Stereco brand record player. A retail store not carrying the brand could lose a considerable amount of business to the competition. Stereco also manufactures a tape deck, but it is not nearly as popular as its record player. To sell more of its tape decks, Stereco tells its retail outlets they must buy one tape deck for each record player purchased. By doing this, it has illegally tied the sale of its tape decks to the sale of its record players. This action discriminates against both retailers and consumers by denying freedom of choice, and limits other sellers of the tied product from competing in that particular market.

Tying arrangements would come under either Section 1 of the Sherman Act or Section 3 of the Clayton Act. Where the tying product is a legal monopoly, such as a patent, the seller is likely to have monopoly control, and the arrangement would constitute a per se violation of Section 1 of the Sherman Act. More likely, the arrangement would come under Section 3 of the Clayton Act, which, whenever there is substantial injury to competition, prohibits the following: (1) the tie-in sale, mentioned in the preceding example; (2) the exclusive dealership, where goods are sold only on the condition the dealer will not handle the goods of a competitor; and (3) the requirement contract, where the sale of a product is made on the condition the customer will buy subsequent products from the seller. However, tying arrangements are allowed when a seller can prove the tied product or service is necessary to maintain the operation of the tying product or service.

The Chicken Delight Case, 1977

Chicken Delight was a fast-food chicken chain that operated through the use of the franchise arrangement. Franchising is a business approach involving permission to use a certain product, including a special name or trademark, and often incorporating a specific set of procedures for creating the product. Chicken Delight had several hundred franchises and required its franchisees to buy a specified number of cookers and frying chickens and other supplies and sauces exclusively from the company. This arrangement was challenged by one of the franchisees who argued that the tying agreement interfered with the right to buy supplies from other sources. Chicken Delight argued that its arrangement enabled it to supervise quality and maintain control over the revenue derived from the sale of its food products and other supplies to its fast-food outlets.

A circuit court ruled that the agreement violated Section 3 of the Clayton Act.[5] It held that Chicken Delight could maintain quality standards over the product on which it had a trademark even if the product were purchased from other suppliers. Trademarks did not immunize a product from antitrust laws. Chicken Delight contended that its income depended solely on the revenues it generated from selling its products to its outlets. However, the court ruled that there were other ways in which it could receive money from its franchises. Royalties based on sales volume are a common form of payment in a franchise arrangement, and they do not involve a tying arrangement or have an undesirable effect on competition.

Exclusive Dealing Agreements

In an exclusive dealing agreement, one firm induces other firms not to deal with the former's competitors. For example, the American Tobacco Company was able to use its economic power to compel wholesalers and retailers of tobacco products to agree to deal only with it and not with its competitors. The effect on competition was appreciable because American Tobacco was able to foreclose on the tobacco market. In general, exclusive dealing agreements that have the effect of eliminating competitors from a particular market have been held to violate Section 3 of the Clayton Act. At one time, the courts generally enforced the rule of Section 3 against exclusive dealing only when a seller dominated a particular market. Today, less than market dominance is sufficient to indicate that a portion of the market can be foreclosed by an exclusive dealership agreement.

Not all exclusive dealership agreements are illegal. They are illegal only when used to eliminate rivals. In many situations, they are socially and economically beneficial. For instance, a buyer and a seller can enter into an agreement for fuel supplies. This agreement may require the supplier to undertake

---

[5] *Siegal v. Chicken Delight,* 448 F. 2d 43 (1971).

capital outlays, which it would be unwilling to do unless assured of a long-term contract. The buyer is assured of a long-term fuel supply. An agreement between a buyer and a seller can also ensure price stability. By guaranteeing a market to the supplier and adequate supplies to the consumer, business costs may be reduced. The nature of a product may also require an exclusive dealership agreement. The product may be so specialized that it has to be sold and serviced by dealers trained to represent the company.

The Standard Oil of California Case, 1949

Standard Oil of California was the largest seller of gasoline in the western part of the United States. In 1946, it had 23 percent of the total gallonage sold in that market, 6.7 percent of which was sold to independent gasoline dealers. Standard Oil had obtained exclusive dealing contracts with 5,397 independent stations, or 16 percent of the total retail gasoline outlets in the western market area. The exclusive dealer contract required the dealers to buy all their gasoline and, in some cases, oil, tires, and batteries from Standard Oil. The government obtained an injunction prohibiting Standard Oil from using the exclusive agreement as violative of Section 1 of the Sherman Act, and of Section 3 of the Clayton Act. The government contended that these contracts foreclosed a substantial amount of the gasoline market and thereby created a barrier to entry for new independent refiners in the gas-refining sector.

A district court found that competition was substantially lessened by these tying contracts because they covered a substantial number of retail gas outlets and a substantial number of products. Standard Oil of California appealed the decision to the Supreme Court, which upheld the decision of the district court.[6] It ruled that the validity of contracts under Section 3 of the Clayton Act can be tested by whether a substantial amount of commerce is affected. The sale of 6.7 percent of the total volume of gasoline sold in the relevant trade area was held to be substantial. Therefore, the Court reasoned that a substantial lessening of competition would be an automatic by-product. The very existence of these contracts denies dealers opportunity to deal in the products of competing suppliers and excludes suppliers from access to the outlets controlled by these dealers. The contracts also create a barrier to entry into the gasoline market by new refiners.

[6] *Standard Oil of California v. U.S.*, 337 U.S. 293 (1949).

Group Boycotts

Group boycotts occur when businesses on the same level of competition agree to deny another business access to business advantages such as supply sources, credit, or advertising. For example, there are three cleaning businesses in a small city. A fourth dry-cleaning business plans to open in two weeks. The owners of the three existing businesses meet at a local restaurant and discuss the impending opening of the new cleaning business. All three, worried about the new firm cutting into their business profits, agree to call their supplier of cleaning fluid, the Jones Supply Company, and threaten to stop buying from it if it sells cleaning fluid to the new business. The Jones Supply Company agrees. The three existing businesses and their supplier of cleaning fluid have entered into an illegal group boycott where the intent is to drive the new competitor out of business.

The three cleaning firms possess market power and are able to exert it to the detriment of consumers and the new entrant into the dry-cleaning business. The boycott is anticompetitive and represents a per se violation of Section 1 of the Sherman Act. Courts have applied a per se prohibition to this type of activity when carried out in commerce. As in price fixing, a key to the illegality of a boycott is the concerted action of its members. This creates a problem, for in many situations a firm may find that sellers refuse to sell to it, but cannot prove there is an agreement not to do so. The following cases illustrate the application of antitrust laws to group boycotts.

The Klor's, Inc. Case, 1959

In this case, it was alleged that a combination of manufacturers, distributors, and retailers had boycotted Klor's, Inc., a small appliance dealer in San Francisco. The dealer operated near one of the branches of Broadway-Hale Stores, a chain of department stores, and brought a suit against the chain, and ten national manufacturers and their distributors, accusing them of a conspiracy of refusing to sell to it. A district court and an appeals court ruled that there was no injury to the public because there were many other appliance dealers in the San Francisco market area. The case was appealed to the Supreme Court, which ruled that the boycott interfered with the natural flow of commerce and was an effort to drive Klor's out of business as a dealer.[7]

---

[7] *Klor's, Inc. v. Broadway-Hale Stores, Inc.*, 359 U.S. 207 (1959).

Reciprocity

A business practice that can come under the jurisdiction of antitrust law is reciprocity, where a buyer uses its power to compel a seller to buy from it. For example, Buyer A, a major customer of Seller B, tells Seller B that since it is a good customer, Seller B should reciprocate by buying from Seller A. The implicit threat of coercion or the mere presence of large purchasing power may convince B to buy from A. In many instances, firms dealing in a variety of products have discovered they are both potential buyers from and sellers to each other; thus, they may tend to implicitly agree to purchase from each other. Reciprocity is not illegal unless its use in some way lessens competition.

Reciprocity has come to be associated with conglomerate mergers. Firm A acquires Firm B. A reciprocal buying arrangement arises when they both sell products that the other buys. If this lessens competition by giving Firm A unfair competitive advantage, there is a violation of antitrust law. For example, Consolidated Foods, a major food processor and retailer, acquired Gentry, a manufacturer of dehydrated onions and garlic. Consolidated Foods was an important purchaser of food products from several food processors, which in turn were large purchasers of dehydrated onions and garlic. Consolidated sent letters to the food processors from which it purchased goods, asking them to buy Gentry products. This action was challenged by the Federal Trade Commission in a court case.[8] The court ruled that the attempt at reciprocity would give Gentry an unfair competitive advantage over other suppliers of dehydrated onions and garlic.

Price Discrimination

If a manufacturer or wholesaler sells a product at different prices to two or more competing buyers, the seller is engaging in price discrimination. The practice is a violation when all the circumstances of the sale are the same, such as grade, quality, and time. Discrimination in price, however, can be justified on the basis of manufacturing or delivery costs, or as a "good faith" attempt by a seller to meet the price of its competitors. For example, Oil Company A supplies gasoline to several competing retail stations in a major city. It drops its price to Retail Station B when the owner complains a competitor, not supplied by Company A, is selling gasoline at a lower price. The oil company agrees to

[8] *Federal Trade Commission v. Consolidated Foods,* 380 U.S. 592 (1965).

lower its price to Station B but not to those stations that compete with B. It did not lower the price to meet its competition but rather to meet Station B's competition; therefore, it is guilty of price discrimination.

Price discrimination can be exercised by a seller only when it has some degree of monopoly control over the market. In a purely competitive market, price discrimination in any form would be impossible. No one seller would have the power to discriminate against other sellers, for sellers are too numerous. Nor could one seller make buyers pay more than the market-determined price, for they have other alternative suppliers. The market price is one that makes trade advantageous to both sellers and buyers, for it is influenced by supply and demand forces. Price discrimination is the opposite of price competition. It is used by a seller to enhance profits and to limit or injure the competitors.

Primary-Line Price Discrimination

There are two main forms of price discrimination—primary line and secondary line. Primary-line discrimination is discrimination in the primary line of commerce, namely, the same line of commerce in which the seller practicing discrimination is engaged. One form of primary-line discrimination is whipsawing, which occurs when a seller operates in several geographic areas and cuts prices in one while maintaining them in the others. This practice gives it an unfair advantage when competing with a seller who operates only in a single geographic area. Unable to maintain its price, the latter has no way to maintain its profits; the former, however, can make up at least a portion of its losses by profits made in other areas. After eliminating one regional competitor by selective price cutting, the seller operating in several areas can turn its attention to another competitor and so on until all regional competitors are eliminated.[9]

An example of primary-line price discrimination is as follows: Seller A is located in City X, and Seller B is located in City Y. Both sell an identical product. Seller A sells the product for $1 a unit in City X, and Seller B sells it for the same price in City Y. The cities are far enough apart to add transportation costs of $0.10 per unit to seller A's product if sold in City Y. Seller A goes into City Y and sells its products for $0.95. It is undercutting Seller B. Given the additional transportation costs of $0.10 per unit, Seller A should be selling the

---

[9] Primary-line price discrimination can also occur in the same geographic area.

product for $1.10 instead of $0.95. Unless Seller A can somehow demonstrate it is actually cheaper for it to sell in City Y than it is for its rival, it is guilty of primary-line price discrimination.

Secondary-Line Price Discrimination

Price discrimination can also be anticompetitive when a seller grants lower prices to some buyers and not to others. Sales to buyers at different prices affect the "secondary" or buyers' level of competition. The pricing abuse most likely to restrain competition at this level is granting rebates or discounts to favored buyers, thus giving them a competitive advantage over their rivals. In many cases, buyers are able to exert pressure on sellers to grant them special discounts. This pressure can occur when the buyer is large enough to use its economic leverage to force favored treatment. The retail price charged by the large buyer can then be lower than the prices charged by smaller buyers that lack the economic leverage to gain discounts from the seller. Secondary-line price discrimination is associated with chain stores that, able to buy in bulk from sellers, demand price concessions not made available to small buyers.

An example of secondary-line price discrimination is as follows: Seller A has several customers. It sells an identical product to each customer for $1 a unit. One of the customers tells Seller A that since it is a large customer, it should be allowed to buy the product for $0.90 a unit. Seller A agrees. This is price discrimination in favor of a large buyer and against the other customers. The initial example of price discrimination in which Oil Company A dropped its gasoline price to one of its retail stations, so that the latter could meet the price of its competitors, is also secondary-line price discrimination because the oil company gave a price break to one of its customers but not to the others.

Section 2 of the Clayton Act, as amended by the Robinson–Patman Act, applies to both primary-line and secondary-line price discrimination. Sellers may not sell goods to different purchasers at different prices if the result is to injure competitors in either the seller's (primary) or the buyer's (secondary) market. In the seller's market, a seller may lower price to meet competition or where it can demonstrate economies of scale. In a buyer's market, a seller may discriminate between buyers to meet the equally low price of a competitor. A seller can also discriminate between buyers if it can justify the price differential by actual cost savings. However, the Federal Trade Commission, which has the primary responsibility for enforcing the Robinson–Patman Act, does have the right to limit quantity discounts.

The Morton Salt Case, 1948

This case involved secondary-line price discrimination, with injury being sustained by customers who were paying a higher price for salt than their competitors. Morton granted substantial quantity discounts to large-scale buyers of salt. The Federal Trade Commission found that the lower prices granted to grocery chain stores constituted price discrimination, and that its effect was to injure competition between small grocery stores and large chains. The company argued that its quantity discounts were openly available to both small and large stores alike and, therefore, were not discriminatory under the Robinson-Patman Act. However, the Federal Trade Commission found that the company had failed to show that the differences in price were justified by cost savings, and an order was issued against the granting of price discounts. Morton appealed, and the case eventually went to the Supreme Court, which held for the FTC. To the argument that the discounts were not discriminatory because they were openly available to all, the Court replied that, in fact, only four or five large buyers were able to use the largest discount. The purpose of the Robinson-Patman Act, it declared, was to deprive a large buyer of any competitive advantage it might secure in lower cost prices, except when the lower prices can be justified by a savings in cost or by a seller's effort to meet a competitor's price.[10] The Morton Salt case established the principle that a seller charged with illegal secondary-line price discrimination must be prepared to justify quantity discounts by showing actual cost savings. This Morton Salt could not do.

The Utah Pie Company Case, 1967

This case involved primary-line, or seller's discrimination. The Utah Pie Company was the leading seller of frozen pies in the Salt Lake City area. Because of its location, it was able to maintain the lowest prices for pies in the market. During the period from 1957 to 1961, it was challenged at one time or another by three major pie competitors, Pet Milk, Carnation, and Continental, all of which operated in several market areas. Each of these competitors sold pies in the Salt Lake City market at prices lower than what they charged in other markets for pies of like grade and quality. In some cases, pies were sold at below costs. Utah Pie brought an action against each of the three

[10] *FTC v. Morton Salt Co.,* 334 U.S. (1948).

competitors, charging them with a violation of Section 2 of the Clayton Act as amended by the Robinson–Patman Act. The evidence suggested the companies had cut into Utah Pie's share of the market.

In lower court, a jury found price discrimination and judgment was entered for Utah Pie. A court of appeals reversed the decision, holding that the evidence was not sufficient to justify any discrimination to Utah Pie because it still remained the major seller of pies in the Salt Lake City market. The case was appealed to the Supreme Court, which ruled in favor of Utah Pie.[11] The Court cited evidence that lower prices of Pet Milk, Carnation, and Continental could not be justified on the basis of cost. It noted that Pet had sent an industrial spy into the Utah Pie plant and that Continental sold its pies in Salt Lake City at below cost, forcing Utah Pie to lower its price, thus creating some financial damage. In this case, there was evidence of predatory intent by each of the three national competitors to lessen competition.

The Boise-Cascade Case, 1988

Boise-Cascade's Office Products Division is the largest distributor of office products in the United States. It is a dual distributor, sometimes selling at retail as well as wholesale. The FTC claimed and ultimately found that Boise-Cascade had violated Section 2(1) of the Robinson–Patman Act by inducing office products manufacturers to give it wholesale discounts on goods that it sometimes sold at retail.[12] The FTC argued that some competing retailers had lost accounts to Boise-Cascade, and that its discounts substantially exceeded the profit margins enjoyed by most competing retailers. However, counterevidence indicated that the retail office products industry was marked by healthy competition, with profits on the rise and with several competing retailers enjoying increased sales.

An administrative law judge and a court of appeals ruled in favor of Boise-Cascade concluding that the evidence did not prove injury to competition.[13] The Morton Salt case, which was used as the frame of reference, established the doctrine that a presumption of injury to competition arises from proof of substantial price discrimination existing over a period of time. The court of

[11] *Utah Pie Company v. Continental Baking Company*, 386 U.S. 685 (1967).

[12] Section 2(f) of the Robinson-Patman Act prohibits any person engaged in commerce, in the course of such commerce, from knowingly or unknowingly inducing a discrimination in price.

[13] *Boise-Cascade Corp. v. FTC*, 54 Antitrust & Trade Reg. Rep. (BNA) 186 (D.C. Cir. Feb. 4, 1988).

appeals held that the FTC had erred because Boise's evidence of healthy competition in the industry was sufficient to rebut the Morton Salt presumption of competitive injury. The Robinson–Patman Act traditionally has been seen as requiring proof only of injury to competitors, not the broader and more abstract injury to competition. The Boise-Cascade case considered sales and profitability of the industry as a whole.

The Matsushita Electric Case, 1986

A second criticism of Reagan antitrust enforcement policy dealt with predatory acts. Primary-line price discrimination is considered a predatory act because one firm is usually trying to put competitors out of business by selling a competing product at a lower price. Standard Oil would go into a competitor's territory, sell a product at below cost, and then raise prices after the competitor was ruined.

The Matsushita case is important for several reasons.[14] First, it represented a ruling of the Supreme Court, which had become increasingly more conservative, as new members were appointed by President Reagan. Second, it involved an application of the Chicago School of Economics approach to antitrust law. Finally, the case involved a foreign competitor, which had entered the U.S. market and which was accused by a U.S. firm of predatory practices. Zenith, the only remaining manufacturer of color television in the United States claimed that Matsushita and other Japanese manufacturers of color television had engaged in predatory pricing in order to dominate the U.S. color television market. Specifically, the Japanese companies were accused of dumping, which is the selling of a product in a foreign market at a price below cost. The Supreme Court ruled in favor of the Japanese companies on the basis that the claim by Zenith was not economically rational. The Court cited such factors as the length of time the alleged practice had been going on, and the fact that the Japanese firms had not been able to dominate the U.S. market to the extent of being able to reap monopoly profits even though their efforts had been going on for some time. In economic theory, the primary rationale for predatory pricing is to reap monopoly profits. The Court ruled in essence that since the scheme of predatory pricing did not achieve its result it didn't happen.

[14] *Matsushita Electric Industrial Corp. v. Zenith Radio Corp.*, 475 U.S. 574 (1986).

There are two major criticisms of the decision in this case.[15] First, it placed economic theory over evidence. If the allegation involved predatory pricing, the first question is whether it happened or not, not whether, if it happened, it made any economic sense. Second, the Court's analysis oversimplified, in the name of economic theory, the complexities of international trade and relations. The Court seemed to assume that Japanese television manufacturers were in fact acting from purely economic motives in their pricing and other business strategies in the United States. However, if the Japanese were always economically rational, they would be eating rice from California; instead, they subsidize domestic rice grown at great expense, for a variety of cultural and other reasons. The fact is that Japanese practices—like anyone else's practices—are governed by a variety of factors having little to do with economics.

ANTITRUST LAWS AND PATENTS, TRADEMARKS, AND COPYRIGHTS

Patents, trademarks, and copyrights convey intellectual property rights to their owners. These rights date back a long time. With the rise of strong nation-states in Europe at the close of the Middle Ages, kings began the practice of granting patents as a reward to enterprises for introducing new processes and products. As an inducement and reward for developing new inventions, patents were granted to inventors, giving them the right to exclude others from making or using the invention for a number of years. Patent rights are recognized in the U.S. Constitution, which specifies that Congress has power to promote the progress of science by securing for limited times to inventors the exclusive right to discovery. This provision on grants of exclusive rights was implemented by statutes. The Patent Act of 1952 was adopted to codify existing patent statutes, particularly concerning conditions for patentability.

Trademarks are also a form of intellectual property. A trademark is a name or symbol used to indicate the source or origin of certain goods. Trademarks, particularly trade names, may be used in a variety of ways. They may be used in advertising that relates to particular products or in institutional advertising that emphasizes the image of a firm. They may be used on product packaging, company letterheads, and even on company buildings. Because of the variety

---

[15] An analysis of this case was provided to the author by William F. Young, who is an antitrust lawyer with Hunton and Williams, a Washington, D.C., law firm, in personal correspondence dated August 9, 1988.

of users and uses possible, effective control of the trademark is difficult. Nevertheless, control is vital to ensure that usage is consistent with the company's image and that the legal rights of the company in its trademark are being protected. Trademarks are registered in the U.S. Patent and Trademark Office and are issued for a period of twenty years. They come under the jurisdiction of the Lanham Act of 1946, which provides the legal right to register any mark that has become distinctive.

Copyrights are particularly relevant to the publishing and entertainment industries. They vest rights in authors and entertainers that prevent others from using their works without permission. Companies argue that copyright laws are necessary for their survival. They depend on the sale of books or music for their existence. Otherwise, competitors could simply copy best-selling works and participate in their continued sale. With the advent of photocopiers, this would be easy to do. Presumably, firms making photocopies could substantially undercut the original publisher because the former would not have to pay for typesetting or editing, nor would they have to pay royalties. Copyrights are issued by the Copyright Office in the Library of Congress and as of 1978 are protected for the life of the author plus fifty years.

Each of the areas of intellectual property law is important to business firms. Without patent law, successful research would be more difficult. Without the protection granted by trademark law, a business firm could not clearly distinguish its name from those of its competitors. A copyright may be very important in protecting a business firm's interest in certain types of products. However, each area conveys a certain monopoly privilege to its owner; often they have been used to eliminate competition. Patents have been used to monopolize the sale of a particular line of goods, and patents and trademarks have often involved the use of tying arrangements to lessen competition. Antitrust law is applicable to the use of patents, trademarks, and copyrights when they are used to lessen competition.

Patents

The patent is a seventeen-year monopoly created by statute. It confers on its holder exclusive rights to processes and products, monopoly power that the government deems appropriate as a means of encouraging inventive initiative. The legal monopoly of a patent can protect only the invention claimed in the patent, nothing else. However, patents have formed the basis of various forms of agreements that have had the effect of restricting competition in the marketplace. Attempts to extend the reach of the patent monopoly beyond its proper scope can lead to charges of misuse of the patent, which can prevent the patent owner from enforcing his or her patent against parties injured by the misuse, or to an antitrust violation if the misuse has had or may have the requisite anticompetitive effect. The antitrust laws place the following types of restrictions on a patent monopoly:

1. An arrangement under which the grant of a license is made conditional on the purchase of unpatented supplies from a specified source is merely a form of illegal tie-in sale because the patent is practically a per se violation of Section 1 of the Sherman Act. In rare cases, if there are legitimate technical considerations in using the patented invention, it may be legal to require the licensee to buy special or specially adapted supplies.

2. An attempt by a patent owner to fix the price at which the licensee may sell articles manufactured under the license is narrowly restricted and in practice is almost impossible to justify.

3. The right of the patent owner to license the patent for specified uses may in some circumstances be legal, although as a general rule it is suspect under the antitrust laws. Licenses may be limited geographically in rare situations, but not without running afoul of the law.

4. The practice of package licensing, in which a licensee accepts a license in a package deal, is proper only when the licensee voluntarily accepts the package; otherwise, it is an illegal tie-in situation

5. The accumulation of patents in a company's portfolio is not in itself illegal, although the purchase of patents may be illegal under the merger provisions of Section 7 of the Clayton Act.

Various sharing devices such as the cross-licensing of patents or the pooling of patents for mutual benefit are not held to be illegal as such, but they generally are declared to be illegal when in the eyes of the courts, they are used as a means of eliminating competition among patent owners and licensees. For example, the Justice Department has challenged long-term agreements between two leading U.S. and Japanese electrical equipment manufacturers, Westinghouse and Mitsubishi, covering both patents and know-how.[16] Each firm has a license to the technology of the other, and each is prevented by the agreement from selling products that use the technology of the other. The broad result has been to keep these two large electrical equipment manufacturers out of each

[16] *U.S. v. Westinghouse Electric Corp.*, Cic. No. 70-852-SAW (April 22, 1970).

other's home markets—an important consideration for the United States, given the concentrated nature of the electrical equipment market and its history of anticompetitive business practices.

The Gypsum Case, 1948

The Gypsum case, decided in 1948, involved price-fixing arrangements among the licensed producers of gypsum wallboard, a product made in accordance with a number of patents. The facts of the case were that the dominant producer, the U.S. Gypsum Company, entered into a separate patent-licensing and price-fixing agreement with each of the principal producers of gypsum wallboard in the United States. U.S. Gypsum had modeled its price-fixing activities precisely on the General Electric precedent, fixing both prices and terms of sale for gypsum board. Since each agreement was an individual one, the company maintained that, on the basis of the General Electric case, its license arrangements were legal. The government charged a violation of the Sherman Act and noted the use by the company of a subsidiary to check on the prices of the various licensees to ensure price compliance.

The Supreme Court upheld the government in the Gypsum case. It stated that the formal separateness of the contracts did not alter the reality of a combination to fix prices. Lawful acts may become unlawful when taken in concert. The General Electric case offers no protection for a patent holder, acting in concert with all members of an industry, to issue licenses under the terms of which the industry is regimented, the class of distributors squeezed out, and the prices on unpatented products stabilized.[17] In essence, the case limited the application of the General Electric case in that restrictive powers given a patent holder were narrowed. (In 1912, General Electric licensed Westinghouse to use its patents to produce and sell lightbulbs at a price set by GE. This was also true of other companies using GE patents, enabling GE to control the lightbulb market. The U.S. government brought suit against GE, accusing it of using its patents to fix prices. In 1926 the Supreme Court ruled in favor of GE.)

Trademarks

Trademarks are also subject to the antitrust laws, particularly when used in restraint of trade. The purpose of a trademark, as originally conceived, was to

[17] *U.S. v. U.S. Gypsum Co.*, 333 U.S. 364 (1948).

identify the origin or ownership of a product. Trademarks are a vitally important component of the operating marketing mix of most successful business firms. Business firms have come to regard trademarks as a strategic device for establishing product differentiation and, through advertising, strong consumer preference. The use of a trade name, a form of trademark, for a wide variety of products will cause the name to become associated intimately with the overall image of the particular business. In this way, firms have sometimes been able to establish a degree of market control that has remained substantially unchallenged for many years. An example is Coca-Cola, which has achieved worldwide recognition. There is nothing wrong with trademarks, provided they are not used to restrict competition in a particular market. Several types of trademark abuses can violate the antitrust laws.

1. Tying agreements in which a trademark owner ties the use of the trademark by other parties to the purchase of goods not normally sold or required under the trademark. In the aforementioned Chicken Delight case, the main issue was a tying agreement in which the Chicken Delight franchises had to purchase cooking equipment, dry-mix food items, and other products from the company as a condition for getting the Chicken Delight trademark. It was ruled that the tying product—the license to use the Chicken Delight trademark—possessed sufficient economic power to lessen competition to constitute a violation of the Sherman Act, The tying restrictions imposed by the company were not essential to the protection of its trademark.

2. Exclusive dealing arrangements in which the trademark owner is able to persuade users to use its product to the exclusion of others. For example, General Electric was able to persuade government procurement agencies to establish specifications requiring the use of Mazada light bulbs. It licensed Westinghouse to use the name, but denied its other licensees the same right. Trademarks have also been used to effect a division of markets among the members of an international cartel, with each member being given the exclusive right to use the trademark in its own territory.

The Parker Brothers Monopoly Case, 1982

The real estate investment game called *Monopoly* was created during the Depression when people had few jobs, little money, and lots of time on their hands. Paradoxically, the game pertained to making money in real estate when money in any form of activity was hard to make. The creator of the game sold it to Parker Brothers, which obtained a trademark on the name *Monopoly* in 1935. The game went on to become the most popular parlor game of all time, making millions of dollars for Parker Brothers, which was eventually purchased by General Mills.

In 1973, a company called Anti-Monopoly, Inc., began producing and selling a game under the name *Anti-Monopoly*. General Mills claimed that *Anti-Monopoly* was an infringement of its trademark rights in *Monopoly*. Anti-Monopoly, Inc., then sought a judgment that *Monopoly* was an invalid trademark, and went to court to cancel General Mills's federal registration.

The court's decision turned on the factual question of whether *Monopoly* had become a generic term primarily denoting the game itself, as distinguished from the game's producer Parker Brothers or General Mills. The court reasoned that if the primary significance of the term *Monopoly* is not the product's but the producer's, then the trademark is valid. But when a trademark primarily denotes a product, not the product's producer, the trademark is lost. Applying this set of reasoning, the court concluded that Parker Brothers and General Mills had promoted *Monopoly* so successfully as the name of the game that its source-identifying function had been lost. Accordingly, the court found that *Monopoly* had become generic and that its registration as a trademark was no longer valid.[18]

The Supreme Court declined to hear the lower court's invalidation of *Monopoly* as a trademark for the famed real estate investment game. As a consequence, *Monopoly* joins *aspirin, linoleum, zipper,* and *thermos* as a generic name unprotected by the federal trademark laws. This case illustrates an important principle of trademark law: a trademark is valid only when it is recognized by the public, not as an identification of the product alone, but as the identification of some particular producer's version of that product. Thus, trademarks are not necessarily forever.

Copyrights

Copyrights have a far more circumscribed use than patents and trademarks in that they are limited primarily to publishing and entertainment. The use of

---

[18] *Anti-Monopoly, Inc., v. General Mills Fun Group, Inc.,* 684F 2d 1316 (9th Cir. 1982), cert. denied, 51 U.S.L.W. 3613 (February 22, 1983).

copyrights as an anticompetitive business practice would most likely take the form of a tying agreement. For example, a movie company might tie the use of a copyrighted film or television to the purchase of other products from the company. However, the enormous advances in photocopying and other forms of reproduction have increased the importance of copyright laws. In response to new technological changes, Congress enacted the 1976 Copyright Act. Among the rights provided for in the 1976 Copyright Act is that the copyright holder is to be the only person to reproduce the copyrighted work or to authorize such reproduction. However, there are exemptions and exceptions to this general grant of monopoly rights. One exception would be where progress and learning are adversely affected by a lack of access to copyrighted work. This exception involves fair use, which is reasonable but unconsented use of copyrighted works despite the owner's exclusive rights.

The Betamax Case, 1984

In 1976, Universal City Studios and Walt Disney Productions sued Sony, the manufacturer of Betamax, for copyright infringement, alleging that Betamax owners had used their machines unlawfully to copy commercially sponsored television programs exhibited by Universal and Disney. The plaintiffs sought monetary damages and an accounting of profits from Sony, as well as an injunction against the manufacture and sale of the Betamax recorders. As such, the case was an attempt to impose copyright liability on a manufacturer of copying equipment and was a direct threat to the viability of the electronic recording industry. The case also posed an indirect threat to the manufacture and sale of other products capable of being used for copying, such as photocopiers and audio tape recorders.

A circuit court of appeals held as a matter of law that home use of video recorders was not a fair use because it was not productive in that it was not undertaken for any purpose other than to record copyrighted material. Moreover, the court distinguished between video recorders, which are sold for the primary purpose of reproducing copyrighted television programs, and audio recorders and photocopiers, which as stable articles of commerce, do not create copyright problems. The court then held that Sony was liable for contributory copyright infringement because it was aware of the fact that owners of the Betamax machine would use it to reproduce copyrighted materials on television. Sony, ordered to pay damages to Universal and Walt Disney, appealed the case to the Supreme Court.

The Supreme Court ruled that Sony's sale of video recorders to the general public did not constitute infringement under federal copyright laws.[19] The Court held that the sale of a video recorder did not constitute an infringement since it is capable of other uses. The Court stated that many copyright owners, including sports, religious, and educational broadcasters, had encouraged copying of their programs for noncommercial home entertainment. Its decision is important for two reasons. First, it makes clear that private noncommercial taping of television programs for later home viewing is a legitimate use of copyrighted materials and, therefore, does not violate copyright laws. Second, and more important, it rejects the proposition that a manufacturer may be held liable for violating copyright law simply by selling a product, capable of a noninfringement use, to a customer who uses the product in a manner that could constitute an infringement.

ANTICOMPETITIVE PRACTICES AND THE REAGAN ADMINISTRATION

The Reagan administration's enforcement of antitrust laws as they pertain to anticompetitive business practices received mixed reviews. The Antitrust Division of the Justice Department was active in prosecuting horizontal antitrust violations, such as price fixing, bid rigging, and market allocation among competitors. During the 1987 fiscal year, the division filed 92 criminal cases involving 119 companies and 116 individuals—the latter a record in the history of the division. During the same period, fines were assessed in the amount of $17.9 million and sentences of 18,488 jail days were imposed, of which 1,994 days were actually served by antitrust violators.[20] In addition, the division recovered $1.1 million in damages suffered by the United States as a result of antitrust violations during the first five months of the 1988 fiscal year, the division filed 38 criminal cases involving 45 corporations and 40 individuals. Fines in the amount of $12.6 million and jail terms of 1,784 days were assessed.

[19] *Sony Corporation of America v. Universal City Studios, Inc.*, 52 U.S.L.W. 90 (January 17, 1984).

[20] Statement of Charles F. Rule, Assistant Attorney General Antitrust Division, Before Department of Justice Subcommittee on Monopolies and Commercial Law, Committee on the Judiciary, U.S. House of Representatives, March 3, 1988.

TABLE 8-1   Antitrust Enforcement in the Area of Vertical Price Fixing

Year	Investigations Opened	Cases Filed
1976	4	1
1977	14	0
1978	4	1
1979	7	1
1980	10	1
1981	1	1
1982	1	0
1983	0	0
1984	0	0
1985	3	0
1986	2	0

Source: U.S. Department of Justice, Office of Legislative and Intergovernmental Affairs, July, 1988.

Criticisms

There were two major criticisms of the Reagan administration's enforcement of antitrust laws pertaining to anticompetitive practices. The first dealt with a lack of enforcement in the area of vertical restraints, and the second dealt with predatory pricing practices. Vertical restraints, or vertical price fixing, typically occur in relationships between manufacturers and distributors. Price fixing, horizontal and vertical, is a per se violation of Section 1 of the Sherman Act. Lack of enforcement, the critics argued, was an attempt by the Justice Department to eradicate per se illegality of vertical restraints of all types. This claim was buttressed by the facts shown in Table 8-1, which presents a tabulation of other vertical price-fixing investigations opened and cases filed by the Antitrust Division for the years 1976–1987.[21]

[21] Testimony of William S. Comanor on Antitrust Enforcement Policies Toward Vertical Restraints Before the Subcommittee, Before the Subcommittee on Monopolies and Commercial Law, Committee on the Judiciary, House of Representatives, February 24, 1988.

The Retail Competition Enforcement Act of 1987

The rationale of the Retail Competition Enforcement Act[22] is to amend the Sherman Act to more vigorously enforce the restraints against vertical price fixing. Proponents of this legislation argue that unless it is enacted discount stores will be driven out of business and the consumer will be the ultimate loser. They point to the *Business Electronics v. Sharp* case in which the Supreme Court confirmed the decision of a lower court that in order for a manufacturer's termination of a distributor to be illegal per se, it must be pursuant to a price maintenance agreement with another distributor. The act would be more specific in dealing with resale price maintenance, which is vertical price fixing. Illegal price fixing would be determined on the basis of two criteria: (1) if a distributor made a request, suggestion, demand, or request to a supplier that the supplier take steps to eliminate or curtail price discrimination; and (2) if because of the suggestion or threat the supplier terminated or refused to supply goods to another distributor.

SUMMARY

Competition is a hallmark of a free enterprise market economy. It requires, among other things, freedom of entry into a market, and open noncollusive pricing based on market factors. Competition creates incentives for business firms to reduce costs while improving products or services. The benefits of competition disappear when business firms agree on prices or engage in other illegal activity that may unfairly force competitors out of business. Antitrust laws generally prohibit business firms from interfering or restricting free and open competition. Not every restraint on competition violates antitrust laws; rather, courts have consistently held that only unreasonable restrictions on competition are illegal. The courts have identified a number of different business practices as anticompetitive. Price fixing is one practice, and price discrimination against sellers or buyers is another. Exclusive dealing, tying arrangements, reciprocity, and group boycotts can also be used to lessen competition. Intellectual property, such as patents, also is subject to antitrust law if used to reduce or eliminate competition.

[22] The Retail Competition Enforcement Act, or a similar version, will probably be enacted into law in the new administration.

QUESTIONS FOR DISCUSSION

1. What economic injury is likely to result from a group boycott?
2. Give an example of a specific cost justification that can be offered for price discrimination under the Robinson–Patman Act.
3. What is a vertical price-fixing agreement? Is it applicable to the Spray-Rite case?
4. What types of unfair business practices were condemned by common law?
5. Why did common law provide no protection against many types of anticompetitive business practices?
6. What is the difference between horizontal and vertical price fixing?
7. Discuss the Morton Salt case of 1948.
8. What is secondary-line price discrimination?
9. Discuss the Utah Pie case of 1967.
10. Discuss the Business Electronics case. Why is it significant?
11. Discuss the Milk Companies case. Is horizontal or vertical price fixing involved?

Chapter 9

Antitrust Laws and International Trade

Almost all large, and many small, U.S. corporations participate in business outside the United States, with trade and investments in many countries. These corporations now have the power to act as agents of change on societies, cultures, and economics. In particular, the multinational corporation has emerged as the most sophisticated type of organization yet developed to globally integrate economic activity. Some multinationals have sales volumes larger than the gross national product of most countries. But size is only one component of their power; they also control the means of creating wealth and make decisions that touch hundreds of millions of people. They have contributed to the internationalization of production, and in this process their investment decisions determine the world's allocation of resources and welfare.

However, the global influence of business is by no means limited to U.S. corporations. European and Japanese business firms also operate all over the world, and have invested in plants and equipment in the United States. These firms operate on an ideological basis quite different from our own. U.S. attitudes toward competition, particularly during the 1980s, will have to be reevaluated in light of increased world competition. Given the dynamic nature of international business, the domestic government regulation of business has become much more complex. In regard to the United States, it has become more difficult to apply antitrust laws written during the last century or the early part of this one to corporations that operate throughout the world. Moreover, countries' varying antitrust policies create conflicts of natural interest because international commerce is subject to overlapping jurisdictions.

Although a number of other Western countries have antitrust laws, they are generally not as far reaching as U.S. law. As a consequence, actions taken by a multinational operating in a foreign country may be legal under the laws of its home nation but illegal in the United States. The American view that a freely competitive economic system is the most efficient, most desirable form of society is not necessarily the view held by other major industrial powers. To compete more successfully with U.S. enterprises, the western European countries and Japan have permitted the use of combinations and cartels of domestic enterprises. One result is that the extent of industrial concentration is greater in many industries in Japan and West Germany than in similar industries in the United States.

APPLICATION OF U.S. ANTITRUST LAWS TO U.S. MULTINATIONALS

U.S. antitrust policy is applicable to any U.S. firm engaged in international business. In regard to foreign commerce in general, U.S. antitrust policy has three separate objectives: to eliminate unreasonable restraints on U.S. exports and imports, to encourage foreign firms to enter the U.S. market, and to prevent U.S. or foreign firms from restraining commerce in the United States through their foreign operations. These objectives are governed primarily by four laws: the Sherman Antitrust Act, the Clayton Antitrust Act, the Federal Trade Commission Act, and the Webb–Pomerene Act. Of these, the Sherman and Clayton acts have had the greatest impact on the multinationals' operations. Through judicial interpretation, the Sherman Act has been extended to apply to both U.S. firms and foreign firms operating in the United States, which permits U.S. courts to govern parties and acts both inside and outside the United States.

Two important concepts pertain to the application of U.S. antitrust laws. One is extraterritorial reach, which is defined as the employment of U.S. domestic antitrust statutes in considering business operations outside U.S. territorial limits. Extraterritorial reach is also the legal basis for controlling the actions of corporations operating outside the United States, thus subjecting worldwide actions to national control. The second concept is the effects test, which means that any action, no matter when or where committed, is subject to U.S. antitrust law if it affects U.S. commerce. This gives the U.S. courts a potentially limitless charter of jurisdiction, because an act committed anywhere in the world conceivably can affect U.S. commerce.

The Sherman Act

The Sherman Act aims primarily at maintaining and promoting interstate and foreign trade or commerce. Both Sections 1 and 2 are applicable to U.S. corporations operating in other countries. Section 1 provides that any contract or combination in the form of a trust or otherwise, or any conspiracy in restraint of trade or commerce among states or with foreign nations, is illegal. Section 2 makes it a crime to monopolize or attempt to monopolize, or combine or conspire with anyone to monopolize, any part of trade or commerce among the states or with foreign nations. To invoke the Sherman Act, involvement in either interstate or foreign commerce is enough. Foreign commerce normally refers to U.S. exports and imports, but the act may also apply to transactions whose impact is entirely outside the limits of the United States if U.S. interests are involved. In the 1968 Pacific Seafarers case, the act set up restraints used solely in shipping between foreign ports, in which any shipments financed by the U.S. government were limited by law to transportation in U.S. ships.[1]

The American Tobacco Case, 1911

The first major international application of the Sherman Act came in the landmark American Tobacco case of 1911.[2] The American Tobacco Company and the Imperial Tobacco Company of Great Britain had agreed to divide markets, with Imperial agreeing not to sell tobacco in the United States except through the American Tobacco Company.[3] The two companies then formed a third corporation, the British-American Tobacco Company, which took over all the foreign business of American and Imperial, though British-American Tobacco could not export to the United States. As a part of its overall decision, the Supreme Court ruled that this allocation of markets illegally restrained trade under the provisions of the Sherman Act. All parties to the agreement, including Imperial Tobacco, were held to have violated the act. The pooling agreement under which the American Tobacco Company and the Imperial Tobacco Company had combined to form the British-American Company was canceled. The Court held that the Sherman Act applied to restraints, including contracts or combinations, that operated to the prejudice of the public by unduly restricting competition.

The Sherman Act has been applied outside the United States by reasons of market power, intent, and effect, although until World War II, the courts required that for an act to be considered a violation of the Sherman Act, it had to be committed within the United States. In 1927, in a case involving the Sisal

---

[1] *Pacific Seafarers, Inc., v. Pacific Far East Lines, Inc.,* 404 F. 2d 804 (D.D.C. 1968).

[2] *U.S. v. American Tobacco Co.,* 221 U.S. 10C, 31 Sup. Ct. 632 (1911).

[3] This was only a part of the American Tobacco Case.

Sales Corporation, the Supreme Court declared a conspiracy to monopolize U.S. foreign commerce to be illegal.[4] The Court emphasized the aspect of unlawful results within the United States and asserted that for an act to be illegal it had to be committed by both domestic and foreign firms within the country. After World War II, however, the courts shifted their position to include acts committed outside the United States. The landmark Alcoa case of 1945 established the principle that the U.S. courts could regulate actions conducted outside the United States that have direct and foreseeable economic consequences inside the United States.[5] In the National Lead case of 1947, American and foreign companies were found to have participated in an international restraint of trade in the production of titanium pigments.[6] A majority of the Supreme Court ruled that the Sherman Act was applicable because the restraint affected U.S. commerce. In the Timken Roller Bearing case of 1951, the Supreme Court ruled that a joint venture between Timken and British and French roller-bearing firms created a cartel arrangement to allocate world markets and restrict imports to the United States.[7] In addition, Timken held 30 percent of the British company's common stock and 50 percent of the French company's common stock.

The test of the applicability of the Sherman Act in both the National Lead and Timken cases came to be known as the *effects test* and enabled an almost unlimited extraterritorial application of the Sherman Act, for almost any commercial enterprise anywhere in the world conceivably could have an effect on U.S. domestic commerce. Agreements made on foreign soil do not relieve a U.S. defendant from the responsibility for restraint of trade. So, at present, proven effects on U.S. commerce may bring totally foreign conduct under the purview of the Sherman Act. No longer is the place where the act occurs the key; rather, when an act or agreement can be shown to have a direct effect on markets within the United States, the Sherman Act will cover it. Of course, it is necessary to have jurisdiction over the party or parties committing the act for this applicability to have any effect. This condition normally presents no problem with a subsidiary of a U.S. corporation, let alone with the corporation itself.

[4] *U.S. v. Sisal Sales Corporation,* 247 U.S. 268 (1927).

[5] The Alcoa case was discussed in Chapter 7.

[6] *U.S. v. National Lead Co.,* 63 F. Supp. 513 (S.D.N.Y. 1945) modified 332 U.S. 319 (1947).

[7] *U.S. v. Timken Roller Bearing Co.,* 83 F. Supp. 284 (N.D. Ohio 1949) modified 341 U.S. 593 (1951).

The Timberlane Lumber Company Case, 1983

Timberlane was a U.S. firm seeking to develop sources of lumber for delivery to the United States from Honduras. Bank of America, which had interests in competing lumber mills, allegedly tried to protect those interests by driving Timberlane out of the Honduran lumber market. The actions of the bank were said to have resulted in attempts to foreclose on mortgages, in the placement of an embargo on the company's property, and in the use of Honduran guards to shut down Timberlane's milling operation. The company's claim relating to the mortgage foreclosure was resolved in the Honduran court system, but it also filed an antitrust action in the United States seeking more than $5 million in damages from Bank of America and its Honduran subsidiaries. The case involved a test of the extraterritorial application of U.S. antitrust law.

A U.S. court decided that jurisdiction over this claim would be based on three points: the determination of the effect or intended effect on the foreign commerce of the United States, the type and magnitude of the alleged illegal behavior, and the appropriateness of exercising extraterritorial jurisdiction over an action committed in another country. The court, stating that the first two points were satisfied in terms of U.S. legal jurisdiction, focused on the last part, the extraterritorial jurisdiction, and came to the following conclusions:[8]

1. Applying the U.S. antitrust laws would potentially conflict with the efforts of Honduras to foster a particular type of business climate.
2. Any judgment against Bank of America could be enforced in a U.S. court.
3. Bank of America's acts were directed primarily toward securing a greater rate of return on its investment in Honduras and were consistent with Honduran customs and practices.
4. The insignificance of the effect on U.S. foreign commerce when compared to the substantial effect in Honduras suggested that U.S. jurisdiction not be exercised.
5. That virtually all the illegal activity occurred in Honduras weighed against the exercise of U.S. antitrust authority.

The suit of Timberlane against Bank of America was dismissed by the court.

---

[8] *Timberlane Lumber Co. v. Bank of America National Trust & Savings Association,* 574 F. Supp. 1453 (N.D. Cal. 1983); also *Timberlane Lumber Co. v. Bank of America,* 549 F. 2d. 597 (9th Cir. 1976).

The Clayton Act

The Clayton Act, particularly Sections 1 and 7, also can be applied to U.S. firms operating abroad. Section 1 includes trade with other nations in its definition of commerce, and Section 7 prohibits one firm from acquiring the stock or assets of another firm when the result may substantially lessen competition or create a monopoly. Section 7 applies to the acquisition of foreign firms by U.S. firms only if the latter are engaged in the foreign commerce of the United States and if the acquisition lessens competition in any part of the country. A transaction that reduces competition does not have to occur within the continental limits of the United States. For example, a U.S. firm could acquire a foreign firm in Argentina that resulted in its controlling the market for a given product in that country. If this control restricted U.S. exports to this market, with adverse effects being felt by a particular part of the United States, then Section 7 would apply. The key is whether or not the acquisition will lessen competition in U.S. markets or among U.S. firms engaged in foreign commerce. Thus, the Clayton Act could be used to promote greater competition in a foreign market if the business activities in some way reduced competition in the United States.

A merger between a U.S. firm and a foreign firm not operating in the United States can be challenged by Section 7 of the Clayton Act when the consequence is to reduce competition. In fact, foreign acquisitions can also be challenged under the doctrine of potential competition. In *U.S. v. Joseph Schlitz Brewing Company,* Schlitz's proposed acquisition of John Labatt, Ltd., a Canadian brewery, was challenged on the grounds that a small California brewer owned by Labatt was a competitor of Schlitz and that Labatt was a potential entrant on a larger scale in the U.S. market.[9] This doctrine was also applied to the Gillette case.

The Gillette Case, 1975

In this case, resolved in December 1975, the acquisition of Braun, a major European electric razor firm, by Gillette, the leading American manufacturer of razors, was challenged on the grounds that potential competition would be eliminated.[10] The rationale behind this challenge was that a potential entrant,

[9] *U.S. v. Joseph Schlitz Brewing Company,* 253 F. Supp. 129 (1966) and 385 U.S. 37 (1966).
[10] *U.S. v. Gillette Co.,* Cir. No. 68-141 (D.C. Mass., 1975).

while standing at the periphery of the market, may significantly affect the performance of an oligopolistic industry.[11] This is true whether the potential entrant is domestic or foreign. Gillette, given the nature of its product, does operate in an oligopolistic industry and probably dominates it. That Braun had not entered the U.S. market was not a deterrent to the merger challenge since the company had the ability to enter the market and provide competition. Thus, the merger was not allowed, and Gillette was ordered to create a new company to market Braun's products in the United States.

The Clayton Act requires only that anticompetitive effects be felt in any line of commerce in any section of the United States. The transaction that causes the effects does not have to occur within the geographic limits of the United States, nor do transgressors have to be U.S. firms. Section 7 of the Clayton Act was amended in 1980 to extend to all transactions affecting the interstate or foreign commerce of the United States; previously it had reached companies only directly involved in such commerce.[12] The amendment provides a firmer basis for the assertion of the broadest possible jurisdiction over international as well as domestic transactions. A merger between two foreign-based companies meets the same statutory standard if it affects competition within the United States.

The Rockwell International Case, 1980

The Justice Department brought an antitrust suit in 1980 against Rockwell International and one of its wholly owned subsidiaries.[13] Rockwell, the largest producer of lubricated tapered plug valves in the United States, and its subsidiary had acquired a stock interest in a British firm that was a principal international competitor of Rockwell's and was also a potential entrant into the U.S. plug valve market. Rockwell and its subsidiary were ultimately required by a consent decree to divest themselves of a 29.7 percent stock interest in the British firm. Pending the divestiture of the stock, the U.S. companies were barred from voting their shares, from attempting to influence the British firm, and from increasing their equity in it. In addition, any acquisition of the assets of the British firm was subject to court approval.

[11] Trade Regulation Report 4.345.19.

[12] H.R. Rep. No. 871, 96th Cong., 2d sess., 1980, pp. 6–7.

[13] *U.S. v. Rockwell International Corp.,* No. 80-1401 (W.D. Pa., 1980).

The Pilkington Brothers Case, 1983

Pilkington Brothers, a British company, is the largest float glass producer in the world. It was challenged by the Federal Trade Commission in 1983 for its acquisition of assets in competing Canadian and Mexican firms.[14] The FTC took the position that the acquisitions lessened competition in the manufacture and sale of float glass in the North American market. Pilkington entered into a consent order requiring divestiture of its shares in the Canadian firm within five years and removal of its representatives from the boards of directors of the Mexican firms it had acquired. Although Pilkington was allowed to retain its shares in one Mexican firm, any attempt to amend its charter was subjected to prior FTC approval. Although Pilkington is a British firm, its activities had an effect on competition within the United States.

Tying Arrangements and Exclusive Dealing

Tying arrangements and exclusive dealing prohibited by Section 3 of the Clayton Act are rarely applied to the foreign activities of U.S. business firms. Congress was concerned that extending prohibitions to sales overseas would hinder the ability of U.S. firms to compete in overseas markets with foreign firms. In *Reisner v. General Motors,* a New York court ruled that Section 3 was not applicable to the plaintiff's claim that General Motors engaged in tie-in sales of automobile engines and components for sale in Europe for automobiles that were to be sold for European consumption.[15] Likewise, Section 2 of the Clayton Act, which prohibits primary-line or "seller's" price discrimination, would have little application to the foreign commerce of the United States.

The Robinson–Patman Act

Section 2 of the Clayton Act, as amended by the Robinson-Patman Act, prohibits the sale of goods of like grade and quality within the United States at discriminatory prices to two or more purchasers, where at least one of the transactions is in interstate commerce. This is secondary-line or "buyer's"

---

[14] Trade Regulation Report (CCH) 22, 167 (FTC June 22, 1984).

[15] *Reisner v. General Motors Corp.,* 511 F. Supp. 1167 (S.D.N.Y. 1981).

discrimination. Unless it can be demonstrated that somehow there is injury to competition within the United States, this provision is not likely to involve foreign commerce.

The Federal Trade Commission and Webb–Pomerene Acts

The Federal Trade Commission Act and the Webb–Pomerene Act also can be applied to multinational corporations. The Federal Trade Commission has concurrent jurisdiction with the Justice Department in dealing with acts that are illegal under antitrust laws. Moreover, Section 5 of the Federal Trade Commission Act supplements the power of Section 7 of the Clayton Act. The Webb-Pomerene Act exempts U.S. firms from the antitrust laws for cooperative participation in export associations. Its purpose is to ensure free access to foreign markets for domestic exports on a basis that will be competitive with foreign exporters. But the act does prohibit the formation of associations when the result is to restrain trade in the United States or to restrain exports of domestic competitors. Section 4 of the Webb–Pomerene Act expands the jurisdiction of the Federal Trade Commission to include unfair methods of competition outside the United States, and Section 5 provides for the registration of all export associations with the Federal Trade Commission.

The Webb–Pomerene Act does not automatically immunize every type of joint export venture from the Sherman Act. There are prohibitions against acts in foreign trade that substantially reduce competition in the United States. In the Minnesota Mining and Manufacturing case of 1950, which involved a joint venture by nine U.S. manufacturers of abrasives to establish an export association and create a joint subsidiary in Europe, the Supreme Court ruled that the move would restrict exports from the United States.[16] The Court reasoned that the association would reduce the firms' zeal for competition in the U.S. market. In general, then, the rule for applying Webb–Pomerene is that participating companies in an export association may agree among themselves on prices and allocate world markets for exports, as long as competition within the United States is not affected. In practice, Webb–Pomerene has proved to be of little practical importance because most joint export arrangements may be carried on under the Sherman Act and because U.S. firms selling highly differentiated products have generally not wanted to merge with their competitors.

---

[16] *U.S. v. Minnesota Mining and Mfg. Co.,* 92 F. Supp. 947, 1958 (D. Mass. 1950).

The Foreign Trade Antitrust Improvements Act, 1982

This act amends the Sherman and Federal Trade Commission acts to exempt from their application export activities that do not have a direct, substantial, and reasonably foreseeable effect on U.S. trade or commerce. The act applies to all U.S. firms engaged in exporting and is supposed to remove antitrust uncertainties by codifying the views of the Antitrust Division of the Justice Department on the proper scope of the Sherman Act with regard to foreign trade. It does not change the fundamental principles that the Sherman Act applies to U.S. export and import trade, as well as purely domestic commerce, and to business conduct outside the United States. Basically, the act requires courts to pay closer attention to antitrust claims than they have in the past to better ascertain their effect on the U.S. economy.

The Industrial Development Corp. Case, 1988

The Sherman Act prohibits activity by two or more entities that unreasonably restrain competition, and monopolization or attempted monopolization by a single entity. The Foreign Trade Antitrust Improvement Act added a new Section 7 to the Sherman Act. This section provides that the Sherman Act applies to foreign trade activities other than imports into the United States only if they have a direct, substantial, and reasonably foreseeable effect on U.S. domestic commerce, or unreasonably restrain competing exporters from the United States.

The American firm, Industrial Development Corp., alleged that a Japanese firm, Mitsui, had engaged in monopolization, attempted monopolization, and restraint of trade by preventing it from going into the logging business in Indonesia. The defendant, Mitsui, asserted that the plaintiff had not established jurisdiction under the Sherman Act, because the logs it intended to harvest in Indonesia would not have been sold in the United States, or even if they had been imported, would have constituted an insignificant portion of the U.S. market. The Fifth U.S. Circuit Court of Appeals issued a decision in favor of Mitsui, which applied the jurisdictional standards added to the Sherman Act by the Foreign Trade Anti-trust Improvements Act. It ruled that Mitsui's conduct did not have a direct effect on commerce into or out of the United States.[17]

---

[17] Industrial Development Corp. v. Mitsui and Co., Ltd., 1988-2 Trade Cas. 68,235 (5th Cir. 1988).

Criticism of U.S. Antitrust Laws

Many U.S. business firms claim that U.S. antitrust laws place them at a disadvantage with foreign firms at a time when competition is becoming increasingly global. They argue that investment and sales opportunities are often avoided in the world marketplace for fear they would attract the attention of the Justice Department or the Federal Trade Commission. They also feel the U.S. antitrust laws are more punitive and restrictive than those used by Japan and other competitors. The latter view is reinforced by a study made by the President's Commission on Industrial Competitiveness that, among other things, compared the antitrust policies of the major industrial countries. Although the primary goal underlying U.S. antitrust policy is the promotion of free competition, other countries have other goals of equal or paramount importance, such as the rationalization of industry and the promotion of the public interest in terms of national goals. In the policy area, the United States is unusual in taking a prohibitory, as opposed to a regulatory, approach in applying per se rules of illegality and a structural test for mergers.

The attitudes of the United States and of other countries toward the role of antitrust laws in regulating various forms of industrial concentration differ. U.S. antitrust law is based on the principle that competition per se is good. The Western European and Japanese governments do not agree, particularly with respect to foreign trade, feeling that industrial concentration and anticompetitive agreements are beneficial, as long as they lead to increased productivity, economic growth, and the advance of technology. European and Japanese antitrust laws are not directed toward breaking up cartels and combinations, but toward regulating and guiding them in the national interest. This approach is to be expected, since government is more directive in most European countries and in Japan than in the United States. Several European countries not only permit but encourage agreements, combinations, and mergers among companies for the purpose of rationalizing production. They have encouraged joint research and joint marketing, have permitted pricing agreements, and also have allowed the formation of export cartels.

The United States is often faced with foreign competitors that are allowed to grow much larger relative to their domestic markets than U.S. firms. For example, when concentration is measured by country using the Herfindahl–Hirschman index, many U.S. industries are less concentrated than those of other major industrial countries. For example, applied to the chemical industry in the United States, the Herfindahl–Hirschman index for the four largest firms in the industry is 682. However, it is 946 for the four largest firms in

TABLE 9-1   Comparative Antitrust Policies

	United States	European Economic Community	Japan
Approach			
Theory	Prohibitory	Regulatory	Regulatory
Practice	Mixed	Regulatory	Regulatory
Exemptions			
Economic-technical	Limited	Yes	Yes
Promote international competitiveness	Limited	Yes	Yes
Enforcement			
Government	Stringent	Mixed	Mixed
Private	Rigorous	Rare	Rare
Damages	Triple	Single	Single
Goals			
Promote competition	Yes	Yes	Yes
Rationalization	No	Yes	Yes
Public good	No	Yes	Yes
Structure			
Degree of enforcement authority independence	High	Low	Low

Source: Report of the President's Commission on Industrial Competitiveness, *Global Competition: The New Reality,* vol. 2 (Washington, D.C.: U.S. Government Printing Office, 1985), p. 191.

Japan's chemical industry, 2,246 for the four largest firms in West Germany's chemical industry, and 6,566 for the four largest firms in the United Kingdom's chemical industry. The index for the four largest firms in the U.S. steel industry is 937, compared to an index of 1,734 for the four largest Japanese steel firms and an index of 1,442 for the four largest West German steel firms.

Table 9-1 presents a comparison of antitrust policy in the United States, the European Economic Community, and Japan. There are five areas of comparison approach, exemptions, enforcement, goals, and structure. The United States differs in its approach to antitrust in that it applies per se rules of illegality and a structural test for mergers. In the area of enforcement, the United States has both rigorous government and private enforcement; for instance, it is the only country to permit triple damages in private antitrust actions. Other countries can grant exemptions from antitrust actions, particularly with respect to mergers, to increase the level of employment or to strengthen domestic enterprises that compete in international markets. Companies in these countries can take advantage of arrangements that would be illegal in the United States.

Antitrust Laws in Japan

The cartel arrangement has been synonymous with the growth of the modern Japanese economy. In 1880, the first Japanese combines, called *zaibatsu,* were formed. These combines dominated the economy to the point that by the beginning of World War II five family-owned *zaibatsu* produced more than one-half of the Japanese gross national product and controlled 80 percent of the total private overseas investment. After the end of the war, U.S. occupation authorities passed an antimonopoly act to dissolve the *zaibatsu* and to create a free market economy. Later, however, the Japanese government enacted various laws to exempt certain industries from the antimonopoly act. Generally, these laws permitted exemptions for three types of cartels—cartels to prevent excessive competition among smaller enterprises, cartels for export and import industries, and cartels for special rationalization in which economies of scale are involved. These exemptions were designed to improve Japan's position as a world exporter, to stimulate its rate of economic growth, and to enable it to compete effectively with U.S. multinationals. Indeed, the present Japanese antimonopoly legislation permits the development of cartels and other forms of combinations to a far greater extent than is permitted by U.S. antitrust laws.

Japanese government policy, however, has stressed consumer protection against such practices as price fixing. The Japanese Fair Trade Commission has taken action against internal price-fixing agreements in such areas as automobile tires, synthetic fibers, petroleum, and household electrical appliances. The commission also has initiated action against false or misleading advertising. With regard to unfair business practices, Japanese antitrust law is as stringent as U.S. law, but with regard to mergers, corporate interlocking directorates, and stockholdings, Japanese law is far more lenient, particularly when international trade is involved. In one merger case, the merger of three firms, each dominant in its field, was allowed on the grounds that it was necessary to meet international competition. But mergers that account for more than 30 percent of a given market may be challenged unless it can be demonstrated that foreign competition must be met or that a company is failing. Almost all mergers in Japan have been between competing enterprises; that is, they have been horizontal mergers.

The Keiretsu

The *zaibatsu* have been reassembled into a group arrangement called the *keiretsu*. There are six *keiretsu* in Japan—Sumitomo, Mitsui, Mitsubishi, Sanwa, Fuyo, and Dai Ichi Kanyo—and most of the largest corporations in Japan are linked to one group or another. The *keiretsu* are enormous in size and consist of companies in many fields. The Sumitomo group, for example, includes firms in banking, electronics, glass, insurance, oil, forestry, and metals.[18] The total volume of business each group does runs in hundreds of billions of dollars. The typical *keiretsu* would have sales of around $300 billion a year, an amount three times as much as General Motors, which is the single largest corporation in the world. There are interlocking directorates in each group, and companies affiliated with a group can own stock in each other. Loans to members of a group can be made at favorable rates of interest by banks that are also group members.

Management of a *keiretsu* is provided by the heads of each company affiliated with it. These executives conduct business strategy for their group relative to the other groups, and they coordinate the policies of member companies with respect to political, business, and world affairs. Members of a group may support each other financially. For example, if one member of a group is in danger of going bankrupt, banks in the group can make low-cost loans to it, and other members may increase their purchases of its product or hire its workers. Members can buy each other's products, thus having a built-in stable market. This helps to reduce risk. The group arrangement also pertains to international trade. Each group develops a trade strategy that pertains to exporting, importing, and investing in other countries. Group loyalty is very important, for when a choice has to be made between a foreign import and a similar product produced by a group member, other members will buy the local product even though the import is much cheaper.[19]

[18] Clyde V. Prestowitz, Jr., *Trading Places* (New York: Basic Books, 1988), pp. 157–159.

[19] Ibid., p. 162.

Needless to say, the *keiretsu* arrangement would not be tolerated in the United States, for it would violate about every provision of all of the U.S. antitrust laws. A comparable U.S. equivalent to a *keiretsu* would involve Chase Manhattan Bank, Inland Steel, Pittsburgh Plate Glass, Reynolds Aluminum, IBM, and Du Pont.[20] There would be an interlocking directorate arrangement, crossing stockownership, and cooperation between each company. They would buy from each other and sell to each other. Chase Manhattan would lend money at favorable interest rates to group members. The chief executives of each firm would hold monthly meetings to discuss business strategy relative to other groups. This approach is the direct antithesis to the American belief in competition in the marketplace.

CORRUPT PRACTICES

Bribery is an accepted way of life in many countries, a way to get things done. In fact, there are special words for bribery—in the Latin countries it is called *mordita,* which literally means "bite"; in the Arab countries, it is called *baksheesh,* which can be translated as "rake-off," and in the Soviet Union it is called *blat,* which means "under the table." The moral implications of bribery are irrelevant in these countries, if, indeed, moral considerations are even considered. To customs officials in a Latin American country, a bribe is regarded as a way to supplement an income that is typically low. Foreigners, then, are often faced with a dilemma—do they play by the rules of the game, give the bribe, and get what they want done; or do they stand on their own principles and refuse to play by the rules of the game? Noble sentiments can be costly in societies that are conditioned to accepting various forms of bribery. One person may be delayed in customs for several days for failing to get a needed appointment, whereas another person, who has played the local game, is immediately cleared through customs and obtains the needed appointment.

The Foreign Corrupt Practices Act

The Foreign Corrupt Practices Act (FCPA) was passed in 1977 in response to scandals arising from the revelation of large payments that U.S. corporations had made to foreign government officials. Although this was hardly a new

[20] Ibid., p. 160.

phenomenon, it did not become a public issue in the United States until the Watergate investigations revealed corporate slush funds through which contributions had been made to President Richard Nixon's campaign fund. The Securities and Exchange Commission found that the slush funds were also being used for contributions to foreign political parties and for bribery of foreign officials.[21] The SEC then began to bring suits against some companies under the disclosure of the material information requirement of the 1933 and 1934 securities acts. When the pervasiveness of the problem was recognized, the commission began a voluntary disclosure program that to a certain extent insulated companies from litigation. In all, about four hundred American companies admitted making payments to officials in various countries. The amounts ranged from a few thousand dollars to over $250 million for Lockheed.

Why Payments Are Made

There are four major categories of payments to foreign countries:

1. *Payments made to obtain or keep business.* Many companies have argued that not making payments puts them at a competitive disadvantage in markets in which payments are a routine part of doing business. For example, Lockheed claimed that any prohibition against payments would cripple its position vis-à-vis Japanese and European firms, affecting not only Lockheed's potential sales but also its backlog orders.[22]

2. *Preventive maintenance.* This category includes averting undesirable events such as the expropriation or nationalization of assets, the expulsion of a company from a country, and the cancelation of existing rights such as drilling concessions. This kind of payment is especially important to oil companies.

3. *Establishing or preserving a favorable business climate.* This phrase means influencing foreign administrative or legislative action in such areas as taxes, price controls, and the extent of government regulation of

---

[21] U.S. Advisory Committee on Corporate Disclosure, *Report on Corporate Disclosure to Securities and Exchange Commission,* Washington, D.C.: U.S. Government Printing Office, November 3, 1977.

[22] Edward D. Herlihy and Theodore A. Levine, "Corporate Crisis: The Overseas Payment Problem," *Law and Policy in International Business* 8 (March 1976): 547–629.

business. More concrete examples are payments to high-level bureaucrats to obtain product registration, import permits, and construction permits.

4. *"Grease."* This term describes payments to low-level officials to expedite performance of routine public services. In less-developed countries, bureaucrats are often paid low salaries, and so many augment their incomes by doing favors for businesspeople and other individuals. In countries where this is a common practice, it is an accepted, although technically illegal, way for bureaucrats to act and for business to be conducted.

Types of Industries

Certain industries are more prone to offer bribes than others are. Huge governmental contracts are often written in heavy capital goods industries such as aerospace. Because any one contract is important to a company and bids tend to be close, companies may be tempted to try to improve their chances of winning a given contract by bribing the decision makers. Similarly, companies selling arms to foreign governments are more likely to make payments. The arms are paid for with public money, and in the absence of a profit motive, the only risk to the bureaucrat is disclosure. In addition, industries closely regulated by foreign government agencies are apt to make payments for such purposes as obtaining product registration. For example, U.S. drug companies were among the top spenders in regard to foreign payments. Finally, the oil industry made foreign payments to avert the possibility of oil expropriation, among other things.

Provisions of the Foreign Corrupt Practices Act

The Foreign Corrupt Practices Act does three things:

1. It sets accounting standards by requiring business firms to keep accurate books and records and to devise and maintain a system of internal accounting controls.
2. It prohibits the corrupt use of the mails or any means of commerce to offer, pay, or promise to pay an authorized or unauthorized payment or gift to any foreign official, foreign political party, officer, candidate, or third party who might have influence with foreign officials or politicians, when the objective is to influence an act or decision favorable to the business firm giving the payment.

3. It provides sanctions for violation: fines of up to $1 million for companies and fines of up to $10,000 and imprisonment for up to five years for individuals.

Attitudes Toward Bribery in Other Countries

Bribery and other forms of payments are by no means the sole preserve of U.S. firms: European and Japanese firms have also made their share of bribes. Siemens, the giant West German electrical equipment multinational, was accused of making payoffs in several countries to obtain lucrative contracts.[23] The Austrian government charged that Siemens used bribes to win a contract to build a hospital in Vienna. In Indonesia, the state company Pertamina alleged that Siemens paid out millions of dollars in illicit payments to a former official of the company. Siemens supposedly made the payments to win contracts to build power facilities at a large Indonesian steel plant. A scandal in Italy resulted in the suspension of Giorgio Mazzanti, the president of ENI, Italy's state-owned oil company, for making payments of $130 million to a go-between in negotiations for a large oil contract in Saudi Arabia. Another European scandal emerged when a Belgian firm, Euro-systems Hospitalies, went bankrupt in 1979. The company had won a bid to build a 500-bed hospital in Saudi Arabia by promising a commission of 30 percent of the original price to influential Saudis. Prince Albert, a brother of the Belgian king, was implicated in the scandal.

More important than the actual bribes are the attitudes of foreign governments toward payoffs made by their multinationals. Companies based in West Germany have something extra going for them when it comes to payoffs. If a payoff is made outside Germany, the German company can consider it a legal and tax-deductible business expense. The same holds true for the United Kingdom. British firms resorting to bribery in overseas business need only report the bribe to Inland Revenue as a cost of doing business. The main competitor of the United States, Japan, also has no legal proscriptions against bribery, and Japanese firms have been involved in payoffs to government officials in Indonesia and the Malay States. French firms, too, are not bothered by anti-bribery laws. The consequence is that multinationals of other countries play by different game rules, with a resultant loss of business to U.S. multination-

---

[23] "West German Concern Faces Bribery Charges in Contracting Abroad," *Wall Street Journal,* February 17, 1981, p. 1.

als. The best solution to the bribery problem would be an enforceable international agreement. According to such an agreement, the firms of all countries would be forced to compete on equal grounds, and the United States would avoid the appearance of trying to export its morality.

Ashland Oil and the Foreign Corrupt Practices Act

As noted, bribery in many forms is a common practice in many countries. It has followed traders from the early Phoenicians to the modern multinational corporation. In many societies, it is accepted as a constant. Ironically, at a time when Congress was set to emasculate the Foreign Corrupt Practices Act because U.S. business firms contended it hurt them in foreign competition,[24] several U.S. companies have found themselves under investigation for foreign bribes. The Justice Department has launched an investigation into payments, reportedly around $55 million, by Northrop to a South Korean official. The money was allegedly tied to Northrop's attempts to sell F-20 fighter jets to the South Korean government.[25] Also, Coca-Cola is under investigation by an Atlanta grand jury for supposedly bribing Soviet officials in order to sell Cokes in the Soviet market.[26] The Goodyear Tire and Rubber Company has admitted paying $1 million in bribes to the Iraqi government to obtain tire contracts.[27]

Ashland Oil is a Kentucky-based oil company, with a total 1987 volume of sales of $6.9 billion.[28] It derives most of its supply of oil from foreign sources, particularly from the Middle East. The Securities and Exchange Commission charged that Ashland Oil violated the Foreign Corrupt Practices Act by paying out millions of dollars in bribes to foreign officials, to get scarce supplies of crude oil, and then tried to cover up the evidence. The company was accused of paying $17 million to an intermediary to bribe a government official in Abu

---

[24] The reporting provisions have been eased. See Foreign Corrupt Practices Amendments in the Omnibus Trade and Competitiveness Act of 1988, pp. 327–337.

[25] *U.S. News & World Report,* June 27, 1988, p. 46.

[26] The son-in-law of the late Soviet leader Leonid Breshnev has been accused of taking millions of dollars in bribes from government officials in Uzbek, a republic in the Soviet Union.

[27] "Former Executives of Ashland Oil Receive Damage Awards," *Roanoke Times,* September 8, 1988, p. C-5.

[28] *Fortune,* The Fortune 500, Vol. 117, No. 9, April 25, 1988, p. D-13.

Dhabi.[29] It was also accused of making payments of $25 million to three representatives of Oman and Saudi Arabia: Tim Landon, a representative of the government of Oman; Yehia Omar, also of Oman; and Hassan Y. Yassin of Saudi Arabia.

What makes this case of particular significance is that two former vice presidents of Ashland Oil contended that they had lost their jobs because they had refused to participate in the conspiracies to cover up the bribes. They provided information to the SEC enforcement staff investigating the bribery charges against the company. The two vice presidents, Bill McKay and Harry Williams, then sued Ashland Oil, claiming that they were wrongfully discharged. A U.S. District Court jury in Covington, Kentucky, awarded damages of $44.6 million to McKay and $24.9 million to Williams.[30] The damages are to be shared by the company and three officials: Orin Atkins, the former chairman and chief executive officer; John Hall, the current chairman and chief executive officer; and Richard Spears, senior vice president for human resources and law.

SUMMARY

U.S. antitrust laws cover much ground. Multinational companies seeking to expand through foreign mergers or acquisitions must be increasingly wary of possible antimerger enforcement. For example, if a U.S. company acquires abroad, or if a foreign company acquires a U.S. competitor, Section 7 of the Clayton Act may be applied. The scope of Section 7 is broad and has been extended to include acquisitions that eliminate potential competition in U.S. markets. Section 1 of the Sherman Act also has widened its application to multinationals. It declares illegal every contract, combination, or conspiracy in restraint of interstate or foreign commerce. The act has been expanded through judicial interpretation to cover parties and acts outside the confines of the United States, which has permitted domestic courts to exercise jurisdiction over foreign nationals and corporations and over U.S. corporations domiciled overseas. The Supreme Court has broadened the interpretation of the Sherman Act to include certain types of conduct that are regarded as illegal per se. Included are price-fixing agreements, agreements among competitors dividing

[29] Morton Mintz, "$17 Million in Fees Prompts Allegations of Kickbacks," *The Washington Post,* Sunday, July 10, 1988, p. H-5.

[30] The difference in the awards was based on the salaries of the two men. McKay made around $140,000 a year and Williams $82,000. Ashland Oil is appealing the decision.

geographic markets or classes of customers, tying agreements, concerted refusals to deal, and certain kinds of reciprocity agreements.

QUESTIONS FOR DISCUSSION

1. Discuss the international application of the Sherman Act in the American Tobacco Case of 1911.
2. What is the effects test? Discuss its application to the Timken Roller Bearing case.
3. What is meant by the concept of extraterritorial reach?
4. What is the significance of the Timberlane case?
5. What is the significance of *Reisner v. General Motors*?
6. How do foreign antitrust laws differ from those of the United States?
7. What is a *keiretsu*? Would it be permitted in the United States?
8. Discuss the objectives of the Foreign Corrupt Practices Act.

RECOMMENDED READINGS

Bureau of National Affairs. *U.S. Department of Justice Antitrust Guidelines for International Competition*. Antitrust and Trade Regulation Report, vol. 54, no. 1369. Washington, D.C.: U.S. Department of Justice, 1988.

Dunfee, Thomas W., and Frank F. Gibson. *Antitrust and Trade Regulation*. New York: Wiley, 1985.

Garson, John R. *Codes of Conduct for Multinational Corporations*. New York: Praeger, 1982.

Neal, A. D., and D. C. Goyder. *The Antitrust Laws of the United States*. 3rd ed. Cambridge, England: Cambridge University Press, 1982.

Rahl, James A. "American Antitrust Policy and Foreign Operations: What Is Covered?" *Cornell International Law Journal* 8 (December, 1974): 1–15.

Townsend, James B. *Extraterritorial Antitrust: The Sherman Act and U.S. Business Abroad*. Boulder, Colo.: Westview Press, 1982.

PART IV

SOCIAL REGULATION OF BUSINESS

The point was made in Part II that there have been three major cycles in the government's regulation of business. The first cycle occurred in the last century and involved the passage of antitrust laws to control monopolies and railroad laws to regulate anticompetitive railroad practices. This cycle continued into the early part of this century and culminated in the passage of additional antitrust laws (Clayton Act) and laws to regulate the sale of electric power. The second cycle came during the Depression of the 1930s and was mainly reformative, including reforms of the banking system and the securities market to prevent abuses that had contributed to the collapse of the stock market and the banking systems. The legal environment for the labor unions was thus greatly improved, and the unions then became a countervailing force to business. The third cycle of regulation began in the late 1960s and early 1970s and was social in nature. We are currently digesting this social regulation, which includes the protection of the environment, consumer protection, and the safety and health of the labor force.

Social regulation, unlike the traditional rate-setting regulation for public utilities, is not subject to the market forces and public opinion that can limit costs. The public reaction to rising utility rates, for example, has been an important constraint on public utility commissions. The disparity between intrastate and interstate airline tariffs, increased the pressure to deregulate the interstate airlines. Because the price of such regulation is visible, it invites a political response. Furthermore when prices are set above the cost of production, many customers will shop for alternative sources of supply. Thus a decision of the Interstate Commerce Commission to allow value-of-service pricing for interstate trucking and generally to permit interstate truck rates to exceed the cost of service led shippers to find other, unregulated forms of transportation. Similarly, improperly set toll rates induced large users of communications to establish their own microwave systems or to obtain them from non-Bell carriers.

The corrective forces of the market and public opinion do not exist in most areas of social regulation. A businessperson has no alternative but to comply with a mandatory standard if the regulatory agency has sufficient enforcement tools. The cost of health, safety, and environmental standards is not directly observable; therefore, the public cannot separate the mandatory costs from the other costs incurred in producing a pound of aluminum or a ton of paper. Social regulation often entails some aspect of human health or safety that can be used by a regulatory agency to incite strong emotional support for its actions, no matter how extreme or costly they may be. After all, who could be so callous as to be opposed to protecting workers from exposure to a cancer-producing agent? What all this means is that much social regulation cannot be subject to rational economic analysis, even though it is costly and inefficient. A peripheral example is the national Social Security program, which was in some danger of running out of funds. Revising it, as President Reagan attempted to do in order to make the fund more solvent, seemed tantamount to the defiling of holy places.

During the 1970s, the federal government extended its involvement in the market system, directing more and more of its effort toward cushioning individual risks and regulating personal and institutional conduct. The cumulative impact of its actions have strongly affected business. In some cases, this was necessary because business was not responsive to public demands for such measures as safer working conditions; in other cases, actions were taken because business became an easy target for the discontent of many special interest groups. There is a conflict between a political system that emphasizes public well-being and economic equality and a business system that adheres to a utilitarian goal of efficiency. Government social regulation proved quite costly, and people came to believe that somehow costs were never taken into consideration and little attention was paid to finding alternative ways of achieving the same social goals. The Carter administration did try to apply sunset measures to regulation of all types and to new procedures that would require federal agencies to show that their rules were beneficial to the economy and society as a whole. The Reagan administration appeared to increase those efforts.

Many regulatory changes were expected from the Reagan administration, particularly in those rules and regulations that do not help business. An unfettered business, like Prometheus unbound, is supposed to save the economy, solve all social problems, restore the virtue of hard work, and create a new "Golden Age." But earlier business in-difference and inaction contributed to many social problems that government then had to try to solve. As noted earlier, President Calvin Coolidge once said "The business of America is business," and many business firms still accept this as an article of faith. We still do not know how business will respond to such problems as protecting the environment and employing minorities without some form of coercion like the threat of losing government contracts. Also, as was evident in the Chrysler bailout, in restrictions on Japanese autos, and in import quotas to protect the steel industry, business is not at all hesitant to ask for government help when its own ox is being gored.

Chapter 10

Issues of Social Regulation

Broad based in its objective and enforcement, social regulation encompasses such areas as occupational health and safety, equal employment opportunity, consumer product safety, and environmental protection, areas that have specific social goals—a cleaner environment, safer consumer products, employment of minorities, and so forth. A number of important regulatory commissions, nearly all of which were created during the 1970s, function to enforce the laws designed to achieve these social goals. The most important commissions are the Consumer Product Safety Commission, the Occupational Safety and Health Administration, the Equal Employment Opportunity Commission, and the Environmental Protection Agency. The jurisdiction of each of these relative newcomers extends mostly to the private sector and at times to productive activities in the public sector. Each of these agencies and commissions has a rather narrow range of responsibility, however. For example, the Equal Employment Opportunity Commission is responsible only for employment policies in a given firm or industry. With deregulation, no agency has the complete responsibility it once had.

Social regulation has an enormous impact on business firms, both large and small. Not much more than a decade ago, most business firms were unregulated private enterprises. They were free to design and produce the products they pleased, subject only to consumer acceptance. Marketing practices were subject to management and control, and pricing policies were devised to yield a rate of return on capital based on a standard volume concept. Antitrust laws did not apply to these business firms except as a deterrent to engaging in certain practices. Public utility regulation ruled only public utilities, and about the most interference any business firm could expect from Washington was with respect to bookkeeping involving Social Security and payroll taxes. Business leaders, of course, complained about Washington, thinking even this amount of interference was excessive, but by and large they were free to manage with few constraints. A businessperson could even hire and promote an in-law if he or she saw fit.

But times have changed, and in instance after instance business firms, both large and small, have been made accountable to the public through legislative or court action, rather than through voluntary action. In great part, the fault was that of business in failing to recognize the changes in U.S. society or, more often, in recognizing the changes but not responding. Another reason was the rise of special interest groups that did not hesitate to alter the political decision-making process to achieve their own goals. The end result was that business firms have become subject to a wide variety of social regulations in a short time. By 1980, they were ruled by detailed government regulations under which almost all phases of their operation were affected. No longer do business firms have complete control over personnel practices; government affirmative action policies have to be considered. Marketing policies have to take into account the possibility of product recall. Today, each auto company now publicly recalls hundreds of thousands of automobiles if serious defects have to be corrected. In many companies, each division has a counterpart agency in Washington with which it must deal—personnel and the EEOC, production and OSHA.

REASONS FOR SOCIAL REGULATION

Justification for social regulation is based partly on the belief that imperfections in the market system are responsible for various social problems. In a market economy, the price mechanism gives people no opportunity to bid against the production and sale of certain commodities and services that they regard as undesirable. Many people would be happier if they could prevent the production and sale of, for instance, alcoholic beverages or the emission of noxious fumes from a chemical plant, and would gladly pay the price if given the opportunity to do so. But there seems to be no way the market price mechanism can take these negative preferences into account, except through government controls on the output of goods deemed deleterious to the public interest.

A second reason for the onset of social regulation is the externalities created by technological advances. Pollution is an externality because one person can impose a cost on another without having to pay compensation.[1] This other person then demands government protection in the form of regulation prohibiting

[1] Lester C. Thurow, *The Zero-Sum Society* (New York: Basic Books, 1980), p. 124.

or limiting the actions of the first person. As our society has become more technologically advanced and congested, one group's meat becomes another group's poison. Airports are necessary to facilitate rapid transportation, but airplane noise damages the environment of those who live near them. So these people coalesce into a group demanding noise abatement measures. Coal is an important, and often the cheapest, source of fuel in the United States, but externalities are involved in mining it—black lung disease for the miners plus the despoliation of the environment, particularly after strip mining. Competitive markets are no solution at all to these externalities: a competitive firm will generate as much, or more, smoke than a noncompetitive one does.[2]

A third reason is the preoccupation with the quality of life. Following World War II, the main concern of most Americans was getting a job and buying a car and a house. Memories of the Great Depression were still fresh, and so their requirements were few. But as money supply and real incomes rose, these basic wants were satisfied, and they turned their interest to the quality as opposed to the quantity of life. By the late 1960s, many people had achieved a level of real income at which they could afford to be concerned about such issues as a clean environment. What fun was it to go to the beach for a vacation if the beach was polluted? This concern about the quality of life extended into other areas as well. Unlike the consumers of the past, who were interested more in the quantity of production to fulfill basic needs, consumers now have come to expect goods and services of better quality and at lower prices; thus laws have been passed in such consumer areas as product warranty and product safety.

A fourth reason for social regulation was a general disenchantment with the U.S. system, resulting from the new social concerns that developed during the latter part of the 1960s. This disenchantment was manifested in several issues. Environmentalists and other groups accused business firms of neglecting their social responsibility to the poor and disadvantaged. Business was also the target of individual crusades, such as Ralph Nader's highly publicized efforts to spearhead improvements in such areas as automobile safety. The criticism of existing institutions, including business, permeated all sections of society. The discontent of the late 1960s did indeed facilitate the passage of social regulation: almost all the major social regulatory commissions, such as the EPA and OSHA, were created in the 1970s, and the principal environmental laws also were passed then. Important consumer laws were also enacted in the early and middle 1970s, the Consumer Product Safety Act of 1972 and the Consumer Product Warranty Act of 1975.

[2] Ibid., p. 125.

Entitlement was a fifth reason, reflecting the changes in social values. The increase in economic growth during the 1950s and 1960s created what Daniel Bell has called a "revolution of rising expectations."[3] In other words, anyone who wants to work should be entitled to a job, even under government auspices if necessary. Anyone who is sick is entitled to medical care, and anyone who wants an education should have it. But, more important, entitlement has come to be expressed on a group basis, particularly in the areas of civil rights and social rights. To put it simply, entitlement has come to mean some form of compensation for a particular group. Because society over time deprived particular groups of their rights, those groups are now entitled to higher incomes and equal representation at all levels of the decision-making process, and there are demands that these disadvantaged groups—blacks, women, and specified national minorities—be given quotas or preferential treatment in hiring. Only in that fashion, it is argued, can these historical injustices be redressed. Attention to merit is regarded with suspicion; proportional representation is more important.

To some extent, entitlement is linked to the egalitarian movement that has long been popular in the United States, particularly in the late 1960s. The concept of equality has meant different things throughout American history. The Jeffersonian concept of equality was more attuned to the relationships among a particular group of people, namely, property owners. In other words, there was an equality of the elect. The Jacksonian idea of equality was somewhat simpler. In essence, it was that any person was just as good as the next one, that no one should put on airs, for that would be emulating the effete aristocracy in England. In fact, spitting on the floor was probably as good a way as any to demonstrate one's democratic and egalitarian instincts. On the positive side, this kind of equality came to mean the opportunity to get ahead regardless of one's origins. The egalitarianism of the late 1960s also was antielitist; in fact, elitism became a pejorative term for any social philosophy opposed to the notion that rigorous egalitarianism was a democratic imperative. Equality was defined in terms of equity; hence the emphasis on equality of result.

THE ADMINISTRATIVE AGENCIES

Almost every type of U.S. business enterprise falls within at least the indirect influence of a number of administrative agencies. It is important to study these

[3] Daniel Bell, *The Cultural Contradictions of Capitalism* (New York: Basic Books, 1976) p. 275.

agencies and their functions, though first some general points should be made. Administrative agencies, regardless of responsibility, acquire their authority to act from the legislative branch of government. Because they do most of the day-to-day work of government, they make many significant policy decisions. Administrative agencies can be divided into two categories: independent regulatory commissions and agencies that are part of the executive branch of government. In many areas of domestic policy formulation, independent agencies exercise more control, although different economic and political needs have produced administrative agencies exercising vast legislative and adjudicative powers that cannot be classified as independent regulatory agencies. Many executive agencies perform regulatory functions as part of their broader responsibility. Administrative functions can be divided into legislative, judicial, and executive categories and are performed by all types of agencies, although the agencies themselves may differ in the reasons for their creation, principal goals, and organizational structures.

Most regulatory agencies that function within the executive departments possess both quasi-legislative and quasi-judicial powers, just as the independent regulatory commissions do. The power to make rules and regulations has been delegated to these agencies by legislative fiat. The only important difference between an agency rule and a law enacted by a legislative body is that the rule may be slightly more susceptible to attack because it was not made by elected officials. Administrative agencies can also implement policy or legislation through a process of initiating and settling specific cases. They also engage in administrative adjudication, which includes procedures used in deciding cases. For many types of cases, the procedures are carefully outlined: hearings are frequently prescribed, records are required, and so on. Furthermore, there often are elaborate provisions for judicial review, which suggests that if the agencies overstep the boundaries of legitimate authority, redress can always be secured in the courts. However, the scope of the judicial review of particular administrative agency decisions is limited, the logic being that the agency rather than the court is supposed to be the expert in the field in which it has been empowered to act.

Administrative agencies, as agents of Congress, reflect group demands for positive action. They are not supposed to be arbiters like the courts; rather, they should be activists and initiate policy in accordance with their policy interests. For example, when the Federal Trade Commission (FTC) ferrets out deceptive business practices, either through its own investigation or through information gained from an outside source, it initiates action in the name of the FTC against the party involved. It then adjudicates the very case it initiates. If the case reaches a formal hearing and goes to a hearing examiner for an initial decision, it is not at that point subject to commission control. But after the examiner renders the decision, the commission may reverse it. The result is that the FTC can control the decisions rendered in almost all the cases it initiates; however, "recourse to appeals" in courts of law is not barred.

Sanctions

Government intervention in business carries with it the threat and the actual application of sanctions to achieve desired economic and social outcomes. When industry survival, industrial externalities such as pollution, or both, are of concern, sanctions may often be positive, taking the form of subsidies, tariffs, and tax incentives. When the target is the undesirable behavior of firms or groups of firms within an industry, negative sanctions are often used to induce compliance. These negative sanctions can designate noncompliance either as a criminal offense requiring the imposition of fines, imprisonment, or both, or as a civil offense involving the deprivation of the right or privilege to engage in economic transaction through the loss of licenses, permits, and franchises. For example, the Clean Air Act of 1970, which is administered by the Environmental Protection Agency, subjects willful polluters to fines of up to $50,000 a day and jail sentences of up to two years. Plants can be shut down and permits to operate canceled if pollution continues. Citizens and interest groups have the right to sue in federal court to force polluters, including the federal government, to cease and desist pollution practices.

In applying negative sanctions, the intent is to use the coercive powers of the state to obtain compliance. This is done by announcing to society or its components, including business, that various actions are not to be carried out and to ensure that fewer of them are. Business firms have no choice other than to comply with a mandatory standard if the regulatory agency has sufficient enforcement tools. In addition, the regulatory agencies are expected to amass facts, to apply the law to these facts, and to impose the appropriate sanctions when noncompliance is found. Thus, the intent and process of regulation is more like adjudication than other types of political action. It can be said that violators of economic regulation differ from violators of criminal law only in the degree of responsibility for societal harm that is attributed to them by policymakers, regulators, and the community as a whole. Firm owners and managers are generally held responsible only for their actions, which are often technical and morally neutral.

The Major Social Regulatory Agencies

The following social regulatory agencies stand in the forefront: the Consumer Product Safety Commission (CPSC), the Environmental Protection Agency (EPA), the Equal Employment Opportunity Commission (EEOC), and the Occupational Safety and Health Administration (OSHA). These and several others of the alphabet-soup variety, in particular the Federal Trade Commission (FTC), are authorized to make rules that have the force of law; in other words, they have quasi-legislative powers. They also possess quasi-judicial power in that they settle disputes and hear and decide on violations of statutes of their own rules. Finally, much of the work of these agencies is administrative, including investigating firms in a particular industry, determining if formal action should be taken, and negotiating settlements.

The Consumer Product Safety Commission (CPSC)

The Consumer Product Safety Act of 1972 created the five-member CPSC, which functions as an independent regulatory commission. The commission is regarded by its critics as the most powerful regulatory agency in Washington.[4] It has jurisdiction over more than ten thousand consumer products and has the power to inspect facilities where consumer goods are manufactured, stored, or transported. The commission can also require all manufacturers, private labelers, and distributors to establish and maintain books and records and to make available additional information as it deems necessary. It can require the use of specific labels that set forth the results of product testing. The greatest impact that this requirement has is in the production process, in which the design of numerous products must conform to federal standards. Since safety standards are formulated at various governmental and independent testing stations, a manufacturer may find that a finished product no longer meets federal standards, and product lines may have to be altered drastically.

The Environmental Protection Agency (EPA)

In July 1970, President Richard Nixon submitted to Congress a reorganization plan to create an independent environmental protection agency. The organization was approved, and the EPA was created in the executive branch.

---

[4] U.S., Congress, Joint Economic Committee, *Hearings on the 1979 Economic Report of the President,* 96th Cong., 1st sess., 1979, p. 32.

Functions that formerly belonged to the Department of the Interior relating to studies on the effects of insecticides and pesticides in the United States were transferred to this agency. Also transferred were functions originally belonging to the Department of Health, Education and Welfare (now the Department of Health and Human Services), including the creation of tolerance norms for pesticide chemicals under the Food, Drug, and Cosmetics Act. The EPA was given supervision over air pollution standards as set forth in the Clean Air Act of 1970 and its subsequent amendments. The EPA also was given jurisdiction over water pollution control programs, particularly those set forth in the Water Pollution Control Act of 1972, including the setting of water quality standards. The jurisdiction of the EPA was later extended to apply to the Noise Control Act of 1972, and it became responsible for setting noise emission standards for products identified as major sources of noise. The EPA has jurisdiction over all the major federal environmental laws passed during the last decade.

The Equal Employment Opportunity Commission (EEOC)

The EEOC was created by the Civil Rights Act of 1964 as an independent commission, and its enforcement authority was greatly increased by the Equal Employment Opportunity Act of 1972. The EEOC now has the power to investigate and act on a charge of a pattern or practice of discrimination, whether filed by or on behalf of the person or group claiming to be aggrieved or by a member of the commission. The EEOC has the right to initiate civil suits against employers, labor unions, and any group accused of practicing employment discrimination. What is more, private individuals and groups have the right to sue under Title VII of the Civil Rights Act of 1964. The EEOC also can investigate company records to see whether a pattern of discrimination exists and to subpoena company records if necessary. Every employer, labor union, and organization subject to the Civil Rights Act and subsequent executive orders must keep records that can determine whether unlawful practices have been committed, and they must furnish to the EEOC a detailed description of how people are selected to participate in job-training programs.

The Federal Trade Commission (FTC)

Few regulatory agencies have had more effect on business than the FTC has. It was created by the Federal Trade Commission Act of 1914 with the intent of preventing unfair business methods of competition. It was given the power to prevent people or corporations, except banks and common carriers subject to the various acts that regulate interstate commerce, from using unfair methods of competition in commerce. It was also given the power to investigate the practices of business combinations and to conduct hearings. The FTC was authorized to issue cease-and-desist orders and to apply to a circuit court of appeals to enforce them. A violation is punishable by contempt of court. In addition to cease-and-desist orders, the commission was given the power to negotiate terms of agreement, known as *consent decrees,* violations of which are cause for court action. The commission was also given joint responsibility with the Justice Department for enforcing certain prohibitions that pertain to various forms of price discrimination.[5]

The FTC has come to be an all-purpose agency. It administers not only the antitrust laws of the United States but a wide variety of other laws as well. The Wheeler–Lea Act of 1938 authorizes the FTC to protect the public by preventing the dissemination of false or misleading food and drug advertisements. Also under the FTC's jurisdiction are various labeling acts such as the Wool Products Labeling Act and the Fur Products Labeling Act. The McCarran Insurance Act of 1948 gives the commission partial jurisdiction over the insurance industry. This responsibility is complex because it varies according to the differences in state law. Then there is the Consumer Credit Protection Act of 1968 or, as it is more commonly called, the Truth-in-Lending Act, which requires that borrowers be made aware of basic information about the cost and terms of credit. Finally, the Consumer Product Warranty Act of 1975 provides minimum disclosure standards for written consumer product warranties and defines federal content standards for these warranties. The act also extended the FTC's consumer protection powers to cover local consumer abuses when state or local protection programs are inadequate.

The Occupational Safety and Health Administration (OSHA)

OSHA was created as an agency of the Department of Labor to administer the Occupational Safety and Health Act of 1970. The purpose of the act is "to assure safe and healthful working conditions for working men and women."[6] It

---

[5] The FTC has jurisdiction over Section 2 of the Clayton Act, which covers primary-line price discrimination, and over the Robinson–Patman Act, which amended Section 2 to prohibit secondary-line price discrimination. This term refers to the sale of the same good to different buyers in the same geographic area at different prices when there is no cost difference.

[6] Robert Stewart Smith, *Occupational Safety and Health Act* (Washington, D.C.: American Enterprise Institute for Public Policy Research, 1976).

requires employers to comply with safety and health standards promulgated by OSHA. In addition, every employer is required to furnish for each of his or her employees a job "free from recognized hazards that are causing or are likely to cause death or serious physical harm."[7] Although this "general duty" clause might appear to be an all-encompassing requirement for the provision of safety, it was clearly Congress's intent that the clause be limited in scope and relied on infrequently. "Recognized hazards" were defined in the congressional debate as those that can be detected by the common human senses, unaided by testing devices, and that are generally known in the industry as hazards.[8] Further, a firm can be penalized under the general duty clause only if the unsafe condition has been cited by an inspector and the employer has refused to correct it in the specified time.

Other Social Regulatory Agencies

Several other federal government agencies also have responsibility for social regulation. One is the Food and Drug Administration (FDA), which was created in 1906. It is responsible for the safety, effectiveness, and labeling of drugs, foods, food additives, cosmetics, and medical devices. The National Highway Traffic Safety Administration (NHTSA) was created in 1970. It is responsible for establishing safety standards for trucks and automobiles and certifies compliance with emission standards for pollution control.[9] The Mine Safety and Health Administration (MSHA) was created in 1973 and is responsible for setting and enforcing mining health and safety standards. A number of government agencies also enforce rules that may have an indirect effect on social regulation. An example is the meat and poultry inspection programs of the U.S. Department of Agriculture (USDA).

It is also important to realize that state and local governments have their counterparts of the federal regulatory agencies. For example, federal laws pertaining to employment practices are not the only laws that affect business; state and local government laws also exist. The degree of state and local laws varies; some state and local governments provide agencies to enforce the laws,

[7] Occupational Safety and Health Act, Section 5a.

[8] U.S., Congress, Senate, Committee on Labor and Public Welfare, *Legislative History of the Occupational Safety and Health Act of 1970,* 92nd Cong., 1st sess., 1971.

[9] There is also the National Transportation Safety Board (NTSB), which sets rules on needed improvements in transportation safety.

whereas others have voluntary enforcement. State and local governments also have environmental regulations. The first consumer protection laws were passed by state and local governments long before consumer protection laws were introduced by the federal government.[10] Regulations governing occupational safety and health and the sale of food and drug products are also among state and local laws.[11]

THE IMPACT OF SOCIAL REGULATION

There is more to social regulation than the creation of a number of new federal government agencies. The laws creating these agencies also defined ambitious health, safety, and equity goals and in some cases established strict deadlines for attaining them nationally. Frequently, the laws restricted agency discretion to moderate regulatory standards in view of economic or other social considerations. They empowered citizen complainants and advocacy groups to sue business firms for damages and government agency officials for failure to promulgate strict rules of enforcement. Business firms were required to undertake extensive recording and reporting of their compliance efforts and of the social and environmental consequences of their operations. Local governments and school districts that failed to meet federally prescribed regulatory requirements concerning affirmative action and other goals were threatened with debarment from federal grants-in-aid and contracts.

Social regulation affects society in three ways. First, income is redistributed; resources are transferred from one income group to another. Second, there are compliance costs, which include the costs of filling out a number of required government reports, adding facilities for handicapped workers, buying equipment to make the environment cleaner, training for minority workers, and making the workplace safer. Finally, social regulation influences business organization. Management must be responsible for the internal monitoring of company operations, including the hiring and promotion of personnel, product evaluation, and other areas. It is also subject to liabilities and restrictions; for example, management has to be responsible for product safety.

[10] State laws date back to before the Civil War.

[11] State and local laws also cover the sale of alcoholic beverages to minors.

Income Redistribution Effects

Environmental protection offers one example of how social regulation results in the redistribution of income. Although most Americans favor a clean environment, the issue itself has been primarily the preserve of the upper-middle classes.[12] Lower-income groups do not rank a clean environment high on their list of priorities because it often threatens their income-earning opportunities, the loss of jobs if plants close. For the lower-income groups, basic needs have to be satisfied; the quality of life does not become important until real incomes rise. For Americans who can afford boats, summer homes, and leisure time at the beaches, a clean environment ranks as a desideratum; for Americans who cannot afford these things, a clean environment is less important.

However, income redistribution is not a one-way street. Equal employment and affirmative action requirements have helped to raise the incomes of low-income groups such as women and minorities. Before equal employment opportunity and affirmative action, women and minority members were systematically shut out of the higher-paying jobs. Few women and minority members attended law or medical schools, and few were employed in such male-dominated occupations as accounting and engineering. Success in the business world was almost exclusively reserved for white men. Social regulation has helped women and minority members increase their incomes by increasing their opportunity to obtain higher-paying jobs. This has had a beneficial effect on the U.S. economy because it has broadened job opportunities, increased productivity, and made the workplace more democratic.

Costs to Business

Social regulation of business involves direct monetary costs. One cost involves the paperwork required for compliance with federal and state rules and regulations. Paperwork adds to the cost of doing business. Another cost is the cost of installing new machinery and equipment. Emission control devices to control pollution, such as smokestack screens and scrubbers, are expensive to install. New hiring and training facilities for handicapped workers have to be provided by the employer. Recruitment of women and minority members is also a business cost. Then there are government administrative costs in social

---

[12] Thurow, *The Zero-Sum Society,* pp. 104–105.

regulation that are paid out of taxes. These costs have increased over the years.[13]

Opportunity costs also have to be considered in measuring the cost of social regulation to business. Since resources are scarce, the decision to use them means that something else must be given up. When resources are used in a certain way, there is a simultaneous choice not to use them another way. The opportunity cost then can be defined as the value of the benefit lost as a result of choosing one alternative over another. It is an important concept because the real cost of any activity is measured by its opportunity cost, not by its outlay cost. Thus, if resources are used to control pollution, society gives up all the other goods and services that might have been obtained from these resources; for example, resources devoted to the production of pollution control equipment might have been used to produce houses instead.

However, there are air and water, less noise, safer products, safer working conditions, and better employment opportunities for women and minority members. New jobs are also created as a result of social regulation. For example, manufacturing companies make pollution control equipment that has to be installed by other companies that are polluters. Few, save the most die-hard free marketers, could argue for the complete elimination of all forms of social regulation and a return to the old status quo. It also might be added that business firms brought most of the social regulation laws on themselves, by maintaining a stance of aloofness that inhibited cooperation with government on social problems.

Impact of Social Regulation on Business Organization

The former chairman of the Council of Economic Advisers, Murray Weidenbaum, identified a "second managerial revolution."[14] The first was noted by Adolphe Berle and Gardiner Means more than four decades ago.[15] These observers of the U.S. corporate scene were referring to the divorce of the modern corporation's formal ownership from its actual management, which occurred

---

[13] For example, total U.S. Budget outlays for the Environmental Protection Agency amounted to $5.1 billion in 1989 compared to $700 million in 1977.

[14] Murray L. Weidenbaum, *Government Mandated Price Increases* (Washington, D.C.: American Enterprise Institute, 1975), p. 82.

[15] Adolphe A. Berle and Gardiner C. Means. *The Modern Corporation and Private Property*, rev. ed. (New York: Harcourt Brace Jovanovich, 1968).

when the corporate form of management superseded the Carnegies, Fords, and Rockefellers of the world and became the dominant business unit by the end of the last century. In the corporate system, the owner of industrial wealth was left with only a symbol of ownership, and the power, responsibility, and substance that had been an integral part of ownership were transferred to a separate management group. In other words, Standard Oil was no longer both owned and operated by the Rockefellers; rather, it was operated by a managerial class, completing the separation of ownership from management.

The second managerial revolution, according to Weidenbaum, came when the decision-making process shifted to Washington. This shift was particularly pronounced in the early 1970s when the federal government took on the unprecedented tasks of coordination and setting priorities. A vast cadre of government regulators can influence and often control the key decisions of the managers of business firms. For example, management has had to accept responsibility for the internal monitoring of company operations, including the hiring and promotion of personnel, personnel safety, product evaluation and safety, and so forth. Government regulation has changed the process of production, one reason being that an increased share of investment became unproductive. Distribution has had to be geared to the possibility of product recalls, and labeling and advertising have had to be reconsidered. Affirmative action has had an impact on employment policies that call for special recruitment, training, and facilities for the benefit of women, minority members, and the handicapped.

Cost-Benefit Analysis

Interest has risen in efforts to determine more precisely the costs and the benefits of government regulation. The motive for incorporating cost-benefit analysis into the regulatory decision-making process is to achieve a more efficient allocation of government resources. In making an investment decision, for example, business executives compare the costs to be incurred with the expected benefits, namely, revenues. Very likely the investment will be pursued only if the expected costs are less than the expected revenues. If an investment will yield $20 and the cost of the investment is $10, the benefits obtained will be $10. Cost-benefit analysis can also be applied to opportunity costs. For example, suppose a business firm has $10 that it wishes to spend on some benefits. Its rational response would be to examine a number of possible uses of the money and ask which of them would yield the greatest net benefit.

Government agencies do not face the same array of benefits and costs. If the cost of an agency action exceeds the benefits, the result may not have an immediate adverse effect on the agency. Because analytical information on economic costs has rarely existed in the public sector, decision makers have largely been unaware of approving a cost-inefficient regulation. An objective of requiring government agencies to perform cost-benefit analyses is to make the regulatory process more efficient and to eliminate actions that, on balance, generate more costs than benefits. This result is not assured by cost-benefit analyses, since political and social considerations often dominate the decision-making process; however, even in those cases cost-benefit analyses can provide valuable assistance.

Cost-benefit analyses must be put in a proper perspective. They are only one tool that can be used to reach a decision concerning a socially desirable action. Critics of cost-benefit analyses contend that, even though costs may outweigh benefits, a project may still be socially desirable. Helping the poor and disadvantaged is an example. The effects of regulatory decisions are distributed unevenly, which inevitably involves the imposition of values and ideology. Nevertheless, with cost-benefit analyses, the question of how much additional cost should be incurred to achieve a specific goal can be more precisely answered.

REFORMING GOVERNMENT REGULATION

Discontent with government social regulation of business developed in the late 1970s and early 1980s. There were several reasons for this discontent. One was the cost of social regulation. A study prepared for Congress's Joint Economic Committee estimated that in the fiscal year 1979 the cost to the public of federal regulations was $102.7 billion—$4.8 billion for the administrative costs of the regulatory agencies and $97.9 billion for the compliance costs by the private sector of the U.S. economy.[16] Another study, done by Paul Sommers of Yale University, determined the annual cost of regulation in 1977 was between $58 billion and $73 billion.[17] He also estimated regulatory costs for eleven sectors of the economy, which were grouped into three categories—

[16] U.S. Congress, Joint Economic Committee, Subcommittee on Economic Growth and Stabilization, *The Cost of Government Regulation of Business,* 95th Cong., 2nd sess., 1978.

[17] Paul Sommers, "The Economic Costs of Regulation: Report for the American Bar Association" (New Haven, Conn.: Department of Economics, Yale University, 1978).

economic, environmental, and health, safety, and product quality. By far the largest cost to society, set at between $30 billion and $45 billion, came from the regulation of health, safety, and product quality.

Another source of discontent with regulation was less tangible than costs. Many people disliked the government's specifying for them the means of achieving protective objectives and requiring constant assurances, in reports and other forms of paperwork, that compliance was taking place. Alienation also occurred when government officials appeared to be overbearing and high-handed. Public discussion of regulation was dominated by horror stories about antagonistic regulatory officials who were out to get business. For example, the Consumer Product Safety Commission did not exactly help its image with business when its chairman was quoted as saying, "If a company violates our statutes, we will not concern ourselves with its middle-level executives; we will put the chief executive in jail. Once we put a top executive behind bars, I am sure that we will get a higher degree of cooperation."[18]

Regulatory Reform Under President Reagan

In 1980 Ronald Reagan promised to get the government off peoples' backs. In this he had widespread support from business and from the public as a whole. Many felt that the regulatory pendulum had swung too far and had reached a point of diminishing returns. It had to be pushed back, and Reagan promised to do that if he were elected. But President Jimmy Carter also implemented regulatory reforms during his presidency and promised to do more.[19] The unanimity with which both candidates attacked overregulation signaled an important change in public philosophy away from what was considered too much regulation for the public good.[20]

---

[18] Gerald R. Rosen, "We're Going for Companies' Throats," *Dun's Review* (January 1973), p. 36.

[19] Regulatory reform had begun when Carter was president. Executive Order 12044 contained requirements for economic impact analysis and set criteria for identifying significant regulations that necessitated regulatory analyses.

[20] Regulation is used in a broader sense. During the Carter administration, airline, trucking, and railroad industries were deregulated.

Executive Order 12291

Regulatory reform was a key element of President Reagan's economic recovery program of the early 1980s, along with government expenditure restraints, tax cuts, and monetary stability. Executive Order 12291, issued on February 17, 1981, directed government agencies to use cost-benefit analysis when promulgating new regulations, reviewing existing regulations, or developing legislative proposals concerning regulation. Administrative decisions on regulations were to be based on adequate information about their need and their economic consequences. Not only did the benefit from regulation have to exceed the cost, but the approach chosen had to maximize net benefits. Regarding major regulation, government agencies were required to publish Regulatory Impact Analyses (RIAs) that set forth conclusions about the cost-benefit balance of feasible alternatives.[21] RIAs had to include a description of the potential costs and benefits of the proposed regulation, as well as a description of feasible cheaper alternatives with an explanation of the legal reasons why such alternatives, if proposed, could not be adopted.

Task Force on Regulatory Relief

President Reagan also created the Task Force on Regulatory Relief, whose responsibility was to review proposed regulations, using the guidelines established by Executive Order 12291. During 1981, the task force earmarked 100 existing rules and paperwork requirements for review, and more than a third of those reviews resulted in action to eliminate or revise the rules and programs involved.[22] Executive Order 12291 also created a new Office of Information and Regulatory Affairs (OIRA) in the Office of Management and Budget (OMB). In effect, OIRA was to become the gate through which all important regulations had to twice pass on their way to becoming law. It must receive all RIAs at least sixty days before an agency's publication of a Notice of Proposed Rule Making (NPRM) and, if unhappy with an agency's draft, it can delay publication of that notice until the agency has responded to its concerns.

---

[21] Majority rules and regulations consisted of those that had any of the three following effects: an annual effect of $100 million or more; a major increase in costs or prices; or a significant adverse effect on a specific industry or on the economy in general.

[22] *Economic Report of the President,* Washington, D.C.: U.S. Government Printing Office, February, 1982, p. 142.

Evaluation of President Reagan's Regulatory Policies

Reactions to the accomplishments of the Reagan administration in reducing regulation—in particular, social regulation—were mixed. During his administration, the airline industry was deregulated. The results, at least so far, have provided some benefit to the American public, although there are critics who advocate enforcement of the antitrust laws. There also was considerable deregulation of financial markets, with commercial banks and savings and loan banks being given considerable latitude in terms of loans and expansion of services. However, there has been an increase in the rate of failure of savings and loan banks.[23] Reagan was subject to the criticism that he did not do enough to enforce environmental protection laws. As for affirmative action, the administration took the side of the defendant in affirmative action cases, holding the position that quotas in any form are wrong.

Although the U.S. public has said it wants government off of its back, it is ambivalent about what it does want from government. Opinion polls continue to show a high level of support for various forms of regulation. An overwhelming majority of Americans support cleaning up the environment even though the end result is a lower rate of economic growth. In a technologically dynamic society, new chemical hazards and new varieties of social injustice will inevitably emerge from time to time. Catastrophic environmental accidents, such as the ones at Bhopal, Chernobyl, and Alaska, fill the evening news and remind people of the need to protect the environment in which they live. Environmentalists and consumer protection groups watch government agencies for signs of ineffectiveness or flagging regulatory zeal, and business firms have generally accepted affirmative action and opposed attempts to modify it.

The Future Course of Regulation

With the Bush administration more regulation of the environment is probable. The summer of 1988 was a summer of discontent. A global heat wave caused scientists to debate whether the greenhouse effect, caused by accumulation of hydrocarbons, had already begun. At U.S. beaches, waste materials replaced seashells and eliminated the summer joy of swimming for many persons. The wholesale destruction of forests in northern India and Nepal caused massive damage from flooding when a monsoon hit Bangladesh, the world's poorest

---

[23] Many failing savings and loan banks are in Texas and Oklahoma, where economies have been affected by declining oil prices.

country.[24] Sturgeon were affected by toxic wastes in the Soviet Union. Earth and its atmosphere are drowning in manmade wastes, a situation that has become so critical it may soon make other issues seem trivial by comparison. The new environmental problems are very complex because they are caused by substances that are necessary to fuel the economies of industrial nations and feed the people of poor countries.

There is also the possibility of new forms of regulation in other social areas. The Civil Rights Restoration Act was passed in 1988, which increased the power of the federal government to enforce antidiscrimination laws. Comparable worth, which involves equal payment to men and women not doing the same jobs, but different jobs to which similar worth is attached, can become an important employment issue. In the area of consumer protection, product liability has assumed increased importance, particularly as applied to the tobacco industry. Increased enforcement of consumer safety laws can also be expected in the future. The pendulum has swung back to increased enforcement of government social regulation of business, in part because the image of business has suffered from such things as stock market scandals.

SUMMARY

Social regulation came into being because society's first line of defense—the market mechanism—had not been effective in eliminating certain social problems. The market mechanism did not prevent air and water pollution, high death rates in highway accidents, unsafe or shoddy consumer products, or the improvement of the economic lot of minority members and women. During the late 1960s and early 1970s, social regulation expanded rapidly. A number of major regulatory laws were passed by Congress, each imposing some kind of limitation on business. Several new federal regulatory agencies were created, including the Consumer Product Safety Commission, the Environmental Protection Agency, and the Occupational Safety and Health Administration. These agencies have the right to regulate certain business activities. This regulation creates compliance costs for business, such as the cost of paperwork and the cost of installing pollution control machinery. The direct costs of running the regulatory agencies are paid out of taxes or from government borrowing.

[24] The Ganges and Brahmaputra rivers, which flow through Bangladesh, originate in northern India and Nepal. Deforestation caused by overpopulation causes soil erosion and a rapid runoff of monsoon rain.

QUESTIONS FOR DISCUSSION

1. Discuss the reasons for social regulation of business.
2. How does social regulation differ from economic regulation?
3. What is opportunity cost?
4. What do *entitlement* and *egalitarianism* mean?
5. Discuss the two types of administrative agencies.
6. Discuss how sanctions can be used to control business activities.
7. What is cost-benefit analysis?
8. What impact does social regulation have on business organization?
9. How do federal regulatory activities affect the U.S. economy?
10. Discuss some of the regulatory reforms established by the Reagan administration.

RECOMMENDED READINGS

Bardach, Eugene, and Robert A. Kagan. *Social Regulation: Strategies for Reform.* San Francisco, Calif.: Institute for Contemporary Studies, 1982.

Breyer, Stephen. *Regulation and Its Reform.* Cambridge, Mass.: Harvard University Press, 1982.

Cegier, Allan J., and Burdelt A. Loomes. *Interest Group Politics.* 2nd ed. Washington, D.C.: Congressional Quarterly Press, 1986.

Clymer, Adam. "How Americans Rate Big Business." *New York Times Magazine,* June 8, 1986.

Jackson, Stewart, and Harris Collingwood. "Business Week/Harris Poll: Is an Antibusiness Backlash Building?" *Business Week,* July 20, 1987.

Kelmen, Steven. "Cost-Benefit Analysis: An Ethical Critique." *Regulation,* January-February 1981.

Noll, Roger G., and Bruce M. Owen. *The Political Economy of Deregulation: Interest Groups in the Regulatory Process.* Washington, D.C.: American Enterprise Institute, 1987.

Reichley, James. "Post-Reagan Politics." *The Brooking Review,* vol. 5, no. 1 (Winter 1987). Washington D.C.: The Brookings Institution, 1987.

Reichley, James. "Post-Reagan Politics." *The Brooking Review,* vol. 5, no. 1 (Winter 1987). Washington D.C.: The Brookings Institution, 1987.

Stone, Alan. *Regulation and Its Alternatives.* Washington, D.C.: Congressional Quarterly Press, 1983.

Zeckhauser, Richard J., and Derek Leebaert, eds. *What Role for Government?: Lessons from Policy Research.* Durham, N.C.: Duke University Press, 1983.

Chapter 11

Equal Employment Opportunity Policies and Their Impact on Business

As mentioned earlier, the newer type of government control differs from the older, more formal type of government regulation of business. It is directed more toward achieving the various social goals of particular interest groups. More important to business is that these controls cut across virtually every kind of private industry. Thus, the Environmental Protection Agency or the Consumer Product Safety Commission has a much broader area to regulate than did the Civil Aeronautics Board, which governed only one industry. The impact of these newer agencies is extensive. Environmental controls apply to all companies, as do requirements for consumer product safety. Moreover, these and other agencies have attempted to bring about social change through the government procurement process—leverage that few business firms can resist.

A third area of the government's social control of business is affirmative action, the federal Equal Employment Opportunity Commission's term for hiring and promoting women and nonwhites. Because business firms are required to meet affirmative action goals, the federal government has intervened in their personnel practices. The purpose of affirmative action is to ensure equal employment opportunities for all people, regardless of race, sex, religion, or national origin. To put it another way, sex, color, and age cannot be used as criteria to deny hiring or promotion. Noncompliance by employers with affirmative action goals can lead to severe penalties; for example, American Telephone and Telegraph had to pay $75 million in 1973 to employees who charged that discrimination had deprived them of past promotions and raises.

To a considerable degree, affirmative action policies are linked to what can be called increased social entitlements. It used to be that economic growth brought rising expectations, which meant simply the desire for higher material living standards. But modern society has come to believe that each person is entitled to at least a minimum and decent standard of living, including the right to a job, protection against the various vicissitudes of life—unemployment, sickness, accidents, and old age—and the right to certain social amenities, such as decent housing. This revolution of rising entitlement has also spread to the areas of civil rights, political rights, and social rights. Disadvantaged groups—blacks, women, and others—demand preferential treatment, arguing that only in this way can historical injustices be redressed. Equality of opportunity is no longer sufficient in itself; equality of representation is the desired goal.

DISCRIMINATION AND THE DISTRIBUTION OF INCOME

The rationale for government intervention in employment policy and education is that equal opportunity is a desideratum of the American democratic system—everyone should have the same opportunity to achieve material success, the usual goal. When opportunity is equal, competition and market forces determine one's worth in the marketplace. The idea behind equality of opportunity is that if everyone is given the same, or substantially the same, starting position in a race, the winners will have achieved their rewards through merit rather than through any favored position. Reward will be based on merit, and the result will be a society formed as a meritocracy.[1] Logically, if everyone is given the same opportunity and there is no discrimination based on sex, age, or other factors, the rewards should be distributed fairly uniformly, without much difference between sexes or among races.

Equality of opportunity has worked better in theory than in practice, however, though the United States has probably done a better overall job of encouraging this equality, particularly by offering mass education, than has any other country. The problem is that a number of impediments hinder achieving true equality of opportunity. Clearly, discrimination—on the basis of sex, color, religion, or any criterion outside professional qualifications—prevents any genuine equality of opportunity. And equality of opportunity is only part of the picture, for opportunity is linked to the distribution of income. In part, income inequality is based on differences in people's abilities; sometimes, however, it is based on sex, race, and age, which have little or no relation to

---

[1] Daniel Bell, "On Meritocracy and Equality," *The Public Interest* 29 (Fall, 1972) pp. 18–21.

ability. First, therefore, it is necessary to discuss the distribution of income in the United States.

Trends in Income Distribution

Recent decades have witnessed no real movement toward greater equality in the distribution of income in the United States. Apparently there is a conflict between the goals of an egalitarian society and the existence of marked income inequality. However, a market economy is bound to have inequality because income distribution is based on institutional arrangements, such as the pricing process, that are associated with this type of system. High prices are set on scarce agents of production and low prices on plentiful agents. In terms of rewards to labor, people whose skills are scarce relative to demand enjoy a high level of income, whereas those whose skills are not scarce do not. In a market economy, people are supposedly rewarded on the basis of their contribution to marketable output, which, in turn, reflects consumer preferences and income.

Table 11-1 presents income distribution in the United States for a period of forty years. The frame of reference is personal income, which includes that part of national income actually received by people or households and income transfers from government and business. Wages and salaries, income from rental properties, interest, and dividends are part of personal income. The table indicates that little change has occurred in the distribution of family income based on quintiles. The lowest fifth of family income recipients received around 5 percent of total personal income during the period, and the highest fifth received around 42 percent.[2] There was also little movement of the in-between groups. For those families in the second quintile, there was a slight decrease in personal income; for those families in the fourth quintile, some increase.

Table 11-2 presents the share of aggregate income of families and unrelated individuals by race for 1987. As the table indicates, greater inequality marks the distribution of income for blacks and other minorities than for whites. In 1987 the poorest fifth of white families received 5.1 percent of aggregate family income compared to 3.2 percent for blacks and other minorities.

---

[2] For perfect equality in income distribution to exist, each quintile would receive exactly 20 percent of personal income. (Perfect income inequality would exist if the highest quintile got 100 percent of personal income.)

TABLE 11-1   Distribution of Family Income in the United States, 1947–1987 (percent)

	1947	1960	1971	1979	1983	1987
Lowest quintile	5.0	4.9	5.5	5.3	4.7	4.6
Second quintile	11.9	12.0	11.9	11.7	11.2	10.1
Third quintile	17.0	17.5	17.3	17.2	17.1	16.9
Fourth quintile	12.1	23.6	23.7	24.4	24.3	24.1
Highest quintile	43.0	42.0	41.6	41.4	42.7	43.7

Source: U.S. Department of Commerce, Bureau of the Census, *Current Population Reports*, "Consumer Income, 1985," Washington, D.C., Table 17, p. 47. "Money Income and Poverty Status in the United States, 1987," Table 4, p. 17, August, 1988.

Conversely, at the other end of income distribution, blacks and minorities received 48.3 percent of family income compared to 42.9 percent for white families. There is also a greater disparity in income distribution for unrelated blacks and other minorities than for unrelated whites. The greater disparity in income distribution for blacks and other minorities can be explained by the fact that more households and unrelated individuals live below the poverty level.

Demographic Characteristics of Income Distribution

Political and economic traditions in the United States have focused on the rights of the individual—equality of opportunity, voting rights, and support for those people who in some sense have fallen below society's norm of acceptability. However, the United States has become a pluralistic society, and a group consciousness has developed, with each group wanting a larger share of the national economic pie. Therefore, a more complete analysis of income based on the demographic characteristics of sex, race, and age is necessary. Income distribution shows disparities related to each of these characteristics.

TABLE 11-2 Share of Aggregate Income in 1987 of Families and Unrelated Individuals by Race

	First Quintile	Second Quintile	Third Quintile	Fourth Quintile	Fifth Quintile	Mean Income
Families						
White	5.1	11.2	17.0	23.8	42.9	$38,200
Black and other races	3.2	8.5	15.3	24.8	48.3	29,486
Black	3.3	8.7	15.5	25.1	47.4	23,292
Unrelated individuals						
White	3.9	9.0	15.2	24.1	47.9	17,581
Black and other races	2.7	7.7	13.5	24.9	51.5	12,590
Black	3.0	7.9	13.5	24.8	50.8	11,906

Source: U.S. Department of Commerce, Bureau of the Census, *Money Income and Poverty Status in the United States, 1987,* Washington, D.C.: U.S. Government Printing Office, July, 1988, Table 4, p. 17.

Affirmative action and comparable worth policies represent a demand for government economic policies that focus attention on eliminating differences based on these characteristics.

Sex

In 1987, the median income of households headed by a man was $26,008, and the median income of households headed by a woman was $16,909.[3] The median income of single men was $17,660, and the median income of single women was $11,250. There were several reasons for these differences in income. A greater percentage of men were in the labor force, and a greater percentage worked full time. Another reason was a greater concentration of men

---

[3] Washington, D.C.: U.S. Department of Commerce, Bureau of the Census. *Money Income and Poverty Status in the United States,* August, 1988, p. 2.

in the higher-paying occupations. Well over one-half of all women in the labor force were concentrated in relatively low-paying clerical and service occupations. Men outnumbered women by three to one in management, professional, and technical jobs. In such high-paying occupations as engineering, accounting, and medicine, men outnumbered women more than four to one.

Moreover, women have not substantially lowered the earnings gap between them and men. In 1960, the median income of women employed full-time outside the home was 61 percent of the median income of men; the 1987 figure was 65 percent.[4] Despite large structural changes in the economy and major antidiscrimination legislation, the economic well-being of women in comparison with that of men also did not improve much in terms of average income. In 1959, women earned on the average 62 cents for every dollar men earned; in 1983, they earned 69 cents for every dollar earned. Although the gap was narrowed during the period 1979–1987 and will continue to be narrowed in the future as women increase their participation in the work force, women have more financial responsibility for children today than in 1959 because many more of them are single heads of families.[5]

Race

In 1987, white median household income was $32,224, whereas black median household income was $18,098, or around 60 percent of white mean income.[6] Hispanic median household income was $20,306, or around 70 percent of that of white households. The much lower black household income can be explained in part by the high concentration of households headed by women. About 43 percent of black households were headed by women, compared to 20 percent for white and Hispanic households. In 1987, 51.8 percent of households headed by a black female had an income below the poverty level.[7] There is also a difference in income between white and black workers who are single. Single blacks had a median income of $10,091 in 1987 compared to a median

[4] Ibid.

[5] Victor R. Fuchs, "Sex Differences in Economic Well-Being," *Science,* April 25, 1986, pp. 459–464.

[6] U.S. Department of Commerce, Bureau of the Census, *Current Population Reports,* 1988, p. 19.

[7] *Economic Report of the President 1988* (Washington, D.C.: U.S. Government Printing Office, February, 1988), table B-29, p. 286.

income of 18,652 for single whites.[8] The difference in income can be explained by a greater percentage of blacks in part-time employment and by their concentration in low-paying jobs.

Age

Both men's and women's income increases in the early years and peaks between the ages of forty-five and fifty-four.[9] For example, the highest average annual income for males with a college education is reached at age forty-nine, after which it declines. This pattern also holds true for college-educated women, for both men and women with high school educations, and for all occupational categories except unskilled workers. This decline in itself does not prove age discrimination, for a number of factors are at work. As family income needs decrease, many men wish to increase their leisure time and are less willing to work overtime. Many women have not participated in the labor force for an extended time, and many interrupt their employment to bear children.

Causes of Income Differences

Differences in the distribution of personal income do not prove discrimination, owing to differences in people's ability, motivation, education, work experience during a given year, and even lifelong work experience. How much income differential, for instance, between men and women, is due to differences in experience or performance on the job, which may be difficult to measure, or due to discrimination is a hard question to answer. The income differential almost disappears when men's and women's earnings are compared within detailed job classifications and within the same plant. In the narrow sense of equal pay for the same job in the same plant, little difference between men and women may exist. But the focus of the problem is only shifted, not eliminated, for then it is necessary to explain why women have a job structure so different from that of men and why they are employed in different types of establishments. This point is made clear in Table 11-3.

---

[8] U.S. Department of Commerce, Bureau of the Census, *Current Population Reports,* 1988, p. 6.
[9] Ibid., p. 24.

TABLE 11-3 Employment in the Ten Largest Occupations for Men and Women, 1980

	Percentage Male	Percentage Female
Ten Largest Occupations for Men		
Managers	73.1	26.9
Truckdrivers	97.7	2.3
Janitors	76.6	23.4
Supervisors, production	85.0	15.0
Carpenters	98.4	1.6
Supervisors, sales	71.8	28.2
Laborers	80.6	19.4
Sales representatives	85.1	14.9
Farmers	90.2	9.8
Auto mechanics	98.7	1.3
Ten Largest Occupations for Women		
Secretaries	1.2	98.8
Teachers, elementary	24.6	75.4
Bookkeepers	10.3	89.7
Cashiers	16.5	83.5
Office clerks	17.9	82.1
Managers	73.1	26.9
Waitresses and waiters	12.0	88.0
Sales clerks	27.3	72.7
Registered nurses	4.1	95.9
Nurses' aides	12.2	87.8

Source: Barbara F. Reskin and Heidi I. Hartmann, eds., *Women's Work, Men's Work: Sex Segregation on the Job* (Washington, D.C.: National Academy Press, 1986), p. 21. Used by permission.

Sex Stereotyping

Beliefs about differences between the sexes play an important role in the organization of any society. They are a part of a society's cultural norms and have existed since time immemorial. In the United States, these beliefs can be divided into three categories.[10] First, the traditional belief about the role of women is that their place is in the home. This assumption is held by employers, parents, men, and women in varying degrees. People invidiously imply that when women work they must do so for pocket money or for diversion from the chores of domestic life. Second, there are stereotyped beliefs about the gender differences relevant to male-female relationships. For example, women are perceived as more governed by emotions than men, which underlies in part the belief that women should be subordinate to men in the workplace. Third, there are beliefs that assume innate differences between the sexes—that women lack aggressiveness and a capacity for abstract thought, for example.

Race Discrimination

In the case of blacks and minorities, income differences can be explained in part by overt discrimination. Over an extended time, blacks have been systematically denied the same educational opportunities as whites, which is reflected in the occupations of blacks. A majority work the low-pay, low-skill jobs. There has also been discrimination in hiring and promotion policies toward minority groups. Often the discrimination is indirect, as in testing, which—although it can be a legitimate device to find out something about employee aptitudes and qualifications—may be culturally biased in favor of certain types of job applicants. Blacks and members of other minorities have been unable to obtain jobs commensurate with their training.

Age Discrimination

The poet Byron once wrote, "The days of our youth are the days of our glory."[11] No society believes that more than Americans, who are firmly committed to the pursuit of youth. Aging is something to be avoided at all cost, for age carries with it certain stereotypes. The notion that older people lose their mental faculties and are unable to perform as well as younger workers is not uncommon in the workplace, where employers have often discriminated against older workers. Employers have also often refused to hire workers because of their age. Older workers have been denied promotions and have been

---

[10] Barbara F. Reskin and Heidi I. Hartmann, eds., *Women's Work, Men's Work: Sex Segregation on the Job* (Washington, D.C.: National Academy Press, 1986), pp. 37–41.

[11] *Stanzas Written on the Road Between Florence and Pisa,* stanza 1.

eased out of their jobs so that employers can hire younger, presumably more productive, workers.

Antidiscrimination Laws

A massive legal and regulatory apparatus exists to protect workers against most forms of discrimination in private firms and government. As Table 11-4 indicates, this apparatus is relatively new. Although the more important laws will be discussed in some detail later, it is important to differentiate between equal employment opportunity and affirmative action. Equal employment opportunity, which stems from the Civil Rights Act of 1964, is a policy ensuring that all applicants for employment, as well as current employees, are treated equally and are not discriminated against on the basis of sex, race, or national origin. Affirmative action is a policy by which employment opportunities for women, minorities, and the handicapped are enhanced. Affirmative action goes beyond equal employment opportunity from the standpoint of hiring and promotion; it is specifically associated with Executive Order 11246 and Executive Order 4.

AFFIRMATIVE ACTION

Affirmative action means active efforts by employers to correct any racial, sexual, or other minority imbalances that may exist in a work force. The general principle behind affirmative action is that a court order to cease and desist from some harmful activity may not be sufficient to undo the harm already done or even to prevent additional harm as a result of a pattern of events set in motion by the previous illegality. For example, racial discrimination is one area in which an order to cease and desist may not be enough to prevent continued discrimination. If a firm has engaged in racial discrimination for years and has an all-white work force as a result, simply to stop explicit discrimination will mean little as long as the firm continues to hire its current employees' friends and relatives through word-of-mouth referral. Clearly, the area of racial discrimination is one in which positive or affirmative steps of some kind appear reasonable—which is not to say that the particular policies actually followed make sense.

Affirmative action is far more comprehensive than simple employment discrimination, which may entail only one person over some issue such as age or

TABLE 11-4 Summary of the Most Common Federal Rules and Regulations

1. *Civil Rights Act of 1964* Prohibits discrimination on the basis of race, color, religion, sex, and national origin regarding civil rights.
2. *Title VI* Prohibits discrimination on the basis of race, color, or national origin under educational programs receiving federal financial assistance. Applies primarily to the student.
3. *Title VII* Prohibits discrimination in employment on the basis of race, color, religion, sex, or national origin.
4. *Pregnancy Discrimination Act* Included as sex discrimination prohibited under Title VII discrimination in employment on the basis of pregnancy, childbirth, or related medical conditions.
5. *Rehabilitation Act of 1973* Is designed to ensure equal opportunities in employment for qualified handicapped persons. *Section 503* Requires government contractors to take affirmative action to employ and advance in employment qualified handicapped people. Applies to employment only. *Section 504* Prohibits discrimination against the handicapped in federally funded programs or activities. Covers employment and students.
6. *Veterans Readjustment Assistance Act of 1974, Section 402* Requires government contractors to take affirmative action to employ and advance in employment qualified disabled and Vietnam era veterans.
7. *Title IX of the Education Amendments of 1972* Prohibits discrimination on the basis of sex in any educational programs receiving federal financial assistance.
8. *Age Discrimination in Employment Act, as Amended 1967* Prohibits discrimination on the basis of age (40–70) in employment.*
9. *Age Discrimination Act of 1975, as Amended* Is designed to prohibit discrimination on the basis of age in programs or activities receiving federal financial assistance. Excludes from its coverage most employment practices.
10. *Equal Pay of 1963* Prohibits discrimination in salaries on the basis of sex.
11. *Executive Order 11246* Prohibits discrimination in employment on the basis of race, color, religion, sex, or national origin in institutions with federal contracts.
12. *Civil Rights Restoration Act of 1988* (P.L. 100-259) Was enacted by Congress to overturn the Grove City College decision, 465 U.S. 555 (1984), which restricted sex discrimination provisions to those university programs directly benefiting from federal financial assistance and not the entire university. The act restores the broad coverage in existence prior to *Grove City*.

* There is no upper age limit now.

sex. It requires employers with a federal contract to evaluate their work forces, to analyze their employment needs, and to solicit actively to obtain more minority employees. Affirmative action programs must meet certain minimal requirements in which the burden is on the employer. A primary requirement is a written description of the efforts being made to achieve equal employment opportunity. A program must contain certain basic information. For example, the work force must be analyzed to determine where minorities are being underused, why they are being underused, and how this situation can be corrected. Goals and timetables must be actual commitments. In addition, an employer must inform all recruiting sources of this affirmative action policy and of the firm's desire to recruit more minority employees, in keeping with its goals and timetables. There also must be a specific objective with regard to promotions; it is insufficient for a firm just to state that it will attempt to promote women or blacks to responsible positions.

The Development of Affirmative Action

The principle of affirmative action goes back much further than the civil rights legislation of the 1960s and extends well beyond questions regarding ethnic minorities or women. In 1935, the Wagner Act prescribed affirmative action as well as cease-and-desist remedies against employers whose antiunion activities had violated the law. Thus, in the landmark *Jones and Laughlin* steel case, which established the constitutionality of the act, the National Labor Relations Board ordered the company not only to stop discriminating against employees who were union members but also to post notices in conspicuous places announcing they would reinstate back pay to unlawfully discharged workers.[12] Had the company been ordered merely to cease and desist from economic retaliation against union members, the effect of its past intimidation would have continued to inhibit the free choice election guaranteed by the National Labor Relations Act.

The Civil Rights Act of 1964

The Civil Rights Act of 1964 was an attempt to eliminate all forms of discrimination in employment. Its genesis was in the Civil Rights Acts of 1866 and

---

[12] Harry A. Millis and Emily Clark Brown, *From the Wagner Act to Taft-Hartley* (Chicago: University of Chicago Press, 1950), p. 97.

1870, both of which were designed to preclude employment discrimination on the basis of race and color.[13] Section 703 of Title VII of the Civil Rights Act of 1964 obligates employers, labor unions, and government agencies not to discriminate on the basis of race, color, religion, sex, or national origin. Section 704 of Title VII provided for the creation of the Equal Employment Opportunity Commission (EEOC), which consists of a five-member board appointed by the president with the approval of the Senate for a term of five years. Section 701 defines an employer subject to the act as a person engaged in an industry affecting commerce who has fifteen or more employees for each working day in each of ten or more calendar weeks in the current or calendar year. The section also puts employment agencies and labor unions under the jurisdiction of the act. Title VI of the act precludes discrimination on the basis of race, color, sex, or national origin in federally aided employment programs.

The Civil Rights Act of 1964 has been criticized on the grounds that it requires compensatory or preferential treatment of minority groups to compensate for past discrimination. In other words, is anything more than equality of treatment justified under the Fourteenth Amendment's corollary statutes? But the intent of Congress in passing the act was reasonably explicit. Senator Hubert Humphrey of Minnesota, one of the drafters of the legislation, pointed out that it did not force employers to achieve any kind of racial balance in their work forces by giving any kind of preferential treatment to any individual or group.[14] He went on to say there must be an intention to discriminate before an employer can be considered in violation of the law. In fact, Section 703 of the Civil Rights Act states that employers, employment agencies, and labor unions are not required to grant preferential treatment to any individual or any group because of race, color, sex, religion, or national origin on account of any imbalance that may exist with respect to the number or percentage of people of any race, sex, religion, or national origin.

Executive Orders

Subsequent executive orders declared it a matter of public policy that affirmative action must be taken to rectify the discrimination against minorities. The policy of affirmative action was first proclaimed by President Lyndon

---

[13] U.S. Equal Employment Opportunity Commission, *Laws and Rules You Should Know* (Washington, D.C.: U.S. Government Printing Office, 1975), p. 91.

[14] U.S. Equal Employment Opportunity Commission, *Legislative History of Titles VII and XI of Civil Rights Act of 1964* (Washington, D.C.: U.S. Government Printing Office, 1969), p. 3005.

Johnson in an executive order in 1965.[15] It states that in all federal contracts or in any employment situation that uses federal funds, employers have to prove they have sought out qualified applicants from disadvantaged groups, must provide special training when necessary if qualified applicants cannot be found immediately, and must hire preferentially from minority group members when their qualifications are roughly equal to those of other applicants. This executive order also applies to women. Another executive order banned discrimination by contractors on the basis of age, and an executive order in 1967 banned discrimination in federal employment on the basis of race, sex, color, and national origin.[16] Directors of federal agencies are required to draw up a positive program of equal employment opportunity for all employees, and to hire more women and minority members at all levels. In the early 1970s, affirmative action was extended to universities, and each school with federal contracts was asked to provide data on the number of women and minority members in each position, academic and nonacademic, and to set specific goals for increasing the number of women and minority members in each classification.

Executive Order 4.   Executive Order 4 of 1971 is the basis of most affirmative action programs. Under this order, affirmative action is required from all employers who hold federal contracts. The type of affirmative action employers must take is determined by the nature of the federal contract they hold. A written affirmative action program, demanded by the Office of Federal Contract Compliance (OFCC) regulations, applies to all nonconstruction contractors and subcontractors of the federal government and to agencies of the federal government that employ fifty or more employees and have a contract in excess of $50,000 a year. All business firms or government agencies that meet these criteria must file a written affirmative action program that contains a statement of good-faith efforts to achieve equal employment opportunity. Such efforts must include an analysis of deficiencies in the use of minorities, a timetable for correcting such deficiencies, and a plan for achieving these goals. In addition, an employer must include an analysis of all major job categories to determine where women and minorities are being underused and an explanation of why they are being underused.

Sanctions can be used to enforce compliance with Executive Order 4. Failure to develop an affirmative action program can lead to possible cancelation

---

[15] Executive Order 11246.

[16] Executive Order 11375.

of existing contracts and elimination from consideration for future contracts. If a contractor has set up an affirmative action program at each of his or her plants, the OFCC will grant a precontract award conference during which every effort must be made to develop an acceptable affirmative action program. If the contractor has no program at all or an unacceptable one, the agency can issue notice, giving the contractor thirty days to show cause why enforcement proceedings under the executive order should not be instituted. If the situation is not remedied within this period, the OFCC will commence formal proceedings leading to the cancelation of all existing contracts or subcontracts the firm may have. It is also possible for the OFCC to initiate lawsuits against contractors who fail to live up to their affirmative action policies.

Revised Order 14.   In July 1974, the Department of Labor gave final approval to its own Revised Order 14 on the procedures that federal agencies must use in evaluating government contractors' affirmative action programs. Among other things, contractors must list each job title as it appears in their union agreements or payroll records, rather than listing only job group, as was formerly required. The job titles must be ranked from the lowest paid to the highest paid within each department or other similar organizational unit. Further, if there are separate work units or lines of progression within a department, separate lists must be provided for each unit or line, including unit supervisors. For lines of progression, the order of jobs in the line through which an employee can move to the job must be indicated. If there are no formal progression lines or usual promotional sequences, job titles must be listed by departments, job families, or disciplines, and in order of wage rates or salary ranges. For each job title, two breakdowns are required. Besides the total number of male and female incumbents, it is also necessary to have the total number of male and female incumbents in each of the following groups: black, Chicanos, American Indians, and Asians.

Grove City and the Civil Rights Restoration Act of 1988

The Civil Rights Restoration Act[17] was passed by Congress to overturn the decision of the Supreme Court in the case of Grove City College. In this case, the court ruled that the sex discrimination provisions maintained in Title IX of the Education Amendments of 1972 were program specific and only applied

[17] P.L. 100-259.

to university programs that received federal financial aid and not to the entire education institution. The purpose of the act is to restore the judicial and administrative interpretations that existed before the *Grove City* decision, and provide for broad coverage not only under Title IX but also Title VI of the Civil Rights Act of 1964, Section 504 of the Vocational Rehabilitation Act of 1973 and the Age Discrimination Act of 1975.[18] The new law allows government agencies administering federal assistance to terminate that assistance if any part of the recipient's operation discriminates based on sex, race, national origin, age, or handicap.

The *Grove City* Case

Grove City is a four-year liberal arts institution in Grove City, Pennsylvania, that did not receive any direct federal aid. However, some of its students did receive financial grants from the U.S. Department of Education.[19] The Department of Education believed that Grove City was a recipient of federal financial assistance because some students received assistance and requested that the college execute an assurance of compliance required by Title IX regulations, namely, that no person would be subject to sex discrimination under any education program or activity receiving federal financial assistance. Grove City refused to comply, and the Department of Education initiated proceedings to declare the college and its students ineligible to receive financial assistance. Grove City filed a lawsuit in the District Court for the Western District of Pennsylvania, which held not only that the grants constituted financial assistance to Grove City but also held that the U.S. Department of Education could not terminate student aid. A court of appeals reversed this decision and found that both direct and indirect aid were covered under Title IX.

The case was then appealed to the Supreme Court, which ruled that the receipt of financial assistance from the federal government by the students at a college would not result in institution-wide coverage under the non-discrimination provisions of Title IX of the Education Amendments Act of

[18] Title VI of the Civil Rights Act of 1964 prohibits discrimination based on race, color, or national origin in a program or activity that receives federal aid; Title IX of the Education Amendments of 1972 bans sex discrimination in educational programs or activities receiving federal assistance; Section 504 of the Rehabilitation Act of 1973 prohibits discrimination against disabled people by recipients of federal funds; and the Age Discrimination Act of 1975 prohibits age-based discrimination by recipients of federal funds.

[19] They were Basic Educational Opportunity grants.

1972.[20] Justice Byron White, who wrote for the majority on the Supreme Court, said that federal money should be considered as financial assistance to the college's own financial aid program, and that program alone could be regulated under Title IX. Thus, the Supreme Court limited coverage to the specific programs that received the financial assistance and not to the entire college. Antidiscrimination laws did not apply to all operations of Grove City College simply because some of its students received financial aid.

Congress overruled the Supreme Court when it passed the Civil Rights Restoration Act. In amending the four statutes prohibiting discrimination in any program or activity receiving federal funds, Congress specified that any program or activity includes all the operations of a college or other organization, any part of which receives federal money. The new law allows government agencies providing federal assistance to terminate that assistance if any part of the recipient's operation discriminates. For educational institutions, if federal aid were provided anywhere within a college or university, the entire institution would be covered. For corporations, the law states that where federal financial assistance is received by the entity as a whole, the antidiscrimination provisions will apply. When a geographically separate plant receives federal assistance, coverage is only applicable to that plant.

Other Antidiscrimination Laws

There also are laws that deal with particular forms of discrimination. The Age Discrimination in Employment Act of 1967 forbids any form of discrimination based on age. Particularly mentioned are those workers between the ages of forty and seventy. Employers cannot discharge or refuse to hire any person on the basis of age, nor can they segregate or classify people on the basis of age when this criterion would deprive them of opportunities for promotion. The Equal Pay Act of 1963 precludes differences in wages based on sex and is applicable to employers with public contracts. The Vocational Rehabilitation Act of 1973 requires federal contractors to take affirmative action in hiring the handicapped. The Equal Employment Opportunity Act amended the Civil Rights Act of 1964 to vest more power in the federal enforcement agencies, particularly the Equal Employment Opportunity Commission (EEOC). The

---

[20] *Grove City College v. Terrel H. Bell, Secretary of the Department of Education,* 465 U.S. 555 (1984).

EEOC can initiate lawsuits against employers believed to be guilty of violating the antidiscrimination laws.

Enforcement of Affirmative Action

The enforcement of affirmative action programs is concentrated in a number of federal agencies, including the Office of Federal Contract Compliance, which is responsible for direct government contracts with business firms, and the Equal Employment Opportunity Commission, which was created by the Civil Rights Act of 1964. Jurisdictions overlap among the Department of Labor, the Department of Health and Human Services, the Department of Justice, the EEOC, and the federal courts. All these agencies also have regional offices, which vary significantly in their practices. Moreover, even though one federal agency approves or requires a given course of action, following such an approved course of action in no way protects the employer from being sued by another federal agency or by private individuals because of these very actions. Indeed, federal agencies have sued one another under the Civil Rights Act.

The Equal Employment Opportunity Commission was created by the Civil Rights Act of 1964 and its enforcement authority was greatly expanded by the Equal Employment Opportunity Act of 1972. The EEOC is empowered to investigate and act on a charge of a pattern or practice of discrimination, whether filed by or on behalf of a person claiming to be aggrieved or by a member of the commission. The commission has the right to initiate civil suits against employers, labor unions, or any group accused of practicing employment discrimination. Private individuals also have the right to sue under Title VII of the Civil Rights Act of 1964. In addition, the commission can investigate company records to see whether a pattern of discrimination exists and to subpoena company records if necessary. Every employer, labor union, or organization subject to the Civil Rights Act and the executive orders must keep records enabling the determination of whether unlawful practices have been committed and must furnish to the commission a detailed description of the manner in which people are selected to participate in job training programs. Employers and labor unions have to keep posted in conspicuous places on their premises notices approved by the commission setting forth excerpts from or summaries of the pertinent provisions of the Civil Rights Act and information pertinent to the filing of a complaint.

Title VII of the Civil Rights Act of 1964, as amended by the Equal Employment Opportunity Act of 1972, allows a person who thinks he or she has been discriminated against to file a complaint, called a *charge,* with the EEOC. The charge has to be filed within 180 days after the alleged discriminatory practice has taken place. The EEOC defers to a state or local agency when such an agency exists. After deferring for the required period, or when the state or local agency completes its process, the EEOC assumes jurisdiction of the charge and notifies the employer or labor union accused of discrimination. Because there has been a backlog of approximately sixty thousand charges, it can be a long time before the EEOC begins investigating the charge. The burden of proving no discrimination is on the employer or union. Records and witnesses have to be provided, which can be time consuming and costly. If the EEOC decides that the charge of discrimination is accurate, it can require corrective measures.

Legal remedies under the Civil Rights Act and related presidential executive orders range from cease-and-desist orders, through individual reinstatement and group preferential hiring, to cutting off all federal contracts to the offending employer. Lawsuits also may be filed under the provisions of the Equal Employment Opportunity Act of 1972. The federal government's most effective means of enforcing compliance with affirmative action goals is the money it spends. One way or another, most business firms derive some part of their revenue from government spending, and the loss of a contract means a loss of revenue. The latter is a virtual sentence of death to a research firm or a university, for they depend on federal money to maintain their competitive standing. Of course, employers also want to avoid lawsuits of the type that led to AT&T's $75 million settlement in 1973 on employees who had charged that discrimination had deprived them of past promotion and raises. The impact of this lawsuit on all firms, and for that matter on unions, has been enormous.

Application of Affirmative Action

From the Civil Rights Act and the executive orders has come the principle of disparate or unequal treatment. There is disparate treatment when members of a minority or sex group have been denied the same employment, promotion, transfer, or membership opportunities as have been made available to other employees or applicants. These people must at least be afforded the same opportunities as had existed for other employees or applicants during the period of discrimination. The result of the principle of disparate treatment has been a series of lawsuits involving affirmative action. The impact of these lawsuits on business firms' personnel practices or, for that matter, on all employers, including educational institutions, is considerable. Some of the more important suits are discussed next.

The AT&T Case, 1970

In 1970, the American Telephone and Telegraph Company asked the Federal Communications Commission for a 9 percent increase in long-distance telephone rates. Lawyers from the Equal Employment Opportunity Commission persuaded the FCC not to act on the request until the company changed its policies with regard to women and minority employees. The EEOC took the position that discrimination had been institutionalized in the company's employment policy and moved to change it to provide more jobs at all levels for women and minority groups. In addition, the commission asked for restitution to compensate workers for past discrimination, according to the principle that payment must be made to certain women and minority group employees, even though they had never applied for better-paying jobs because they knew it was company policy not to give them those jobs.

The results of this case had far-reaching implications for business. AT&T agreed to promote 50,000 women and 6,600 minority workers and to hire 4,000 men to fill such jobs as operators and clerks, jobs traditionally held by women.[21] By 1974, AT&T had also agreed to pay $75 million in compensation to groups that the government said had been victims of discrimination. Some 1,500 women college graduates who held management jobs between 1965 and 1971 but who were, according to the government, kept out of certain training programs received $850,000; 500 switchroom helpers at Michigan Bell received $500,000; and 3,000 women in craft jobs received up to $10,000 each.[22] AT&T also agreed to use an elaborate system of goals and timetables to ensure fair representation in the employment of women and minority groups in the future. A planned utilization of women and minority members had to be specified for fifteen affirmative action job classifications covering all the Bell System's subsidiaries.

[21] See U.S. District Court, Eastern District of Pennsylvania, Civil Action No. 73-149, Consent Decree, 1973.

[22] Diane Crothers, "The AT&T Settlement," *Women's Rights Law Reporter* 1 (Summer 1973): 8–12.

The Weber Case, 1979

The United Steelworkers Union and Kaiser Aluminum entered into an agreement covering an affirmative action plan designed to eliminate racial imbalance in the Kaiser Aluminum plants. Black hiring goals were set for each plant equal to the percentage of blacks in the respective local labor forces. To enable plants to meet these goals, on-the-job training programs were established to teach unskilled workers the skills necessary to become craft workers. For black employees, the plan reserved 50 percent of the openings in these newly created in-plant training programs. Selection of craft trainees was made on the basis of seniority with the provision that at least 50 percent of the new trainees were to be black until the percentage of black skilled craft workers in the plant in question approximated the percentage of blacks in the local labor force.

The Kaiser plant in Gramercy, Louisiana, initiated a program to train workers for skilled craft positions. Twenty white workers and twenty black workers were selected to participate in the program. Brian Weber ranked twenty-first among the white workers. Arguing that he was discriminated against on the basis of race and that he had more seniority than some of the black workers selected for the program, he filed suit under Title VII of the Civil Rights Act of 1964. A district court ruled for Weber, holding that the plan violated Title VII, and enjoined Kaiser from denying whites access to on-the-job training based on their race. A court of appeals affirmed the decision, holding that employment preference based on race violated Title VII prohibitions against racial discrimination in employment.

The decision was appealed to the Supreme Court, which by a vote of five to two, overruled the lower court and upheld the quota system for the training program.[23] As to Title VII of the Civil Rights Act of 1964, the Court found that Congress's primary concern in enacting the prohibition against racial discrimination was with the plight of the blacks. The crux of the problem was to open employment opportunities for blacks in occupations traditionally denied to them. The Court stated that had Congress meant to prohibit all race-conscious affirmative action, it would have provided that Title VII not permit racially preferential integration efforts; instead, it merely prohibited requiring such efforts. The Court found it significant that the plan was only temporary and was not intended to maintain racial balance, but rather to eliminate racial imbalance. It also held that the company was making a good-faith effort to correct past discrimination.

[23] *U.S. Steelworkers v. Brian Weber,* 61 U.S. 480 (1979).

The Stotts Case, 1984

Carl W. Stotts, a black member of the Memphis Fire Department, filed a class action suit in a federal district court charging that the department and city officials were basing hiring and promotion decisions on race in violation of Title VII of the Civil Rights Act of 1964. A consent decree was entered with the purpose of remedying the department's hiring and promotion policies with respect to blacks. However, when the city announced that projected budget deficits would require the layoff of some firefighters, the district court enjoined the fire department from following the seniority system in determining who would be laid off. A layoff plan, designed to protect black employees who had less seniority than white employees, was presented by the city and approved by the court, and layoffs were carried out. White employees with more seniority were then laid off. The decision was appealed and the case went to the Supreme Court, which overturned it.[24]

The decision of the Supreme Court upheld the seniority system. There was no finding that any of the blacks protected from the layoff had been a victim of discrimination, nor had there been any award of competitive seniority to any of them. Title VII of the Civil Rights Act protects bona fide seniority systems, and it is inappropriate to deny an innocent employee the benefits of his seniority. Moreover, the lower court ignored an agreement between the union representing the firefighters and the City of Memphis concerning seniority. The Supreme Court also stated that there was no merit to the argument the district court ordered nor to that which the city could have done by way of adopting an affirmative action program. The case indicated that the Court would look with disfavor on affirmative action remedies for past discrimination where whites were victims of reverse discrimination.

The Jackson School Board Case, 1986

In a case that can be interpreted in many ways, the Supreme Court ruled that broad affirmative action plans that include hiring goals are permissible as long as they are carefully tailored to remedy past discrimination.[25] The case was a reverse discrimination case. At issue was a voluntary arrangement between a teacher's union in Jackson, Michigan, and the local school board to lay off white teachers before laying off black teachers with less seniority. The Court

---

[24] *Firefighters Local Union No. 1784 v. Stotts*, U.S. No. 82-206 (1984).

[25] *Wygant v. Jackson Board of Education*, 54 USLW 3339 (1986).

said that the Jackson plan was unacceptable because school officials failed to provide evidence of past discrimination in the school system. However, the importance of the ruling stems from the language of the individual justices on the Court. Justice Sandra Day O'Connor stated that the Court agreed that public employers could have affirmative action plans to remedy past discrimination as long as the rights of innocent people were not trampled on. This means that broad hiring goals or quotas tend to provide job opportunities for whole classes of minorities—individually victimized by discrimination or not.

Justice Lewis F. Powell, writing for the majority of the Court, said that the Jackson plan was invalid because school officials did not justify it with careful findings of past discrimination and because layoffs of white teachers were too drastic to be used in affirmative action plans. The Jackson plan could not be justified by generalized claims of societal discrimination. In cases involving valid affirmative action goals, the burden borne by innocent people is considerably diffused among society. In contrast, layoffs impose the entire burden of achieving racial equality on particular people. The Jackson case reaffirmed affirmative action on terms of the adoption of hiring goals, but opposed layoff plans that discriminate against innocent people. However, Justice O'Connor, who voted with the majority in most of the ruling, disagreed that layoffs would never be permissible under an affirmative action plan.

The Cleveland Firefighters Case, 1986

On July 2, 1986, the Supreme Court ruled on two more affirmative action cases.[26] In the Cleveland firefighters case, the justices upheld by a six-to-three vote a lower-court-approved settlement between the city of Cleveland and minority firefighters that initially called for the promotion of one minority member for one white, with the goal of increasing to a certain percentage the number of black officers in each rank. The plan, agreed to by the city to settle a lawsuit brought by black firefighters, was opposed by the majority-white firefighters union. They argued that the plan amounted to reverse discrimination and was put into effect over their objections. Justice William Brennan, writing for the majority, said Title II of the Civil Rights Act of 1964 does not prohibit voluntary agreements ratified in court consent decrees. He stated that it was the intent of Congress for voluntary compliance to be the preferred means of achieving the objectives of Title VII.[27]

[26] *The Washington Post,* July 3, 1986, pp. 1, 11, and 14.

[27] *IAFF v. Cleveland,* 54 USLW 3573 (1986).

The New York Sheetmetal Union Case, 1986

In this July 2, 1986, case, the justices upheld by a five-to-four vote a federal court order for a local sheetmetal workers union in New York to meet specific minority hiring targets of 29.23 percent. This case involved a twenty-two-year battle to integrate the sheetmetal workers union in the New York area. Justice Brennan stated that a federal judge correctly ordered a 29 percent minority hiring goal to rectify what he called pervasive and egregious discrimination by the union. The union, joined by the Justice Department, argued that the precise percentage hiring formula was a forbidden quota. Brennan, speaking for the majority, said it was not. Justice Sandra Day O'Connor viewed the hiring percentage differently, saying it was not a goal but a racial quota and therefore impermissible under Title VII of the Civil Rights Act. She stated that even racial preferences short of quotas should be used only when clearly necessary, but not if they benefited victims of discrimination at the expense of innocent nonminority workers.[28]

The Reagan Administration and Affirmative Action

The Reagan administration was generally opposed to affirmative action, in particular to what it calls "hiring by the numbers." Its position was that employers can achieve true fairness in hiring workers only by ignoring race and sex altogether. It argues that preference of any kind is illegal except for people who have been discriminated against as individuals. It bases its argument in part on the decision in the Stotts case, where the Supreme Court ruled that racial quotas do not supersede seniority as a basis for who gets laid off. However, these three major affirmative action cases may be viewed as a defeat for the Reagan administration's civil rights policies for several reasons. The Supreme Court in the Jackson case did not forbid the voluntary use of numerical goals in affirmative action. In the two subsequent cases, the Court said federal judges may set goals and timetables requiring employers who have acted in a discriminatory manner to hire and promote specific numbers of minorities. It also gave states and cities broad discretion to agree to similar racial quotas for their work force. It rejected the administration's arguments that federal civil rights laws and the Constitution prohibit the use of affirmative action remedies based on race or color.

[28] *Sheetmetal Workers of N. Y. Local 28 v. EEOC*, 54 USLW 3596 (1986).

The Johnson Case, 1987

This case is the most important of all of the cases involving affirmative action in that the Supreme Court laid to rest the last remaining doubts about its endorsement of limited preferential treatment for women and minorities. The court upheld the decision of the Transportation Agency of Santa Clara County, California, to promote Diane Joyce to road dispatcher, a position never held before by a woman, instead of Paul Johnson, who had scored two points higher than Joyce on a qualifying interview.[29] Both were among seven applicants who had applied for the job. Johnson tied for second on his interview, while Joyce was third. Johnson claimed that he had been denied the promotion that went to Joyce solely because of his sex. A district court ruled in his favor, but the Ninth U.S. Circuit Court of Appeals reversed the decision. With Reagan administration backing, Johnson appealed to the Supreme Court.

By a six-to-three majority, the Supreme Court ruled against Johnson. Justice William J. Brennan, in speaking for the majority, said that it was appropriate to take into consideration the sex of Diane Joyce in determining that she should be promoted to the job of road dispatcher as part of an affirmative action plan. Drawing on the decision made in *United Steelworkers of America v. Weber,* he noted that the transportation agency's plan was valid for the same reason that the Weber plan was valid: it did not require white men to be fired and replaced by blacks or women. It did not impose an absolute bar to advancement by white men; and it was a temporary remedy. It was noted that women comprised 36 percent of the labor force in Santa Clara County, but held none of the 238 dispatchers' jobs—an obvious imbalance that, according to Brennan, the agency was trying to correct.

In dissenting, Justice Antonin Scalia criticized the decision of the majority. He said that the court by its decision had replaced the goal of a discrimination-free society with a different and incompatible goal of proportional representation by race and by sex in the workplace. He further said that the only losers in the affirmative action process are the Johnsons of the world, for whom Title VII of the Civil Rights Act of 1964 had not been merely repeated but actually inverted. He said that the true losers in this case were those individuals who were unaffluent, unknown, and unorganized. He also said that it was absurd to think that certain jobs were segregated because of a systematic exclusion of women. Instead, they were male-dominated because women themselves have not regarded them as desirable.

[29] *Johnson v. Transportation Agency, Santa Clara County, California,* 55 USLW 3078 (1982).

The Watson Case, 1988

Clara Watson was a black bank employee at the Fort Worth Bank and Trust who tried without success to obtain several promotions.[30] The bank relied on the subjective judgment of a supervisor as to who would receive promotions. Watson filed a suit but a trial court dismissed the action after finding that Watson had failed to prove racial discrimination under the standards of disparate or unequal treatment. Under disparate treatment, an employer may be liable if he or she impermissibly differentiates among employees or applicants, or treats some unfavorably, based on their race, color, sex, religion, or national origin. In order to prove disparate treatment, a plaintiff has to prove that he or she is a victim of intentional discrimination. However, Watson argued that disparate impact analysis should have been applied in her case and appealed the court's decision to a higher unit.

Disparate impact analysis is designed to eliminate racially neutral employment practices that have a disproportionate impact on members of a protected class and that cannot be justified by legitimate business considerations. The focus is on the effects of an employer's practices, not the intent in establishing those practices. To establish proof of disparate treatment, a plaintiff has to prove that a practice or system adversely affects employment opportunities of a protected class when compared to the effect that practice has on the opportunities of other classes. This proof usually takes the form of a statistical analysis. For example, if fifteen workers are doing the same job, e.g., shoveling walks, and no worker is a black, this in itself would constitute disparate treatment.[31] If the adverse impact is established, the burden is shifted to the defendant to explain that the use of the practice is necessary.

The higher court also ruled against Watson, who took the case to the Supreme Court, which unanimously ruled in her favor. In an opinion written by Justice O'Connor, the Court ruled that subjective employment practices could be analyzed under the disparate impact approach. Thus an employee may support an individual claim of discrimination with statistical evidence showing that women or minorities are underrepresented in the workplace instead of having to prove intentional discrimination. However, a plurality of the Court indicated that plaintiffs cannot automatically assume that statistics in itself is proof of discrimination under disparate impact analysis. This case poses a new dilemma for employers seeking to avoid discrimination cases.

---

[30] *Watson v. Fort Worth Bank and Trust*, No. 86-6139 S.C., June 1988.

[31] See *Griggs v. Duke Power* on p. 287. The cases are related.

City of Richmond v. J. A. Croson Co., 1989

This case involves what many people feel is the most important affirmative action ruling handed down by the Supreme Court. It marks the first case of a new era. The balance of power in affirmative action cases has moved to Justice Sandra Day O'Connor and a conservative majority on the Supreme Court. In 1980 the court, speaking through five separate opinions, voted to uphold a congressional statute requiring that a certain percentage of federal funds for construction be set aside for minority contractors. But when Richmond, Virginia attempted to enact a similar ordinance, setting aside 30 percent of city construction funds for minority businesses, the Supreme Court found the ordinance invalid on a six-to-three vote, with Justice Sandra Day O'Connor writing the key opinion and announcing the judgment of the court. Her views are likely to prevail in future affirmative action cases.

The decision actually found unconstitutional a set-aside program that was no longer in use. A contractor, J. A. Croson Co., had bid on a city contract, but was rejected on the grounds that it had not made sufficient effort to find minority subcontractors.[32] J. A. Croson Co. argued that it had made a good-faith effort, but was unable to find qualified minority subcontractors. The firm took the case to court where a lower federal court struck down the program in 1987, and the city took the case to the Supreme Court. Justice O'Connor modified her previous position when she and three other justices argued that affirmative action programs could be justified only on the basis of evidence of prior discrimination by the government unit involved. In *City of Richmond v. J. A. Croson Co.*, she held that in appropriate circumstances, a city would have the constitutional right to use affirmative action to combat the effects of discrimination by others within its jurisdiction.

However, she stressed that this discrimination must be specific and identifiable, and it is on this point that she faulted the Richmond ordinance. To establish specific discrimination as distinct from a general societal discrimination, she concluded that one should not compare the percentage of the general population made up by minorities, but rather the proportion of all qualified contractors made up of qualified minority contractors. This, she contended, was not what the city of Richmond did. She would require a government

---

[32] *City of Richmond v. J. A. Croson Co.*, 57 Law Week 9132 (January 23, 1989).

agency to show evidence of a significant disparity between the proportion of qualified minority contractors and the proportion of total funds received by such contractors. Such a disparity does not in itself prove illegal discrimination, but it does constitute a prima facie case.

Impact of Affirmative Action on Business

As the preceding cases demonstrate, the impact of affirmative action programs on the personnel practices of employers is considerable. The cost of compliance for an employer begins with paperwork. A document of employer affirmative action policies must be sent to the EEOC, and other forms must be sent to other federal agencies. There is also the cost of litigation, for at any one time a large company may have several discrimination suits filed against it. Training costs also can be expensive, and so can facilities that must be installed for handicapped workers. The point is not that affirmative action is undesirable, but that costs are involved. In a very real sense, federally mandated rules governing personnel practices can add to the employer's cost of labor. Then this cost is reflected either in the selling price of the goods that the firm provides or it is shifted backward to the employees in the form of lower wages.

However, this does not mean all employers are opposed to affirmative action. One survey of corporations listed in *Fortune*'s 500 indicated that an overwhelming majority of chief executive officers supported affirmative action as a part of company objectives.[33] There are practical reasons why companies may support affirmative action. It can enlarge the pool of talent that employers draw on, and it has practical value in terms of customer relations with women and minorities. In some companies, almost all of their customers are women. Moreover, once a company has an affirmative action program in force, it is less likely to stir grievances and impair morale among women and minorities on the payroll. The problem of litigation is also reduced. If affirmative action were voluntary, there likely would be an increase in the number of lawsuits brought by impatient employees.

---

[33] Anne B. Fisher, "Businessmen Like to Hire by the Numbers," *Fortune,* September 16, 1985, pp. 26–30.

RECRUITMENT AND SELECTION OF EMPLOYEES

Affirmative action is only a part of equal employment opportunity. Employers also are affected by laws concerning the recruitment and testing of employees. In advertising for workers, it is unlawful for an employer to print or publish an advertisement relating to employment that expresses a preference based on sex, except where sex is a necessary qualification for employment. Somewhat similar requirements have been applied to application forms with respect to race, though it quickly became apparent that if there were no records concerning race, there would be insufficient statistical data on which to prove discrimination or the lack of it. Thus, the EEOC has had to grapple with the fact that the logical time and place to gather certain significant information about a person's qualifications is also the time when there is the greatest likelihood of discrimination in recruitment and hiring at the preemployment stage. Nevertheless, almost all data that employers requested routinely in the past now either are scrutinized by the EEOC or are denied as permissible questions.

Employment Interviews

In the process of hiring workers, business firms can run afoul of Title VII of the 1964 Civil Rights Act or other legislation regulating employment practices. One of the greatest areas of potential problems is in the employment interview, since virtually all business firms use it. There are basically three types of questions that are illegal. First, it is illegal to ask questions about race, sex, or age in the employment interview unless they are relevant to the job. Second, questions asked of one group but not another are generally illegal; for example, asking a woman applicant how many children she has without asking the same question of male applicants is usually illegal. Third, questions that would have an adverse effect on employment should not be asked unless they are job related. Illegal employment questions have resulted in large numbers of lawsuits against employers.

Testing

Certain personnel problems confronting business are quite subtle. The entire area of testing is an excellent example of how genuine efforts at compliance with civil rights laws can still be construed as noncompliance. The courts have held that inquiries into a prospective employee's criminal record would be racially discriminatory unless the inquiry and the answer it was designed to elicit were somehow directly related to the total assessment of the employee. The same is true of all other types of preemployment testing and standards, such as aptitude tests, IQ tests, and educational achievement tests. That there was no intent to discriminate does not matter. If the effect is discriminatory, it will be disallowed.

Griggs v. Duke Power

In the landmark Griggs case the plaintiffs attacked the use of the Wonderlic and Bennett tests.[34] The company justified the use of the Wonderlic and Bennett tests on the basis of increasing business complexity. In the lower court case, it was held that a test developed by professional psychologists need not have a demonstrable relationship between testing and job performance so long as there was no intent to discriminate and there was a genuine business purpose for the test. Finding no intent to discriminate, the court relied on the employer's contention of genuine business purpose. But the Supreme Court reversed the decision on the grounds that there was no satisfactory relationship between the tests and job performance and concluded that if there was no such relationship, then the tests were discriminatory if their effects were discriminatory, regardless of their intent. The Supreme Court included the company's past record of racial discrimination as a reason why it could not use tests that eliminated more black job applicants than white job applicants; that is, tests that had no demonstrated relationship to actual job performance. The decision is particularly noteworthy in view of the findings by the Educational Testing Service that carefully administered preemployment tests can fairly gauge the ability of prospective employees. These findings came from a six-year study conducted in cooperation with the Civil Service Commission. The study concluded that people who do poorly on job-related tests, regardless of race, do not do well at work either.

Under the general guidelines of *Griggs v. Duke Power,* no question that does not have a clear business necessity may be asked either in a preemployment application or of a prospective applicant. It is also forbidden to ask questions not related to the job, even without discriminatory intent, when the inquiry might enable discrimination on the basis of race, color, sex, age, or national origin. Thus questions dealing with infant children, number of

[34] *Griggs v. Duke Power Co.,* 401 U.S. 424 (1971).

dependent children, willingness to relocate, and whether or not one is now or plans to become pregnant can get an employer into trouble. Employers also are required to prove that hiring, promotion, or assignment criteria for jobs are job related. Physical requirements are no exception. If physical strength is required for the performance of a job, all prospective employees must be given an opportunity to prove they have this capability. Educational requirements also are governed by the Griggs case. For example, educational requirements such as the possession of a business or technical degree may discriminate against women or blacks. It is incumbent on the employer to demonstrate the necessity of the requirement; that is, that persons possessing this type of degree are more successful than others in the performance of the job for which it is required.

SEXUAL HARASSMENT

Sexual harassment is a very important subject, for employers may find themselves in related lawsuits even though they were not aware that harassment was going on. It is a form of discrimination and falls within the statutory prohibitions against sex discrimination. Such harassment is covered by the Civil Rights Act of 1964. Section VII of the act prohibits discrimination on the basis of race, color, religion, sex, or national origin in any employment conditions, including hiring, firing, promotion, transfer, compensation, and admission to training programs. Title VII also includes behavior that affects the work environment. This has come to include any verbal, nonverbal, or physical behavior that has an adverse effect on work conditions. Personnel with supervisory responsibilities are required to take immediate and appropriate action when incidents of alleged sexual harassment are brought to their attention.

Sexual harassment is defined as unwelcome sexual advances, requests for sexual favors, and other verbal, nonverbal, or physical conduct of a sexual nature when

1. Submission to such conduct is made, either explicitly or implicitly, a form of condition of an individual's employment.
2. Submission to or rejection of such conduct by an individual is used as the basis for employment.
3. Such conduct has the purpose or effect of unreasonably restraining or interfering with an individual's work or creating an intimidating, hostile, or offensive work environment.

Meritor Savings Bank v. Vinson[35]

Michelle Vinson was hired by Meritor Savings Bank as a teller-trainee. She progressed in the bank's hierarchy, but after using up approximately two months of sick leave, she was discharged for excessive use of leave time. She brought action against her supervisor, claiming that she had been subject to constant sexual harassment in violation of Section VII of the Civil Rights Act. She stated that she was forced to have intercourse with him on numerous occasions, and that he had fondled her in front of other employees. She stated that she had not reported these and other abuses to his supervisors because she was afraid of him. Her extended use of leave time was caused by the emotional stress that she had gone through as a result of her sexual abuses.

Vinson asked for injunctive relief as well as compensatory and punitive damages against her supervisor and the bank. There were countercharges by the supervisor and the bank. One was that Vinson dressed provocatively, and another was that she had engaged in sexual fantasies. The bank stated that if her supervisor had sexually harassed her, it was unknown to the bank and was engaged in without its consent or approval. Vinson alleged that unwelcome sexual advances that create an offensive or hostile working environment violated Title VII, but Meritor contended that Title VII was aimed at addressing a tangible loss of an economic nature, not a psychological aspect of the workplace environment. Therefore, it should not be held responsible for the action of the supervisor.

This case is of paramount importance because it addressed four issues.[36] First was the voluntariness of Vinson's sexual behavior toward her supervisor; second, notice to the bank of the supervisor's behavior; third, evidence of Vinson's dress and personal fantasies; and fourth, employer liability for the conduct of the supervisor. In addressing these issues, a district court labeled Vinson's relations with her supervisor as voluntary and that it had nothing to do with her employment advancement. It also found that, even if the supervisor had harassed Vinson, Meritor was not liable for his actions; and held that evidence of Vinson's dress and personal fantasies was admissible. The lower court ruled in favor of Meritor. Vinson then took the case to an appeals court, which ruled in her favor. It determined that sexual advances must be

[35] *Meritor Savings Bank, FSB v. Vinson,* 106 S. Ct. 2399 (1986).

[36] Maria Morlacri, "Sexual Harassment Law and the Impact of *Vinson,*" *Employee Relations Law Journal* 13 (Winter 1987/1988): 501–519.

unwelcome and must in some way amount to an explicit or implicit condition of the individual's employment.

The Supreme Court upheld the court of appeals, finding that Vinson's voluntary sexual relationship was not a defense to a sexual harassment suit. The Supreme Court's decision strengthened the hostile environment theory of sexual harassment, namely, the severe or pervasive effect of the workplace that affects the victim. Vinson was the victim of a hostile environment created by her supervisor and unwittingly maintained by the bank. The court, in its decision, upheld the litigability of this form of discrimination under Title VII of the Civil Rights Act. In additional, the decision also eased the burden of proof by employees of sexual harassment, by indicating that economic harm; such as the loss of a job, need not be established in a hostile environment case. Thus, if a woman can prove she was a victim of hostile environment sexual harassment, Title VII is applicable.[37]

Application of *Meritor v. Vinson*

Catherine A. Broderick was employed as an enforcement attorney in the Washington office of the Securities and Exchange Commission. When initially employed, her performance rating was high, but later she was criticized for a poor attitude and tardiness. She complained that her emotional state was caused by sexual harassment on the job. She contended that the head of the SEC's regional office got drunk at a party and fondled her and tried to undress her. A supervisor had an affair with his secretary and arranged for the secretary to receive special consideration and promotions. A third SEC executive also had a relationship with his secretary. This woman received a cash bonus, a superlative performance rating, and two in-grade promotions.

Her complaint resulted in a district court finding of sexual harassment. Even though her employment benefits were not directly affected, the court was clear. It said that the record established that Broderick and other women were for obvious reasons reluctant to voice their displeasure, and, when they did, management treated them in a hostile manner. While there was no

---

[37] Cynthia F. Cohen, "Implications of *Meritor Savings Bank, FSB v. Vinson*," *Labor Law Journal* (Chicago: Commerce Clearing House) (1987), pp. 243–247.

direct tie between the sexually hostile environment and the employment of Broderick, the court ruled that she was a victim of sexual harassment.[38]

STATE FAIR EMPLOYMENT LAWS

Federal laws pertaining to employment practices are not the only laws that affect business; there also are state laws. In fact, federal laws are often designed to stimulate activity by the states under their existing laws. The Civil Rights Act of 1964 directs the EEOC to defer to the states for a reasonable time when there is a charge of discrimination. A number of local governments also have antidiscrimination laws. Both state and local laws vary in their effect and enforcement. Almost all state laws provide for an administrative hearing and the judicial enforcement of orders of an administrative agency or official and carry penalties for violating the laws. Some states do not provide for any type of administrative agency or judicial enforcement of orders but do make discrimination in employment a misdemeanor. Other states have voluntary statutes and no enforcement provisions. State laws are applied to all employers, unions, and employment agencies located within a state without being restricted to those engaged solely in intrastate operations. This application of the state laws to interstate employees has been upheld by the Supreme Court.

State laws vary in their coverage but generally prohibit discrimination on the basis of race, sex, color, and religion, unless a necessary occupational requirement.[39] Some states forbid job discrimination based on age, and sex discrimination laws may collide with other state laws prohibiting the employment of women in certain types of work and regulating the hours of work. For example, an employer may reject a qualified applicant for a job that requires overtime solely because a state law says that women may not work more than eight hours a day in such jobs. However, the EEOC has ruled that protective laws conflict with Title VII of the Civil Rights Act. Apart from laws governing the employment practices of business firms, many states have separate laws requiring equal pay for equal work by male and female employees. These laws are limited to eliminating discrimination in wage differentials and do not touch other forms of job discrimination. In addition to the equal pay laws,

---

[38] *Broderick v. Ruder,* no. 86-134 (D.D.C. 5/13/88).

[39] Bureau of National Affairs, *Key Provisions in State Fair Employment Practice Laws,* no. 274, 1975.

discrimination in compensation based on sex also is barred, either specifically or by implication, in states that include sex bias in their employment practice laws.

COMPARABLE WORTH

Comparable worth is one of the most controversial subjects to appear in a long time. It is a compensation policy whereby employers pay equally for jobs of comparable worth or equal value, regardless of market wage rates and other factors. Is, for example, the work of nurses as valuable as the work of truck drivers? Nurses, as a group, make less than truck drivers. The great majority of nurses are women, and the great majority of truck drivers are men. Comparable worth is not the same thing as equal pay for women and men who are doing the same job as is required in the Equal Pay Act of 1963. However, although the Equal Pay Act required equal pay for equal work, men and women seldom did the same work. That men and women are frequently employed in sex-segregated occupations (such as nurses and truck drivers) and that they are paid different wages for this different work were not situations addressed by the Equal Pay Act.

The concept of comparable worth rests on several principles. First, workers should be paid in proportion to the worth of their jobs. Second, nonmarket methods exist or can be developed for determining the worth of jobs. Third, these nonmarket methods for evaluating jobs are preferable to the market, can be based exclusively on measures of worth, and can exclude the effects of sex discrimination. The most commonly used nonmarket measure relies on professional job evaluation systems that assign different points to different jobs based on the measurement of factors thought to be generic standards for any job—factors such as skill, effort, responsibility, and working conditions. These methods involve subjective judgments. Someone decides what factors are relevant to an evaluation of job worth, the weight to be attached to those factors, and the wages to be assigned to the various jobs after they are rated.

Before proceeding to discuss comparable worth in more detail, it is necessary to discuss the operation of a market economy. Resources, including labor, are allocated on the basis of the price mechanism. Prices are determined by supply and demand. Resources that are scarce relative to demand should command a high price in the marketplace; resources that are not scarce relative to demand should command a low price in the marketplace. Resources flow into markets where prices are high, and away from markets where prices are low.

The market is supposed to be an impersonal allocation of resources. As to the distribution of income, it is necessary to discuss the marginal productivity theory of income distribution.

The Marginal Productivity Theory of Income Distribution

The most basic concept underlying income distribution in a market economy is the marginal productivity concept.[40] This concept can be applied to the distribution of both labor and property incomes. Accordingly, the income received by the owner of a productive resource is determined by supply and demand under competitive conditions, thus equaling the marginal contribution that the resource is able to make to the exchange value of goods and services. With respect to labor income, it is best for employers to hire the number of workers that makes their marginal revenue product equal to their wage. Marginal revenue product, to put it simply, is the revenue added to the total firm revenue by each additional unit of labor, which in turn determines the demand for labor. A firm will hire that number of people at which the addition made to total revenue by a one-unit increment of labor equals the addition made to total cost by that same increment.

The marginal productivity concept is based on the law of diminishing returns, which holds that an increased amount of a resource applied to a fixed quantity of other resources will yield a diminished marginal product. Thus if employers were to hire so many workers that their marginal revenue product was not worth the wage that had to be paid, they would soon find that number excessive. The number of workers that any employer would want to take on is the number that maximizes profit, and that number is determined by the equality of wages to the marginal revenue of the last worker employed. Below this point, an employer would be reducing revenue more than costs and so diminish profits; above this point, profit is not being maximized. Each unit of labor is worth to the employer what the last unit produces. From the standpoint of the individual business firm, costs are the key determinant of the supply function. The most important cost element in the short run is marginal cost, defined as the cost of producing an additional unit of output. Since marginal cost represents costs associated with changes in output, it is apparent that understanding the behavior of marginal costs is crucial to understanding the behavior of

---

[40] See John M. Hicks, *The Theory of Wages* (New York: Peter Smith, 1948), chap. l.

prices in response to changes in output. In the short run, with fixed plant capacity, marginal cost is the same thing as a change in variable costs, which are costs that vary directly with changes in output. The most important variable costs are the wages of labor and the cost of materials.

Criticisms of Marginal Productivity Theory

The marginal productivity theory of income distribution can be debated. It assumes that there is a truly competitive market economy and that all units of an economic resource are basically alike and so may be interchanged in production and may contribute to the output of a number of goods and services with different exchange values. Actually, much of the labor market is characterized by imperfect rather than perfect competition. Thus, labor tends to be relatively immobile, and in some markets, one or a few firms, rather than several, may be buying labor inputs. Marginal productivity theory assumes that there is equality of bargaining power between the suppliers and demanders of any productive agent such as labor and that there is no outside interference in the distribution process. If this assumption holds, the price for all the factors of production, including labor, is determined exclusively by the market forces of supply and demand.

However, in a complicated market economy, it is inconceivable that marginal productivity analysis is sufficient to explain the distribution of income. Moreover, there may not be a close correlation between the income received by resource owners and the value of marginal revenue product of the resources they provide. If the resource they provide is scarce relative to demand, their marginal revenue product should be high, as should their income. Discrimination can circumvent their reward. For example, in comparison with other occupations, nurses and secretaries are usually in short supply. Nurses and secretaries are usually women, and the income they receive is often lower than in comparable worth occupations dominated by men. Given a limited supply and a high demand for nurses, their income is not commensurate with their marginal revenue product.

Nevertheless, a business firm has to make some comparisons between what a worker contributes to total output and what it costs to employ the worker. No employer will pay more for a unit of output, regardless of whether it is labor, land, or capital, than it is worth to the firm. An employer will continue to employ an input as long as each unit purchased adds more to total revenue than to total cost; otherwise, the opportunity for profit would not be maximized. In general, a firm's demand for labor is a derived demand based on the productivity of labor, the price of the final product, and the price of labor relative to the price of other factors.

The AFSCME Case, 1983

In 1974, the state of Washington commissioned a management study to determine whether or not a wage disparity existed between employees in jobs held predominantly by men and jobs held predominantly by women. The study examined sixty-two job classifications in which at least 70 percent of the employees were women, and fifty-nine classifications in which at least 70 percent of the employees were men. For jobs considered of comparable worth, it found a wage disparity of about 20 percent against employees in jobs held mostly by women. Comparable worth was calculated by evaluating jobs under four criteria: knowledge and skills, mental demands, accountability, and working conditions. To each category, a maximum number of points was assigned: 280 for knowledge and skills, 140 for mental demands, 160 for accountability, and 20 for working conditions. Every job was assigned a numerical value under each of the four criteria.

In July 1982, two unions, the American Federation of State, County, & Municipal Employees (AFSCME) and the Washington Federation of State Employees (WFSE), initiated a class action suit against the state of Washington on behalf of some 15,000 workers in jobs held primarily by females. In December 1983, the Federal District Court for the state of Washington awarded damages of $800 million to $1 billion to female state employees.[41] This ruling, decided under the theory of comparable worth, represented the largest damage award ever handed down under the equal employment laws. In this case, decided under Title VII of the Civil Rights Act of 1964, the court found that the state had underpaid women in female-dominated state jobs compared to what women were paid in male-dominated state jobs. The damages assessed by the court represented the amount it thought necessary to correct the effects of past discrimination in the state's pay system. In addition, the state was required to adjust women's salaries upward by as much as 30 percent to eliminate the possibility of future discrimination.

In September 1985, a federal appeals court reversed the district court order. In overturning the decision, the appeals court noted that basing salaries on the market is not in itself a proof of unintentional discrimination. The appeals

---

[41] *AFSCME v. State of Washington,* No. C-82-465T (W.D. Wash. 1983).

court said that market pricing is a method too complex even to prove discriminatory, and that employees must challenge more clearly delineated practices. Further, the court said that AFSCME failed to prove the state was guilty of intentional discrimination because it did not create the market disparity, and that Congress did not mean Title VII to abrogate fundamental economic principles to prevent employees from competing in the labor market.[42] Because AFSCME and the other plaintiffs never testified to specific incidents of discrimination, the court deemed the evidence too meager to prove that the core principle of the state's market-based compensation system was adopted or maintained with a discriminatory purpose.[43]

Impact on Employers

That employers, both public and private, will face increased pressure from unions and other groups to develop comparable worth plans or to negotiate the inclusion of pay comparability in labor agreements cannot be doubted. For example, AFSCME and the state of Minnesota ratified an agreement including a comparable worth provision, and other state legislatures have taken similar actions. Private employers, too, have to be concerned with the issue of comparable worth or some variation of it. Pay disparity between the sexes will continue to be an issue for several reasons. First, women's already large presence in the labor force will continue to increase. Women accounted for the majority of the growth in the U.S. labor force between 1975 and 1985, and the Bureau of Labor Statistics projects that they will make up two-thirds of the new entrants between 1985 and 1995.[44] Second, women's earnings continue to lag behind those of men, even though they account for an increasing share of the labor market. This earnings gap is cited by advocates of women's equality as continued existence of wage discrimination.

SUMMARY

In recent years, the focus of government regulation has been on social goals. An example is regulation pertaining to the employment of women and mem-

---

[42] In a 1984 decision, that was upheld by the U.S. Supreme Court, the appeals court had ruled that basing salaries on the market does not prove discrimination. See *Spaulding v. University of Washington* (740 F. 2d C8C).

[43] The state of Washington has already implemented a revision of its pay system.

[44] *The Washington Post*, April 18, 1986, p. 10.

bers of minority groups. In 1964, the Civil Rights Act was passed to prevent discrimination based on race, color, sex, religion, or national origin. Other acts also were passed to prevent discrimination based on age and to provide equal pay for equal work. Executive orders in 1965 and 1967 introduced the idea of affirmative action, which has come to be identified with the hiring and promotion of certain numbers of women and nonwhites. An affirmative action program now is required of all employers with federal contracts. Thus, even without any complaint of prior discrimination, an employer must analyze the composition of each department and compare it with the relevant available pool of women and designated minority groups. If the department's composition reveals a significant underuse of the pool of women and minority groups, the employer is required to establish certain goals, usually expressed as statistical changes in the composition of the work force reflecting an increase in the percentage of female or minority employees.

The impact of affirmative action on an employer can be considerable, and noncompliance can lead to severe penalties, including the probable loss of federal contracts, on which many business firms and universities depend. Employers also want to avoid lawsuits that demand payment of restitution to employees who charge that discrimination has deprived them of past promotions and raises. But there also is the problem of paperwork. The sheer volume of resources required to gather and process data, formulate policies, make huge reports, and conduct interminable communications with a variety of federal officials is a large, direct, and unavoidable cost to any employer—whether or not the employer is guilty of anything and whether or not any legal sanction is ever imposed. The hiring has been changed by outside pressures so that it now generates much more paperwork as evidence of "good faith."

QUESTIONS FOR DISCUSSION

1. What is meant by affirmative action? What is the difference between affirmative action and equal employment opportunity?
2. Explain some of the reasons for the differences in income between men and women and between whites and blacks.
3. What are the functions of the EEOC?
4. Discuss the Weber case.
5. When is testing illegal as an employment practice?
6. Discuss the Jackson School Board case. Why is it important?

7. Discuss *Griggs v. Duke Power*.
8. In what ways do affirmative action policies directly affect business?
9. "Affirmative action can benefit business firms in several ways." Discuss this statement.
10. Discuss *Johnson v. Transportation Agency*, Santa Clara County, Cal.
11. Discuss the Grove City case.
12. Discuss the Stotts case.
13. What is sexual harassment?
14. Discuss *Meritor v. Vinson*.
15. What is comparable worth?

RECOMMENDED READINGS

Bielby, William T., and James N. Baron. "Men and Women at Work: Sex Segregation and Statistical Discrimination." *American Journal of Sociology* 91 (January 1986): 4–13.

Cohen, Cynthia F. "Implications of *Meritor Savings Bank, FSB v. Vinson*." *Labor Law Journal* (Chicago: Commerce Clearing House). (April 1987), pp. 243–247.

Fisher, Anne B. "Businessmen Like to Hire by the Numbers." *Fortune,* September 16, 1985, pp. 26–30.

Fuchs, Victor. Sex Differences in Economic Well-Being. *Science* 232 (April 25, 1986): 459–464.

Olson, Craig, and Brian E. Becker. "Sex Discrimination in the Promotion Process." *Industrial and Labor Relations Review* 36 (July 1983): 624–641.

Reskin, Barbara F., and Heidi I. Harmann, eds. *Women's Work: Men's Work: Sex Segregation on the Job.* Washington, D.C.: National Academy Press, 1986.

Rix, Sara. *The American Woman, 1988–89.* Washington, D.C.: Women's Research and Education Institute, 1988.

Sindier, Allan P. *Equal Opportunity: On the Policy and Politics of Compensatory Racial Preferences.* Washington, D.C.: American Enterprise Institute, 1984.

Chapter 12

Government and the Consumer

Consumerism as a political movement can be divided into three distinct cycles. The first cycle began around the turn of this century and was concerned with pure food and drug laws. The second cycle began in the 1930s and included the passage of several disclosure laws designed to protect consumers against fraudulent advertising, mislabeling, and so forth. The third cycle began in the late 1960s when product safety laws were passed to protect consumers. But the term *consumer movement* is used rather loosely here, for unlike other movements of the past such as the Grange movement, which pertained only to farming, the consumer movement has been a conglomerate of rather disparate interest groups, each with its own set of concerns but able to coalesce and form temporary alliances on particular issues. This coalition of interest groups is expressed from time to time in efforts to bring pressure on government to pass consumer laws.

Consumer protection covers a rather broad category of laws that must be separated on the basis of objectives. Each law in its own way has had an effect on business. Take, for example, the U.S. automobile industry. Before the 1960s, it was largely unregulated by the federal government and pretty much free to do as it pleased as long as consumers were willing to buy its cars. By the end of the 1960s, however, a series of product safety laws were passed that imposed requirements on the automobile industry. Before discussing these and other laws, we must first discuss the reasons for government protection of the consumer.

CONSUMER SOVEREIGNTY AND FREEDOM OF CHOICE

In a capitalistic market economy, consumer sovereignty is an important institution because consumption is supposed to be the basic rationale of economic activity. As Adam Smith said, "Consumption is the sole end and purpose of all production; and the interest of the producer ought to be attended to only as far as it is necessary for promoting that of the consumer." Consumer sovereignty assumes, of course, there is a competitive market economy in which consumers are able to "vote" with their money by offering more of it for products in demand and less of it for products not in demand. There will be shifts in supply and demand in response to the way in which consumers spend their money. In competing for the consumers' dollars, the producers will produce more of those products in demand (for the price will be higher) and fewer of those products not in demand (for the price will be lower). Production is the means; consumption is the end. On the one hand those producers that effectively satisfy the wants of the consumers are rewarded by large monetary returns, which in turn enable them to purchase the goods and services they require in their operations. On the other hand, those producers that do not respond to the wants of the consumers will not remain in business long.

Freedom of choice is linked to consumer sovereignty. In fact, one defense offered for the market mechanism is the freedom of choice it offers consumers in a capitalistic economy. Consumers are free to accept or reject whatever is produced in the marketplace; thus, they are paramount, since production ultimately is oriented toward fulfilling their desires. Freedom of choice is consistent with a laissez-faire economy. It is assumed that consumers are capable of making rational decisions, and in an economy dominated by a large number of buyers and sellers, this assumption has some merit. Since the role of the government is minimal, the principle of *caveat emptor,* "Let the buyer beware," governs consumer decisions to buy.

These statements, however, should be qualified in regard to the position of the consumer in today's marketplace. First, the statements assume some sort of parity between consumers and producers, at least with respect to product knowledge. They also assume that consumers are capable of making rational, dispassionate choices in the marketplace based on information about a particular product. True consumer choice, taking into account that the buyer must be wary, is all very well in a society in which consumers are generally equipped with at least the minimum of technical information necessary for enlightened choice. Indeed, in a far less complex time than now, it was possible for consumers to be relatively well informed about products and markets. In the last century, the range of products from which consumers had to choose was small. The products were generally simple and were in everyday use. Intelligent buyers had the expertise to make a reasonable evaluation of the products, and if they needed credit, the sources to which they could turn, although limited, were at least well known. Consumers in the last century were faced with few choices not within their range of personal experience.

Today the situation is different. Consumers are confronted with many products and not enough information to make the most rational or optimum choice. The average person—in fact, even the most intelligent—has neither the ability nor the time, nor probably the inclination to be an expert in the intricacies of the many products industry provides. To many consumers, differences in the qualities of goods are a mystery. If consumers do recognize differences in the quality of certain goods, they face the almost impossible task of determining whether or not a given item is sufficiently superior to another article to justify a higher price. The relation of price to quality is further complicated when retailers sell the same article at different prices or when merchants offer at so-called bargain prices articles that are in reality set at their regular price or even higher. Even in purchasing relatively simple products, such as food, consumers are confronted with added considerations such as weight, color, and chemical substances.

Probably the most important qualification is that producers influence the choice of consumers. First, producers take the initiative in changing the techniques of production that increase the variety and volume of consumer goods. Second, producers use skilled marketing methods, including advertising, that influence the consumer's choice of goods. It can be argued that the purpose of advertising is to provide product information for the consumer, but it also can be argued that the purpose of advertising is to entice consumers into buying products they for the most part do not need. The so-called educational benefit of advertising may be designed merely to stimulate conspicuous consumption, such as a new car every year or the emulation of certain living standards. Consumers are goaded into maintaining superficial appearances at the expense of more fundamental needs. The overall effect of the producers' influence on consumers cannot be determined accurately; to consumers, there are both gains and losses.

Cigarette advertisements are a case in point. They suggest sex, youthfulness, virility, and elegance. The theme of the Marlboro cigarette commercial is virility as epitomized by "the Marlboro man," a rugged outdoorsman. There is no question but that this commercial theme has made Marlboro cigarettes the world's most popular brand. Then there is the Virginia Slims cigarette with its theme of the liberated woman who has come a long way from the days when an outraged father or husband threatened horsewhipping for smoking. Some cigarette brands, Newport and Parliament, for example, promote popularity or escape. The best way to maintain the smoking population or encourage people, particularly teenagers, to begin smoking is to reinforce the reason to smoke. With nearly $3 billion in annual advertising, cigarettes are promoted twice as much as automobiles or alcohol, the two next most advertised products.

The market and price mechanism never asks consumers to specify for which commodities and services they would like the scarce resources of society used. The most important choices are made by business managers who decide what commodities and services should be placed on the market, and consumers can choose among only those options offered to them. Consumers are not totally passive, however; they can exercise a considerable degree of selectivity despite the persistent advertising aimed at them. So some freedom of choice exists, but it is related to the alternatives available. Different market structures may determine the degree of choice. For example, the responsiveness of the market to consumer demands is less than ideal when monopolistic elements are present, whereas a competitive market structure necessarily must respond more to consumer demands. The consumer, although less sovereign than capitalist theory would have it, does have more freedom of choice than in a centrally planned economy, such as in the Soviet Union. There the state reduces choice to a minimum by presenting only a narrow and biased range of alternatives.

GOVERNMENT AND THE CONSUMER

The laws protecting the consumer are of infinite variety, but it is possible to divide them into several categories. The first includes laws designed to protect consumers from the adulteration, misbranding, or mislabeling of food, drugs, and cosmetics. In fact, the original focus of government consumer regulation was in this area. Its first piece of consumer legislation, the Food, Drug, and Cosmetics Act of 1906, was passed in response to public demands to curb these abuses. The second category includes laws to protect consumers from unfair competition, such as false or misleading advertising or various forms of product misrepresentation. Of particular importance in this category is the Wheeler-Lea Amendment to the Federal Trade Commission Act. The third category of consumer protection laws is product safety, which has become even more important in recent years. In essence, the purpose of product safety legislation is to protect consumers from themselves. Implicit in product safety legislation is that the concept of consumer sovereignty is inadequate if there are external costs in a product's consumption or production, or both, that the consumer does not account for in the consumption decision. As a result of this market failure, the government has intervened to control product quality standards and relations so as to upgrade product quality and repairability.

Both the federal and state governments participate in consumer protection. The Federal Trade Commission Act of 1914 created the Federal Trade Commission to protect both business and consumers against unfair competition. The commission has since expanded its responsibilities so that it is now the primary regulatory agency concerned with consumer protection. Some of the acts that the FTC administers are the Wheeler–Lea Act of 1938, the Wool Products Labeling Act of 1939, the Fur Products Labeling Act of 1951, the Textile Fiber Labeling Act of 1958, the Cigarette Labeling and Advertising Act of 1965, the Fair Packaging and Labeling Act of 1966, and the Consumer Product Warranty Act of 1975. The FTC also has jurisdiction over certain provisions of the Packers and Stockyard Act, as amended in 1958. In addition, Section 6 of the FTC Act gives the commission the right to collect and make available to the public factual data about various business practices. The FTC has investigated the meat-packing, cereal, oil, and telephone industries; chain stores; and farm implements manufacturers.

Pure Food, Drugs, and Cosmetics Legislation

The passage of pure food and drug laws was related directly to the consumers' welfare. In the last century, hygienic standards were very low, and many sellers, particularly in the cities, sold goods unfit for human consumption. Adulteration of foodstuffs was a common practice among the bakers and grocers of the 1880s, who met the growing demands of an increasing population by diluting their raw materials with a variety of additives.[1] Milk was often diluted with water, and to improve the color of milk from diseased cattle, dealers often added chalk or plaster of paris. Meat and other perishable goods were displayed on unrefrigerated racks, subject to the vagaries of the weather. Spoilage was common, but the meat was still sold to the public. Fruit was not covered by inspection laws, and rotted on the counters. In 1872, *Harper's Weekly* stated that in the markets of New York City there were cartloads of decayed

[1] Cited in Otto L. Bettman, *The Good Old Days—They Were Terrible* (New York: Random House, 1974), pp. 77–85.

fruit, which, if eaten, would almost certainly cause death.[2] Even the growth of the food-canning industry did not necessarily reduce the danger of spoilage, for chemicals often were used to mask the signs of food decay. In fact, many American soldiers died during the Spanish-American War from eating decayed meat packaged in tin cans.

State and local governments were the first to pass laws to protect the consumers' interest. Sanitary regulations, inspection of weights and measures, and the like were established public functions at the beginning of the nation's history. State laws to protect consumers against the adulteration of food and drugs were first passed in Virginia in 1848 and in Ohio in 1853. As production methods became more sophisticated, leading to the development of large-scale food and drug enterprises, state regulation did not work as efficiently. Products sold in interstate commerce were difficult to subject to state regulation, and as the problem of consumer protection became more complex, federal action became inevitable. One catalyst for this action was *The Jungle,* a novel written by Upton Sinclair in 1906,[3] which described conditions in the meat-packing industry. The following represents one of its more blatant graphic descriptions:

> It was only when the whole ham was spoiled that it came into the department of Elzbieta. Cut up by the two-thousand-revolutions-a-minute flyers, and mixed with half a ton of other meat, no odor that ever was in a ham could make any difference. There was never the least attention paid to what was cut up for sausage; there would come all the way back from Europe old sausage that had been rejected, and that was mouldy and white—it would be dosed with borax and glycerine, and dumped into the hoppers, and made over again for home consumption. There would be meat that had tumbled out on the floor, in the dirt and sawdust, where the workers had tramped and spit uncounted billions of consumption germs. There would be meat stored in great piles in rooms; and the water from leaky roofs would drip over it, and thousands of rats would race about on it. It was too dark in these storage places to see well, but a man could run his hand over these piles of meat and sweep off handfuls of the dried dung of rats. These rats were nuisances, and the packers would put poisoned bread out for them, they would die, and then rats, bread, and meat would go into the hoppers together.

[2] Ibid., p. 88.

[3] Upton Sinclair, *The Jungle* (New York: Doubleday & Page, 1906), p. 321.

The Pure Food and Drug Act of 1906

Unquestionably, *The Jungle* was one reason why the Pure Food and Drug Act passed. Theodore Roosevelt read the book and was as aroused by its disclosures as was the general public. He immediately ordered an investigation of the meat-packing industry, and a pure food bill that had been bottled up in Congress took a new lease on life and was passed with only a few opposing votes. The Pure Food and Drug Act is considered the first significant piece of consumer protection legislation in the nation's history. Its main provisions were as follows:

1. The federal Food and Drug Administration was formed to administer and enforce the provisions of the act.

2. The law prohibited interstate commerce in adulterated or misbranded foods and drugs. Adulteration was defined as the hiding of damage or inferiority through artificial color or coating, the addition of poisonous or other deleterious ingredients injurious to health, and the inclusion of decomposed or diseased animal or vegetable substances.

Foods and drugs were declared to be misbranded if their packages or labels bore statements that were "false or misleading in any particular" or if one were sold under the label of another. Food also was considered misbranded if its weight or measure was not plainly shown, as were drugs if their packages or labels bore false claims of their curative effects.

The Food, Drug, and Cosmetics Act of 1938

The Food, Drug, and Cosmetics Act of 1938 strengthened the Pure Food and Drug Act of 1906. It expanded consumer protection by enlarging the range of affected commodities, broadening the definitions of adulteration and misbranding, increasing penalties, and making special provisions for particularly dangerous substances. Cosmetics and therapeutic devices also were included in its terms. Food was defined as adulterated if it contained any poisonous or deleterious substances; if it was colored with coal tars not approved by the Food and Drug Administration; if it was prepared under conditions that might result in contamination with filth or injury to health; or if it was packed in containers composed of substances that might make it injurious. The definition of adulterated cosmetics was similar to that for food, with special provisions for coal tar hair dyes. However, no provision was made for the establishment of standards for cosmetics, and the disclosure of ingredients was not required.

Other provisions of the Food, Drug, and Cosmetics Act of 1938 were as follows:

1. A food sold under the name of another had to be marked clearly as an imitation, and foods bearing proprietary names had to be labeled with the common or usual name of the food and with each ingredient.

2. The Food and Drug Administration was authorized to inspect factories producing food, drugs, and cosmetics and was empowered to license manufacturers and establish standards of sanitation for granting licenses when the processing of foodstuffs might involve a risk of contamination that would make it a menace to public health.

3. Drug firms developing new drugs were required to obtain approval from the Food and Drug Administration before putting them on the market, and the FDA was authorized to deny approval of drugs that had not been tested or that had been found to be unsafe.

Drug Amendments of 1962

The Food, Drug, and Cosmetics Act of 1938 was amended in 1962 to extend the authority of the Food and Drug Administration, particularly in the area of drugs. The initial impetus for changing the 1938 law came from hearings begun in 1959 by Senator Estes Kefauver's Antitrust and Monopoly Subcommittee.[4] Underlying these hearings was a belief that the prevailing regulation permitted the introduction of new drugs of dubious efficacy that were sold at high prices. This loophole was said to result from a combination of patent protection for new chemical formulas, consumer and physician ignorance, and weak incentives for physicians to minimize the cost of drugs for patients. It was argued that drug companies devoted inordinate time and research to the development of patented new drugs that represented only a minor modification of existing formulas. The companies would then exploit the patent protection through expensive promotion campaigns in which extravagant claims for the effectiveness of the new drug were impressed on doctors. Even when patent protection was weak, as for new products that were combinations or

---

[4] Sam Peltzman, *Regulation of Pharmaceutical Innovation: The 1962 Amendments* (Washington, D.C.: American Enterprise Institute for Public Policy Research, 1974), pp. 8–27.

duplicates of existing chemical formulas, consumer ignorance and weak cost minimization incentives made artificial product differentiation an attractive market strategy.

The hearings characterized much drug innovation as socially wasteful. The waste was said to arise from product differentiation expenditures in an imperfectly competitive market permeated by physician and consumer ignorance. Product differentiation expenditures were incorporated in prices that therefore did not reflect the "true value" of the drug to the consumer. It was argued that only in hindsight would doctors or patients discover that claims for new drugs were exaggerated and that consumers would have been better off if they had used the low-priced old drugs instead of the high-priced new ones. It was apparent that accurate information about new drugs would be provided only if the federal government regulated the manufacturers' claims of effectiveness. Thus, the primary feature of the 1962 amendments to the 1938 act is that a manufacturer must prove to the satisfaction of the FDA that a drug has the curative powers the manufacturer claims for it. No drug can be put on the market unless approved by the FDA, which also can remove a drug from the market if it has evidence that the drug carries a threat to health.

Other Food and Drug Laws

The Meat Inspection Act of 1907 was a companion to the Food and Drug Act of 1906. It provided that a veterinarian from the Department of Agriculture must inspect the slaughtering, packing, and canning plants that ship meat in interstate commerce. The use of adulterates to hide meat decay or to color the meat was prohibited. Animals had to be inspected before slaughter and the carcasses after slaughter. The Wholesome Meat Act of 1967 amended the 1907 act. It is designed to force states to raise their inspection standards to those of the federal government. If the states failed to meet federal standards within two years after the passage of the act, the Department of Agriculture had the right to impose federal standards. The Poultry Products Inspection Act of 1957 gave the Department of Agriculture the right to inspect poultry sold in interstate commerce. In addition, the department was to supervise the sanitation and processing of poultry for sale in interstate commerce. The Wholesome Poultry Act of 1968 offers federal aid to the states so that they can establish their own inspection programs for intrastate poultry plants and meet federal inspection standards. States were given two years to comply with federal standards. Intrastate poultry-processing plants that posed a health problem were to be cleaned up or shut down.

There are some weaknesses in enforcing the existing pure food and drug laws. One is that the FDA is given far less money than are those agencies with smaller responsibilities but greater political support. The FDA, like many older, well-established agencies, has been accused by consumer interest groups of being more concerned with maintaining the status quo than with protecting the consumer. The increased use of chemicals in many foods and cosmetics has raised some hazards to health and has strained the capacity of the FDA. Chemicals may be added to foods without prior tests: only when the FDA has investigated and found the chemical to be unsafe may its use be banned. Only a small fraction of all the establishments processing or storing foods, drugs, and cosmetics can be inspected in any one year, and an even smaller fraction of their products can be tested. In many cases, gross adulteration of food, such as visible filth or decay, goes undetected until noticed by the consumer.

Beech-Nut Case, 1988[5]

A federal judge in New York sentenced the former chief executive of the Beech-Nut Nutrition Corporation and a former vice president of the company to a year and a day in prison for distributing bogus apple juice intended for babies. Each was also sentenced to pay fines totaling $100,000. The chief executive officer was found guilty of 358 counts of violating the Food, Drug, and Cosmetic Act. Each count carried a possible three-year prison term and $10,000 fine. The vice president was convicted of 429 counts of violating the Food, Drug, and Cosmetic Act, 18 counts of mail fraud, and one count of conspiracy. Each of the mail fraud and conspiracy counts carried possible five-year prison terms. In rejecting pleas that the two men not be sent to prison, the judge said their actions were too unwarranted to merit any leniency.

Beech-Nut, which is a subsidiary of Nestlé's of Switzerland, is the nation's second largest baby food maker after Gerber. It had to pay a $2 million fine, by far the largest ever imposed under the Food, Drug, and Cosmetic Act of 1938. It also had to pay a $7.5 million consumer class action suit for selling the phony apple juice. What the company did was to buy, with full knowledge, misbranded and adulterated apple juice concentrate from several suppliers, which were also named as co-defendants in the suit. The apple juice concentrate was more water than apple juice. The company purchased the apple juice

[5] *New York Times,* February 18, 1988, p. D-3.

concentrate at a price 20 to 25 percent below that of competing apple juice concentrates and sold it as apple juice to consumers at the regular price. The company gained $750,000 a year over a five-year period from the sale of the apple juice.

Advertising and Other Forms of Disclosure

A second area of government involvement in consumer protection is the various forms of disclosure such as advertising and warranties. This area is rather broad, but generally the practices that come under its purview are covered by Section 5 of the Federal Trade Commission Act of 1914, which gives the FTC the right to prevent unfair competitive practices, including those that affect consumers adversely. A rather common practice over the years has been false or misleading advertising. But a study of advertising by no means takes in the entire subject of disclosure. First, there are various product labeling requirements designed to protect consumers against misrepresentation and fraud. There also are laws designed to protect consumers against excessive credit charges. Since 1969, federal law has required that creditors disclose to borrowers basic information about the cost and terms of credit. Finally, there are consumer product warranties. Consumers usually are not aware of the warranty coverage on purchased products until after the sale is consummated and some defect or problem with the product directs their attention to the terms of the warranty.

The rationale for advertising is that for markets to work effectively, buyers must have accurate information about the quality and other characteristics of products offered for sale. Otherwise, the market is unlikely to enable consumers to make purchases maximizing their welfare within the limits of their resources. The provision of information about products is of fundamental importance to a market system. Without individuals or firms producing and selling product information to consumers, almost all information about products would have to be generated by the sellers and, to a lesser extent, by the consumers. As a result of the increases in the complexity and variety of products and in the value of people's time, there has been a major shift from consumer to seller in the comparative advantages of supplying consumer product information. But this increased reliance on sellers for information about products does not mean the information disseminated will be truthful. A seller's general purpose is to provide information that, if believed, will induce consumers to buy this product in preference to other sellers' products.

Several market situations can predispose a seller to use false or misleading information about a product:[6]

1. The first situation is monopoly. This market arrangement is conducive to the use of false or misleading advertising for two reasons. First, there is little likelihood of effective consumer retaliation when the deception is discovered, for consumers have no close substitutes they can turn to Second, the incentive of other sellers to correct false advertising is weak, for the false claim is unlikely to have much effect on them. By definition there is no close substitute for a monopolized product, and so any sales loss will be a small one distributed among the producers of a variety of distant substitutes.

2. Another market situation is oligopoly, in which a few sellers practice product differentiation through advertising. One seller, in an attempt to gain a competitive advantage over rivals, may make false claims about his or her products. False claims aside, a certain level of industrial concentration is necessary before it becomes profitable for a firm to engage in large-scale product promotion. By and large, only the largest firms in an industry can afford the high costs of advertising, particularly on television. A good example of concentration is the cereal industry, with the three largest firms—Kellogg, General Foods, and General Mills—together accounting for about 85 percent of total industry sales. Advertising is a way of life to the cereal industry, for some form of product differentiation is necessary to facilitate consumer choice among a myriad of products. Thus, each company is compelled to make exaggerated claims for its cereals to maintain its market position and to achieve some payoff on advertising expenses, which amount to around fifteen cents out of every sales dollar.

3. A third market situation is created when the performance of a product is highly uncertain, making false claims difficult to challenge, or when the seller can terminate business quickly and at low cost. The first category covers many restorative services, ranging from automobile repair to medicine, and the second includes various "fly-by-night" operations in which the seller does not have a substantial investment that would be jeopardized if customers, having discovered the falseness of the seller's claim, ceased to deal with him or her.

---

[6] Richard A. Posner, *Regulation of Advertising by the FTC* (Washington, D.C.: American Enterprise Institute for Public Policy Research, 1974), pp. 22–24.

The Federal Trade Commission Act and False Advertising

The first demands for the control of advertising came at the turn of this century, as a result of the false claims made by the many charlatans who populated the food and drug industries. Although the early postal laws were meant to deal with the wholesale distribution of false advertising by mail, it was not until 1914, when the Federal Trade Commission Act was passed, that broad federal legal weapons against false or misleading advertising came into existence. As mentioned earlier, Section 5 of the act declared that unfair methods of competition in commerce were unlawful and gave the Federal Trade Commission the authority to prevent persons or corporations from using unfair methods of competition in commerce. So preoccupied were the framers of the act with the commission's role in supplementing antitrust enforcement that the intended role of the commission as an agency for protecting consumers against fraud was left wholly undefined. The intention of Section 5, however, went deep, for it authorized the commission to proceed against various forms of antisocial business conduct over and above the unfair practices proscribed by the Sherman and Clayton acts; for example, price fixing and boycotts.

The FTC did attempt to prosecute consumer fraud cases. To circumvent objections that a mandate to prevent unfair methods of competition did not include efforts to protect consumers, the commission claimed that the fraudulent practice harmed the honest competitors of the defendant by diverting sales from them. In 1931, the Supreme Court overturned an FTC ruling that Raladam, the manufacturer of Marmola, cease and desist from representing its product as a remedy for obesity.[7] The Court found misrepresentation common among vendors of such nostrums and concluded that no damage had been done to Raladam's competitors. The Court held that in the absence of proof of such an effect, the FTC could not act against consumer fraud. This decision led to proposals to amend the original Federal Trade Commission Act.

The Wheeler–Lea Amendment

In 1938, the Wheeler–Lea Amendment to the Federal Trade Commission Act changed Section 5 to direct the FTC to prevent "unfair or deceptive acts or practices" as well as "unfair methods of competition," thereby making it the commission's explicit duty to protect consumers against fraud in the form of false or misleading advertising when no harmful effect on other sellers can be

---

[7] *FTC v. Raladam Co.*, 283 U.S. 643 (1931).

established. The amendment also forbids specifically false or misleading advertisements for food, drugs, cosmetics, and therapeutic devices sold in interstate commerce. The term *false advertising* means an advertisement, other than labeling, that is false or misleading in a material sense. When injuries to health ensue from customary or advertised uses of the commodity being falsely advertised, the advertiser becomes subject to the same criminal penalties as those under the Food, Drug, and Cosmetics Act of 1938. The importance of Wheeler–Lea is that it made of equal concern before the law the consumer who may be injured by an unfair trade practice and the merchant or manufacturer injured by the unfair methods of a dishonest competitor.

With Wheeler–Lea, it has become possible to prosecute for deceptive advertising without having to show that competition has been restrained. The amendment, however, has failed to define what is "unfair" or "deceptive" with respect to a practice, nor does it have any provisions for monetary damages, compensatory or punitive. The commission's inability to award monetary reparations to victimized consumers has had two effects. First, it has weakened the consumer's incentive to lodge complaints of deception with the commission, and second, it has weakened the seller's incentive to comply with the statutes enforced by the commission. The only consequence of violation is that if apprehended and successfully prosecuted, a fraudulent seller will be prevented from continuing, or repeating, the violation. But the seller is permitted to keep any of the profits obtained during the period of violation.

Enforcement Proceedings

As mentioned earlier, there is only one standard procedure by which the FTC can act to prevent deceptive practices such as false advertising although it can encourage and promote voluntary compliance. That is, the commission will, in certain instances, settle cases by accepting adequate assurance that a given business practice has been discontinued and will not be resumed. The FTC also can make a formal complaint against a business firm engaged in deceptive acts and practices. The business firm, which is the respondent, or accused party, is given an opportunity to enter into a consent settlement without formal litigation. If the respondent decides to contest the complaint, the matter is set for trial before an administrative law judge, or hearing examiner, appointed by the FTC. The commission and the respondent each are represented by their own attorneys. At the conclusion of the hearings, the judge issues his or her findings and an initial decision, which, if it goes against the prosecution, can be appealed to the full commission. The respondent can also appeal if the decision goes against him or her. A judicial review of the commission's decision is available only to the respondent.

The Wheeler–Lea Amendment provides that if a respondent plans to appeal an order of the commission, he or she must do so within sixty days, or the order becomes final and binding. If the respondent is judged guilty, either by the administrative law judge or the full commission, an order is entered directing him or her to cease and desist from the unlawful conduct. Like an injunction, it need not be wholly negative in its terms: it may spell out particular requirements that the respondent must follow. Once the cease-and-desist order has become final, either because the court of appeals has affirmed the commission or because the respondent has not sought a judicial review, any subsequent violation of the order subjects the respondent to contempt proceedings and a civil penalty of up to $5,000 for each day of continuing violation or for each separate offense. This fine—technically a civil rather than a criminal penalty—is enforced through federal court actions brought by the Department of Justice.

Deceptive Advertising

A Supreme Court justice once said about pornography that he couldn't define it, but he would know it when he saw it. The same can be said of deceptive advertising. The legal definitions of deceptive advertising are rather abstruse. The Federal Trade Commission Act contains a general prohibition of deceptive advertising and a definition of false advertising that makes clear that false representations are illegal and that failure to disclose material facts can be illegal. The Federal Trade Commission has used the following criteria in determining whether an advertisement is illegal:[8] An advertisement is illegal (1) if it deceives a significant number of customers, (2) if a false representation or mission relates to facts important to consumers in their purchasing decisions, and (3) when a false implication relates to facts that consumers use in their purchasing decisions.

Deceptive advertising can be considered antithetical to the public interest for two reasons.[9] First, it harms consumers by causing them to have false beliefs about the nature of the products being advertised and thereby causes

[8] Lewis W. Stern, and Thomas L. Eovaldi, *Legal Aspects of Marketing Strategy. Antitrust and Consumer Protection Issues* (Englewood Cliffs, N.J.: Prentice-Hall, 1984), pp. 371–372.

[9] Thomas L. Carson, Richard E. Wokutch, and James E. Cox, Jr., "An Ethical Analysis of Deceptive Advertising," *Journal of Business Ethics* 4 (1985): 99–101.

some consumers to make different purchasing decisions than they otherwise would have. For example, a consumer may select Product A because it promises to make him or her a more skillful athlete, even though Product B is the better product. Second, it can be argued that, apart from its immediate bad consequences, deceptive advertising can lower the general level of trust essential to the proper functioning of a free market economy. Consequently, there is a strong feeling against deception even when it does no immediate harm.

Deceptive advertising takes many forms. One example is a Rise Shaving Cream commercial of more than a decade ago, in which the manufacturer, Colgate-Palmolive, claimed that the cream had such a softening effect that even the toughest beards could be shaved. To prove this point, Rise was applied to sandpaper, and then a razor was used to "shave" the sandpaper. The lesson to be learned was that if Rise could soften sandpaper, it could surely soften any beard. What the public did not know, however, was that the sandpaper had been soaked in water for a number of hours before the "test" was made. Naturally, the sand did not adhere to the paper after the soaking, and the razor would have taken it off without the Rise.

Labeling

Advertising is by no means the only problem in the area of disclosure. In fact, the FTC is responsible for administering several laws regulating various types of disclosure. The Wool Products Labeling Act of 1939 is an example. The purpose of the act is to protect merchants and consumers against deception and unfair competition with regard to articles made from wool. Many abuses prompted the passage of this act. Reused wool was sold as new wool, and products sold as "all wool" often contained less than 5 percent wool. The 1939 act provided that all wool garments must disclose on a label attached to the merchandise the percentage of each fiber contained in the product. The Fur Products Labeling Act of 1951 was passed to protect consumers from the mislabeling of furs, such as rabbit fur being called mink. Manufacturers are required to attach labels to a garment showing the true name of the animal that produced the fur and indicating whether the fur is bleached or dyed. The Textile Fiber Products Identification Act of 1958, which covers the labeling of textiles and fibers, protects consumers by requiring a disclosure on the label and in advertising of the exact fiber content of all textile fibers other than wool marketed in interstate commerce. All products must have a label that shows the exact fiber content, the identity of the product, and the name of the product's manufacturer.

Then there is the Cigarette Labeling and Advertising Act of 1965, which requires that cigarettes sold in interstate commerce be packaged and labeled with the warning that cigarette smoking may be hazardous to health.[10] Certain drug products, such as aspirin, are required to carry on the label the warning that the product should be kept out of the reach of children. Some drugs may also be required to carry the notice that their use may be habit forming. Still other drugs must state on their label that they ought not to be taken by pregnant women without first consulting a physician.

Truth in Lending

The Consumer Credit Protection Act of 1968 or, as it is more commonly called, the Truth-in-Lending Act, requires that creditors disclose to borrowers basic information about the cost and terms of credit. The purpose of these disclosures is to encourage competition in financing by making debtors aware of specific charges and other relevant credit information, thus encouraging them to shop for the most favorable terms of credit.[11] Before the act was passed, borrowers had no way of knowing the true percentage rate they were being charged for credit. Often they believed the interest rate was less than what they actually paid, for creditors had ways to obfuscate the issue by using a variety of methods in quoting rates. The effect of using a variety of methods was to make it impossible to compare the rates of competing creditors. The act restricts the garnishment of wages by creditors and provides penalties for exorbitant credit charges.

Other Credit Laws

Other credit laws also are designed to protect consumers. The Fair Credit Reporting Act was passed in 1970 to give consumers more rights in the area of consumer reporting. It requires consumer-reporting companies to provide the consumer with information in his or her file to verify whether the credit

[10] The subsequent Public Health Smoking Act of 1969 required the warning on cigarette packages to read "Warning: The Surgeon General Has Determined That Cigarette Smoking Is Dangerous to Your Health."

[11] U.S. Congress, House Committee on Banking and Currency, *Report on the Consumer Protection Credit Act,* 90th Cong., 1st sess., 1967.

information is accurate or inaccurate.[12] If a consumer is denied credit, he or she must be advised as to the origin of the credit report. The Equal Credit Opportunity Act was passed in 1974. Its purpose is to prevent any bias in lending by requiring that credit has to be extended to all creditworthy applicants regardless of their age, race, sex, or national origin.[13] It also limits the amount of credit that a creditor can require in processing a loan application. The Fair Credit Billing Act was passed in 1975. Its purpose is to deal with billing errors involving credit card transactions. A credit card holder who feels that he or she has been erroneously billed must complain to the biller within 60 days of receipt of the bill. The biller must acknowledge the complaint within 30 days, and must acknowledge or deny the error within two billing cycles.[14]

The Credit Card Disclosure Act of 1988

More than 105 million people in the United States hold 800 million credit cards. Consumers constantly receive letters in the mail that state how lucky they are to be the recipients of new credit cards with special low rates of interest. All they have to do is to fill out the enclosed application and send it to a particular bank or department store that will then send them their new credit card, usually carrying a high interest rate. On October 20, 1988, The Credit Card Disclosure Act was passed. It requires banks, department stores, and other issuers of credit cards to disclose clearly their interest rates, fees, method of calculating interest charges, and the grace period before interest charges begin to accrue. The new disclosure law is stricter than current federal laws and most state laws. The act specifically aims at bulk mail credit card solicitations that tempt potential customers while not disclosing application fees. The act will make it easier for consumers to shop around for lower interest rates.

---

[12] Consumers may receive damages if a reporting agency does not comply with the act. Noncompliance or coercion by an agency can result in fines of up to $5,000 and jail sentences of up to a year.

[13] The act provides for actual damages and punitive damages of up to $10,000 for those people who are discriminated against by creditors.

[14] The act provides that a cardholder, erroneously charged, can collect the amount in question and any additional finance charges.

Warranties

A warranty is a promise, either expressed or implied, that affirms a fact or makes an affirmation related to the goods sold. Consumers attempting to have a product repaired under a warranty have often confronted problems; for example, the warranty may fail to cover a particular part, or it may not cover the cost of labor. State laws on warranties have conformed to the Uniform Commercial Code (UCC), which follows the theory of the common law that a product when sold carries with it the promise that it is fit for ordinary use. The UCC provides that a sale by a merchant is accompanied by an implied warranty of title and an implied warranty of merchantability, together with any expressed warranties, oral or written, that the seller makes as part of the law. The UCC has followed the theory of the common law that a buyer and seller may bargain freely over the terms of the warranty and sale.

The Consumer Product Warranty Act, passed by Congress in 1975, is important for two reasons: (1) it provides minimum disclosure standards for written consumer product warranties, and (2) it strengthens the capabilities of the Federal Trade Commission to function as the protector of consumer rights when deceptive warranties and other unfair acts and practices are found to exist. The act was passed because consumers had become increasingly dissatisfied with product warranties and had resorted to the courts for redress. Generally this dissatisfaction centered on such problems as the purchase of a product that turned out to be a "lemon," delays in making repairs, excessive labor charges, the failure of companies to honor guarantees, unscrupulous service operators, and the consumer's seemingly total lack of power to compel performance.

The act's major provisions can be divided into two categories. The first category pertains to consumer warranty provisions. To increase the product information available to purchasers, prevent deception, and promote competition in the marketplace, any warrantor offering a written warranty for a consumer product must disclose the terms of the warranty in simple and easily understood language. The FTC is directed to require that the terms and conditions of warranties be made available to consumers before the product is sold. The second category extended the FTC's consumer protection powers to prescribe rules regulating unfair or deceptive practices to apply to national banks. It was given the authority to move against local consumer abuses when state or local consumer protection agencies are ineffective. With respect to defective warranties, the FTC was given the power to seek injunctions against offenders and to represent itself in litigation. In addition, the FTC can initiate civil suits against offenders that knowingly engage in an act or practice determined to be unfair or deceptive.

Product Safety

Until recently, national product safety legislation consisted of a series of isolated statutes designed to remedy specific hazards existing in a narrow range of product categories. Moreover, enforcement authority was divided among a number of federal agencies. For example, the Flammable Fabrics Act of 1953 was passed after serious injuries and deaths had resulted from the ignition of clothes made from synthetic fibers. The act prohibits the sale of highly flammable apparel and empowers the FTC to issue appropriate rules and regulations, to conduct tests, and to make investigations and reports. Enforcement measures include cease-and-desist orders, seizure of offending goods, and criminal penalties of a year's imprisonment or fines of up to $5,000 for willful violations. Tests of flammability are established by the Bureau of Standards. The act was amended in 1967 to cover also interior furnishings, fabrics, and materials.

Also, the Federal Hazardous Substances Labeling Act of 1960 mandates warnings on the labels of potentially hazardous substances such as cleaning agents and paint removers. This act is administered by the Food and Drug Administration. The Child Protection Act of 1966, also administered by the FDA, prevents the marketing of potentially harmful toys and other articles intended for children. The FDA is supposed to remove the potentially dangerous products. The National Traffic and Motor Vehicle Safety Act of 1966 specifically concerns automobiles. Under its provisions, safety standards were set for new automobiles, which include such features as an impact-absorbing steering wheel and column, safety door latches and hinges, safety glass, dual braking system, and impact-resistant gasoline tanks and connections. Tires must be labeled with the name of the manufacturer or retreader and with certain safety information, including the maximum permissible load for the tire. The Public Health Smoking Act of 1970 extends warnings about the hazards of cigarette smoking, and the Poison Prevention Packaging Act of the same year authorizes the establishment of standards for child-resistant packaging of hazardous substances. In 1971, the Lead-based Paint Elimination Act was passed to assist in developing and administering programs to eliminate lead-based paints.

The Consumer Product Safety Act of 1972

One of the most important laws with a direct impact on business to be passed in a long time is the Consumer Product Safety Act. Fragmentation of legislation and generally ineffective controls over product hazards prompted the federal government to introduce new product safety legislation to protect the consumer. The act was a result of congressional findings that unsafe consumer products are widely distributed, and hence consumers are frequently unable to anticipate and guard against the risks entailed in their use. Findings presented before the Senate Committee on Commerce indicated more than 20 million Americans are injured by consumer products annually.[15] Of this total, 110,000 people are permanently disabled, and 30,000 lose their lives. The annual cost to consumers is around $5.5 billion. It has been estimated that 20 percent of these injuries could have been prevented if the manufacturers had produced safe, well-designed products.

The origins of the Consumer Product Safety Act are in the common law in that the manufacturer or seller is liable for injuries to a buyer or others caused by a defective or hazardous product. The common law imposed liability on a broad group of people involved in the marketing process, including suppliers, wholesalers, and retailers. Many product liability cases have been based on the landmark case of *MacPherson v. Buick Motor Company,* which held that the manufacturer of an automobile with a defective wheel is liable for negligence, even though the customer had no direct contact with the manufacturer.[16] Liability is assumed for injuries to the consumer when the results of such injury are reasonably foreseeable, regardless of whether the product itself is dangerous or harmful. A consumer need not prove that a manufacturer was guilty of negligence.

Provisions of the Act

The Consumer Product Safety Act is broad in scope and affects those consumer products not already regulated by the federal government. When compared with earlier consumer-oriented legislation, the act not only possesses

---

[15] U.S. Senate Committee on Commerce, *Hearing of National Commission on Product Safety,* 91st Cong., 2nd sess., 1972, p. 37.

[16] *MacPherson v. Buick Motor Company,* 217 N.Y. 382, 111 N.E. 1050 (1916).

more effective legal and administrative sanctions but also allows an application of safety standards. Its basic provisions may easily be summarized as follows:

1. It created a five-member Consumer Product Safety Commission, which functions as an independent regulatory agency. A major function of the commission is the gathering and dissemination of information related to product injuries. In addition, the commission is empowered to create an advisory council of fifteen members to provide expert information on product safety.

2. Section 14 of the act requires manufacturers to conduct a testing program to assure their products conform to established safety standards. After the products are tested, a manufacturer must provide distributors or retailers with a certificate stating that all applicable consumer product safety standards have been met. Section 14 also holds the manufacturer accountable for knowing all safety criteria applicable to the product and requires that safety standards be described in detail. The manufacturer also is obligated to maintain technical data relating to the performance and safety of a product. This information may have to be given to the consumer when purchasing the product.

3. The Consumer Product Safety Commission also can require the use of specific labels that set forth the results of product testing. This requirement will have its most significant impact on the production process, in which the design of numerous products must conform to new federal standards. Since safety standards will be formulated at various governmental and independent testing stations, a manufacturer may find that a finished product no longer meets federal standards, and product lines may have to be altered drastically.

4. Section 15 requires a manufacturer to take corrective steps if he or she becomes aware that a product either fails to comply with an applicable consumer product safety rule or contains a defect that could create a substantial product hazard. The manufacturer has to inform the Consumer Product Safety Commission of the defect. If, after investigation, the commission determines that a product hazard exists, the manufacturer—or distributor or retailer, for that matter—may be required to publicize the information to consumers. The commission can compel a manufacturer to refund the purchase price of the product, less a reasonable allowance for use, or to replace the product with a like or equivalent product that complies with the consumer product safety rule.

DECLINE OF CONSUMERISM

The last cycle of consumerism reached its apogee around 1975 with the passage of the Consumer Product Warranty Act. More consumer protection laws were passed between 1965 and 1975 than between 1890 and 1965. Consumer groups also lobbied for a federal consumer protection agency that would have had the authority to represent and advocate consumer interests before federal agencies and courts, and a bill to create such an agency was introduced in Congress. In 1975, the legislation to create an independent consumer agency within the executive branch of government, designed to represent consumers' interests, was passed by both the House and the Senate but was vetoed by President Gerald Ford. When Jimmy Carter was elected president in 1976, he promised to create a consumer protection agency along the lines proposed by Congress. But the legislation introduced to create the agency failed to clear Congress, giving consumers cause to worry that consumerism as a viable political factor had already begun to lose its force. How was it possible that such progress in consumer protection suddenly took a turn in the opposite direction?

There were several reasons for the decline of consumer regulation. First, a mood favoring deregulation had begun to develop in Congress, a feeling that there was already too much regulation and less, not more, was needed. In 1978, measures designed to deregulate the airline and natural gas industries cleared Congress and were approved by President Carter. Second, consumerism lacked an effective spokesperson. Ralph Nader, the self-appointed advocate of consumerism, began to lose the influence he once had had, when he took on other social issues. He also lost his influence with Congress when he published his own ratings (mostly bad) of its members. Third, many, including the respected late senator from North Carolina, Sam Ervin, felt that consumers could be overprotected. They believed consumers had to assume some responsibility for their actions and were intelligent enough to make rational choices. Fourth, and most important, was the ability of business to organize and lobby effectively against any proposed legislation it did not like. There is no question but that effective business lobbying was the catalyst that killed the consumer protection agency, even though impartial observers at the time considered it unnecessary.

Business has traditionally disdained government, being preoccupied with its own affairs. As special interest groups began to organize and lobby effectively for legislation they wanted, business decided it could no longer remain aloof.

Consumerism and the Reagan Administration

The Consumer Product Safety Commission faced an uncertain future when Ronald Reagan was elected to his first term in office, particularly since he had stressed in his campaign that he was going to reduce the role of government. Opponents of consumer protection regulation had raised some valid arguments. They claimed that regulation increased the cost of goods to consumers, limited their freedom to make significant choices by themselves, and led to bigger and more restrictive government. Some people in the Reagan administration proposed the outright elimination of the commission, but that did not happen. Changes were made in that the commission has been required to use cost-benefit analysis in setting industry regulations and to encourage industry-imposed standards.

The new federalism of the Reagan administration placed more reliance on state agencies to protect consumer interests. This shift does not mean a return to the principle of *caveat emptor,* which was more appropriate in the last century when consumers could be expected to know more about a product. Consumerism is far from dead. It is represented by a conglomerate of disparate interest groups, each with its own set of consumer concerns. Included are senior citizen groups, credit unions, consumer education organizations (such as Consumers Union), and other organizations with related interests. These groups may form a coalition to bring pressure on business and government. However, the action now centers more on the state level of government, and consumer groups that once lobbied Congress to take action on specific consumer measures, have now focused their attention on lobbying activities before state legislatures.[17]

Consumer expectations have risen over the years and will surely continue to rise. Our standards about the products we consume are higher than ever. People favor regulation that promotes safety and protection. High prices, high interest rates on credit cards, and the poor quality of products draw common consumer complaints. The failure of many companies to live up to their advertising claims also draws complaints. Product safety, such as the installation of air bags in cars, has become an issue. Credit availability is likewise a consumer concern. Deregulation of banks has made it easier to move capital from

---

[17] In government, there are 390 state, county, and municipal consumer protection offices. Business has hundreds of consumer affairs departments. The Society of Consumer Affairs Professionals in Business (SOCAPB) has more than 1,500 members. There are 150 Better Business Bureaus, which provide consumer information and report on the reliability of companies.

one area to another. Capital is often moved to more profitable markets, leaving smaller areas with less available credit. Advances in telecommunications have also made worldwide capital transfer easier. And finally, another issue of concern to consumer groups is customer service, particularly error resolution.[18]

CONSUMER PROTECTION AND ITS IMPACT ON BUSINESS

The impact of consumer protection requirements on business is considerable. One has only to read the daily newspapers to be aware of this impact. For example, in June 1986 the *Roanoke Times & World News* announced that Volkswagen was recalling 132,000 Audi 5000s in the 1984–1986 model years, to reposition the vehicles' brake and accelerator pedals.[19] General Motors recalled 98,000 cars to inspect headlight switches for defects. The Consumer Product Safety Commission moved to recall 1.6 million crib toys sold by Johnson & Johnson, claiming that the toys are a strangulation hazard. The toys—Soft Triplets, Piglet Crib Gym, and Triplets Marching Band—consist of three soft figures holding hands in a line held together by elastic. The CPSC claimed that two babies were strangled on the string used to tie the toys across baby cribs. The company, which plans to fight the recall, claimed that the parents of both babies did not follow the instructions included with the toys.

Automobile safety regulation provides an example of the impact of consumer protection regulation on business. Federal safety standards promulgated in the 1960s involved accident avoidance, crash protection, and postcrash survivability.[20] Accident avoidance standards were set for braking systems, tires, windshields, lamps, and transmission controls. Occupant protection standards included requirements for safety belts; head restraints; and highly penetration-resistant windshield glass. Exterior protection standards included the absorption capacity of front and rear bumpers. These and other standards for automobiles are presented in Table 12-1.

[18] Meredith M. Fernstrom, *Consumerism: Implications Financial Services,* Office of Public Responsibility, American Express Company, 1986.

[19] *Roanoke Times & World News,* Monday, June 16, 1986, p. C-6.

[20] Robert W. Crandall, Howard K. Gruenspecht, Theodore E. Keeler, and Lester B. Lave, *Regulating the Automobile* (Washington, D.C.: Brookings Institution, 1986), p. 47.

TABLE 12-1   Safety Standards for Passenger Cars

Standard	*Effective Date*
Occupant protection in interior impact	1968
Head restraints	1969
Impact protection for driver from steering control	1968
Door locks	1968
Safety belt assemblies	1968
Windshield-wiping system	1968
Child seating system	1971
Side door strength	1973
Roof crash resistance	1973
Flammability of interior material	1972

Source: Robert W. Crandall, Howard K. Gruenspecht, Theodore E. Keeler, and Lester B. Lave, *Regulating the Automobile* (Washington, D.C.: Brookings Institution, 1986), p. 48. Used by permission.

Costs and Benefits of Safety Standards

Using the automobile industry as an example, there are both costs and benefits of safety standards. The costs of safety standards are the original cost of meeting them as well as the costs of complying with them after the companies have had sufficient time to redesign the vehicles to accommodate the standards at the lowest cost. There is the cost of variable inputs required to produce such safety devices as safety belts, padded dashboards, and other interior protection devices. There is also the cost of external production devices, including the installation of safer, more durable bumpers. An important part of safety standards cost is the fuel penalty that motorists have to pay as a result of the weight added to cars, which is due in part to bumper standards.[21] There also may be a loss in the driving quality of cars imposed by tight regulatory deadlines.

Benefits also accrue to individuals and to society as a whole as a result of safety standards. One benefit is the reduction in the number of injuries and fatalities caused by automobile and other accidents. There has been a reduction in the number of highway deaths per 100 million vehicle miles driven.

[21] Ibid., p. 47.

TABLE 12-2   Estimates of the Benefits and Costs of Automobile Safety Regulation

Benefits	
Reductions in premature deaths	23,400
Reductions in all deaths	35,100
Value at $1 million per fatality avoided (in billions of dollars)	$ 35.1
Value at $300,000 per fatality avoided (in billions of dollars)	$ 10.5
Costs	
Cost per car (1981 dollars)	$ 671
Annual cost (in billions of dollars)	$ 7.0
Annual cost without bumper standards (in billions of dollars)	$ 4.9
Benefits less costs—first estimate = 35.1 less 7.0 =	$ 28.1
Benefits less costs—second estimate = 10.5 less 7.0 =	$ 3.5

Source: Robert W. Crandall, Howard K. Gruenspecht, Theodore E. Keeler, and Lester B. Lave, *Regulating the Automobile* (Washington, D.C.: Brookings Institution, 1986), p. 77. Used by permission.

In 1965, the highway deaths were 5.52 per 100 million vehicle miles driven; in 1983, there were 2.70 highway deaths per 100 million vehicle miles driven.[22] In 1965, the highway deaths for passenger-car occupants were 4.58 per 100 million vehicle miles driven; in 1983, the highway deaths were 1.92 per 100 million vehicle miles driven.[23] These reductions can be attributed in part to improved safety standards for automobiles but also in part to other factors such as driver education and the 55 mph speed limit.

Table 12-2 presents an estimate of the costs and benefits of automobile safety regulation. The costs include the various forms of safety devices that must be installed in automobiles. The benefits include a reduction in premature deaths, a large portion of which occurs among teenagers and young adults. It is difficult to assign values to the reduction in early fatalities: the estimates range from $300,000 to $1,000,000. As the table indicates, the benefits far outweigh the costs of safety regulation, regardless of what type of estimate is used.

[22] Ibid., p. 46.

[23] In 1965, there were 32,500 highway deaths in passenger cars compared to an estimated 28,000 for 1988.

PRODUCT LIABILITY

The United States is a litigious society, which explains why it has more lawyers than the rest of the world combined. One area of litigation is product liability. Each year between 60,000 and 70,000 Americans sue manufacturers
in a broad array of industries, alleging they were injured by unreasonably dangerous products, including asbestos, drugs, medical devices, cars and trucks,
toxic chemicals, and toys. Almost all plaintiffs settle out of court. Of the small
proportion who go to trial, more than half win damage awards—multimillion-
dollar sums in a few cases. Two companies, A. H. Robins, manufacturer of the
Dalkon Shield, and Johns-Manville, maker of building supplies including asbestos products, have been forced into or are in the process of filing for bankruptcy as a result of product liability suits against them.

Product liability is a part of tort law, a set of principles developed by judges
as part of the common law. This field of the law is concerned with compensat-
ing one person for harm caused by the wrongful conduct of another. Courts
impose monetary liability on firms whose products have caused personal
injury. Liability originally depended on showing that a firm had acted negli-
gently, which meant a firm had failed to exercise that degree of due care as
would be reasonably expected in similar circumstances. However, liability
has become stricter in that the fault or negligence of the manufacturer is irrelevant; liability is now imposed if the product is defective and the defect is
unexpected by the consumer and causes injury. Moreover, product liability
has been extended to apply to any purchaser of a product, to members of the
purchaser's family, and even to people having no relation to the purchaser. In
the aforementioned *MacPherson v. Buick* case, the company was held liable
when a defective wooden spoke in a wheel collapsed and MacPherson was injured as a result.[24] He sued the company, but it claimed that he had bought the
car from a dealer, and that it was no longer liable. A judge ruled otherwise,
holding the company liable for the defect because it was negligent when it had
not properly inspected the wheel before putting it on the car. The significance
of *MacPherson v. Buick* is that plaintiffs in a suit can go directly to the producer and bypass any intermediary such as a retailer or wholesaler. Before
MacPherson, a person injured by a defective product could sue only the dealer
from whom he or she had bought the product. Then the dealer could sue the
wholesaler, and the wholesaler the producer.

---

[24] *MacPherson v. Buick Motor Company.*

The Cigarette Industry and Product Liability

Not one smoker who has sued a cigarette manufacturer has been paid a penny in damages,[25] despite estimates by the U.S. Surgeon General that smoking kills 350,000 Americans annually, mainly from lung cancer, emphysema, and heart disease. Although many of these people started smoking before cigarette packages were required to carry a warning label, others started after the label first appeared in 1966. The latter group will have to show that the "Dangerous to Your Health" warning was not adequate to warn them of addiction. The warning, it is argued, warned only of the physical danger of smoking; it failed to mention the additional dangers of dependency in that a vast majority of smokers became rapidly addicted to cigarettes. Numerous health and psychiatric associations have also recognized the dependency-producing characteristics of cigarettes, some equal to the dependency produced from using addictive drugs.[26] In *Hudson v. R. J. Reynolds Tobacco Co.*, the plaintiff failed to prove that the risk of cigarette-induced lung cancer was foreseeable by the defendant tobacco company at the time the cigarettes were sold.[27] In *Green v. American Tobacco*, the jury found that Green's lung cancer and subsequent death was caused by smoking Lucky Strikes.[28] However, a federal court of appeals found in favor of the American Tobacco Company, ruling that the plaintiff (Green's widow) had to prove that Lucky Strikes killed more smokers than just Edwin Green.[29] In *Pritchard v. Liggett & Myers Tobacco Co.*, the jury determined that Pritchard's lung cancer was caused by smoking but also found he had assumed the risk.[30]

Plaintiffs in cigarette manufacturer liability suits advance several arguments. The first is misleading advertising. Most smokers begin smoking in high school because it is the thing to do or because of peer pressure. This tendency is reinforced by seductive multimillion-dollar advertising campaigns

---

[25] Tobacco companies *have* been held civilly liable when their products contained foreign objects such as human toes, mice, small snails, nails, and firecrackers, none of which are related to tobacco smoke.

[26] See, for example, *1979 Surgeon General's Report* (Washington, D.C.: U.S. Government Printing Office), chap. 12, p. 6.

[27] *Hudson v. R. J. Reynolds Tobacco Co.*, 427 F. 2d 541 (5th Cir. 1970).

[28] *Green v. American Tobacco Co.*, 154 So. 2d 169 (Fla. 1963).

[29] *Green v. American Tobacco Co.*, 391 F. 2d 97 (5th Cir. 1968).

[30] *Pritchard v. Liggett & Myers Tobacco Co.*, 295 F. 2d 292 (3d Cir. 1961).

that suggest smoking is sophisticated. A second argument is that cigarette smoking is addictive and creates a dependency not easily broken. When the dependent smoker attempts to stop smoking, a variety of unpleasant things may happen.[31] In addition to experiencing a craving for tobacco, the dependent smoker may become irritable and restless, with accompanying sleeplessness and gastrointestinal disturbances.[32] Concentration and judgment may be impaired as well. Third, it is argued that when warning labels first appeared on cigarette packages, they did not go far enough but should have included an explicit, unequivocal warning of addiction.

The tobacco companies advance the following counterarguments.[33] One is freedom of choice, which is a basic consumer right in a free market economy. As consumers, we are free to smoke or not to smoke. Second, the defendants can argue that Congress has preempted the entire field of cigarette information under the 1965 Cigarette Labeling and Advertising Act and the subsequent Public Health Smoking Act of 1970. The label requires a cigarette warning, but it requires no specific statement relating to health. A third defense is that of comparable fault in product liability.[34] The comparable fault doctrine looks at the plaintiff's conduct in determining the extent to which he or she has caused his or her own harm. It is expected that a consumer notice or be aware of a risk. For example, many young smokers understand when they first begin to smoke that certain risks may be involved. Comparable fault permits a jury to hold the plaintiff responsible for some degree of risk conduct.

The Rose Cipollone Case

The Rose Cipollone case has to be considered a classic tobacco liability case because it marks the first loss for the tobacco industry.[35] Cipollone, a New Jersey housewife, started smoking when she was sixteen and quit smoking a year before her death of lung cancer at the age of fifty-eight in 1984. She started smoking because she had seen movie stars such as Joan Crawford and Barbara

---

[31] The cigarette liability suits involved smokers who started smoking before there was a ban on cigarette advertising on television and before the warning labels appeared on packages.

[32] *1979 Surgeon General's Report,* chap. 16, p. 14.

[33] Garner, pp. 1448–1454.

[34] *Butaud v. Suburban Marine and Sporting Goods,* 555 P. 2d 42 (Alaska 1976).

[35] The case is on appeal. The decision could be overturned. I think it will be.

Stanwyck smoking in the cigarette ads in magazines.[36] She said they were so glamorous and always appeared in evening dresses. She continued to smoke as an adult, despite efforts of her husband and children to make her stop. However, in 1955 she switched from Chesterfield straight to L&M filters, which were advertised at the time as "Just What the Doctor Ordered!" A picture of Rosalind Russell, another glamorous movie star, appeared on the advertisement.[37] She kept smoking even after a malignant tumor forced removal of part of her lung in 1981, and her whole lung was removed in 1982. When she did quit, she and her husband filed a liability suit, which was pursued after her death.

In June 1988, the lawsuit made national headlines. It was heralded as the tobacco industry's first loss, and it was predicted that many new suits against tobacco companies would occur. A six-member jury ordered the Liggett Group, makers of Chesterfield and L &M, to pay Tony Cipollone $400,000 in compensatory damages for his wife's death. However, New Jersey law states that product liability awards can be given only if the defendant is at least 50 percent to blame. The jury was not fully persuaded that it was the fault of the tobacco company and decided that Rose Cipollone's illness and subsequent death was 80 percent her fault and 20 percent the fault of Liggett & Myers.[38] Cipollone's estate received nothing, even though the husband received the compensatory award.

Lawyers for the plaintiff blamed the tobacco companies. They sought to portray her as helplessly addicted to cigarettes. They contended that her failure to quit despite her encroaching cancer was proof positive of her inability to shake the habit. They also accused the tobacco companies of conspiring to withhold studies that they themselves had commissioned that showed that cigarette smoking could be hazardous to one's health. The lawyers for the tobacco companies argued that Rose Cipollone smoked of her own free will and that she could have given it up sooner had she really tried, as many other smokers had managed to do. They also argued that the health hazards of cigarette

[36] Joan Crawford died of cancer; Barbara Stanwyck is still alive.

[37] Rosalind Russell died of cancer.

[38] Three of the six-member jury have subsequently been quoted as saying they made a mistake and if they had it to do over, they would have awarded nothing to Tony Cipollone. They said that they awarded compensatory damages because one member of the jury was very adamant about it. Rose Cipollone herself was less than an ideal subject. She refused to stop smoking even when her husband and children begged her to stop. She told them to mind their own business.

smoking were known when Rose first started smoking.[39] Finally, they reiterated doubts about a causal relationship between cigarette smoking and the type of cancer that killed Rose Cipollone.

There are two main issues in this case. Rose Cipollone had a choice to smoke or not to smoke, and she chose the former, with all its attendant risks. Her husband's lawyers tried to portray her as the helpless victim of seductive advertising by malevolent tobacco companies, who hid the truth from her. But she did not stop smoking even when a warning was placed on cigarette packages, and even when nearly every magazine and newspaper in the country was devoting considerable attention to the hazards of cigarette smoking. Conversely, it can be argued that Rose Cipollone was misled by advertising. For example, there was the L&M advertisement, "Just What the Doctor Ordered!" Barbara Stanwyck and Rosalind Russell gave testimonials for this new miracle cigarette, which had a new alpha cellulose filter that was supposed to be "Just what the doctor ordered."[40] It was supposed to filter out nicotine. It can be argued that Rose Cipollone was given an express warranty when she switched to L&Ms that the product was safe. Therefore, Liggett & Myers should be held responsible for her death.

SUMMARY

One of the fundamental tenets supporting a market economy is consumer sovereignty, which is based on the idea that ultimate decisions as to what will be produced rest with the consumer. This presupposes that consumers have the information necessary to make rational choices in the marketplace. If this is

---

[39] In a product liability suit involving the R. J. Reynolds Tobacco Company, a federal judge in Knoxville, Tennessee, dismissed the suit before a jury had reached a verdict. The judge stated that the issue in the case is not what the specific plaintiff knew or did not know about the dangers of smoking, but what an ordinary consumer would be expected to know. Tobacco has been used for more than four hundred years, and its characteristics and qualities are well known. Therefore, there was no way an average consumer would not know the potential risks of smoking cigarettes. In fact, there was even a popular song in 1947 called "Smoke, Smoke, Smoke That Cigarette," which included the words "Puff, puff, and if you smoke yourself to death."

[40] Rosalind Russell stated in her testimonial, "I wanted a cigarette with a filter I could depend on and a flavor I could enjoy. I read the letter below from Dr. F. R. Darkis, director of Liggett & Myers Research, and changed immediately to L&M filters." The letter itself said that extensive research had found a material that effectively filtered the smoke. This was a cellulose that removed over one-third of the smoke. When you smoked the L&M cigarette, you supposedly drew into your mouth much less nicotine.

true, consumer expenditures guide resource allocation into chosen products. But in a complex industrial society, it is difficult for consumers to have the expertise necessary to distinguish among the many products. In addition, consumers are subject to the external pressures of advertising. It can be argued that consumers are led by advertising to make product choices on the basis of subjective factors—conspicuous consumption, envy, and emulating one's peer group, for example. Therefore, laws have been passed to protect consumers against those practices considered deleterious to their interests.

Consumer protection reached a new peak in the late 1960s and early 1970s when the federal government began to increase its support of consumer welfare. This support reflected the mood of the times, with consumer interests coalescing into group pressure for the passage of new laws. Business firms often have lacked innovation or have been slow to respond to consumers' needs. But many felt regulation in the consumer area was carried too far and proved costly and inefficient. The basic issue before the public today is whether consumers can be best protected by relying on voluntary standards set by business, by transferring responsibility to state consumer protection agencies, by relying on existing federal agencies such as the Food and Drug Administration, or by allowing consumers to act for themselves.

QUESTIONS FOR DISCUSSION

1. What is meant by "consumer sovereignty"? Are consumers really sovereign?
2. What is considered false or deceptive advertising?
3. What control does the Federal Trade Commission have over false or deceptive advertising?
4. Discuss the main provisions of the Consumer Product Safety Act of 1972.
5. Discuss the main objectives of the Consumer Product Warranty Act of 1975.
6. What philosophy did Congress adopt for controlling rates of credit in the Truth-in-Lending Act of 1969?
7. There are costs as well as benefits in consumer protection legislation, but the costs are often overlooked. Discuss.
8. What is product liability? Should the tobacco companies be held liable for deaths and injuries that occur from the consumption of tobacco?

9. Discuss the impact of the consumer movement on business.
10. What is the future of the consumer movement?
11. What is comparable fault? Was it an issue in the Cipollone case?
12. If you had been on the jury, how would you have voted in the Cipollone case?

RECOMMENDED READINGS

Baily, Mary Ann, and Warren I. Gikins, eds. *The Effects of Litigation on Health Care Costs.* Washington, D.C.: Brookings Institution, 1985.

Bloom, Paul N., and Stephen A. Greyser. "The Maturing of Consumerism." *Harvard Business Review* 59 (November–December 1981): 130–139.

Carson, Thomas L., Richard E. Wokutch, and James E. Cox, Jr. "An Ethical Analysis of Deceptive Advertising." *Journal of Business Ethics* 4 (1985): 93–104.

Crandall, Robert W., Howard K. Gruenspecht, Theodore E. Keeler, and Lester B. Lave. *Regulating the Automobile.* Washington, D.C.: Brookings Institution, 1986.

Fernstrom, Meredith. *Consumerism: Implications and Opportunities for Financial Services.* New York: American Express, 1986.

Grabowski, Henry G., and John M. Vernon. *The Regulation of Pharmaceuticals: Measuring the Risks.* Washington, D.C.: American Enterprise Institute, 1983.

Pertschuk, Michael. *Revolt Against Regulation: The Rise and Pause of the Consumer Movement.* Berkeley: University of California Press, 1982.

Viscusi, W. Kip. *Regulating Consumer Product Safety.* Washington, D.C.: American Enterprise Institute, 1984.

Chapter 13

Environmental Policies and Their Impact on Business

The year 1988 was a bad year for the world environment. In fact, *Time* departed from its usual tradition of naming its man, or occasionally its woman, of the year. Instead, *Time* named Earth as the planet of the year.[1] Many bad things happened to the planet earth. Floods hit Bangladesh, leaving thousands homeless in one of the poorest countries in the world, and hurricanes devastated Jamaica and parts of Mexico and Central America. Famine occurred in northern Africa and many people died of starvation. Pollution remained a worldwide problem. The United States, too, had its share of environmental problems. It experienced the hottest weather in this century, with much damage done to the food crops in the Midwest. Many of its beaches were polluted by waste materials that drifted ashore. Its cities were crowded as usual, and gridlock occurred on the highways. In Los Angeles, drivers took out their frustrations by shooting at each other. All in all, 1988 was not a good year for the environment.

Pollution of the environment is by no means a recent phenomenon. In one form or another, it has existed throughout recorded times. In the Middle Ages, human effluvia was dumped in the streets, thus contributing to such epidemics as the Black Plague, which killed at least one-third of Europe's population.[2] Natural disasters, such as the volcanic eruption of Krakatoa in 1883, caused their share of environmental damage. In the United States, pollution as we know it today is a by-product of industrialization, which was stimulated by the Civil War. Industrial cities, such as Chicago and Pittsburgh, were cited by foreign visitors to the United States early in this century as being particularly

---

[1] *Time*, "Planet of the Year, Endangered Earth," January 2, 1989, pp. 26–73.

[2] Barbara W. Tuchman, *A Distant Mirror* (New York: Ballantine Books, 1978), pp. 92–125. The disease was bubonic plague, which is transmitted by rat fleas.

foul.[3] The largest assemblage of stockyards in the world added a mephitic flavor to Chicago's air, as if a poisonous or foul-smelling gas were being emitted from the earth. Natural drainage was nonexistent, flooding was habitual, and the surface of the Chicago River was so thick with grease that it looked like a liquid rainbow.[4]

ENVIRONMENTAL PROBLEMS

Clemenceau, premier of France during the latter part of World War I, once said that war was too important to be left to the generals. By the same token, the environment is too important to be left in the hands of business or any other group, because it belongs to everyone. Threats to the environment exist everywhere and take many forms. In the United States, radon, which is an odorless, colorless radioactive gas, has created an environmental threat because it is associated with lung cancer. The gas is considered one of the worst health hazards in the United States. The gas, which is produced by the decay of uranium in rocks and soils, can cause lung cancer if it seeps up from the ground into houses through cracks in foundations and drains. A number of studies, including data collected from uranium mines, have indicated that radon causes between 5,000 and 20,000 deaths from lung cancer each year, making it the second leading cause of that form of cancer after smoking.[5] (According to the 1989 Surgeon General's Report, there were about 350,000 deaths from smoking.)

The Greenhouse Effect

At one time there was talk in the United States about the beginning of a new Ice Age that would rival the Little Ice Age, which lasted from about the fourteenth century to the eighteenth century. The Little Ice Age was caused by an advance of polar and alpine glaciers and caused years of cold weather that reduced the production of grain and other food products.[6] But times have changed and the new Ice Age has not arrived. Instead, in the latter part of the

[3] Rudyard Kipling, *Actions and Reactions* (New York: Doubleday and Page, 1909).

[4] Louis Mumford, *The City in History* (New York: Harcourt, Brace and World, 1961), p. 469.

[5] *Time,* September 26, 1988, p. 56.

[6] Tuchman, *A Distant Mirror,* p. 24.

twentieth century, there is now talk of a warming effect that bodes ill for the future of the world. The two extremely hot summers of 1987 and 1988 have lent credence to the belief that the world is getting warmer. Scientists generally agree that the world is getting warmer, and that the resulting change could harm food and energy production. This change is called the "greenhouse effect."

The greenhouse effect is caused by a series of related circumstances. Carbon dioxide from the burning of fossil fuels such as oil, coal, and gasoline—all concomitants of higher living standards—is accumulating in the atmosphere.[7] So are other gases like chlorofluorocarbons, which are less abundant but equally as devastating. These and other gases come from a variety of man-made sources such as vehicle exhausts and industrial solvents. In Earth's atmosphere, the gases act like the glass in a greenhouse, which lets in sunlight but traps heat. By absorbing rather than reflecting the infrared radiation that produces heat, they are bringing about the warming of the world. As heat rises from Earth's surface, it strikes molecules of carbon dioxide and other gases, setting them vibrating. The gas molecules reflect some of the heat back to Earth, which intensifies the warming or "greenhouse effect."

There are many possible adverse outcomes of the "greenhouse effect."[8] First, the melting of the polar ice cap can produce more icebergs that can endanger shipping.[9] Second, lower water levels on the world waterways can increase shipping costs and reduce the generation of hydroelectric power. Third, farming in the midwestern United States as well as elsewhere can be damaged by hotter and drier summers. Fourth, India and Bangladesh, which are already adversely affected by flooding, will have more flooding. The same could hold true in China, the world's largest country, but the central area of the country, by receiving more rain, would be able to increase its rice yield. In Canada, less rain could cause crop failure in the rich farmlands of Ontario, and in a worst-case scenario water levels of the Colorado River could drop, thereby disrupting water supplies and the generation of power to eight states, including California.

[7] The United State accounts for about one-fifth of the world's carbon dioxide emissions, and 98 percent of these come from burning fossil fuels.

[8] Anthony Ramirez, "A Warming World: What It Will Mean," *Fortune,* July 4, 1988, pp. 104–105.

[9] The sinking of the *Titanic* after hitting an iceberg is an example.

The Ozone Layer

In the past two decades, the depletion of Earth's ozone layer has become a great environmental concern. The destruction of the layer by chemical pollutants has been linked to an increased incidence of skin cancer and has led to the regulation of many chemical products. The ozone layer protects living organisms by using up ultraviolet and other high-energy forms of radiation through a cycle of chemical reactions. Atmospheric oxygen (O_2) is converted to and from ozone (O_3) via high-energy radiation. The radiation is consumed and is dissipated harmlessly as heat and cannot reach the earth's surface. When the ozone layer is weakened, ultraviolet radiation interacts with genetic material, damaging it and increasing the incidence of melanoma and other forms of skin cancer.[10] That is why it has become of increased importance that people should not spend time in the sun without some protective covering.

The ozone layer, which has been taken for granted by society, is indeed one of the factors that has allowed life to exist and thrive on earth since the beginning of time. With the evolution of oxygen-producing organisms, such as algae and plants, ozone was generated from a reaction between this oxygen and ultraviolet radiation. Once the layer was built up, more complex life forms were able to exist. The chief culprits in the destruction of the layer are the freons. These gases are commonly used as solvents, refrigerants, and aerosol propellants. The production of freons began in the 1930s and by the 1970s had reached almost two billion pounds per year. In 1975, a study by the National Academy of Sciences indicated that freons were damaging the ozone layer. Freon reacts with ozone by converting it to atmospheric oxygen and thereby reducing the amount available to interact with ultraviolet radiation.[11]

Acid Rain

Acid rain is caused by acid deposition in the atmosphere. (Acids can also occur in snow, as well as clouds, dew, and fog.) The major chemicals involved in

[10] Since the 1930s, the occurrence of malignant melanomas has risen from 1 in 100,000 to 1 in 250 in 1980. Occurrences of nonmelanoma skin cancer have increased just as rapidly. Besides skin cancer, eye cataracts and suppression of the immune system may also be caused by the effects of ultraviolet radiation.

[11] The ozone depletion and the greenhouse effect are closely coupled because ozone itself is a greenhouse effect gas, and because the same gases that are predicted to modify ozone are also predicted to contribute to a climate warming.

acid rain are sulfuric acid and nitric acid. However, neither of these is emitted directly into the atmosphere in significant quantities. Rather, they are formed in the atmosphere by the oxidation of sulfur dioxide, emitted primarily by coal-fueled electric utilities; nitrogen oxides, emitted by motor vehicles and electric utilities; and a variety of volatile organic compounds, released during petroleum refining, chemical manufacturing, and paint and solvent used by a number of atmospheric oxidants. These transformations can occur in clean air or in clouds, near or far from the location of emission. The eventual acid deposition into rain is influenced by prevailing meteorological conditions and earth surface characteristics.

Acid rain can harm the environment in several different ways. First, metals, paint systems, stones, and other materials are sensitive to acid rain or any other form of acid deposition. Second, acid rain can affect the growth of forests. Evidence of diminished growth in forests have heightened concern over causal factors, one of which may be acid rain. Third, agricultural crops may be affected by acid rain.

However, other factors also affect crop yield and it is difficult to separate acid rain from these factors. Finally, lake and stream acidification, which can damage aquatic organisms, may result from acid rain. Surface water chemistry can change either over the long term or during episodes, such as the spring melting of snow. Again, it is hard to separate acid rain from other factors that can cause aquatic pollution.

Pesticides and Hazardous Wastes

The rise of pesticide use in developing countries is essential to the maintenance and promotion of agricultural production as well as for the control of diseases. However, pesticides are hazardous to some forms of life. They can be misused by individuals, or stored near food or when containers are improperly used for other purposes. Misuse can also lead to environmental contamination. Pesticides can also be ingested by humans because some may get into food products. DDT, a pesticide that is now banned, got into streams and lakes, poisoning fish and the people who ate them. Any pesticide that is water soluble can get into food crops, which are then consumed by humans. Pesticides are exported from industrialized countries to developing countries and then can be reimported as residues on food back to the industrial countries.

There are two types of hazardous waste—solid and toxic. Solid waste is the by-product of production and consumption. It includes garbage, disposable cartons and other effluvia emitted by consumers. In the summer of 1988 from New Jersey to Long Island, incoming tides washed up an array of human detritus on the public beaches.[12] Included were plastic tampon applicators, balls of sewage two inches thick, drug paraphernalia, prescription bottles, stained bandages, vials of blood (three of which tested positive for hepatitis), and containers of surgical sutures. Toxic waste includes various by-products of industrial production. An example is nitrous acid, which is released by the production of fertilizers. This waste is usually disposed of in barrels that are buried in the earth. Wastewater from factories and sewage treatment plants includes such toxic substances as heavy metals, including lead and mercury. Chemical pollutants have been held responsible for the decimation of oysters, lobsters, and crabs in Chesapeake Bay. And Seattle's Elliott Bay is contaminated with a mix of copper, lead, zinc, arsenic, cadmium, and polychlorinated biphenyls (PCBs).[13]

Nuclear Accidents and Radiation

During the late 1970s there was a very popular television show called *The Incredible Hulk,* in which a wimpy scientist who was exposed to gamma rays was transformed into a monster resembling a Russian weight-lifter in green leotards. This transformation occurred when someone was picking on him or other people whom he had befriended. The radiation to which he had been exposed caused the mutation to a muscle-bound version of Robin Hood. After he had wreaked havoc on various assorted bad guys, he then reverted back to his old wimpy self. Although *The Incredible Hulk* was far-fetched, it was part of the genre of movies and television shows, going back to *Godzilla,* that dealt with the impact of nuclear testing or nuclear accidents on the environment.

The meltdown of a nuclear reactor at a nuclear power plant in Chernobyl in the Soviet Union illustrated the potential environmental damage that can occur from the misuse of nuclear power. It was an embarrassment to the Russians, who had suggested that anything bad that happened, environmental or otherwise, could only occur in capitalist countries. But Chernobyl illustrated that environmental disasters had nothing to do with political and economic ideologies. It caused a number of fatalities among workers who were employed at the plant; it caused radiation damage that has had and will continue

---

[12] *Time,* "Our Filthy Seas," August 1, 1988, p. 44.

[13] Polychlorinated biphenyls (PCBs) are chemicals used by the electrical equipment industry.

to have far-reaching effects on both the people and the economy of that area of the Soviet Union; and radiation was carried by the clouds to surrounding countries. Finland, Sweden, and Norway reported an increase in radiation activity, with some contamination occurring in milk.

Pollution Is a Global Problem

The two previous chapters discussed subjects that are limited to the United States. Consumer protection laws apply to American consumers, and equal employment-affirmative action policies apply to American workers, but pollution is a global problem that transcends national boundaries and from which no country is immune. Modern civilization's capacity for manipulating and modifying nature, and the rapidity with which new means and methods of production are being discovered and implemented, make it important to look for both national and global solutions to problems of the environment. The subject of pollution is very complex and cuts across many disciplines—biology, geology, chemistry, sociology, and economics. An attempt to alleviate one environmental problem can sometimes create others even more troublesome. What is more, since the quality of the environment is not subject to market forces, allocational efficiency is difficult to attain.

Most countries of the world depend on the seas for their livelihood and recreation. The seas are polluted, and the problem is global. Recreational boaters, fishermen, and ocean-going ships dump their garbage overboard. Marine debris entangles many different marine species throughout the world, including marine mammals, seabirds, marine turtles, and fish. In addition, some species, including endangered species of sea turtles and many species of marine birds, ingest ocean debris such as plastic bags and small plastic pellets.[14] Many causes of sea pollution are difficult to trace, because they may occur hundreds of miles from the sea. Nutrients, such as nitrogen and phosphorus, can enter rivers from a variety of sources. Eventually these pollutants find their way to the sea. For example, in the early 1970s a chemical plant in Strasbourg, France, dumped mercury into the Rhine River, killing fish for a distance of 300 miles. The Rhine flows into the North Sea and forms an estuary with the Meuse River in the Netherlands. From the estuary, the mercury found its way into the waters of the sea, thus depleting the fish supply.

[14] Council on Environmental Quality, *Environmental Quality 1985*, 16th Annual Report of the Council on Environmental Quality (Washington, D.C.: 1987), p. 246.

TABLE 13-1   Marine Fish Catch by Region: 1975–1983 (millions of metric tons)

Year	North Atlantic	Central Atlantic	South Atlantic	Indian Ocean	North Pacific	Central Pacific	South Pacific	Total
1975	15.8	6.3	3.4	3.1	19.5	6.4	4.7	59.1
1976	16.5	6.5	3.6	3.2	20.0	6.8	6.1	62.7
1977	15.5	6.3	4.0	3.6	20.0	7.2	4.5	61.1
1978	14.5	6.4	4.8	3.6	20.3	7.5	5.9	63.1
1979	14.7	6.1	4.4	3.5	20.3	7.5	7.3	63.8
1980	14.7	6.9	3.9	3.7	20.8	7.9	6.6	64.4
1981	14.5	6.8	4.0	3.7	21.9	8.5	7.2	66.6
1982	13.6	7.2	4.3	3.9	22.6	8.2	8.3	68.0
1983	13.8	7.3	4.3	4.1	23.6	7.8	6.6	67.6

Source: From Council on Environmental Quality, *Sixteenth Annual Report* (Washington, D.C.: 1987), p. 443.

Human activities have had an adverse impact on the marine environment. Overfishing has depleted populations of some commercial fish species. Marine pollution has already damaged many ecosystems and certain living marine resources in coastal areas. Table 13-1 presents marine fish catch by world regions for 1975 to 1983. As the table indicates, fish catches for certain regions have actually shown a decline or have remained about the same over the time period. This does not augur well for the future. If human population continues to grow at the rate it is growing now, the pressure of a declining food supply will increase. Although the fish catch showed an increase in the Indian Ocean, the countries of that region are among the poorest in the world and have a very high rate of population growth.

Deforestation

Probably the most important environmental problem the world faces is deforestation, because trees provide oxygen and prevent soil erosion. The forest ecosystem is biologically rich, containing about one-half of all species of plants and animals. The major forests of the world are the tropical rain forests, which are located at the equator. The rain forests of the Amazon River and equatorial Africa are disappearing at an alarming rate. A worst-case scenario, based on the assumption that the rain forests are disappearing at a rate of 2 percent a year would lead to a prediction that by the year 2000 half of the rain forests would be gone.[15] A more optimistic scenario is that the rain forests are disappearing at a rate of less than 1 percent a year. However, that is not the whole point, because in many regions of the world rain forests containing unique endemic wildlife populations are in danger of being depopulated. Again, the problem is that deforestation occurs in the poorest areas of the world, where people eke out a marginal existence. The end result is a food supply reduced by the leaching of the soil, polluting water supplies and making land less arable.

CAUSES OF POLLUTION

The reasons for pollution are varied and cannot be attributed solely to the operations of business firms, as some critics of U.S. society contend. One reason is the concentration of population in the United States and in other industrial countries into urban areas. The geographic distribution of population densities and the volume of pollution have an important relationship to each other. More than half the people in the United States live in 1 percent of the total land area; two-thirds live in 9 percent of the area. On this basis, the United States is one of the most overpopulated countries in the world. Such clustering of population greatly intensifies the problem of pollution: the very process of living generates wastes—wastes that, for the most part, nature can cope with efficiently until population density becomes quite high. Thus, at least part of the pollution problem can be attributed to the concentration of a large population in a relatively small land area. The larger the population is, the greater the volume of waste it will create—all other things being equal.

A second reason for pollution is the widespread affluence of Western industrial society. This affluence has created effluence, since many people have the money to demand a wide variety of goods and services, while discarding articles that often are still usable. In the United States and other overdeveloped countries, millions of cars and billions of bottles and cans are junked annually. Demand patterns have shifted to require more convenience goods and services. Parents who themselves walked to school transport their children by auto day after day. In the past, one automobile was enough for most families; today, two cars per family is common. The increased demand for creature comforts is also a part of the changing lifestyles. Few churches today expect their congregations to keep cool on a summer's day with paper fans from the local funeral parlors as in the past, even though the generation of electricity to operate air conditioning may add to the pollution of the environment.

A third reason for pollution is industry itself. Undeniably, dramatic examples of industrial pollution can readily be found, in part because much of this pollution is highly visible. One has only to look at the effluvia dumped into the rivers and lakes near any industrial city. Lake Erie is an excellent example, for it is one of the most polluted water areas in the world, polluted by industrial wastes from Cleveland's steel mills as well as industries in other cities. Moreover, today's rapidly advancing technology constantly creates new problems of pollution; the very processes that improve the ordinary person's lot as a consumer may have the reverse effect on the ecological balance. As one example, when most steelmakers changed from open hearth methods to the more efficient oxygen process, the demand for scrap metal dropped, since the oxygen process mainly uses iron ore and taconite pellets. Consequently, the incentive for junk dealers to salvage old cars became so low that some dealers actually insisted on being paid for accepting the vehicles. The inevitable result was that cities began to face the expensive chore of disposing of old automobiles. This situation raises the question of who the polluter is: the steelmaker who changed to a new process, the auto manufacturer who builds a car that fails to disintegrate readily, or the auto owner who behaves in an antisocial way by abandoning the car?

Government is the fourth source of pollution.[16] Localities must contend with two major kinds of potential pollutants: sewage and solid wastes such as garbage, sometimes on an incredibly large scale. All too often, localities have taken the most economical approach, letting raw sewage pour into the nearest river and dumping the garbage at the city dump and then burning it, thus polluting the air. In addition, cities that operate their own public utilities and conduct other quasi-business activities are often as guilty of polluting the environment as their counterparts in private industry are. A city that operates a public utility is going to use the same fuels and emit the same fumes as does a privately owned public utility. Federal government facilities also have contributed to pollution.[17]

[16] Pollution may also emanate from other sources. One source is agriculture, which adds to pollution through wastes from feedlots, pesticides, and sediments carried by erosion.

[17] For example, the Aberdeen Proving Ground, a federal military facility, is a major polluter of the Chesapeake Bay. (*The Washington Post,* Sunday, June 1, 1986, p. 15.)

GOVERNMENT ROLE IN POLLUTION CONTROL

Several public policy approaches can be used to control pollution—direct regulation; charges for emissions, including taxes; subsidies; and other government activities. Combinations of these approaches also can be used. Each approach has advantages and disadvantages, and because there are different kinds and sources of pollution, many of which are not well understood, it is impossible to say which is best. Hence, a method of control that might effectively curb air or water pollution might not be suitable for reducing noise levels or the misuse of land.

Regulation

Legislation can be used to establish appropriate standards for air, water, noise, and land use: the Clean Air Act of 1970 sets standards for air quality, and there is similar legislation for water. In addition, regulation can require licenses, permits, zoning regulation, and registration. The formulation of air and water standards implies a value judgment about the reasonable degree of control that can be achieved through regulation. A rationale for regulation is that similar standards are established for all business firms. Requiring every steel mill to meet similar effluent standards is considered fair not only among individual firms but also among communities. Proponents of uniform or similar standards contend that unless these standards are applied everywhere, the rules will be neither fair nor effective in reducing pollution. Firms polluting in one area would move to locations where standards are lower, and firms in areas with high standards would be treated unfairly. Communities with high standards also would be at a disadvantage in attracting and holding industry, and pollution would continue to come from communities with low standards.

An objection to regulation is that it leads to rigidities and, in many cases, unwieldy and inefficient forms of control. For example, uniform emission standards produce certain problems. One problem is that differences exist among firms in the same industry and differences in environmental conditions among geographic areas. Different firms have different requirements in the use of the environment. The discharge of waste into a river is an example. Some firms want to discharge more waste because their cost of waste treatment is higher; other firms may have lower costs. A firm might be permitted to discharge more waste if the damage done by such waste is lower because few or no people live downstream from the point of discharge. Environmental conditions also may vary considerably among geographic areas, and these differences will be reflected in the prices of the goods produced. An area with natural resources that absorb waste discharges may be prevented from using this absorptive capacity because of uniform national standards for environmental quality. Thus, a law that sets a standard pollution level may cause a misallocation of resources.

Emission Charges

Another method of controlling pollution is to levy emission charges in the form of taxes or fees against polluters. For example, in copper smelting sulfur oxides are among the principal pollutants produced. Rather than requiring copper companies to reduce the sulfur oxides by a given percentage, such companies could be taxed according to the amount of sulfur oxide they actually do release into the atmosphere. Each polluting firm could then decide for itself how much control it wants to provide. A firm that, for one reason or another, has higher costs for control presumably would release more pollutants than a firm with relatively low control costs. Emission charges would become part of a firm's costs of operation and would cause the firm to calculate both the costs of waste and the costs and benefits of pollution abatement. Since emission charges would take advantage of differences in control costs among polluters, it would be possible to reach an average air standard at a lower cost to society than would be possible by applying a uniform emission standard through law. Another advantage of emission charges is that the government could charge lower emission fees in sparsely populated areas and higher fees in more densely populated areas, thus spreading pollution more evenly throughout the country and encouraging industrial dispersion. This approach would have the net effect of decreasing total pollution. Furthermore, the fees would provide revenue that could be used for various social purposes, including the construction of waste treatment facilities or research on pollution abatement.

The implementation of a tax or any form of use charge requires an evaluation of the damage done by the emission of an incremental quality of pollution at any given time or place. After this evaluation, an emission charge is assessed to the responsible parties based on the amount of damage. Presumably, those firms with the capabilities to reduce emissions at a cost less than the pollution charge will do so, and the proper amount of abatement will be obtained by the least costly means. If the tax or charge is too low, it will not be an adequate inducement to reduce the wastes disposed; if the price is too high, it will impose more control than necessary and will be uneconomic in its effect. The experience gained through using some sort of charge might resolve this problem; however, charges have yet to be tried extensively, even though numerous task forces and studies have specifically recommended their experimental use.

Subsidies

A third public approach to pollution control would be to award subsidies to business firms to defray the cost of compliance with pollution control standards. A rationale for such subsidies is that business firms are being forced to treat their effluents at least in part so that others may benefit, and therefore, they should be compensated for the benefit. Subsidies could take several forms. First, a tax credit might be given to compensate for the cost of acquiring pollution abatement equipment. This credit would be deducted from the tax a firm would pay on net income after total business deductions. Thus, a $100 tax credit for pollution control equipment would reduce by $100 the amount of tax due. Second, outright cash payments could be made to reduce the level of pollution. Third, accelerated depreciation allowances could be used to reduce the cost of pollution control equipment. Specifically, accelerated depreciation would permit business firms to write off the cost of equipment in a shorter time than would standard depreciation provisions, increasing the cash flow of these firms in the process. Fourth, state and local governments could allow property tax exemptions on pollution control equipment.

Subsidies do have disadvantages.[18] If firms are given aid for their cost of waste treatment or for the purchase of pollution abatement equipment, less pressure is on them to find alternative ways of dealing with the pollution problem. Subsidies in the form of tax relief based on the purchase of abatement equipment favor capital-intensive waste treatment. A firm must respond to varying consumer tastes, which means manufacturing different products that in turn give rise to different forms of waste. Subsidies for capital equipment reduce its cost to the firm and encourage the firm to substitute fixed for variable costs, and economic inefficiency in waste treatment may result. It also can be argued that subsidies, particularly if they are financed out of general tax

[18] Tax Foundation, *Pollution Control: Perspective on the Government Role* (New York: Tax Foundation, 1971), pp. 11–25.

revenues, violate the benefit principle of equity. According to this principle, the cost of pollution control should be part of the cost of production, and consumers who buy products should pay the antipollution costs just as they pay for labor, capital, and other inputs.

Other Government Activities

Government carries on several activities regarding the protection of the environment. Both the federal and state governments have become regulators, establishing laws, setting standards, and monitoring and supervising compliance. Thus, the Clean Air Act as amended in 1970 provides standards of air quality; there is similar legislation for water. The government also offers special tax assistance and subsidies by underwriting or engaging directly in research related to environmental problems. Virtually all the states now have enacted legislation that establishes a legal basis for controlling the sources of pollution. Besides writing laws to regulate pollution and provide subsidies, the government has also had to cope with its own harmful by-products.

Federal legislation for pollution control dates back as far as the turn of the century, when the Refuse Act of 1899 prohibited the discharge of waste materials into navigable waters. The Oil Pollution Act of 1924 forbade the discharge of oil into coastal waters, and in 1948 the Water Pollution Control Act was passed. Asserting that pollution problems were better handled at the local level, the act nonetheless authorized the Public Health Service to coordinate research, provide technical information, and—on request from the states involved—provide limited supervision of interstate waterways. The Water Pollution Control Act of 1956, along with amendments of 1961, 1965, 1966, and 1970, considerably extended federal involvement, both regulatory and financial, in water pollution control. The Water Quality Act of 1965 created the Water Pollution Control Administration, which almost immediately was transferred to the Department of the Interior. Responsibility for air pollution, however, remained with the Department of Health, Education and Welfare (now the Department of Health and Human Services).

Federal laws concerned with air pollution were first instituted in 1955, when Congress authorized technical assistance to states and localities, as well as a research program. In 1963, the Clean Air Act was passed to give states grants both to improve pollution control programs and to provide for federal enforcement in interstate pollution cases. The 1963 act also expanded federal research, particularly in connection with pollution from motor vehicles and from the burning of coal and fuel oil, and emphasized the need for controlling pollution from facilities operated by the federal government. A 1965 amendment authorized federal regulation of motor vehicles through standards that became effective in 1968. In 1966, an amendment broadened the federal aid program, making grants available for state and local control programs. The Air Quality Act of 1967 directed the Department of Health, Education and Welfare to delineate broad atmospheric areas for the entire country, as well as air quality control regions. The act continued and strengthened most of the provisions of the earliest legislation and provided for special studies of jet aircraft emissions, the need for national emission standards, and labor and training problems. The 1967 law also established the Presidential Air Quality Advisory Board.

The Clean Air Act of 1970

Probably the most important of all federal laws governing pollution is the Clean Air Act of 1970, which contains a series of provisions that have a direct impact on the operations of business firms. The more important provisions are as follows:

1. The act required that by 1975 new cars be virtually pollution free and specified that emissions of hydrocarbons and carbon monoxide gases had to be 90 percent less than levels permissible in 1970. At the insistence of the automobile manufacturers, who contend that compliance is a costly proposition, the date was extended to 1981. The act also requires manufacturers to offer a 50,000-mile warranty on automobile emission control devices and establishes strict controls for fuel additives.[19]

2. The 1970 act also sets national standards for air pollution, with the states required to establish and enforce programs that meet national standards within four to six years. The federal government has the right to establish minimum ambient air standards for the entire country.

The Clean Air Act directed the Environmental Protection Agency to set national ambient air quality standards for pollutants covered in the act. It also authorized the EPA to set two types of standards, primary and secondary, without considering the cost of compliance.[20] Primary standards were to protect human health with an added margin of safety for vulnerable segments of

---

[19] It should be noted that compliance dates and emission standards were amended in 1977. The original hydrocarbon and carbon monoxide standards were put off until the 1980 model year.
[20] The functions of the EPA were discussed in Chapter 10.

the population, such as the elderly and infants. Secondary standards were to prevent damage to such things as crops, visibility, buildings, water, and materials. The EPA was also directed to determine maximum emission limits for plants and factories, called "new source performance standards." These standards were to be set on an industry-by-industry basis for states to use as a guideline in deciding on more specific emission restrictions for individual factories. Regions that violated standards for any of the pollutants covered by the act were designated as nonattainment areas for those pollutants, and the states had to limit new construction of pollution sources until the air in these regions was brought up to federal standards. Companies wanting to build plants in these regions were required to install equipment that limited pollution to the least amount emitted by any similar factory elsewhere in the country.

The Water Pollution Control Act of 1972

The Water Pollution Control Act amends previous acts pertaining to water pollution, including the Water Quality Act of 1970, which extended federal control standards to oil and hazardous substance discharges from onshore and offshore vessel facilities. The Water Pollution Control Act is divided into five categories: research and related programs, grants for construction of treatment works, standards of enforcement, permits and licenses, and general provisions. Responsibility for the enforcement of the act is vested in the EPA and in state governments. Some of the more important provisions of the act are as follows:

1. Manufacturers are required to monitor discharges at point sources of pollution and to keep records of the results of their efforts to reduce water pollution. The EPA or the state is authorized to inspect records to determine whether or not the act is being violated.

2. The act extended federal water pollution control to all navigable waters. When there is a violation, EPA can issue an order requiring compliance or notify the appropriate state of the alleged violation. If the state does not begin an appropriate enforcement within thirty days, the EPA can issue a compliance order requiring the violator to comply with a conditional or limited permit, or it can bring a civil action or begin criminal proceedings.

3. Both the Clean Air Act and the Water Pollution Control Act give citizens the right to bring suits to enforce standards set under the acts. Anyone having an interest that is or may be adversely affected by pollution may sue in

the judicial district in which the offending source is located, and the U.S. district courts are given jurisdiction without regard to citizenship or amount in controversy.

The Noise Control Act of 1972

Although air and water pollution have been the targets of corrective legislation for a long time, recent efforts have been directed at abating noise to create a quieter environment. The Noise Control Act of 1972 places noise in the formal category of a pollutant. Congressional findings indicated that inadequately controlled noise presented a danger to the health and welfare of the nation's population, particularly in the urban areas. Noise adversely affects human blood pressure and heartbeat and causes other detrimental physiological changes.[21] Although its immediate consequences are usually transitory, the effects of sustained noise can accumulate in an almost imperceptible manner, causing permanent injury to the human body. Harmful noise is often difficult to define, since the degree of annoyance depends on the person's response to the source of irritation.

The Noise Control Act offers federal regulatory guidelines for controlling noise pollution. Although primary responsibility for control of noise rests with state and local governments, federal action provides national uniformity of treatment. The act is intended to facilitate the establishment of federal noise emission standards for commercial and consumer-oriented products and to allow the federal government to preempt the field of noise control, though not depriving the states of local control and autonomy. The provisions of the act are basically as follows:

1. The act's most important provision is noise emission standards for a wide variety of product categories. The act is designed to control and abate aircraft noise and sonic boom as well as establish railroad, aircraft, and motor carrier emission standards. The EPA is required to establish noise emission standards for newly manufactured products that have been identified as being major sources of noise. Such standards will limit the noise emissions from each product, as is necessary to protect the public health, safety, and welfare. Effective noise emission standards have to be established for all products identified as major noise sources within eighteen months after the passage of the act.

[21] Robert A. Baron, *The Tyranny of Noise* (New York: St. Martin's Press, 1970).

2. Criminal sanctions under the act parallel those of the Clean Air and Water Pollution Control acts. Fines of up to $25,000 per day of violation, or imprisonment for up to one year, or both, are authorized for the first offense. Subsequent offenders are liable for fines of up to $50,000 for each day of violation or for imprisonment of up to two years, or both. Each additional day of violation constitutes a separate offense.

3. The act also authorizes citizens to sue in the federal district courts for any violations of noise control requirements. Citizens are also permitted to sue the administrator of the EPA for an alleged failure to perform his or her duties under the act, and also to sue the administrator of the Federal Aviation Administration, for similar reasons.

4. Technical assistance can be given to state and local governments to develop and enforce ambient noise standards.

5. The act authorizes labeling requirements for any product that emits noise capable of adversely affecting the public health and welfare or that is sold on the basis of its effectiveness in reducing noise. When a product is labeled, purchasers or users must be informed of the level of noise the product emits or its effectiveness in reducing noise, whichever the case may be.

Other Environmental Legislation

The Toxic Substances Control Act of 1976 gives the EPA broad regulatory authority over chemical substances during all phases of their life cycles, from before their manufacture to their disposal. It directs the EPA to make an inventory of the approximately 55,000 chemical substances in commerce; to require premanufacture notice to the EPA of all new chemical substances; and to enforce recordkeeping, testing, and reporting requirements so that the EPA can assess the relative risks of chemicals and regulate them. In December 1980, the Comprehensive Environmental Response, Compensation, and Liability Act became law. This legislation created a $1.6 billion fund for the cleanup of both spills of hazardous substances and inactive hazardous waste disposal sites. The Resource Conservation and Recovery Act of 1976 requires the safe disposal of hazardous wastes. Regulations define hazardous waste and establish standards for generation and transportation of hazardous wastes, as well as permit requirements for owners and operators of facilities that treat, store, or dispose of hazardous wastes. A waste generator has to prepare a manifest for hazardous wastes that is to track movement of the wastes from the point of generation to the point of disposal. If a waste is hazardous, it must be properly packaged and labeled.

The Hazardous and Solid Waste Amendments of 1984 provide for the protection of groundwater, which is increasingly seen as a vulnerable source because it is used so widely for drinking water. The amendments place restrictions on the treatment, storage, and disposal of hazardous waste in land-management facilities. They provide new regulations for underground tanks that store liquid petroleum and chemical products. They also create new and more stringent requirements for land disposal facilities that now exist and for those that will be created. Land disposal of hazardous wastes contaminate ground and surface waters, thus resulting in adverse human health effects. The amendments require the EPA to develop standards before November 1986 governing the burning of hazardous waste fuel mixtures. They also require producers and distributors of hazardous waste fuels to place a warning label on the invoice or bill of sale.

Numerous bills were introduced in Congress in 1988 to provide more environmental protection. Ocean dumping of sewage sludge off of the New Jersey coast would be prohibited after 1992 under a measure (HR4338) approved by the House Public Works and Transportation Committee. Legislation has been introduced to control radioactive radon gas. The House Energy and Commerce Subcommittee on Health and the Environment approved a bill (HR2837) authorizing $42 million over three years for federal grants to help states reduce radon in homes and schools. The Senate Environmental Committee introduced a bill (S1516) that would protect groundwater from pesticides, protect farmers from liability for damages caused by improperly applied pesticides, and regulate unsafe pesticides. A proposed clean air bill (S1894) would reduce sulfur dioxide, the main ingredient in acid rain by providing funds for technology to burn coal more cleanly. The House Interior Committee approved a bill (HR2504) that would allow the Energy Department to load nuclear waste into salt caverns 2,200 feet below New Mexico.

International Cooperation on the Environment

Many international agreements have been developed to prevent or regulate ocean pollutants by certain contaminants. The London Dumping Convention came into force in 1975 and regulates wastes loaded on ships with the express intent of dumping them at sea. The agreement prohibits the dumping of certain substances, including mercury, DDT, PCBs, oil, and certain plastics, and requires special permits for certain other wastes, such as low-level radioactive wastes. The Regional Seas Program of the United Nations Environmental Program encourages countries to develop regional action plans. An example is the Barcelona Convention, which prohibits the dumping of certain substances, such as mercury and radioactive wastes, into the Mediterranean. The United States is a participant in the Cartagena Convention, which is designed to reduce petroleum contamination of the Caribbean Sea and to control land-based sources of marine pollution.

There are also international agreements pertaining to the Antarctic seas, which are among the most biologically productive in the world. These seas hold many tons of krill, a crustacean which is a food source that feeds penguins, seabirds, fish, squid, seals, and whales. The Antarctic region also holds nonliving resources. Ninety percent of the world's freshwater supply is locked in the ice cap, which affects the world's climate. The region also holds an abundance of minerals, including platinum, copper, lead, and zinc. The development of these and other minerals could pose a major threat to Antarctic marine life, so international conventions govern activities in Antarctica. The Antarctic Treaty of 1959 prohibits use of the continent for nuclear explosion. The Convention of 1982 requires a comprehensive ecosystems approach to controlling the use of living marine resources. Restrictions on harvests must protect the species being harvested and other species that depend on the harvested species for food.

COSTS AND BENEFITS OF POLLUTION ABATEMENT

The subject of the environment is very controversial, although to argue against a clean environment is almost impossible. Suggestions that environmental laws should be modified to make them less costly to business or perhaps that more public land should be opened up for mineral exploration elicit the wrath of environmental groups and their supporters. If there is a complaint that a certain environmental requirement may cost a firm $10,000 a year per worker, the response may be that the possibility of cancer is reduced or that the life of the worker is lengthened. Such a response does not address the wisdom of the rule, nor does it consider more viable alternatives, but it is virtually impossible to argue against in any public forum. To make prudent choices about resource allocation, costs need to be weighed against benefits.

Costs of Pollution Abatement

Few things come free in this world, and cleaning up the environment is certainly not one of them. For example, emission control standards, as required by the Clean Air Act, decrease the economy of a car because they require the operation of auxiliary devices, such as air pumps, and the returning of the engine to less than optimal fuel efficiency. Emission controls can also reduce the reliability of a car and thereby increase total repair costs. Therefore, it is necessary to examine some of the costs involved in pollution abatement regulations. These costs can be divided into several categories: opportunity costs, economic costs, and the actual monetary outlays involved in cleaning up the environment.

Opportunity Costs

Opportunity cost can be considered a part of environmental regulation. For example, the money spent for cleaning up the environment could have been spent in modernizing industrial plants to better meet foreign competition. As Table 13-2 indicates, the total pollution abatement expenditures for 1983 amounted to $62.7 billion. In this case, opportunity cost can be applied to the whole economy because it is limited in what it can do with its resources, including its technological ability. Tradeoffs are involved in terms of how much of one good or service must be given up to gain a certain quantity of another good or service. In the case of the $62.7 billion expenditure on pollution abatement, there are many alternative combinations of uses involving expenditures on other goods or services. There might have been an alternative combination that would have used the $62.7 billion better.

Economic Costs

An example of an economic cost is when a plant shuts down as a result of environmental compliance costs and jobs are lost. This sort of thing has happened. EPA records kept from 1971 through early 1977 showed that 107 plants employing 20,318 workers were closed by companies that considered pollution control costs too high to merit keeping the plants open.[22] Plants have been closed down since that time also; for example, Youngstown Sheet and Tube, a

[22] See annual reports of the Council on Environmental Quality for 1975 and 1977.

TABLE 13-2   National Expenditures for Pollution Abatement and Control, 1972–1983 (billions of dollars)

Year	Air	Water	Total
1972	$ 6.4	$ 8.7	$ 18.4
1973	8.3	10.1	21.9
1974	10.4	11.6	26.3
1975	12.8	13.6	30.9
1976	14.2	15.5	34.7
1977	15.6	16.8	38.0
1978	17.3	19.9	43.4
1979	21.0	21.8	49.9
1980	24.9	22.4	55.4
1981	28.1	21.8	58.9
1982	27.4	22.1	58.9
1983	29.2	23.6	62.7

Source: Council on Environmental Quality, *Environmental Quality 1984*, pp. 614–617.

steel mill in Youngstown, Ohio. Almost all the plants shut down were marginal in terms of profitability and may have been eventually shut down anyway. Economic costs are larger than the profit loss from the closing down of a plant. The tax base of the community decreases and the quality of social services it can provide declines.

Monetary Costs

In addition to opportunity costs and economic and social tradeoffs, actual monetary outlays are related to pollution control. Table 13-2 presents the costs of pollution control for the two main categories of pollution, air pollution and water pollution for the period 1972–1983. This spending includes only federally mandated pollution control requirements. There are also expenditures made in response to state and local regulations, as well as voluntary expenditures. Air pollution expenditures have accounted for almost one-half of total national expenditures for pollution abatement and control during the 1972–1983 period.

Benefits of Pollution Abatement

Benefits also accrue to the individual and to society from cleaning up the environment. The benefit of any environmental improvement can be defined as the sum of the monetary values assigned to the effects of that improvement by all people directly or indirectly affected by the action. These monetary values can be defined in terms of the willingness of people to pay to obtain the effects of the environmental improvement or in terms of the sums people would have to receive to induce them to accept voluntarily the adverse effects of pollution.[23] Benefits can be divided into several categories, the first of which is human health. Also, economic and esthetic benefits can accrue to people and to society as a result of a clean environment.

Health Benefits

Air pollution, water pollution, and other forms of pollution can have adverse effects on health. Exposure to some form of air pollution has been associated with an increase in the mortality rate and also with respiratory ailments, particularly among older people. Outbreaks of infectious diseases have been traced to contaminants in municipal water supplies. Certain chemicals in water supplies have been linked with increased rates of cancer, and there is also a relationship between air pollution and the incidence of lung cancer. Health, then, can be improved by a reduction in the amount of pollution. One study estimated that approximately 25 percent of mortality from lung cancer could be saved by a 50 percent reduction in air pollution.[24] Several measures can be used to place a value on the premature loss of life. One measure uses an opportunity cost approach that values a life lost as the present value of the expected stream of future earnings for that person had his or her death been avoided. Lawyers attempt to place a value on life when there is a suit.

Economic Benefits

Pollution can have an adverse effect on such economic activities as agriculture and commercial fishing. Agricultural production can be harmed by rising acidity in the soil. The environmental fallout from the Chernobyl nuclear plant

[23] A. Myrick Freeman, *Air and Water Pollution Control* (New York: Wiley, 1982), pp. 3–5.

[24] Lester B. Lave and Eugene P. Seskin, "Air Pollution and Human Health," *Science* 169 (August 21, 1970): 722–733.

disaster has harmed agricultural production in Eastern Europe. Sale of agricultural products to the West has been banned by a number of Western countries, with a resultant loss of revenue to Poland and other Eastern European countries. In our country, lowered water control standards have had an adverse effect on commercial fishing production. Pollution in the Chesapeake Bay has reduced or destroyed almost all the fish supply and has put many commercial fishermen out of business.[25] Shellfish beds have been closed to commercial harvesting because of both bacteria and chemical contents, and rockfish, considered a delicacy, has all but disappeared.

Esthetic Benefits

Esthetic benefits, though less tangible than health and economic benefits, are also important to personal welfare. Air and water pollution can cause odors and tastes that affect people's ability to function well; the smell of a paper mill is a good example. Both forms of pollution can also be unsightly. Oil slicks on a beach or fish killed by a chemical spill destroy amenities. Noise pollution also offends the senses. Visibly unpleasant pollutants can have an adverse effect on property values in that they can reflect price differentials. To summarize, the esthetic benefits of a location increase as air, water, and noise pollution decrease.

Cost-Benefit Analysis: Lead in Gasoline

An example of cost-benefit analysis can be applied to leaded gasoline.[26] Lead in gasoline has been regulated by the EPA since the Clean Air Act of 1970, with a reduction in lead required through various ratings. A new rule, issued in 1984, required that lead in gasoline be reduced from 1.1 grams per leaded gallon to 0.5 grams per leaded gallon by July 1985, and to 0.1 grams by January 1986. The benefits to be derived from the reduction of lead in gasoline included improvement in the health of children and a reduction in high blood pressure for adults. Lead results in the emission of various forms of air pollutants—hydrocarbons, nitrogen oxides, and carbon monoxide. Lead in gasoline

---

[25] *The Washington Post,* June 1, 1986, p. 14.

[26] Council on Environmental Quality, *Fifteenth Annual Report* (Washington, D.C.: U.S. Government Printing Office, 1985), pp. 231–237.

TABLE 13-3   Costs and Benefits of Decreased Lead in Gasoline (millions of dollars)

	1985	1986	1987
Benefits			
Children's health effects	$ 223	$ 600	$ 547
Conventional pollutants	0	222	222
Maintenance	102	914	859
Fuel economy	35	187	170
Total benefits	360	1,924	1,799
Total cost	96	608	558
Net benefits	264	1,316	1,241

Source: Council on Environmental Quality, *Fifteenth Annual Report*, 1987, p. 235.

raises blood lead, which is linked to high blood pressure. Lead also corrodes engines and exhaust systems, which causes excess emissions of pollutants from misfueled vehicles.

There is also a cost involved in reducing the lead content of gasoline. Since the 1920s, refineries have added lead to gasoline as an inexpensive way of boosting octane. To meet octane requirements with little or no lead, refineries must engage in additional processing, which raises costs, or use other additives, which are more expensive than lead. The EPA estimated the cost of reducing lead by specifying the cost of the 1984 lead limit of 1.1 grams per leaded gallon. Then it computed the cost of specifying a tighter lead limit. Based on its analyses, the EPA estimated the rule would cost less than $100 million in the second half of 1985, when the standard was 0.5 grams per leaded gallon, and just over $600 million in 1986, when the standard became 0.1 grams.

Table 13-3 presents the monetary estimates of costs and benefits for the period 1985–1987. Excluded from the table are benefits that cannot be monetarily quantified; for example, there are blood pressure benefits. Since gasoline lead is linked to blood lead, which is linked to blood pressure, reduced lead in gasoline should reduce blood pressure levels. This change would cause a decline in cardiovascular diseases, reducing the number of heart attacks, strokes, and deaths related to high blood pressure. Monetary benefits in the table were limited to the positive health effect on children that will accrue from a decline in lead in gasoline. These benefits are based on EPA estimates of the reduction of blood lead and the increased health effects on children.

POLLUTION CONTROL AND ITS IMPACT ON BUSINESS

Pollution control costs are by far the most important regulatory costs imposed on business. First there is the incremental cost; that is, the cost of anything that must be done to comply with a regulation that would not have been done otherwise. Emission control devices, such as smokestack screens, are an example. Paperwork costs are also part of the incremental costs. In addition to the incremental costs of regulation, there are also secondary effects that incur costs to business and society. These costs may exceed the incremental cost of compliance. Examples of secondary effects are opportunity costs, changes in productivity, and costs of regulation-imposed delays. One example of a regulation-imposed delay is the Trans-Alaska Pipeline, which was delayed more than four years. In those four years, the cost of construction was estimated to have increased by $3.4 billion.[27]

The Environmental Protection Agency has made some efforts to decrease the cost of environmental regulation. It introduced the "bubble concept," which is based on the idea that it is often possible to reduce emissions of a given pollutant from one source far less expensively than from another. Thus, instead of compelling each source to meet a certain standard, a "bubble" is placed over the plant or geographic area, and private decision makers are allowed to decide the standard for the area at the lowest cost. For example, a number of smokestacks or even plants could be grouped together and treated as though they were enclosed by one large bubble. Thus, instead of being concerned with emissions from each smokestack, one can deal with the cumulative emissions from that bubble. This approach allows firms to undercontrol those stacks where control is expensive while overcontrolling stacks where control is cheap.[28]

[27] Arthur Andersen and Company, *Cost of Government Regulation Study: Project for the Business Roundtable* (New York: Business Roundtable, 1979), p. 27.

[28] Council on Environmental Quality, *Fifteenth Annual Report 1985* (Washington, D.C.: U.S. Government Printing Office, 1987), p. 60.

Cost Shifting

Business firms will regard the cost of pollution control as a part of the total cost of doing business and will attempt to shift it forward to consumers via price increases, backward to stockholders in the form of lower dividends, or to workers in the form of lower wages. The actual extent to which prices change in a given market as a result of the inclusion of pollution control costs in production will depend on a complex set of variables, including the price elasticities of demand and supply and the degree of competition in a given market. When a business firm must buy pollution abatement equipment, this purchase represents an addition to total fixed costs and average fixed costs at all levels of output. Marginal costs also will increase. Firms with sharp increments in costs associated with small increases in output are less likely to shift pollution costs forward, because profit will decline on incremental amounts sold.

Elasticity of Demand

If the demand for a product is absolutely or relatively inelastic, consumers will purchase the same or similar quantities at a higher price than the original market equilibrium price. There is an inelastic demand for a product when there are few, if any, close substitutes and the product is inexpensive—the smaller the fraction of total expenditures consumers allocate for a good is, the more inelastic the demand for it is likely to be. Thus, all other things being equal, firms confronted with an inelastic demand for their product would be able to incorporate pollution abatement costs into a higher price for the product, and with the quantity demanded decreasing at a rate slower than that of the increase in price, consumers would incur the cost of pollution control. On the other hand, if the demand for the product is elastic, an increase in price to cover the pollution control cost will be accompanied by a more than proportionate decrease in demand, and revenue will fall.

The Nature of the Market

In general, the more competitive a market is, the more difficult it will be for firms to pass pollution abatement costs on to consumers. Under pure competition, it is impossible, for sellers have no control over the price of their product. The price is determined in the market by supply and demand, and sellers can only react to it. In the short run, a firm can vary its output but not its plant capacity, and hence will have some variable and some fixed costs. Firms will have to absorb the pollution control costs themselves, and some will go out of business. In the long run, a firm can vary not only its output but also its plant capacity and therefore has no fixed costs. In industries characterized by oligopoly, the market situation is somewhat different. In other market situations, including monopoly, price is determined by how firms react to their cost situation in light of the individual firm's demand curve. The sum of these reactions gives the supply response, which sets the price in combination with total market demand. In oligopoly, however, the situation is not so simple, primarily because the individual firm cannot act without considering the reactions of its rivals. Thus, demand, as seen by the individual firm, is not independent of the reactions of rival firms, as in other market situations. The precarious position of the individual firm under oligopoly gives it an incentive to move in concert with other oligopolistic firms or to follow a price leader.

There are not many monopolies in the United States, primarily because there are few commodities or services for which there are absolutely no close substitutes. But local or regional monopolies of various kinds are relatively common. A monopolist tends, under any given condition of demand and productive capacity, to limit output to the volume at which the marginal cost of producing the good is equal to the marginal revenue derived from its sales. Since such an output is ordinarily well short of that at which the price just covers the average cost of production per unit of output, the productive results of operations under monopoly conditions are quite different from those under competitive conditions. The monopolist has more leverage and more opportunity to push the cost of pollution control onto the consumer by simply readjusting output to a different point on the demand curve for the product and by charging a higher price. In the case of natural monopolies, such as electric power companies, the cost of air and water pollution control equipment is considerable. But for the most part, pollution control costs to power companies are reflected in higher rates to consumers, who thus pay the major part of the cost of cleaning up the environment.

The market mechanism through which changes in prices tend to reflect the inclusion of pollution cost can be illustrated with a simple diagram of market price determination. (See Figure 13-1.) A business firm will treat the pollution abatement cost the same as it would any other cost of operations and include it in the final price of the product. In the figure, DD and SS represent the respective demand and supply curves before the imposition of pollution cost. Market price is at P_1 and output at Q_1. After the cost, the supply curve shifts to S_1S_1, the vertical distance between SS and S_1S_1 representing the cost of installing pollution control devices. Since demand (DD) is less than perfectly elastic, the

FIGURE 13-1   Market Price Determination of Inclusion of Pollution Control Cost

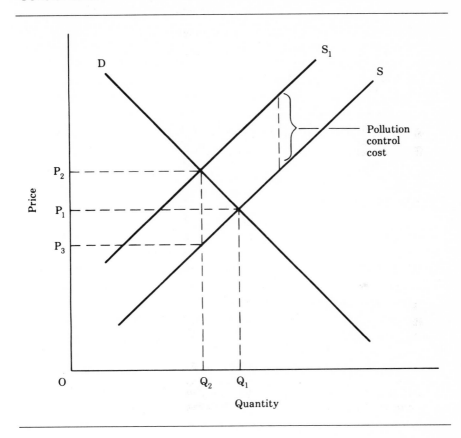

price in the marketplace has risen by less than the full cost of pollution control, in other words, the distance P_1P_2. This means that the cost is borne partly by the consumer and partly by the producer; the exact manner in which the cost is divided depends on the relative elasticities of demand and supply.

Environmental Regulation and the Automobile Industry

In a relatively short period, the automobile industry has become one of the most regulated industries in the United States. Federal regulation of the automobile began in the 1960s when the government imposed safety and emission standards on new vehicles. The Clean Air Act of 1970 imposed additional emission standards on the industry, which contributed to the cost of producing automobiles. The Energy Policy and Conservation Act Amendments of 1975 provided a set of corporate average fuel economy (CAFE) standards for new cars produced in the United States, which required car companies to achieve a sales-weighted, fleet-average fuel economy of 27.5 miles in the 1985 model year. These federal laws resulted in increased investments in the auto industry on emission control equipment. Emission costs per automobile, which can be divided into emissions equipment costs and other costs including fuel penalties, are presented in Table 13-4 for the period 1968–1984.

Effects on Business

The costs to business of compliance with pollution control requirements may be overemphasized, since there also are benefits to business from the esthetic value of a clean environment. Fulfilling pollution control requirements does increase business's expenditures. Installing and maintaining pollution control equipment necessitate additional bricklayers, electricians, iron workers, operating engineers, carpenters, and plumbers. Additional off-site labor is required to produce or transport the materials and equipment used in the actual construction of a project, as well as the engineering and technical labor needed to design, plan, and evaluate the operational performance of the pollution control systems. Jobs also are created in the pollution abatement industry. All this activity can stimulate employment. Nonetheless, that increased employment also can be offset by the closing down of plants that cannot comply with the cost of cleaning up the environment.

Apart from the cost of pollution control, other problems confront business firms. One problem is the regulatory infrastructure that has been built up at the federal and state levels of government to administer pollution control laws. To conform to pollution abatement requirements, business firms have to deal directly with these regulatory agencies. But there is more to regulation of the environment than conformance to required standards of abatement. Government also is making an effort to control other areas that are in some way related to environmental pollution—land use, energy, and urban transportation; all directly affect business operations. Land use in particular has an impact on business location. Local governments have adopted land use controls that require the dispersion or isolation of new factories and power facilities from centers of

TABLE 13-4 The Cost per Automobile of Emissions Regulations, Model Years 1968–1984 (current dollars)

Year	Cost
1968	$ 14
1969	15
1970	24
1971	25
1972	195
1973	532
1974	690
1975	306
1976	323
1977	466
1978	502
1979	559
1980	906
1981	1,551
1982	1,582
1983	1,607
1984	1,601

Source: Robert W. Crandall, Howard K. Gruenspecht, Theodore E. Keeler, and Lester B. Lave, *Regulating the Automobile* (Washington, D.C.: Brookings Institution, 1986), pp. 30, 38. Used by permission.

population. Local control over urban transportation designed to meet air quality standards would also affect industrial dispersion and business costs. Even the energy crisis is unlikely to alter materially the total impact of clean air requirements on industry.

SUMMARY

Problems related to environmental pollution have attracted widespread attention only in recent years. This is not to say, however, that pollution is a relatively new phenomenon; on the contrary, pollution was already a part of the American industrial and municipal scene during the last century. Recognition of this problem was expressed in the Refuse Act of 1899, which prohibited the discharge of waste into navigable waters. Nevertheless, most laws governing pollution are of recent vintage. The basic Water Pollution Control Act dates only from 1948, and the first Clean Air Act dates from 1956. The most important laws governing pollution were passed during the 1970s—the Clean Air Act of 1970 and the Water Pollution Control Act of 1972, both of which are amendments to the basic acts, and the Noise Control Act of 1972, which adds an entirely new dimension to the whole area of pollution control, with noise considered for the first time a major environmental pollutant. The Toxic Substances Control Act of 1976 regulates chemical substances, and the Hazardous and Solid Waste Amendments of 1984 protect groundwater.

Pollution abatement entails both costs and benefits to society. There are three types of costs: opportunity, economic, and monetary. Monetary costs include the use of emission control devices. Air pollution expenditures account for almost half of total pollution abatement expenditures. The benefits that accrue to society from pollution abatement include improved health from the reduction of respiratory diseases. There are also economic and esthetic benefits. Economic benefits include an improvement in agricultural production as soil acidity is reduced. Esthetic benefits pertain to the senses. Air pollution creates offensive odors, and water pollution creates unsightly refuse on beach shores.

QUESTIONS FOR DISCUSSION

1. What is the "greenhouse effect"? What impact can it have on the world?
2. What is the ozone layer? Why is it being damaged?
3. Discuss how pesticides and hazardous wastes cause pollution.
4. Discuss the causes of sea pollution.
5. What impact does deforestation have on the environment?
6. How is the term "opportunity cost" applied to the cost of cleaning up the environment?
7. What are some of the costs and benefits of cleaning up the environment?
8. What are the basic causes of pollution?
9. Give an example of cost-benefit analysis as applied to cleaning up the environment.
10. What are some forms of international cooperation on the environment?

RECOMMENDED READINGS

Bresnahan, Timothy, and Dennis A. Yao. "The Nonpecuniary Costs of Automobile Emission Standards." Technical Report 33. Stanford, Calif.: Center for Economic Policy Research, Stanford University, 1984.

Caldwell, Lynton K. *International Environmental Policy: Emergence and Directions.* Durham, N.C.: Duke University Press, 1984.

Council on Environmental Quality. *Fifteenth Annual Report.* Washington, D.C.: U.S. Government Printing Office, 1987.

Crandall, Robert W., Edward K. Gruenspecht, Theodore E. Keeler, and Lester B. Lave. *Regulating the Automobile.* Washington, D.C.: Brookings Institution, 1986.

Epstein, Samuel, Lester O. Brown, and Carl Pope. *Hazardous Waste in America.* San Francisco: Sierra Club Books, 1982.

National Academy of Sciences. *Petroleum in the Marine Environment.* Washington, D.C.: 1984.

National Research Council. *The Polar Regions and Climatic Change.* Washington, D.C.: Polar Research Board, 1984.

"Planet of the Year; Endangered Earth." *Time.* January 2, 1988, pp. 26–73.

Ramirez, Anthony. "A Warming World: What It Will Mean." *Fortune,* July 4, 1988, pp. 104–105.

Worldwatch Institute. *State of the World 1988.* Washington, D.C.: 1989.

PART V

DEREGULATION OF BUSINESS

A major development during both the Carter and Reagan administrations was the deregulation of a number of industries that had been formerly regulated. The Civil Aeronautics Board (CAB), which long regulated interstate air transportation, determining rates that would be charged and services that would be provided by carriers, is no longer in existence, and airline companies are now free to compete on the basis of price. Substantial price and service deregulation has also occurred in the natural gas, trucking, railroad, and banking industries, to encourage more price and service competition. The move toward deregulation of industries previously regulated reflected a shift in attitudes toward the proper role of government, and belief that regulation has hampered productivity and job creation in the U.S. economy.

However, some people now feel that deregulation went too far. A case in point is the failure of some savings and loan banks during the latter part of the 1980s, many of which can be attributed to mismanagement. In 1982 Congress allowed the S&Ls, which traditionally had been home lenders, to venture into the riskier but potentially more profitable areas of commercial real estate and consumer lending. The idea was to allow the institutions to earn more on their investments so that they would afford to pay higher interest on deposits. There is also some support for regulation of the airline industry on the grounds that services to a number of localities have been abandoned, and that mergers have created an oligopoly market, reducing competition. Although complete deregulation is unlikely, a certain degree of reregulation will occur, particularly with respect to the S&Ls.

Chapter 14

Deregulation and Airline Competition

Competition is regarded as a principal desideratum of a market economy. It is thought to maximize productivity, encourage research and development, improve the position of the small businessperson, prevent excessive concentration of economic power, provide for attainment of consumer interests, and eliminate arbitrary barriers to market entry. There is also an interrelationship between competition in a free enterprise market economy and a democratic political structure, in that competition is supposed to prevent the growth of excessively powerful economic units, regardless of whether they are business or labor. This preventive aspect of competition will, it is believed, help maintain basic democratic institutions. In *Wealth of Nations* (1776), Adam Smith wrote that self-interest works not only in the interest of the individual but also in the social interest; that is, it promotes the ends of society as well as those of the individual as long as there is competition in the economic system. When pure competition exists, no one person or firm can exercise economic control, for economic power comes from the ability to influence or control prices.

Competitive market structures sometimes can cause inefficient resource allocation and a socially undesirable market performance. This can happen when economies of scale are so extensive in relation to the size of the market that only one firm can operate efficiently within that market. It is not feasible to remedy this situation by means of structural modifications intended to create conditions. Instead, direct regulation under the laws governing public utilities has been used. Certain industries, including transportation, electricity, gas, telephone service, and the broadcast media, are exempted from the direct application of the antitrust laws on the theory that a regulatory agency protects the public interest and thus there was no rationale for redundant intervention by antitrust enforcement agencies. But regulation differs greatly among the industries in which conditions of natural monopoly may exist, and public utility regulation often has been applied in cases in which a natural monopoly clearly does not exist. In an important minority of industries—transportation, communications, and electric and gas services—government intervenes actively and regulates business decisions more closely than in most private enterprises. These industries, classified under the general category of public utilities, provide all of us with services as essential to today's lifestyle as, perhaps, food or shelter. Yet, unlike the food or shelter industries, utilities are in a unique business category. From a legal standpoint, utilities are distinguished as a class of business affected with a deep public interest, which therefore makes them subject to regulation. What sets this segment of industry further apart is that in most areas it is considered desirable for a utility to operate a controlled monopoly. As such, a utility is obligated to charge fair, nondiscriminatory rates and to render on demand satisfactory service to the public. The tradeoff is that a utility generally is free from direct competition and is permitted, though not assured of, a fair return on its investment.

The logic behind this kind of operating environment is reasonably straightforward. Utilities operate most efficiently as monopolies because they usually offer a single service or a quite limited number of services. A utility's operations are localized and limited by the necessary direct connection between the production plant and each piece of customer equipment. To a large degree, a utility plant can be used only for the service for which it is intended. Concentration within a territory permits the use of larger and more efficient equipment, hence a lower average expense per unit of output. Direct competition would be uneconomical because it would require duplicate investment and would clutter public property with distribution lines. This could lead to unnecessarily high rates or insufficient earnings—both unacceptable alternatives to the public and to the investor as well. There is some competition, but it is relatively diluted. Thus, a public utility operates under an exclusive franchise granted by a governmental unit.

ECONOMIC CHARACTERISTICS

Regulated industries such as public utilities have two economic characteristics. The first is that they generally are very capital intensive, since there is a very high ratio of fixed assets to total assets. A railroad has almost all its assets concentrated in rolling stock, terminals, and warehouses; an electric company has almost all its assets in power plants and transmission lines. These fixed assets lead to the second economic characteristic of regulated industries, namely, fixed costs that do not vary with output. Examples of these are rental payments, depreciation of plant and equipment, property taxes, wages and salaries of a skeleton staff that a firm would have to employ as long as it stayed in business—even if it produced nothing—and interest payments on debt. The last category is particularly important to a public utility, given the nature of its debt structure. Fixed costs are those costs that a firm would have to bear even if the plant were completely closed down for a time. A railroad, for example, has a tremendous investment in land, rolling stock, and repair shops. The expense of maintaining these properties continues regardless of the amount of traffic hauled by the railroad.

Because of certain technical factors, the expenses of many utility companies, particularly those in gas and electric power, decrease as the size of the plant increases. In most market areas the demand for electric power is insufficient to justify the construction of the optimum-sized production and distribution system. A firm considering building a new plant must decide on its size. A relatively small plant would have higher average costs than a larger plant would. For the firm, the average total costs usually drop over a certain range as the scale of operations is increased, then reach a minimum, and then increase when the scale of operations becomes too large. But since the total fixed cost remains the same regardless of output, the fixed costs are spread over more units of output, and consequently, each unit of output bears a smaller share of the fixed costs. Therefore, the average fixed cost curve is downward, sloping to the right throughout its entire length, and so firms with large fixed costs— railroads, for example, with their tremendous fixed costs for roadbeds and rolling stock—can substantially reduce their fixed costs per unit by producing larger outputs.

It is evident that firms operating very small plants are likely to be inefficient—that is, expensive to operate—in almost any line of production. The production unit is too small to take full advantage of the specialized labor and equipment. A good example of inefficient single-plant firms are small farms. They have proved to be inefficient in comparison with larger farms because they are not large enough to use mechanized equipment efficiently. It would hardly pay a wheat farmer with a ten-acre plot to purchase the combine that the farmer with a thousand-acre plot could use. But it also is true that firms operating very large plants are likely to be inefficient in almost any line of production. The production unit simply becomes too large for the job to be done properly. We can conclude, therefore, that the average total costs for the single-plant firm fall as the plant size is increased, reach a minimum, and then begin to increase as the plant grows larger. This curve is shown in Table 14-1.

Decreasing-cost industries are those for which the demand curve (represented by demand price) lies to the left of the point at which the average total

TABLE 14-1   Cost and Price Figures of a Decreasing-Cost Firm (dollars)

Output (units)	Total Fixed Costs	Total Variable Costs	Total Cost	Average Total Cost	Marginal Cost	Demand Price
0	$1,000	$ 0	$ 0	$ 0	$ 0	$ 0
100	1,000	400	1,400	14.00	4.00	9.00
200	1,000	750	1,750	8.75	3.50	8.00
300	1,000	1,050	2,050	6.83	3.00	7.00
400	1,000	1,300	2,300	5.60	2.50	6.00
500	1,000	1,500	2,500	5.00	2.00	5.00
1,000	1,000	2,400	3,400	3.40	1.80	3.00
2,000	1,000	4,000	5,000	2.50	1.60	2.00
3,000	1,000	6,000	7,000	2.33	2.00	1.00
4,000	1,000	9,000	10,000	2.50	3.00	.80
5,000	1,000	13,000	14,000	2.80	4.00	.60

$$\text{Average total cost} = \frac{\text{Total cost}}{\text{Output}} = \frac{\$1,400}{100} = \$14.00$$

$$\text{Marginal cost} = \frac{\text{Increase in total cost}}{\text{Increase in output}} = \frac{\$1,400 - \$1,000}{100} = \$4$$

costs are the lowest—that is, in the example, at an output of three thousand units. This means there is room for only one firm in this hypothetical industry. Under the existing conditions of demand, two or more firms would have such small outputs that their average total costs would be much higher than those of the single firm. Hence, they would probably be eliminated in a competitive struggle, until only one firm remained. If, on the other hand, the demand price were larger than the average total cost at three thousand units, there would be room in the industry for a number of competing firms to operate at their lowest average total cost output.

Figure 14-1 illustrates the points just made. A company considering building a new plant must decide on its size. A relatively small plant, as for example a_1, would have higher average total costs than would a larger plant, a_2. The optimum-size plant would be a_5, which would produce an output of OL at an average cost per unit of OK. Past this point, average total costs will increase. If

FIGURE 14-1   Natural Monopolies and Economies of Scale (LRAC = Long Run Average Cost)

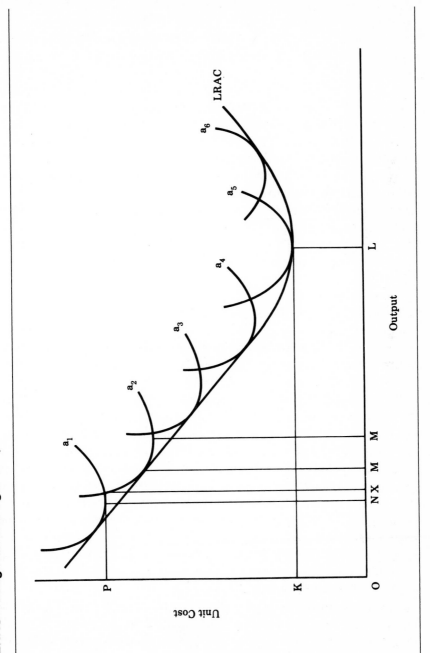

the market is too small to justify a plant of this size, a smaller one should be constructed. If it is expected that fewer than OX units will be sold per period, Plant a_1 is preferable to Plant a_2. If the expected output is OM, that output can be produced by Plant a_2 at a lower average cost than by a plant of any other size.

Let us assume the market is currently being served by a firm with a plant of the a_1 size. If demand is sufficient and a new company builds a plant of A_2 size, it will be able to undersell the first plant. This, of course, requires a lengthy period in which changes in plant capacities are possible. At any price below OP, the first plant will be selling below cost, whereas the larger plant will be able to sell at a price somewhat below OP and will enjoy a considerable profit. If competition is allowed to operate without restriction in this situation, either the first company will be forced out of business or the two companies will get together and agree on a price that will bring monopoly profits to one or both firms. In neither case will the interest of consumers be protected by allowing the market forces to compete freely.

ECONOMIC PRINCIPLES OF RATE MAKING

Monopoly is a market situation in which a single firm sells a product for which there are no close substitutes. There are no similar products whose price or sales will influence the monopolist's price or sales, and cross-elasticity of demand between the monopolist's product and other products will be either zero or small enough to be neglected by all firms in the economy. Indeed, the monopoly is the perfect industry from the producing point of view, and the market demand curve for the product is also the demand curve faced by the monopolist. Thus, the monopolist is able to exert some influence on price, output, and demand for the product. It is in a position to ascertain that point on the industry demand curve at which profits will be maximized. This control has important implications for resource allocation because output restriction and higher prices are the end result. Long-run profits can be achieved under monopoly because little or no entry is possible into monopolized industries. When there are profits, consumers pay more for products than is necessary to hold the resources for making those products.

Figure 14-2 represents the short-run marginal cost (MC) and the marginal revenue (MR) curves for a regulated monopoly. If the monopoly is allowed to operate under monopoly market conditions and attempts to maximize profits, it will produce OM units of output and sell them at a price of MP per unit. To

FIGURE 14-2   Monopoly Price, "Fair" Price, and Socially Optimum Price for a Public Utility

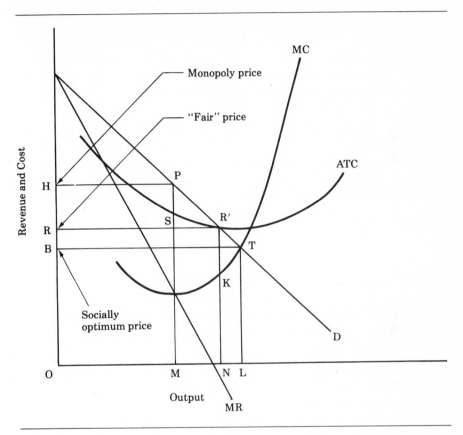

maximize profits, the monopoly will produce at exactly the rate at which marginal cost and marginal revenue are equal. Up to this point, marginal revenue exceeds marginal cost, and it would continue to be profitable to produce any unit of output that adds more to revenue than it adds to cost; in other words, any unit for which marginal revenue exceeds marginal cost. Beyond this rate, marginal cost exceeds marginal revenue, and it would be pointless to produce additional units of output. At the output OM and the price MP, the monopoly is making a profit per unit of PS and a total profit of HPSR. From an economic and social point of view the result is undesirable, because consumers get less and pay more than would be the case under pure competition. This is so because the price under pure competition tends to equal the marginal cost of production, whereas the price under monopoly exceeds the marginal cost.

A fair rate of return, as allowed by a public utility commission, can be represented by the point OR, since this is the rate at which price equals average total cost (ATC), assuming that average total cost includes a normal or fair rate of return on capital investment. In economic theory, competitive long-run cost is defined to include the opportunity cost of all factors employed—what they could earn in their best alternative employment. In the case of capital supplied to a public utility, this inclusion means the rate of return should be comparable to that which could be earned in alternative investments. In Figure 14-2, output under government regulation would be MN units greater than that which would exist in an unregulated monopoly situation, and the price would be lower by PS. Although the regulated price, NR', is equal to average total cost, it is greater than marginal cost. The price represents what can be called full cost or average cost pricing, the price at which the utility covers all its costs, both fixed and variable, and earns a normal profit.

The price OR is not the socially optimum price, however, for it is above marginal cost. Marginal cost at output ON is only NK. This level indicates that output is still too low in terms of the ideal allocation of resources. This is true because marginal cost represents the amount of additional resources required to put an additional unit of service in the market; price represents the amount that consumers are willing to pay to secure the additional unit. As long as price is above marginal cost, more resources should be devoted to producing the service. The price OB illustrates marginal cost pricing, the price at which the utility's marginal cost equals its demand (D), or average revenue. Production is carried to the point at which marginal cost is equal to demand price and there are no customers to which the service is worth more than the additional cost of production. The marginal cost price is therefore the socially optimum price—the price that maximizes society's welfare—because at this price the value of the last unit to the marginal user is equivalent to the value of the resources used to produce that unit.

Under pure competition price equals marginal cost, and the optimum allocation of resources is achieved. But, under pure competition, price is also equal to average cost, and in the long run, firms neither make abnormal profits nor incur losses. Rate regulation for public utilities, therefore, poses a policy dilemma. If prices are set at average total cost levels (OR in the figure), the output of the utility may be restricted below that which is most desirable socially for consumer sovereignty. But if the price is set at marginal cost levels, the utility company may be unable to cover average costs and therefore suffer losses, or it may make monopoly profits. In the diagram, marginal cost pricing would cause the utility company to incur losses, since the price falls below the average cost. If, however, the demand curve were to intersect the marginal cost curve somewhere to the right of the lowest point on the average cost curve, marginal cost pricing would enable the utility to secure an above-normal return.

CRITICISMS OF REGULATION

Criticisms of government regulation took a number of forms. Some critics felt the regulatory agencies acted more in the interest of the regulated firms than in the interest of the public. Regulatory agencies were blamed for "bending with the wind," changing policies and taking actions designed to curry favor whenever commissioners saw political tides going in a particular direction. Other critics thought there was too much regulation by the commissions. The results, they said, were that the individual, the economy, and in fact, society as a whole, were stifled. Often commissions, supposedly the experts, made decisions that hurt both regulated business and the consumer. For example, the Interstate Commerce Commission was accused of following policies detrimental to the interests of the railroad industry. Even though it was clear by the 1930s that the nineteenth-century concept of the railroads being responsible for offering complete service to every locality along every mile of track had become obsolete, the ICC refused to allow them to abandon unprofitable services.

There were other, more esoteric complaints about the regulatory agencies. In some agencies, the agency personnel not only made the rules and served as the judges but also decided to bring action. One highly esteemed American political tradition is the separation of legislative, judicial, and executive power; this tradition would seem to be violated when the decision to bring an action is not separated from its adjudication. In other agencies, the commissioners who made the ultimate decisions were removed from the actual fact finding. Thus, they never really knew what was going on because they saw only a summary report when they made their decisions. They acted only on the basis of facts found by a trial or a hearings examiner of some kind, but they did not hear the actual testimony.[1]

[1] For a summary of the reasons for deregulation, see *The Economic Report of the President 1983* (Washington, D.C.: U.S. Government Printing Office, 1983), pp. 100–102.

Finally, critics have decried the effects of regulation on the efficiency of the market as a resource allocator. A price kept below the market price by regulation has the effect of creating a system of nonprice rationing in which excluded customers are forced to pay higher prices for substitutes. In some cases, price regulation leads to an excessively high level of some service characteristics because firms are prevented from competing on the basis of price. Because of price regulation by the Civil Aeronautics Board, for example, airlines competed primarily through frequency of flights, which led to low load factors and considerable excess capacity. Regulation of oil and natural gas prices has on occasion kept prices too low, causing shortages and inefficient choices among competing fuels.

DEREGULATION

A major deregulation effort was underway in the United States by the 1970s, which culminated in the passage of the Airline Deregulation Act of 1978, the Natural Gas Policy Act of the same year, and the Motor Carrier Act and the Staggers Railroad Act of 1980. These acts reflected a general distrust of big government, and regulatory agencies were part of the big government syndrome. With deregulation in such industries as air transportation and natural gas, firms have been able to set prices based on market demand but are constrained by competition. Further steps toward deregulation of industry occurred during the early 1980s, with the deregulation of the commercial banking industry. This deregulation has changed the nature of commercial banking and the competitive environment in which it operates.

Table 14-2 lists the various deregulatory initiatives that occurred during the Carter and Reagan administrations. A major objective of the Reagan administration was to roll back regulation. A number of major acts were passed to accomplish this end. The Garn–St. Germain Depository Institutions Act was passed, which gave the savings and loan industry far more latitude in terms of the types of loans they could make to customers. This created repercussions in the industry when a number of savings and loan institutions made bad loans and became insolvent. Antitrust merger guidelines were changed in the same year. Probably the most important initiative that occurred during the Reagan period was the break-up of AT&T into two separate parts, AT&T, which has become more of a manufacturing company, and seven independent regional telephone companies.

TABLE 14-2   Deregulatory Initiative, 1978–1988

Year	*Initiative*
1978	Airline Deregulation Act
	Natural Gas Policy Act
	Standards revocation (OSHA)
	Emissions trading policy (EPA)
1979	Deregulation of satellite earth stations (FCC)
	Urgent-mail exemption (Postal Service)
1980	Motor Carrier Reform Act
	Household Goods Transportation Act
	Staggers Rail Act
	Depository Institutions Deregulation & Monetary Control Act
	International Air Transportation Competition Act
	Deregulation of cable television (FCC)
	Deregulation of customer premises equipment & enhanced services (FCC)
1981	Decontrol of crude oil & refined petroleum products (Executive order)
	Truth-in-lending simplification (FRB)
	Automobile industry regulation relief package (NHTSA)
	Deregulation of radio (FCC)
1982	Bus Regulatory Reform Act
	Garn–St. Germain Depository Institutions Act
	AT&T settlement
	Antitrust merger guidelines
1984	Space commercialization
	Cable Television Deregulation Act
	Shipping Act
1986	Trading of airport landing rights
1987	Sale of Conrail
	Elimination of fairness doctrine (FCC)
1988	Proposed rules on natural gas and electricity (FERC)
	Proposed rule on price caps (FCC)

Source: *Economic Report of the President 1989* (Washington, D.C.: U.S. Government Printing Office, January 1989), p. 196.

Deregulation of Air Transportation

The main issue in the air transportation industry was whether competition or regulation would bring about more socially desirable results. When commercial aviation in the United States began, some feared that ineffectively regulated competition would become cutthroat competition, to the detriment of both safety and the development of a commercial fleet that might serve as a national defense transport reserve. Originally, Congress intended to place the airline industry under the jurisdiction of the Interstate Commerce Commission, but Congress then decided that the ICC was too close to the railroads and too judicial and regulatory in its approach to be able to provide the leadership necessary to promote a new means of transportation. In 1938, the Civil Aeronautics Act was passed, which created the Civil Aeronautics Board (CAB) and gave it regulatory authority over entry, routes, rates, airmail payments, and subsidies of common carriers. It was also empowered to grant or withhold the certificates of convenience or necessity needed for operating specific routes, as well as to approve mergers or pooling arrangements.

The CAB followed a general policy of fostering a mixture of competition and monopoly, mostly the latter. The competition was over service rather than price. As traffic grew on existing routes, the CAB approved applications from existing airlines to extend their routes and add new ones, thereby strengthening the weaker systems and permitting the duplication of service on major routes. The CAB was authorized to regulate domestic airlines and rates and to control entry into the air transportation industry. Its entry policy was restrictive with regard to the entrance of new airlines into the industry but permissive with respect to entry by existing carriers into specific markets. Thus the regulatory policies of the CAB were somewhat analogous to those that would be followed by a cartel—an agreement between legally independent enterprises that restrains competition. Except for self-imposed restraints on output, sales, or prices, the activities of the cartel members remain independent. Entry barriers are created and enforced by legal sanction, the market is divided formally among participants, and internal price competition is discouraged. As in an oligopoly, a cartel needs other forms of competition. In the airline industry, this competition was primarily service—an excessive number of routes and product differentiation, elaborate cuisines, and attractive attendants.

The greatest criticism of the CAB's regulation of the air transportation industry was that it encouraged inefficient airline operation. In essence, the CAB established the fares that could be charged in various markets, and then the airlines tended to compete away the profits they could make through changes in scheduling. The absence of any real form of price competition, coupled with higher than competitive rates, works to the disadvantage of many consumers of air travel. Many passengers would prefer to be able to select airlines on the basis of price as well as type of service. Moreover, comparisons of CAB-regulated airlines with less-regulated intrastate airlines indicated that the latter were generally more efficient and could provide transportation over similar routes at a lower cost. A case in point was the Texas intrastate market, in which Southwest Airlines, a carrier licensed by the Texas Aeronautics Commission, directly competed with Braniff Airways, a CAB-regulated trunk carrier, and Texas International Airways, a CAB-regulated local service carrier. Despite having its service introduction postponed for nearly four years because of judicial challenges by Braniff and Texas International, Southwest Airlines was eventually allowed to serve the so-called golden triangle of Dallas, San Antonio, and Houston. It made a profit, charging fares that ran as much as 50 percent below comparable CAB fares.[2]

The Airline Deregulation Act of 1978

This desire to deregulate air transportation and return it to a competitive market resulted in the passage of the Airline Deregulation Act of 1978. One purpose of the act was to eliminate legal barriers to market entry, thus promoting competition. If profits are made in a competitive market, new firms will be attracted into the industry. These new firms will endeavor to obtain a share of the profits by providing the same goods at lower prices, improved goods at the same price, or a combination of the two. Furthermore, should the industry have the productive characteristics that allow a purely competitive market structure to be approximated, the marginal cost of output will eventually equal the price of each good, thereby yielding economic efficiency in production and exchange. Consumers are better served, since they can get the same goods at a lower price, but a firm loses when new firms enter and reduce profits through competition. However, the surviving firms benefit in the long run by earning a market rate of return equal to what they would get if they were producing their next highest-valued alternative product.

The Airline Deregulation Act of 1978 had the following provisions:

1. The Civil Aeronautics Board was to be eliminated by 1985 (which it was), with economic regulation to be phased out by that time and other CAB

---

[2] Few frills were provided, and many flights were scheduled at off-hours.

functions were to be transferred to other agencies, such as the Federal Aviation Administration (FAA).

2. The act was designed to allow existing interstate carriers to enter new markets, and to make it easier for new firms to enter the air transportation industry.

3. The act allowed domestic airlines to cut or raise fares in single markets.[3] This freedom increased during a transition period, until, on January 1, 1983, all regulations on fares were eliminated.

Results of Air Transportation Deregulation

The interstate air transportation industry was deregulated with the intent of promoting competition between air carriers. Prior to deregulation, the major interstate airlines had been protected from competition by the Civil Aeronautics Board. Since its creation in 1938, the CAB had seventy-nine applications from companies that wanted to become long-distance interstate airlines; not one was approved. During the time they were protected from competition, the regulated airlines had become high-cost unionized operations. There was no incentive to become cost efficient, for increased costs could be readily absorbed by rate increases granted by the CAB. The Airline Deregulation Act of 1978 had as its intention the elimination of legal barriers to market entry, thus promoting competition from new entrants into the air transportation industry.

However, things did not work out quite as well as the regulators had hoped. Right after the deregulation, the major airlines were at a severe cost disadvantage. New entrants into the airline industry were able to use cheaper nonunion labor and smaller crews on their aircraft. This efficiency gave them a competitive cost advantage over the major airlines, which were stuck with union contracts negotiated during regulation. There were a number of new entrants into the airline industry; most went broke. Some 150 airlines went broke during the period 1978–1986, and there were years when the industry lost money. This trend appears to have changed somewhat during 1987 and 1988. In 1987 operating profits for the major airlines amounted to $41.97 billion, with 1988 operating profits estimated at $2.5 billion.

---

[3] The act allowed domestic interstate airlines to cut fares in individual markets by as much as 50 percent in one year or to raise them by as much as 5 percent in fifty-eight days without CAB approval. This variability is now a thing of the past.

The Airline Deregulation Act has created dramatic changes in the airline industry. Before 1978, the regulatory climate within which the airline industry operated was one in which competition on prices and entry was severely restricted. After 1978, the airline industry has experienced significant restructuring. The act sparked dramatic changes in the industry, particularly in the manner in which airlines provide service. Airlines generally took advantage of the opportunities afforded them under the act to radically alter their routes and pricing structure in order to attract passengers. So it is important to evaluate the results of deregulation from the standpoint of changes in route structure; mergers and acquisitions, which have reduced the number of air carriers; air fares and their impact on consumer welfare; service, which has drawn complaints; and air safety.

Route Structure

One structural change that has resulted from the competitive environment created by deregulation has been the airlines' creation of hub-and-spoke systems. The airline industry, like other transportation industries, discovered that there were often enormous efficiencies from establishing networks. The airlines realized these gains by creating hubs at one or more airports. The airlines have found that by scheduling flights at these hub airports in banks—a number of flights come into an airport within a short period of time and a number leave a short time later—they are able to offer passengers from many origins one-stop flights to many destinations. This method of scheduling inbound and outbound flights has enabled carriers to make efficient use of their facilities and to provide service on many previously unserved routes out of the hub airport.

In addition, hub carriers have been affiliated with commuter carriers in many cities to serve smaller markets on an efficient scale, and several have developed multiple hub systems to provide more regional service. Thus, with the development of hub and spoke systems, a process that has historically entailed a substantial investment of time, planning, and facilities investment on the part of the hubbing carrier, carriers have grown from local to regional or regional to national as they offer passengers an increasing array of destinations on a single carrier. The development of a hub-and-spoke system has become an important marketing tool in that passengers much prefer single-carrier service to having to change airlines in mid-journey. The ability to offer single-carrier service to connecting passenger was limited under regulation

TABLE 14-3 Airline Acquisitions Consummated in 1986 and 1987

Buyer	Target	Value of Acquisition (millions of dollars)
U.S. Air	Piedmont Aviation	$1,600
Northwest	Republic	884
Delta	Western	860
Texas Air	Eastern	607
TWA	Ozark	250
Texas Air	Frontier	197
Texas Air	People's Express	125

Sources: From *USA Today*, September 12, 1986; *Fortune*, February 1, 1988, p. 37, ©1988 Time, Inc., all rights reserved. Reprinted by permission.

because of entry restrictions. Note that airlines with an efficient hub-and-spoke system increase the scale of entry requirements for new competitors.

Mergers

Some people see a parallel between the airline industry of the 1980s and the railroad industry during the latter part of the last century. Faced with heavy fixed costs and recurring recessions, the railroad industry struggled for survival. Price wars were frequent and there were many bankruptcies or last-ditch mergers. By the end of the last century, six major railroad companies controlled most of the railroads in the United States. Similarly, airlines have gone bankrupt and an increase in the number of mergers has occurred. The airline industry is well on its way, if not already there, to becoming an oligopoly. But this situation in itself does not constitute proof of a lessening of competition. In fact, a well-developed commuter network in a more concentrated competitive environment may actually bring greater benefit to travelers on low-density routes.

The Airline Deregulation Act of 1978 created a procedure for the review of proposed airline mergers that differs from the procedures used for mergers in most industries. Airlines must seek approval from the U.S. Department of Transportation (DOT) before merging with other carriers. Although not the deciding agency in approving or disapproving mergers, the Antitrust Division of the Department of Justice must be notified of proposed mergers, and usually participates in airline merger hearings before DOT administrative law judges. On several occasions, DOT has approved mergers to which the Justice Department was opposed.

Table 14-3 presents the major airline acquisitions for the period 1986–1987. All the acquiring firms are survivors in the shakeout that has hit the airline industry. With these acquisitions, the four largest firms have around 60 percent of the total air passenger market.

The Federal Aviation Act was revised in 1985 to increase the regulatory responsibilities of the Department of Transportation. Section 408 of the revised act provides the framework for DOT consideration of mergers and acquisitions. Under this provision, it is unlawful, without prior approval, for any air carrier to acquire control over another air carrier in any manner whatsoever. The act set two standards for the approval of mergers and acquisitions: an antitrust standard and a public interest standard. Under the antitrust standard, a merger that would violate Section 7 of the Clayton Act, by lessening competition substantially in any region of the United States, may not be approved by DOT unless it finds that the anticompetitive effects are outweighed in the public interest by benefits accruing from meeting increased transportation needs. The public interest standard provides that DOT must determine whether or not a merger is in the public interest.

Table 14-4 presents the market shares of passenger revenue miles held by the seven largest air carriers in 1987. During the period from 1985 (when DOT was given responsibility for airline mergers) through 1987, there were thirteen mergers, none of which were opposed by DOT. As the table indicates, there has been an increase in the market share of the seven major carriers during the period. Moreover, it is conceivable that Pan American and TWA will be bought out during 1988 by one of the other major carriers, or by some corporate raider.

Two attendant criticisms of airline consolidation are as follows:

1. Some critics allege an anticompetitive effect of computer reservation systems that are dominated by the major air carriers. The majors' CRS systems are said to be the root cause of excessive market domination. As Table 14-5 indicates, these systems and their inherent biases can seriously impede entry into new markets and compromise the ability of new airlines to grow larger. As the table indicates, the five largest carriers own the five computer systems that are in the marketplace and thus control over 86 percent of revenue passage miles flown.

TABLE 14-4   Market Shares for the Major Airline Carriers 1985 and 1987 (percent)

Carrier	1985	1987	Change in Share
American–Air Cal.	12.92%[a]	14.44%	+1.52%
United	19.00	17.02	+2.02
Texas Air Group	10.59[b]	18.32	+7.73
Delta–Western	9.19[c]	12.04	+2.85
TWA–Ozark	8.46[d]	7.73	−0.73
Northwest–Republic	6.49[e]	10.02	+3.53
Pan Am	8.85	6.49	−2.36
Total	71.50	86.06	+14.56

[a] For American only. It had not acquired Air Cal.
[b] For Eastern Airlines, which had not been acquired by Texas Air.
[c] For Delta. It had not acquired Western.
[d] For TWA. It had not acquired Ozark.
[e] For Northwest. It had not acquired Republic.

Source: U.S. Senate, *Sunset of DOT Merger Authority & Airline Service Issues,* Hearings Before the Subcommittee on Aviation, 100th Cong., 1st sess., April 23, 1987, p. 97.

2. With increased consolidation and concentration that have occurred, the problem of airport access—be it in the form of gates, slots, ticket counterspace, or restricted access to an airport in the guise of noise regulation—has increased substantially, thus seriously compromising the ability of new airlines to enter markets.

The airline industry has gone from an unconcentrated to a clearly oligopolistic industry as a result of the mergers. It can be suggested that ease of market entry, which is a requisite for a competitive market, is not present in the airline industry except for short-distance hauls in low-density markets. For the denser markets, air carriers require time and must absorb sunken costs to obtain gate space and establish patronage. Establishing patronage can be particularly difficult when competing against carriers that offer frequent flier programs, which effectively increase the cost of switching carriers, and that develop computer reservation systems that bias information in favor of their

TABLE 14-5 Carrier Groups, Reservation Systems, and Market Share of Revenue Passage Miles (RPM) Flown

Carrier/Carrier Group	Reservation System	Market Share of RPM
American–Air Cal/Pan Am	Sabre	20.93%
Texas Air Group	Sodas	18.32
TWA–Ozark/Northwest–Republic	Pars	17.75
United	Apollo	17.02
Delta–Western	Datas II	12.04

Source: U.S. Senate, *Sunset of DOT Merger Authority & Airline Service Issues,* Hearings Before the Subcommittee on Aviation, 100th Cong., 1st sess., April 23, 1987, p. 98.

flights. There are no market-oriented public policies that can eliminate this bias, because CRS owners can set excessive access charges for their services as to discourage other carriers from participating in their systems.

Impact of Deregulation on Passenger Fares

Proponents of deregulation predicted that the elimination of restrictions on pricing and entry would cause average ticket prices to decline. Under regulation, the CAB set ticket prices, discouraged competition, and restricted entry. In many markets, fares were deliberately set to exceed the costs of service. Although technological advances frequently caused airline costs to fall, rate controls often prevented ticket prices from falling to reflect these lower costs. When the CAB decided which carrier would serve a new route, it generally did not attempt to determine which applicant could provide service at the lowest cost. Under CAB regulations, a limited number of major airlines was permitted to serve the important routes. Local service airlines were restricted to providing services between smaller cities, between smaller cities and major traffic centers, and to major routes within their regional service areas.Typically, no more than two or three carriers were allowed to serve a given route. This policy induced a regional specialization among the carriers, and thereby impeded the development of a lower-cost, nationally integrated route structure.

Although average ticket prices have fallen since deregulation, they have not fallen by the same amount everywhere. Long-distance flights, such as those from coast-to-coast, have dropped 35 percent in real terms.[4] Price reductions have also dropped to the big city markets. Fares have generally increased in small city markets because the CAB had determined fares almost totally on the basis of mileage and, unlike a competitive market, did not take into account the lower costs of operating in markets with high passenger volume. This situation created a fare structure that subsidized travelers in short-distance, small city markets, who were charged a price exceeding cost. This policy is known as "cross-subsidization." Fares in all markets now correspond more closely to the cost of providing services. The ending of regulated below-cost fares increased average fares between 22 and 35 percent in short-distance markets, with a concomitant decrease in the number of passengers.[5]

However, consumers have benefited overall, despite higher fares for short-distance services.[6] The lower prices that airlines can charge customers in long-distance markets make them better off. People who could not afford to fly at the old, artificially inflated prices now can fly. Those who could have flown at the higher prices are also better off, because they have more income to spend on other things. Consumers in some short-distance markets have to pay a higher price, and are thus worse off because of deregulation. Some people in these markets may choose to fly less, or not at all. Most of these consumers, however, are being asked to pay for the true cost of the service. Moreover, consumers in these markets do have alternatives, such as automobile travel, trains, buses, and smaller planes. Many planes, as well as other resources that served these short-distance markets, have been redirected to other uses, where they will continue to benefit customers who place a higher value on them.

Service

The complaints of air travelers regarding service are epitomized in the true experience of an irate traveler. Apparently, a man and his wife wanted to travel

[4] Steven Morrison and Clifford Winston, *The Economic Effects of Airline Deregulation* (Washington, D.C.: Brookings Institution, 1986), p. 24.

[5] Thomas Moore, "U.S. Airline Deregulation: Its Effects on Passengers, Capital, and Labor," *Journal of Law and Economics* 29 (1986): 8–9.

[6] Jonathan D. Ogur, Curtis L. Wagner, and Michael G. Vita, *The Deregulated Airline Industry: A Review of the Evidence,* (Washington, D.C.: Bureau of Economics, Federal Trade Commission, January 1988), pp. 7–8.

from Washington, D.C., to Sarasota, Florida to spend a weekend. They drove to Dulles Airport to catch an 8:45 A.M. flight to Sarasota. The plane arrived fifteen minutes late, and after boarding, the couple sat in the airplane for two hours with the heat off while efforts were made to repair a defective window defroster. At 11:00 A.M. the flight was canceled, and the couple was shifted to another airline whose plane was to leave for Sarasota at 11:40 A.M. However, it was announced that the plane had defective weather radar, so the couple had to wait in the lounge for four hours until the flight was canceled at 3:30 P.M. The next flight was to leave for Tampa at 7:30 P.M. with ground transportation provided to Sarasota. The couple gave up, but lost one bag in the process, while the other bags ended up at Sarasota.

This experience is not exactly an endorsement for air travel. However, there is an extenuating circumstance, namely, that air transportation has become so affordable that anyone can fly, and thus the terminals are crowded.[7] In the past, railroad and bus terminals were crowded, and it was not uncommon for Union Station in Washington, D.C., to handle 25,000 passengers a day. But railroad and bus passenger service is largely a thing of the past. The number of passengers flying by airplanes has almost doubled since deregulation,[8] placing more of a burden on terminal facilities and on the use of airplanes. It might be added that U.S. railroads, in their heyday, were not known for their service. They were usually late, dirty, crowded, and they were regulated by the ICC.[9]

Table 14-6 presents frequency of delays calculated as a percentage of operations from 1982 to the period January–September 1987. Delays as used in the table occur only after a plane is ready to leave the gate; delays that occur before planes are ready to leave the gate are not included.

The two most important reasons for delay are the problems of peak load, and weather and mechanical troubles.[10] The peak load problem results from leaving at the most desirable hours during the day. Business travelers in particular desire to leave at specific times. To accommodate business travelers, airlines offer more flights at peak periods. The greater volume of flights

---

[7] Flight delays can result from two fundamental factors: First, the traveling demands of the public affect delays. Consumers want to travel at particular times of the day. This is true for both business and pleasure travel. Second, existing capacity of the airport and airway system is inadequate, and better air traffic control is needed.

[8] In 1987, the number of revenue passengers flown was 450 million; in 1977, 207 million.

[9] Airline delays reached a six-year low in August 1988. It was reported that 90 percent of all interstate carriers arrived on time.

[10] Ogur, Wagner, and Vita, *The Deregulated Airline Industry,* pp. 34–38.

TABLE 14-6   Frequency of Delays as a Percentage of Total Operations

Years	Delays	Operations	Delays/ Operations
1982	332,321	7,372,778	0.045
1983	242,840	7,880,090	0.031
1984	404,285	8,665,542	0.047
1985	333,817	8,878,892	0.038
1986	417,644	9,225,836	0.045
1987 (Jan.–Sept.)	280,501	7,042,284	0.040

Source: Jonathan D. Ogur, Curtis L. Wagner, and Michael G. Vita, *The Deregulated Airline Industry: A Review of the Evidence* (Washington, D.C.: Bureau of Economics, Federal Trade Commission, January 1988), p. 33. Reprinted by permission.

during peak periods causes the demand for airport services to reach a peak at the same time. In addition to requiring the services supplied by airports, airlines require the services produced by one or more of the Federal Aviation Administration (FAA) control centers. Each of those centers controls the airspace in its part of the United States, guiding aircraft through the sectors under its control. Peaking of consumer demand for air travel also causes peaking of demand for the services of some en-route centers. For the first eight months of 1987, 12 percent of all delays were caused by congestion at en-route centers.[11]

Weather and mechanical problems are a second reason for delay. In the aforementioned experience of an irate passenger, mechanical failure was the reason for the flight delays. Weather factors can create problems. The crash of an Air Florida plane into the Potomac River was a direct result of snow and ice conditions at Washington National Airport. When weather is poor, airports and en-route centers cannot handle the same traffic volume as under normal weather conditions. A massive snowstorm, heavy rain, or a thick fog can shut down an airport completely. Weather delays at an airport in one region can affect the entire system. Many carriers operate route networks in which several flights arrive at an airport within a short period of time to connect with several

[11] Federal Aviation Administration, *Air Traffic Activity & Delays Report for August 1987*, Washington, D.C.: FAA, September 18, 1987, pp. 1–5.

**TABLE 14-7   Safety Records of Commercially Scheduled Airlines
1965–1975 and 1976–1986**

| | Total Accidents Involving Commercially Scheduled Airlines | |
	1965–1975	1976–1986
Cause		
Pilot error	32	12
Weather	18	8
Traffic control	9	5
Aircraft engines	7	4
Maintenance	2	1
Airport facilities	0	2

Sources: From *Safe Skies for Tomorrow: Aviation Safety in a Competitive Environment*, July, 1988. Reprinted by permission of The Brookings Review. Congress of the United States, Washington, D.C.: Office of Technology Assessment, *Safe Skies for Tomorrow: Aviation Safety in a Competitive Environment*, May 1988, p. 5.

departing flights. For the first eight months of 1987, approximately 70 percent of all delays were caused by bad weather.[12]

Probably the most important aspect of airline deregulation has to do with passenger safety. We all read about air disasters—the crash of a Pan American jet near New Orleans during a thunderstorm, which killed every passenger, and the crash of a Delta Airlines jet at the Dallas-Fort Worth Airport, which was attributed to windshear—come immediately to mind. But when airline fatalities are compared to the number of passengers who fly, the airlines are quite safe. Table 14-7 presents a comparison of total accidents involving commercially scheduled airlines for two time periods, 1965–1975 and 1976–1986. As the table indicates, the number of airline accidents actually has decreased during the latter period, despite the increase in the number of airline passengers and an increase in the number of planes in use.

Table 14-8 presents the number of accidents, fatal accidents, and number of fatalities before and after deregulation. Major scheduled airline fatality rates, which are fatalities per 100 million revenue passenger-miles fell from 0.133 during 1971–1978 period to 0.043 during the 1979–1987 period. This compares to an average of 3.57 fatalities per 100 million passenger-miles in pas-

[12] Ibid., p. 2.

TABLE 14-8 Accidents, Fatal Accidents, and Fatalities for Major Airlines Before and After Deregulation

| | Before Deregulation | | |
Year	Accidents	Fatal Accidents	Fatalities
1971	43	7	194
1972	46	7	186
1973	36	8	221
1974	43	7	460
1975	29	2	122
1976	21	2	38
1977	19	3	78
1978	20	5	160

| | After Deregulation | | |
Year	Accidents	Fatal Accidents	Fatalities
1979	23	4	351
1980	15	0	0
1981	25	4	4
1982	16	4	234
1983	22	4	15
1984	13	1	4
1985	17	4	197
1986	21	2	5
1987	33	4	231
1988P	29	3	285

P = Preliminary data.

Source: Data provided by the National Transportation Safety Board, Washington, D.C., March 1989.

senger car travel: air travel is safer than automobile travel. Estimates reveal that 800 lives are *saved* each year when travelers go by air instead of by car.

Although accidents and fatal accidents have decreased since deregulation, the rate of near mid-air collisions has increased, as Table 14-9 indicates. Most of the near collisions reported on nightly news programs do not involve commercial aircraft, but small private planes or military operations. Small private

TABLE 14-9 Near-Airline Collisions, 1981–1986

Year	Hazardous	Critical [a]	Potential [b]	Unclassified [c]	Nonhazardous
1981	317	85	230	2	77
1982	24	56	191	0	64
1983	391	98	283	10	84
1984	474	127	317	30	115
1985	625	180	423	22	133
1986	642	162	473	7	199

[a] *Critical* means that the planes came within 100 feet of each other.

[b] *Potential* means that the planes came within 100 to 500 feet of each other.

[c] *Nonhazardous* means that a collision was found to be unlikely.

Source: Jonathan D. Ogur, Curtis L. Wagner, and Michael G. Vita, *The Deregulated Airline Industry: A Review of the Evidence* (Washington, D.C.: Bureau of Economics, Federal Trade Commission, January 1988), p. 78. Reprinted by permission.

planes do constitute a danger to commercial planes. The crash of a Mexican Airline plane near San Diego, which killed every passenger, was caused when a private plane flew into it. Near collisions involving only commercial airlines made up approximately 4 percent of the total. In the table, "hazardous" consists of "potential," "critical," and "unclassified."

EVALUATION OF AIRLINE DEREGULATION

Alfred Kahn, who was chairman of the Civil Aeronautics Board when Jimmy Carter was president and who was the driving force behind airline deregulation, feels that it has been a success. He has said that if airlines had not been deregulated, it probably would have been impossible to deregulate trucking, railroads, and buses.[13] He has stated that airline deregulation has been successful in that average fares today are running at levels that represent savings to

[13] *The Washington Post,* September 25, 1988, p. 66.

travelers on the order of $20 billion a year.[14] He also states that deregulation has not worked perfectly. Many travelers who can't stay over a weekend are paying high fares, especially if they live in small towns. And the skies are too crowded—although accident rates are down 35 percent compared with regulated levels. He concludes by saying that if he had to do it all over again, he would have deregulated the airlines.

The Federal Trade Commission in its major study of airline deregulation concludes that it has been a success. It bases its conclusion on several factors.[15] First, there has been an improvement in air safety, particularly by the major airlines. The absolute number of accidents, fatal accidents, and fatalities on scheduled airlines have declined substantially. Fares have fallen and the total number of air flights has increased as a result of deregulation. Consumers have gained as a result of lower fares, totaling $100 billion since deregulation. Total passenger airline industry profits have been higher than they would have been in the absence of deregulation. More people now travel by air than ever before. Flight frequency has increased and the total number of passenger-miles flown has almost doubled since deregulation. Congestion, although a serious problem, could be solved if there were a reduction in the number of commercial and general aviation flights using airports during "peak" times. In general the frequency of flights to small cities has increased since deregulation.

Morrison and Winston, in their Brookings Institution study, estimated the total benefit of airline deregulation to be $15 billion a year. Most of these benefits have been in the form of direct savings to consumers. They calculated that in 1977 alone had airlines been deregulated, consumer benefits would have equaled $10.3 billion, while airline profits would have been $4.7 billion.[16] Actual and potential competition in high-density markets should remain sufficient to maintain the level of benefits achieved under deregulation, and the increased importance of a well-developed commuter network in a more concentrated competitive environment may actually bring greater benefits to travelers on low-density routes. The evolution of the deregulated capital and industrial structure of U.S. airlines is likely to enhance improvements already generated under deregulation. In years to come, deregulation will be regarded as a spur to the airline industry's continued development.

[14] In 1987, 21 percent of all passengers traveled on discount tickets, at an average discount of 62 percent. Since deregulation, coach fare classifications and discount fares have proliferated.
[15] Kirk, Wagner, and Vita, *The Deregulated Airlines Industry*, pp. 6–31.
[16] Morrison and Winston, *The Economic Effects of Airline Deregulation*, pp. 51–67.

However, some people do not share Morrison and Winston's optimism. There is the problem of traffic control, for example. In October 1988, the U.S. Senate passed emergency legislation ordering the Federal Aviation Administration to resolve an air traffic control crisis at Chicago's O'Hare International Airport.[17] The resolution, which was approved without any objection, instructed the FAA to report to Congress on its plans to reduce pressure on air controllers and alleviate flight delays at the nation's busiest airport. However, the problem is more attributable to federal budgetary constraints and Reagan administrative policies carried out by the DOT than to deregulation. These difficulties have slowed FAA regulatory processes and procurement; eliminated many expert technical personnel, who have chosen more rewarding jobs in industry; and prevented modernization of traffic control equipment.[18]

A more specific criticism of airline deregulation has to do with mergers. The rationale for airline deregulation was to promote competition in the airline industry, which would be achieved by easing market entry for new airlines. However, a series of mergers has turned the airline industry into an oligopoly, dominated by a half-dozen major airlines. Hobart Rowen, a business columnist for *The Washington Post,* stated that the airline industry has changed from a regulated oligopoly to an unrestrained oligopoly.[19] Each firm in the oligopoly operates out of its own hub and is served by commuter or feeder lines. Thus, in ten major cities, including St. Paul, Minneapolis, and Newark, two-thirds of the traffic is controlled by a single airline. In Atlanta and Chicago, two lines divide three-quarters of the market.

It is certainly true that mergers and takeovers of all types have been a fact of life during the Reagan administration. In October 1988, Carl Icahn made a bid to acquire Eastern Airlines from Texas Air, Eastern's corporate parent, and then changed his mind. During the Reagan years, the Department of Transportation approved eleven out of eleven proposed mergers, despite the fact that the Justice Department was opposed to three of them. What is needed is a more vigorous enforcement of the antitrust laws and a transfer of authority to administer them from the Department of Transportation to the Justice

---

[17] *The Washington Post,* October 18, 1988, p. 2.

[18] U.S. Senate Committee on Commerce, Science, and Transportation, *Reports on Aviation Safety,* Hearings Before the Subcommittee on Aviation, 100th Cong., 2nd sess. (Washington, D.C.: U.S. Government Printing Office, 1988), pp. 60–62.

[19] Hobart Rowen, "Airline Deregulation at 10: Did the Theory Fail?" *The Washington Post,* October 18, 1988, p. H–1.

Department. It is quite possible that closer enforcement of antitrust laws with regard to airline mergers will occur in the Bush administration. Also, more attention will be placed on airline safety, even though fewer accidents and fatalities have occurred since deregulation. It is felt that airlines, under the pressure of competition, have been cutting corners on safety.

Hubbing

Hubbing is a by-product of deregulation and has transformed the airline industry and the way in which airlines compete. A hub is simply a center point for airlines to fly into and out of. An example is Atlanta's Hartsfield Airport, which is one of the busiest airports in the United States. Passengers fly into it on many flights and depart from it on other flights. There is a hubbing arrangement by which a bank of flights is scheduled to arrive and depart within a short period of time. Passengers fly into a central point in the airport, change planes, and fly on to a particular destination. For example, at Baltimore–Washington International Airport, twenty-five Piedmont Airlines flights arrive daily from 8:09 A.M. to 8:25 A.M. and twenty-nine flights depart daily from 8:10 A.M. to 9:15 A.M.[20] There are several advantages of hubs. First, there is less layover time; prior to hubs, airlines would stop at several cities to fill planes. Second, there are lower fares because planes fly with a higher percentage of filled seats. Third, there are more nonstop destinations.

There are also some disadvantages to hubbing. There is concern that one or two airlines have come to dominate a particular hub, thus creating a potential monopoly of air service into and out of it. The end result is that passengers have to pay higher airfares. A Transportation Department study showed that ticket prices at seven airports dominated by one or two carriers outstripped average fare increases at airports served by many airlines. Another study found that after a merger with Ozark Airlines, Trans World Airlines' share of passengers boarding at Lambert–St. Louis International Airport increased to 83 percent. It also found that TWA's St. Louis fares increased more than fares at another hub where the merger had little impact on TWA's market share.[21]

---

[20] *The Washington Post,* "The Hubbing of America: Good or Bad?" Sunday, February 5, 1989, p. H1.

[21] Ibid., p. 2.

SUMMARY

The Airline Deregulation Act of 1978 ended forty years of regulation of the fares, rates, schedules, and routes of passenger airlines in interstate commerce. The rationale for the act was to promote more competition in the airline industry. Prior to 1978 fares, service, and market entry was determined by the Civil Aeronautics Board (CAB). Critics of airline regulation argued that it worked against the efficiency of the market as a resource allocator in that it kept prices below the market price, which created a system of nonprice rationing. Also, regulated carriers competed primarily through frequency of flights, which led to excess capacity. The Airline Deregulation Act phased out the Civil Aeronautics Board, eased entry into the airline industry, and allowed domestic airlines freedom to lower or to raise rates.

It has now been ten years since the airlines have been deregulated. Several problems have developed, one of which is the number of mergers that have occurred and that could ultimately lead to a lessening of competition. A second problem is the overcrowding of airports, which is attributable to the fact that airline travel is far more popular today than it was ten years ago. Finally, less air service is provided to certain areas of this country, but it is necessary to remember that those services were subsidized by consumers. However, on balance it can be argued that airline deregulation has been a success. Consumers are paying lower fares, particularly on long-distance flights. A greater improvement in air safety has been achieved by the major commercial airlines. There has been an improvement in the accident rate, although new technology is a contributing factor. Service has also improved in many areas through the use of hub and spoke operations.

QUESTIONS FOR DISCUSSION

1. What are the characteristics of regulated industries?
2. Why was the airline industry deregulated?
3. What is a hub-and-spoke system?
4. What are some problems of airline deregulation?
5. Have fares gone up or down as a result of airline deregulation?
6. What are some causes of airline delays?
7. Are airlines safer today than before deregulation?

8. Are consumers better off or worse off as a result of deregulation?
9. What were the major provisions of the Air Deregulation Act of 1978?
10. "The airline industry of today resembles an oligopoly." Discuss.

RECOMMENDED READINGS

Bailey, Elizabeth E., David R. Graham, and Daniel P. Kaplan. *Deregulating the Airlines*. Cambridge, Mass: MIT Press, 1985.

Carlton, Dennis W., William M. Sandes, and Richard A. Posner. "Benefits and Costs of Airline Mergers: A Case Study." *Bell Journal of Economics,* vol. 11 (Spring 1980), pp. 65–83.

Graham, David R., Daniel P. Kaplan, and David S. Sibley. "Efficiency and Competition in the Airline Industry." *Bell Journal of Economics,* vol. 14 (Spring 1983), pp. 118–138.

Kahn, Alfred E. "I Would Do It Again." *Regulation.* No. 2 (Spring 1988), Washington, D.C.: American Enterprise Institute, 1988.

_____. *Testimony Before the U.S. Senate Committee on Commerce, Science and Technology,* September 1988.

Kaplan, Daniel. *The Changing Airline Industry.* Congressional Budget Office, Washington, D.C., 1985.

Levine, Michael. "Airline Competition in Deregulated Markets." *Yale Journal of Regulation,* vol. 4 (Spring 1987), pp. 393–494.

Moore, Thomas. "U.S. Airline Deregulation: Its Effect on Passengers, Capital, and Labor." *Journal of Law and Economics,* vol. 29 (Apr. 1986), pp. 1–28.

Morrison, Steven and Clifford Winston. *The Economic Effects of Airline Deregulation.* Washington, D.C.: Brookings Institution, 1986.

Ogur, Jonathan D., Curtis L. Wagner, and Michael G. Vita. *The Deregulated Airline Industry: A Review of the Evidence.* Bureau of Economics, Federal Trade Commission, Washington, D.C., 1988.

U.S. Senate, Subcommittee on Aviation. *Sunset of DOT Merger Authority and Airline Service Issues.* 100th Congress. 1st sess. Washington, D.C.: U.S. Government Printing Office, 1987; and *Reports on Aviation Safety.* 100th Congress. 2nd sess. Washington, D.C.: U.S. Government Printing Office, 1988.

Chapter 15

Deregulation of Financial Institutions

Much business news in the latter part of 1988 was devoted to the problems of the U.S. savings and loan industry. The savings and loan crisis is not just limited to the industry itself—it may also hamper efforts to reduce the federal deficit. The losses experienced by savings and loan institutions are growing by an estimated $35 million each day, so the issue is becoming how to keep their problems from affecting the economy like a virus, depressing the value of the U.S. dollar, throwing the budget out of balance, and reducing the effectiveness of monetary policy. The savings and loan crisis threatens to make depositors lose faith in the government's ability to control the problem. Such a loss of public confidence could lead to depositors making runs on these institutions, triggering a cash crisis like the one that caused the federal government to declare a bank holiday during the Great Depression. The savings and loan industry of 1989 seems to have come full circle back to the early 1930s.

However, many commercial banks are also in financial trouble. The number of failed banks rose from 10 in 1980 to 184 in 1987. Predictions for the 1988 total were 200 including two of the largest banks ever to fail, First Republic of Texas and M Corp. For the first time in four decades, total reserves held by the insurer of bank deposits—the Federal Deposit Insurance Corporation (FDIC)—is expected to fall below $3 billion. Insolvent banks and thrift institutions can bleed their competitors, just as in the Depression. To remain liquid, depository institutions with little or no capital must offer high interest rates on their deposits to attract funds. But their efforts bid up the cost of funds for their soundly capitalized competitors and thus impair the health of both the bank and thrift industries.

This chapter will explore the problems of the banking and thrift industries, both of which were deregulated in the early 1980s. Their problems can only partially be blamed on deregulation. Other factors were at work, not the least of which was the collapse of the oil-producing economies of the southwestern states. We'll begin at the beginning, by discussing the regulation of both the banks and the savings and loan institutions during the early part of the Depression. The regulation of commercial banking has already been discussed in some detail in Chapter 3; we now need to focus on it more sharply. We will also discuss the insurance instruments of the banking and savings and loan industries, the Federal Deposit Insurance Corporation (FDIC), and the Federal Savings and Loan Insurance Corporation (FSLIC).

THE COMMERCIAL BANKING INDUSTRY

Federal government regulation of the banking industry actually goes back almost to the beginning of the United States as a country,[1] but the collapse of banking during the Depression provided the rationale for much of the regulation. Several important laws were passed to regulate the activities of banks. The Glass–Steagall Act created the Federal Deposit Insurance Corporation (FDIC) to guarantee depositors' accounts, and it separated commercial banking from investment banking activities. The Banking Act of 1935 extended government control over banking by connecting it with monetary and fiscal policies of the Federal Reserve and the U.S. Treasury. It also created the Federal Reserve Board of Governors, which was given greater control over such tools of monetary policy as rediscounting and legal reserve requirements of commercial banks against consumer demand and time deposits.

The Federal Deposit Insurance Corporation (FDIC)

The FDIC was created by the Glass–Steagall Act of 1933 as an independent regulatory commission. The existence of this and other commissions is justified on the ground that the complexity of modern society demands economic regulation to avoid economic anarchy, monopoly, and irresponsibility. It has been argued, for example, that the advent of such phenomena as nuclear energy and jet aircraft calls for greater government surveillance in order to allocate resources to meet the goals of modern society. Independent commissions regulate specific activities. The regulation of stock exchanges has been delegated to the Securities and Exchange Commission; the regulation of interstate commerce has been the domain of the Interstate Commerce Commission; the

---

[1] Massachusetts created a commission to regulate state banks in 1838. The Federal Reserve System was created in 1913.

regulation of electric power and natural gas used in interstate commerce is the responsibility of the Federal Energy Regulatory Commission; and the regulation of banking is the responsibility of the FDIC.

When the FDIC was created in 1935, it replaced the Temporary Deposit Insurance Fund, which was set up in 1933 to bail out ailing commercial banks. This measure proved inadequate. As bank failures continued, Congress created the FDIC with the intent of protecting bank depositors from losses and of restoring and maintaining confidence in the stability of the private banking systems. Runs on banks by depositors who were anxious to get their money contributed to the collapse of the banking system. The FDIC insures deposits up to $100,000 per deposit in all banks belonging to the Federal Reserve System[2] and in all other mutual savings or commercial banks that so desire. It finances itself with assessments, originally set at 1/12 of 1 percent of deposits, levied on assessed banks. Today, each insured bank pays for the cost of the insurance through semiannual assessments based on the volume of the bank's deposits. The deposit insurance fund consists of those assessments and of income from investing the fund's balances.

FDIC Procedures for Failed Banks

The FDIC does not have the power to close a bank. That power rests with the chartering authorities—either a state banking commission if the bank has a state charter, or the Office of the Comptroller of the Currency if the bank has a national charter. After a bank is closed, the FDIC is appointed receiver and is responsible for settling the affairs of the bank. However, several alternatives are available to the FDIC in handling the affairs of a failed or a failing bank. These alternatives have been provided by various laws that were passed in the 1980s. The Garn–St. Germain Act of 1982 expanded the authority of the FDIC to arrange mergers between healthy and failing banks. In August 1987, President Reagan signed an omnibus banking bill called the Competitive Equality Banking Act, which expanded the options available to the FDIC to deal with failed banks. The following alternatives are available to the FDIC:

1. One of the more important alternatives available to the FDIC to deal with failed banks is called a *purchase and assumption contract*. Under this approach, a buyer steps forward to purchase all or some of the bank's failed

---

[2] All types of deposits are insured, including checking deposits, savings deposits, deposits in NOW accounts, Christmas savings, and time certificates of deposit.

assets and to assume its liabilities. The usual procedure is for the FDIC to invite a number of possible buyers to a bidders' meeting. A transaction is consummated with the highest bidder.

2. A second approach is called a *deposit payoff*. As soon as a bank is closed by the chartering authority, the FDIC is appointed receiver and steps in to pay all depositors the full amount of their insured claims and begins to liquidate the assets of the failed bank. Uninsured depositors and other general creditors of the bank generally do not receive either immediate or full reimbursement on their claims. Soon after the bank is closed, they receive what are called *receiver's certificates,* which entitle the holders to proportionate shares of the collections received on the failed bank's assets.

3. Another alternative is called a *bridge bank*. This solution is temporary. It merely provides a bridge until a more permanent solution can be found. The idea is that when a bank fails, the FDIC may prefer to keep it operating briefly until prospective purchasers have had enough time to assess the bank and can make a reasonable offer for it. If kept operational, the bank can retain much of its value. Moreover, less community disruption is likely to occur if the bank can be kept open.

4. A fourth solution is called an *insured deposit transfer*. In this approach, only the insured deposits and secured liabilities are transferred to another institution. Uninsured and unsecured liabilities remain in receivership. Sufficient cash is paid by the FDIC to the institution that accepts the failed bank's insured and secured liabilities, to equal the amount of these liabilities. Generally, the acquiring institution will use some of its cash to purchase certain of the failed bank's assets.

5. Finally, there is what is called *open-bank assistance,* which means that a transaction occurs before the failing bank is declared insolvent and closed. Generally, the FDIC provides enough money to cover the difference between the estimated market value of the bank's assets and its liabilities. New capital is provided by private investors.

THE DEREGULATION OF COMMERCIAL BANKING

There were several reasons for the deregulation of commercial banking during the early 1980s. First, precedent for deregulation had already been established when the airline industry was deregulated in 1978 and the railroad and trucking industries were deregulated in 1980. The pendulum had swung away from regulation toward more reliance on the free market. Second, consumer groups argued that interest ceilings, which dated back to the regulations passed in the 1930s on time and savings accounts, discriminated against small savers, including the elderly. They advocated the elimination of interest ceilings so that banks could pay market-determined rates of interest. Technological change was a third reason for commercial bank deregulation. With the developments that have occurred in electronic communication and transportation, the geographic scope of the market for financial services broadened greatly, encompassing the entire United States. Regulatory constraints limited the ability of depository institutions, such as banks, to install the latest electronic equipment available.

Other reasons were related to the financial state of the U.S. economy during the late 1970s and early 1980s. Wild fluctuations in interest rates occurred during both the Carter and Reagan administrations as the Federal Reserve tried to put a clamp on inflation. Interest rates on mortgages, which had been around 8 percent during most of the 1970s, shot up to around 14 to 15 percent. Banks and savings and loan associations, which were locked into old mortgage rates, found that they had to pay more money to attract funds. However, the interest they could pay to depositors was fixed. Thus, banks as a group sought legislative changes that would allow them to compete with unregulated competitors. Money market funds, in particular, were able to offer higher rates of interest. Many depositors took their money out of banks where interest rates were fixed at around 5 percent, and put it in money market funds, where they could earn a much higher rate of return.

Depository Institutions Deregulation and Monetary Control Act of 1980 (DIDMCA)

The centerpiece of deregulation for banks and other depository institutions is the DIDMCA. This legislation authorized NOW accounts nationwide, established uniform reserve requirements for all depository institutions, and empowered them to pay interest on demand deposits. Title I of the act provided for the gradual elimination of the limitations on interest payable on accounts in depository institutions covered by the act. Interest rate regulations had been criticized as discriminatory against small savers. Title III of the act authorized all depository institutions to provide checking services. The act also contained other provisions, including the following:

1. It authorized automatic transfer systems (ATSs) accounts, which provide for automatic funds transfer from interest-bearing to demand accounts, and negotiable order of withdrawal (NOW) accounts and share drafts for individual depository organizations.

2. It authorized mutual savings banks to make business loans and to accept demand deposits from business customers.

3. It eliminated the effects of state usury laws on certain types of loans, specifically agricultural, business, and mortgage loans.[3]

The Garn–St. Germain Depository Institutions Act of 1982

The basic reason for the passage of the Garn–St. Germain Act was that managers of savings and loan associations and other thrifts feared their institutions would collapse because the high rates of interest they had to pay to attract capital often exceeded the rates they earned on their portfolios. People feared that if savings and loan associations fail in large numbers, such a failure could result in a run on the commercial banking system, which could harm the entire financial system of the United States. Congress was also concerned about the potential effects of a savings and loan industry collapse on the availability and cost of mortgage credit.

The Garn–St. Germain Act has a number of important provisions. In Title I and Title II of the act, regulatory agencies were given the power to deal with troubled banks and thrifts. The Federal Deposit Insurance Corporation (FDIC) and the Federal Savings and Loan Insurance Corporation (FSLIC) can make loans or purchase assets of any insured financial institution to prevent closing or to restore normal operations. For example, if an insured commercial bank closes and has assets of $500 million or more, the FDIC, as receiver, may sell the closed bank to an instate depository institution owned by an out-of-state bank or bank holding company. By expanding the geographic and institutional barriers that constrained such mergers, this and other provisions of the act alleviated the problems faced by regulatory authorities in finding and acquiring firms to take over failing financial institutions.

---

[3] This provision was important because when the act was passed, the prime rate was 18 percent, which was above the usury rate that many states allowed.

Interstate Banking

In 1970, changes in the Bank Holding Company Act permitted most banking-related services to be offered interstate, except for deposit taking. The 1970 changes also narrowed the definition of "bank" to include only institutions that both accepted deposits and made commercial loans. As a result, bank holding companies and others were able to establish an interstate network of consumer financing companies, mortgage companies, and the like that escaped regulation either by not accepting deposits or not making commercial loans. The Garn–St. Germain Act empowered bank regulatory agencies to permit the acquisition of failing institutions across state lines. States then passed laws to facilitate interstate banking. In 1983 South Dakota passed a law that allowed out-of-state bank holding companies to own state-chartered banks, which can own insurance companies. Massachusetts passed an interstate banking law that allowed local banks into other New England states on a reciprocal basis. Other states have followed suit.

The Financial Modernization Bill of 1988

This bill, introduced by Senator William Proxmire, who was the chairman of the Senate Banking Committee,[4] would have amended the Glass–Steagall Act, which barred a mingling of the securities and banking industries. This mingling was blamed for contributing to the speculation that preceded the 1929 stock market crash. The bill, which passed by a vote of 94–2 in the Senate,[5] would have gradually torn down barriers between banks and securities firms and forced banks and other financial service companies to spell out in simple English the costs and potential interest income of checking and savings accounts, certificates of deposit, and other products that banks sell to the public. The bill would have permitted a company that owns a bank to also own a securities company, as long as the two subsidiaries were operated separately. The activities of the various subsidiaries would have been regulated by existing federal agencies, with the Securities and Exchange Commission policing securities operations and the banking regulatory agencies overseeing the commercial banking operations.

---

[4] Senator Proxmire retired from the Senate in 1988.

[5] The bill did not have support in the House of Representatives.

Effects of Banking Deregulation

Changes in banking laws, plus recent advances in communications and data processing technologies that have appeared to reduce the costs of managing multibranch banks, have led to a substantial increase in the level of interstate banking. Clearly, technological and economic forces, in conjunction with deregulatory actions and a new pattern of competition, have resulted in nothing less than a revolution in the market for financial services. The banking sector of the U.S. economy has been supplanted by a financial services industry of which depository institutions are only a segment. The regulatory environment for commercial banks and thrift institutions was narrowed considerably by the landmark legislation of DIDMCA and the Garn–St. Germain Act. State banking laws have also been passed that have reduced the regulation of banking.

Supply of Financial Services

Developments in the electronic computer industry have served to reduce greatly the costs of transmitting, storing, and processing information. Computer advances have made electronic banking feasible. This state of the art incorporates automated clearinghouses, automated teller machines, and point-of-service terminals into an electronic funds transfer system (EFTS) which is now spreading rapidly. The development of an EFTS involves substituting capital for labor and, to a considerable extent, substituting fixed for variable costs. The equipment needed to efficiently operate an EFTS involves a substantial monetary outlay. Expensive EFTS and other technological advances clearly require economies of scale. Larger institutions have an advantage in being able to muster the capital resources necessary to meet the equipment requirements mandated by the new technology.

Nonbank institutions have expanded into the financial services industry. This competition has energized both the credit and deposit markets. In the credit market, competition is particularly intense for consumer loans. For example, the single largest consumer lender in the United States is General Motors, through its GMAC (General Motors Acceptance Corporation). Sears is also a large consumer lender, as is Ford. Nonbank lenders also provide business loans. Competition from nonbank organizations is also intense for commercial mortgage loans. Nonbanks also compete for sources of funds. Money market funds have offered the widest substitute for deposits. Deregulation of financial institutions reflected the growth in competition from nonbank firms and enabled banks to compete against them in interest rates for loanable funds.

Before deregulation, several restraints were placed on banks, one of which limited the price of deposits. Deregulation has virtually eliminated pricing restrictions on entry and expansion into financial markets as well as on the scope and nature of financial activities. Before deregulation, restrictions limited geographic expansion, but these, too, were eased. Constraints on entry and geographic expansion had acted to limit competition among the suppliers of such services. It encouraged vertical integrated operations[6] in which banks both produced and distributed financial services. Relaxing the geographic restraints and deregulating activities were intended to allow depository institutions to use new strategies in providing financial services.

Deregulation and Commercial Bank Failures

For most of the history of the Federal Deposit Insurance Corporation, there was little or no public interest in the cost of bank failures. Few banks failed, and few creditors suffered any loss of their deposits. The losses sustained by the FDIC were negligible in comparison to its total income. Only in the 1980s have bank failures and their cost become significant enough to cause concern. Table 15-1 presents the number and deposits of FDIC-insured failed banks for the period 1970 through August 1988. As the table indicates, more banks failed in 1984 than in the entire decade of the 1970s. Not included in the table are the number of banks on the FDIC problem list. In 1973, there were 155 banks on the FDIC problem list; in 1987, there were 1,559 banks on its problem list.

The most common way in which the FDIC has handled banks that fail is through purchase and assumption. In 1987, for example, 132 out of the 184 banks that failed were handled by a purchase and assumption transaction.[7] Generally, a purchase and assumption transaction is preferable to a deposit

---

[6] Dwight B. Crane, Ralph C. Kimball, and William T. Gregor, *The Effects of Banking Deregulation,* Association of Federal Reserve City Bankers (July 1983), pp. 1–12.

[7] F. Jean Wells. "The Federal Deposit Insurance Funds: Their Financial Condition and Public Policy Proposals." Economics Division. *Congressional Research Service.* Washington, D.C.: Library of Congress. September 27, 1988, CR5-2–CR5-4.

TABLE 15-1 Number and Deposits of FDIC-Insured Failed Banks, 1970–1988 (deposits in thousands of dollars)

Year	Failed Banks	Deposits
1970	7	54,806
1971	6	132,058
1972	1	20,480
1973	6	971,296
1974	4	1,575,832
1975	13	339,574
1976	16	864,859
1977	6	205,208
1978	7	854,154
1979	10	110,696
1980	10	216,300
1981	10	3,826,022
1982	42	9,908,379
1983	48	5,411,608
1984	79	2,883,162
1985	120	8,136,786
1986	138	6,553,400
1987	184	6,251,700
1988 to August	148	23,636,100

Source: Pauline H. Smale, "Bank Failures: Recent Trends and Policy Options," Economics Division, *Congressional Research Service* (Washington, D.C.: Library of Congress, September 23, 1988), CR5-3.

payoff by the FDIC, particularly if the volume of uninsured liabilities is not high. It is less disruptive to a community, because it ensures that many of the failed bank's former borrowers and lenders will have another institution with which they are able to conduct business. In fact, the failed bank's deposit customers rarely notice any inconvenience whatsoever. The bank may be closed on an afternoon after the close of one business day and reopened at its regularly scheduled time on the next business day. The only apparent difference from the viewpoint of most customers is that there is a new name on the building.

Reasons for Bank Failures

There are a number of reasons for bank failures. One of the more important reasons has to do with depressed economic conditions in a particular region of the country. The agricultural and energy industries in the United States have had their share of problems. Of the 184 banks that failed in 1987, 95 were located in the energy-depressed states of Texas, Louisiana, and Oklahoma.[8] When the world price of oil was around $35 a barrel, these states prospered. Houston was considered the oil capital of the world, and many thousands of people moved there from the depressed industrial states of the Midwest. But the world price of oil dropped to less than $10 a barrel. This fall depressed the economies of these states, and also of Mexico, one of the major oil-producing countries in the world. Thousands of people lost their jobs, and real estate values in Houston and other cities plummeted. Banks that had lent money on real estate found that they could not recoup their losses by selling real estate.

Farm bank failures accounted for 54 of the total 184 bank failures.[9] These banks were concentrated in the agricultural states of Iowa, North Dakota, South Dakota, and Nebraska. What happened here had its genesis in the 1970s, when the value of agricultural land was increasing. Farmers took out loans to buy more farm land as speculation, or to buy expensive new farm equipment. Some people argue that banks encouraged farmers to take out new loans, using their land as collateral. An agricultural recession hit the farm states in the early 1980s. The price of agricultural products dropped, and farmers had less money to pay off their loans. Foreclosures became common, and thousands of farmers lost their land. Some banks, faced with real estate that could not be sold and a declining farm economy, simply did not have the resources to remain solvent.

Other banks that failed or were on the FDIC list of problem banks made loans to less developed countries during the 1970s. Mexico is a case in point. Major oil discoveries in the early 1970s made Mexico one of the major oil-producing countries in the world. Mexico mortgaged its economy to the hilt, based on the prosperity that oil exports brought to the economy. It borrowed some $102 billion from U.S. and other foreign banks, using oil exports as its collateral to finance its economic development. All went fine until the world

[8] Ibid., CR5-4.
[9] Ibid., CR5-4.

price of oil hit rock bottom during the 1980s. Since Mexico had predicated its loan repayments on revenue from its oil exports, serious financial problems developed and still remain. It became difficult for Mexico to pay the interest on its foreign debt, much less to pay the principal. All Mexico could do was to borrow to pay interest and roll over the principal that came due. United States banks that had Mexican debt in their portfolios encountered serious financial problems.

Fraud and insider abuse frequently play a part in bank failures. Such conduct contributed to one-third of the bank failures in 1986, 1987, and through August 1988.[10] Analysts estimate that outright criminal conduct was responsible for 12 to 15 percent of bank failures. For example, from January 1985 through the end of 1987, 98 of the 354 banks that failed were cited by examiners as showing at least some sign of fraud or insider abuse. Those 98 failed banks had assets of $2.7 billion and cost the FDIC nearly $676 million. The FDIC has taken several steps to deal with fraud and abuse. It is publishing a time-tested list of "red flags" and other warning signs of fraud and abuse to be used as an aid to examiners and auditors. Some fifty FDIC examiners have received special training in spotting fraud and insider abuse. This training focuses on criminal motivation and early detection.[11]

However, few bank failures are the result of a single cause. The U.S. banking system has had to adjust to dramatic changes resulting from financial deregulation. A broad goal of deregulation was to enable depository financial institutions (commercial banks, savings and loan associations, mutual savings banks, and credit unions) to compete more effectively with each other and with nondepository financial institutions. The increased level of competition has placed new pressures for bank management. The management of an individual bank must decide what is feasible for its successful operation. This decision involves considering the bank's market and competitors. The more sophisticated and complicated the decisions become, the easier it may be to make the wrong choice, which will adversely affect the safety and soundness of a bank.

Table 15-2 presents the percentage share of assets held by private domestic financial institutions for two time periods, 1975 and 1987. The declining asset

---

[10] Testimony of L. William Seidman, Chairman of the Federal Deposit Insurance Corporation, *Condition of the Federal Deposit Insurance Funds,* Hearings Before the Committee on Banking, Finance, and Urban Affairs, House of Representatives, 100th Cong., 2nd sess., August 3, 1988, p. 338.

[11] Ibid., p. 339.

TABLE 15-2   Distribution of Assets Among Private Domestic Financial Institutions, 1975–1987 (in percentages)

	1975	1987
Commercial banks	38.8%	32.5%
Savings and loan associations	15.5	15.8
Mutual savings banks	5.7	3.3
Credit unions	1.7	2.9
Life insurance companies	13.0	11.4
Other insurance companies	3.6	4.0
Private pension funds	8.6	10.9
State and local government retirement funds	4.9	6.3
Finance companies	4.6	5.3
Mutual funds	2.0	4.3
Money market funds	0.2	3.1
Other	1.4	0.2
Total	100.0	100.0

Source: U.S. House of Representatives, *Condition of Federal Deposit Insurance Corporation Funds,* hearings before the Committee on Banking, Finance, and Urban Affairs, 100th Congress, 2nd session (Washington, D.C.: U.S. Government Printing Office, 1988), p. 402.

growth rate in commercial banking, along with the decrease in the overall number of commercial banks, has resulted in a decline in the market share in the private domestic financial services industry. Between 1975 and 1987, the share of total private financial institutions' assets declined from 38.8 percent to 32.5 percent.

Technological change has provided many advances in state-of-the-art banking, but these innovations have also added pressures to the banking industry. Advances in the delivery of services have increased competition. Using new technology, individual banks have extended their areas of operations and increased the variety of financial products they offer. The startup and maintenance costs associated with new equipment can be substantial. The competition of other forms of financial services and the cost of new technology creates problems for bank managers. This technology represents a fixed cost that smaller banks can find difficult to cover. Often these small banks are located in depressed agricultural areas. When the economy of the area is bad, small banks don't have the resources to cover fixed costs.

The First Republic Bank of Texas—Anatomy of a Bank Disaster[12]

As of the end of 1987, the First Republic Bank Corporation was the fourteenth largest bank holding company in the United States, with over 160 banking offices throughout Texas. It was also the largest bank with headquarters in Texas and the Southwest, with $28.4 billion in assets as of March 31, 1988. First Republic's subsidiary banks had a strong presence in the market areas of Dallas, Fort Worth, Houston, Austin, and San Antonio. In addition, First Republic owned a bank in Delaware, which was primarily a credit card operation. The First Republic banks had major correspondent relationships with almost 1,100 banks located throughout the United States, but concentrated primarily in the Southwest. They acted as depositories for their correspondents and provided check clearing, funds transfer, loan participation, and custodial clearance and investment advisory services.

In December 1987, First Republic announced that it expected to suffer a loss of between $325 million to $350 million for the fourth quarter of that year. As a result of the announcement, the holding company and the lead banks in Dallas and Houston began to experience even more significant funding problems. In late January 1988, First Republic announced that it had suffered a fourth-quarter loss of $347 million, bringing the 1987 losses to a total of $656 million. It also announced that $3.9 billion in loans, which represented 16 percent of all its loans, were nonperforming at the end of 1987. By late February 1988, First Republic Bank of Dallas began experiencing a depositor run. In a five-day period, the customers of the Dallas bank had withdrawn their deposits by $750 million, or approximately 15 percent of the bank's total deposits. By March 1, the First Republic's banks as a whole had lost $1.8 billion since the beginning of the year. On March 15, 1988, as a result of continuing outflows, the Dallas bank's funding needs exceeded its $2 billion line of credit

---

[12] This case is primarily based on the following source: U.S. Senate Committee on Banking, Housing, and Urban Affairs, *The First Republic Bank of Texas Assisted Merger*. Hearings on the Merger of the North Carolina National Bank and the First Republic Bank of Texas, 100th Cong., 2nd sess., August 11, 1988 (Washington, D.C.: U.S. Government Printing Office, 1988).

with other holding companies and was about to fail when First Republic sought assistance from the FDIC.

On March 17, 1988, the FDIC, after consulting with the Federal Reserve and the Comptroller of the Currency, announced an interim assistance plan for the First Republic Bank Corporation, involving a $1 billion six-month loan to the two largest banks in the First Republic system. The announcement included an assurance to depositors and general creditors of the First Republic banks that in resolving the situation, bank depositors and bank creditors would be protected and that services to customers would not be interrupted. The FDIC specifically provided no assurance to the creditors of the First Republic holding company or other banking subsidiaries. In exchange for the financial assistance, the First Republic holding company guaranteed the $1 billion loan by pledging the shares of 30 of its bank subsidiaries. First Republic also agreed to substantial restrictions on its operations, management, and policies.

Acquisition by the NCNB Corporation

On July 29, 1988, the Texas subsidiary banks of First Republic Bank Corporation were closed, and the FDIC agreed, after considering several bid proposals, to sell the banks to North Carolina National Bank (NCNB), a holding company based in Charlotte, North Carolina. The FDIC provided $4 billion—the biggest bailout in bank history. NCNB was picked because it had strong management and the support of prominent Texas business interests, particularly those of billionaire H. Ross Perot, who agreed to back it if it could not raise the more than $200 million it needed within three months. The key to consummating the deal was a ruling by the Internal Revenue Service granting NCNB tax relief on FDIC assistance and on profits made from its Texas acquisition. The FDIC then organized a bridge bank, NCNB Texas National Bank, to assume the closed bank's deposits and other liabilities and to acquire certain of the bank's assets. The bridge bank will be run under contract by NCNB Texas National Bank. Eventually NCNB will have a majority interest in the bank.

NCNB has gained access to the third largest banking market in the United States, and it has five years to decide whether it wants to buy the banks in the First Republic Bank system. For its money, NCNB gets control of a $26.8-billion array of Texas banks. The deal will roughly double NCNB's size. It had to put up only $210 million to get a 20 percent share of the new bank, NCNB Texas National Bank, while the FDIC put up $4 billion to get an 80 percent interest. NCNB will have operational control, and it will have the exclusive right to purchase the government's 80 percent share in the bank from the FDIC over a five-year period. Regulatory officials estimate that the FDIC will recover $1 billion of its $4 billion. Meanwhile, NCNB will get roughly a $700 million tax break for its $210 million investment.

The Role of the FDIC

The FDIC arrangement with NCNB is similar to its bailout of Continental Illinois National Bank and Trust in July 1984. Until the assistance to First Republic Bank, that has stood as the most expensive bank bailout in U.S. history. The FDIC pumped about $4.5 billion into Continental Illinois, and it has recovered all but about $1.7 billion. The idea behind arrangements of this type is that a bank, which can be revived with federal money, will flourish and grow, allowing new management ultimately to buy out the government. Unfortunately, that has worked better in theory than in practice. The FDIC, for instance, continues to hold stock in Continental Illinois. The cost of the arrangement with NCNB will plunge the FDIC into the red for the first time ever, surpassing the $2 billion to $3 billion from the insurance fees it receives annually from member banks. The arrangement is by no means a guaranteed success. Banking experts point out that the Texas economy is still fraught with risk.

The Role of the Taxpayer

Very few things come free in this world, and the bailout of First Republic Bank is not one of them. There are costs to the U.S. taxpayer. The first cost involves the $700 million tax break that NCNB got for putting up $210 million of its own money to acquire First Republic. This break deprives the U.S. Treasury of money at a time the budget is running an enormous deficit. The tax break is supposed to be made up out of future earnings. The bank put in $210 million, got a tax break of $700 million, and doubled its assets. If the acquisition is a success, it wins; if it is not, somebody will have to pay and that somebody is the taxpayer. Second, the FDIC is an independent agency and is financed out of the federal budget. If the FDIC runs a loss, which it is expected to do, the taxpayer, not the FDIC, will have to pay. Money that goes to the FDIC has to come from someplace else, and it could well come out of education and health care.

Deregulation and the Free Market

Several points can be made about First Republic Bank. First, it was created by a merger between two large bank companies, Republic Bank and Interfirst Corporation, both of which had been losing money before the merger. Second, although the tired economy of Texas contributed to the demise of First Republic Bank, it was not the only factor. The great majority of Texas commercial banks had a more conservative loan policy and did not get into trouble. Third, some of the larger banks, including First Republic Bank, got involved in the real estate and building boom, and made a number of loans based on the assumption that Texas oil would always sell at $30 a barrel. Deregulation had little to do with their problems; they rolled the dice and lost.

THE SAVINGS AND LOAN INDUSTRY

Will Rogers once said, "The business of government is to keep the government out of business, that is, unless business needs government aid." Well, one business apparently needs government aid in a big hurry, and that is the savings and loan industry. L. William Seidman, chairman of the Federal Deposit Insurance Corporation, stated that the federal government would need at least $30 billion in cash in 1989 to close the 500 weakest savings and loans that are costing taxpayers millions of dollars every day that they remain open.[13] He also said that as much as $70 billion in additional cash will be needed in 1990 and the years beyond to close hundreds of other troubled savings and loans that are healthier than the worst 500 cases. Seidman also said that before any money is spent, however, the agency that regulates the savings and loan industry—the Federal Home Loan Bank Board, and its insurance arm, the Federal Savings and Loan Insurance Corporation (FSLIC)—should be overhauled to eliminate conflicts of interest that many banking experts believe helped create the savings and loan crisis.

The Development of the Savings and Loan Industry

Movie actor Jimmy Stewart has made many movies, including *Mr. Smith Goes to Washington* and *The Philadelphia Story* (for which he won an Oscar),

---

[13] Statements of L. William Seidman on TV's "MacNeil–Lehrer Report," November 30, 1988.

but the one for which he will always be remembered is *It's a Wonderful Life*, which is regularly shown on television during the Christmas holidays to make us feel good about ourselves.[14] Stewart plays the part of a savings and loan executive who has been wrongly accused of misplacing funds. He attempts to drown himself in the river, but is saved by his guardian angel who makes him see what the world would have been like if he hadn't been born. In one memorable scene, he explains how a savings and loan operates.[15] It is neighbors lending to neighbors, he said. You bring your money to us, and we will lend it to those who want to build homes. The whole thing is based on mutual trust. However, the savings and loan institutions of that time period are long since gone. Today they are into all sorts of activity, and that diversity is where the problem lies.

The structure of the savings and loan industry is a product of the Depression. Difficulties affecting every aspect of the nation's debt structure were aggravated by special features of the mortgage market. They included the inflation of real estate values during the boom of the late 1920s; loss of income by homeowners during the Depression; unsatisfactory short-term unamortized mortgages; and the inability of local sources of credit to meet the needs of the mortgage market. In 1933, a thousand foreclosures were being ordered every day. The response of Congress to the housing problems of the Depression was the creation, beginning in 1932, of a series of interrelated corporate agencies, which included the Federal Home Loan Bank, federal savings and loan associations, and the Federal Savings and Loan Insurance Corporation.

The Federal Home Loan Bank Act of 1932

The Federal Home Loan Bank Act of 1932 sought to improve the mortgage system and provide home-financing institutions better able to serve borrowers. It created a structure modeled after the Federal Reserve System and consisted of a central Federal Home Loan Bank Board appointed by the President, twelve Federal Home Loan Banks, and numerous member savings and loan institutions. The loan banks are authorized to borrow funds by issuing deben-

---

[14] *It's a Wonderful Life* was produced in 1946 by RKO. Frank Capra directed, Donna Reed co-starred, and Henry Travers played the guardian angel.

[15] In those days, the savings and loans were called "building and loans." They were locally owned and operated—depositors and borrowers were from the same town or area. They lent money on mortgages.

tures or bonds guaranteed by the United States and to make loans to their member institutions on the security of mortgages. The member institutions, in turn, can make mortgage loans to homeowners. All federal savings and loan associations must become members of the system, and other financial institutions may join on the purchase of back stock and by conforming to the system's regulations.

The Federal Savings and Loan Insurance Corporation (FSLIC) is the federal agency that insures deposits for most of the nation's savings and loan associations.[16] It is under the supervision of the Federal Home Loan Bank Board. The FSLIC insures individual accounts up to $100,000 per deposit, and is financed by assessments on its members. Its financial condition has been of great interest and concern to Congress in recent years as the number of failed savings and loan institutions with which it has had to deal has increased. The Competitive Equality Banking Act[17] recapitalized the FSLIC fund by creating the Financial Corporation (FICO), a new financing facility capitalized from the earnings of the Federal Home Loan Banks. Funds are raised by the FICO in the long-term credit markets and invested in FSLIC stock. FSLIC can use the proceeds, in addition to its other income, to close insolvent S & Ls.

Deregulation of the Savings and Loan Industry

Times were different when Jimmy Stewart ran his savings and loan bank. Depositors could earn about 2 to 3 percent on their savings, and the savings and loans would charge 4 to 5 percent on their mortgage loans. This is actually the way it was after the post-World War II housing boom and up through the 1950s and middle 1960s. The rate of inflation was very low, averaging a little more than 1 percent annually during the 1950s and the first half of the 1960s. But times changed, and the rate of inflation increased during the Vietnam War and hit double digits during the 1970s. The savings and loans, as well as commercial banks, were locked in by regulation in terms of what they could pay depositors. As inflation increased, the savings and loans found themselves stuck with old 5 and 6 percent mortgages at a time it cost them more to borrow. Depositors began to shun the savings and loans because they could earn higher interest in money market accounts.

---

[16] As of November 1988, there were 3,028 federally insured Savings and Loans.

[17] P.L. 100-86.

As has been mentioned previously, the Depository Institutions Deregulation and Monetary Control Act (DIDMCA) of 1980 and the Garn–St. Germain Act of 1982 deregulated the savings and loans. The first act provided for the gradual elimination of the limitations on interest payments in depository institutions, and expanded the authority of the savings and loan associations to expand their consumer loan business. The second act permitted savings and loan associations to have a much greater access to commercial loans by allowing them to invest up to 55 percent of their assets in such loans. Meanwhile, state laws were also passed that deregulated financial institutions, including the savings and loans, making mergers easier and permitting them to expand across state lines. But deregulation itself was not responsible for the troubles that have beset many of the savings and loans institutions.

Causes of Savings and Loan Failures

The crisis in the savings and loan industry has been caused by several factors, not the least of which has been poor management and corruption on the part of some savings and loan executives. Deregulation took the lid off what savings and loans could do, so many managers were inspired to lend money for practically any purpose, including such chimerical schemes as California windmill farms. There is also some evidence of corruption on the part of savings and loan managers. For example, evidence of corruption forced the closing of the North American Savings and Loan Association in California, and Federal Home Loan Bank Board regulators had to pay depositors $209 million. In another example, Congressional investigators found that FBI reports on the status of criminal probes of certain California savings and loans were routinely ignored by the San Francisco branch of the Federal Home Loan Bank Board. In fact, the reports were filed away in a back office.

A second reason for the problems of the savings and loans is economic. Like their commercial bank counterparts, many of the failed or failing banks are in the Southwest. Table 15-3 presents the location of 504 insolvent FSLIC-insured savings and loans. Three states—Texas, Oklahoma, and Louisiana—whose economies are affected by low oil prices, accounted for one-third of the insolvencies. Also presented is the loss in net income for the insolvent savings and loans.

Loose state regulation is a third reason for the problems of some of the savings and loans. State deregulation of state-chartered savings and loans occurred after the Depository Institutions Deregulation and Monetary Control

TABLE 15-3   Number of FSLIC-Insured Insolvent Savings and Loans, by State, as of March 31, 1988

State	Number of Insolvencies	Net Income (in thousands)
Texas	133	$–3,358,131
Illinois	54	–67,547
California	32	–250,520
Louisiana	29	–78,319
Florida	20	–61,395
Ohio	19	–20,324
Oklahoma	19	–77,894
U.S. Total	504	–4,579,294

Source: U.S. House of Representatives, *Condition of the Federal Deposit Insurance Funds,* Hearings Before the Committee on Banking, Finance, and Urban Affairs, l00th Cong., 2nd sess. (Washington, D.C.: U.S. Government Printing Office), 1988, p. 197.

Act (DIDMCA) of 1980. Without constraints on what could be paid by funds, persuasion at the state level could be used by savings and loan institutions in states such as California, Florida, and Texas, to get state legislators to enact laws to attract deposits, which were used to fund high-risk and poorly underwritten investment schemes.

Table 15-4 presents the estimated cost of resolving the financially troubled savings and loans as of the second quarter 1988. The banks are divided into two categories—those that have been resolved and those that are unresolved and unprofitable.

What Should Be Done About the FSLIC Problem?

The savings and loan industry has created a serious problem—there are projections that the U.S. government could spend as much as $112 billion to restore it to health. The number of insolvent savings and loans increased during 1988, and many will be placed in receivership. The repossession of real estate from failed savings and loans could exacerbate problems in the depressed Southwest and Midwest. So what is going to happen if FSLIC runs out of

TABLE 15-4 Estimated Cost of Resolving Financially Troubled S & Ls, 1984–1988 ($ billions)

S & L Group	2:1988[1]	1:1988	4:1987	4:1986	4:1985
Resolved					
Number	133	14	N/A	N/A	N/A
Total Assets	$62	$1.6	N/A	N/A	N/A
Residential Mortgage Assets[2]	$29	$0.8	N/A	N/A	N/A
Mortgage Assets-to-Total Assets	46.8%	50.0%	N/A	N/A	N/A
Estimated Loss	$22.1	$0.7	N/A	N/A	N/A
% of Assets	35.6%	43.8%	N/A	N/A	N/A
FSLIC Loss Estimate	$23.7	$0.45	N/A	N/A	N/A
Insolvent, Unprofitable					
Number	338	503	489	394	310
Total Assets	$163	$221	$209	$131	$94
Residential Mortgage Assets	$69	$96	$93	$46	$40
Mortgage Assets-to-Total Assets	42.3%	43.4%	44.5%	35.1%	42.5%
Estimated Loss	$46.8	$62.6	$52.8	$37.0	$19.5
% of assets	28.7%	28.4%	25.3%	28.2%	20.7%
Total					
Number	471	517	489	394	310
Total Assets	$225	$223	$209	$131	$94
Residential Mortgage Assets	$98	$97	$93	$46	$40
Mortgage Assets-to-Total Assets	43.6%	43.5%	44.5%	35.1%	42.5%
Estimated Loss	$68.9	$63.3	$52.8	$37.0	$19.5
% of Assets	30.6%	28.4%	25.3%	28.2%	20.7%

[1] Data for 1985 through the first quarter of 1988 are for S & Ls open at the end of the quarter indicated. Data for 2nd quarter 1988 are for S & Ls open at 10/20/88. Merger and liquidation data for 2nd quarter 1988 are for all mergers and liquidations occurring in 1988 for which data are available.

[2] Permanent loans on 1–4 family dwellings, mortgage-backed securities, and home equity loans, net of a fraction of S & Ls' contra asset accounts corresponding to the fraction of these items on the balance sheet.

Source: Data provided by the Senate Banking Committee, December, 1988.

money? The answer to this question was provided by Senator William Prox-mire (erstwhile chairman of the Senate Committee on Banking, Housing, and Urban Affairs), who stated, "We have pledged the full faith and credit of the United States Government and when it comes to a situation where either FSLIC or FDIC can't do it, there is no question but what Congress will have to do it."[18]

Several things can be done. First, the Federal Reserve can be authorized by Congress to expedite mergers between solvent and insolvent savings and loans. This arrangement is somewhat similar to that between NCNB and First Republic Bank. The Federal Reserve could provide U.S. government securi-ties to a healthy savings and loan to offset the bad debts it would acquire from the acquisition of an insolvent savings and loan. Second, the FSLIC could raise money from the Treasury. The latter would sell debt obligations in the open market and lend the proceeds to the FSLIC to pay off the debts of the insolvent savings and loans. This tactic would increase interest payments on the federal debt, which would have to be paid by taxpayers. Third, the Com-petitive Equality Banking Act of 1987 authorized the creation of a special fi-nancing corporation[19] to sell bonds in the capital market to raise funds for the FSLIC. This corporation is authorized to raise $10.8 billion for the FSLIC, but spending from the fund is limited to $3.75 billion a year. However, more than this amount is needed. Fourth, the FSLIC can be merged into the FDIC.

The last alternative would involve putting the savings and loans under the FDIC. However, to move into the FDIC and become a bank, a savings and loan has to give up its franchise, which in many cases has boosted prosperity for the community in which it operates. Such a decision also depends on how willing the institution is to go down a new road. The rationale for merging the FSLIC into the FDIC is that the latter is in a far stronger financial position. There is a problem here in that two industries would be merged regulatorily, but two separate pools of money with disparate assessments on the industry to repre-sent the higher risks from the savings and loans as opposed to the lower risks in the commercial banks. Merging the two funds under a single regulator still does not obviate the need to go out and get additional funds to bail out all the insolvent or troubled savings and loans. There is also the question of whether or not the savings and loans would come in under the same one-twelfth of 1 percent assessment on deposits that the FDIC requires of commercial banks. A merger of the FSLIC into the FDIC is unlikely.

---

[18] U.S. Senate, *The First Republic Bank of Texas Assisted Merger,* p. 34.

[19] This is the Financial Corporation (FICO).

THE BUSH ADMINISTRATION AND THE SAVINGS & LOAN INDUSTRY

The first major problem confronting the Bush administration is the collapse of the savings and loan industry. Bank failures are spreading like a tidal wave across the United States. Each day brings news of new insolvencies. On Friday, February 17, bank regulators placed 25 insolvent savings and loan institutions under government control, and President Bush has ordered the Federal Deposit Insurance Corporation to take over another 224 insolvent S & Ls by the end of March.[20]

Comparisons are being made to the 1930s, when thousands of banks failed and depositors made runs on banks in the hope that they would at least get some of their money back. But there is a difference today in that there are no longer long lines of depositors anxiously clutching savings passbooks and waiting for their S & Ls to open. Instead, there are electronic runs, where wealthy investors transfer their funds by computers from a problem S & L to other areas of investment.

The Case of Bwana Ed

The crisis is occurring amid revelations of scandals and fast buck schemes that have contributed to the insolvency of a number of savings and loan institutions. These schemes have been facilitated by deposit insurance that was set up to stabilize commercial banks and savings and loan institutions during the 1930s. The insurance allows savings and loan owners to put up a little of their own money, take in a lot of deposits usually by paying high interest rates, and gamble on risky loans. This is what happened in Louisiana, where Herman Beebe created a $150 million financial empire by buying banks and S & Ls and using them to finance high-risk money-making schemes, including building polo fields and time-sharing condominiums.[21] Another person, Ed McBirney bought Sunbelt Savings in Stephensville, Texas for $6 million and turned it into a $3.2 billion empire before it collapsed.[22] Through Sunbelt Savings, he financed hundreds of high-risk loans for land, housing and apartment projects,

[20] *Roanoke Times & World News,* "25 More S & L's Placed Under Conservatorship," Saturday, February 18, 1989, p. A10.

[21] Barbara Rudolph, "Finally the Bill Has Come Due," *Time,* February 20, 1989, p. 71.

[22] Thomas Moore, "The Bust of '89," *U.S. News & World Report,* January 23, 1989, p. 40.

shopping centers, and for other activities including the purchase of 84 Rolls-Royces.

In a 1980s version of "It's a Wonderful Life Texas Style," McBirney paid homage to the ethical and moral values of the decade by grabbing and spending. At a Halloween party, his wife served up lion, antelope, and pheasants, while McBirney masqueraded as a king, a regular Texas version of Louis XVI and Marie Antoinette, except that there were no peasants around to demand their heads. At another party, which was ostentatious even for Texas, she created a jungle, hired a live elephant and cast her husband as Bwana Ed, complete with pith helmet and binoculars. Unfortunately for Bwana Ed, his financial empire came tumbling down and the FSLIC is seeking to recover over $500 million from him and other Sunbelt officers plus $100 million in punitive damages from him. He and other Sunbelt officials are also reported to be under investigation by the Justice Department.

The Bailout Plan of the Bush Administration

The Bush Administration has been put in the unenviable position of having to try to solve the savings and loan crisis. His plan will require taxpayers and S & Ls to share a bailout that will cost an estimated $125 billion during the next decade. Taxpayers will be called on to pay $60 billion of the cost that will be contained in the federal budget. The federal government would borrow another $50 billion by issuing 30-year bonds to be repaid from revenues collected from S & Ls. Then, there is the interest that has to be paid on the borrowing, part of which has to be borne by the taxpayer, that will add to the cost of the bailout. In addition, the federal government is obliged to spend another $40 billion to pay for the bailout of 205 S & Ls that it closed in 1988. The approximately 300 remaining insolvent S & Ls would be placed under a newly created agency called the Resolution Trust Corporation, which would auction off their assets.

There would also be regulatory reform. The savings and loan industry would be brought under the supervision of the U.S. Treasury Department, and the Federal Home Loan Bank Board would be replaced by a chairman who would report to the Treasury. The Federal Savings & Loan Insurance Corporation would be under the supervision of the Federal Deposit Insurance Corporation. The healthy S & Ls, which number around 2,500, would assist in the bailout by increasing their insurance premiums from the current $2.08 per $1,000 of deposits to $2.30 from 1991 to 1994, after which it would decline to

$1.80. The rate for banks would also increase from $.83 per $1,000 to $1.20 in 1990 and $1.50 in subsequent years. The rationale for raising bank premiums is to keep them from gaining a competitive advantage over the S & Ls.

SUMMARY

From the early 1930s to 1980, commercial banks and savings and loan institutions were subject to legal and regulatory requirements imposed on them by the government. The assets of savings and loan associations were limited to government securities and fixed-rate, long-term mortgages. Virtually all their liabilities were subject to deposit rate ceilings. Commercial banks were as equally circumscribed in terms of how they could invest and the interest they could pay on deposits. However, the financial services industry has undergone unprecedented changes. Recently, these changes have been nothing short of revolutionary. Technological innovations, changes in the law, increased competition among different types of financial institutions, changing demographics, and consumer demands have placed significant pressure on all depository institutions. In no segment has this pressure been greater than in the savings and loan industry.

One of the more important problems confronting the financial services industry in the latter part of the 1980s is the increase in the number of insolvent commercial banks and savings and loan associations, particularly the latter. Several factors have contributed to this problem. One is the debt of the Third World countries. Some U.S. banks have too much of their assets tied up in loans with Mexico, Brazil, and other debtor countries. A second factor is the depressed oil economy of the Southwest. Many commercial banks and savings and loans have failed in Texas, Louisiana, and Oklahoma. A third factor is the depressed economy of the Midwest farm states. A fourth factor is poor management and, in some cases, fraud on the part of bank and savings and loan managers. When deregulation ended constraints on what banks and savings and loans could do with their money, many unwise loans were made.

QUESTIONS FOR DISCUSSION

1. What is the difference between the Federal Deposit Insurance Corporation and the Federal Savings and Loan Insurance Corporation?
2. Why were the commercial banks and savings and loan institutions deregulated?

3. What were the major provisions of the Garn–St. Germain Act?

4. What are the ways in which the FDIC can deal with banks that fail?

5. Discuss some of the changes that have occurred in commercial banking in recent years.

6. Discuss the major reasons for the increase in the number of bank failures in the 1980s.

7. Discuss the issues in the First Republic Bank case. What is a bridge bank?

8. Who ultimately may have to pay most of the cost of bailing out the savings and loan industry? Why?

9. Was it a mistake to deregulate commercial banks and savings and loan institutions? Explain your answer.

10. How can the problems of the savings and loan industry be resolved?

RECOMMENDED READINGS

Bonvenzi, John F. and Arthur J. Murton. "Resolution Cost of Bank Failures." *FDIC Banking Review*, Vol. 1, No. 1 (Fall, 1988), pp. 1–11.

Bowser, Charles A. *Resolving the Savings and Loan Crisis*. Testimony Before the Committee on Banking, Housing, and Urban Affairs, U.S. Senate, 101st Cong., 1st sess., Washington, D.C.: U.S. General Accounting Office, February, 1989.

Moore, Thomas. "The Bust of 1989." *U.S. News & World Report*. January 23, 1989, pp. 36–43.

Rudolph, Barbara. "Finally, the Bill Has Come Due." *Time,* January 20, 1989, pp. 69–73.

Smale, Pauline H. "Bank Failures: Recent Trends and Policy Options." Economics Division. *Congressional Research Service,* Washington, D.C.: Library of Congress. September 23, 1988.

U.S. General Accounting Office. *Failed Thrifts*. Washington, D.C.: December, 1988.

U.S. Senate. *Strengthening the Safety and Soundness of the Financial Services Industry*. Hearings Before the Committee on Banking, Housing and Urban Affairs, 2nd sess., Washington, D.C.: U.S. Government Printing Office, 1988.

U.S. Senate. *The Conclusions & Recommendations of the President's Working Group on Financial Markets.* Hearings Before the Committee on Banking, Housing, and Urban Affairs. 100th Cong., 2nd sess., Washington, D.C.: U.S. Government Printing Office, 1988.

U.S. Senate. *The First Republic Bank of Texas Assisted Merger.* Hearings Before the Committee on Banking, Housing, and Urban Affairs, 100th Cong., 2nd sess., Washington, D.C.: U.S. Government Printing Office, 1988.

U.S. Senate, *Final Oversight Hearings on the Savings & Loan Industry in the 100th Congress.* Hearings Before the Committee on Banking, Housing, and Urban Affairs, 100th Cong., 2nd sess., Washington, D.C.: U.S. Government Printing Office, 1988.

Wells, F. Jean. "Federal Savings and Loan Insurance Corporation: Current Estimates of Future Costs of Resolving Problem Institution Cases." Economics Division. *Congressional Research Service.* Washington, D.C.: Library of Congress, July 27, 1988.

Wells, F. Jean. "The Federal Deposit Insurance Funds: Their Financial Condition and Public Policy Proposals." Economics Division. *Congressional Research Service.* Washington, D.C.: Library of Congress, September 27, 1988.

Wolf, Frederick D. "Budgetary Implications of the Savings & Loan Crisis." Statement for the Committee on the Budget, U.S. Senate. 100th Cong., 2nd sess., Washington, D.C.: U.S. General Accounting Office, October 5, 1988.

PART VI

THE UNITED STATES IN THE POST-REAGAN ERA

The Reagan era was one of the more controversial eras in U.S. history. To those persons who supported him, he will be remembered as the president who brought back respect to the United States after a decade of self-doubt, achieved the longest running period of prosperity in American history, and improved relations with the Soviet Union. However, Reagan also had many critics. They pointed to the fact that the national debt more than doubled during his eight years in office. The United States became the leading debtor nation in the world, while Japan became the leading creditor nation. Consumption was financed by borrowing from abroad. The United States also ran a deficit in its merchandise trade account, and the gap particularly widened with Japan. Critics predicted a day of reckoning which would call on future generations of taxpayers to pay for the profligacy of the Reagan administration.

The United States enters the decade of the 1990s with a set of problems that need to be addressed. They come under the subject of U.S. competitiveness in the world. The decline in the economic significance of national boundaries and the increased globalization of markets are fundamentally changing the way in which the United States does business at home and abroad. We have to compete in a global economy in which Japan is our leading competitor. But in order to compete, it is necessary that the United States attend to certain problems at home. Education is one of them. In international comparisons of student achievements on a variety of subjects, U.S. students rank down at the bottom. The national debt and budget deficit reduce saving which is necessary for capital formation and creates more dependence on borrowing from abroad. Recent experience has shown that in an open economy such as the United States, international capital mobility has altered the way in which fiscal and monetary policy work.

Chapter 16

Industrial Competitiveness

Paul Kennedy, author of the 1988 best seller *The Rise and Fall of the Great Powers,* states, "In the largest sense of all, therefore, the only answer to the question increasingly debated by the public of whether the United States can preserve its existing position in *no,* because it has simply not been given to any one society to remain permanently ahead of all the others. That would imply a freezing of the differentiated patterns of growth rates, technological advancements, and military developments which have existed since time immemorial."[1]

Clyde V. Prestowitz, author of *Trading Places,* states: "Monday, October 19, 1987 marked the end of the American century twelve years before its time. This date signaled as clearly as any bugle call the most serious defeat the United States has ever suffered."[2] By *trading places,* Prestowitz is referring to Japan. In industry after industry, whether it is in semiconductors or machine tools or automobiles, the United States has ceded first place to Japan.

The first writer is part of a group of declinist theorists who contend that the United States in particular and the West in general are in a process of decline. Kennedy traces the rise and fall of Spain, France, and other powers, ending with the United States. In each case, the reason for their decline is imperial overreach. The problem with Spain was that its expenditures on military conquests overreached its capacity to pay for them; the problem with the United States today is the same in that it is playing military policeman for the world and it no longer is capable of doing so. Kennedy is joined by another decline theorist, Mancur Olsen, who wrote *The Rise and Fall of Nations.*[3] He contended that mature societies start to decline when layers of powerful

[1] Paul Kennedy, *The Rise and Fall of the Great Powers* (New York: Random House, 1987), p. 533.

[2] Clyde V. Prestowitz, Jr., *Trading Places* (New York: Basic Books, 1988), pp. 4–5.

[3] Mancur Olsen, *The Rise and Fall of Nations.* New Haven: Yale University Press, 1983.

special-interest groups succeed in impeding the normal "creative destruction" of capitalism.[4] In order to hold onto what they have, they resist change. But society pays for obsolescence and inefficiency, and the result is decline.

Prestowitz belongs to the Japan-will-win school. He and others cite Japanese feats in the area of high technology, once exclusively the preserve of the United States. In a relatively short period of time, Japan has transformed itself into a world superpower through hard work and a social organization so cohesive and well managed that it is the envy of much of the world. With methodical precision, it has assumed leadership in industry after industry, moving from heavy industry to high technology. Now, the yen has replaced the dollar as the symbol of financial strength, and Japan is buying up assets in the United States and the rest of the world. Moreover, during the 1980s, Japan became the leading creditor nation in the world and the United States became the leading debtor nation. Japan has now become a financial powerhouse. In *Yen! Japan's New Financial Empire and Its Threat to America*[5] Daniel Burstein develops a future scenario of America battered by debts and prolonged economic crisis, electing a president who will get tough with Japan.

Finally, there is the "God is in his heaven and all is right with America" school, which is epitomized by *The Wall Street Journal* in two separate articles entitled "The 1990s and Beyond."[6] The United States is still the economic colossus of the world and will remain so for the foreseeable future. The problems it faces now are just temporary blips that will be ironed out. As for Japan, it has too many problems of its own to seriously challenge the United States for economic leadership. It is a one-dimensional power, whose economic might is not bolstered by military, political, and ideological clout. It is not particularly loved, especially in its own backyard, where China and other Asian countries remember past Japanese aggressions. Japan also is vulnerable to what happens in its foreign markets, while the enormous domestic markets of the United States virtually guarantee self sufficiency for it industries.

---

[4] The term "creative destruction" is associated with the economist Joseph Schumpeter, who predicted the end of capitalist civilization. To Schumpeter, the entrepeneur was the creator, the one who got things done, and who moved society. This creative dynamism was responsible for change, with the new replacing the old. Eventually, however, bureaucracy and other groups replace individual action and economic progress then begins to decline as society becomes more inflexible.

[5] Daniel Burstein, *Yen! Japan's New Financial Empire and Its Threat to America* (New York, Simon & Schuster, 1988).

[6] *The Wall Street Journal,* Monday, January 23, 1989, p. A1 and A5; Monday, January 30, 1989, p. A1 and A8.

IS THE U.S. ECONOMY DECLINING?

Harvard sociologist Daniel Bell wrote a book called *The Coming of Post Industrial Society*.[7] His premise was that the United States was in the process of changing from an industrial economy to a service economy. The same held true for other industrial countries. Developing countries, with lower labor costs, would be the emerging industrial societies. According to Bell, this was an inevitable concomitant of economic development. In the United States today, 70 percent of all workers are employed in service jobs. In West Germany, Japan, and other major industrial countries, a majority of workers are employed in service jobs. As the world moves from material-based production to knowledge-based production, the traditional heavy industries, such as steel, will continue to decline, particularly in the employment of blue-collar workers.

The U.S. Service Sector

Because of the boom in the service sector, the United States has been creating more jobs over the past decade than at any other time in its history, and far more than in Western Europe and Japan. The United States creates more jobs in one year than all of Western Europe in a decade. Moreover, many of these jobs pay well and are very unlike the hamburger-flipping jobs normally associated with service employment. The service sector comprises a broad array of activities, including health, legal, education, repair, and personal and business services. In fact, the four fastest-growing occupations from 1972 to 1987 were as follows:[8]

Profession	*Percent*
Executive, Administrative, Managerial	83%
Professionals: doctors, lawyers, and others	63
Technicians	74
Sales	59

[7] Daniel Bell, *The Coming of Post-Industrial Society* (New York: Basic Books, 1976).

[8] "Employment by Occupations, 1972–1987." Washington, D.C.: U.S. Department of Labor, Bureau of Labor Statistics 1988.

TABLE 16-1   Unemployment Rates for 1987 and for July 1988 for Major Industrial Countries (percent)

Countries	Unemployment Rate 1987	Third Quarter 1988
United States	6.2	5.5
Canada	8.9	7.9
Japan	2.9	2.5
France	10.8	10.7
West Germany	6.9	6.9
Italy	7.8	7.8
United Kingdom	10.3	8.1

Sources: *Economic Report of the President 1989* (Washington, D.C.: U.S. Government Printing Office, 1989), Table B-110, p. 435.

The Rate of Unemployment

One important measure of an economy is its ability to provide jobs for those who seek work. The rate of unemployment in the United States is lower than in all other industrial countries, with the exception of Japan. In fact, other countries look at the United States as the "great job machine," an economy that is constantly able to create jobs. Table 16-1 presents unemployment rates for the United States and other countries for the third quarter of 1988. The unemployment rate for the year 1987 is also included.

The Federal Deficit

The federal deficit can be regarded as a drag on the U.S. economy because it keeps interest rates higher than they should be. This effect occurs because the government is constantly competing against private firms for the supply of loanable funds. However, the relationship of the federal deficit to gross national product (GNP) provides a frame of reference. This ratio can be used as a measure of a country's capacity to carry its debt. As Table 16-2 indicates, the

TABLE 16-2   A Comparison of Government Deficits to Gross National Products for Major Western Countries for the Fiscal Year 1988 (percentages)

Country	Percent of Deficit to Gross National Product
United States	3.3
Japan	2.5
West Germany	1.7
France	2.2
United Kingdom	1.8
Italy	9.9
Canada	3.3

Sources: Office of Management and Budget, Executive Office of the President, *Budget of the United States Government, Fiscal Year 1989*, p. 3a-1; Bundesministeriums der Finanzen, *Finanzpolitische Mitteilungen 1988*, p. 2; *Annual Report of the Japanese Ministry of Finance*, Tokyo, 1987; Chancellor of the Exchequer, *Financial Statement & Budget Report*, 1987–1988; and Ministre de l'Economie et des Finances, *Le Budget de 1988*.

United States does not differ much from the other major industrial countries in regard to running budget deficits. A comparison is made for the fiscal year 1988 of the relationship of government deficits to gross national products for the seven major Western industrial countries. However, it must be mentioned that the rate of saving is higher in such countries as West Germany and Japan, meaning that there is a larger supply of loanable funds and a lower rate of interest for them.[9]

U.S. Manufacturing Output

Those who argue that the United States is not declining competitively contend that the move from manufacturing to services is a natural one, which is occurring in all advanced countries; and also that U.S. manufacturing is increasing

[9]This discount rate set by the (West German) Deutsche Bundesbank for July 1988 was 3 percent; for Japan, it was 2.5 percent; and in the United States, 6.5 percent.

TABLE 16-3   Manufacturing Output in the United States and Other Countries, 1980–1987 (1977 equal to 100%)

	United States	Japan	West Germany	France	United Kingdom
1980	108.6%	119.2%	108.0%	106.0%	99.8%
1981	111.0	120.4	106.2	106.0	96.4
1982	103.1	120.9	103.1	104.0	98.2
1983	109.2	125.1	104.1	104.0	101.7
1984	121.4	138.9	107.6	105.0	103.2
1985	123.7	145.1	112.9	106.0	107.9
1986	125.1	144.5	115.1	106.0	109.5
1987	129.8	148.4	115.4	107.0	111.2
1988*	138.4	159.6	120.9	117.0	116.6

*Third Quarter

Source: *Economic Report of the President 1989* (Washington, D.C.: U.S. Government Printing Office, 1989), Table B-109, p. 432.

in output in absolute terms, even though blue-collar employment is declining. That is a natural trend as the world moves from material-based to knowledge-based production. Table 16-3 can be used to buttress the claim that manufacturing production in the United States has increased both absolutely and also relative to industrial production in other countries.

The Inherent Dynamism of the U.S. Economy

It also can be argued that the U.S. economy is so large and variegated that some regions and sectors are likely to be growing at the same time that others are declining. Therefore, to say that the economy is in decline is a sweeping generalization. For most of the 1980s, the steel-producing states have been referred to as the Rust Belt, where companies have shut down and thousands of highly paid steel workers have lost their jobs.[10] However, an article in *Fortune*

[10] The Rust Belt includes the steel-producing areas of Pennsylvania and the industrial Midwest.

magazine, "The Resurrection of the Rust Belt," states that manufacturing has made a comeback and that steel and other industries are more competitive than ever.[11] For the first time in a decade, USX (U.S. Steel) can export steel profitably. This goal was not achieved easily: it shut down the seven least efficient of its 12 steel mills, and reduced its work force from 75,000 to 20,000. Other industries have also developed in the Rust Belt states, and the unemployment rate, which averaged 12 percent in 1982, has been cut in half.

YES, THE UNITED STATES IS LOSING ITS COMPETITIVE EDGE

There are a number of rather convincing reasons advanced to prove that the United States is losing competitively to other countries. First, the United States lags behind other industrial countries in the rate of saving and investment. Second, the United States standard of living has not increased as rapidly in the United States as in other countries. Third, the United States is getting beaten in the high-tech area. Fourth, the United States has a lower rate of productivity growth in manufacturing than other countries. Finally, the United States has shown a relative decline industrially, as measured against world production, not only in manufacturing, such as textiles, iron and steel, shipbuilding, and basic chemicals, but also it is losing its global share of the market for automobiles, robotics, machine tools, and computers. We need to explore in depth each of these reasons.

Saving and Investment

The United States has not had a high rate of savings in comparison with other countries. Large federal budget deficits have absorbed more than two-thirds of private saving in recent years, and national saving has averaged less than 3 percent of GNP. A low rate of national saving hurts manufacturing in two ways. First, it reduces the supply of capital and chokes off much-needed investment. This restriction hurts manufacturers in their role as producers of capital equipment, and discourages them from making productivity-enhanc-

[11] Myron Magnet, "The Resurrection of the Rust Belt," *Fortune,* vol. 118, no. 4, August 15, 1988, pp. 40–47.

TABLE 16-4 A Comparison of U.S. and Japanese Saving and Investment Rates (percent)

| | United States | | Japan | |
	Saving	Investment	Saving	Investment
1975	2.8	2.1	19.4	19.9
1980	4.4	4.2	18.3	19.5
1981	5.3	5.2	18.5	18.6
1983	2.0	3.2	17.0	15.5
1985	3.2	6.2	16.7	13.0
1987	6.2	5.5	16.5	13.1

Source: Rudiger Dornbusch, James Poterby, and Lawrence Summers, *The Case for Manufacturing in America's Future* (Rochester, New York: Eastman Kodak Company, Communications & Public Affairs, 1988), p. 15. Reprinted courtesy of Eastman Kodak Company.

ing investments. Second, the low national saving rate forces the United States to borrow from abroad in order to finance investment. This outreach makes trade deficits inevitable. Part of this borrowing comes from Japan, which is the world's leading creditor nation and the major industrial competition to the United States. As Table 16-4 indicates, the Japanese have a much higher rate of saving and investment.

U.S. Living Standards

Since 1972, the U.S. standard of living has increased one-fourth as fast as West Germany's and one-seventh as fast as Japan's although in absolute terms the United States still has the highest standard of living. In 1987 America's standard of living continued to grow more slowly than other industrial countries. A rising standard of living is the ultimate goal of any nation. A comparison of changes in living standards for major countries is presented in Table 16-5. It focuses on workers rather than on the overall population. It shows, per worker, how much income is generated, plus or minus any change in what is owed to foreigners. By taking into account changes in foreign debt, the measure gives insight into future living standards.

TABLE 16-5   A Comparison of Standard of Living Indexes for the United States and Other Countries, 1980–1987 (percent)

Country	1980	1981	1982	1983	1984	1985	1986	1987
United States relative to Summit countries*	83.6	83.0	80.5	80.8	81.2	80.5	79.8	78.9
U.S. index	101.0	101.9	100.3	102.7	105.5	106.8	107.7	108.3
Summit index*	120.9	122.7	124.5	127.0	129.9	12.7	134.9	137.4
West Germany index	123.5	124.6	125.4	129.7	131.8	133.8	136.0	137.6
Japanese index	129.0	132.9	135.3	137.3	143.3	149.0	151.3	155.9

*The Summit countries are the United States, United Kingdom, France, West Germany, Italy, and Japan.

Source: Council on Competitiveness, Competitiveness Index (Washington, D.C.: 1988), p. 6. Reprinted by permission.

High Technology

Probably the most serious challenge to U.S. competitiveness is in the area of high technology, which represents the future. The United States has blown its lead in high technology, and the problem could become a crisis. Foreign competition has ruined Silicon Valley, once considered the Mecca of high technology. In 1987, the U.S. trade deficit with Japan in electronics was almost as large as it was for automobiles. Between 1970 and 1988, the U.S. share of the U.S. consumer electronics market fell from 100 percent to under 5 percent; color TV sales share fell from 90 percent to 10 percent; and share of phones from 99 percent to 25 percent. Now the Japanese have developed high-definition television, which can transmit about six times more information to the screen and video receivers to movie screen proportions, bringing more colorful, detailed pictures into the home. Japan has seized the world lead in an emerging multibillion-dollar technology. The new technology could prove decisive in the United States' attempt to maintain a healthy semiconductor industry, since high-definition television will consume large quantities of chips.

Semiconductors are the fundamental building blocks of modern electronics. These are small, rectangular chips of the element silicon. Each chip is the size of a fingernail and is crammed with microscopic circuits capable of storing and processing enormous amounts of information. Semiconductors operate products ranging from digital watches and videocassette recorders to supercomputers and the telephone network. In addition, they are essential to advanced weapons systems. The semiconductor industry, founded in the United States and consummate symbol of U.S. dynamism, has come to represent the rise of Japan and the decline of the United States in the latter part of the twentieth century. But more than just semiconductors is involved. The Japanese have come to dominate virtually all the high-technology industries, including disk drives, robots, printers, optical fiber electronics, satellite ground stations, and advanced industrial ceramics. Many products associated with U.S. companies, such as personal computers, are made in Japan.

In the two decades following World War II, U.S. firms dominated the commercial application of technology. Over time, however, foreign firms assimilated and improved state-of-the-art technology, often American in origin, generated their own products and processes, and skillfully brought them to market. Table 16-6 presents the commercial challenge to U.S. technology. Since World War II, technology has been a leading U.S. export strength. However, since 1970 many U.S. industries have lost their dominance in foreign markets and in U.S. domestic markets to foreign competitors. U.S. firms once controlled much of the domestic market. Today even though the market is large, U.S. firms have been displaced to an important extent by foreign competitors. Nowhere is that displacement more obvious than in the production of color television sets, where U.S. firms now have only 10 percent of a $14 billion domestic market.

During the 1960s and 1970s, U.S. companies dominated the world market for the design and manufacture of semiconductors and computers. However, in the 1970s Japan targeted semiconductors as a strategic industry. By 1983, Japan-based firms' share of the world market equaled that of U.S.-based firms. By 1986, the Japanese had taken 65 percent of the world market, while the U.S. share had fallen to 30 percent. As Table 16-7 indicates, these market shifts are even more dramatic for dynamic random access memory (DRAM) products, which constitute a core semiconductor technology. Combining their edge in memory technology with aggressive pricing policies, the Japanese have made a clean sweep of the world DRAM market.

TABLE 16-6   The Erosion of the U.S. Manufacturers' Share of U.S. Technology Markets, 1970–1987

Technology	Pioneered by	*U.S. Companies' Share of U.S. Markets*			
		1970	*1975*	*1980*	*1987*
Phonographs	United States	90%	40%	30%	1%
Television					
Black and white	United States	65	30	15	2
Color	United States	90	80	60	10
Audio tape recorders	United States	40	10	10	1
Video cassette recorders	United States	10	10	10	1
Machine tools					
Numerically controlled lathes	United States	100	92	70	40
Machining centers	United States	100	97	79	35
Telephone sets	United States	99	95	88	25
Ball bearings	Germany	88	83	71	71
Semiconductors					
Manufacturing equipment	United States	100	90	75	75
Semiconductors	United States	89	70	65	64

Source: Council on Competitiveness, *Picking Up the Pace: The Commercial Challenge to American Innovation,* Washington D.C.: 1988, p. 15. Reprinted by permission.

Foreign countries have made inroads into a number of industries pioneered and dominated by U.S. firms. Consumer electronics is one area. Since 1970 the United States has lost virtually the entire consumer electronics market to Japan and other countries. In 1987 it had less than 5 percent of its own domestic market estimated at $25 billion.[12] This situation has repercussions for other parts of the electronics industry. The connection has been likened to the biological food chain in that when one link is weakened, other links feel the

---

[12] Council on Competitiveness, *Picking Up the Pace* (Washington, D.C.: 1988), p. 16.

TABLE 16-7   World Shares of Dynamic Access Memory (DRAM) Products (percentages)

Year	1975	1980	1987
United States	95.8%	55.6%	17.9%
Japan	4.2	39.4	73.0
Europe	—	5.0	2.0
Rest of the world	—	—	2.1

Source: Council on Competitiveness, *Picking Up the Pace: The Commercial Challenge to American Innovation,* Washington, D.C.: 1988, p. 17. Reprinted by permission.

injury. Although the United States continues to enjoy a market presence in related fields, such as home computers, telephones, and calculators, the erosion of the United States position in consumer electronics could harm the U.S. lead in other electronics markets.

Lower Manufacturing Productivity

Another measure of industrial competitiveness is how U.S. manufacturing is doing compared with other nations in productivity trends. Low productivity affects a country's cost competitiveness and the standard of living. It implies that real wages cannot rise as fast as they can in high-productivity countries. Lower productivity also has an impact on exports and imports. It has contributed in part to the unfavorable balance in the U.S. merchandise trade account, and has resulted in import penetration, which is defined as the share of imports in apparent consumption; that is, production less exports. Rising imports in the U.S. capital goods sector have been particularly dramatic in 1987; for example, nearly 40 percent of all manufacturing equipment was imported. In Japan, which is the United States' number one trade competitor, productivity growth has been higher than in any industrialized country. Table 16-8 presents a comparison of annual percent changes in manufacturing productivity for the Summit countries from 1960 to 1986.

Labor productivity is another way to measure manufacturing performance. This can be done by using gross domestic product per worker, which also includes services and government activities as well as manufacturing. Table

TABLE 16-8   Annual Changes in Manufacturing Productivity for the Summit Countries (percentages)

Year	Output per Hour						
	United States	Canada	Japan	France	Germany	Italy	United Kingdom
1960–1986	2.8%	3.3%	7.9%	5.2%	4.6%	5.7%	3.6%
1960–1973	3.2	4.5	10.3	6.5	5.8	7.5	4.2
1973–1979	1.4	2.1	5.5	4.9	4.3	3.3	1.2
1979–1986	3.5	2.3	5.6	3.1	2.7	4.3	4.5

Source: Office of Technology Assessment, Congress of the United States, *Paying the Bill: Manufacturing & America's Trade Deficit* (Washington, D.C.: U.S. Government Printing Office, 1988), p. 45.

16-9 presents a comparison of average annual changes in real gross domestic product per employed person. The rate of productivity growth in the U.S. economy has only recovered slightly from the low-growth period of the 1970s. Conversely, Japan has put an enormous effort into increasing productivity in industries such as steel, autos, and electronics that have been central to their export-led growth strategy. In many areas, the Japanese have forged ahead of the United States in terms of productivity. For example, the International Motor Vehicle Program found that in the mid-1980s it took, on average, 19.1 hours to build a car in Japanese assembly plants. In U.S.-managed plants, the average time for assembly was 26.5 hours.[13]

U.S. Decline in World Production

Again, it is necessary to emphasize the fact that America's economic decline is only relative, not absolute. It is not becoming poorer, and its economy, which increased at a growth rate close to 4 percent in 1988, is hardly weak. The gross national product of the United States for 1988 is around $4.5 trillion, far surpassing second-place Japan's $2.1 trillion. But the United States has ceased to dominate the world economy as it did for nearly four decades after World

[13] United States Congress, Office of Technology Assessment, *Paying the Bill: Manufacturing & America's Trade Deficit* (Washington, D.C.: U.S. Government Printing Office, 1988), p. 49.

TABLE 16-9 Average Annual Changes in Real Gross Domestic Product Per Employed Person in the Summit Countries, 1960–1986 (percentages)

Year	United States	Canada	Japan	France	Germany	Italy	United Kingdom
1960–1986	1.2	1.9	5.5	3.6	3.1	3.7	2.2
1960–1973	1.9	2.6	8.2	4.9	4.1	5.8	2.9
1973–1979	0.0	1.3	2.9	2.7	2.9	1.7	1.3
1979–1986	0.8	1.0	2.8	1.9	1.6	1.6	1.7

Source: United States Congress, Office of Technology Assessment, *Paying the Bill: Manufacturing & America's Trade Deficit* (Washington, D.C.: U.S. Government Printing Office, 1988), p. 48.

War II. The United States still remains first among a group of increasingly assertive industrial countries. However, Japan has come to dominate some of the growth industries of the future. It produces 70 percent of the world supply of robots. In thirty-one areas of high technology, it is ahead in twenty-five.[14] It produces most of the world's supply of memory chips. Foreigners have invested more money in the United States economy than Americans have invested abroad, and foreign banks have replaced U.S. banks as the world's largest. Japan has become the world's leading creditor country, and the United States has become the world's largest debtor nation. International competition will now determine America's place in the world.[15]

REASONS FOR DECLINING INDUSTRIAL COMPETITIVENESS

A well-known quote from Shakespeare's play *Julius Caesar* can be paraphrased as follows: "The fault, dear America, is not in Japan or South Korea, but in ourselves, that we are losing ground in economic competition."[16] It is, of

[14] Council on Competitiveness, Competitiveness Index (Washington, D.C.: 1988), p. 27.

[15] C. Michael Aho and Marc Levinson, *After Reagan: Confronting the Changed World Economy* (New York: Council on Foreign Relations, 1988), p. 6.

[16] The correct quote is "The fault, dear Brutus, is not in our stars, but in ourselves, that we are underlings."

course, easy to blame Japan for all our problems. In part, this attitude goes back to World War II when we were the good guys and they were the bad guys, who never would fight fair and would get their comeuppance at the hands of John Wayne or Errol Flynn. Today we blame our trade problems on the Japanese, who (we say) don't play fair and don't open their export markets to us. We also accuse the Japanese of copying our technology and picking the brains of our best scientists.[17] To some extent this accusation is true, but it is also patronizing because it assumes that the Japanese are incapable of original thinking, and that we have a monopoly on the world's "smarts." Both assumptions are false.

Four reasons can be advanced to explain the decline in U.S. competitiveness. To some extent, they are interrelated. The first comes under the generic name *self-indulgence,* and includes crime and drugs. The second is euphemistically referred to as "the British disease," which suggests that Americans have lost the Protestant work ethic, a loss that carries with it a concomitant decline in productivity. The third holds U.S. management responsible for the U.S. competitive decline because U.S. managers are too interested in short-term objectives and are not conditioned to compete in global markets. The fourth reason is that it was only a matter of time that other countries, whose economies were destroyed by World War II, would catch up to the United States.

An Uncompetitive Society

Richard Lamm, a former governor of Colorado, offers a rather interesting explanation for why the United States is losing its competitive edge.[18] Better education and better management are not enough to restore America's competitive position because of several internal handicaps, as follows.

First, no modern industrial society has such high rates of drug addiction, teenage pregnancy, and functional illiteracy as we do. Drug abuse provides a consummate example of what is wrong with U.S. society today. The cost of drug abuse to the U.S. economy is $200 billion a year, and is steadily climb-

---

[17] Joel Dreyfuss, "How Japan Picks America's Brains," *Fortune,* December 21, 1987, vol. 116, no. 14, pp. 79–89.

[18] Richard Lamm, "The Uncompetitive Society," *U.S. News & World Report,* April 25, 1988, p. 9. Lamm is now director of the University of Denver's Center for Public Policy.

ing.[19] Drugs are an epidemic that is seeping into American life. They are the prime cause of crime, absenteeism in the workplace, and increasing hospitalization and other health care costs. According to the National Council on Alcoholism, 10 percent of the U.S. population over age fifteen is chemically dependent on alcohol. The economic impact of drug abuse is illustrated by the 1984 figures from the Division of Substance Abuse Services of the state of New York. According to these statistics, the average active drug addict costs the state $32,700 a year: $26,800 in theft losses, $3,300 in law enforcement costs, and $2,600 in health expenses.[20] Drug abuse has been estimated to cost national business firms between $20 to $35 billion annually. The cost is due to absenteeism, theft, poor performance, and higher health care costs.

The cartoon character Pogo (created by Walt Kelly) once said, "We have met the enemy, and it is us." It is rather absurd to be talking about meeting foreign competition until we get our own house in order. Take, for example, education. One-fifth of U.S. adults are functionally illiterate, and 30 percent of U.S. teenagers drop out of high school before they graduate, compared to 2 percent in Japan.[21] In international student achievement comparisons, Americans do poorly in math and sciences.[22] One-third of U.S. secondary schools do not offer their students enough mathematics to qualify them to enter accredited engineering schools. College-bound students in Europe and Japan usually have had two more years of math and science than their U.S. counterparts. The ability of the United States to retain leadership in emerging technologies and the jobs they create depends on a better-educated work force.

Table 16-10 presents an international comparison of the performance of twelfth-grade students in thirteen countries in math and sciences. It shows the poor performance of U.S. students in comparison with foreign students. United States students take fewer science and math courses in high school than do students in other industrial countries. Consequently, they score lower on international tests in these areas, and fewer are prepared to pursue higher education in these fields. America's ability to compete in technology is linked

---

[19] Joint Economic Committee, Congress of the United States, *The Cost to the U.S. Economy of Drug Abuse,* Hearings before the Subcommittee on Economic Goals and Intergovernmental Policy, 99th Cong., 1st sess., 1986, p. 3.

[20] Ibid., p. 4.

[21] World Bank, *1988 Statistical Yearbook* (New York: Oxford University Press, 1988), p. 392.

[22] Joint Economic Committee, Congress of the United States, *International Student Achievement Comparisons and Teacher Shortages in Math and Science,* 98th Cong., 1st sess., 1983 (Washington, D.C.: U.S. Government Printing Office, 1983), pp. 3–7.

TABLE 16-10   U.S. Ranking on International Math and Science Achievement Tests

	Rank		
	United States	*Japan*	*Hungary*
Geometry	11	2	12
Biology	13	10	3
Algebra	12	1	11
Physics	9	4	3
Calculus	11	2	12
Chemistry	11	4	5

Source: *Changing America, The New Face of Science and Engineering, Task Force on Women, the Handicapped and Minorities in Science and Technology* (Washington, D.C.: International Association for Evaluation of Educational Achievement, 1988), p. 9.

closely to its supply of skilled technical workers. It is evident that the nation faces significant human resource problems. By the year 2000, the number of jobs requiring college degrees will increase. However, the educational system is failing to produce the number of scientists and engineers needed to meet future demand. Also, 40 percent of all college faculty engineering teachers are foreigners who have been educated in the United States.[23]

The results of the comparison are rather revealing. The only communist country evaluated was Hungary, and twelfth-grade students in that country generally did better than U.S. students. It can be concluded that Russian students also score better than U.S. students in math and science tests. West Germany and France were also not included in the test comparisons, but both countries have excellent educational systems, where students on average attend classes for 240 days, compared to 180 days for U.S. students. Students from the East Asian countries do far better than their U.S. counterparts on math and science tests. The competition in the future will come from the highly literate, well-educated labor forces of the East Asian countries.

[23] Paul Doigan and Mack Gilkeson, "ASEE Survey of Engineering Faculty and Graduate Students, Fall 1985," *Engineering Education,* October 1986, pp. 51–56.

The National Alliance for Business provides some statistics that create concerns about America's most important asset, its human resources.[24]

1. Twenty-three million adults are functionally illiterate in America today; another 47 million are borderline illiterates.
2. Eighty percent of all new entrants to the labor force in the 1990s will be minorities, women, and immigrants, traditionally those who have the least preparation for work.
3. Over one million young people drop out of high school each year. The dropout rates of many urban schools are close to 50 percent.
4. Each year's dropouts cost the United States $240 billion in lost earnings and foregone taxes over their lifetimes.
5. By the year 2000, 50 percent of all jobs in America will require education beyond high school and 30 percent will require a college degree.

Second, a character in Shakespeare's play *King Henry VI* said, "The first thing we'll do, let's kill all the lawyers." The United States is the most litigious society in the world. Two-thirds of the lawyers on the planet Earth live in the United States. There are more lawyers in Washington, D.C., than there are in Japan. All of the other countries in the world combined do not spend as much time in court as we do. Warren Burger, who was once a Supreme Court Justice, once made the statement that America had too many lawyers and they and the myriad of lawsuits constituted a drag on U.S. productivity. To put it another way, Japan produces engineers and the United States produces lawyers.

Third, the United States is the most crime-ridden, violent society in the world. More homicides are committed in a year in the United States than in all Western Europe and Japan combined. Many of the major cities in the United States are battle zones in which no one dares to appear at night. Teenage gangs prey on each other and on innocent bystanders. Many crimes are drug related. In Baltimore, for example, 243 drug addicts committed 500,000 crimes over an eleven-year period.[25] Then, too, there is the U.S. preoccupation with guns. Carrying guns is an inalienable right, according to the National Rifle Association, which wraps itself in the Constitution and the flag. According to the NRA, it is not guns that kill, but people.

---

[24] *The Road Ahead* (New York: National Alliance for Business, 1988), p. 1.

[25] Joint Economic Committee, Congress of the United States, *The Cost to the U.S. Economy of Drug Abuse*, p. 27.

The United States Has Caught the "British Disease"

The "British disease" is not the name of a social disease, but a pejorative term that Americans have applied to the British—and now the Japanese are applying it to us. Basically, it means the lack of desire to work hard, and an overdependence on the welfare state. New entrants into the U.S. labor force are less skilled and motivated than their international competitors; they come out of an educational system that deemphasizes merit, excellence, and discipline as it levels elitist values. Our society focuses on short-term consumer values and entitlements, and ignores producer values and the requisite of increased productivity. United States manufacturers do not insist on product quality and manufacturing excellence, but on quantity and profit margins.

The Harvard sociologist Daniel Bell once made the statement that the Protestant work ethic disappeared with the advent of the credit card. The Protestant work ethic is one of the fundamental institutions of Western capitalist societies.[26] It was a driving force in the economic development of this country. It stressed hard work and thrift, and postponing the consumption of goods until you could pay for them. God rewarded you in direct proportion to what you contributed in this world, so John D. Rockefeller was able to ascribe his monetary success to the fact that God had rewarded him because he worked hard. Generations of Americans were raised to believe in the Protestant work ethic, that hard work would get you ahead and that indolence, as in the fable of the ants and the grasshopper, would get you nowhere. But times have changed and it can be argued that the Asian nations, not the United States, now follow the work ethic.

Poor Management

A third explanation for the decline in U.S. competitiveness lays the blame on U.S. managers. U.S. companies are overstaffed and managers think only in terms of short-term objectives. This orientation is linked to U.S. society, which is interested in immediate solutions to every problem. Managers are judged successful if profits continue to rise and dividends are increased each year. United States management also places more emphasis on marketing than

[26] See R. H. Tawney, *Religion and the Rise of Capitalism* (New York: Harcourt, Brace, & World, 1926), and Max Weber, *The Protestant Work Ethic and the Spirit of Capitalism* (New York: Charles Scribner and Sons, 1930).

on manufacturing and invests too little in the future. U.S. managers are out-hustled abroad because they have not really had to compete until recently, because for thirty years after the end of World War II they have had domestic and world markets to themselves. Now the rest of the world has caught up to the United States. Finally, most American managers—like most Americans—know little or nothing about foreign cultures.

The criticism of U.S. managers extends into the area of labor-management relations. Critics argue that management practices, such as the assembly line, have become obsolete, and that the more flexible management techniques, such as quality circles, used by Japan and other countries, are superior.[27] Japanese managers allow more participation by workers in the decision-making process.[28] This participation makes the workers feel they are part of the team. However, it is difficult to attribute the high productivity of Japanese industry to that one factor alone. High productivity in Japanese industry is due to a number of factors, including the high literacy of Japanese workers and cultural factors. However, some U.S. business firms have been spurred to take corrective action, which has ranged from emphasizing product quality and improving employee relations, to sharply reducing white-collar staff.[29]

Convergence

It is important to remember that the economies of Western Europe and Japan were damaged by two major world wars. During World War I, most of the fighting was done in western and central Europe, with the United States a participant at the very end of the war. The industrial base of the western European countries was damaged; the United States was untouched and came out of the war as the leading creditor nation. During the interwar period, the United States did not have a particularly high growth rate in comparison to other industrial countries. World War II had a more devastating impact on other industrial countries.[30] The economies of France, Germany, the Soviet Union,

---

[27] Bruce R. Scott, "National Strategies," in Bruce R. Scott and George C. Lodge, eds., U.S. Competitiveness in the World Economy (Boston, Mass.: Harvard University Press).

[28] William Ouchi, *Theory Z* (Reading, Mass.: Addison-Wesley, 1981).

[29] Raymond Vernon, "Can U.S. Manufacturing Come Back?" *Harvard Business Review* 69 (July–August 1984): 98–106.

[30] Edward F. Dennison, *Why Growth Rates Differ: Post-War Experiences in Nine Western Countries* (Washington, D.C.: The Brookings Institution, 1967).

TABLE 16-11   Comparison of Average Annual Increase in Per Capita GNP for Major Industrial Countries, 1965–1986 (percentages)

Country	*Increase*
Italy	2.6
West Germany	2.5
France	2.8
Japan	4.3
Canada	2.6
United Kingdom	1.7
United States	1.6

Source: World Bank, *World Development Report 1987* (New York: Oxford University Press),   p. 203; reprinted with permission.

Italy, and Japan were literally destroyed by the war, while the United States remained untouched. Germany was split into three parts, with West Germany created out of one part. The major world competitors to the United States had to rebuild their economies from scratch, and it was only a matter of time before they caught up with us.

Table 16-11 presents the average annual rate of growth in per capita GNP for the major industrial countries for the period 1965–1986. As the table indicates, the growth rate of the United States was lower than the other industrial countries.

HOW TO INFLUENCE COMPETITIVENESS

Competitiveness has a simple meaning, and it presents a genuine dilemma for the United States economy which now is irrevocably tied to a larger world economy. Simply put, the issue is whether U.S. goods and services can be made as efficiently and productively as those of other nations. If not, the United States must grow both relatively poorer and absolutely poorer, as the logic of an open world economy relentlessly causes advanced efficient production to gravitate elsewhere. If it takes the United States 80 worker-hours to make a Ford and Japan 40 worker-hours to make a comparable Toyota, economic logic does not dictate that the United States gets to make half as many cars as Japan; it dictates that the United States makes no cars, unless the U.S. wants to subsidize car manufacture through protectionist measures.

The real issue is not whether competitiveness matters, for it does, but what to do about it. Here, expert opinion divides between the free marketers and the planners. The planners are further divided into those who think that government should be a strategic player in the economy, versus those who think that the government should mop up the social mess left by the inevitable dislocation of a healthy capitalist economy. For the free market advocates, the least government intervention will produce the best outcome. America's uncompetitiveness reflects the many years when it had no competition. Its sheltered industries, overpriced labor, and mediocre education, compounded by trade deficits, federal deficits, and an overvalued dollar, are problems that must be solved before the United States can be truly competitive. These problems are addressed in subsequent chapters.

INDUSTRIAL POLICY

Industrial policy involves choosing an industry or industries to emphasize at a point in time. There is nothing particularly unique about industrial policy. The Soviet Union has always incorporated such policy in its five-year economic plans. The French use it in their four-year economic plans. For example, the French Ninth Plan, which lasted from 1984 to 1988, stressed the development of the aircraft and electronic industries, and aimed at increasing investment from 11.1 percent of French GNP in 1982 to 12.3 percent in 1988. Japan and South Korea have also achieved significant economic success through the use of industrial policy. Japanese industrial policy has followed a sequential development strategy since the end of World War II. First, Japan sought to develop the shipbuilding industry to carry exports. Export earnings were used to modernize the steel industry, and Japan became a steel exporter. Then priority was given to the automobile industry, which the Japanese came to dominate worldwide. The current strategy is to make Japan dominant in the high-tech area.

What Is Industrial Policy?

Industrial policy is a form of strategic planning. It outlines the basic strategy a nation intends to follow to achieve economic growth and meet foreign competition. It analyzes how changes in technology and human needs are going to alter the industrial structure. The role of government usually increases in three ways:

1. A government agency is created to partially fund private investment research on new products or new products in process.
2. The government systematically seeks to reduce the costs and increase the availability of capital to industrial firms. Included are tax incentives and measures designed to reduce the cost of capital by increasing saving. To stimulate saving in Japan, interest income on deposits up to $13,700 is tax exempt.
3. A government has a systematic procedure for dealing with declining or financially troubled industries. This can be done through rationalization (a British term for gradually closing down inefficient plants) or the granting of aid.

Problems with Industrial Policy

The implementation of industrial policy in the United States could prove difficult for several reasons:

1. What works well in Japan, France, or South Korea may not work well in the United States, which has a far more heterogeneous population and a far more decentralized form of government. Geographically, Japan and South Korea combined are not much larger than California. In France, the banking system is owned by the government, which can allocate resources to industries that are to be stimulated under the four-year plans.
2. Another problem is to identify industries that will be successful in the future. What criteria do you use to determine success?
3. Finally, it is subject to manipulation by special interest groups. In the United States, as is evident by the number of Political Action Committees (PACs), interest groups dominate the political decision-making process, although on rare occasions, Congress manages to rise above itself.[31]

[31] In Virginia, for example, in the race for the U.S. Senate, Democrat Charles Robb received $2.7 million in contributions. His Republican opponent received $165,000.

Industrial Policy in Japan

One of the biggest mistakes the United States ever made was in 1853, when Commodore Matthew Perry opened up Japan to the West and exposed it to capitalism. Capitalism took hold in Japan as deeply as the Catholic religion took hold in South America after it was conquered by Spain in the sixteenth century and Jesuit missionaries were sent to convert the Indians to the "true faith." Japan realized early that it had to learn how to compete in the world in order to survive. Its industrial policy stems back to 1867. First, it intended to industrialize. To do so, Japan had to have capital. It had two choices—get it abroad as the Americans did, or generate it from within. The latter is what they did and what they still do. To acquire the necessary technical skills, they sent their brightest students to foreign universities, and they still do that. Also, foreign firms were invited to Japan to set up factories. By 1914, Japan could be considered a world power.

Japanese industrial development is thoroughly discussed in Prestowitz's book *Trading Places*.[32] A brief description follows:

1. A group of government agencies develop industrial policy. They are the Industrial Structure Council of the Ministry of International Trade and Industry, the Telecommunications Advisory Council of the Ministry of Posts and Telecommunications, and similar groups established to advise other industries.

2. At the policy execution stage, the ministries have many tools at their disposal to encourage the development of specific industries. Special depreciation rates, tax incentives, and government-sponsored research and development are standard devices. Beyond these are other measures, such as the creation of the Japan Electronic Computer Corporation, the government-supported leasing company.

3. The control that the Ministry of International Trade and Industry (MITI) exercises over the establishment of industrial standards constitutes another industrial policy tool.[33] When a Japanese industry establishes industrial standards different from those of other nations, it is automatically protected from invasion by foreign producers without the necessity for a tariff or quota. Guidance to banking and financial institutions on preferred areas of loan activity can strongly influence industrial developments as can such things as delay in granting patents.

[32] Prestowitz, *Trading Places,* chap. 5, pp. 124–150.
[33] Ibid., pp. 129–131.

4. The government-controlled Japan Development Bank makes low-interest loans to special projects. By long tradition, this bank's loans and other government institution loans signal the financial institution at large that it should prefer these targeted projects in its own lending.

5. There are such devices as legal cooperation agreements between companies on the types of goods to be produced. These devices have one thing in common: they induce investment and sometimes disinvestment by reducing risk.

SUMMARY

Competitiveness is the most pressing U.S. economic problem today. The word *competitiveness* regularly appears in corporate advertising extolling the virtues of free enterprise and free trade. However, it is often the same corporations that seek protection from foreign competitors, claiming they don't play fair. It is a complex subject and linked to it are the federal deficit, the trade deficit and the status of the United States as the world's leading debtor nation, all of which will be discussed in subsequent chapters. Although balancing the federal budget is a solution for competitiveness, it is by no means the only solution. We can begin with such social problems as drug abuse and a mediocre educational system. Also, our competitors, particularly the Japanese, play by different rules of the game. They plan more explicitly than we do, and all use variants of "corporatism," which is deliberate business-government collaboration aimed at achievement of specific economic goals.

QUESTIONS FOR DISCUSSION

1. What is meant by the term "industrial competitiveness"?
2. What are some of the reasons for the decline in U.S. competitiveness?
3. What impact does the deficit in the federal budget have on industrial competitiveness?
4. Explain how a low rate of saving can affect industrial competitiveness.
5. What role does education play in world competition between the industrial countries?
6. How does the United States rate in science and math education compared to other countries?

7. Do you agree with Richard Lamm's reasons as to why the United States is an uncompetitive society? Explain.
8. Why is poor American management considered a reason for the decline in U.S. competitiveness?
9. What is industrial policy? How does it work in Japan?
10. How can the competitive position of the United States be improved?

RECOMMENDED READINGS

Aho, C. Michael, and Marc Levinson. *After Reagan: Confronting the Changed World Economy*. New York: Council on Foreign Relations, 1988.

Council on Competitiveness. *Competitiveness Index*. Washington, D.C.: 1988.

Council on Competitiveness. *Picking Up the Pace*. Washington, D.C.: 1988.

Dornbusch, Rudiger, James Poterba, and Lawrence Summers. *The Case for Manufacturing in America's Future*. Rochester, N.Y.: Eastman Kodak, 1988.

Finan, William F., Perry D. Quick, and Karen M. Sandberg. *The U.S. Trade Position in High Technology, 1980–1986*. Report for the U.S. Joint Economic Committee, 1988 (Washington, D.C.: U.S. Government Printing Office, 1988).

Kennedy, Paul. *The Rise and Fall of the Great Powers*. New York: Random House, 1987.

Magnet, Myron. "The Resurrection of the Rust Belt." *Fortune,* vol. 118, no. 4, August 15, 1988.

Prestowitz, Clyde. *Trading Places*. New York; Basic Books. 1988.

U.S. Congress Office of Technology Assessment. *Paying the Bill: Manufacturing and America's Trade Deficit*. Washington, D.C.: U.S. Government Printing Office, 1988.

U.S. Joint Economic Committee, Congress of the United States. *Competitiveness and the Quality of the American Work Force*. Parts 1 and 2, Hearings Before the Subcommittee on Education and Health. 100th Cong., 1st sess. Washington, D.C.: U.S. Government Printing Office, 1987.

Chapter 17

The United States as a Debtor Nation

Twenty years ago, U.S. business firms dominated the world. Investment was a one-way street, flowing from the United States to the rest of the world. In Europe, many people feared an impending takeover of the European economy by U.S. business firms. This fear was encapsulated in a book called *The American Challenge,* published in 1967, by the French journalist-politician Jean Jacques Servan-Schreiber.[1] Investments by U.S. corporations had produced an economic revolution in European management and technology and stimulated an upsurge in income and technology. However, Servan-Schreiber objected to the control of European industry by U.S. firms. He felt that these firms were acquiring dominance over the European economy; worse, they were exporting American culture—or lack of culture—to Europe.

How times have changed in twenty years! The United States is now the leading debtor country in the world, and Japan, which was not really a strong force in world economic competition in 1967, is now the world's leading creditor country. Servan-Schreiber has now written a book called *The Japanese Challenge,* which applies to the whole world, not just to part of it.[2] At the end of 1987, foreign individuals, companies, and governments held $368.2 billion more in U.S. assets than the total of all U.S. assets abroad.[3] Conversely, Japan held a surplus of $240 billion in foreign assets. Concerns once held by Europe twenty years ago have now become U.S. concerns. Is the United States being taken over by foreigners, particularly by the Japanese? To some Americans, that is about as palatable as being taken over by the Mongol hordes of Genghis Khan.

---

[1] Jean Jacques Servan-Schreiber, *The American Challenge* (New York: Atheneum, 1968).

[2] Jean Jacques Servan-Schreiber, *The Japanese Challenge* (New York: Simon & Schuster, 1980).

[3] *The Washington Post,* July 1, 1988, p. 1.

TABLE 17-1   U.S. Assets Abroad and Foreign Assets in the United States, 1980–1987 (billions of dollars)

	1980	*1985*	*1986*	*1987*	*Percentage Change 1980–1987*
U.S. assets					
abroad	$607	$949	$1,071	$1,168	92%
Portfolio	392	719	811	859	188
Direct	215	230	260	309	44
Foreign assets in					
the United States	501	1,061	1,341	1,536	207
Portfolio	418	876	1,121	1,274	205
Direct	83	185	220	262	216

Source: Congressional Economic Leadership Institute, *American Assets: An Examination of Foreign Investment in the United States* (Washington, D.C.: Linda M. Spencer, 1988), p. 49. Reprinted by permission.

FOREIGN INVESTMENT IN THE UNITED STATES

There are two types of investment—direct and portfolio. Direct investment involves investment in companies, factories, and real estate. In contrast, portfolio investment involves the purchase of government securities and the stocks and bonds of private companies. By the end of 1987, total foreign investment in the United States amounted to $1.54 trillion and total U.S. investment in foreign countries amounted to $1.16 trillion.[4] Foreign direct investment in U.S. companies, factories, and real estate amounted to $262 billion at the end of 1987, while U.S. direct investment abroad amounted to $309 billion. Foreign portfolio investment in the United States amounted to $1,274 billion, and U.S. portfolio investment abroad amounted to $859 billion. Moreover, as Table 17-1 indicates, the shift from being a creditor nation to being the world's leading debtor nation began during the decade of the 1980s.

[4] U.S. Department of Commerce, *Survey of Current Business,* June 1988 (Washington, D.C.: Bureau of Economic Analysis), p. 3.

FOREIGN DIRECT INVESTMENT IN THE UNITED STATES

Direct investment is more tangible and visible than portfolio investment. Many U.S. firms have been acquired by foreign investors: for example, Standard Oil of Ohio, CBS Records, A&P, Hardee's, Baskin-Robbins, Howard Johnson, Celanese, Firestone, Brooks Brothers, Peoples Drug Stores, Grand Union, and Smith-Corona, among many others. In Washington real estate, foreign investors have acquired the buildings housing the U.S. Justice Department and the Federal Communications Commission; in New York, they have acquired the Exxon Building and half of Citibank's headquarters complex. Foreign investors own 46 percent of the commercial property of Los Angeles, 39 percent of Houston's, and one-third of Washington's.[5] Foreign investors own 12.5 million areas of U.S. farmland.[6] In banking, foreign banks with branches in the United States account for around 25 percent of all U.S. commercial and industrial lending in the United States. In New York, foreign branch banks account for 53 percent of all commercial and industrial lending; in California, they account for 43 percent.[7]

Foreign direct investment accounted for 6 percent of U.S. direct investment in 1987.[8] However, U.S. direct investment abroad is decreasing relative to foreign direct investment in the United States. In 1960, the ratio of U.S. direct investment abroad to foreign direct investment in the United States was 4.6 to 1. In 1972, the ratio had increased to 6.5 to 1; by 1978 it had decreased to 4.2 to 1; and by 1987 the ratio was 1.2 to 1.[9] It must be pointed out that the rise and fall of the U.S. dollar relative to the pound, yen, mark, and other foreign currencies has had an impact on direct investment. When the dollar is strong relative to other currencies, it is cheaper for U.S. firms to acquire assets in other countries: when the dollar is weak relative to other currencies, it is cheaper for foreign firms to buy assets in the United States.

[5] James K. Jackson, *Foreign Direct Investment in the United States,* Congressional Reference Service (Washington, D.C.: Library of Congress, 1988), p. 3.

[6] J. Peter De Graaf, *Foreign Ownership of U.S. Agricultural Land Through December 31, 1987* (Washington, D.C.: U.S. Department of Agriculture, 1988), pp. 5–8.

[7] Bank for International Settlements, *38th Annual Report* (Geneva: 1988), p. 121.

[8] U.S. Department of Commerce, "International Transactions," *Survey of Current Business,* Bureau of Economic Analysis, June 1988, p. 1.

[9] Ibid., p. 2.

TABLE 17-2   U.S. Direct Investments Abroad and Foreign Direct Investment in the United States, 1975–1987 (billions of dollars)

Year	U.S. Direct Investment	Foreign Direct Investment
1975	$14.2	$2.6
1976	11.9	4.3
1977	11.9	3.7
1978	16.1	7.9
1979	25.2	11.9
1980	19.2	16.9
1981	9.6	25.2
1982	2.4	13.8
1983	0.4	11.9
1984	2.8	25.4
1985	17.3	19.0
1986	28.0	25.1
1987	38.6	40.1

Source: U.S. Department of Commerce, "International Transactions," *Survey of Current Business*, June 1988.

Table 17-2 presents the flows of U.S. direct investments to foreign countries and foreign direct investment to the United States for the years 1975 through 1987. As the table indicates, the flow was one-sidedly in favor of the United States from 1975 to 1980. Then the recession in 1981 and 1982 and the declining value of the dollar contributed to the inflow of foreign investment. The subsequent rise and fall in the value of the dollar did little to curb the inflow of foreign investment. This sharp increase in foreign direct investment in the 1980s concerns some people because it coincides with a trade deficit, low savings rates, and a devalued dollar, which could mean that the United States is selling off its assets too cheaply.

There has been a major redistribution of direct investment in the world. In particular, the position of the United States has changed with respect to outflows and inflows of direct investment. In 1967, the United States had 50 percent of the total outflow of direct investment to other countries, but only 9

TABLE 17-3   Inflow and Outflow of Foreign Direct Investment for Selected Countries (billions of dollars and percent of world foreign investment abroad)

	Outflow of Investment				Inflow of Investment			
	1967	1984	1967	1984	1967	1984	1967	1984
United States	$57	$238	50%	40%	$10	$165	9%	27%
United Kingdom	16	85	14	14	8	47	8	8
West Germany	3	46	3	8	4	36	3	6
Netherlands	11	41	10	7	5	16	5	3
Switzerland	2	25	2	4	2	13	2	2
France	6	32	5	5	3	16	2	2
Japan	1	38	1	6	1	5	3	1
Canada	4	32	3	5	19	62	18	10
Other developed countries	9	45	9	8	21	89	21	15
Developing countries	3	18	3	3	32	154	31	26
Total	112.3	600	100	100	105	603	100	100

Source: Congressional Economic Leadership Institute, *American Assets: An Examination of Foreign Investment in the United States* (Washington, D.C.: Linda M. Spencer, 1988), p. 17. Reprinted by permission.

percent of the inflow. By 1984, U.S. outward investment had decreased to 40 percent of direct investment to other countries, while the inflow had increased to 27 percent. As Table 17-3 indicates, Japan increased its share of investment outflows to other countries from 1 percent in 1967 to 6 percent in 1984, while the inflow of investments from other countries remained at 1 percent for both 1967 and 1984.

Contrary to popular belief, the largest foreign direct investment in the United States is not done by the Japanese or Arabs, but by Canadians and Europeans, particularly the latter. This was also the case in the last century, when the U.S. rise to global economic power was initially financed by imports of European capital. At the end of 1987, the United Kingdom was the largest direct investor, with $75 billion, followed by the Netherlands with $47 billion. Total direct investment from Europe amounted to $158 billion. Total direct investment from Japan amounted to $33 billion. However, as is indicated in

TABLE 17-4   Foreign Direct Investment in the United States by Countries in 1987 (billions of dollars)

Country	Total	Percentage Change 1980–1987
United Kingdom	$75	431%
Netherlands	47	146
Japan	33	611
Canada	22	78
West Germany	20	158
Switzerland	14	180
France	10	176

Source: Congressional Economic Leadership Institute, *American Assets: An Examination of Foreign Investment in the United States* (Washington, D.C.: Linda M. Spencer, 1988), p. 49. Reprinted by permission.

Table 17-4, Japanese direct investment in the United States is increasing at a more rapid rate than that for other countries. Most of the Japanese direct investment has been concentrated in real estate, which has been facilitated by the declining value of the U.S. dollar relative to the yen.

Reasons for Foreign Direct Investment in the United States

There are a number of reasons for the inflow of foreign direct investment into the United States:

1. The United States has the single largest market for goods and services in the world. Per capita income and purchasing power of Americans are high, and the United States is consumer oriented. Also, direct investment circumvents the application to foreign imports of such protectionist measures as import quotas and tariffs.

2. A second reason for the influx of foreign capital is the relationship of the U.S. dollar to other currencies. The Japanese yen, the German mark, the

British pound, and other foreign currencies have risen in value relative to the dollar. This differential makes it cheaper for foreigners to buy assets in the United States. Other major countries, in particular Japan, have a higher rate of savings than the United States, giving them a surplus to invest elsewhere.

3. Foreign banks have some important advantages over U.S. banks. For example, U.S. banks have to maintain a higher ratio of capital to assets than do foreign banks. Also, foreign banks can acquire U.S. banks, while U.S. banks cannot acquire foreign banks. Foreign banks can pay their depositors a lower rate of interest than can U.S. banks. Japanese banks, which have benefited from Japan's status as the world's leading creditor nation, are the largest in the world and have enormous amounts of excess capital to invest abroad.

4. The United States is one of the more politically stable countries in the world. Political unrest is continuous in many other countries. Even in Western Europe, a change in governments could result in a changed business environment.

5. Finally, as Clyde Prestowitz, author of *Trading Places,* argues, the Japanese invest in the United States as a part of their global competitiveness strategy. Aided by a very high rate of saving, the Japanese can streamline production and compete industrially in this country. They use the most modern equipment, financed at very low rates of interest by Japanese banks, which have a surplus of funds drawn from a national savings rate of $1 billion a day, to create a separate economy in the United States.

Issues Concerning Foreign Direct Investment in the United States

Measuring the effect of foreign direct investment on the U.S. economy is difficult, because it entails some offsetting factors. For example, direct inflows of foreign capital provide an immediate benefit to the U.S. balance of payments. But, as in the case of U.S. investments abroad, the initial inflow ultimately causes outflows of dividends, interest, and royalties, as foreign investors receive returns on their investments. These direct flows are only a starting point for assessing the balance of payments effect. In addition to the capital-related impact, foreign direct investment has secondary and even tertiary effects on the U.S. trade accounts. It may cost import substitution by replacing imports with products made in the United States.

Does the United States benefit from foreign direct investment? Obviously the great majority of state governments must think so, because they spend a considerable amount of time and effort to attract foreign investment. As governor of Kentucky, Martha Collins, went to Japan fourteen times to attract investment into her state. Her efforts paid off, for a major Japanese automobile company built a plant in Kentucky. States often offer generous incentives in bidding wars against one another for foreign investments. Many states maintain overseas offices, the primary purpose of which is to attract foreign investment into the United States. Localities also bid for foreign investment as the best hope of restoring jobs and prosperity. U.S. firms also count on foreign investors. The benefits that states, localities, and business firms hope to derive from foreign investment are as follows:[10]

1. There is a positive effect on employment, which has been concentrated in industries such as automobiles, chemicals, electrical equipment, and machinery in which wages are about the national average. At the end of 1986, some three million Americans were employed by foreign-owned firms. In South Carolina and New Jersey, 5 percent of the labor force works for foreign-owned firms. Firms from the United Kingdom and Canada are the leading employers of U.S. workers.

2. Imported foreign technology is often superior to that of the United States. Such technological innovations as the radial tire, the Wankel engine, and prestressed concrete all have come from foreign research and development efforts. At a minimum, these factors taken by themselves increase competition in U.S. markets.

3. New management techniques are introduced into the U.S. market. Foreign managers, particularly Japanese and German, rely on worker motivation techniques that are different from their U.S. counterparts. An example is Theory Z, or Japanese-style management, which uses worker participation in the decision-making process. Quality circles and other techniques are designed to help workers feel useful and a part of the company.

4. Increased tax revenues result from foreign direct investment. The tax base of states and localities is broadened. Locating the Nissan plant in Smyrna,

---

[10] Linda M. Spencer, *American Assets: An Examination of Foreign Investment in the United States* (Washington, D.C.: Congressional Economic Leadership Institute, 1988), pp. 35–38.

Tennessee, increased income in that area, which is essentially rural. The higher income increased sales, income, and property taxes, thus enabling the community and state to provide better services.

5. Foreign investment increases capital formation, which would otherwise have had to come from saving in the United States.

Conversely, a number of concerns have been raised about the role of foreign direct investment in the United States:

1. Both foreign direct and portfolio investment in the United States result in an outflow of income from this country, thus contributing to an unfavorable trade balance and increasing the foreign debt of the United States. (The same complaint was voiced by foreigners when the United States was the leading creditor nation of the world.)

2. Some people are concerned that foreign investment in the United States may mean eventual domination of certain sectors of the economy by other countries. Foreign companies and investors now hold a majority interest in such industries as concrete and consumer electronics, and significant portions in others, such as machine tools, chemicals, and auto parts. There is also concern over foreign control of a considerable part of U.S. bank assets, and prime real estate in some major U.S. cities. Foreign creditors also hold an estimated 20 percent of the federal debt. Any precipitous withdrawal of these funds could raise our interest rates and provoke a recession.

3. The U.S. market is the most open in the world, while other countries impose numerous restrictions on U.S. investments. For example, Japan prohibits investment that it believes will adversely affect the interest of national security. Canada also places restrictions on foreign investment: certain industries, such as oil and gas, are off limits to foreign investors.[11]

4. Some people oppose the grants and tax subsidies that state and local governments are using to attract foreign investment. Kentucky, for example, offered Toyota benefits that included 1,500 acres of free land, $47 million in new roads, and $65 million for an employee-training program.[12] This and other incentive programs agitate established U.S. companies that have not been given similar assistance. Such companies argue that they are placed at a competitive disadvantage in their own country.

[11] Ibid., pp. 21–22.

[12] Ibid., p. 47.

5. Japanese investment in the United States is criticized on several grounds. First, it is being used to reinforce Japan's strong market position by creating assembly plants, with high technology being held at home. Second, there is the export of the *keiretsu* system to the United States. The Toyota plant in Kentucky was built by a Japanese construction company. Suppliers were also Japanese companies, financing was done by a Japanese bank affiliated with Toyota in the same *keiretsu*.[13] Third, there has been a mutual direct investment flow between (1) the United States and (2) Europe and Canada, while with Japan it has been a one-way street.

6. Finally, there is a certain amount of U.S. hubris regarding other industrial countries, particularly Japan. It is inconceivable to many Americans that their country cannot be number one in everything forever. But, as Paul Kennedy contends in his bestseller *The Rise and Fall of the Great Powers,* no country can expect to be dominant forever.[14]

FOREIGN PORTFOLIO INVESTMENT IN THE UNITED STATES

Although more importance has been attached to the role of foreign direct investment in the United States, foreign portfolio investment is actually much larger. In 1987, it amounted to around $1.3 billion. In fact, were it not for portfolio investment, the United States would still be a creditor nation because U.S. direct investments abroad exceed foreign direct investments in the United States. Historically, foreign investors have preferred portfolio investment to direct investment. In 1987, portfolio investment amounted to 84 percent of total foreign investment in the United States. This situation conforms to a pattern that has been maintained for more than a century, when foreign investors provided the finance capital necessary to build railroads and steel mills in the United States. The end result was that by 1914, the United States was the leading debtor country in the world, but it had an industrial base to show for it. World War I proved propitious for the United States because it could both sell its goods and lend its money to the Allies. By the time the war was over, the United States had become the world's leading creditor country.

---

[13] Clyde Prestowitz, *Trading Places* (New York: Basic Books, 1988), p. 308.

[14] Paul Kennedy, *The Rise and Fall of the Great Powers* (New York: Random House, 1987).

The willingness of foreigners to purchase U.S. Treasury obligations has helped finance the deficit in the federal budgets, thus enabling America to live beyond its means. There are several reasons why U.S. Treasury obligations—such as bonds, notes, certificates of deposit, and bills—are popular with foreign investors. The first reason is that the real rate of interest, which is the difference between the money rate of interest and the inflation rate, is higher in the United States than in other industrial countries.[15] A Japanese investor, shopping for alternative investments, can earn a higher rate of return on U.S. Treasury securities than on comparable investments in Japan. Instant electronic communication makes it very easy to purchase securities in other countries. The second reason is that the debt obligations of the U.S. Treasury are considered the safest form of investment in the world. This will continue to hold true as long as the United States government maintains its high credit rating.

Table 17-5 presents portfolio investment inflows and portfolio investment outflows for the United States during the period 1980–1987. It can be seen from the table that foreign investment in U.S. corporate securities showed a marked increase during the period 1984–1987. Contrariwise, U.S. investment in foreign corporate securities showed an actual decline during the period. U.S. bank liabilities also showed a far greater increase than U.S. bank assets abroad. Foreign investment in U.S. Treasury securities also increased during the period 1984–1987, while U.S. investment in foreign government securities was negligible. As the table indicates, portfolio investment has helped make the United States a debtor nation.

There are two types of portfolio investment—debt and equity. Debt investment includes government bonds and other forms of debt obligations; private bank debt instruments; corporate and other bonds; and liabilities of other private institutions. Like direct investment, foreign capital inflows to the stock market are an equity investment, with no guaranteed returns. Foreigners traditionally have found the highly developed U.S. stock market a profitable place for their funds, while the relatively underdeveloped equity markets of other countries provided fewer opportunities for U.S. investors. The debtor position of the United States can be attributed in part to the rush of foreign investors to the U.S. stock market during the 1980s. For foreign investors, the rising dollar

---

[15] In August 1988, the U.S. prime rate of interest was around 9.5 percent, compared to the Japanese prime rate of 3.5 percent.

TABLE 17-5   Portfolio Investment Inflows and Outflows for the United States (billions of dollars)

Portfolio Inflows to the United States

	Total	U.S. Treasury Securities	Corporate Securities	Bank Liabilities
1980	$28.4	$12.3	$5.5	$10.6
1981	48.2	7.9	6.9	33.4
1982	62.8	12.8	6.1	63.9
1983	74.7	15.7	8.2	50.8
1984	74.7	27.7	12.6	34.4
1985	112.2	19.6	51.0	41.6
1986	191.2	43.0	70.8	77.4
1987	158.7	38.8	42.1	77.9

Portfolio Outflows from the United States

	Total	Foreign Securities	U.S. Bank Assets	Other Outflows
1980	$65.9	$3.6	$46.8	$16.5
1981	101.4	5.7	84.2	11.5
1982	118.7	8.0	111.1	−0.4
1983	49.1	6.8	29.9	12.7
1984	19.5	4.8	11.1	3.6
1985	14.1	7.5	1.3	5.3
1986	68.0	3.3	59.0	5.7
1987	25.6	3.7	33.4	−11.5

Source: U.S. Department of Commerce, "International Transaction," Bureau of Economic Analysis, *Survey of Current Business*, June 1988.

TABLE 17-6   Total Portfolio Investment, 1975–1987 (billions of dollars)

Year	Corporate Stock			Debt Instruments		
	Assets	Liabilities	Net	Assets	Liabilities	Net
1975	$10	$ 36	$ –26	$150	$ 158	$ –8
1976	10	43	–33	189	190	–1
1977	10	40	–30	211	232	–21
1978	11	42	–31	262	287	–25
1979	15	48	–33	297	313	–16
1980	19	65	–46	362	353	9
1981	8	64	–56	463	406	57
1982	19	76	–58	587	487	100
1983	26	96	–70	630	551	79
1984	27	94	–67	647	632	15
1985	40	124	–84	668	752	–84
1986	51	167	–116	746	955	–209
1987	55	125	–70	804	1,149	–345

Source: U.S. Department of Commerce, "International Transactions," Bureau of Economic Analysis *Survey of Current Business,* June 1988.

enhanced the already attractive stock market. Ironically, the stock market crash of October 1987 resulted in the lowering of United States foreign indebtedness because the value of this form of portfolio investment was reduced.

Table 17-6 presents a breakdown of portfolio investment by debt instruments and corporate stock for the period 1975–1987. Corporate stock had a negative balance for each of the years, while debt instruments had a negative balance for eight of the thirteen years. The negative balances were offset by surpluses from direct investment, but as foreign direct investment in the United States increased relative to U.S. direct investment abroad, the surplus was more than offset by the negative portfolio investment balance. This time period is when the United States became a debtor country. In Table 17-6, U.S. portfolio investment abroad is shown as an asset, and foreign portfolio investment in the United States as a liability.

THE SIGNIFICANCE OF EXTERNAL DEBT

The growing interdependence of the world economy poses some risk for the U.S. economy in the future. A collapse of the dollar, driven by a loss of investor confidence and capital flight, could force interest rates sharply higher and send the United States into a deep recession, even as the unfavorable exchange rate requires the United States to produce more for each Japanese car it wants to buy. The default of a developing country with billions of dollars in foreign debt could threaten the survival of U.S. banks and with them the world banking system. Financial instability in foreign markets can be transferred to markets in New York, or vice versa. The stock market crash of October 1987 is a case in point. From the close of trading on Tuesday, October 13, to the close of trading on Monday, October 19, the Dow-Jones Industrial Average declined by almost one-third, representing a loss in the value of all outstanding U.S. stocks of almost $1.0 trillion. This collapse was not limited to the U.S. stock exchanges. It occurred throughout all of the major stock markets in the world.

High-speed computers and communications technology came into wide use during the 1980s. With their development, each nation's separate securities and banking industries coalesced into a single worldwide financial market in which political boundaries have ceased to exist. Thus, foreign investors can buy the stocks of U.S. corporations on the exchanges in Frankfurt and Tokyo, and U.S. investors can buy stock in Japanese companies on the New York Stock Exchange. Foreign investors can hedge against a fall in the price of their shares by acquiring stock options in New York and can minimize their exposure to changes in the value of the dollar by selling exchange rate futures contracts in London or Chicago—all within a matter of seconds, without moving from their computer terminals.[16]

The 1987 stock market crash illustrated how vulnerable any country is to world forces.[17] These forces are wide ranging and affect all markets. They include economic recovery, improvement in corporate earnings, changes in exchange rates, trade deficits, increases or decreases in financial liquidity, the

---

[16] Michael Aho and Marc Levinson, *After Reagan: Confronting the Changed World Economy* (New York: Council on Foreign Relations, 1988), p. 5.

[17] *Report of the Presidential Task Force on Market Mechanisms* (Washington, D.C.: U.S. Government Printing Office, 1988), p. 1-1.

TABLE 17-7   Stock Market Performance in October 1987 Versus Underlying Economic Conditions—An International Comparison (percentages)

Country	October Price Decline	Inflation Rate	Unem- ployment Rate	Growth Rate	Trade Deficit[a]	Govern- ment Deficit[a]
United States	–21.5%	4.1%	6.9%	5.2%	–3.3%	–5.3%
Australia	–44.7	8.1	NA	NA	–1.1	–1.0
Canada	–22.2	4.2	9.4	4.4	1.4	–4.2
United Kingdom	–21.7	4.0	11.8	3.8	0.1	–2.2
France	–18.6	3.3	10.7	1.1	1.0	–2.6
West Germany	–17.7	0.6	7.5	2.2	5.8	–1.5
Italy	–12.3	4.3	6.1	3.3	0.5	–12.2
Japan	–7.5	0.2	2.9	5.0	4.4	–4.9

[a] Percentage of GNP.

Source: *Report of the Presidential Task Force on Market Mechanisms* (Washington, D.C.: U.S. Government Printing Office, 1988), Table 1-4, p. 11-5.

relative appeal of financial versus fixed assets, and the growth of derivative products. These and other phenomena affect each market differently. They also interact with local factors that affect stock markets. An example is the provision of tax incentives for investment, shifts in institutional investing patterns, and the development of hedging strategies. These and other factors affect the flow of funds from one country's market into another. In the United States, other factors attract or deter the participation of foreign investors in the stock or bond markets, such as the level of interest rates and the value or anticipated value of the dollar.

Table 17-7 presents a comparison of the stock performance in various countries for October 1987. It is very difficult to identify fundamental causes that can explain the rate of stock market decline in these countries. The table does illustrate how interdependent the stock markets in these countries are. What happens on the Tokyo Stock Exchange can affect the New York Stock Exchange, and vice versa. An increase in the U.S. monthly trade deficit can adversely affect stock prices on the New York Stock Exchange.[18] If foreign investors lose confidence in the ability of the U.S. government to reduce the federal deficit, they can unload their U.S. direct and portfolio investments.

Foreign Banks

As has already been pointed out, there is an enormous amount of foreign investment in the United States. As the United States has run unprecedented deficits in the federal budget, totaling $1.3 trillion from 1981 to 1987, it has relied on foreigners to provide the capital it needs. At the end of 1987, an estimated $290 billion in U.S. Treasury securities were in foreign hands, as well as $171 billion in corporate bonds, $540 billion in bank deposits, and $261 billion in direct investment. For the most part, these investments are passive. Their owners have no particular desire to own U.S. debt simply because it is U.S. debt; they have placed their money here because this is where they can earn the greatest return, given the risk they are prepared to tolerate. This preference can change at any time. Exchange rate fluctuations can affect that return. If the U.S. dollar falls relative to other currencies, and if the difference between the U.S. interest rate and other countries' interest rates does not offset the change in exchange rates, investors will sell U.S. securities and go elsewhere.

An integral part of the new global financial market is currency trading, which is expedited by large multinational banks. The equivalent of over $300 billion was exchanged from one currency to another during a typical day in 1987.[19] Japan has replaced the United States as the world's leading creditor nation, and its banks are the largest in the world. Table 17-8 presents the assets of the ten largest banks in the world, none of which are American and eight of which are Japanese. These banks hold a part of the U.S. portfolio debt. Some, like the Sumitomo Bank, are part of the Japanese *keiretsu,*

---

[18] There was an increase in the U.S. trade deficit for September 1988. This was announced on a Thursday. The next day the Dow-Jones Industrial Average went down 31 points. The trade deficit for the year was $137.2 billion.

[19] Aho and Levinson, *After Reagan*, p. 7.

TABLE 17-8   The Ten Largest Banks in the World, 1987 (millions of dollars)

Bank	Country	Assets
Dai-Ichi Kangyo Bank	Japan	$288,337.3
Sumitomo Bank	Japan	270,212.1
Fuji Bank	Japan	263,069.1
Mitsubishi Bank	Japan	245,333.0
Sanwa Bank	Japan	238,109.4
Industrial Bank of Japan	Japan	222,463.3
Credit Agricole	France	214,864.6
Norinchukin Bank	Japan	186,334.3
Banque Nationale de Paris	France	183,086.3
Mitsubishi Trust & Banking	Japan	173,398.8

Source: *Fortune,* vol. 118, no. 3, August 1, 1988, pp. D41, D42. © 1988 Time Inc. All rights reserved.

which is an amalgamation of various Japanese banks and companies into one business group.

GOVERNMENT REGULATION OF FOREIGN INVESTMENT

Foreign investment has become a very important issue as the United States has changed from being the world's leading creditor nation to being the world's leading debtor nation. It entered into the debate in both the House and Senate on the Omnibus Trade Bill of 1988. Many feel that the United States must do more to regulate the inflow of foreign investment. As mentioned earlier, most other countries—developed and developing—impose numerous constraints on foreign investment, while the United States has been open to foreign investment. Therefore, it is necessary to review U.S. law and proposed reforms as they apply to foreign investment. Such a review will include U.S. antitrust laws, laws pertaining to reporting and disclosure, and laws pertaining to reciprocity.

The Omnibus Trade and Competitiveness Act of 1988

The Omnibus Trade and Competitiveness Act of 1988 contains provisions concerning mergers, acquisitions, and takeovers of U.S. firms by foreign firms.[20] The act amends Title VII of the Defense Production Act of 1950 to give the president of the United States or someone else designated by the president to investigate the effect of mergers, acquisitions, and takeovers of U.S. firms by foreign firms. If they adversely affect the national security of the United States, or increase foreign dominance of a particular industry, the president has a right to prohibit such action. The president can also direct the attorney general to seek appropriate antitrust relief, including divestiture, in the U.S. district courts.

Application of U.S. Antitrust Laws to Foreign Investment

Most foreign direct investment outlays in the United States are for the acquisition of existing firms rather than for the creation of new ones. In 1987, the largest acquisition of a U.S. firm by a foreign firm was consummated when British Petroleum purchased for approximately $8 billion 45 percent of the common stock of Standard Oil of Ohio, a company in which it had already owned 55 percent of the stock.[21] Unilever, a British-Dutch conglomerate purchased the U.S. firm Chesebrough-Pond for $3.1 billion. The West German chemical company Hoechst acquired the U.S. firm Celanese for $2.9 billion. In 1987, foreign investors spent around two-thirds of their total outlays, or $26 billion, to acquire 306 U.S. firms, while spending only $5 billion to establish 251 new business firms.[22] However, Japanese direct investment in the United States is very likely to involve the construction of branch plants, such as the construction of the Nissan truck plant in Smyrna, Tennessee.

[20] Omnibus Trade and Competitiveness Act of 1988, House of Representatives, 200th Cong., 2nd sess., April 20, 1988, pp. 337–339.

[21] William E. Sheeline, "Deals of the Year," *Fortune,* February 1, 1988, vol. 117, no. 3, p. 34.

[22] Bureau of Economic Analysis, U.S. Department of Commerce, "Foreign Investors' Spending to Acquire or Establish U.S. Businesses Remains Strong" (Washington, D.C.: May 1988).

Application of U.S. Antitrust Laws to Foreign Multinationals

Antitrust laws are applied equally to U.S. and foreign corporations to preserve competitive market structures and to forbid specific anticompetitive business practices. It is argued that by maintaining a competitive market, such laws do not discourage foreign investment in the United States, but rather make it more attractive than other countries to the foreign investor. In fact, foreign competition has proved particularly important to U.S. consumers in two situations. The first is when all or almost all the goods originate abroad, and the second is an oligopolistic situation in which outside competition is needed. As a result, such products as small cars and stainless steel razor blades have become available in the United States largely because of the pressure of the foreign firms selling them here. It is an important goal of antitrust policy to preserve this kind of foreign competition in the U.S. market.

Section 7 of the Clayton Act is the principal statute safeguarding against further industrial concentration in the United States. It prohibits any merger or acquisition that may substantially reduce competition or create a monopoly in any line of commerce in any section of the United States. Foreign direct investment is subject to antitrust scrutiny when such investment involves a purchase, merger, or joint venture with an existing U.S. firm. The antitrust laws are applicable in the following situations: the merger of actual competitors in the U.S. market, the merger of potential competitors in the U.S. market and joint ventures between potential competitors in the U.S. market. The acquisition of a U.S. company may be the easiest way to enter the U.S. market, but the antitrust laws may prevent the particular acquisition because of its effect on actual or potential competition. A merger between an important exporter to the United States and a significant domestic company will be treated in much the same way as would the merger of two U.S. companies with corresponding shares of the market.

The General Motors–Toyota Joint Venture, 1984

In March 1983, General Motors, and Toyota—the first and third large automobile companies in the world—announced plans to establish a joint venture to build a four-passenger subcompact car in the United States. Under the agreement, which was approved by the Federal Trade Commission in late 1984, the firms began producing 200,000 cars annually at an idle General Motors plant in Fremont, California. The design and engineering of the subcompact was based largely on Toyota's successful compact car. Toyota contributed $150 million to the venture, and General Motors contributed $120 million and the plant. For each company, there were potential gains. General Motors gained in two ways: it learned how the Japanese produce subcompacts with such a big cost advantage, estimated at $1,500 to $2,000 over comparable U.S. cars, and it learned the subtleties of the management style that has contributed to the Japanese edge in the world automobile market. Toyota gained in that it established a beachhead in the United States at a time when protectionist sentiment against Japanese imports was high.

Any foreign entity that chooses to do business in the United States must do so in accordance with U.S. law, including U.S. antitrust laws. The General Motors–Toyota joint venture is a good example of the global nature of competition in many industries. The rationale for prohibiting the joint venture on antitrust grounds was that it would have a significant adverse effect on competition in the U.S. automobile market by decreasing competition between General Motors and Toyota. By the same token, approval of the joint venture was premised on the market's remaining competitive notwithstanding the combination of the joint venture partners, or indeed, being made more competitive as a result of the better products produced by the joint venture. In the automobile industry, a joint venture between General Motors and Toyota was considered permissible and judged to be not an infraction of antitrust rules because of the presence of a number of other foreign competitors; for example, Nissan, Honda, Renault, and others.

Legislative Initiatives

Congress has shown some interest in enacting measures that concern foreign direct investment in the United States. The issue of foreign direct investment was discussed in the debate on the Omnibus Trade Bill that was passed in 1988. The debate focused on five major issues, as follows:[23]

1. Reporting, which would improve the collection of information about

---

[23] Spencer, *American Assets,* pp. 25–31.

foreign direct investors, including who they are, the industries in which they invest, and the balance sheets and income statements of foreign-owned companies in the United States.

2. Disclosure, which would require public disclosure of foreign investment data.

3. Screening, which would establish a more formal screening mechanism to review potential investments for their possible effect on national security.

4. Reciprocity, which would tie foreign access to U.S. markets directly to U.S. access to foreign markets.

5. Benefits and incentives, which would restrict the use of federal, state, and local funds, including loans and direct subsidies, by foreign investors.

Regulating the Securities Markets

Regulation of portfolio investment would be much more difficult than the regulation of direct investment. It is easy to pass laws limiting the amount of land foreigners can acquire in Iowa or Ohio, but it would be extremely difficult to keep foreigners from buying U.S. stocks and bonds. There is a vast global community of investors, and the United States is simply one part of a global financial market in which hundreds of billions of dollars change hands every day. Foreigners buy U.S. debt obligations because the U.S. government runs a deficit and has to borrow money from someone to finance its spending. But they are not buying debt to please the United States; they are buying because, for the moment, they can earn more here than elsewhere, given the degree of risk they want to accept.

The obvious solution is to balance the federal budget. This is easier said than done, for it would require a decrease in government spending, or an increase in taxes, both of which would be painful to the voters of the United States. Both the trade deficit, which is the subject of the next chapter, and dependence on foreign capital can be ended only if personal savings can be increased through decreased consumption. The dissaving by the government in the form of deficits has exceeded the personal savings of individuals for most of the 1980s. Congress cannot increase personal savings by passing a law. In order to free up more goods and services to service foreign-owned debt and increase saving for business investment, there is no alternative but for the budget deficit to decrease.

SUMMARY

The United States has come full circle in a short period of time. In 1980, it was the leading creditor nation in the world; in 1987 it was the leading debtor nation in the world. The U.S. government ran up $1.3 trillion in deficits in the federal budget, and it relied on foreigners for much of the money to finance its operations. This situation puts more constraints on the ability of the president of the United States to direct the national economy. In an open economy, as the United States has been, the traditional economic instruments of monetary and fiscal policy are blunted because capital can move in or out of the country in response to interest rates. Instant electronic communication has facilitated movements of capital. Capital has ceased to have national characteristics, and national capital markets are no longer separate and distinct, as they once were.

Some people are concerned that foreigners, in particular the Japanese, are taking over America. In the case of Japan, some Americans feel that the "yellow peril," as the Japanese were once called during the days of Theodore Roosevelt, are conducting some covert takeover of the United States. However, foreign investment in the United States obviously cannot be all bad, for state governments vie with each other to attract foreign factories. Jobs are created, and new technology is imported. A very small part of manufacturing is owned by foreigners. Foreign direct investors see the purchase of production capacity in the United States as a way to expand their activities in the U.S. market, just as U.S. direct investors see the purchase of production capacity in foreign countries as a way to expand their activities abroad.

QUESTIONS FOR DISCUSSION

1. What is the difference between direct and portfolio investment?
2. What are some reasons why the United States has become the leading debtor country in the world?
3. Discuss some reasons why foreign direct investment is beneficial to the U.S. economy.
4. Discuss some reasons why foreign direct investment is not beneficial to the U.S. economy.
5. Why are some people concerned over Japanese direct investment in the United States?

6. What is the relationship between foreign portfolio investment in the United States and the deficit in the U.S. government budget?
7. What are the various types of portfolio investment?
8. There is now a single worldwide financial market. What is its significance for the U.S. stock market and the financial stability of the U.S. economy?
9. Japan is now the leading creditor nation of the world. What significance does this fact have for the U.S. economy?
10. Should foreign direct investment in the United States be restricted?

RECOMMENDED READINGS

Aho, C. Michael and Marc Levinson. *After Reagan: Confronting the Changed World Economy*. New York: Council on Foreign Relations, 1988.

Bureau of Economic Analysis, *Survey of Current Business,* Washington, D.C.: U.S. Department of Commerce, August 1988, pp. 65, 90.

Burstein, Daniel. *Yen! Japan's New Financial Empire and Its Threat to America.* (New York: Simon & Schuster, 1988).

Jackson, James K. *Foreign Direct Investment in the United States.* Congressional Research Service. Washington, D.C.: Library of Congress, 1988.

Joint Economic Committee, U.S. Congress of the United States. *The 1988 Joint Economic Report.* Washington, D.C.: U.S. Government Printing Office, 1988.

Lipsey, Robert E. *Changing Patterns of International Investment in and by the United States*. National Bureau for Economic Research (NBER) Working Paper No. 2240. Cambridge, Mass.: NBIR, 1988.

O'Leary, James J. *Trends in Foreign Investment in the United States and the Implications*. New York: United States Trust Company of New York, 1988.

Tolchin, Martin and Susan. *Buying into America: How Foreign Investment Is Changing the Face of the Nation*. New York: Random House, 1988.

Report of the Presidential Task Force on Market Mechanisms. Washington, D.C.: U.S. Government Printing Office, 1988.

Spencer, Linda M. *American Assets: An Examination of Foreign Investment in the United States*. Washington, D.C.: Congressional Economic Leadership Institute, 1988.

Chapter 18

International Trade Policies

The reasons for the importance of international trade between nations have been recognized by economists since the time of Adam Smith. He attacked the mercantilist view that only exporting countries gained from trade. More recently, political scientists and international affairs specialists have come to recognize the political and strategic importance of foreign trade to a country's national security. Exports of goods and services that are highly valued by consumers around the world, and that can be produced by one country more efficiently than it can produce other goods, raise a nation's productivity and create employment. Imports of goods from other countries increase the choices of consumers and raise a nation's standard of living. Exports and imports are linked together in that each contributes to economic growth and rising living standards throughout the world.

For thirty years after the end of World War II, most of the world existed under a Pax Americana, like the peace (pax romana) imposed by the Roman empire of old. American economic and political dominance extended over a wide area. But times have changed, worldwide competition has been growing more severe, and the relative competitive strength of the United States has declined. The rest of the industrial world has either caught up with or is in the process of catching up with the United States. Thus, U.S. business firms no longer have a monopoly on business conducted in the world or even in the United States. German steel, Japanese cars and Chinese textile products compete with U.S. industry in its own home territory. Furthermore, foreign competition in the U.S. domestic market has expanded rapidly during recent years, particularly in certain product areas. An example is the automobile market, where Japanese imports now account for more than one-fifth of automobile sales.

One of the major political issues that has developed in the United States is a demand for protection against the import of certain foreign products. Segments of the U.S. economy have taken a beating from foreign competition.

Factories ranging from textile plants in North Carolina to machine tool plants in Ohio have shut down. In many cases, older installations have been replaced by hundreds of smaller, more competitive plants, but many industrial towns are dying, and the number of blue-collar jobs has dramatically declined. The villain is foreign competition, and restrictive trade measures, aimed at sheltering a wide variety of U.S. industries from foreign competition, have been introduced in Congress. Some argue that deindustrialization of key U.S. industries such as steel will occur unless they are protected, and that protectionism is necessary to rebuild the competitiveness of U.S. manufacturing. However, it also can be argued that deindustrialization is not occurring—that there is, instead, a shift from large and heavily unionized companies to smaller, more productive enterprises in which labor plays a less important role.

THE RATIONALE FOR INTERNATIONAL TRADE

If there were no restrictions on the free movement of productive factors from one region to another or from one nation to another, the total world production of goods and services would be maximized when the marginal products of similar units of each production factor were equal in all uses and all places. Resources are attracted to those areas in which they are the most productive, and the total output of goods and services is maximized when similar units of resources produce marginal products of equal value in all regions. So it is easy to see that if the whole world were one economic unit and the maximization of world production were accepted as the appropriate policy goal, the same principles would apply. This suggests that from the consumer's standpoint, free international trade is beneficial, contributing to higher living standards. The interest of the consumers and the general welfare would be identical if there were free mobility of resources from one area to another.

Of course, in the real world, productive resources do not readily move across international boundaries in response to economic concerns. Rather, the impetus for trade across national boundaries increases, because differences in the efficiency and proportion of labor and capital make it profitable for nations and regions to specialize in the production of those goods and services for which the resource situation is the most advantageous. A major benefit of trade between nations is that it allows them to capitalize on any advantage they may have in cost of production. This advantage may be absolute or comparative, and each plays a significant role in foreign trade theory.

Absolute Advantage

The law of absolute advantage states that there is a basis for trade when one nation can produce a good or service more cheaply than another nation can. The latter should buy from the former. To put it simply, if the Japanese can produce automobiles more cheaply and of better quality than the United States, we should buy their automobiles; conversely, if the United States can produce farm products more cheaply and of better quality than the Japanese, they should buy our farm products. Consumers in both countries stand to benefit from the specialization of trade, though the U.S. auto producers and the Japanese farmers do not. By concentrating on that one thing it does best, each country gains. Resources are allocated to those areas in which they can be used most efficiently and away from those areas in which they are used inefficiently.

Comparative Advantage

The law of absolute advantage ought not to be confused with the law of comparative advantage. The latter holds that if one country enjoys an advantage over another country in the production of several goods, it should produce the good in which it has the greatest advantage and buy the good in which it has the least advantage from the other country.[1] For example, assume Brazil has an advantage over the United States in producing both coffee and sugar. Brazil can produce five units of coffee for every unit of coffee produced by the United States, and Brazil can produce two units of sugar for every unit produced by the United States. Brazil has a greater advantage over the United States when it comes to producing coffee, and the United States has less of a disadvantage when it comes to producing sugar. Therefore, Brazil should produce coffee, and the United States should produce sugar. The exchange between the two countries should be coffee for sugar.

The principle here is that a country should not produce all the goods it can make cheaper but only those it can make cheapest. Even if a country is inefficient, it should not cease all production simply because labor and other costs

---

[1] David Ricardo, an important classical economist of the last century, is associated with the concept of comparative advantage.

are more expensive. It should drop only those lines in which its performance is most expensive. In the example, Brazil has a five-to-one advantage over the United States when it comes to producing coffee and only a two-to-one advantage when it comes to producing sugar. Brazil would specialize in the commodity it could make with the greatest relative efficiency, and the United States would concentrate on the commodity it could produce with the least relative inefficiency.

Restraints on Trade

In the real world, U.S. auto companies and Japanese farmers are not going to stand by idly while their respective competitors win. Each will ask its government for assistance, and that is precisely what has happened. The U.S. auto industry has lobbied extensively for protection against Japanese auto imports, and Japanese farmers have demanded and received government protection from U.S. farm imports. U.S. business firms may praise the virtue of free competition in their annual reports to their stockholders and in their pronouncements to the general public, but all too often they lobby in Washington for protection against foreign competition. Competition thus has a double standard: it is fine if we win but wrong if foreigners win. Trade restrictions are by no means limited to the United States; other countries also use them.

Forces and events have created a world much different from the one that existed thirty years ago. Before discussing U.S. foreign trade policies, it is necessary to examine the changes that have taken place in the world and how they have affected the U.S. economy. As other economic processes have emerged, it has become progressively more difficult for the United States to continue to ignore economic practices that have taken their toll on the economy. But U.S. government policies to protect U.S. industries further undermine the whole process of trade.

THE UNITED STATES AND THE NEW ECONOMIC ORDER

Since its inception, the United States has generally followed a policy of trade protection designed to protect domestic producers from foreign competition. In this respect, it is no different from other countries. Trade protection reached its peak during the Depression of the 1930s, when all the major industrial countries used tariffs and other restrictive devices to restrict imports. This strategy was self-defeating, for as soon as one country restricted the imports of another country, the other country would retaliate. The rationale of protection was to protect home industries and workers from the impact of the worldwide Depression, but the benefits of trade protection on unemployment were short-lived because the retaliatory protection measures offset any short-term gain. The Depression also brought about the use of many different kinds of trade restrictions, including exchange controls and import quotas.

The General Agreement on Tariffs and Trade (GATT) was signed in 1947 by twenty-three countries, including the United States. Its purpose was to reduce the trade barriers between countries by reciprocal trade agreements and to ensure that all nations would be treated the same. The objectives of unrestricted and nondiscriminatory trade were intended to increase economic efficiency. Since production costs and production structures in the various advanced countries were thought to converge, it was believed that expanded trade would result in greater specialization. Consequently, trade between nations could grow without the pains of economic dislocation. The implication was that countries should produce what they could make most efficiently, and should trade for the rest. Product specialization and higher incomes for all trading nations would result from expanded exchange.

The world monetary system also was reordered after the end of World War II. The gold standard was replaced by a mixed standard under the Bretton Woods Agreement of 1945. Countries that signed the agreement agreed to maintain stable exchange rates, to abstain from exchange controls, and to avoid competitive currency devaluation. All member currencies were freely convertible against the dollar, which was the only currency backed by gold. The exchange rates of other currencies were linked to the dollar. Each nation established a par value for its currency, with the price of gold the yardstick by which par value was measured. In this way, exchange rates could fluctuate only within limits.[2] However, the mixed standard was eventually abandoned in favor of floating exchange rates where supply and demand forces determine the value of a country's currency.

---

[2] Under the gold standard, the exchange rate for the currency of a country was fixed in terms of gold into which the currency could be converted. Gold inflows and outflows were the correction mechanism that held fluctuations in exchange rates to a minimum.

The Changing World Economy

The liberal economic order in which trade between countries could move freely and exchange rates would remain stable has been affected by a number of changes that have occurred in the world. The task of promoting free trade between countries has become more difficult because of state-centered practices that have developed in response to changes in production and in the international division of labor, as well as to the economic problems of the 1970s and 1980s. State strategies to shape world markets have become more prevalent, more powerful, and more central to the future shape of the world economic order. It is desirable to look at some of the changes that have occurred and how they have had an impact on the U.S. economy.

The Oil Crisis of 1973

The oil crisis of 1973 caused the greatest transfer of wealth in the history of humankind; the surplus of the oil-exporting countries was channeled into those importing countries that had the greatest need. Meanwhile, countries that imported oil soon developed large trade deficits, which set off a round of double-digit inflation. The high rate of inflation made floating exchange rates inevitable. Under floating exchange rates, a decrease in the price of a nation's currency relative to other currencies would encourage that country's exports and discourage its imports; an increase in the price of its currency relative to other currencies would have the opposite effect. Since the market determines the value of currencies, some are overvalued and some undervalued. In countries whose currencies become undervalued, import prices rise and export prices fall; in countries whose currencies become overvalued, import prices fall and export prices rise. A good example of the latter effect has been the strength of the U.S. dollar relative to other currencies. Imports have increased, and exports have declined.

Government Economic Development Strategies

A second factor that has undermined the objective of the free trade order of the GATT system was the development of government strategies to shape markets. Japan is a case in point. Since the end of World War II, it has pursued policies that have moved the economy from the production of labor-intensive goods such as textiles, to capital-intensive goods such as steel, through consumer durables such as television sets and automobiles, to the advanced technology sectors of computers. Japanese economic development can be catalogued in periods.[3] During the 1950s, emphasis was placed on the development of the shipbuilding industry. The central purpose was to facilitate the external development of Japan through exports. In the 1960s, priority was given to the development of a modern world-class steel industry, which was to provide the industrial base required for the expansion of the entire economy. The development strategy of the 1970s involved the expansion of the Japanese automobile industry; by the end of the decade, Japan was the world's largest producer of automobiles. The strategy for the 1980s is the development of the high-technology industries.

It is one thing to have a development strategy and quite another to implement it. But the Japanese have succeeded in their strategy and in the process have incurred the animosity of their trading partners, who accuse them of unfair trading practices and of blocking all competing foreign products from entering the domestic Japanese market. There is an enormous imbalance in trade with the United States. In 1987 alone, Japanese exports to the United States exceeded imports from the United States by close to $60 billion. Japan has also become the world's major creditor nation and by degrees is becoming the nexus of the world banking system. It has achieved this success in a relatively short time and is serving as a model for other East Asian countries such as South Korea, Singapore, and Taiwan.

Japan is an example of state-directed capitalism. The government has played an important role in the development of the Japanese economy but not the paramount role, as many Americans think. One thing that has contributed to the success of Japan is savings—government, corporate, and personal. The savings rate of the Japanese is the highest of all major industrial countries (the United States is the lowest). In part, this can be attributed to government tax policies designed to encourage savings, which are funneled through government-owned investment banks to industry.[4] The close working relationship between business and government dates back to their last century.[5] This relationship has resulted in working to achieve common ends. Japanese exports

[3] Ezra Vogel, *Comeback* (Cambridge, Mass.: Harvard University Press, 1985), chapter 2.

[4] Peter F. Drucker, "Behind Japan's Success," *Harvard Business Review,* vol. 59, no. 1, January–February 1981, pp. 83–90.

[5] There are far more businesspeople in politics in Japan than there are in the United States.

are encouraged through the use of tax breaks.[6] At the same time, domestic industries are protected by an elaborate system of tariffs and quotas.[7]

The Developing Industrial Countries

A number of countries are in the process of achieving industrial development. South Korea is one example, and Brazil is another. These and other developing countries have attempted to achieve a state-directed comparative advantage in the production of such goods as steel and automobiles.[8] The capacity of governments to act as players in the market in pursuit of development goals rests on the provision of specific financial and administrative arrangements. Traditional trade theory, which is based on the assumption of pure competition, does not take into consideration the role that a government can play in creating comparative advantage. It can define and pursue detailed industrial goals, setting not only general objectives but also specific ones involving the organization of particular sections. A government-dominated financial system also allows state intrusion into the marketplace, as does the government budget.

The developing industrial countries have affected the advanced industrial countries such as the United States in several ways. First, they have cut into the exports of those countries. Brazil and South Korea have made a conscious effort to develop a steel industry. Given an advantage of low-cost labor, exports of steel from these countries have cut into the shares of the world steel market held by such producers as Japan and West Germany. Second, they have substituted domestic production for imports from the advanced industrial countries. Mexico, for example, has pursued a policy of import substitution—restricting imports to encourage the development of domestic manufacturing. This strategy obviously reduces the market available to the advanced industrial countries. Third, these and other development strategies have enabled the developing countries to concentrate on making low-cost producer and consumer goods, which they can sell to less developed countries.

---

[6] The United States, Canada, and the Western European countries also do this.

[7] The Japanese domestic economy is highly competitive, with an element of social Darwinism involved. It is a sort of training ground for international competition. But few outsiders are allowed to compete.

[8] The South Koreans are now able to undercut the Japanese in terms of price, and the quality of their products is equally good.

Excess Capacity

The entry of producers from the developing industrial countries increases the world output of many manufactured goods. The end result is excess capacity for industries in both the developed and developing industrial countries. When there is a drop in world demand for a product such as steel, producers must battle over a diminishing market. Each country, developed and developing, is going to take some sort of action to preserve jobs and protect its industries. Subsidies, import protection, and currency devaluation are devices that can be used to preserve jobs and company earnings, while exporting the problem elsewhere. But these actions violate the principles of free trade in that each country raises its trade barriers to protect its own industries.

The developing countries have a production cost advantage over the developed countries because their labor costs are lower. This effect is particularly true in producing such products as shoes and textiles. This advantage enables them to increase their exports to the markets of the developed countries, which has critical implications for profitability of home industries and for employment for each country. Each country may react in a different way. Western European countries protect their industries through the use of subsidies or through market sharing arrangements. U.S. policy response is usually effected through some form of external protection such as a tariff or import quota. Internal readjustment occurs as a result of shifts in resources from one sector to another, as firms leave industries affected by excess capacity, or as a result of shifts in competitive advantage. Given the changing world economy, export and import policies have become an important component of government economic policy.

POLICIES TO PROMOTE EXPORTS

Several types of government policies are used to promote exports. Of these, tax policies are probably the most important. A government can manipulate taxes to grant exemptions and special rates to certain types of activities, corporations, or people. Favorable tax treatment of certain types of income can influence shifts in economic behavior.[9] Governments also sponsor exports through loans financed out of budget revenues or by commercial banks. Subsidies may also be used to aid export industries. Export cartels—international

---

[9] Tax incentives were discussed in Chapter 16.

associations of firms in the same industry—are often used to set prices in foreign markets and to restrict output.

Subsidies

Most governments, including the United States, subsidize some exports. Export bounties have been paid by some European governments on one product or another since the seventeenth century. Some countries subsidize the output of farm products. Europe, a major importer of sugar on the world market since 1976, has turned into one of the largest subsidizers in the world, second only to Cuba. Farmers in the European Community countries received a subsidy in 1985 of 18 cents a pound for their sugar, which was sold in the world market for 5 cents a pound.[10] Sugar production in the United States is also subsidized. The United States sells beef to Brazil at 30 cents a pound. The economic effect of these and other subsidies is that a country's resources are allocated less efficiently than would be the case if competition and the free flow of resources were permitted among countries. According to World Bank estimates, subsidies of farm products for export cost taxpayers in the United States, Western Europe, and Japan $104.1 billion in 1985, almost twice the $55.6 billion the farmers of these countries gained from farm exports.[11]

Cartels

A cartel is an agreement, formal or informal, entered into by firms situated in different countries or in one country and doing business across international boundaries when the purpose of the agreement is to increase profits by reducing or eliminating competition. Firms may enter into an agreement to control prices. They may also allocate markets among their members, or they may assign sales to an international trade association. They may exchange patents and secret processes. They may also control the use of trademarks, with each cartel member granted the right to use a trademark in its territory. The European countries and Japan tend to manage excess capacity at home through cartels or similar arrangements, which have government support. These cartels

[10] World Bank, *World Development Report 1986* (New York: Oxford University Press, 1986), p. 8.

[11] Ibid., p. 24.

operate in international markets. In the United States, such arrangements are legally more difficult in most cases.[12]

IMPORT POLICIES

International trade is a two-way street. Countries export goods and services to other countries, and import goods and services from them. Consumers gain because there are a wider variety of goods and services from which to choose. Although consumers gain from imports, domestic producers can lose from increased competition because they will sell less, and they may have to sell at a lower price. Competition is a hard taskmaster, for there are losers as well as winners. Over time, individuals and groups have altered the rules of the competitive marketplace when they didn't like the results. Chrysler is one example of a company that sought government help, but it is hardly the only one. Because foreign competition causes some domestic firms, their employees, and their suppliers to lose, they have an incentive to seek government protection from imports, and this is where the whole concept of free trade breaks down. Governments must respond to the demands of their various constituencies.

Since the end of World War II, the United States has led the world toward a more open and free world trading system. But times have changed, and protectionist sentiment is stronger in the United States than at any time since the Depression. It is necessary to discuss in some detail the cause of this sentiment; the use of various import restriction devices, such as tariffs and import quotas; and the effect of these restrictions on consumers, for they will bear the impact.

THE TRADE DEFICIT

The "trade deficit," as reported on the nightly news and in the newspapers, refers to the merchandise trade deficit, which is the difference between goods imported into the United States and exports from the United States to other countries. However, it is only one of the balances commonly used to express the position of the United States in international flows of goods and services.

---

[12] The Export Trading Company Act of 1982 permits a form of cartel called the *export trading company*. The law, which is designed primarily to benefit small and medium-sized companies, grants antitrust immunity to a trading company as long as the foreign operations do not inhibit U.S. competition or undercut domestic prices.

These flows are a part of the U.S. balance of payments statements. A balance of payments is simply an account of the value of goods and services, capital loans, gold, and other items coming into and out of a country. A balance of payments and a corporate balance sheet are similar in that each is a summary in monetary terms of the result of business activity over a period of time. Accounting procedures for the two are also similar in that each uses double-entry bookkeeping. In the balance of payments accounts, a debit is any transaction that results in a money outflow or payment to a foreign country, and a credit is any transaction that results in a money inflow or receipt from a foreign country.

The balance of payments can be broken down into four categories: current account, capital account, unilateral transfers, and net gold exports or imports. The current account summarizes the difference between total exports of goods and services and total imports of goods and services. It is the "stuff" of which international economic relations are composed. A country can run a surplus or a deficit in its current account. The capital account is long- and short-term capital movements into and out of a country. A country can also run a surplus or deficit in its capital account. Unilateral transfers involve capital movements and gifts for which there are no return commitments or claims. Gold exports or imports reflect the position of current and capital accounts. A deficit is accompanied by an outflow of gold; a surplus, by an inflow.

Current Account

The current account is the most important part of a country's balance of payments because it measures all income-producing activities that go into foreign trade. It consists of exports and imports of goods and services. Exports are a credit in the current account and are represented by a plus (+) symbol, and imports are represented by a minus (−) symbol. The current account includes merchandise trade and service transactions. The latter can be divided into several categories: transportation, which includes that rendered by U.S. and foreign transport facilities; travel expenditures, which include those made by Americans abroad and those made by foreigners in the United States; interest and dividends received from abroad by Americans and received by foreigners from the United States; banking and insurance services rendered by U.S. and foreign institutions; and government expenditures by the U.S. government abroad and by foreign governments in the United States.

TABLE 18-1   A Simplified U.S. Balance of Payment Statement

Credits (+)	Debits (−)
Current Account	*Current Account*
U.S. merchandise exports	U.S. merchandise imports
U.S. services sold to foreigners	U.S. services bought from foreigners
Tourist expenditures here	U.S. tourist expenditures there
Fees and royalties from abroad	Fees and royalties to foreigners
Interest, dividends, and earnings	Interest, dividends, and earnings
	from abroad to foreigners
Transportation, insurance,	Transportation, insurance,
and other services	and other services
Capital Account	*Capital Account*
Net change in investment by	Net change in U.S. investments
foreigners in the United States	abroad
Direct investment	Direct investment
Portfolio investment	Portfolio investment
Unilateral transfers received	Unilateral transfers sent
from abroad	abroad
Private remittance from abroad	Private remittance from United
	States
Pensions from abroad	Pensions from United States
Grants from other governments	Grants from U.S. government
Official Reserve Account	*Official Reserve Account*
Gold from abroad	Gold from United States
Foreign currency	U.S. currency
Total Credits	*Total Debits*

Capital Account

The capital account summarizes long- and short-term movements of capital
into and out of a country. It is divided into direct investment, portfolio invest-

ment, and short-term capital flows. Direct and portfolio investment involve
financial assets with a maturity of more than a year; short-term capital movements consist of financial paper with a maturity of less than one year. Direct
investment means both ownership and control of assets, and portfolio investment means only control of assets. U.S. direct investment abroad means an
outflow in the U.S. balance of payments; foreign investment in the United
States represents an inflow in the U.S. balance of payments. The same holds
true for portfolio investment. United States purchases of foreign securities
would represent an outflow in the U.S. balance of payments; conversely, foreign purchases of U.S. securities would represent an inflow in the U.S. balance
of payments.

Table 18-1 presents a simplified version of the balance of payment
accounts. The entire balance of payment account must, as the name implies,
balance. The key entries are U.S. merchandise exports and U.S. merchandise
imports; U.S. services sold to foreigners and services purchased from foreigners; U.S. receipts from investments abroad and foreign receipts from investments in the United States; and U.S. direct and portfolio investment abroad
and foreign direct and portfolio investment in the United States. The position
of the United States as the world's leading debtor country is linked to the trade
deficit, and both are linked to the deficit in the federal budget. It should be emphasized that foreign investment flows into the United States because the real
interest rate, which is the difference between the money rate of interest and the
rate of inflation, has been high. For this reason foreign investors cannot continue indefinitely to invest larger and larger amounts of money in the United
States.

The U.S. Merchandise Trade Deficit

For 1987 the merchandise trade deficit for the United States was $171.9 bil-
lion. Merchandise exports amounted to $252.9 billion and merchandise im-
ports amounted to $424.1 billion. Table 18-2 presents the ten leading country
markets for U.S. exports and the ten leading U.S. suppliers of exports for 1987.
The major part of the total deficit is concentrated in two major trading areas:
the East Asian countries and Canada. In fact, half of the merchandise trade
deficit for 1987 was with three East Asian countries: Japan, Taiwan, and South
Korea. Demand for protection has been directed against imports from these
countries.

TABLE 18-2   Major U.S. Export Markets and Import Suppliers for 1987 (billions of dollars)

Export Markets	Amount	Import Suppliers	Amount
Canada	$59.8	Japan	$88.1
Japan	28.2	Canada	71.5
Mexico	14.6	West Germany	28.0
United Kingdom	14.1	Taiwan	26.4
West Germany	11.7	Mexico	20.5
Netherlands	8.2	United Kingdom	18.0
South Korea	8.1	South Korea	18.0
France	7.9	Italy	11.7
Taiwan	7.4	France	11.2
Belgium and Luxembourg	6.7	Hong Kong	10.5
World Total	$252.9	World Total	$424.1

Source: U.S. Department of Commerce, International Trade Administration, *Business America*, Vol. 109, no. 9, April 25, 1988, p. C.

The U.S. Service Trade

Services such as data processing, computer programming, scientific research, and engineering and consulting are important and rapidly growing elements in international trade. The application of new technologies in communications, data processing, and transport has made it increasingly possible to perform a wide variety of services at a distant geographical location, and this mobility has opened up new trade. International trade in traditional services such as shipping, aviation, communication, banking, and insurance has always been important to trade in goods, and, in fact, could not take place without them. There is, of course, an interrelationship between trade in services and trade in goods, and restrictions on trade in goods impacts on trade in services and vice versa. Surpluses from service trade have reduced the deficits from merchandise trade, but these surpluses have declined in recent years, as Table 18-3 indicates.

TABLE 18-3 U.S. Service Trade for 1981 and 1987 (billions of dollars)

| | U.S. Exports (+) | | U.S. Imports (−) | |
	1981	1987	1981	1987
Business services				
Travel	12.9	15.4	32.2	56.2
Passenger fares	3.1	4.6	11.5	20.8
Other transportation	12.6	16.5	12.5	19.4
Fees and royalties	7.3	8.1	6	1.2
Other private services	6.6	12.4	3.2	6.8
Private receipts and payments of income				
Direct	32.5	47.9	6.9	12.6
Portfolio	50.2	46.5	28.5	48.8
U.S. government transactions				
U.S. services	0.5	0.5	1.3	1.8
U.S. receipts and payments	3.7	5.3	16.9	24.0
Military sales and transfers	10.0	11.9	11.2	14.0
Total	139.4	169.3	97.1	157.3

Source: U.S. Department of Commerce, International Trade Administration, *Business America,* Vol. 109, no. 9, April 25, 1988, p. 5.

Manufacturing goods account for most of the merchandise trade deficit. Among these goods, by far the most important deficit item is motor vehicles, parts, and engines. The deficit in automotive imports was $53 billion in 1987, having risen more than tenfold since 1976. It amounts to one-third of the trade deficit. But automobile imports are not the sole cause of the deficit, for other industrial sectors are also running sizable deficits. The worsening trade deficit has not spared high-technology products. Between 1980 and 1987, the U.S. trade balance surplus in high technology shrank from $27 billion in 1980 to

TABLE 18-4   Trade Deficits in Selected Manufacturing Industries in 1987 (billions of dollars)

Durable goods	
Motor vehicles	$–53.3
Electronic, computing, and office equipment	–21.6
Iron and steel	–8.5
Nonferrous metals	–6.0
Industrial machinery	–6.7
Aircraft and other transportation equipment	–12.5
Nonmetallic mineral manufactures	–6.8
Nondurable goods	
Textile and apparel	–20.8
Footwear	–7.4
Paper	–4.4
Chemicals	–9.6
Total Manufacturing	–137.7

Source: U.S. Congress of the United States, Office of Technology Assessment, *Paying the Bill: Manufacturing & America's Trade Deficit* (Washington, D.C.: U.S. Government Printing Office, June 1988), p. 108.

$600 million in 1987.[13] Between 1985 and 1987, for example, the positive trade balance in computers and automatic data processing machinery dropped by $2.8 billion to about $1 billion. The total trade deficit in manufacturing in 1987 was $137.7 billion, and the deficit in major industrial components is presented in Table 18-4.

CAUSES OF THE TRADE DEFICIT

There is no one single cause of the trade deficit; rather, a complex set of factors is responsible. These factors can be divided into several categories. The first one, commonly advanced, is that the deficit is the fault of other countries, in particular Japan, because they don't play by the rules of free trade. The second

[13] Office of Technology Assessment, Congress of the United States, *Paying the Bill: Manufacturing and America's Trade Deficit* (Washington, D.C.: U.S. Government Printing Office, June 1988), p. 67.

reason is much more complex. Macroeconomic forces, which include the federal budget deficit and the overvalued dollar, cause the trade deficit. The key is the federal deficit, for once it is balanced, the rest will fall into place. The final reason has to do with the declining competitiveness of U.S. manufacturing. U.S. manufacturers have been losing their share of both domestic and foreign markets for some time. Even U.S. exports of high-technology products have lost world market shares.

Unfair Trade Relations

Imports from the East Asian countries account for over half of the U.S. trade deficit. In 1987, U.S. imports from Japan amounted to $88.1 billion, while U.S. exports to Japan amounted to $28.2 billion; and U.S. imports from Taiwan amounted to $26.4 billion, while U.S. exports to Taiwan amounted to $7.4 billion. Given these deficits, U.S. trade relations with Japan and the other East Asian countries have not been smooth. They are criticized for taking unfair advantage of the free trade policies that the United States has attempted to maintain since the end of World War II. Conversely, they have used many restrictions to keep U.S. firms from selling their products in their home markets. Japan, which is responsible for one-third of the trade deficit, is held up as the main example of unfair trade practices, which are as follows:[14]

1. Dumping is the practice of selling a product in a foreign market at a price below the domestic price. For example, assume that it cost the Japanese $1,000 to make a ton of steel and the freight cost from Japan to the United States is $300 a ton. If the Japanese sell the steel in the United States at a price lower than cost plus freight, that is considered dumping. The Japanese have been accused of dumping steel, television sets, and other products in the United States at prices below costs.

2. Restrictions on market entry are used by Japan to make it difficult for foreign firms to penetrate its domestic markets. For example, Reynolds Tobacco found that it was difficult to penetrate the Japanese cigarette market. First, a tariff was levied against cigarette imports. Second, an excise tax was imposed on U.S. cigarettes once they were sold in Japan. Third,

[14] Joint Economic Committee, Congress of the United States, *Impact on the U.S. Economy of Imbalances and Unfair Trade Relations. The Case of Japan,* Hearing before the Subcommittee on Economic Goals and Intergovernmental Policy (Washington: D.C.: U.S. Government Printing Office, 1985).

the distribution of U.S. cigarettes was limited to about 10 percent of the total number of sales outlets in Japan. Fourth, advertising expenditures on Japanese television were based on the number of Reynolds cigarettes sold in Japan.[15]

3. Combines, which control 75 percent of Japanese manufacturing, make it hard for U.S. firms to enter the Japanese markets. The member firms trade with each other even though U.S. firms can offer a lower price. The Japanese antitrust laws are not applied to these combines. As a matter of policy, Japanese firms do not buy foreign products if Japanese products are available.

4. Financial subsidies, which provide a competitive advantage for Japanese firms in the world export markets. The Japanese banks and government lending agencies provide low interest rates or even outright cash grants for developing new products. It is possible to get loans that don't have to be paid back unless the product is successful.

5. Import restrictions, which include tariffs, quotas, and investment restrictions. In industrial targeting, critical industries are identified. Then restrictions are placed on the import of competing goods into Japan. These barriers enable Japanese manufacturers to develop a large volume of production of whatever those products are, in order to be economically successful at home and abroad.

However, it is necessary to make two points. First, Japan is not the only country in the world to subsidize exports and use import restrictions. The United States subsidizes its beet producers, even though beet sugar is far more expensive than cane sugar imported from abroad. It subsidizes export firms through the provision of tax incentives and through loans from the Export–Import Bank. Second, even if all barriers to U.S. imports were completely lifted in Japan, it is estimated that the U.S. trade deficit with Japan, which was $62 billion in 1987, would at most be reduced by $12 billion. As Prestowitz has pointed out in his book *Trading Places,* the whole rubric of the Japanese economy and society is so totally different from that of the United States that opening it up to U.S. trade would be very difficult.[16]

---

[15] There are no proscriptions against tobacco advertising in Japan. Cigarette sales amount to about $20 billion a year.

[16] Clyde V. Prestowitz, *Trading Places* (New York: Basic Books, 1988), pp. 127–141.

The U.S. Dollar

The value of the U.S. dollar relative to other foreign currencies has been a major cause of the trade deficit.[17] There is a direct relationship between the value of the dollar and the federal deficit. During the period 1982 to 1985, the trade deficit tripled. Budget deficits and a generally restrictive monetary policy raised inflation-adjusted interest rates, which attracted large inflows of foreign capital, increasing the value of the dollar. As the value of the U.S. dollar went up relative to the Japanese yen, the West German mark, and other foreign currencies, U.S. exports increased because Americans could acquire more foreign goods with fewer dollars; conversely, foreigners had to give up more of their currencies to acquire U.S. dollars with which to buy U.S. goods. The strength of the U.S. dollar also meant that dollar-dominated costs of production here in the United States became higher than the costs of production in Europe and Japan. As a result, the U.S. trade deficit rapidly increased.

The problem of the overvalued dollar was supposed to be rectified in the fall of 1985 when central banks in Japan, West Germany, and other major Summit countries flooded the world markets with U.S. dollars. The rationale for this move was to drive down the value of the U.S. dollar relative to the yen and other currencies. The purpose of depreciating the U.S. dollar was to make it cheaper, thus increasing U.S. exports and decreasing U.S. imports. Protectionist sentiment was strong in the United States, particularly against Japan, and the central banks' depreciation of the dollar was considered a way to reduce it. Table 18-5 shows the value of the U.S. dollar relative to the yen, the mark, and other foreign currencies for the period 1981–1988.

Although the central banks of the major foreign industrial countries made a concerted effort to drive down the international value of the U.S. dollar, the end result had little impact on the U.S. trade deficit. The value of the yen more than doubled relative to the value of the U.S. dollar in 1986 and 1987, yet the U.S. trade deficit with Japan did not shrink. One reason was that the price of Japanese exports to the United States rose far more slowly in dollar terms than was anticipated. Japanese producers were willing to reduce profit margins in order to maintain profit margins. The currencies of South Korea and Taiwan, two major exporters to the United States, were pegged to the value of the U.S.

[17] Joint Economic Committee, Congress of the United States, *Impact of the Dollar on U.S. Competitiveness,* Hearing before the Subcommittee on Economic Goals and Governmental Policy, 99th Cong., 1st sess. (Washington, D.C.: U.S. Government Printing Office, 1985).

TABLE 18-5   A Comparison of U.S. and Foreign Exchange Rates, 1981–1988

| | | | (U.S. = $1) | | |
Period	France (franc)	West German (mark)	Japan (yen)	Canada (dollar)	United Kingdom (pound)
1981	5.4	2.3	220.6	1.2	0.5
1982	6.6	2.4	249.0	1.2	0.6
1983	7.6	2.6	237.6	1.2	0.7
1984	8.7	2.8	237.4	1.3	0.8
1985	9.0	2.9	238.5	1.4	0.8
1986	7.0	2.1	168.4	1.4	0.7
1987	6.0	1.8	144.6	1.3	0.6
1988	6.0	1.7	122.2	1.2	0.5

Source: *Economic Report of the President 1989* (Washington, D.C.: U.S. Government Printing Office, 1989), Table B-108, p. 431.

dollar. As the U.S. dollar moved, their currencies maintained the same proportionate relationship. Foreign exporters can lock in an exchange rate in the futures market, thus reducing their exposure to the declining dollar. Finally, U.S. consumers are willing to pay more for foreign products.

Declining Competitiveness of U.S. Manufacturing

A third reason for the U.S. trade deficit is the declining competitiveness of U.S. manufacturing. Table 18-4 presented the merchandise trade deficits in various areas of manufacturing. Moreover, U.S. manufacturers have been losing their share of both domestic and foreign markets for some time. Between 1970 and 1980, the U.S. share of world imports increased from 12.1 percent to 12.5 percent, while its share of world exports declined from 13.6 percent to 10.9 percent. Between 1980 and 1986, U.S. exporters' sales of manufacturing fell 15 percent, while other countries were increasing their imports from all sources by 22 percent.[18] U.S. exports of high-technology products, an area the United States has dominated, have lost world market shares. Of ten high-technology sectors, only two—office, computing, and accounting machines and agricultural equipment—gained in world market shares between 1960 and 1980. Seven high-technology industries have lost market shares.

A second indicator of a decline in manufacturing competitiveness was the slow response of imports and exports to a fall in the value of the dollar. In 1987, over two years after the dollar began to fall, the merchandise trade deficit set a new record of around $170 billion. Even for 1988 the merchandise trade deficit is expected to be well over $100 billion. These facts suggest that U.S.-made goods are less attractive than foreign-made goods. In some cases, the attractiveness of foreign products reflects lower labor costs or government subsidies; in other cases, it arises from high quality and reliability. Productivity growth of U.S. manufacturing has lagged, especially when compared to Japan's. However, not all indicators are negative. Some U.S. industries have performed much better than others; the United States is by no means at the bottom of the list among nations in competitive performance.

THE UNITED STATES GOVERNMENT AND THE TRADE DEFICIT

It was apparent that the U.S. trade deficit was not a major issue in the 1988 campaign for president. Exit polls in California indicated that only 4 percent of the voters in that state rated the trade deficit as the most important issue and three-fourths of the 4 percent voted for George Bush. The deficit in the federal budget was rated by California voters as the most important issue, but both deficits are linked together. Also President Reagan's veto of the bill that required sixty-day notice of plant closings had little impact on the election. Nevertheless, a major trade bill was passed in 1988 that gave the president increased power to deal with countries with whom the United States had a large unfavorable trade balance. Government reaction to trade deficits can also take the form of such protectionist measures as tariffs and import quotas. Economists are generally opposed to these measures on the grounds that they raise the price of imported goods for U.S. consumers.

---

[18] United Nations, *1987 Yearbook of International Trade Statistics,* Vol. 1: *Trade by Country* (New York: Department of International Economic and Social Affairs Statistical Office, United Nations, 1987).

Protective Tariffs

The tariff is probably the most common device used by the United States and other countries to restrict foreign trade. It is simply a tax levied on foreign goods coming into the country. The result is to make imported goods more expensive than comparable domestic goods, which, of course, are not subject to the tax. If the tariff is sufficiently high, U.S. consumers will find imported goods too expensive to buy; if they buy at all, they will probably buy the domestic goods. The main effect of a tariff is that it raises the prices of the commodities protected by it; if it did not raise prices, it would afford no protection. The increase in prices represents a gain to domestic producers, at least in the short run, and a loss to consumers. The higher price for the product is likely to mean a greater income for producers and a reduction in living standards for consumers, for consumers are denied the opportunity of buying foreign goods, which could come into this country at a lower cost and with greater quality than comparable U.S. goods.

Import Quotas

Compared with tariffs, which have been used by countries since the days of mercantilism, import quotas are relatively new. Introduced in France in the 1930s as an antidepression measure, the import quota has become a significant part of most countries' international commercial policy. As the name implies, a quota places limits, numerical or other, on the amount of a product that can be imported. For example, one country decides to restrict its auto imports from another country to two million cars a year. An import quota is generally considered more restrictive than a tariff. With a tariff, there is still the option of buying the foreign product, albeit at a higher price, but the import quota limits even this option. Prices cannot be forced by a tariff to rise by more than the amount of the tariff, but there is no upper limit to the price increase that can result from a quota. The prices to consumers are raised, and the restrictions placed on imports take away the incentive of domestic producers to innovate and promote efficiency.

The Automobile Industry and Import Quotas

In 1981, the U.S. auto companies asked Congress and the Reagan administration for quotas against the Japanese automobile industry. At stake, the U.S.

auto industry claimed, was the survival of the industry and the necessity to preserve jobs. Import quotas would provide a time out or respite, so to speak, while the auto industry could recuperate, retool, and develop new cars that could compete successfully against Japanese cars. Precedents for import quotas had already been established. Beef quotas have assisted cattle raisers, sugar quotas have kept high-cost domestic sugar cane and sugar beet growers in business, and quotas and other forms of support have been used to protect domestic steel producers from further losses to Asian and European steel producers. The Reagan administration made a compromise in that it reached an agreement with Japan whereby Japanese auto companies would voluntarily limit their exports to the United States. These quotas, set at 1,680,000 cars a year over a three-year period, ended in March 1984. A new quota, which raised the number of cars the Japanese could ship to the United States to 1,850,000 cars, was applied from April 1, 1984, to March 31, 1985. The allocation of import shares among Japanese automobile manufacturers was determined by the Japanese government on the basis of each company's shares of the U.S. market before the quota was imposed. The breakdown of the market was as follows:[19]

Toyota	31%
Nissan	27
Honda	21
Mazda	9
Mitsubishi	7
Subaru	4
Isuzu	1

Results of the Import Quota on Japanese Cars

The import quota had a number of results, few of which were of benefit to U.S. consumers. As the market allocation indicates, the quota benefited those Japanese auto firms that had already established a market for their cars in the United States. Toyota was assured of a market share of around one-third of the quota. Conversely, Japanese car companies that had not established a market share before the quota were virtually shut out of the U.S. car market. U.S. consumer choice was limited to a choice of the cars produced by Toyota, Nissan, or Honda, or the U.S. cars, or the cars of countries to which the import quota did not apply. However, the import quota on Japanese cars also had other

[19] Information provided by the Office of the U.S. Special Trade Representative.

effects on U.S. consumers:[20]

1. It raised the prices of both American and Japanese cars to U.S. consumers. One estimate was that the price of Japanese imports increased an average of $920 to $960 per car in the 1961–1982 period. Since restrictions were placed on Japanese cars, the companies shipped their top-of-the-line models. It was estimated that Japanese producers and their dealers benefited by as much as $2 billion a year during the quota.

2. The prices of U.S. automobiles also increased by an estimated $1,300 for each new U.S. car sold during the period 1981–1983. The estimated additional costs to consumers for new U.S. and Japanese cars was $4.3 billion in 1983.

3. One benefit of the import quota was to protect U.S. jobs. An estimated 20,000 to 25,000 jobs were saved in the automobile industry, at a cost to consumers of $160,000 a year per job.

4. Another purpose of the import quota was to enable the U.S. car companies to improve the quality of their cars. There is little evidence that such improvements have been made.

5. The U.S. automobile companies increased their market shares and made record profits. In 1984, Chrysler's profits were the highest in its history. Automobile industry profits were $6.3 billion for 1983 and close to $10 billion in 1984.

6. With such profits, the automobile companies paid their executives and some employees substantial bonuses. Chairman Philip Caldwell of Ford Motor Company received a 1983 salary and bonus of $1.4 million plus $5.9 million in long-term compensation. Chrysler Chairman Lee A. Iacocca received stock options valued at $17 million.

The Omnibus Trade and Competitiveness Act, 1988

The Omnibus Trade and Competitiveness Act joins the Bible and *Gone with the Wind* as one of the longest publications ever written.[21] It is 1,115 pages long and contains something for everyone. The purpose of the act is to develop coherent trade policy in dealing with countries with whom the United States

---

[20] Robert W. Crandall, "Import Quotas and the Automobile Industry: The Costs of Protection," *The Brookings Review* 2, no. 4 (September 1984): 11–16.

[21] H.R. 3, 100th Cong., 2nd sess., April 20, 1988.

has an unfavorable trade deficit, thus preventing future declines in the U.S. economy. In the past, U.S. presidents have preferred to handle trade on an ad hoc basis, with each issue left to the political and economic circumstances of the moment. But no trade dispute can be separable from many other kinds of issues. Congress wants future presidents, beginning with President Bush, to give more weight to trade in their foreign policy and to make their perform-ance more consistent. However, nearly all the provisions in the act give the president the right to do nothing when he (or she) considers that to be in the country's best interest.

The most important provision of the act is Section 1102, which states that the president, on finding that import restrictions of other countries have an ad-verse effect on the foreign trade of the United States, is to negotiate to reduce them.[22] The principal negotiation objective is to improve the provisions of GATT and nontariff measure agreements in order to define, deter, and dis-courage the use of unfair trade practices including subsidies, dumping, and ex-port targeting practices. Agreements entered into by the president are valid only if he (or she) informs Congress of his intent to enter into them. The presi-dent must also inform Congress if the United States provides reciprocal bene-fits under a trade agreement. Other purposes of the act are to provide increased cash assistance and job training for U.S. workers who lose their jobs as a result of foreign competition; restrictions against certain imports that threaten na-tional security; and increased funding to improve foreign language teaching in the United States.

The Worker Adjustment and Retraining Act, 1988

In July 1988, Congress passed (over President Reagan's veto) the Worker Ad-justment and Retraining Act or, as it is more commonly called, the "Plant Closing Act." President Reagan vetoed the bill on the grounds that it directly infringed on the right of private property owners to do with their property as they saw fit. There was also opposition to the bill on the grounds that it would tie the hands of business firms when they needed to close a plant that was no longer profitable. Supporters of the bill argued that workers should not be forced to bear the brunt of plant closings. It is only fair to inform workers who had invested time in their jobs of a pending plant closing so that they would have the time to find other jobs. Moreover, other industrial countries, includ-

[22] Ibid., pp. 23–27.

ing Japan, require that advance notice be given workers before plants were shut down.

The basic provision of the act is Section 3, which states that an employer must notify workers sixty days in advance of a plant closing. It applies to employers with 100 or more employees, excluding part-time employees; or employers with 100 or more employees, who in the aggregate work at least 4,000 hours a week excluding overtime. The term "plant closing" means the permanent or temporary shutdown of a single plant, or more than one plant in the same area of employment if the shutdown results in an employment loss during any thirty-day period for 50 or more workers. If an employer orders a plant closing in violation of Section 3, it is liable for back pay for each day of violation at a compensation rate based on the higher of the average regular pay rate over the last three years of employment, or the final regular rate received by employees.

SUMMARY

Everyone is in favor of trade between countries as long as the results are of equal benefit to all concerned. However, this is not usually the case. Although to consumers, trade between countries clearly contributes to higher living standards, some producer groups may be adversely affected. Those whose sales are reduced by foreign competition, and those whose incomes are reduced if foreign goods are made available to domestic consumers, will want protection against foreign imports. It is important to keep in mind that any change generates a conflict among economic groups in any country. Policymakers in the field of international trade have to determine what groups are to be helped at the expense of other groups.

The U.S. merchandise trade deficit constitutes a very important problem. Even though the U.S. dollar has declined in value relative to the Japanese yen and other major currencies, the trade deficit still remains high. The declining value of the U.S. dollar stimulated U.S. exports, but U.S. consumers are still willing to pay higher prices for foreign imports. The greatest imbalance in the merchandise trade account is with Japan and other East Asian countries. The latter have been able to score major trade gains as a result of tying their currencies to the U.S. dollar. In addition, lower labor costs have given them a competitive edge in their exports to the United States. Demand for protection against Japan, South Korea, and other East Asian countries has been strong in the United States, and the Omnibus Trade and Competitiveness Act was passed by Congress in 1988.

QUESTIONS FOR DISCUSSION

1. What are some reasons why world trade has turned away from the principles of free trade as promised by GATT?
2. What is the principle of absolute advantage? How would it apply to the U.S. and Japanese auto industries?
3. What is comparative advantage? Can a country create comparative advantage?
4. What is meant by a country's balance of payments?
5. What is the merchandise trade account?
6. Give some reasons for the deficit in the U.S. trade account.
7. What impact does the U.S. dollar have on the trade deficit?
8. What is an import quota? What effect does it have on consumers?
9. Why is it difficult for U.S. firms to penetrate the Japanese market?
10. What is a tariff? What effect does it have on consumers?

RECOMMENDED READINGS

Aho, C. Michael and Marc Levinson. *After Reagan: Confronting the World Economy*. New York: Council on Foreign Relations, 1988.

Council on Competitiveness. *Picking Up the Pace: The Commercial Challenge to U.S. Innovation*. Washington, D.C.: 1988.

Dornbusch, Rudiger, James Poterba, and Lawrence Summers. *The Case for Manufacturing in America's Future*. Rochester, N.Y.: Eastman Kodak Company, 1988.

Finan, William F., Perry D. Quick, and Karen M. Sundberg. *The U.S. Trade Position in High Technology: 1980–1986*. Washington, D.C.: Quick, Finan, and Associates, 1987.

Frost, Ellen. *For Richer, For Power: The New U.S.–Japan Relationship*. New York: Council on Foreign Relations, 1987.

Joint Economic Committee, Congress of the United States. *Impact of the Dollar on U.S. Competitiveness.* Hearings before the Subcommittee on Economic Goals and Intergovernmental Policies. 99th Cong., 1st sess. Washington, D.C.: U.S. Government Printing Office, 1985.

Joint Economic Committee, Congress of the United States. *Impact on the U.S. Economy of Imbalanced and Unfair Trade Relations—The Case of Japan.* Hearings before the Subcommittee on Economic Goals and Intergovernmental Policies, 99th Cong., 1st sess. Washington, D.C.: U.S. Government Printing Office, 1986.

Meyer, Stephen A. "Trade Deficits and the Dollar: A Macroeconomic Perspective." *Federal Reserve Bank of Philadelphia Business Review,* September–October 1986, pp. 1–5.

Office of Technology Assessment, Congress of the United States. *Paying the Bill: Manufacturing and America's Trade Deficit.* Washington, D.C.: U.S. Government Printing Office, 1988.

Prestowitz, Clyde V. *Trading Places.* New York: Basic Books, 1988.

Restoring International Balance: Japan's Trade and Investment Patterns. Staff Study prepared for the Joint Economic Committee (Washington, D.C.: Joint Economic Committee, July, 1988).

U.S. International Trade Commission. *U.S. Global Competitiveness: The U.S. Textile Industry.* Report to the Committee on Finance, U.S. Senate. Washington, D.C., US17C Publication 2048, 1987.

Chapter 19

The U.S. Government Budget

The budget of the U.S. government can be defined as an accounting of the current federal financial position, which mainly includes income, expenditures, and debt. Income is composed of the sources of revenue that are used to finance government operations; expenditures reflect government spending priorities; and debt is composed of loans borrowed to finance government programs that are not covered by tax revenues. The budget also represents the president's recommended programs, including appropriations sought for the coming fiscal year. The federal budget is also commonly seen as a measure of the breadth of economic and social activities carried on by the government, and the amount of public funds used by the government to finance its operations. This meaning is implied when people refer to the growth of the federal budget.

However, a simple clinical explanation of the federal budget does not do justice to its very important role in the U.S. economy. Public policy can be implemented through the budget. It can be used as a flywheel to change the level of economic activity in the United States. Both changes in taxes and government expenditures can be used to manipulate the level of aggregate demand. The budget is the single most important force affecting the contemporary economic, political, and social scene in the United States. Taxes, expenditures, and debt management policies are now major determinants of both internal and external economic development. Given the increased role of the federal government in the U.S. economy, people have come to expect future economic progress as a right, as well as many entitlements such as Social Security, veterans' benefits, Medicaid, aid to farmers, and other forms of income transfers.

The deficit in the federal budget is the single most important issue confronting the new Bush administration. It is linked to the problems of the U.S. trade deficit, the status of the United States as the world's leading debtor nation, and

U.S. industrial competitiveness. During his election campaign, President Bush promised not to raise taxes; it remains to be seen whether or not he can carry out this promise. There are only two ways in which the federal budget can be balanced: by raising taxes and by cutting government expenditures— neither of which is likely to be popular with U.S. voters. However, before discussing what the federal deficit is and how it can be reduced, we need to discuss in some detail why the deficit is so important to the economy.

THE FEDERAL BUDGET DEFICIT

A budget deficit occurs when a government spends more than the revenues it takes in. When this occurs, the government may resort to borrowing to make up the difference. Budget deficits did not begin with Reagan; through most of U.S. history, the federal government has incurred budget deficits, first to finance wars, and then to finance defense and entitlement expenditures. However, a peacetime deficit was a product of the Depression, and since 1929 it has been balanced only six times. The federal debt, which is really a total of all the fiscal deficits run by the government, has also shown a marked increase, particularly in recent years. Table 19-1 presents the budget deficit, the federal or national debt, GNP, and the national debt expressed as a percentage of GNP for selected years beginning in 1929. The first real jump in deficits and debt occurred during World War II, and the second real increase took place during the period 1980–1989.

The federal deficit and debt exert an enormous impact on the U.S. economy. The federal deficit is the paramount issue today. Less than one week after the presidential election was over, the U.S. stock market went down 47 points in one day, the sharpest one-day decline in a year.[1] The decline reflected concern that the Bush administration would not act decisively enough in reducing the deficit, and that the U.S. dollar would decrease further in value relative to other currencies. So we need to examine some problems associated with the federal deficit. Several have been discussed in the preceding chapters, but deserve further mention. These problems are linked to the federal deficit and debt. For example, a higher federal debt causes higher federal interest expenses, making it even more difficult to balance the budget the next fiscal year.

---

[1] The decline occurred on November 11, 1988.

TABLE 19-1 The Federal Deficit, Debt, GNP, and Debt Expressed as a Percentage of GNP for Selected Years (billions of dollars)

Year	Deficit	GNP	Debt	Debt as a Percentage of GNP
1929	+$ 0.7	$ 103.9	$ 16.9	16.2%
1939	−2.8	91.3	48.2	53.6
1945	−47.6	212.4	260.6	122.7
1950	−3.1	266.8	256.9	96.3
1960	+0.3	506.7	290.9	57.4
1970	−0.8	990.2	382.6	38.6
1980	−73.8	2,670.6	914.3	34.1
1985	−212.3	3,943.4	1,827.5	46.3
1988	−129.5	5,023.3	2,825.3	56.2

Source: *Economic Report of the President 1988* (Washington, D.C.: U.S. Government Printing Office, 1988), Table B-76, p. 337.

Debt Management

The U.S. Treasury is the government agency that is responsible for both borrowing and managing the federal debt. It can borrow by issuing three different types of debt obligations, ranging from the sale of short-term Treasury bills to long-term Treasury bonds. Treasury bills, which are usually issued for periods of three months up to a year, are the most widely held and most popular income-earning liquidity investment in the United States. They are held for the short-term investment of funds by financial institutions of all types and by individuals. One common reason for holding them is in anticipation of tax payments. Treasury notes are intermediate-term debt obligations, with maturity dates of from one to ten years, are less liquid than Treasury bills, and carry a higher rate of interest. Treasury bonds are long-term debt obligations: they are the least liquid of the three types and carry the highest rate of interest.

The term *debt management* refers to the U.S. Treasury handling of the national debt when securities are issued and when they become due. When part of the federal debt becomes due, as happens very frequently, the Treasury rolls it over and replaces it with new debt. This means that the Treasury is constantly in the money market to borrow loanable funds to refinance the maturing debt and the fiscal year deficit. Treasury debt operations not only influence the government securities market, but also affect the markets for all other types of securities. The approach of a major Treasury financing operation affects trading for other securities. The terms set by the Treasury can sharply influence all other interest rates. Business firms that borrow are affected by the interest rate the Treasury must pay to refinance the debt.

Debt management policy can make monetary policy more difficult to implement. The Federal Reserve is restricted in its freedom of policy action by the frequency and size of Treasury financing operations. The size and frequency of such operations can make it necessary, both on cash and refinancing operations, for the Federal Reserve System to pump more money into the economy by providing more reserves to commercial banks to absorb more Treasury issues. A tight money policy run by the Federal Reserve means higher interest rates. The Treasury, in refinancing the debt or financing the deficit, would not want to lock itself into paying higher interest rates on intermediate or long-term debt obligations. Instead, it would issue the short-term Treasury bills, which are a highly liquid form of investment and which can be used to increase the money supply.

Table 19-2 presents a breakdown of the national debt by kinds of debt obligations for the period 1980–1988. The debt obligations are broken down into two categories—marketable and nonmarketable. The marketable debt obligations include Treasury bills, Treasury notes, and Treasury bonds; the nonmarketable debt obligations include U.S. savings bonds, bonds sold to foreign governments, and government account series. As the table indicates, the national debt increased from $906 billion in 1980 to $2.6 trillion in 1988. Most of the gain was in marketable debt securities, in particular sales of Treasury notes. All this means is that interest payments on the national debt have also increased and are a fixed cost that must be met out of federal government budget expenditures. It also means increased U.S. Treasury borrowing, which keeps interest rates high.

Saving

Americans are not known for their frugality. In fact, U.S. consumer debt reached an estimated $1.5 trillion in November 1988. Given the fact that the U.S. government is a big borrower and U.S. consumers are also big borrowers, the pressure on the supply of available loanable funds is considerable. In U.S. national income and product accounts, there are three sources of saving. The

**TABLE 19-2   U.S. Debt Obligation by Kind, 1980–1988
(billions of dollars)**

| Year | Total | Marketable | | | Nonmarketable | | |
		Bills	Notes	Bonds	Savings Bonds	Foreign	Government Account
1980	$ 906	$199	$ 311	$ 84	$ 73	$25	$190
1981	996	223	364	96	68	20	201
1982	1,141	278	443	104	67	15	210
1983	1,376	341	557	126	70	11	235
1984	1,560	357	662	158	73	9	259
1985	1,821	384	776	200	77	7	314
1986	2,123	411	897	242	86	4	366
1987	2,348	378	1,005	278	97	4	441
1988	2,600	398	1,098	299	106	6	536

Source: Economic Report of the President 1989 (Washington, D.C.: U.S. Government Printing Office, 1989), Table B-84, p. 406.

first is personal saving, which is disposable income minus consumption. Personal saving averages around 4 percent of disposable income. The second source of saving is corporate retained earnings, and the third source of saving is a surplus in the federal government's budget. A federal government deficit reduces the supply of available saving. For example, if personal saving is $10 billion and retained earnings are $10 billion, and the deficit in the budget is $–10 billion, then total savings equal $20 billion, and the government dissaves $10 billion.

Table 19-3 presents total gross saving for the period 1980 to 1987. Gross saving includes personal saving, gross business saving,[2] and federal and state and local government's surplus or deficit in the national income and product account. As the table indicates, the size of the federal deficit reduces the rate of saving in the United States. For example, in 1986 the federal government had a deficit of $204.7 billion in the national income and product account, which

---

[2] Gross business saving includes the capital consumption allowance, which is saving for replacement of capital goods that are obsolete or have been destroyed or damaged. It also includes undistributed corporate profits. Net saving would be retained earnings.

TABLE 19-3   Gross Saving in the United States, 1980–1987 (billions of dollars)

| Year | Total | Gross Private Saving | | Government Surplus or Deficit | |
		Personal Saving	Business Saving	Federal	State and Local
1980	$445.0	$136.9	$341.5	−$61.3	$26.8
1981	522.0	159.4	391.1	−63.8	34.1
1982	446.4	153.9	403.2	−145.9	35.1
1983	463.6	130.6	461.6	−176.0	47.5
1984	568.5	164.1	509.5	−169.6	64.6
1985	531.3	127.1	537.2	−196.0	63.1
1986	532.0	130.6	549.3	−204.7	56.8
1987	566.0	120.2	553.4	−152.6	54.4

Source: *Economic Report of the President 1989* (Washington, D.C.: U.S. Government Printing Office, 1989), Table B-28, p. 340.

was offset to some extent by a surplus of $56.8 billion in the national income and product account contribution of state and local governments. There was a total government deficit of $147.8 billion, which reduced private sector saving from $679.8 billion to a total saving of $532 billion. Total gross saving in 1986 amounted to around 12 percent of GNP, compared to around 18 percent in 1979.[3]

Interest

The federal budget deficit reduces the supply of saving available for investment. In Table 19-3, the federal deficit reduces gross savings by $152.6 billion. This loss affects interest rates. As already noted, high real rates of interest attracted investment from abroad. This investment contributed to the status of the United States as the world's leading debtor country and also to the trade deficit. It can be said that Americans financed higher living standards through

[3] *Economic Report of the President 1989* (Washington, D.C.: U.S. Government Printing Office, 1989), Table B-1, p. 248, and Table B-28, p. 280.

foreign borrowing. Interest rates were not only high during the early 1980s, but they were also volatile. Volatile interest rates have generally negative effects on business investment planning, although they create opportunities for speculation in the capital market. It may be added that even lower interest rates and a depreciated U.S. dollar have done little to halt the flow of foreign investment in the United States, or to lower the trade deficit.[4]

The U.S. Dollar

The link between federal budget deficits and the U.S. dollar is as follows: deficits reduce the supply of loanable funds, which increases interest rates. Foreign investors, attracted by higher real interest rates and the size of the U.S. market, invest in the United States. This investment increases the value of the U.S. dollar, making exports more expensive and imports cheaper. An increase in the flow of foreign imports has an adverse impact on certain industries, such as textiles and lumber. Then U.S. business firms and workers demand protection against foreign imports, particularly those from East Asia. Even though there has been a dramatic fall in the value of the U.S. dollar from its high in 1985 to a low point against the yen and mark in November 1988, the stock markets of the world are jittery for two reasons. First, investors in the United States think that inflation and interest rates will rise, and, second, foreign investors lack confidence in the ability of the United States to balance the budget.

REAGANOMICS

It is necessary to go back to the 1970s to understand Reagan economics, or Reaganomics, as it was popularly called. This decade witnessed the worst combination of unemployment and inflation in modern U.S. experience. The average rate of unemployment ranged from a high of 8.5 percent in 1975 to a low of 5.3 percent in 1973. The unemployment rate for the decade, however, was over 6 percent—the highest rate for any decade since the 1930s. During the same decade, the inflation rate was the worst for any decade in this century.

---

[4] The merchandise trade deficit for September 1988 was $10.6 billion.

In fact, the rate of inflation was 12 percent in 1974, the highest peacetime rate since the Civil War. The rate of inflation decreased to less than 6 percent by 1976, but was back to double-digit levels by 1978. By 1980, the misery index—a term coined by former President Carter—was more than 20 percent—an unemployment rate of 7.8 percent plus an inflation rate of 12.4 percent.

Supply Side Economics

Supply side economics received considerable attention in the early 1980s. The term "supply side economics" represented a reaction against the "demand side" economics of John Maynard Keynes, which has guided government stabilization policies in most Western countries since the end of World War II. The Keynesian prescriptions—tax tinkering and government spending to stimulate aggregate demand—became articles of faith in the West. Everything was fine when demand was slack and unemployment was on the increase. But during the 1970s, stagflation—a term applied to a combination of low growth and inflation—was the problem in the United States. Supply-siders wanted to place more attention on the supply side of the economy to stimulate investment and growth. They wanted to reduce taxes, thus increasing the rate of saving and investment. Given the right incentives, they felt the free market would do a better job than government in stimulating the rate of economic growth.

Reaganomics, the term used to describe the economic policies instituted since the election of Ronald Reagan, had five components—a large across-the-board tax cut, a cut in social welfare spending, an increase in defense spending, less government regulation, and restricted growth in the money supply. The tax cut reflected a belief in the efficacy of supply side economics. The cuts were designed to favor people who made $50,000 or more annually, for they provide the bulk of savings in the United States. Savings were supposed to increase and be channeled into investment. This created a tax cut flow from savings to investment to increased productivity. Cuts in social welfare expenditures were designed to limit increases in entitlement programs. Increases in defense spending were not designed for economic reasons but had the effect of increasing the deficit in the federal budget because they were larger than cuts in civilian spending. Antitrust and other forms of government regulation were relaxed because they discouraged investment and were too costly to business. The slow rate of growth in the money supply was designed to reduce inflation.

The Economic Recovery Tax Act of 1981

The cornerstone of Reagan's tax policy was the Economic Recovery Tax Act, ERTA, which was signed into law in August 1981. The act legislated sweeping changes in both the individual and corporate income taxes. It provided for an across-the-board reduction in individual income tax rates amounting to 23 percent over three years, and an immediate cut in the top bracket from 70 to 50 percent. These reduced marginal rates were designed to increase the incentive to invest. There was a shift in emphasis away from using the tax system to redistribute income and toward the creation of national income through economic growth. The corporate income tax was also reduced from 48 to 46 percent, and ERTA allowed accelerated depreciation of new capital assets and a system of tax credits for investment. Both provisions decreased the effective tax burden on new investment.

Changes in Federal Expenditures

The composition of federal expenditures by the Reagan administration reflected its objectives. As a share of GNP, defense expenditures grew from 4.9 percent in 1980 to 6.3 percent in 1985, as total federal expenditures increased from 21.6 percent of GNP in 1980 to 22.1 percent in 1988. The federal deficit rose from 2.7 percent of GNP in 1980 to 5.3 percent in 1985. Changes in tax laws reduced receipts as a share of GNP to the range that had existed during most of the 1970s—from 21.1 percent in 1981 to an estimated 19.4 percent in 1988.[5] Given the increase in expenditures and the decrease in tax revenues, it is obvious why the federal budget deficit increased. However, without tax law changes, GNP growth during the 1983–1985 recovery would probably have been lower.

Monetary Policy

There were four changes in monetary policy in the period from 1981 to 1985. The first change, which extended to mid-1982, saw the Federal Reserve pursue a restrictive monetary policy designed to reduce inflation. The second

[5] Office of Management and Budget, *Budget of the United States Government, Fiscal Year 1989* (Washington, D.C.: U.S. Government Printing Office, 1988), pp. 48–57.

change began in the late summer of 1982. Prompted by accumulating evidence that the recession would be deeper and longer than had been expected, the Federal Reserve began to ease credit and the money supply. Interest rates fell sharply as the growth in the money supply accelerated in 1982 and early 1983. The third change began in the spring of 1983 and ran to the latter part of 1984. The concern was that too rapid a recovery of the economy would lead to inflation. Interest rates were permitted to rise, and money supply growth was substantially reduced. The fourth change began in late 1984 and continued through late 1988. Fear that the economic recovery was running out of steam led the Federal Reserve to increase the money supply, and interest rates fell to one of their lowest points in the decade. In the last months of the Reagan administration monetary policy tightened.

Regulatory Policies

A number of federal regulatory agencies were created during the 1970s, and regulation increased in such areas as consumer protection and the environment. But by the end of the decade, the feeling was there was too much regulation of the U.S. economy. During the election campaign of 1980, Reagan promised to get the government off the people's backs. Regulatory approaches to environmental and health and safety problems raised production costs and created considerable uncertainty because rules and regulations continually changed. It was also felt that antitrust regulation was out of step with the times and that concentration of output in the hands of a few large firms in a given industry could not automatically be considered bad. The Reagan administration did not eliminate any of the major regulatory agencies, but it did attempt to cut back on the extent of their enforcement. In the area of antitrust policy, a number of major mergers were permitted, including mergers involving Standard Oil of California, Gulf, Texaco, and Getty, four of the largest oil companies in the United States.

The Laffer Curve

The centerpiece of supply side economics is the Laffer curve and its concept of incentive effects. Figure 19-1 illustrates the Laffer curve. Its shape, which bends backward, is based on the concept that if government levies no taxes, it collects no revenues. If it levies 100 percent taxes, however, it also collects no

FIGURE 19-1 The Laffer Curve

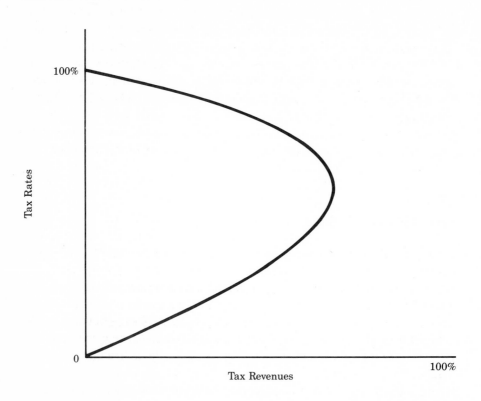

revenues because no one would work. Tax rates are plotted on the vertical axis, and tax revenues on the horizontal axis. As tax rates first rise, so do government revenues. However, the curve eventually bends backward as increased taxes cause a decline in work and investment enough to reduce tax revenues. The assumption was made that the U.S. economy was at an upper point on the curve. The increase in income that a tax cut was supposed to generate would raise government tax revenues so much that the loss of revenue from the tax cut would be more than offset. However, this plan did not work; instead, the budget deficit increased.

The Results of Reaganomics

President Reagan will probably be regarded as one of the most popular and charismatic U.S. presidents of this century but there is much controversy concerning his performance as president. Those who think that he has been an outstanding president point to the economic prosperity of the country and to improved relations with the Soviet Union. His critics point to the massive increase in the federal debt, the Iran-Contra scandal, and increased inequality of income distribution. They contend that the federal deficit problem is a direct legacy of Reaganomics. The truth, as in most controversies, lies somewhere in the middle. So it is important to examine the impact of Reaganomics on the U.S. economy.

When Ronald Reagan was first elected president in 1980, the most important problem confronting the U.S. economy was the rate of inflation. The consumer price index increased at a rate of 13.3 percent in 1979 and 12.4 percent in 1980. The U.S. economy had performed poorly during the 1970s and the average U.S. family was no better off at the end of the decade than it was at the beginning of it. President Carter had said that Americans could not automatically take rising living standards for granted. Our relations with the Soviet Union were poor, and President Carter refused to let U.S. athletes participate in the 1980 Olympic games held in Moscow. Some people also felt that the Carter and previous administrations had so neglected defense expenditures that the Russians were vastly superior to us in military strength.

Table 19-4 presents the rate of inflation, the rate of unemployment, and the real rate of U.S. economic growth during the eight years Reagan was in office. Probably the single most important accomplishment of the Reagan administration was the reduction of the inflation rate. This goal was achieved at some cost. The tight money policy of the Federal Reserve increased interest rates, and contributed to a major recession in 1982 and 1983. The unemployment rate increased to 9.7 percent in 1982. There was also a decline of 2.5 percent in the real rate of growth in GNP for the same year. The real rate of economic growth, although unspectacular, was higher than the real rate of growth for other countries, with the exception of Japan. There was a sustained increase in economic growth during the last six years of the Reagan administration, and unemployment declined. Also presented in the table are corporate profits expressed as a percentage of GNP.

However, it can be argued that this coin has a reverse side. The six years of uninterrupted prosperity have been financed by increasing the federal budget

TABLE 19-4 Comparison of Economic Indicators in the 1980s and 1970s (percent)

Years	Unemployment	Economic Growth	Inflation	Profits Related to GNP
1970–1979	6.2%	2.8%	7.1%	7.9%
1980	7.1	−0.2	13.5	6.5
Reagan Years				
1981	7.6	1.9	10.4	6.2
1982	9.7	−2.5	6.1	4.7
1983	9.6	3.6	3.2	6.3
1984	7.5	6.8	4.3	7.1
1985	7.2	3.0	3.6	6.9
1986	7.0	3.0	1.9	6.7
1987	6.2	2.9	3.7	6.6
1988	5.8	3.0	4.1	6.6
Reagan Average	7.6	2.7	4.2	6.4

Source: Congress of the United States, Congressional Budget Office, *The Changing Distribution of Federal Taxes: A Closer Look at 1980* (Washington, D.C.: U.S. Government Printing Office, 1988), p. 12.

deficit. Although running a budget deficit is standard Keynesian economic policy, ideally deficits should be run by a government during a recession, when resources are underused and when aggregate demand needs to be stimulated. Conversely, a government should run a surplus when the economy is healthy. The total of budget deficits run by the Reagan administration is $1.3 trillion, as shown in Table 19-5.

BALANCING THE BUDGET

On November 20, 1988, Comptroller General Charles Bowsher of the General Accounting Office reported that the federal deficit for the 1988 fiscal year was $155 billion.[6] He said that new taxes would be needed as part of an effort to

[6] Report of the Comptroller General's Office, Washington, D.C., November 19, 1988.

Table 19-5   Federal Budget Deficits and Gross Federal Debt, 1981–1989 (billions of dollars)

Fiscal Year	Deficit	Gross Federal Debt
1981	−78.9	994.3
1982	−127.9	1,136.8
1983	−207.8	1,371.2
1984	−185.3	1,564.1
1985	−212.3	1,817.0
1986	−221.2	2,120.1
1987	−149.7	2,345.6
1988	−155.1	2,600.8
1989 estimate	−161.5	2,868.8

Source: Executive Office of the President, Office of Management and Budget, *Budget of the United States Government, Fiscal Year 1990* (Washington, D.C.: U.S. Government Printing Office, 1989), p. 10-38.

solve the nation's budget problem. He also indicated that the deficit would have been $252 billion had it not been for contributions of $97 billion in the surplus contributions to Social Security, civil service, and military retirement funds. Bowsher stated that the government faces much new spending that is not included in official deficit projections, and some of which is unavoidable. He reported that it would cost $50 billion to deal with 500 insolvent savings and loan institutions, with a significant amount of money coming from the taxpayers, and $100 to $300 billion spread over many years to clean up and rebuild the government's nuclear weapons plants.

Bowsher also chided George Bush and Michael Dukakis. Bush's proposal to freeze spending will not work because most government spending is concentrated on politically sensitive programs such as Social Security, and because some spending—mainly the interest the government pays on the national debt—is locked into the budget. Dukakis's proposal to forgive taxpayers who will simply pay uncollected revenue would have made no impact on the deficit. Bowsher's report also rejected the Gramm-Rudman-Hollings law, which set a deadline for balancing the budget by 1993, in part because Congress and the administration have already shown a willingness to extend the deadline and in part because mechanical processes will not work.

The inevitable concomitant, the report states, is that Congress and the Bush administration need to raise taxes. But this move also presents problems. Higher income taxes could jeopardize the improvements achieved by the 1986 overhaul of the tax system, and a national sales tax would affect the poor more than the rich.

So what can be done about the federal deficit? The starting point is to look at the Gramm-Rudman-Hollings Act and what it is supposed to accomplish. Second, it is important to look at the major revenue and expenditure items in the federal budget to see what can be done to lower the federal deficit. Then we need to see what new taxes must be levied in order to increase federal government revenues. The choice is rather limited. It is highly unlikely that the U.S. economy will grow out of the deficit with an increased GNP, so the probable solution is to raise the so-called "sin" taxes, such as taxes on alcohol and cigarettes. There may also need to be an increase in users' fees, plus selected cuts in expenditures.

The Gramm-Rudman-Hollings Antideficit Law

In December 1985, Congress—unwilling and unable to take the steps necessary to balance the federal budget—took the historic step of binding itself to five years of forced deficit reduction, with the goal of balancing the budget by October 1990. The Gramm-Rudman-Hollings Act[7] was passed, thus letting both Congress and President Reagan off the hook. Congress did not want to have to make decisions to make cuts in the favorite entitlement programs of voters, and President Reagan did not want to cut defense expenditures. The Gramm-Rudman-Hollings law took the reduction decisions out of their hands by mandating a series of expenditure cuts that were supposed to balance the budget by 1990, using the following measures:

1. It required that federal budgets must not have a deficit exceeding $171.9 billion in the fiscal year 1986, $144 billion in fiscal 1987, $108 billion in fiscal 1988, $72 billion in fiscal 1989, $36 billion in fiscal 1990, and zero in fiscal year 1991.

2. It exempted from automatic cuts Social Security, interest on the federal debt, veterans' compensation, veterans' pensions, Medicaid, Aid to Families with Dependent Children, and several other entitlement programs.

---

[7] HJ Res 372-PL 177, December 1985.

3. It required across-the-board cuts of nonexempt programs by a uniform percentage to achieve deficit targets if regular budget and appropriations actions fail to reach deficit goals.

A new version of Gramm-Rudman-Hollings was passed in September 1987 because the U.S. Supreme Court in 1986 struck down the law's original automatic cut procedure on the grounds that it was unconstitutional.[8] The new version eased the deficit targets of the 1985 law and promised a balanced budget by 1993. It increased the debt ceiling from $2.1 trillion to $2.8 trillion. Under the new version,[9] a deficit reduction of $23 billion was to be required for the fiscal year 1988, leaving a deficit in the federal budget of $144 billion.[10] For the fiscal years 1988–1993, the new version established an automatic spending cut procedure to reduce the estimated deficit to specific targets.

Revenue Sources

The federal government budget is financed from two income sources, taxes and borrowing. Table 19-6 presents budget revenue by sources for fiscal 1989. The two most important revenue sources are personal income and Social Security taxes. The Tax Reform Act of 1986 nominally reduced the number of personal income tax rates to two, 15 percent and 28 percent,[11] but the advantages of the lower first-bracket rate and the personal exemptions are phased out for high-income taxpayers. In the phaseout range, the marginal tax rate is actually 33 percent. Beyond the phaseout range, the effective tax rate is a flat 28 percent of adjusted gross income less deductions. With the bulge, a rate structure beginning in 1988 will have four brackets with rates of 15, 28, 33, and 28 percent.

At one time, the corporate income tax was the most important source of federal government revenue. During World War II, the personal income tax supplanted the corporate income tax as the most important revenue source and has remained so ever since. From 1941 to 1967 corporate income tax receipts were second only to those of the personal income tax, but they were overtaken by payroll taxes in 1968 and have been declining in importance ever since. They

---

[8] It was ruled unconstitutional on the grounds that automatic cuts could be made only if approved by both chambers of Congress and the President.

[9] HJ Res 324, September 1987.

[10] The actual deficit was $155 billion.

[11] This act is also called the Packwood-Bradley Act, after its two major Senate sponsors.

TABLE 19-6 Federal Revenue by Sources, Fiscal Year 1989 (billions of dollars)

Source	Amount
Personal income taxes	$412.4
Corporate income taxes	117.7
Social Security taxes	354.6
Excise taxes	35.2
Estate and gift taxes	7.8
Custom duties	17.2
Miscellaneous receipts	19.8
Total	$964.7

Source: Executive Office of the President, Office of Management and Budget, *Budget of the United States Government,* Fiscal Year 1989 (Washington, D.C.: U.S. Government Printing Office, 1988, p. 4-3.

accounted for approximately 11 percent of total receipts for the 1989 fiscal year. The corporate tax rate has been reduced from a high of 52 percent for the period 1952–1963 to a low of 34 percent under the Tax Reform Act of 1986, which also eliminated the investment tax credit and lengthened the allowances for depreciation.

Payroll taxes were introduced into the federal revenue system by the Social Security Act of 1935 and have increased in importance to the point where they are now second to the personal income tax as a source of revenue, accounting for 32 percent of federal revenue for the fiscal year 1989. Payroll taxes are earmarked, through trust funds, to finance Social Security programs, of which there are two types. The first type is a federal system of old age, survivors, disability, and health insurance benefits (OASDHI), which is financed by payroll taxes collected from employees and employers in equal amounts. The second type is a federal and state system of unemployment compensation, which is financed mainly by payroll taxes on employers. Payroll taxes constitute a significant part of the tax payments made for lower income groups. In 1988, the employees' and employers' taxes for OASDHI reached 15.02 percent of wages up to $45,300.

Excise taxes are a minor source of federal government revenue, accounting for 3 percent of total revenue for fiscal 1989. Excise taxes are consumption taxes and are levied on the sale of a particular commodity. Excises are levied on gasoline, alcohol, tobacco, and other products. They can be employed as "user charges" to collect part or all of the cost of services enjoyed by specific groups of taxpayers. Gasoline taxes are a good example. Excise taxes levied on alcohol and tobacco are called "sin taxes" because they are used to discourage the consumption of these products as well as to raise money. Excise taxes are regressive because they are likely to represent a larger burden to low-income taxpayers than to those with higher incomes. Excises are usually the first taxes to be raised in a national emergency, and the deficit in the federal budget can be considered exactly that.

The difference between federal government revenues and expenditures is made up by borrowing. It is an easy way out for politicians and for the public. Politicians can spend money, and the public can "eat their cake and have it too," in that they can postpone payment until a later date. But, as mentioned, living beyond one's means does create a problem. Borrowing has affected the trade deficit, has made the United States the world's leading debtor nation, and has made fiscal, monetary, and debt management policies more difficult to implement.

Types of Expenditures

There are three major types of government expenditures—national defense, entitlements, and interest on the national debt. Combined, they amount to 84 percent of federal government expenditures. Table 19-7 presents the types of budget expenditures for the 1989 fiscal year. The Reagan administration placed priority on increasing national defense expenditures, which had fallen from 44 percent of total federal budget expenditures in 1970 to 24 percent in 1980. During the Reagan administration, national defense expenditures increased to 27 percent of total budget expenditures. As a share of GNP, outlays on national defense increased to 6.4 percent for 1988, compared to 5.0 percent for 1980. Interest payments on the national debt increased from 2.0 percent of GNP in 1980 to 3.0 percent in 1988, and entitlements increased from 10.4 percent of GNP in 1980 to 10.6 percent of GNP in 1988. The single largest expenditure in the federal budget is in benefits for the elderly and retirees, with most expenditures for Social Security and Medicare. These expenditures will increase as life expectancy increases.

The first major area of federal government expenditures is national defense. The four major components of national defense expenditures are military personnel operations and maintenance, procurement, and research and

TABLE 19-7   Federal Outlays by Functions, Fiscal Year 1989 (billions of dollars)

Outlays	*Amount*
National defense	$294.0
Entitlements	511.5
Retirement and unemployment	315.9
Medical care	116.6
Low-income programs	45.5
Agriculture	19.8
Other mandatory programs	13.7
Net interest	151.8
Grants to states and localities	110.2
Other	27.6
Total	$1,094.2

Source: Executive Office of the President, Office of Management & Budget, *Budget of the United States Government, Fiscal Year 1989* (Washington, D.C.: U.S. Government Printing Office, 1989), Tables 2 and 3, pp. 6g-8 and 6g-9.

development. Together they account for over 90 percent of total national defense expenditures. Most defense expenditures have a direct impact on business. For example, in the 1989 fiscal budget, the Army is going to buy 545 Abrams tanks and 581 Bradley fighting vehicles. It also plans to modernize its helicopter forces. The Navy has plans to buy three guided missile destroyers, three attack submarines, and other ships. The Air Force also has a shopping list. It wants to buy 36 F-15 aircraft and 180 F-16 multimission bombers. These and other expenditures by the military provide business for U.S. factories and shipyards and jobs for thousands of U.S. workers.

The largest federal government expenditure is on entitlements. One major entitlement program is Medicare, which will amount to an estimated $84 billion for the 1989 fiscal year. In 1989 Medicare will provide health insurance for an estimated 33 million people who are aged, disabled, or suffer from a terminal disease. Then there are the general income security programs, which will amount to around $136 billion for fiscal 1989. An example is the family support programs. Veterans benefits represent a third entitlement program. An example is service disability compensation, which will amount to around

$11 billion for fiscal 1989. The largest and most important component of entitlement expenditures is Social Security. Social Security represents about one-fifth of estimated total federal government outlays for fiscal 1989 and provides benefits to one out of every six Americans.

The third major areas of federal government expenditures is net interest on the national debt. The federal government engages in both borrowing and lending, and as a result it both pays and receives interest. Interest payments on the national debt will amount to an estimated $220 billion for fiscal 1989. However, interest received from off-budget trust funds, one-budget trust funds, and other sources reduce government interest payments to a net $151.8 billion for fiscal 1989. The Federal Reserve System owns U.S. government securities for the purpose of implementing monetary policy. The Treasury pays interest on these securities but virtually all the interest the Federal Reserve receives is returned to the Treasury. This returned interest is subtracted from the net interest payment, which shows the net budgetary effect of interest transactions with the public.

How to Cut the Budget Deficit

Former Senator Russell Long, who was once the chairman of the Senate Finance Committee, used to say in jest, "Don't tax you, don't tax me, tax that man behind the tree." Most Americans would heartily agree—few people like to pay taxes; even fewer want their taxes raised. Most people are for government expenditures—*if* the expenditures benefit *them*. So how is the budget going to be balanced? After all, President Bush said, "Read my lips" and "no new taxes" when asked if he was going to raise taxes if elected president.[12] How are expenditures going to be cut when special-interest groups adamantly oppose suggested cuts. Then there are the losses of the failed savings and loan banks, which could cost as much as $60 billion to the federal government. Here are four possible ways in which the federal deficit can be cut:

1. Reduce defense expenditures by $20 billion. There is a lot of waste in Pentagon expenditures on such things as $600 toilet seats, exotic weapons of doubtful value,[13] and proposed expenditures for Strategic Defense

[12] Former presidents Ford and Carter met with president-elect Bush in mid-November 1988 and urged him to consider a combination of tax increases and expenditure cuts that would reduce the deficit by $40 billion.

[13] The Stealth bomber and the B-1 bomber are two examples.

Initiative (SDI) (nicknamed "Star Wars" from the movie). Our NATO allies and Japan should be called on to share a greater burden of the cost of maintaining defense in Western Europe and Asia. Fewer U.S. military personnel and their dependents would be needed in those parts of the world. Finally, military pay increases could be limited to 2 percent a year. The military might well not approve, but these cuts are the best place to begin.

2. Increase taxes on gasoline, alcohol, and tobacco. Gasoline taxes can be increased by 10 cents per gallon annually over a four-year period. This increase would raise government revenues by $40 billion by the fourth year. The "sin taxes" on tobacco and alcohol can also be raised, which could increase tax revenues by as much as $7 billion a year. (Even gasoline could be considered an "ecological sin.")
    The problem with raising excise taxes is their regressive nature. A Congressional Budget Office study found that excise taxes accounted for 40 percent of taxes paid by the lowest 20 percent of U.S. income earners, while excise taxes paid by the top 20 percent of income earners represented only 4 percent of their total taxes.[14]

3. Impose a national value-added tax similar to the one used in most industrial countries. This tax could raise as much as $80 billion annually. A value-added tax falls on the increase in value of output at each stage of production. The type in most common use around the world falls on the difference between the value of output and the cost of goods and services purchased from other countries. The main objection to the value-added tax is that it is regressive, falling on the poor and the elderly.[15] State and local governments in the United States are likely to oppose federal use of the value-added tax on the grounds that it would interfere with their ability to levy general and selective sales taxes.

4. Other ways to reduce the federal deficit would include the reduction of cost-of-living increases in Social Security benefits.[16] Limiting them to the annual consumer rate of inflation less two percentage points would save

---

[14] Congress of the United States, Congressional Budget Office, *The Changing Distribution of Federal Income Taxes 1975–1990* (Washington, D.C.: U.S. Government Printing Office, 1988), p. 67.

[15] Henry J. Aaron, "The Value-Added Tax: Sorting Through the Practical and Political Problems," *The Brookings Review*, 6, no. 3 (Summer 1988): 10–16.

[16] Benjamin M. Friedman, *Day of Reckoning*, Aspen Institute (New York: Random House, 1988).

$22 billion annually by 1992. President Bush opposes this measure, and it has no chance in Congress. A second way is to cap mortgage interest deductions at $20,000 per couple and $12,000 for a single person. This would increase revenues by $10 billion annually. A third way would be to tax those people who have high incomes at a higher rate. For example, couples with taxable incomes above $89,500 would be required to pay a rate of 33 percent.[17] A fourth way to raise revenue is to increase the annual deductible for Medicare enrollees from $75 to $200, a move that would save the government $2.4 billion annually. The politicians won't touch this one.

One thing is certain—the deficit in the federal budget has to be cut. It remains to be seen how President Bush and a Democratic Congress proceed in cutting it. There are no painless solutions, and none address the long-term questions confronting the U.S. economy, such as how to encourage saving and investment, how to reduce drug use and crime, and how to improve education.

FEDERAL LOAN AND TAX POLICIES THAT AFFECT BUSINESS

The federal government runs a number of programs that offer financial assistance to private enterprise. Some of these programs are of a permanent nature, whereas others are of limited duration and are intended to help a firm or industry through a temporary crisis. The permanent programs give assistance to agriculture, housing, transportation, small business, and banks, among others. Many federal programs are an important source of credit for certain sectors of the economy. For example, the housing industry relies on the various federal mortgage credit programs and the Federal Home Loan Board for a good portion of its funds, particularly when money is tight. Agriculture receives credit assistance from the Farmers Home Administration and government-sponsored credit corporations such as the Federal Land Banks and Federal Intermediate Credit Banks. Exporters also can obtain financial assistance from the Export-Import Bank (Eximbank). Many of these programs were created during the 1930s to help various sectors of the economy through the Depression. Instead of being abolished after this economic crisis, they have continued to operate and have become an important part of the nation's credit structure. The

[17] There are currently two standard rates, 15 percent and 28 percent, but upper-income wage earners pay a 33 percent rate on a portion of their taxable incomes.

temporary programs, though, have not become an institutionalized source of funds and, with the ending of a particular financial crisis, have lapsed.

Taxation is another area in which government affects business. It can be used to stimulate or deter methods of doing business or the kind of business being done. A tax can be used as a subsidy or a negative tax to encourage a specific course of action. The agricultural price support program is a large-scale example. Other examples are subsidies to airlines and to the merchant marine. Then there are tariffs that protect domestic industries from foreign competition, though this approach goes against the grain of competition. The consumer pays higher prices for protected goods, and efficiency may suffer because the producer is spared the necessity of striving to reduce costs. There is much public support for protection, however, because many people regard themselves as having primarily a producer's rather than a consumer's interest. They are, therefore, more concerned about the possibility of losing profits or becoming unemployed because of foreign competition than they are about being able to buy the imported commodity at a lower price.

Tax incentives are used to stimulate many activities. At the federal level, tax credits and accelerated depreciation have been used to encourage business investment. Depletion allowances are used to encourage oil and mining companies to explore for new sources of energy. The foreign tax credit is said to be an incentive for U.S. firms to invest abroad. At the state and local level, there are also a variety of tax incentives, the most common being an exemption from the property tax as an inducement to encourage the location of industry. In fact, states use this device to compete against one another in attracting industry. The exemption of interest on state and local bonds for federal income tax purposes also has been used to stimulate industrial development, with states or localities using the proceeds from tax-exempt bonds to build a plant to be leased to industry. Both the federal and state governments grant special tax concessions to firms that comply with environmental protection laws by acquiring pollution control equipment. Some states permit the deduction of pollution control costs as a credit against state income taxes. Federal loan programs exist to erase imperfections from the direct market, to provide subsidies for socially desirable activities, and to stimulate the economy when there are idle resources. Imperfections in the credit market occur because borrowers differ in size, geographic location, and types of activity. Federal loans are designed to fill certain gaps in the private lending market. In addition, many economic transactions benefit not only the principal participants in the transaction but other members of society as well. Home ownership, which increases social stability, and education, which increases productivity and economic growth, are two examples of activities with external benefits. When there is a difference between the total costs and benefits and the private costs and benefits, federal loan programs can supply credit for socially desirable purposes at less than the market interest rates. This has a subsidy effect, in that subsidies reduce the private cost of a particular transaction. By setting the subsidy at an appropriate level, the government can induce the level of activity that would prevail if social benefits were taken into consideration by the market process.

Direct Loans

Direct federal loans have several characteristics. First, they are designed to promote socially useful activities rather than to remove imperfections in the credit market. Second, they contain a subsidy element. For example, loan programs of the Rural Electrification Administration and loans for the construction of higher education facilities and college housing offer borrowers subsidies at around 50 percent of the total value of the loan. Third, direct loans are financed directly out of the federal budget. Through the tax transfer mechanism of the federal budget, the government can influence the amount—and presumably the allocation—of credit extended in the private market. Fourth, foreign loans are by far the largest single component of direct loans, accounting for more than 40 percent of the total loans outstanding in 1988. In quantity, the most important types of outstanding foreign loans are development loans and loans of the Export-Import Bank. Both types create a foreign demand for the products of U.S. business. An example of a foreign loan that benefits business is the military sales credit extended to countries to help them purchase military equipment from the United States, which benefits firms making aircraft, tanks, and so forth.

Table 19-8 presents the amount of new direct federal loans made by major government agencies for 1988. Excluded from the table are the loans of the federally sponsored agencies that are also not included in the federal budget. Government-sponsored agencies were originally financed by subscriptions of government capital, but this capital now has been retired and the agencies are entirely privately owned. Direct loans financed out of the federal budget include business loans made by the Small Business Administration, loans made by the Economic Development Administration of the Department of Commerce, and loans made for ship construction by the Maritime Administration.

TABLE 19-8   New Direct Loans by Sector, 1988 (millions of dollars)

Sector	Amount
Agriculture	$19,335
Business	5,900
Education	62
Housing	3,470
Other	50
Total of direct loans	$28,817

Source: Executive Office of the President, Office of Manpower and Budget, *Budget of the U.S. Government, Fiscal Year 1989* (Washington, D.C.: U.S. Government Printing Office, 1988), p. 6g-43.

In addition, the Export-Import Bank, a federally owned enterprise, lends directly to exporters and importers and insures and guarantees loans extended by private lenders.

Economic Impact of Direct Loans

Since direct loans are included in the federal budget, we shall examine their possible economic impact. The method of financing used in the budget is important. If there is a deficit in the budget, the whole process, including the loans, can have an income-generating effect, particularly if new money is created to finance the deficit. This would affect both consumption and investment. The impact on consumption may be divided into income and wealth effects. The income effect comes about because the government spends and consumers receive income. The wealth effect comes about because savings accumulate as income increases. Assuming that income and consumption continue to expand for a long enough period, consumption increases also will produce increases in investment. And because the deficit was created by means of new money, interest rates will remain low, which also should encourage an increase in investment spending unless, of course, the investment schedule is interest inelastic.

One issue in the federal credit programs is the existence of subsidies. Many of these credit programs offer loans or insurance at rates below those that would be charged by a private firm for such services and at rates below those that the government itself would have to pay to borrow money. The subsidy can be defined as the difference between the amount the borrower has to pay for a government loan and the price he or she would have to pay for a similar loan from a competitive private lender. In essence, the subsidy circumvents the forces of the free market. In the market for loanable funds, the interest rate is supposedly determined by the interaction of the supply of funds with the demand for the funds. An equilibrium point is reached when supply and demand are in balance at a given rate of interest. In a competitive market economy, borrowers are free to obtain loans at the going interest rate. If this market rate is 6 percent and the government charges 2 percent to a specific set of borrowers, the subsidy, in the final analysis, is paid by the taxpayers. The effectiveness of the market as an allocator of loanable funds is circumvented.

The Small Business Administration and the Export-Import Bank are examples of agencies that make direct loans to business. In 1988, the total loans of the Small Business Administration (SBA) amounted to more than $1 billion, and the loans of Eximbank amounted to $705 million.[18] Both agencies were created to achieve specific economic objectives, the SBA to offer loans and assistance to small business firms and the Eximbank to stimulate business involvement in foreign trade.

The Small Business Administration

The principal governmental agency concerned with the problems of small business is the Small Business Administration. The SBA was created by the Small Business Act of 1953, which had as its objective the assistance of small business firms, to ensure fair competition. The common problem of small business firms is securing capital, and so the act authorized the SBA to provide two types of financial assistance to small firms—loans for plant construction and the acquisition of land, equipment, and materials, and disaster loans to business concerns that suffer financial loss from floods, hurricanes, drought, or other natural catastrophes. In addition, the SBA was responsible for helping small business firms secure a larger share of government contracts for materi-

---

[18] Executive Office of the President, Office of Manpower and Budget, *Budget of the U.S. Government, Fiscal Year 1989* (Washington, D.C.: U.S. Government Printing Office, 1988), pp. 6g–11.

ials, construction, and research and development. The SBA was also supposed to provide counseling for small firms. In applying for a loan, a small business concern must submit credit data, and in evaluating these data, SBA officials often are able to advise on alternative ways of solving a problem.

In 1958, the Small Business Investment Act was passed by Congress to help small businesses secure additional equity capital and long-term loan capital. This law, which is administered by the SBA, provides equity capital and long-term capital through privately owned and operated small business investment companies and state and local development corporations. Small business investment companies operate by supplying equity capital in exchange for convertible debentures under conditions approved by the SBA. These securities give the investment company the privilege of converting such debentures into the small business firm's common stock. The investment company also may make long-term loans to small business concerns for up to twenty years, with provision for an additional ten years for repayment. State and local development corporations have been formed to assist the development of small business, and loans made to them by the SBA are used to make loans to small business firms. In its community development work, the SBA works closely with the Department of Commerce's Economic Development Administration to establish, expand, and assist in financing local industries in areas designated for redevelopment.

The Export–Import Bank (Eximbank)

The Export–Import Bank (Eximbank) is a wholly federally owned enterprise, and its mission is to promote U.S. exports. It does this by making direct loans to exporters and importers and by insuring and guaranteeing loans made by private lenders. It is authorized to have outstanding at any one time dollar loans, guarantees, and insurance in an aggregate amount of not in excess of $40 billion. Since it concentrates on areas where private financing is not available and on meeting foreign competition, its programs are generally intended to supplement private credit financing. To match the special terms that foreign governments provide to subsidize their exporters, terms and credits on the use of its funds are more favorable than those available in the private sector. Eximbank receives its financial support from the federal budget, with authorizations in the 1989 fiscal budget set at $326 million.

Direct loans extended by Eximbank are dollar credits made to borrowers outside the United States for the purchase of U.S. goods and services. Disbursements under the loan agreements are made in the United States to the suppliers of the goods and services, and the loans plus interest must be repaid in dollars by the borrowers. The purposes for which the loans can be used are as follows:[19]

1. To supplement private sources of financing when the private financial source is unwilling or unable to assume the political and commercial risks under current conditions
2. To extend credit on terms longer than those private lenders can provide
3. To enable U.S. suppliers to provide terms on major projects that are competitive with those offered by government-sponsored export-financing institutions in other exporting countries

In addition, Eximbank has financial guarantee programs under which it can guarantee, backed by the full faith and credit of the United States, the repayment of credits extended by private lenders to foreign purchasers of U.S. goods and services. In this respect, the bank's role is comparable to that of the many foreign institutions that provide guarantees and insurance to aid their countries' exporters and safeguard them from undue risk from overseas sales. Under the financial guarantee loan authority, the Eximbank will unconditionally guarantee repayment by a borrower of up to 100 percent of the outstanding principal due on such loans, plus interest equal to the U.S. Treasury rate for similar maturities, plus 1 percent per annum, on the outstanding balances of any loan made by a U.S. financial institution to a buyer in another country for the purchase of U.S. goods and services.

Insured Loans

From the standpoint of the amount of money involved, insured loans are by far the most important segment of federal government credit. In 1988, insured loans by the federal government amounted to $550 billion, compared with $222 billion for direct federal loans.[20] The government may either insure or guarantee loans made by private lenders. The best-known example of the former is the Federal Housing Administration mortgage insurance, in particular, the Veterans Administration's mortgage guarantee program. The major dif-

---

[19] Export-Import Bank, *Description of Eximbank Export Financing Programs and Services,* 1983, pp. 5–8.

[20] Executive Office of the President, Office of Manpower and Budget, *Budget of the United States Government, Fiscal Year 1989* (Washington, D.C.: U.S. Government Printing Office, 1989), p. 10-41.

ference between loan insurance and loan guarantees is that a fee generally is charged for insurance.

Loan insurance is of particular importance in the housing market. In fact, when FHA mortgage insurance was introduced, it led to a revolution in home mortgages and home ownership. Before its introduction, home mortgages for the average family were difficult to obtain. The typical home mortgage was a medium-term loan—on the average of three to five years—and covered only a relatively small portion of the price of the house. In addition, these mortgages were typically nonamortizable, that is, the monthly mortgage payments covered only interest on the loan and these payments did not reduce the principal of the loan. The FHA insurance permitted private lenders to extend mortgages with much higher loan-to-value ratios than before, without incurring any more risk than they assumed by making uninsured mortgage loans of considerably less value. The higher loan-to-value ratio associated with the FHA mortgages implied that a correspondingly lower down payment would be required to take possession of a house, and the mortgages thus undoubtedly stimulated the demand for, and the construction of, private housing.

Federal loan insurance is subject to fiscal offsets, just as direct federal loans are. For those types of insurance that carry a premium and are just self-supporting, the premium itself is not an offset. Funds collected as premiums are used to cover administrative costs and to settle claims. The settlement of claims does not offset the income and loan-generating effects of loan insurance; it redirects these effects. Premiums are collected from one group of lenders and distributed to another group of lenders. It is in the case of loan guarantees, in which no premiums are charged and losses are financed out of general revenues, and in the case of loan insurance programs that do not break even, that the possibility of fiscal offsets arises. The analysis of offsets to insured loans is identical with that made for direct loans.

Table 19-9 on the following page presents new loan guarantees by sectors for 1988. Almost all the loan guarantees were made by two agencies—the Department of Housing and Urban Development (HUD) and the Veterans Administration (VA). The Small Business Administration and the Export-Import Bank are also in the business of making loan guarantees.

Government-sponsored Financial Institutions

A third way in which the federal government allocates credit, although indirectly, is through privately owned government sponsored financial

TABLE 19-9   New Loan Guarantees by Sector, 1988 (millions of dollars)

Sector	Amount
Agriculture	$ 8,389
Business	26,603
Education	9,926
Housing	78,137
Other	178
Total new loan guarantees	$123,233

Source: Executive Office of the President, Office of Manpower and Budget, *Budget of the U.S. Government, Fiscal Year 1988* (Washington, D.C.: U.S. Government Printing Office, 1988), Table 6g-43.

enterprises. These enterprises have been created by the government to perform specialized credit functions. Three of them, the Federal National Mortgage Association (Fannie Mae), the Federal Home Loan Mortgage Bank (Freddie Mac), and the Federal Home Loan Banks, serve the housing financial market. The Farm Credit System finances agriculture, and the Student Loan Market Association (Sallie Mae), makes a secondary market in federally guaranteed student loans. Each issues securities and uses the proceeds to finance its lending activities, and their earnings are exempt from state and local income taxes. They have greatly increased their activities in the domestic credit market in the past few years. In 1980, lending by government sponsored enterprises amounted to $153.4 million; by 1987 it increased to $581 billion.[21] These enterprises affect the national economy and business in several ways:

1. Government-sponsored loan enterprises can borrow at interest rates significantly lower than even the best-rated private borrowers. Thus, they can make loans at interest rates below prevailing market rates. This provides a subsidy to borrowers.

2. The loans have some impact on business. More than half of their total amount has gone to support housing construction, which benefits a variety of industries.

[21] Executive Office of the President, Office of Manpower and Budget, *Budget of the U.S. Government, Fiscal Year 1989*, p. 6b-1.

3. By creating a national market for mortgages, Fannie Mae and Freddie Mac have provided a method for diversifying away much of the geographically specific risk in mortgage lending, thereby lowering the cost of return required by the lender.

Other Forms of Financial Assistance

Government aid to business extends far beyond credit assistance. There are also direct cash benefits that the federal government pays to a particular firm or industry to accomplish a particular objective. For example, the government pays the sugar beet and sugar cane growers a subsidy to produce sugar even though sugar could be purchased far more cheaply from foreign countries. Cash payments are also used to help support the privately owned U.S. merchant marine. For financial and security reasons, the federal government has determined that it is necessary to have a domestic merchant marine capable of carrying a part of the U.S. oceangoing trade. Nearly every aspect of the merchant marine industry is affected by a public measure, such as paying of seamen's wages, instruction costs, and mothballing, intended to promote the U.S. fleet. Without subsidies, there would probably be no U.S. fleet and no U.S. shipbuilding industry; with the subsidies, the cost of U.S. ships is more than double the price of those built in foreign shipyards.[22]

Government research and development expenditures also have an impact on business. There are expenditures on basic research in science and engineering. Then there is space research, which will amount to $10.6 billion in 1989[23] in space science and the application of space technology. There are also weapons research and development expenditures, a part of national defense, which will amount to an estimated $33 billion in 1989.[24] Government procurement expenditures were $81 billion in 1989 and go for a wide variety of expenditures, including the purchase of planes, aircraft carriers, tanks and other military hardware, all of which is produced by private industry. Funding for the construction of highways, set at $13.7 billion for fiscal 1989 benefits private construction firms. Government expenditures on airports and airways benefit business firms, as do expenditures on aeronautic research and technology.

---

[22] Operating subsidies for the U.S. maritime industry amounted to $249 million in 1989.

[23] Executive Office of the President, Office of Manpower and Budget, *Budget of the U.S. Government, Fiscal Year 1989*, p. 5-83.

[24] Ibid., p. 5-8.

TAXATION AND THE CONTROL OF BUSINESS

Taxation is often used as an instrument of regulation to supplement the state's police power. Every tax necessarily exerts some kind of effect on the ability or willingness of an individual or a business firm to undertake an economic act. If an individual or firm pays the tax, there is less purchasing power to use for other things. If the tax is avoided by a decision not to perform a taxable action, the tax has conditioned the action of the individual or firm. Usually a tax is used to combine revenue and regulation. In some cases, however, the revenue and regulatory aspects of a tax conflict. An example would be a moderate tax on the undistributed profits of corporations. The effect of such a tax might be to increase dividends, but not to eliminate undistributed profits altogether. Therefore, some revenue would be collected, but at the same time, revenues would be sacrificed if the firms responded to the tax by declaring dividends.

The Tax Reform Act of 1986

The Tax Reform Act of 1986 dealt with many parts of the tax code that created widespread opportunities to avoid taxation and distorted the flow of investment into wasteful uses. By closing many tax loopholes, the act enabled reductions in personal and corporate income taxes. One objective of the act was to increase the efficiency of investment. The previous tax law favored certain types of investments over others. The law contained a variety of provisions that made tax shelters possible. Shelters worked especially well for investments in assets such as commercial real estate, multifamily housing, horse farms, and other shelters with low investment productivity. This distortion hindered growth in output and cost the U.S. Treasury billions of dollars in lost revenue. The new law reduced tax shelters in three ways. First, it repealed the investment tax credit; second, it stretched out depreciation on commercial real estate; and third, it curtailed the deductibility of investment interest.

The act also increased taxes on industries that previously had tax breaks such as depletion allowances. Examples are petroleum extraction and other mining industries. For other industries, the effective rate of tax on investment increased from 38 to 41 percent. This increase resulted from the repeal of the investment tax credit and amended depreciation deductions offset by a lower corporate income tax rate. Restrictions were also placed on the foreign tax credit that some U.S. firms had used to reduce their payments of the U.S. corporation income tax to zero. Limitations were placed on the deductions for meals, travel, and entertainment, and sales tax deductions were repealed. Although there will be a higher cost of capital to corporations, it will be offset by an increased efficiency in its use.

SUMMARY

The number one problem confronting the Bush administration is the federal budget deficit that is in part a legacy from the Reagan administration. It remains to be seen how well the deficit is handled, but economic growth will not eliminate it, and Gramm-Rudman-Hollings represents a sort of last-chance solution. Some options are available for cutting the budget, but each is unpalatable to one group or another. One possibility is to make the other NATO countries share more of the cost of maintaining defense readiness in western Europe. Another option is to impose a national value-added tax, which could raise as much as 80 billion dollars a year but discriminates against the poor. Its use is extremely unlikely. A third option is to increase the gasoline taxes and the "sin taxes" on alcohol and tobacco. A fourth option is to reduce national defense expenditures or entitlements, or a combination of both.

QUESTIONS FOR DISCUSSION

1. Discuss the impact that the federal budget deficit has on the U.S. economy.
2. What is the difference between the federal deficit and the federal debt?
3. Describe Reaganonomics. Was this approach successful?
4. What are the major sources of revenue in the federal budget?
5. Why is the net interest on the public debt a burden to taxpayers?
6. Federal loans to business often contain a subsidy element. Discuss.
7. Distinguish between the objectives of direct loans and those of insured loans.
8. What types of risks are covered by federal loan insurance?
9. Discuss the effect of the Tax Reform Act of 1986 on business.
10. What is the purpose of government-sponsored financial institutions such as the Federal National Mortgage Association?

RECOMMENDED READINGS

Aaron, Henry J. "The Value-Added Tax: Sorting Through the Practical and Political Problems." *The Brookings Review*. (Washington, D.C.) 6, no. 3 (Summer 1988): pp. 3–10.

Blinder, Alan S. *Hard Heads, Soft Hearts*. Reading, Mass.: Addison-Wesley, 1987.

Bowsher, Charles. *Report on the Deficit by the Comptroller General's Office*. (Washington, D.C.: U.S. General Accounting Office, 1988.)

Congressional Budget Office, Congress of the United States. *The Changing Distribution of Federal Taxes: 1975–1990*. Washington, D.C.: U.S. Government Printing Office, 1988.

Congressional Budget Office, Congress of the United States. *Trends in Family Income: 1970–1986*. Washington, D.C.: U.S. Government Printing Office, 1988.

Economic Report of the President 1989. Washington, D.C.: U.S. Government Printing Office, 1989.

Executive Office of the President, Office of Management and Budget. *Budget of the United States Government, Fiscal Year 1989*. Washington, D.C.: U.S. Government Printing Office, 1988.

Ferguson, Charles R. "From the People Who Brought You Voodoo Economics." *Harvard Business Review* 66, no. 3 (May–June 1988): 55–61.

Friedman, Benjamin. *Day of Reckoning*. New York: Random House, 1988.

Gilder, George. "The Revitalization of Everything: The Law of the Microcosm." *Harvard Business Review* 66, no. 2 (March–April 1988): 43–50.

Pechman, Joseph A. *Federal Tax Policy*, 5th ed. Washington, D.C.: Brookings Institution, 1987.

Richman, Louis S. "Are You Better Off Than in 1980?" *Fortune*, vol. 118, no. 8. October 10, 1988, pp. 38–44.

Chapter 20

Business and the Bush Administration

In November 1988, George Bush was elected president of the United States, receiving 54 percent of the popular vote and 426 out of 538 electoral votes. However, the Democrats picked up one Senate seat and two House seats and maintained control over the Senate and House of Representatives. It can be said that voters opted to maintain the status quo by choosing a Republican successor to Ronald Reagan and by leaving Congress in control of the Democrats. But the status quo is unlikely to be maintained, for too many problems confront the country. Sooner or later, but probably sooner, President Bush and Congress must address the problem of how to reduce the federal budget deficit. The increasing insolvency of many savings and loan associations, the trade deficit, corporate takeovers, and industrial competitiveness in a global economy are also important issues. These and other problems are the subject of this chapter.

Business will probably not continue the privileged status that it enjoyed under the Reagan administration. The pendulum has swung back from the probusiness climate of the Reagan years, and business may well find itself on the defensive. There are several reasons why. First, scandals on Wall Street and the October 1987 collapse of the stock market have made people wonder if tighter securities regulation is not needed. Second, corporate takeovers accelerated during the later years of the Reagan administration, and have culminated in the largest takeover ever consummated, namely, the acquisition of RJR-Nabisco by Kohlberg, Kravis, and Roberts. Third, the political atmosphere seems to favor an expansion in government economic and social activities. Minimum wages are very likely to be raised, over the objections of business. Proposals that cause concern to business, but that are likely to be passed by Congress, include temporary work leave for parents of newborn babies, and mandatory notification to employees of safety risks associated with the workplace.

Then there is the position of the United States in the world economy. The most important point is that the major countries of the world have become interdependent. What happens in the New York financial market affects the Tokyo financial market, and vice versa. Fiscal or monetary policy decisions made in Washington affect the West German economy, and vice versa. The value of the dollar in foreign exchange markets can be affected by central bank policies made in West Germany and Japan. No longer does the U.S. economic colossus dominate the world. In fact, it has now become the world's largest debtor nation, because it has borrowed heavily from abroad to finance a consumption binge that has lasted throughout the 1980s.

THE BUDGET DEFICIT AND OTHER PUBLIC POLICY ISSUES

The status of the U.S. economy, which is linked to the deficit in the federal budget, is the most important problem confronting President Bush or Congress. The dearth of national savings and capital accumulation can be directly attributed to the deficit. President Bush has two choices with respect to the overspending of consumers and government. First, he can reduce the budget deficit to slow down domestic spending and raise the nation's savings rate; second, he can let the Federal Reserve curb spending through a restrictive monetary policy. If he opts for the first alternative, the growth in consumer expenditures could be reduced through a tax increase and the growth in government spending could be cut back. Interest rates would then fall, reflecting lower federal borrowing. Lower interest rates, in turn, would produce a lower overseas value for the U.S. dollar and hasten the decline of the trade deficit.

Tax Increases

Corporate executives and ordinary individuals agree on one thing: they will support tax increases as long as the increase does not touch the personal income tax. Sixteen percent of corporate executives and 15 percent of consumers polled in two separate polls favored increases in personal income taxes as a way to reduce the budget deficit! Conversely, both groups support raising taxes on alcohol and tobacco; however, corporate executives favored raising gasoline taxes, while consumers in the other group were opposed to it.[1] Currently, the federal government levies 9.1 cents per gallon on gasoline. In addition, states levy a tax on gasoline, ranging from 7.5 cents a gallon in Georgia to 20.9 cents in Wisconsin. Even if Congress increased the federal gas tax 20 cents per gallon over a five-year period, motor fuel taxes would be considerably lower than those in other countries.

Then there is the matter of Social Security. Although most civil service and private pensions are taxable, Social Security benefits are completely tax free for couples with adjusted gross incomes under $32,000 and individuals under $25,000. Couples above the thresholds pay taxes on no more than 50 percent of their benefits. There is a surplus in the Social Security trust funds. Congress has several options with respect to Social Security. First, it can increase the taxable portion of Social Security for people above the cutoff point.

Such a change could boost government revenues by as much as $15 billion a year. Second, it would be possible to cut payroll taxes, which are highly regressive because they exclude earnings over the current wage ceiling of $45,000, and increase the personal income tax rate. Social Security benefits to the wealthy would have to be reduced.

Spending

In December 1988, Congress made a move toward reducing spending by proposing to close some thirty-four military installations, most of which served no useful purpose. Defense expenditures are a prime target for reduction, particularly with the improved political relationship between the United States and the Soviet Union. As mentioned in an earlier chapter, defense expenditures can be reduced in several ways, beginning with scrapping the Stealth bombers, which cost $500 million each to build. Another military toy that can be eliminated is the F-15E fighter plane that is supposed to destroy enemy airfields. Star Wars research can be eliminated, and wasteful everyday procurement expenditures on such things as toilet seats and hammers should be monitored.

---

[1] The corporate executive poll appeared in *Fortune,* January 16, 1989, p. 75. A Cable Network News (CNN) poll involving 611 individuals was published on December 30, 1988, on p. 8 of the *Roanoke Times*.

Government expenditures can also be reduced in other areas. Cost-of-living adjustments (COLAs) for Social Security can be suspended or capped. A one-year suspension would reduce benefits by $20 billion a year. Agricultural expenditures can, but probably won't, be cut. Policies that encourage overproduction cost taxpayers billions of dollars annually. Congress has guaranteed farmers certain prices. For example, the target price for 100 pounds of rice was $11.25 at the end of 1988. The rice producer can get only half of that on the market; the government pays the producer the difference. Reducing the target price by one cent on rice and other farm products could save $100 million annually. Expenditure reductions can also be made in a myriad of other areas, including Medicare and other health programs. Reimbursement fees to doctors can be reduced.

Education

President Bush wants to be known as the education president, and education is certainly an area that can stand improvement. On December 15, 1988, ABC aired a program called *Losing the Future,* a comprehensive survey of reasons for America's decline as a world technological power. Education, business, and government have fumbled the ball and are letting other countries, especially Japan, run with it. A *USA Today* poll conducted in July 1988 found that 27 percent of U.S. teenagers could not find the United States on a world map and 57 percent could not find the state of Massachusetts. The Joint Council on Economic Education surveyed 8,000 U.S. high school students and found that 75 percent of them didn't know what *profit* meant. Other reports have found U.S. schools to be breeding grounds for a nation of illiterates, not only in geography and economics, but also in science, mathematics, writing, and foreign languages.

Quality education costs money, and there is the question of how to pay for it at a time when the top priority is to balance the budget. President Bush has proposed to expand Head Start, the preschool program for lower-income children to include all eligible four-year-olds. A crucial shortage of math and science teachers has to be addressed. Over the next five years, 20,000 new teachers will be needed, ten times more than are expected to enter the profession. Another problem is the high school dropout rate, which is the highest for all industrial countries. One solution is to improve vocational education, which is often of poor quality because of different state and local standards. A part of increased government expenditures on education can be financed by a crackdown on student loan defaults, which are estimated to cost the federal government $1.8 billion in 1989.[2]

Takeovers

Some people feel there is an ominous parallel between the takeover mania of the 1980s and the nineteenth century "robber barons" who grabbed up most of America's industries, which led to the eventual passage of the Sherman Antitrust Act of 1890. Mergers, acquisitions, and leveraged buyouts have become common in the U.S. business world of today. Headline-making marriages between corporate giants and corporate takeovers by corporate raiders spark fears of monopoly power: rising prices, diminishing choices and a sense of isolation from the megacompanies that offer goods and services people rely on every day. Buyouts have imposed new dimensions on the U.S. economy. Decapitalization of U.S. business, through the substitution of new debt for outstanding equity, is proceeding rapidly. From 1984 to 1988, the debt of U.S. nonfinancial corporations has gone up by an estimated $840 billion, and the equity position has contracted by nearly $300 billion.[3] In the process, interest payments made by U.S. financial corporations have been increased to the point where they absorb more than a quarter of internal cash flow.

The federal government is also affected by buyouts in that an adverse revenue effect affects the Treasury from substituting tax-deductible debt for equity. The government is thus subsidizing the decapitalization of U.S. industry. Buyouts, then, will become a top congressional priority. Congress and the SEC will be expected to consider requiring fuller disclosure, passing conflict-of-interest laws, and reducing the tax advantages of these transactions. Under current tax law, the interest paid on borrowing to finance corporate buyouts is tax deductible. If the tax advantage is taken away, the number and size of corporate buyouts would decrease. In addition, bondholders in the existing securities subject to a leveraged buyout could be given the legal right to sue the organizers of the buyout for damages resulting from the downgrading of their bonds. Stricter enforcement of antitrust laws is another approach.

[2] *Fortune*, January 1989, p. 82.
[3] *Washington Post*, Sunday, December 25, 1988, p. B1.

The Savings and Loan Industry

Another problem confronting the Bush administration is the insolvency of many savings and loan associations. In 1988, 217 savings institutions were insolvent, the highest number since the Depression year of 1938 when 277 savings and loans failed. The total cost of these 1988 insolvencies was $38 billion, much of which will ultimately have to be paid by the federal government. All the savings and loans closed in 1988 and sold to purchasers had been technically insolvent for some time, but the Federal Home Loan Bank Board had been forced to keep them open because its insurance agent, the Federal Savings and Loan Insurance Corporation lacked sufficient funds to close the institutions and pay off depositors. A spate of bailouts occurred on the last two days of 1988, as purchasers wanted to take advantage of tax breaks.[4] During this time, the Federal Home Loan Bank Board accepted packages that provided almost $5 billion in assistance to purchasers of insolvent savings and loans.[5] As the savings and loan industry headed into 1989, 400 S & Ls, out of the remaining 3,000, were technically insolvent, and others were close behind.

There is much criticism of the savings and loans bailouts. Various members of Congress have complained that the deals have saddled taxpayers with billions of dollars in open-end obligations, raising objection to tax provisions that will give investors more in tax breaks than they are putting up to acquire the savings and loans. Estimates of bailing out the savings and loans range from $50 billion, the estimate provided by the Federal Home Loan Bank Board, to $112 billion, the latest projection by the General Accounting Office. It is expected that the cost of bailing out insolvent savings and loans will average $1 billion a month in 1989. Senator Lloyd Bentsen, chairman of the Senate Finance Committee, has scheduled early 1989 hearings on the state of the savings and loans, and the Bush administration is expected to draft a plan to help these institutions within three months after his inauguration.

Stock Market Regulation

There is a distinct similarity between the stock market of the 1980s and the stock market of the 1920s. Both enjoyed an enormous boom for almost a

---

[4] The tax breaks were effectively cut in half on January 1, 1988.

[5] Five savings and loans were closed on the last day of 1988, four in California and the last in North Dakota.

decade, and both crashed. The stock market crash of 1929 caused investors to lose billions of dollars they never regained, and was a precursor to the Depression, which lasted a decade. The stock market crash of October 1987 had an even more harmful effect on investors, at least in the short run. In four days of trading the Dow-Jones Industrial Average fell by 769 points, and the value of all outstanding U.S. stock decreased by almost $1.0 trillion. Because the stock market is considered to be a harbinger of things to come, many people believed that a serious recession would occur in the near future. But it did not occur and the stock market did rebound, although the Dow-Jones Industrial Average is well below the high of 2,722 that it reached in August 1987.[6]

A second parallel between the stock market of the 1980s and the stock market of the 1920s is that they both had their share of individuals and companies who tried to manipulate the market for personal gain.[7] The 1920s had its Whitneys and Insulls, who used insider information on the stock exchange or who used fake holding companies to make fortunes and who went to jail when discovered. The 1980s had its Ivan Boeskys and other sterling products of America's business schools, who also used insider information and other devices to make fortunes in the stock market and who are also serving time in prison. And then there is Drexel Burnham, the investment banking house that agreed to pay a $650 million fine for alleged machinations in the securities market. Specifically, Drexel Burnham was accused of using a complex network of contacts to manipulate securities prices, and an executive, Michael Milken, was indicted in 1989 on criminal charges for securities violations.

Several major studies focused on the October 1987 stock market crash, and recommendations were made on how to prevent a recurrence. A staff report published by the Securities and Exchange Commission recommended greater cooperation between the SEC and the Commodity Futures Trading Commission (CFTC), with the former being given greater regulatory authority over both the stock and futures markets. The SEC should also be given emergency authority to order trading halts and other steps to restore order to the markets. A General Accounting Office staff report recommended the creation of contingency plans involving the Federal Reserve, the stock and future exchanges, the SEC and the CFTC. The Presidential Task Force on Market Mechanisms (Brady Commission) recommended that one agency should coordinate the crucial regulatory issues that have an impact on the securities and futures mar-

[6] The Dow-Jones Industrial Average as of June 1, 1989, was around 2,450.

[7] President Calvin Coolidge said that "the business of America is business." President Ronald Reagan, who had a picture of Calvin Coolidge on a White House wall, concurred.

kets. It also recommended the creation of circuit breaker mechanisms, such as price limits and uniform trading halts to protect the securities market.[8]

The Environment

The year 1988 was not a good one for the world environment. Hurricanes did considerable damage to Mexico and Central America, and floods inundated most of Bangladesh. In Soviet Armenia, an earthquake devastated cities and killed thousands of people. Pollution closed beaches on the Mediterranean, the North Sea, and the English Channel. The United States, too, had its share of environmental problems. A prolonged drought parched the soil in the Midwest, reducing the country's grain harvest by 31 percent and killing thousands of head of livestock. Pollution closed beaches in New York and New Jersey. A heat wave lasting for more than a month raised fears about the greenhouse effect. A lack of rain encouraged forest fires in California and Yellowstone National Park. It was revealed that federal weapons-making plants had recklessly and secretly littered large areas with radioactive waste. The further depletion of the atmosphere's ozone layer testified to the continued use of atmosphere-destroying chlorofluorocarbons.

President Bush campaigned as a supporter of the environment. He inherits the record of the Reagan administration on the environment, which was at best mixed. James Watt, Reagan's first Secretary of the Interior, and Anne Gorsuch, his first director of the Environmental Protection Agency, were not exactly considered friends of the environm nt. During the latter years of the Reagan administration, environmental enforcement improved. In December 1988, the EPA announced that it planned to levy fines totaling nearly $1.5 million against 25 companies in thirteen states for failing to report chemical emissions. Nevertheless, the environment remains both a national and global problem. Although the United States contains less than 5 percent of the world's population, it is the single largest polluter in the world. Each American produces an average of 3 pounds of trash a day.

The Bush administration must deal with environmental issues in both a national and global context. Priority can be given to encouraging waste recycling, by setting national goal standards for recycling. Also, funding can be increased for the testing of chemicals to determine their toxicity and cancer-causing potential. It is also likely that auto fuel efficiency requirements will be

[8] Presidential Task Force on Market Mechanisms, *Report of the Presidential Task Force on Market Mechanisms* (Washington, D.C.: U.S. Government Printing Office, 1988), pp. 69–73.

changed by Congress from the current average of 26 miles per gallon to a fuel efficiency target of 27.5 mpg.

More international initiative must be aimed at solving population problems. Third world countries produce too many people and have too little food and space. This pressure mandates increased funding for research and development of new methods of birth control that are easier to use or are more acceptable in some cultures than are current techniques.

Legislation Affecting Business

Congress can be expected to take action in two areas that directly affect business. First, after a hiatus of eight years, it is likely that the minimum wage will be raised from the current level of $3.35 an hour. Bills to increase the minimum wage were introduced in the 100th Congress, but were opposed by business groups and the Reagan administration on the grounds that U.S. business firms would be adversely affected in competition with foreign firms that have lower labor costs. Second, although it is likely to be strongly opposed by business, a bill permitting family and medical leave for any worker who needs to take time off from work to care for a newborn, newly adopted, or seriously ill child will very possibly be passed by Congress. The Bush administration, which appears to be more pragmatic and less ideological than the Reagan administration, is likely to reach an accommodation with Congress on these measures.

Minimum Wage

The minimum wage was a part of the Fair Labor Standards Act of 1938. It was first set at $0.40 an hour in 1939. The rationale for its inclusion in the act was to provide a minimum standard of living for all full-time workers. It was passed during the Depression, when $0.25 an hour was considered good pay for anyone who could obtain work. Along with Social Security, it was designed to help maintain income. The minimum wage has been changed a number of times, the last in 1981 when it was set at $3.35 an hour. The Minimum Wage Restoration Act of 1989 would have raised the minimum wage in three steps. Beginning on January 1, 1989, it would have been raised to $3.75 an hour; on January 1, 1990, it would have been raised to $4.15 an hour; and on January 1, 1991, it would have been raised to $4.55 an hour. Congress did not act on mini-

TABLE 20.1   Minimum Wages from 1939 to 1988 (dollars per hour)

Year	Amount
1939	$ .40
1949	.75
1955	1.00
1961	1.15
1963	1.25
1967	1.40
1968	1.60
1974	2.00
1975	2.10
1976	2.30
1977	2.50
1978	2.65
1979	2.90
1980	3.10
1981	3.35
1988	3.35

Source: U.S Senate, Committee on Labor and Human Resources, Minimum Wage Restoration Act of 1988 (S.737). 100th Congress, 2nd sess., 1989, pp. 2–7.

mum wage legislation in 1988 because it was an election year. However, a new version of the Minimum Wage Restoration Act will be introduced in the 101st Congress.[9]

Business firms and many economists are opposed to increasing minimum wages.[10] Some feel that such an increase involves direct government intervention in the marketplace. They say it will increase unemployment, particularly among unskilled workers, because employers will not pay them a wage above what they add to output. And these economists say unemployment will increase for those people who need jobs the most, teenage dropouts and inner-city blacks. Some estimate that a 10 percent increase in the minimum wage will result in the loss of 100,000 to 200,000 jobs. It would be better to train workers for more skilled jobs than to pay them minimum wages to remain in a

[9] U.S. Senate, Committee on Labor and Human Resources, Minimum Wage Restoration Act of 1988 (S. 737), 100th Congress, 2nd Sess., 1988.

[10] See the minority report on S. 737, the Minimum Wage Restoration Act of 1988, pp. 43–47.

dead-end job. Second, increasing the minimum wage won't reduce poverty because most workers who would receive the increase do not come from poor families. Finally, some critics say that increasing the minimum wage would increase labor costs and the inflation rate.

Those who favor an increase in the minimum wage argue that the gap between rich and poor has increased in the United States during the 1980s.[11] Increasing the minimum wage can increase living standards of low-income workers and stimulate more purchasing power. They argue that increasing the minimum wage will not have a deleterious effect on unemployment. States that have raised their minimum wage above the national average have not experienced increased unemployment. An example cited is California, which had a state minimum wage of $4.25 an hour but has an unemployment rate below the national average. They also argue that the relationship of minimum wages to average hourly earnings of production has shown a decline from a high of 46.5 percent in 1980 to a low of 37.3 percent in 1988.

FAMILY AND MEDICAL LEAVE

In 1988 bills were introduced in both houses of Congress to allow workers to obtain unpaid family and medical leaves.[12] These bills have several things in common. They would guarantee job security for any worker who needs to take leave from work to care for a newborn, newly adopted, or seriously ill child. They also guarantee job security, seniority, and health benefits for any worker who takes leave to recover from a serious medical operation. Employers must provide unpaid leave, although there is no prohibition against employers providing paid leave with the same job security provisions. Under family leave, an employee could take up to ten weeks of unpaid leave over a 24-month period on the birth or adoption of a child or on the serious illness of a child or parent. Under medical leave, an employee could take up to fifteen weeks of unpaid leave over one year when seriously ill. The bills would cover twenty or more employees.

Many business firms are opposed to family and medical leave legislation on the grounds that it would lessen productivity by depriving them of workers

---

[11] See the majority report on the Minimum Wage Restoration Act of 1988, pp. 10–17.

[12] The Parental and Temporary Family Leave Act of 1988 (S. 2488), introduced by Senator Christopher Dodd and Senator John Chafee; and the Family and Medical Leave Act of 1987 (H.R. 925), introduced by Representative William L. Clay and Representative Patricia Schroeder.

when they are needed. These firms would also face the cost of hiring someone on a temporary basis while a worker is on leave. Several arguments are advanced to support this legislation. The first is that it provides job security to workers who have to take leave. Second, most women work out of economic necessity, and cannot afford to leave their jobs when they bear a child. In addition to child care responsibilities, families may have to care for elderly parents. The legislation provides job security. Third, other industrial countries, including Japan, are far more liberal than the United States when it comes to providing family and medical leave. Some countries provide up to six months paid leave for women who have had a baby.[13]

THE U.S. ROLE IN THE WORLD ECONOMY

Like it or not, the United States has now become a part of a larger global economy. For thirty years after the end of World War II, the United States was the undisputed industrial power of the world. U.S. technological know-how and marketing skills once dominated world markets: but now it finds itself in the position of competing for world business with new competitors. In addition, the United States has been spending more than it produces, with much of the money going for imports. The government has also been living beyond its means, with the end result of a federal budget deficit of around $150 billion, and a trade deficit that has been in excess of $100 billion since 1984. Moreover, during the 1980s the United States has been transformed from the world's largest creditor nation to the world's largest debtor nation. It has now become more dependent on foreign capital and is much more affected by the risk of volatility in foreign currencies and financial markets. The U.S. share of world manufacturing output has come full circle since 1913. In that year, the United States' share of world manufacturing output was 31.2 percent; in 1987, it was 31.4 percent.[14] Helped to some extent by World War I and by the prosperity of the 1920s, the U.S. share of output increased to 39.5 percent in 1928, but during the world depression of the 1930s, fell to 31.1 percent. In 1953 the U.S. share reached an all-time high of 49.1 percent, but has declined ever since. However, while the U.S. share of global manufacturing output has declined, it is important to remember that output is much larger today than it was

---

[13] For example, France allows sixteen weeks for parental or maternity leave. The employer, business, or government has to pay 90 percent of the normal wage. Japan allows twelve weeks at 60 percent of the normal wage.

[14] *U.S. News & World Report,* January 2, 1989, p. 82.

in 1913 and 1953. The United States may make only a third of the world's automobiles today compared to 65 percent in 1928, but that does not mean that Americans are making and buying fewer cars; rather, foreigners are making and buying more cars.

Nevertheless, several problems confront the United States in the world economy. One problem is our industrial competitiveness, which is linked to a low rate of savings and investment and a low rate of productivity growth. If the United States is to improve its living standards over the long run, it must improve its productivity. To do so, it has to improve its educational system in ways that maximize the potential of the work force. A second problem is foreign competition, particularly from Japan and other East Asian countries. Some people think that the United States is losing its world economic supremacy to Japan. The third problem is the debt owed us by many of the third world countries, particularly those in Latin America. Such countries as Argentina, Brazil, and Mexico face social unrest and political turmoil if their massive foreign debts are not reduced.

U.S. Economic Performance in a Global Economy

The late famous baseball pitcher Leroy "Satchel" Paige used to say, "Never look back, for you don't know who might be gaining on you." Although U.S. living standards are higher than those of other major industrial countries, those nations are gaining on us. One reason is that productivity is growing faster in other countries than it is in the United States.

Table 20-2 presents annual average rates of gross domestic product per worker in the major capitalist industrial countries, for selected time periods. Since 1950, growth in gross domestic product per worker in the United States has been consistently below that of other countries, especially during 1970–1979. Of course, in the years immediately after World War II the other countries were starting from a lower point.

Growing productivity means that available resources—labor, land, materials, plants, and equipment—can produce more than before. It means that less time is required to produce a more efficient, safer, and more convenient automobile, to prepare a more nutritional meal, or to take a coast-to-coast trip. It also means that resources are freed to produce other goods and services that could not otherwise have been produced. It means more leisure, but, more important, productivity growth means a rising standard of living. Since 1973 the growth in U.S. productivity, as measured by output per hour of labor, has

TABLE 20-2 Annual Average Rates of GDP Growth Per Worker for Major Industrial Countries, 1951–1988

	1951–1960	1961–1973	1974–1979	1980–1987
United States	2.0%	1.9%	0.0%	0.8%
Canada	2.4	2.6	1.3	1.0
Japan	6.5	8.2	2.9	2.8
France	4.4	4.9	2.7	1.9
West Germany	5.7	4.1	2.9	1.5
Italy	5.7	5.8	1.7	1.9
United Kingdom	2.1	2.9	1.3	1.8

Source: Barry P. Bosworth and Robert Z. Lawrence, "America in the World Economy," *Brookings Review* 7, no. 1 (Winter 1988–1989): 44.

slowed significantly, and the real earnings of U.S. workers have stagnated. Real income per worker increased by 2.6 percent a year for the period from 1950 to 1973; 0.6 percent for the period from 1973 to 1979; and 0.5 percent for the period from 1979 to 1987.[15] It has been estimated that if productivity had continued to grow throughout the postwar period at the 3.25 percent rate recorded between 1948 and 1965, output in 1987 would have been 50 percent higher than it was.[16] The median family income of the U.S. family, which was roughly $30,000 in 1987, would have been about $45,000.

Determinants of Productivity

A number of factors help determine productivity. Two of the more important are education and savings. The productivity of any nation depends on the skill of its labor force, which in turn is influenced by education. If a nation wants to increase its productivity, it has to improve its educational system in ways that will maximize the potential of the labor force. That is not happening in the United States. It is good at turning out lawyers, but lawyers do not increase

[15] Barry P. Bosworth and Robert Z. Lawrence, "America in the World Economy, *Brookings Review* 7, no. 1 (Winter 1988–1989): 43.

[16] Robert E. Litan, Robert Z. Lawrence, and Charles L. Schultze, "Improving American Living Standards," *Brookings Review* 7, no. 1 (Winter 1988–1989): 28–29.

productivity; in fact, they probably reduce it. What is much more important is producing a skilled labor force that is capable of handling new technology in an ever-changing economy. Unfortunately, many U.S. workers do not have the skills to compete for an increasing number of jobs that require basic mathematical skills or the ability to solve even simple problems.

Productivity also depends on savings, which are a necessary requisite for capital formation. The rate of savings in the United States has been low compared to other industrial countries. During the 1980s, the United States has been spending more than it has been producing, and importing more than it has been exporting. The deficit in the federal budget has reduced the rate of net national savings to around 2 percent a year, well below the rate of 6 to 7 percent that prevailed in earlier decades. It has depended on foreign borrowing to finance consumption and investment, but in the process has become the world's largest debtor nation. So the prescription for less dependence on foreign borrowing is to increase the rates of savings and productivity growth. To do so, excessive consumption must be reduced and the rate of savings increased.

Japan

In his book on Japan called *Yen! Japan's New Financial Empire and Its Threat to America,* Daniel Burstein projects the world of November 2004. Japan has replaced the United States as leader of the capitalist world just as the United States replaced Great Britain in the previous century.[17] It is no longer morning in America, but twilight, and in a national election a xenophobic leader has just been elected president of the United States by a landslide based on a campaign of getting tough with the Japanese, who have all our money and are our leading creditors. The U.S. dollar has been replaced by the yen as the world's leading currency, and the United States, like Argentina, has found itself borrowing increasingly in the currency of Japan. The newly elected president, in a fit of hubris, has threatened to repudiate America's debt to Japan. This scenario has changed from the 1980s, when Rambo saved the United States from Red hordes; now, it must be saved from rapacious Japanese bankers who want to collect their debts.

Clyde V. Prestowitz, Ezra Vogel, and other U.S. experts on Japan have focused on its manufacturing strength, planning strategies, and social cohesive-

---

[17] Daniel Burstein, *Yen! Japan's New Financial Empire and Its Threat to America* (New York: Simon & Schuster, 1988), pp. 1–19.

ness,[18] but Burstein focuses on Japan as a financial colossus that dominates the world of finance. In 1987 the total value of all stocks listed on the Tokyo Stock Exchange surpassed total value of all stocks listed on the New York Stock Exchange. The Osaka Stock Exchange is larger than the American Stock Exchange. Japan replaced the United States as the world's leading creditor nation in 1986; as noted earlier, the United States is now the world's leading debtor nation. Seventeen of the twenty-five largest banks in the world are Japanese; only two are American. As recently as 1980, only two Japanese banks were among the twenty-five largest banks in the world. The Japanese securities company, Nomura, is the largest in the world and, in terms of market capitalization, is twenty times larger than Merrill Lynch, the largest American brokerage house. In 1987, Japanese banks controlled nearly 10 percent of U.S. retail banking assets.

This apocalyptic view of the future of America may not even occur. It assumes two things—first, that Japan will continue its uninterrupted march toward world economic and financial supremacy, and second, the United States will do nothing to correct the problems that have contributed to its relative economic and financial decline. The United States still remains first among equals in the world. The future of U.S. living standards and its competitive position in the world depends, as it always has, on domestic productivity and savings. To accomplish this, the federal deficit must be reduced to increase the rate of savings, and the quality of education must be improved. The dominant issue for U.S. economic policy is how to reduce the growth of consumption, both to eliminate the need to borrow abroad and to provide the investment necessary to improve U.S. living standards in the future.

The Latin American Debt

The Latin American debt problem affects the United States in several ways. First, there is the possibility that a country or countries may default, thus creating problems for U.S. and other banks that hold the debt. Although a collapse of the international banking system is unlikely, some banks may have to write off heavy losses. Second, and more important, the debt is increasing social tensions in Latin America. It has contributed to inflation, which has increased by as much as 1,700 percent a year in Peru and 400 percent a year in Argentina. In order to pay the annual interest, much less the principal, on their debt, Latin

---

[18] Clyde V. Prestowitz, Jr., *Trading Places* (New York: Basic Books, 1988); Ezra Vogel, *Japan as No. 1* (Cambridge, Mass.: Harvard University Press, 1979).

TABLE 20-3   Foreign Debt for the United States and Latin American Countries for 1987 (in billions of dollars and percent of GDP)

Country	Foreign Debt	Percentage of GDP
United States	$368	8.0
Brazil	121	37.0
Mexico	106	76.0
Argentina	55	79.0
Venezuela	36	73.0
Chile	21	113.0
Peru	18	49.0
Colombia	17	47.0
Ecuador	11	103.0
Uruguay	6	79.0
Bolivia	5	89.0

Source: *Economic Report of the President 1988* (Washington, D.C.: U.S. Government Printing Office, 1988), Table B-12, p. 262 (New York: Morgan Guaranty Trust, *Monthly Report,* November 1988), p. 1.

American countries have had to sacrifice spending on social programs, thus increasing the division between rich and poor. This situation is made to order for politicians of both the right and left who can stir up nationalist sentiment against the United States. It also encourages various Marxist groups.

Table 20-3 presents the debt of various Latin American countries and the relationship of the debt to gross domestic product (GDP) for each country. A frame of reference is the U.S. foreign debt of approximately $360 billion in 1987. Although the United States is the largest debtor nation in the world, its debt equals less than 10 percent of its gross domestic product. The United States, then, is far more capable of carrying its foreign debt than Mexico or Brazil. The latter countries depend far more on exports to finance debt repayment than does the United States. Also, the flight of capital is a major problem. This loss can be attributed to a considerable degree to political instability.

There remains the problem of what to do with the Latin American debt. One approach is for banks holding the debt to write it off as bad loans. This loss would be hard on banks that have a considerable amount of Latin debt in their loan portfolios. It also lowers the credit rating of the Latin American countries, and would work against their capacity to borrow in the future. Another approach is to allow Latin American countries to declare a moratorium on their debt and pay what they can. A third approach is to allow an international agency such as the International Monetary Fund to buy the Latin debt at a discount. Regardless of the solution to the debt problem, the United States, for economic and security reasons, has to be involved.

Global Financial Markets

Probably the most important world development of the 1980s that affects the United States has been the internationalization of financial markets. Capital has ceased to have national characteristics, and national capital markets are no longer separate and distinct. U.S. stocks and bonds are now traded on the Tokyo, London, Frankfurt, and other foreign stock exchanges. In the currency market, on any given day more than $300 billion are changed from one currency to another. High-speed computers and communications technology make it easy to execute complex arbitrage strategies—buying in one market and almost simultaneously selling in another market halfway around the world to take advantage of price differences. Banking activities across national borders have expanded dramatically. Loans made by banks in one country to nonbanking companies in other countries amounted to $1.1 trillion in the first six months of 1987, while cross-national deposits of nonbank companies amounted to $1.0 trillion during the same period.[19]

So any nation could feel the adverse effects of a financial collapse caused by the imprudent actions of another. A case in point is the stock market crash of October 1987, which was truly global in nature, starting in Tokyo and Hong Kong, spreading to Europe and only then, as markets opened in the United States, causing the value of stocks on the New York Stock Exchange to fall 22 percent in one day, which then caused the London Stock Exchange to experience a sharp drop the next day because U.S. investors were trying to sell their stocks in the London market.[20] A second example of interdependence could involve banks. The U.S. dollar is in widespread use for borrowing and investment around the world. The Federal Reserve and the New York Clearing House Association handles most U.S. dollar-denominated transactions,

---

[19] E. Gerald Corrigan, *Financial Market Structure: A Longer View* (New York: Federal Reserve Bank of New York, 1987), p. 16.

[20] Nicholas de B. Katzenbach, *An Overview of Program Trading and Its Impact on Current Market Prices* (New York: New York Stock Exchange, 1987), p. 20.

regardless of the country. A failure by a major bank abroad could place U.S. financial institutions in jeopardy.

Given the interdependence of financial markets, there is obviously the need for some form of international regulation. The securities market is becoming more international by the day, but individual countries regulate their securities market in different ways. Accounting standards, margin requirements, and mandatory disclosures vary greatly from one country to another. What is needed is more international cooperation in order to prevent a repeat of October 19, 1987. For example, there are no international agreements on margin requirements, which regulate the degree to which a securities transaction can be financed by money borrowed from a broker. The margin requirement is an important regulatory tool. A lower margin requirement in one country as opposed to another encourages (1) speculation and (2) the movement of money to the country that has the lower requirement.

SUMMARY

The Reagan era is over and the Bush administration faces a number of problems, some inherited from the previous administration. The budget deficit is the number one problem, and many other problems, including the trade deficit, stem from it. It has contributed to a decrease in saving, which in turn has caused a reliance on foreign borrowing to finance capital formation. Foreign capital has been attracted to the United States by high real interest rates that had to be paid on the rapidly rising debt. In the process of borrowing from abroad, the United States became the world's largest debtor country. In addition to the budget deficit, the Bush administration will also have to confront other issues, such as improving the quality of U.S. education. A more immediate issue has to do with the problem of the savings and loan industry. There is also public concern over the pervasive takeover mania and the continuing scandals on Wall Street. Finally, we need to improve environmental regulation.

The United States also confronts a changed world economy. Its dominance of the world economy has slipped, and Japan has become the world's leading creditor country. The U.S. rate of productivity growth has lagged in comparison with other countries. Japan, in particular, has become a major economic competitor. Some feel that world economic dominance by Japan is inevitable. The debts of the Latin American countries also pose a problem. A default by one of the major debtor countries could threaten the survival of major U.S. banks. A loss of investor confidence in the U.S. dollar could result in capital flight, drive interest rates higher, and send the United States into a recession.

QUESTIONS FOR DISCUSSION

1. What changes can business expect from the Bush administration?
2. What is the relationship between education and the position of the United States as a world industrial power?
3. Discuss some of the legislation likely to be passed during the first year of the Bush administration. Is family leave a good thing for business?
4. Discuss the arguments for and the arguments against increasing the minimum wage.
5. What environmental policies should the Bush administration pursue in conjunction with other countries?
6. Low productivity and a low rate of saving have contributed to the decline in dominance of the United States in the world economy. Discuss.
7. The stock market crash of October 1987 showed that not only the United States but other countries as well are vulnerable to financial shocks. Discuss.
8. The Latin American debt crisis poses serious problems for the United States. Discuss.
9. The spread of banking and security market activities across national boundaries create problems of regulation. Why? Can anything be done about it?
10. Japan may have lost World War II to the United States, but it is entirely possible that Japan will have won the economic and financial battle with the United States by the end of this century. Discuss.

RECOMMENDED READINGS

Aho, C. Michael, and Marc Levinson. *After Reagan: Confronting the Changed World Economy*. New York: Council on Foreign Relations, 1988.

Blumenthal, Michael. "The World Economy & Technological Change." *Foreign Affairs* 66, no. 3 (Winter 1988): 529–550.

Bosworth, Barry P., and Robert Z. Lawrence. "America in the World Economy." *Brookings Review* 7, no. 1 (Winter 1988–1989): 39–52.

Burstein, Daniel. *Yen! Japan's New Financial Empire & Its Threat to America*. New York: Simon & Schuster, 1988.

Feldstein, Martin, ed. *The United States in the World Economy*. Chicago: University of Chicago Press. 1988.

Friedman, Benjamin. *Day of Reckoning*. New York: Random House, 1988.

Kennedy, Paul. *The Rise and Fall of the Great Powers*. New York: Random House, 1987.

Litan, Robert E., Robert Z. Lawrence, and Charles L. Schultz. "Improving America's Living Standards." *Brookings Review,* 7, no. 2 (Winter 1988–1989): 23–38.

Markey, Edward J. "Give the Markets Regulatory Cohesion." *International Economy* 2, no. 3. (May–June 1988): 15–23.

"Planet of the Year: What on Earth Are We Doing?" *Time*. January 2, 1989, pp. 24–73.

Resolving the Global Economic Crisis: After Wall Street, A Statement by 33 Economists from 13 Countries. Washington, D.C.: Institute for International Economics, 1987.

Appendix A

Federal Regulatory Commissions

TABLE A-1   Regulation of Banking and Finance

Organization	Year Established	Primary Regulatory Functions
Office of the Comptroller of the Currency	1863	Licenses and regulates national banks
Board of Governors of the Federal Reserve System	1913	Determines monetary and credit policy for the system and regulates member commercial banks
Federal Home Loan Bank Board	1932	Provides credit reserves for and regulates federally chartered savings and home-financing institutions
Federal Deposit Insurance Corporation	1933	Insures deposits of eligible banks and supervises certain insured banks
Federal Savings and Loan Insurance Corporation	1934	Insures savings in thrift and home-financing institutions
Securities and Exchange Commission	1934	Requires financial disclosure by publicly held companies; regulates practices of stock exchanges, brokers, and dealers; regulates certain practices of mutual funds, investment advisors, and public utility holding companies

TABLE A-1 (continued)

Organization	Year Established	Primary Regulatory Functions
National Credit Union Administration	1970	Charters, supervisors, and examines all federal credit unions
Farm Credit Administration	1971	Supervises and regulates all activities of credit disbursed through the Farm Credit System
Commodity Futures Trading Commission	1975	Licenses all futures contracts and the brokers, dealers, and exchanges trading them
International Trade Commission (formerly U.S. Tariff Commission, established in 1916)	1975	Investigates and rules on tariff and certain other foreign trade regulations

TABLE A-2   Regulation of Energy and Environmental Matters

Organization	Year Established	Primary Regulatory Functions
Army Corps of Engineers	1824	Issues permits for all construction in navigable waterways; constructs and maintains rivers and harbor improvements
Mississippi River Commission	1879	Approves plans for and constructs flood control projects in lower Mississippi River Basin

TABLE A-2 (continued)

Organization	Year Established	Primary Regulatory Functions
Bureau of Reclamation	1902	Establishes criteria for use, development, and pricing of resources obtained from reclamation projects
Forest Service	1905	Manages U.S. forest preserves by determining amounts of land eligible for harvest, conditions of cutting, need for reforestation, etc.
National Forest Reservation Commission	1911	Rules on requests from Secretary of Agriculture for authority to acquire or exchange national forests
Federal Power Commission	1930	Regulates wholesale rates and practices in interstate transmission of electric energy and regulates transportation and sale of natural gas
Tennessee Valley Authority	1933	Operates river control systems and sets rates for power generated from TVA hydroelectric projects
Bonneville, Alaska, And Southeastern and Southwestern	1937 (abolished 1967)	Sets prices and markets federall generated hydroelectric power
Bureau of Land Management	1946	Classifies, manages use of, and disposes of all federal lands
Delaware River Basin Commission	1961	Develops and/or approves all plans for control and utilization of water resources in Delaware River Basin

TABLE A-2 (continued)

Organization	Year Established	Primary Regulatory Functions
Environmental Protection Agency	1970	Develops environmental quality standards, approves state abatement plans, and rules on acceptability of environmental impact statements
Federal Energy Administration	1970	Develops and/or approves all plans for utilization and control of watershed resources in Susquehanna River Basin
Susquehanna River Basin Commission	1973	Regulates price and allocation of certain petroleum products under emergency energy legislation
Mining Enforcement and Safety Administration	1973	Sets and enforces mine safety standards
Nuclear Regulatory Commission (formerly Atomic Energy Commission, established in 1946)	1975	Promotes and regulates civilian use of atomic energy
Ocean Mining Administration	1975	Supervises leasing of ocean resources and regulates ocean mining

TABLE A-3 Regulation of Commerce, Transportation, and Communications

Organization	Year Established	Primary Regulatory Functions
Patent and Trademark Office	1836	Administers patent and trademark laws

TABLE A-3 (continued)

Organization	*Year Established*	*Primary Regulatory Functions*
Interstate Commerce Commission	1887	Regulates rates, routes, and practices of railroads, trucks, bus lines, oil pipelines, domestic water carriers, and freight forwarders
National Bureau of Standards	1901	Establishes standards of measurement in trade, public safety, technical, and scientific performance
Coast Guard	1915	Sets and enforces safety standards for merchant vessels and navigable waterways
Federal Communications Commission	1934	Licenses civilian radio and television communication, and licenses and sets rates for interstate and international communication by wire, cable, and radio
Foreign Trade Zones Board	1934	Grants authority to public or private corporations to establish and/or utilize foreign trade zones within United States
Federal Maritime Commission	1936	Regulates fares, rates, and practices of steamship companies engaged in U.S. foreign commerce
Maritime Administration	1936	Determines eligibility for merchant marine subsidies, and regulates construction and operation of certain merchant ships

TABLE A-3 (continued)

Organization	Year Established	Primary Regulatory Functions
Civil Aeronautics Board	1938	Promotes and subsidizes air transportation, and regulates airline routes, passenger fares, and freight rates
Appalachian Regional Commission	1965	Approves state plans for projects in Appalachian area before requests for funds can be considered by federal departments
Federal Highway Administration	1966	Determines highway safety standards and administers federally funded highway construction programs
Federal Railroad Administration	1966	Administers high-speed railroad development program and the railroad and oil pipe-line safety programs formerly administered by the ICC
Office of Telecommunications Policy	1970	Sets standards for broadcast technology and performance and assigns federal telecommunication frequencies

TABLE A-4 Regulation of Food, Health, and Safety, and Unfair or Deceptive Trade Practice

Organization	Year Established	Primary Regulatory Functions
Federal Trade Commission	1914	Administers some antitrust statutes, and laws concerning advertising misrepresentation, flammable fabrics, packaging, and labeling of certain products
Packers and Stockyards Administration	1916	Regulates fair business practices in livestock and processed meat marketing
Food and Drug Administration	1931	Administers laws concerning purity, safety, and labeling accuracy of certain foods and drugs
Commodity Credit Corporation	1933	Finances and determines farm price supports and administers production stabilization programs
Social Security Administration	1933	Determines eligible medical expenses under Medicare/ Medicaid
Agriculture Marketing Service	1937	Sets grades and standards for most farm commodities, inspects egg production, administers product and process safety acts, licenses and bonds warehouses
Agricultural Stabilization and Conservation Service	1953	Administers commodity stabilization programs, and rules on eligibility of participants
Animal and Plant Health Inspection Service	1953	Sets standards, inspects and enforces laws relating to meat, poultry, and plant safety

TABLE A-4 (continued)

Organization	Year Established	Primary Regulatory Functions
Federal Aviation Administration	1958	Certifies airworthiness of aircraft, licenses pilots, and operates air traffic control system
Federal Insurance Administration	1968	Sets standards for all insurance programs related to natural disasters and similar occurrences
Office of Interstate Land Sales Registration	1968	Requires disclosure and regulation for interstate sales of land in quantities of over fifty lots
Interim Compliance Panel	1969	Grants permits for noncompliance with health standards in underground coal mines
National Highway Traffic Safety Administration	1970	Establishes safety standards for trucks and automobiles and certifies compliance with emission standards for pollution control
Occupational Safety and Health Review Commission are	1970	Adjudicates all enforcement actions when OSHA rulings contested
Consumer Product Safety Commission	1972	Establishes mandatory product safety standards and bans sale of products that do not comply
Occupational Safety and Health Administration	1973	Develops and enforces worker safety and health regulations
Professional Standards Review Organization	1973	Reviews and sets private medical practice and health care standards

TABLE A-4   (continued)

Organization	Year Established	Primary Regulatory Functions
Foreign Agricultural Service (absorbed Export Marketing Service, established in 1969)	1974	Determines eligibility price and terms of payment for commodities allocated to export market
National Transportation Safety Board	1974	Investigates transportation accidents, and rules on needed improvements in airline, rail, and highway safety

TABLE A-5   Regulation of Labor, Housing, and Small Business

Organization	Year Established	Primary Regulatory Functions
Civil Service Commission	1833	Sets job standards and classifications for most federal employees and enforces Equal Employment Opportunity Act within federal government
National Mediation Board	1926	Conducts union representation elections and mediates labor-management disputes in the railroad and airline industries
Employment Standards Administration	1933	Sets and administers standards under laws relating to minimum wages, overtime, nondiscrimination, etc.

TABLE A-5 (continued)

Organization	Year Established	Primary Regulatory Functions
Unemployment Insurance Service	1933	Reviews state unemployment insurance laws to ensure compliance with federal standards
Federal Housing Authority	1934	Sets and enforces standards for federally insured residential and commercial properties
National Labor Relations Board	1935	Conducts union representation elections and regulates labor practices of employers and unions
Railroad Retirement Board	1935	Administers retirement and insurance acts for railroads, and rules on eligibility of retiring or disabled workers
General Services Administration	1949	Establishes critical needs for national stockpile and regulates purchase/sale of required/surplus materials
Renegotiation Board	1951	Sets standards for private contracts with federal government and rules on contractors' liabilities
Small Business Administration	1953	Makes loans and gives advice to small businesses
Labor-Management Services Administration	1963	Determines (with Treasury) eligibility of employee welfare and pension plans and sets standards for financial disclosure
Equal Employment Opportunity Commission	1964	Investigates and rules on charges of racial and other discrimination by employers and labor unions

TABLE A-5   (continued)

Organization	Year Established	Primary Regulatory Functions
Federal Labor Relations Council	1969	Oversees and prescribes regulations pertaining to labor-management relations programs in federal government
Cost Accounting Standards Board	1970	Promulgates rules and regulations for implementation of cost accounting standards to be included in federal defense contracts and subcontracts

Appendix B

The Exxon Valdez:
An Environmental Disaster

Since the building of the Alaska pipeline 15 years ago, environmentalists have expressed concern that an ecological disaster could occur. The pipeline carries oil from the North Slopes to Valdez harbor for shipment by tanker to West Coast markets. The supposedly impossible disaster happened with devastating consequences for the environ. Millions of gallons of oil flowed into Prince William Sound and then spread southward, polluting both water and beaches.

The oil spill happened in the wrong place at the wrong time and created an incalculable loss of fish and wildlife. It spread over rocky beaches and inland coves killing salmon and other fish that spawn in the shallows. Waterfowl by the thousands were destroyed and their natural habitat damaged for years to come. Many sea animals were also destroyed by the oil spill, and pictures on the nightly news showed sea otters and other animals covered with oil. Then, there was also the resulting financial damage to the livelihoods of fishermen and the economies of small fishing towns that depended on fishing. But the catastrophe did not stop there nor was it limited to a short time period because oil deposits that sink to the bottom will act as time-released capsules for years to come. Microorganisms will ingest oil and then be ingested by small fish which will be ingested by larger fish, right up the food chain.

It is an article of faith that is held by believers in the free market that business is far more efficient than government and can do anything better. Exxon proved them wrong. Its response to the handling of the oil spill appeared inept and inefficient. Instead of acting immediately and decisively as business firms presumably are supposed to do, it was as slow as any government bureaucracy in the world. It issued assurances right after the spill that help was on the way. This was hardly the case; in fact, little was done by Exxon until several weeks had elapsed. Local villagers and the U.S. Coast Guard were the first to get involved in cleaning up the oil spill, and the Soviet Union sent a vessel that could skim oil. Finally, Exxon responded belatedly and ineffectively.

Union Carbide had its Bhopal disaster, which hurt its image and pocket-book, but that was nothing when compared to the Exxon Valdez fiasco. It is safe to say that Exxon will pay out hundreds of millions, and maybe billions, of dollars on claims and lawsuits before things get back to normal. The price of gasoline went up by an average of $.15 a gallon within a month after the oil spill and Exxon was blamed for it. The price increase occurred at a time when there was a world oversupply of oil and Mexican oil was selling for around $11 a barrel. The Senate Commerce, Science and Transportation Committee held hearings on the oil spill, with Exxon placed on the defensive.

Finally, as far as the environmentalists were concerned, the Exxon Valdez disaster touched off a worst-case scenario of a marine nightmare, the destruc-tion of an aquatic ecosystem. This environmental issue transcends Alaska, where more stringent laws can be expected; it will probably give conserva-tionists the edge over those who wish to make the U.S. less dependent on foreign sources of oil. It will probably be more difficult to drill for oil in the coastal waters of other U.S. states because of environmental opposition. Congress can be expected to pass more conservation legislation. For example, higher mileage standards could be raised for automobiles. If the average auto-fuel consumption were raised from the present 26.5 miles per gallon to 40 mpg over the next 20 years, it would save 15 billion barrels of oil by the year 2020.

Appendix C

Price Waterhouse v. Hopkins

On May 2, 1989, the Supreme Court ruled on a "second generation" job discrimination case that focused not on barriers to entry to the workplace but on more subtle barriers to promotion into managerial positions. By a 6-3 vote, the Court ordered further lower court hearings in a suit against the accounting firm of Price Waterhouse by a former employee, Ann Hopkins, who contended that she was denied a partnership because she acted too much like a man. The issue is whether women should act feminine in the workplace, or should they be openly assertive and competitive. When women adopt behavior considered desirable in the business world, they risk being branded as undesirable, unfeminine, and unladylike.

Hopkins was the only woman among 88 candidates proposed for partnership at Price Waterhouse in 1982.* She had the best record of all the candidates in obtaining government contracts and thereby generating new business. Clients had been impressed with the quality of her work. She was not one of the 47 persons who were appointed to partnership. Several partners in the firm said that she was overly aggressive, harsh, profane, impatient with her staff, and difficult to work with, qualities that can be applied to many men in the workplace. She claimed that a partner in the firm told her that she could improve her chances for promotion if she walked, talked, and dressed more femininely. He also suggested she wear makeup and jewelry and have her hair styled. Another partner suggested she attend charm school, and a third partner described her as "too macho."

Hopkins sued under Title VII of the Civil Rights Act of 1964, claiming that Price Waterhouse judges her on criteria different from the male candidates. A trial court and federal appeals court ruled in her favor saying that the firm had to show clear and convincing evidence that it had not discriminated against her. The Supreme Court said that it was enough for the firm to present a

*The company had seven women among its 662 partners.

preponderance of evidence that it did not discriminate. Under the preponderance standard, the employer would only have to present more evidence for its position than against it. Justice William F. Brennan, in writing the lead opinion, said that the firm may avoid a finding of liability only by proving that it would have made the same decision even if it had not taken gender into account. Justice Sandra Day O'Connor, while agreeing with Brennan on most of the case, said that employees must present direct evidence that discrimination was a factor in the employer's decision before the employer could be made to act on it.

Index